The Origin of the Samaritans

Supplements

to

Vetus Testamentum

Edited by the Board of the Quarterly

H.M. BARSTAD – R.P. GORDON – A. HURVITZ – G.N. KNOPPERS
A. VAN DER KOOIJ – A. LEMAIRE – C.A. NEWSOM – H. SPIECKERMANN
J. TREBOLLE BARRERA – H.G.M. WILLIAMSON

VOLUME 128

The Origin of the Samaritans

By

Magnar Kartveit

BRILL

LEIDEN • BOSTON
2009

This book is printed on acid-free paper.

Library of Congress Cataloging-in-Publication Data

Kartveit, Magnar, 1946-
  The origin of the Samaritans / by Magnar Kartveit.
      p. cm. – (Supplements to Vetus Testamentum ; v. 128)
  Includes bibliographical references and indexes.
  ISBN 978-90-04-17819-9 (hardback : alk. paper)
  1. Samaritans–Origin. 2. Josephus, Flavius–Knowledge–Samaritans. I. Title. II. Series.

  BM910.K37 2009
  296.8'17–dc22

                                                                    2009023695

ISSN   0083-5889
ISBN   978 90 04 17819 9

PRINTED IN THE NETHERLANDS

Dedicated to Professor Dr Magne Sæbø on his 80th birthday,
23 January 2009

CONTENTS

Preface XI
Abbreviations XIII

1. Introduction 1

2. The Legacy from Josephus 17
   2.1. Josephus' Version of the Origin of the Samaritans 17
   2.2. The Church Fathers 20
   2.3. The Samaritan Version of the Origin: The Chronicles 22
        Background in Josephus 23
        The *Tolidah / Chronicle Neubauer* 24
        The *Kitab al-Tarikh* by Abu'l Fath 27
        The *Arabic Book of Joshua* 34
        The New Chronicle / Chronicle Adler 37
        Chronicle II 39

3. State of the Question 45
   3.1. The Impact of the Samaritan Version 45
   3.2. Josephus' Version Mirrored in Scholarship 49
        The Cross-Purvis Hypothesis 59
        R. J. Coggins' Model: Estrangement, and no
          Reconciliation 68
        "Cain and Abel" 69

4. Josephus on the Origin of the Samaritans 71
   4.1. Terminology and Sources 71
   4.2. Josephus' *Tendenz* 80
        Opportunism 82
   4.3. The First Story: An Eastern Origin 85
   4.4. The Second Story: Origin from Jerusalem and
        Construction of the Temple 90
   4.5. The Third Story: Sidonians 96
   4.6. The Destruction of the Temple 100
   4.7. Further Information on the Samaritans 103
   4.8. Summing up so Far 104
   4.9. Genesis 34 in Josephus' Rendering 106

5. Josephus' Predecessors 109
   5.1. Genesis 34 111
   5.2. Genesis 34 Interpreted in the LXX 117
   5.3. Demetrius the Exegete and Chronographer 119
   5.4. Theodotus 122
   5.5. Sirach 50:25–26 140
   5.6. *Jubilees* 30 149
   5.7. *4QNarrative and Poetic Composition*$^{a-c}$ 160
   5.8. *Aramaic Levi Document* and *Testament of Levi* 171
   5.9. Judith 182
   5.10. *Joseph and Aseneth* 189
   5.11. Philo 192
   5.12. Pseudo-Philo 194
   5.13. Genesis 34 in the Samaritan Pentateuch 194
   5.14. Conclusions 199

6. Samaritan Inscriptions and Related Texts 203
   6.1. Excavations 203
        Shechem / Tell Balatah 203
        Tell er-Ras 205
        Mount Gerizim / Jabal at-Tur 206
   6.2. The Inscriptions from Mount Gerizim 209
   6.3. The Inscriptions from Delos 216
        Excursus: Later Samaritan Inscriptions 225
   6.4. Texts with "Argarizein" 228
        2 Maccabees 5:23 and 6:2 236
        Josephus' *War* 1.63 240
        Masada Fragment 10 241
        Pseudo-Eupolemus 243
   6.5. Summary 256

7. The Pentateuch that the Samaritans Chose 259
   7.1. The Samaritan Pentateuch in the West 259
   7.2. The Predecessors of the Samaritan Pentateuch in Qumran   263
   7.3. The Major Expansions 265
        4QExod-Lev^f = 4Q17 267
        4QpaleoExod^m = 4Q22 267
        4QNum^b = 4Q27 270
        RP = 4Q158: a, 4Q364: b, 365: c, 366: d, 367: e 271
        4Q175 272

7.4. Explanations 273
7.5. A Layer of Major Expansions 276
7.6. Script 288
7.7. The Samaritan Tenth Commandment 290
7.8. Moses as a Prophet in the Durran 296
7.9. Conclusion 299
    Excursus: Deuteronomy 27:4 in the Old Greek Papyrus
    Giessen 19 and in the Old Latin Lyon Manuscript,
    and the Altar-Pericope in Joshua 8:30–35 300
    Chart 1: Major Expansions in the Samaritan
    Pentateuch: Gen 1–Exod 11 310
    Chart 2: Major Expansions in the Samaritan
    Pentateuch: Exod 12–Deut 34 311

8. The Samaritan Attitude to the Prophets 313
8.1. A Prophet like Moses 313
8.2. The Canon of the Prophets 316
8.3. The *Ascension of Isaiah* 317
    Literary Analysis 317
    The Oldest Stratum 325
    The Accusations against Isaiah 329
8.4. *4QList of False Prophets ar* / 4Q339 337
8.5. False Prophets from the North 344
8.6. True and False Prophets 346
8.7. Conclusion 348

9. The Origin of the Samaritans 351
9.1. The Construction of the Temple............................ 353
9.2. The Biblical Evidence 362

Bibliography 371
Indices
Index of Ancient Sources 393
Index of Modern Authors 399
Subject Index 403

PREFACE

As a student I had the privilege in 1969 of meeting the Samaritan High Priest, Amram Ben Yitzhaq Ben Amram, and this meeting made a lasting impression on me. Some years later Professor Magne Sæbø of Oslo suggested that Samaritan studies would be an interesting field for scholarly work, as it indeed has proved to be. The book is dedicated to him in appreciation for his suggestion and continuous support. The School of Mission and Theology (Misjonshøgskolen), has made it possible to pursue the subject, especially during sabbaticals of varying length in 1977–1978, 1993, 1999, 2001 and 2006. Initial studies were made during a stay at the University of Göttingen in the fall of 1977 and the spring of 1978, for which I received support from the Norwegian Research Council for Science and the Humanities (Norges Almenvitenskapelige Forskningsråd). After years devoted to other tasks Samaritan studies were taken up again in the library of the Pontifical Biblical Institute in Rome in the summer of 1993 with support from the University Funds in Stavanger (Universitetsfondet i Stavanger). A new grant was provided by the Research Council of Norway (Norges forskningsråd), for work in Jerusalem and Cambridge, UK, in the fall of 2001. I am much obliged to these research funds for their support. To the staff of the university libraries in Göttingen, Cambridge, Jerusalem and Oxford, as well as of the libraries of the Pontifical Biblical Institute and the École biblique et archéologique française de Jérusalem, of Tyndale House, Cambridge, and Campion Hall, Oxford, I express my deepest thanks. Above all, I am indebted to the School of Mission and Theology for the continued support and to the library staff for generous help.

Presentations of some of the topics covered in this book were given at the following congresses of the Société d'Études Samaritaines: the fifth, Milan 1996, the sixth, Helsinki 2000, and the seventh, Pápa, Hungary, 2008. Further presentations were given at the conferences of Nordic Network in Qumran Studies, Oslo 2004, Jerusalem 2005, and Copenhagen 2006, and at the Annual Meetings of the Society of Biblical Literature in Washington in 2006, and in Boston in 2008. Drafts of some of the parts were presented at the OT seminars of the universities of Cambridge and Oxford in 1999, and at the Collegium Judaicum annual meeting in Oslo in 2005. Presentations of related topics were given at the first and second

Mandäer- und Samaritanertagung in Berlin in 2003 and 2008. Some of these presentations have been published or will be published; for details readers are referred to the bibliography. Many thanks to the participants of the various congresses and conferences, who have provided valuable suggestions and necessary corrections.

The Research Council of Norway (Norges forskningsråd), has provided a grant for improving the language of my manuscript and Dr Walter Houston has carried out this task, and made several additional suggestions. Both the man and the council deserve my gratitude. I am deeply indebted to Brill for accepting the manuscript for publication and for publishing it in the series Vetus Testamentum Supplements. Also, I am grateful to Charles V. Crowther and Steve Mason for their comments on my discussion of the Delos inscriptions and of the Josephus material.

Documentation follows the guidelines of *The Chicago Manual of Style*, fifteenth edition, Chicago and London: The University of Chicago Press, 2003, and P. H. Alexander et al., eds., *The SBL Handbook of Style: For Ancient Near Eastern, Biblical and Early Christian Studies*, Peabody, Mass.: Hendrickson, 1999. Articles in encyclopaedias, dictionaries or lexicons are referred to in the footnotes only, where they are also supplied with the volume number and, if the publication of the encyclopaedia etc. in question extended over several years, the year of publication. The bibliography contains full documentation of the encyclopaedias etc. As a rule, only initials are used for given names. Some abbreviations are used in addition to those provided by *The SBL Handbook of Style*, and these are explained in a separate list. Unless otherwise noted the NRSV is used.

Magnar Kartveit
Stavanger, February 2009

ABBREVIATIONS

Abbreviations are according to the system in P. H. Alexander et al., eds., *The SBL Handbook of Style: For Ancient Near Eastern, Biblical and Early Christian Studies*, Peabody, Mass.: Hendrickson, 1999. In addition, the following abbreviations are used:

A.H.   Anno Hegirae
BHQ   Biblia Hebraica Quinta
DSS   Dead Sea Scrolls
EDSS   *Encyclopedia of the Dead Sea Scrolls*
HB   Hebrew Bible
JSJSup   Journal for the Study of Judaism in the Persian, Hellenistic and Roman Periods: Supplement Series
JSSSup   Journal of Semitic Studies: Supplement Series
LXX   Septuagint
OG   Old Greek
OT   Old Testament
RVV   Religionsgeschichtliche Versuche und Vorarbeiten
SJSHRZ   Studien zu den jüdischen Schriften aus hellenistisch-römischer Zeit
SP   The Samaritan Pentateuch
SSLL   Studies in Semitic Language and Linguistics
TSAJ   Texts and Studies in Ancient Judaism / Texte und Studien zum antiken Judentum
TTPS   Text and Translations: Pseudepigrapha Series
WdF   Wege der Forschung

CHAPTER ONE

INTRODUCTION

Many Bible readers will think that chapter 17 of the second book of Kings refers to the origin of the Samaritans. According to the Authorized Version we read about "the Samaritans" in verse 29, and a number of translations reveal the same understanding of the Hebrew הַשֹּׁמְרֹנִים. On closer inspection, however, it turns out that 2 Kgs 17:29 does not refer to the Samaritans, but to the "people of Samaria," whose relation to the Samaritans is not immediately clear.

The understanding of 2 Kgs 17 as dealing with the Samaritans has its earliest attestation in the works of Josephus. He offers a story where he describes them as "Chouthaioi," a group which was brought by the Assyrian king Salmanasser from "Chouthas" in Persia into Samaria after the occupation and subsequent depopulation of that area, *Ant.* 9.278 f., 288–291. This version takes us back to the eighth century B.C.E., and it has led scholars and lay people to believe that the Samaritans were deportees from the East, brought into Samaria in this early period; in Samaria they remained through the ages, and perhaps they mixed with the local population—a situation which most likely resulted in syncretism.[1] The story resembles 2 Kgs 17 and this has led to reading the chapter as referring to the origin of the Samaritans.

---

[1] See e.g.: "The Jews despised the Samaritans because they were heretical descendants of the mixed population in the North: Israelites who had survived the Assyrian destruction of the Northern Kingdom in 722 B.C. and intermarried with the pagan peoples from Mesopotamia who had settled there (cf. 2 Kgs 17:24–41). The Jews, who considered the Samaritans spurious worshippers of Yahweh, detested them even more than pagans." A. A. Di Lella and P. W. Skehen, *The Wisdom of Ben Sira: a New Translation with Notes, Introduction and Commentary* (AB 39; Garden City, N.Y.: Doubleday, 1987), 558; "... according to [2 Kgs 17:24–34] the Samaritans were not related to the Israelites, but were people brought to Samaria by the Assyrians in the eighth century B.C.E.[...] In the Talmud they are indeed named 'Kutim', that is, men from Kutah, a region in Assyria (cf. 2 Kgs 17:24)." E. Tov, *Textual Criticism of the Hebrew Bible* (2. rev. ed., Minneapolis, Minn.: Fortress, 2001), 82 f.; "The Samaritans were a 'mixed race' contaminated by foreign blood and false worship." *The Hodder and Stoughton Illustrated Bible Dictionary* (Nashville: Nelson; Dunton Green: Hodder and Stoughton, 1986), s.v. "Samaritans"; and "... dem Charakter des Volkes ... Aus der Vermischung assyrisch-babylonischer, medisch-persischer, syrisch-phönikischer und israelitischer Bestandtheile

Josephus adds to this account a narrative about a priest who was forced to leave Jerusalem and move to Samaria because of his exogamous marriage. In this involuntary exodus he was followed by other Jerusalemites who were in a similar situation in regard to their marriages. This migration to Samaria led to the building of the temple on Mount Gerizim at the time of Alexander the Great, and thus provided the "Chouthaioi" with their sanctuary, *Ant.* 11.302 f., 306–312. This description of events would explain the existence of the temple and provide a rationale for connections between the Samaritans and the population in Jerusalem. It is perhaps less generally known than the former account, but scholars often refer to it.

To these reports from Josephus one may add the Samaritans' own story of their origin. It is found in the Samaritan chronicles *Kitab al-Tarikh* and the *Arabic Book of Joshua*. These documents were created in the late Middle Ages, in 1355 and 1362/3 respectively, and they provide us with an origin story which assumes that the Samaritans represent the true Israel from the time of Jacob, whereas the Jews split off from this true Israel by following the aberrant priest Eli. This version of their origin is standard among the Samaritans themselves, and a limited number of scholars have relied on the main elements in this story in the quest for their origin.

On the one hand, therefore, we are provided with several narratives about the origin of the Samaritans. These narratives could be a natural point to start a search for their origin. One might take one or more of these stories, adjust for possible unhistorical idiosyncrasies, and locate the result in a larger historical framework. In chapter 3 I will survey some attempts made in this direction. On the other hand, these stories might complicate the matter, as they cannot at the outset be acquitted of the suspicion of having their own agenda and therefore blur the question.

---

hervorgegangen, liebäugeln sie bald mit Juden, bald mit Heiden, rühmen sich bald hebräischer (Jos. Ant. XI 8, 6), bald phönikischer Abkunft (das. XII 5, 5); üben gewisse Vorschriften des mosaischen Gesetztes strenger als selbst das jüdische Volk (Berach. 47b; Chulin 4a) und weihen ihren Tempel dem Ζεὺς ξένιος (2 MB 6,2; Jos. Ant. XII 5, 5); verehren den Einen Gott Israel's und sind es, aus deren Mitte der heidnische, jüdische und christliche Lehren durcheinander werfende Simon Magus und sein Anhang hervorging." J. Freudenthal, "Hellenistische Studien: Heft I: Alexander Polyhistor und die von ihm erhaltenen Reste jüdischer und samaritanischer Geschichtswerke," *Jahresbericht des jüdisch-theologischen Seminars "Fraenkel'scher Stiftung"* (Breslau: Grass, 1874), 96.

The version presented by Josephus in *Ant.* 9, for example, carries strong similarities to 2 Kgs 17. It therefore either depends on the reliability of that story as regards the origin of the Samaritans, or—if it used 2 Kgs 17 as a literary model only—it must be trusted on its own merit. In chapter 4 of the present book it is argued that the description presented by Josephus suffers from the taint of contemporary polemics against the Samaritans, and therefore cannot be taken at face value. In addition to this, 2 Kgs 17 could be polemical in its various layers, and its polemics may have been directed against opponents belonging to the various times of composition.

The core of Josephus' story in *Ant.* 11 reminds the reader of the brief autobiographical remark made by Nehemiah according to Neh 13:28, only Josephus is speaking of an event taking place in the century following Nehemiah, the century of Alexander the Great. *Ant.* 11 presupposes the story of the deported "Chouthaioi" in *Ant.* 9, and its value for tracing the origin of the Samaritan temple seems to be dependent upon the reliability of that earlier story and the reliability of Neh 13:28. If read as historical information built upon Neh 13:28 it poses in addition the problem of being relocated to a different century. Again, if Josephus only used Neh 13:28 as a literary inspiration for his own narrative, we have to evaluate him on his own premises, and his polemical slant must be taken into account. The material presented by Josephus contains several conundrums, and a separate chapter, chapter 4, is dedicated to these questions.

If we turn to the Samaritan story of their own origins, it purportedly takes place at the time of the judges in Israel. The historicity both of the Books of Samuel and of the Samaritan chronicles is at issue here and these questions are not easily dealt with. In chapter 2 it will be argued that the story was created in self-defence. The author seems to have taken one of the stories of Josephus—*Ant.* 11 could be the material used—turned it on its head, slightly changed the plot, and directed the resultant story against the Jews. The suggestion made in that chapter is that this version is more relevant for the time of its composition than for an earlier period, in particular for the origin of the Samaritans or the Jews. It seems to be aimed at strengthening the home morale and weakening that of the adversaries, but not at finding historically reliable information. Still, it has attracted the attention of scholars, and gained the approval of some of them, as described in chapter 3.

The material most apparently relevant for investigating the origin of the Samaritans, found in the origin stories, on first inspection reveals itself as a web of related texts, all of them polemical, and none of them intended to represent unbiased historical information. The kind of material for which a modern investigator would look is not prominent in these expositions.

The Samaritans owe their fame in the Christian world to the NT. The NT is another ancient source with information on them, and the scholar might turn in this direction to find help. The "Samaritai" are mentioned several times there, most notably in Matt 10, Luke 9, 10, 17, Acts 8, and John 4, but these texts have no information on their origin or background. The attitude towards them varies in these texts, but on the whole they are seen as a contemporary phenomenon, the origin of which is not further explained or explored.

The Mishnah mentions the Samaritans several times under the name "Kuthim," and this name seems to reveal that the origin was supposed to be as narrated by Josephus in *Ant.* 9, where the "Chouthaioi" are described. The Mishnah is concerned with the relationship between Jews and Samaritans in terms of *halakhah*, and their origin is not discussed or drawn into the *halakhic* deliberations, only—perhaps—presupposed. Their supposed background did not hinder every contact with them, but occasioned a precise ruling for different cases of ritual contact between Jews and Samaritans. Josephus' possible influence on the Mishnah in this respect is a topic in chapter 2.

If the origin stories confront us with a network of polemical texts, dependent upon each other, the material in the NT and in the Mishnah presents no extra information on origins. Further, there is no foundation document for the Samaritans; and no specific event resulting in their formation is recorded apart from the three origin stories in Josephus and the Samaritan chronicles. The question of their origin seems hampered at the outset by possibly biased accounts and by a lack of independent sources. Scholars must therefore consider other tools for tracing it.

One might for instance think that the name "Samaritans" would lead us to the origin.[2] "Samaritan" as a term comes from the Greek noun or adjective Σαμαρίτης, in the feminine Σαμαρῖτις, whose oldest occurrence is the Septuagint translation οἱ Σαμαρῖται of the Hebrew term

---

[2] For an overview of the relevant material, see J. Zsengellér, "Kutim or *Samarites*: A History of the Designation of the Samaritans," in *Proceedings of the Fifth International Congress of the Société d'Études Samaritaines, Helsinki, August 1–4, 2000* (ed. H. Shehadeh & H. Tawa; Paris: Paul Geuthner, 2005), 87–104.

השמרנים, 2 Kgs 17:29. Both the Hebrew term and the Greek word are *hapax legomena* in the HB/OT. In the LXX, Σαμαρῖτις is used in 1 Macc 10:30; 11:28.34 in the sense "the area of Samaria," as this area was conceived in the second century B.C.E. As a translation for the city and region of Samaria in earlier periods (שׁמרון), the LXX uses Σαμάρεια. Josephus uses Σαμαρεῖται, but also Σαμαρεῖς (from Σαμαρεύς), in such a way that both may refer to the Samaritans, as we will see in chapter 4. As already mentioned, he also uses Χουθαῖοι, "Chouthaioi," and we will meet other designations in the chapter on Josephus. The NT uses Σαμαρῖται only, and we encounter it especially in the Lukan and Johannine literature, and then as a name for a people or a community.[3] It appears together with the name for the region Samaria, for which the NT employs the most common term in the LXX, Σαμάρεια.[4] A preliminary conclusion from this material would be that there are no obviously relevant terms until the time of Josephus and the NT. Before that, the HB and the LXX designate as השמרנים or οἱ Σαμαρῖται the inhabitants of the region of Samaria; no more specific group is referred to by these names. The region or city of Samaria is referred to by the names שׁמרון and Σαμάρεια or Σαμαρῖτις.

The fact that a name for a people or a community is related to the name of a region would on first observation seem unproblematic, but modern scholarship has made this more complicated. Today's scholarly literature makes a distinction between "Samaritans" as a religious group on the one hand, and the region "Samaria," whose inhabitants are called "Samarians," on the other. But this prompts the question, who are the Σαμαρ(ε)ίται in the ancient sources? According to John 4 Jesus arrives in Σαμάρεια and meets a Σαμαρῖτις. Is she a "Samarian" or a "Samaritan"?

This question of names is addressed by R. Pummer in his *Early Christian Authors on Samaritans and Samaritanism* (2002):

> In the past, the term "Samaritan" was used indiscriminately for all inhabitants of the region of Samaria. Gradually the problematic nature of such usage became clear, and now terminological and substantive distinctions are made between "Samaritans" on the one hand and "Samarians" on the other. The first term signifies members of that religio-ethnic group that has its roots in Judaism, but split off from the latter, rejected the temple of Jerusalem and regarded its own temple on Mount Gerizim as the only legitimate sanctuary; eventually, they became an independent religion. The Samaritan Bible consists of the Pentateuch only, and rabbinic

---

[3] Luke 9:52; 10:33; 17:16; Acts 8:25; John 4:9, 39 f.; 8:48. A single extra occurrence at Matt 10:5 brings the total number of NT occurrences to nine.

[4] Luke 17:11; Acts 1:8; 8:1,5,9,14; 9:31; 15:3; John 4:4 f.,7.

writings are not part of the Samaritan tradition. Research during the last three to four decades has shown that the split between Judaism and Samaritanism occurred gradually. In this process, the destruction of the temple on Mt. Gerizim by John Hyrcanus in 111 B.C.E. must have been a momentous event, even if it was not the end of the mutual relationships between the two branches of the biblical religion(s). The textual form of the Samaritan Pentateuch is proof that Samaritanism and Judaism developed along different lines out of their common heritage, beginning in the Hellenistic-Roman period. A comparison with the biblical texts found in Qumran shows that the version used by the Samaritans was one among the various text-forms that were current among Jews around the turn of the era.

The term "Samarians" applies, in principle, to all inhabitants of the district of Samaria, not only to Samaritans in the narrow sense, but also to the Jewish, the "pagan" and the Christian population of Samaria. In practice, "Samarians" is used for Jewish and "pagan" inhabitants of Samaria. The ancient sources, of course, do not make such clear terminological distinctions. Thus, the Greek term Σαμαρεῖς may refer to Samaritans or to Samarians. The same is true of other terms, either Greek or Latin, such as Σαμαρεῖται and *Samaritae*. It has to be decided on a case by case examination which of the two—Samarians or Samaritans—is intended by a given author. This work is concerned only with "Samaritans" in the sense of the religio-ethnic group described above, and not with "Samarians."[5]

From the same year comes the discussion by R. T. Anderson and T. Giles on the designations:

> The origin and early history of the Samaritan sect are problematic in almost every respect. Trouble begins with the designation of the group as "Samaritans." This term now means a well-defined and self-conscious religious sect employing a version of the Pentateuch called the Samaritan Pentateuch as its sacred text and honoring Mount Gerizim as the proper place of worship ... In some texts, including the Old Testament, the meaning of the term "Samaritan" is not clear ... Consequently, we cannot assume that every mention of "Samaritans" taken from an ancient text refers to the religious sect ... Very likely, the designation "Samaritan" has had a long history of referents and only gradually became identified with a religious sect based in Samaria."[6]

---

[5] R. Pummer, *Early Christian Authors on Samaritans and Samaritanism: Texts, Translations, and Commentary* (TSAJ 92; Tübingen: Mohr Siebeck, 2002), 1 f., footnotes omitted. Similarly, idem, "The Samaritans and their Pentateuch," in *The Pentateuch as Torah: New Models for Understanding Its Promulgation and Acceptance* (ed. G. Knoppers and B. M. Levinson; Winona Lake, Ind.: Eisenbrauns, 2007), 251.

[6] R. T. Anderson and T. Giles, *The Keepers: An Introduction to the History and Culture of the Samaritans* (Peabody, Mass.: Hendrikson, 2002), 9.

In line with modern scholarly parlance we should distinguish between a proto-history of the Samaritans and the Samaritan sect.

> The movement from proto-history to history, that is, the formation of the Samaritan sect, will be identified when three criteria are met: (1) a self-awareness as a religious sect, (2) the use of the Samaritan Pentateuch as the holy text, and (3) the preference for Mount Gerizim as the proper place of worship.[7]

To come to terms with the material, scholarship sometimes looks for "pre-" or "proto-Samaritans" at an earlier stage in history, and for "Samaritans" at a later stage. These are seen as distinct from the other inhabitants of Samaria, the "pagan" and Christian Samarians.

Scholars find such a distinction between pre- or proto-Samaritans and Samaritans helpful, and to accord well with what one might expect: a development from earlier to later.[8] The pre- or proto-Samaritans were people living at the time of Ezra and Nehemiah, carrying on Yahwistic traditions from an earlier age. The assumption behind this distinction is a teleological understanding of history. The pre- or proto-Samaritans ended up as Samaritans, and wherever we find early elements of Samaritanism, there must be pre- or proto-Samaritans. To use "Samaritan" in combination with "pre-", "proto-" or other elements is suggestive of a somewhat linear development in one specific direction.

Similarly, R. Egger in her study of the terminology in Josephus defines the "Samaritans" as *die Samaritanische Religionsgemeinschaft*, "the Samaritan religious community," a group believing in YHWH, regarding Mount Gerizim as the chosen place, sacrificing to YHWH in the temple there, and regarding the Pentateuch only as holy scripture.[9] Only a few texts in Josephus provide information on this group.

A. D. Crown introduces some of the various expressions possibly used for Samaritans in the ancient sources, of which "Israelites" in the Delos inscriptions and "Ephraim" in 4Q169 in his view do refer to the Samaritans—in the last case against the common understanding of "Ephraim" as a sobriquet for the Pharisees.[10] Only one of the expressions *Samareis*, *Samareitai, Chutaioi* and "Sidionians," found in Josephus, the rabbinic literature and 4Q550, is used for the Samaritans: *Samareitai*.[11]

---

[7] Ibid., 9 f.

[8] F. Dexinger, "Samaritaner," *TRE* 29 (1998): 750–756.

[9] R. Egger, *Josephus Flavius und die Samaritaner: eine terminologische Untersuchung zur Identitätsklärung der Samaritaner* (NTOA 4; Freiburg: Universitätsverlag, 1986), 20.

[10] S. L. Berrin, "Pesher Nahum," *EDSS* 2: 653–655.

[11] A. D. Crown, "Samaritans," *EDSS* 2: 817 f.

These four examples from recent scholarly literature may serve to show the current usage even if not all scholars adhere to such precise language. The definition of the "Samaritans" is reached through a summary of recent research on them, and involves more than a regional name converted into the group's name. First, there is the combination of religion and ethnicity: a "religio-ethnic group" (R. Pummer as quoted above). Secondly, scholarly theories are represented in the notion that the Samaritans actively split off from the Jewish religion, especially by rejecting the Jerusalem temple and by considering the Gerizim sanctuary as the only legitimate one. On the other hand, John Hyrcanus was also an active agent through his campaign against the temple on Mount Gerizim—"a momentous event" according to R. Pummer, who dates it to 111 B.C.E. In addition to these two active agents, there was a development and a process: the "split ... occurred gradually. In this process ..." (R. Pummer). A. D. Crown also seems to use a modern understanding of the Samaritans as the criterion for evaluating the ancient usage.

A modern, scholarly based understanding of Samaritanism is what Anderson and Giles are looking for in antiquity. At the moment when this understanding is discernible, we have the Samaritans. Apparently, the name is no clue to this phenomenon, since Anderson and Giles mention other possible ancient referents for "Samaritans": "residents of Samaria" and "people with a political bent in competition with the political authorities in Jerusalem (rather than to an identifiable religious sect)."[12] Anderson offers another definition of "Samaritans" in *ABD*: "The people who dwelt in Samaria, particularly in the tribal regions of Manasseh and Ephraim, and who have maintained a unique identity to the present. Subsequently the form of Israelite religion that developed in the area centred around Mount Gerizim."[13] Here, the term "Samaritans" in an older age refers to the "Samarians" in R. Pummer's usage, and to the "Samaritans" in a later period. Anderson cautions though that

> The Samaritans are not easily brought into sharp focus. Sources are often contradictory, sketchy, or nonexistent. It is problematic how distinct the Samaritans are from the Jews of different periods, what constitutes the basic distinguishing focus, or how much interaction existed between the Samaritans and other sects based on the Mosaic Pentateuch. The geo-

---

[12] Anderson and Giles, *Keepers*, 9.
[13] R. T. Anderson, "Samaritans," *ABD* 5: 940.

graphic origin of the people called Samaritans has been seen in Mesopotamia and both N and S Palestine, raising the question whether their basic characterization is geographical, ethnic, or doctrinal.[14]

It is understandable that scholars define their technical terms, but what is striking about these definitions is how much is built into them: a summary of recent research defines the two names "Samaritan" and "Samarian." It is clear that these definitions cannot be a tool for finding the origin of the Samaritans. That would be a circular investigation based upon modern, and therefore anachronistic, criteria. The danger is that modern distinctions used by scholars are read into the sources. It will be argued in chapter 4 that the study by R. Egger demonstrates the problematic nature of such an approach. Modern definitions are necessary in order to make clear what we are discussing, but may represent an impasse for us in finding the origin of the Samaritans. Or, perhaps more adequately, these definitions and terminological discussions may serve as a warning against using the terms as a lead in the investigation. In view of the scarcity of old cases of the terms, the discussions may even seem exaggerated. Josephus' works necessitate such a discussion, but the earlier material offers a limited number of texts with the relevant terms.

Another problem with the definitions is succinctly described by R. Pummer, as quoted above: "The ancient sources, of course, do not make such clear terminological distinctions ... It has to be decided on a case by case examination which of the two—Samarians or Samaritans—is intended by a given author." One would then need an independent, ancient source to ascertain the validity of the interpretation, but it is hard to find such a source.

J. Zsengellér has reviewed the names used for the Samaritans in the early sources, and conjectures that the name "Kuthim" was first used in an interpretation of 2 Kgs 17:29 in connection with the Roman conquest of Palestine and Herod's rebuilding of Samaria.[15] He finds it surprising that the corresponding Greek designation was not used in the Greek sources of the first century C.E., but rather "Samaritai." Another, and simpler, explanation is that the use of "Kuthim" was initiated at the time of Josephus, who in fact is the earliest author to employ this term.

This survey of the earliest testimony for the name "Samaritan" and of the modern understanding of it reveals that one cannot follow the name

---

[14] Ibid., 941.
[15] Zsengellér, "Kutim or *Samarites*," 87–104.

backwards to its earliest use and find the beginning of Samaritanism in
this way. When we encounter the terms "Samaritans" and "Chouthaioi,"
the group referred to already existed, and may have had a history prior
to the texts that mention them. The Samaritans may well have existed
for some time under other names or without a fixed nomenclature. One
should probably look for a phenomenon which does not present itself
under a certain name. When we come, in chapter 5, to discussing some
of the material older than the turn of the era, this possibility will be kept
in mind.

In this book the term "Samaritans" is used in a broad way without
any precise definition. I have not attempted to distinguish between pre-
or proto-Samaritans on the one hand and Samaritans on the other, nor
to distinguish between "Samarians" and "Samaritans." Instead, "Samaritans" is used for the group described by Josephus, for the group attacked
in the second century B.C.E. texts, and for the group emerging in an earlier
period. This loose usage will, perhaps, annoy some readers or bring criticism upon the author. The reason for this choice is to take the evidence
into account without having to refer to some definition of the term, a definition which would have to differ according to the diverse evidence. As
the understanding of the situation in each period is what we are searching
for, it seems better to use the term in the general sense which readers will
apply to it than to start with definitions and have to constantly modify
them according to the evidence. Only one criterion will be used for finding the Samaritans: the temple on Mount Gerizim. From the moment
this was erected, we have the Samaritans; before that we may have the
same population, but without the distinguishing mark of the Samaritans.
Therefore, no attempt is made here to trace the origin of this population,
and the following discussion will clarify why I think such an attempt is
futile.

A notion which often occurs in connection with the groups existing
around the turn of the era in Palestine is referred to by words like
"race" and "ethnicity." R. Pummer defines the "Samaritans" as a "religio-
ethnic group" in the passages quoted above and we saw that R. Anderson
mentions that "The geographic origin of the people called Samaritans
has been seen in Mesopotamia and both N and S Palestine, raising the
question whether their basic characterization is geographical, ethnic, or
doctrinal."

When F. Dexinger surveyed the research in 1991, he organized the different opinions around this question: How did the Samaritans acquire

their Jewish-monotheistic religion, yet are not Jews?[16] He finds three different possibilities for their origin—he uses the expression "ethnicity" in this connection—they may have been pagan colonists, northern Israelites, or dissidents from the south. He then combines these possible backgrounds with five possibilities for religious influence: from northern Israelites, from pagan colonists, from southern dissidents, from the repatriated priest, or from Judeans; and a sixth possibility is that they were without any influence. There are then twelve possible answers to the question raised.

Perhaps these scholars—and others—are on the right track in considering the Samaritans a separate race or an ethnic group?

Such a procedure might seem warranted on the showing of the ancient documents, which mention "race" or "ethnos." We have seen that Josephus speaks of mixed marriages between Jerusalemites and Northerners. Ethnicity seems to be referred to in the Talmudic tractate *Masseket Kuthim*, when the question of mixed marriages and *mamzerot* is raised in connection with the Samaritans.

But the researcher soon learns to avoid following leads such as expressions in ancient documents. In chapter 5 I will discuss the poem attributed to Theodotus, in which it is stated that circumcision was the criterion for belonging to the Hebrew race (γενεά, fragment 4). This gives an impression of how different their thinking was from ours, and shows how difficult it is to use the ancient terms. If ethnicity was based on phenomena like circumcision we have to be careful in approaching the words in question. In addition, it may be that the ancient understanding of the relevant terms was broader than ours, and more imprecise, and they may have been terms that played a part in polemics rather than in neutral description.

If "ethnicity" in antiquity was indeed understood on the basis of religious affiliation, it would be nearer to some modern popular views than to a precise scholarly definition of ethnicity which takes into account several factors. On the other hand, these expressions may be considered as one type of ancient polemics, polemics that can help us understand some of the thinking and the development. The contents of the polemics cannot form the basis of any modern (e.g. biological) investigation.

---

[16] "Wie sind die Samaritaner zu ihrer jüdisch-monotheistischen Religion gekommen und sind trotzdem keine Juden?" F. Dexinger, "Der Ursprung der Samaritaner im Spiegel der frühen Quellen," in *Die Samaritaner* (ed. F. Dexinger and R. Pummer; WdF 604; Darmstadt: Wissenschaftliche Buchgesellschaft, 1992), 69.

Understanding the mechanism of polemics is different from believing in
its surface sense and using it as a lead in the work. Chapter 5 will investigate some texts concerned with exogamous marriages and "ethnic" affiliation, not as part of a modern approach to ethnicity, but as a window
into polemics, revealing the contemporary scene. R. Pummer's expression "religio-ethnic group" might be close to such an ancient understanding where religion plays a major role in the understanding of ethnicity
and in the polemics of the time. A modern scholar should respect the
view of the insiders and not press modern concepts upon the material.[17]

This said, modern science may produce tools to tackle this question on
the basis of genetics. Historical genetics is a growing field in science, and
one may expect reliable results to come from it. At the moment, however,
there are no such studies on the Samaritans, and to pursue the question
of ethnicity from this angle is therefore not possible at the moment.

The twentieth century saw an abuse of the term "race" that has led
to a decline in its use in the social sciences. In a parallel development,
the term "ethnicity" seems to be favoured by scholars. F. Barth speaks of
ethnic groups and boundaries and of the social organization of cultural
differences.[18] This approach takes up an important point in the ancient
understanding: the relation between different entities. This relational
aspect is taken into account by S. Jones, inspired by T. Hylland Eriksen:

> In what follows, a similar processual and relational approach to the def-
> inition of ethnicity is adopted. *Ethnic groups are culturally ascribed iden-*
> *tity groups, which are based on the expression of a real or assumed shared*
> *culture and common descent* (usually through the objectification of cul-
> tural, linguistic, religious, historical and/or physical characteristics.). As
> *process* ethnicity involves a consciousness of difference, which to varying
> degrees, entails the reproduction and transformation of basic classifica-
> tory distinctions between groups of people who perceive themselves to be
> in some respect culturally distinct (Eriksen 1992: 3). The cultural differ-
> ences informing ethnic categories are, to varying degrees, systematic and
> enduring, because they both inform modes of interaction between peo-
> ple of different ethnic categories, and are confirmed by that interaction;
> that is, ethnic categories are reproduced and transformed in the ongoing
> processes of social life.[19]

---

[17] T. N. Headland et al., eds., *Emics and Etics: the Insider/Outsider Debate* (Frontiers
of anthropology 7; Newbury Park, Cal.: Sage), 1990.

[18] F. Barth, *Ethnic Groups and Boundaries: The Social Organization of Culture Differ-*
ence (Bergen etc.: Universitetsforlaget, 1969).

[19] S. Jones, *The Archaeology of Ethnicity: Constructing Identities in the Past and Present*
(London and New York: Routledge, 1997), 84, with reference to T. Hylland Eriksen, *Us*

The consequence for archaeology is that,

> If archaeologists persist in assuming that there is only one ethnic meaning
> or association to be 'extracted' from a particular monument or a particular
> style of material culture then they will never be able to understand the
> multiple strands of practice involved in the reproduction and maintenance
> of ethnicity in the past.[20]

The shift in social sciences from essentialist understandings of "race" and
"ethnicity" to a culturally based, relational approach is to be welcomed
from our point of view: the origin of the Samaritans cannot be sought in
groups understood in essentialist terms. It is difficult to use Dexinger's
taxonomy, if understood in essentialist terms. The ancient understandings of "ethnos" or similar expressions cannot be followed as leads in our
search for the groups we are looking for in modern research. Also, they
do not provide us with all the relevant material for a relational approach,
either. Not every aspect of the modern understanding of "ethnicity" can
be investigated, as the necessary material from the Samaritan group itself
at an early stage is not available to us. But there is material for understanding the friction between groups, and thus we may sense the social
boundaries of the time. Chapter 5 will look at some texts from the second
century B.C.E. where the presence of such boundaries is felt. The understanding of F. Barth, T. Hylland Eriksen, and S. Jones referred to here
may be helpful also in an investigation of the ancient sources, although
we cannot use individual terms as our lead.

Archaeology is also in focus in much modern study of the period
before the turn of the era, and the warning from S. Jones will be kept
in mind as we survey the relevant excavations in Samaria in chapter 6.
Fortunately, some inscriptions have turned up during the excavations on
Mount Gerizim, and these will be brought into the discussion. Archaeology does not provide us with simple truths, any more than texts do, but
we will have to see what information can be gleaned from these types of
evidence, and if and how it can help to draw a picture of the historical
development.

It is often said that the European cognizance of the Samaritans started
in 1616 when Pietro della Valle bought a copy of the SP and one of

---

*and Them in Modern Societies: Ethnicity and Nationalism in Mauritius, Trinidad and
Beyond* (Oslo: Scandinavian University Press, 1992).
    [20] Jones, *Archaeology of Ethnicity*, 141.

the Samaritan Targum in Damascus and brought them to Europe.[21] But it probably started in 1537 with G. Postel.[22] Since 1616, however, the study of the Samaritan Pentateuch has been part and parcel of textual criticism of the HB. This approach was boosted when manuscripts from Qumran with a text reminiscent of the SP were found and published around the middle of the twentieth century. The study of these proto- or rather pre-Samaritan texts is still going on, and chapter 7 is devoted to this topic. It is surmised that the major differences between the Masoretic and the Samaritan text are a clue to early Samaritan theology, or even pre-Samaritan theology.

The focus on the Pentateuch among the Samaritans has its counterpart in the lack of interest in prophets, at least in the early days of the group's existence.[23] The attitude to prophets has been difficult to assess, due to the lack of early evidence, but a text from Qumran may reveal that there was a discussion about false and true prophets before the turn of the era. It contains a list of false prophets, one of whom, Zedekiah, is also found in the oldest part of the *Ascension of Isaiah*. This latter text is often thought to contain an early Jewish nucleus, around which the later Christian version of the *Ascension of Isaiah* was spun, and in this Jewish legend the false prophet from Samaria appears, a follower of Zedekiah. Chapter 8 explores this material and makes suggestions on the early Samaritan attitude towards the biblical prophets.

When H. G. Kippenberg wrote his important study on the Samaritan traditions in 1971 he noted that the Samaritans during the preceding years had dropped below the level of awareness for theologians and historians of religion.[24] Not so any more: in the meantime there have appeared many studies of the Samaritans and this community is regularly

---

[21] Text and translation of della Valle's report on the purchase in M. Gaster, *The Samaritans: Their History, Doctrines and Literature* (Schweich Lectures on Biblical Archaeology 1923; München: Kraus Reprint, 1980), appendix.

[22] T. Harviainen and H. Shehadeh "How did Abraham Firkovich acquire the great collection of Samaritan manuscripts in Nablus in 1864?" *StudOr* 73 (1994): 167–192.

[23] M. Kartveit, "Die älteste samaritanische Kanonauffassung," in *"Und das Leben ist siegreich!" "And Life is Victorious!" Mandäische und samaritanische Literatur / Mandaean and Samaritan Literatures: Im Gedenken an Rudolph Macuch / In Memory of Rudolph Macuch (1919–1993)* (ed. R. Voigt; Mandäistische Forschungen 1; Wiesbaden: Harrassowitz, 2008), 219–226.

[24] H. G. Kippenberg, *Garizim und Synagoge: Traditionsgeschichtliche Untersuchungen zur samaritanischen Religion der aramäischen Periode* (RVV 30; Berlin, New York: Walter de Gruyter, 1971), 1.

taken into account in general publications on antiquity. One of the factors behind this development is the formation of the Société d'Études Samaritaines (SES) in Paris in 1985. Through congresses in 1988, 1990, 1992, 1996, 2000, 2004 and 2008 and many publications the members of this society have contributed substantially to the development of the field—together with many other scholars. The time is now ripe for a new assessment of the available material. The approach adopted in this book is to venture into some uncharted territory where there is a chance of making new finds. But first it is necessary to evaluate the methods often used for finding the origin of the Samaritans. Traditional views are influenced by Josephus to such an extent that we may not be aware of it any more. The following two chapters will make this influence visible.

CHAPTER TWO

THE LEGACY FROM JOSEPHUS

The works of Josephus have been a great source of information on the Samaritans, ever since they were created. Even today—with an increased amount of material—Josephus constitutes a most valuable source from antiquity on this question. He refers to the Samaritans as he deems it appropriate throughout his account of history, and, taken together, this is a wealth of material. It will be considered in a separate chapter, and where it is needed in other chapters. In this chapter the focus is on the legacy from him. He has influenced the image of the Samaritans in several ways, even their own image of themselves.

2.1. *Josephus' Version of the Origin of the Samaritans*

Josephus does not comment upon the origin of the Samaritans in the *Jewish War*, but the classic description of their origin is found in the *Antiquities*. The following story has influenced the understanding of this question until our own time, directly and indirectly.

> He [Salmanasser] utterly exterminated the leadership of the Israelites, and transported the entire people to Media and Persia, among them also King Osees [Hoshea] whom he took alive. Moving other nations from a certain river called the Chouthas—for there is a river in the country of the Persians bearing this name—he settled them in Samareia and the country of the Israelites.[1]   (*Ant.* 9.278 f.)

Compared to the corresponding description in the HB (2 Kgs 17), a novelty here is the assertion that the leadership of Samaria was exterminated and the land emptied of its inhabitants and completely resettled by a foreign population. In the HB there are indications of such an understanding of the situation, but it does not specify that the leadership was exterminated and that "the entire population" was deported. These are notions

---

[1] Translated by C. T. Begg and P. Spilsbury, *Flavius Josephus: Judean Antiquities Books 8–10* (vol. 5 of *Flavius Josephus: Translation and Commentary*; Leiden: Brill 2005), 200. Explanations in brackets are added.

that developed after the HB, perhaps because Josephus wanted to create
parallel accounts of the destruction of Jerusalem, as in 2 Kgs. 25:18–21,
and that of Samaria.[2] Out of the five locations of origin for the deportees
in 2 Kgs. 17:24 Josephus singles out Choutas, corresponding to the name
for the Samaritans used by the Mishnah. A little later in the same context,
Josephus elaborates on the topic:

> Now those who were settled in Samareia were the "Chouthaioi" (Χου-
> θαῖοι), for they are called by this name until today because they were
> brought in from the country called "Chouthas"; this is Persia, where there
> is a river that has this name. Each of the nations—there were five of them—
> brought its own god to Samareia. By adoring these, as was their ancestral
> [custom], they aroused the greatest God to wrath and rage. For he inflicted
> them with a plague, by which they were afflicted. Ascertaining no cure for
> their calamities, they learned by way of an oracle that, if they worshipped
> the greatest God, this would be [a source of] safety to them. They there-
> fore dispatched messengers to the king of the Assyrians and begged him
> to send them priests from those he had taken captive when he warred
> against the Israelites. Upon his sending these and their being taught the
> ordinances and reverence for this God, they worshipped him lavishly and
> the plague immediately ceased. Even now the name "Chouthaioi" contin-
> ues to be used for these nations in the Hebrew language, whereas in Greek
> they are called "Samareitai" (Σαμαρεῖται). Whenever, by turns,[3] they see
> things going well for the Judeans, they call themselves their relatives, in
> that they are descendants of Josep [Joseph] and have family ties with them
> in virtue of that origin. When, however, they see that things are going badly
> for them [the Judeans], they say that they owe nothing to them and that
> they have no claim to their loyalty or race. Instead, they make themselves
> out to be migrants of another nation (ἔθνος). But about these matters we
> shall have to speak in a more suitable place.[4]   (*Ant.* 9.288–291)

Josephus here identifies the group as "Samaritans" (Σαμαρεῖται) in Greek
and "Chouthaioi" (Χουθαῖοι) in Hebrew. The Greek name Σαμαρεῖται
and the name of the area where they were settled, Σαμάρεια, are related.
In the same way, the name Χουθαῖοι (corresponding to the Hebrew
כותים) reminds one of the place of origin, Χουθα in Persia (correspond-

---

    [2] Ibid., n. 1084.
    [3] Πρὸς μεταβολὴν is translated in different ways. If it is taken as an expression of the
Samaritans' behaviour, the translation may be "Adapting their behaviour;" if it describes
the circumstances, it will be as R. Hanhart's translation "je nach der Lage," R. Hanhart,
"Zu den ältesten Traditionen über das samaritanische Schisma," *ErIsr* 16 (1982): 106*-
115*. C. T. Begg and P. Spilsbury connect the expression "even now" (ἔτι καὶ νῦν) to the
names, and the expression πρὸς μεταβολὴν is connected to the following sentence.
    [4] Translated by Begg and Spilsbury, *Judean Antiquities Books 8–10*, 202 f. Greek words
in brackets are added. Compare the different translation provided in chapter 4, p. 82.

ing to כותה in Hebrew). Even if he calls the Samaritans "Chouthaioi," here, as in 9.278 f., he knows of the five nations mentioned in 2 Kgs 17:24.

This story has been taken to describe the origin of the Samaritans, and it is perhaps necessary to note some allegations Josephus does not make, as he is often understood to say more than he does. He does not say that they were syncretists. He is not clear on the question whether they gave up their own religions and worshipped the greatest God only, and he also does not specify whether they kept their old religions along with the new one, but he does not make any explicit allegation of syncretism. Further, there is no indication here of their being a mixed race. But he mentions that they sometimes called themselves foreigners, from another race (ἔθνος). This story of Josephus cannot be taken as a witness in favour of the allegations of syncretism and racial impurity made again and again.

In the Mishnah, the designation "Kuthim" is the only name used for the Samaritans, possibly a legacy from Josephus, as no earlier sources use this designation for them. Another possibility is that this designation was in use at the time of Josephus, and he took over the expression. In the Mishnah this designation was used because it had simply become common parlance, examples of which are found in *m. Ber.* 7:1; 8:8; *m. Demai* 3:4; 5:9; 6:1; 7:4. A more general statement is found in the Talmudic tractate *Masseket Kuthim*, where we read the following:

> Why are the Kuthim prohibited from participating in [the congregation of] Israel? Because they are mixed (ערב II, Hitp.) with the priests for the sacrificial places (במות). Rabbi Ishmael said: in the beginning they were real converts (גרי צדק). Why are they [then] forbidden? Because of the *mamzerot* and because they do not observe the levirate marriage.[5]

The stringency of this dictum on the question of Samaritan participation in the Jewish community rests on the assumption that the Samaritans were mixed with "the priests for the sacrificial places." If the name "Kuthim" indicates that the tractate considered the Samaritans to be descended from the deported peoples mentioned in 2 Kgs 17 as interpreted by Josephus, the novelty here is the idea that the deportees intermarried with the priests of the "high places." This latter expression is similar to כהני במות in 2 Kgs 17:32, and corresponds to the use of במה in 4Q372 for the temple on Mount Gerizim, which was considered

---

[5] Translated from A. Cohen, *Minor Tractates Translated into English with Notes, Glossary and Indices* (vol. 29 of *Hebrew-English Edition of the Babylonian Talmud* ed. I. Epstein; London: Soncino, 1984), 122.

illegitimate. I will return to 4Q372 in chapter 5. This combination of foreigners and illegitimate priests was deemed by Rabbi Ishmael to result in
mamzerot—a logical conclusion. *Masseket Kuthim* is an early attestation
of the idea that the Samaritans were a mixed race. Rabbi Ishmael added
that the "Kuthim" were genuine converts, evidently presupposing their
foreign origin and conversion as told in 2 Kgs 17, and this is in line with
the story in *Ant.* 9.

2.2. *The Church Fathers*

Already in antiquity, Josephus influenced the understanding of the origin
of the Samaritans. Some examples of this may be found in the church
fathers. Origen (c. 185 – c. 254), *Commentarii in evangelium Johannis*
20.35.321: "... the king of the Assyrians sent them [τοὺς Σαμαρεῖς] to be
guards of the land of Israel after the captivity." Here, the name of the group
differs from that of *Ant.* 9.278 f., 288–291, but Σαμαρεῖς can be found in
a number of places in Josephus, and constitutes no surprise. The story is
evidently based on *Ant.* 9; however, the interpretation of their name as
guards of the land of Israel is new. This name plays on another name for
the group, the Hebrew equivalent to Σαμαρεῖς or Σαμαρεῖται, שמרונים,
and this Hebrew name is supposed to refer to the meaning "guard" of the
root שמר. Such an understanding of their name became popular in later
times, but it is interesting that it is found as early as Origen.

Eusebius of Caesarea (c. 260 – c. 340), *Onomasticon* 160.26–27: "Seph-
pharouem. From where the invading Assyrians colonized Samaria; and
from them (are descended) the Samaritans [οἱ Σαμαρεῖται]. Isaiah mentions it also." This explanation of the origin is also based on Josephus. It is
unclear what the reference to Isaiah has in mind, unless Eusebius thinks
of Is 36:19, where the gods of Sepharvaim seem to reside in Samaria:
"Where are the gods of Hamath and Arpad? Where are the gods of
Sepharvaim? Have they delivered Samaria out of my hand?" "Sepharvaim" is one of the five places mentioned in 2 Kgs 17:24 but not repeated
by Josephus. If Is 36:19 lies behind the remark by Eusebius, he considered
the Samaritans of his age to be idolaters.

Epiphanius of Salamis (c. 315–403) presents us with a picture with
other interesting elements. In *Haereses* (or *Panarion*) 8.8.10–11 the Samaritans are considered settlers from Assyria, but added to this is the
allegation that Ezra was the one to create the Samaritan religion: "...
They gave him (i.e., the king) one (i.e., a copy of the Law) without demur,

and with the Law also sent a priest named Ezra, a teacher of the Law, from Babylon, to instruct the Assyrian settlers in Samaria—the Cutheans [Κουθαίους] and ⟨the⟩ others—in the Law of Moses. This took place in about the thirtieth year of the captivity of Israel and Jerusalem. So Ezra and his successors taught the nation in Samaria; and those who had received the Law through Ezra, who came from Babylon, were called Samaritans (Σαμαρεῖται)." A similar picture emerges from his *Anacephalaiosis I* 9,1 9.1–3:

> Samaritanism (Σαμαρειτισμὸς) and the Samaritans (οἱ Σαμαρεῖται) who belong to it, which is derived from Judaism. The occasion for it came at the time of Nebuchadnezzar and the captivity of the Jews, before the establishment of sects among Greeks and the rise of their doctrines, but after there was a Greek religion and during the period of Judaism. Samaritans were immigrants from Assyria to Judaea and had received Moses' Pentateuch only, since the king had sent it to them from Babylon by a priest named Ezra. All their opinions are the same as the Jews', except that they detest gentiles and will not touch certain persons, and that they deny the resurrection of the dead and the other prophecies, the ones after Moses.

Similarly, we read the following in *De XII gemmis* 88.23: "... the tribe of the Samaritans were from the land of the Babylonians and of the Assyrians; they were brought in by Nebuchadnezzar and settled in the land of the Galileans and of the Palestinians, when Nebuchadnezzar led the sons of Israel into captivity."[6] Despite the assumption that the Samaritans were Assyrian settlers, the deportation into Palestine is supposed to have happened at the time of Nebuchadnezzar, and not in Assyrian times. The last text, though, makes them settlers from the land of the Babylonians and of the Assyrians. On the one hand, Epiphanius builds on 2 Kgs 17, but on the other the interpretation of this chapter as revealing the origin of the Samaritans dates to Josephus. An interesting feature here is that Samaritanism was created by Ezra and constituted a form of Judaism. This reveals an outsider's view, and it reads strangely in the light of the Samaritan negative attitude to Ezra. Epiphanius is aware of the problem with dating "Ezra who is the son of Salatiel, the son of Zorobabel" to the time of Nebuchadnezzar, and therefore states that this is "another called by this name, and this Ezra had been a priest in the land of Israel," *De XII gemmis* 188.4–7.[7] Neh 12:1 mentions an Ezra who was the contemporary of Zerubbabel, and if Epiphanius is thinking of this Ezra, it would bring

---

[6] All quotations from Pummer, *Early Christian Authors*, Origen, 74; Eusebius, 102; Epiphanius, *Anaceph.*, 146; *Haer.*, 147; *De gem.*, 178.
[7] Translation from Pummer, *Early Christian Authors*, 178.

him closer to the time of Nebuchadnezzar, but the problem is not solved. On the other hand, this story takes into account that the Samaritans also lived according to the Pentateuch. We note Epiphanius' information that the Samaritans rejected the prophets after Moses, a topic which is treated in chapter 8.

What is clear from these quotations is that the origin in Assyria (in the last text Babylonia and Assyria) was considered the important element, not the priests and laymen moving from Jerusalem. Thus, Josephus' interpretation of 2 Kgs 17 found resonance with the early church fathers, but not his story of the emigration from Jerusalem. Epiphanius locates the deportation from Assyria to the exile after the conquest of Jerusalem, and has a name for the priest coming from the East to teach the Law of Moses: Ezra. Ezra's teaching explains why the Samaritans' religion is so close to that of the Jews. Apart from this, the story is the same as in Josephus' understanding of 2 Kgs 17.

This interpretation of 2 Kgs 17 was often adopted by later authors, including modern scholars, as if it were a natural, maybe even necessary, interpretation of the text.[8] It is therefore important to keep in mind that it is a clearly datable interpretation of the text, and—perhaps—no author before the latter part of the first century C.E. explicitly presents a similar interpretation. 2 Kgs 17 in itself is clearly negative with regard to the inhabitants in Northern Israel at the time of its composition, as well as at the time of the additions and the redaction. This includes the claim that the imported population became syncretists, 2 Kgs 17:33. Josephus, perhaps surprisingly, does not repeat this claim. The several parts of 2 Kgs 17 may refer to earlier inhabitants of the area, but these do not automatically correspond with Josephus' understanding of what the Samaritans were, or even with modern theories about them.

2.3. The Samaritan Version of the Origin: The Chronicles

The Samaritans do not have to explain their origin, as they envisage themselves as descendants of the original Israel. Instead, the existence of the Jews demands explanation and this is found in the Chronicles. The background for their story seems to have been provided by Josephus.

---

[8] Examples are given in the next chapter; see also J. D. Purvis, *The Samaritan Pentateuch and the Origin of the Samaritan Sect* (HSM 2; Cambridge, Mass: Harvard University Press, 1968), 89; see however ibid., 94–96.

Background in Josephus

Josephus has more to say about the origin of the Samaritans than what the church fathers have adopted. Neh 13:28 reads, "And one of the sons of Jehoiada, son of the high priest Eliashib, was the son-in-law of Sanballat the Horonite; I chased him away from me." This short note is expanded by Josephus into a longish story about an exodus from Jerusalem by temple personnel, and relocated to the time of Alexander the Great:

> When Joannes departed this life, he was succeeded in the high priesthood by his son Jaddus. He too had a brother, named Manassēs, to whom Sanaballetēs—he had been sent to Samaria as satrap by Darius the last king, and was of the Cuthean race from whom the Samaritans also are descended ... gladly gave him his daughter, called Nikasō, in marriage ...
>
> (*Ant.* 11.302f.)

> Now the elders of Jerusalem, resenting the fact that the brother of the high priest Jaddus was sharing the high priesthood while married to a foreigner, rose up against him, for they considered this marriage to be a stepping-stone for those who might wish to transgress the laws about taking wives and that this would be the beginning of intercourse with foreigners. They believed, moreover, that their former captivity and misfortunes had been caused by some who had erred in marrying and taking wives who were not of their own country. They therefore told Manassēs either to divorce his wife or not to approach the altar. And, as the high priest shared the indignation of the people and kept his brother from the altar, Manassēs went to his father-in-law Sanaballetēs and said that while he loved his daughter Nikaso, nevertheless the priestly office was the highest in the nation and had always belonged to his family, and that therefore he did not wish to be deprived of it on her account. But Sanaballetēs promised not only to preserve the priesthood for him but also to procure for him the power and office of high priest and to appoint him governor of all the places over which he ruled, if he were willing to live with his daughter; and he said that he would build a temple similar to that in Jerusalem on Mount Garizein—this is the highest of the mountains near Samaria—, and undertook to do these things with the consent of King Darius ... But, as many priests and Israelites were involved in such marriages, great was the confusion which seized the people of Jerusalem. For all these deserted to Manassēs, and Sanaballetēs supplied them with money and with land for cultivation and assigned them places wherein to dwell, in every way seeking to win favour for his son-in-law.[9] (*Ant.* 11.306–312)

---

[9] Translated by R. Marcus, *Jewish Antiquities Books IX–XI*, (LCL 326; Cambridge, Mass.: Harvard, 1937, repr. 1995), 461–467.

It is my contention that this story provided the raw material for the Samaritan version of the origin of the Jews. Texts that are relevant for the question of origins are the *Tolidah*, the *Kitab al-Tarikh*, the *Arabic Book of Joshua*, all coming from the late Middle Ages, and some texts from the early twentieth century, of which the *New Chronicle* and *Chronicle II* may serve as examples. Without entering into the discussion on which texts may appropriately be termed "chronicles," in the following I take into consideration texts listed as "chronicles" in more recent presentations.[10] Despite the many open questions in the research on this literature, enough material is available to give an impression of the topic addressed here.

The Tolidah / Chronicle Neubauer

The oldest chronicle is the *Tolidah* ("Genealogy"). The text is known from a manuscript dated 1797 and one from 1859, and a number of later manuscripts.[11] The edition by M. Florentin in 1999 is based upon a larger number of manuscripts than the earlier editions.[12] M. Florentin supposes that the latest version of the text comprises several different parts, some composed in Hebrew, of which much is in hybrid Hebrew, and some parts in Aramaic, which together with the contents indicates that the material is very different in nature and from different times. According to the text itself, much of it was written in A.H. 747, 1346 C.E., based on an earlier text from A.H. 544, 1149 C.E. It has been updated up to the time of the latest manuscripts.[13] First published by A. Neubauer in 1869 (therefore sometimes called "*Chronicle Neubauer*") and by M. Heidenheim in 1870, it was republished in a supposed original form by J. Bowman in 1954.

---

[10] P. Stenhouse, "Samaritan Chronicles," in *The Samaritans* (ed. A. D. Crown; Tübingen: Mohr, 1989), 218–265; F. Niessen, *Eine samaritanische Version des Buches Yehošuᵃ und die Šobak-Erzählung* (Hildesheim: Olms, 2000); M. Florentin, *The Tulida: A Samaritan Chronicle: Text. Translation. Commentary* (Jerusalem: Yad Izhak Ben-Zvi, 1999).

[11] Stenhouse, "Samaritan Chronicles," 218 f.; Florentin, *Tulidah*, [17]–[30].

[12] A. Neubauer, "Chronique samaritaine suivie d'un appendice contentant de courtes notices sur quelques autres ouvrages samaritains," *JA* 14 (1869): 385–470; M. Heidenheim, "Die samaritanische Chronik des Hohenpriesters Elasar aus dem 11. Jahrhundert, übersetzt und erklärt," *Deutsche Vierteljahrsschrift für englische theologische Forschung* 4 (1870): 347–389; J. Bowman, *Transcript of the Original Text of the Samaritan Chronicle Tolidah* (Leeds: Leeds University Oriental Society, 1954); Florentin, *Tulida*.

[13] Stenhouse, "Samaritan Chronicles," 218 f.

An English translation of the first part of it was made by J. Bowman and published with a short introduction and notes in 1977.[14]

M. Florentin has investigated the language of the text, and his analysis points in the same direction as the dates given by the author. Most of it is written in a hybrid Hebrew, containing many Aramaisms and Arabisms. This language is termed by him "Hybrid Samaritan Hebrew," by Z. Ben-Hayyim "Shomronit" or "Late Samaritan Hebrew," by A. Tal "Neo-Samaritan Hebrew."[15] It was created at a time of cultural revival in the fourteenth century. The linguistic analysis must be considered a valuable tool for dating texts, though it can only provide us with the era of the text, not a precise date. To detect possible archaizing features one has to look for signs betraying the mother tongue and linguistic milieu of the author. The investigation by Florentin is an important step in this direction. A similar undertaking is the linguistic analysis by F. Niessen of a manuscript relevant in connection with the so-called *Chronicle II* (see below), namely JR(G) 1142 = Ryl. Sam. MS 259, a portion of which he has published under the siglum HS2, or "Samaritanische Chronik Nr. II, Handschrift 2."[16]

Bowman's edition of the *Tolidah* is mainly concerned with proving that the pentateuchal manuscript "Sefer Abisha" did not exist in 1149, but that in 1346 it did. The reason for this is that "Sefer Abisha" is not mentioned in the running text of the Nablus manuscript, but the story about it is presented in a marginal note to the left of the name Abishua on p. 11. Bowman published p. 11 of the Nablus manuscript as the last page of his edition. In the Bodleian manuscript, however, "Sefer Abisha" appears in the running text of the introduction to the genealogy of high priests, p. 7. If the Nablus manuscript represents the *Grundschicht* from 1149, then the "Sefer Abisha" did not exist at the time, but was created later.[17]

The main feature of the *Tolidah* is that the Samaritans were interested in a defence for their Torah, for Gerizim and Shechem, for the correct line of high priests, and for the Samaritan calendar. It is a self-defence concentrated on the calendar.

---

[14] J. Bowman, *Samaritan Documents Relating To Their History, Religion and Life: Translated and Edited by John Bowman* (Pittsburg Original Texts and Translations Series 2; Pittsburg, Penn.: Pickwick, 1977), 37–61.

[15] M. Florentin, *Late Samaritan Hebrew: A Linguistic Analysis of its Different Types* (SSLL 43; Leiden: Brill, 2005), 93.

[16] Niessen, *Eine samaritanische Version des Buches Yehošuᵃ*, linguistic analysis 19–37.

[17] Bowman, *Samaritan Documents*, photograph of the Nablus manuscript opposite 37, translation 47.

The *Tolidah* contains "a deliberate polemic against" *Jubilees* on the question of the calendar, according to R. H. Charles.[18] The direction of the criticism is clear in such expressions as ארורי שלם, "Cursed Shalem" for "Jerusalem."[19] *Jubilees* emphasizes that calendrical calculations should be made according to the 364 days' cycle, divided into twelve months of 30 days with one extra day at the beginning of each quarter of a year, totalling four extra days. This system was revealed to and first practised by Noah after the flood.[20] The *Tolidah* says that a different and correct system was revealed by God to Adam and transmitted to the patriarchs and the priest independently of the HB, and for the first time written down in the *Tolidah*. The calculation in the *Tolidah* is directly from God because it was not to be found in the Torah.[21] Its year is a lunisolar year of 354 days with twelve months of 29 or 30 days, and an intercalary month decided by the Samaritans.[22] As for "the antediluvian patriarchs, their respective ages on the birth of their eldest sons agree in both books [*Jubilees* and *Tolidah*] in every instance except in that of Seth."[23] "The genealogy of the high priests of Jerusalem in the lineage of the Zadokites in I Chronicles [5:27–41] shows an amazing similarity to the corresponding part of the *Tolidah*."[24] The simplest explanation for these facts is that the *Tolidah* reproduced and polemicized against earlier literature. Whether it reproduced or polemicized, it is dependent upon it. It constitutes a self-defence based upon HB texts, Jubilees, and, possibly, other texts.

In the *Tolidah* there is no information on the origin of the Jews, only a brief reference to the ending of the era of Divine Favour, *Rawuta*. "In the 25th year of the priesthood of Uzzi YHWH hid the holy Mishkan which Bezalel made. From Adam until YHWH hid the holy Mishkan [there were] 3055 years. And these are the names of the High Priests who

---

[18] R. H. Charles, *The book of Jubilees, or, The little Genesis* (London: Adam and Charles Black, 1902), lxxvi; cf. lxvii for the identification of the *Tolidah* as Charles' "The Samaritan Chronicle."

[19] Florentin, *Late Samaritan Hebrew*, 364, n. 17; ibid., 52, n. 25; idem, *Tulida*, 8B₁₀₉.

[20] *Jub.* 6:18–38; A. Jaubert, "The Calendar of *Jubilees*," in *The Date of the Last Supper* (transl. I. Rafferty; Staten Island, N.Y.: Alba House, 1965), 15–30.

[21] Cf. the opening sentences in Bowman, *Samaritan Documents*, 39.41.

[22] *Tolidah*, 1,7–2,1; S. Powels, "The Samaritan Calendar and the Roots of Samarian Chronology," in *The Samaritans* (ed. A. D. Crown; Leiden: Brill, 1989), 691–742.

[23] Charles, *Book of Jubilees*, lxxvi–lxxvii.

[24] J. Bowman, *The Samaritan Problem: Studies in the Relationships of Samaritanism, Judaism, and Early Christianity* (PTMS 54; Pittsburg, Penn.: Pickwick, 1975), 14.

officiated as priests after YHWH hid the Mishkan."[25] Nothing more is said about the priesthood of Uzzi, a priesthood in which later texts place the schism between Jews and Samaritans.

It is significant that the *Tolidah* does not include an account of the origin of the Jews. On the one hand, this may be due to the purpose of the text, which is to defend the Samaritan calculation of festivals and jubilees, their list of High Priests, their understanding of Moses and their Torah, against other texts, viz. the Jewish versions.[26] On the other hand, it is probable that the lack of information on the split between Samaritans and Jews stems from the fact that such an account had not yet been created in 1346 C.E. If it had existed, one would expect it to have been included in such a polemical text. Possibly, it was created very soon afterwards; it is found in the *Kitab al-Tarikh*, written in 1355.

The Kitab al-Tarikh *by Abu'l Fath*

The oldest Samaritan text about the origin of the Jews is found in Abu'l Fath's Arabic work *Kitab al-Tarikh*. The date of composition of *Tarikh* is given by the author as A.H. 756 (Introduction, p. 2) = 1355 C.E., and this date is accepted by scholars.[27] For his edition and translation P. Stenhouse used 31 manuscripts, the oldest of which is dated 1502. E. Vilmar first published the text in 1865, but the edition by P. Stenhouse now gives new access to the text.[28] This chronicle covers history from Adam to Muhammad.[29]

The background of the book is given as "the lack of any familiarity [among the Samaritans] with the affairs of past generations … [and of] any recent presentations of what took place after the death of the

---

[25] Florentin, *Tulida*, [76]; cf. Bowman, *Samaritan Documents*, 49.

[26] The list of high priests may build on Josephus, *Ant.* 5:361 f.; it is not a parallel text to Josephus, as Kippenberg thinks, Kippenberg, *Garizim und Synagoge*, 64.

[27] P. Stenhouse, "The Kitab al-Tarikh of Abu 'l-Fath" (Ph.D. diss., Sydney University, 1980); idem, *The Kitab al-Tarikh of Abu 'l-Fath Translated into English with Notes by Paul Stenhouse* (Studies in Judaica 1; Sydney: Mandelbaum Trust, 1985).

[28] E. Vilmar, *Abulfathi Annales Samaritani quos ad finem codicum manu scriptorum Berolinensium Bodleijani Parisini edidit et prolegomenis instruxit Eduardus Vilmar* (Gothae: Sumtibus Frederici Andreae Perthes, 1865).

[29] In the Bibliothèque Nationale Ms. Samaritain no. 10 there is a continuation to the Tarikh, published by M. Levy-Rubin, *The* Continuatio *of the Samaritan Chronicle of Abū l-Fath al-Sāmirī al-Danafī: Text, Translation and Annotated by Milka Levy-Rubin* (Studies in Late Antiquity and Early Islam 10; Princeton, N.J.: Darwin, 2002). She describes this text as different in character from the *Tarikh*, covering history after Muhammad. It is therefore of no relevance here.

Messenger of God. . . . vast numbers of them [the Samaritans] and their community were in scattered and dispersed circumstances; and that their Chronicles were in a similar state of disarray."[30]

The purpose of Abu'l-Fath might be understood from this, but also from the ending of the book, which focuses on the relation with the Muslims: "(T)Sarma(t)sa went to Mu(k)hammad and received treaties of peace and protection. . . . Muhammad (himself) never mistreated any of the followers of the Law . . . it was said in a tradition of the ancestors concerning Mu(k)hammad, 'Mu(k)hammad was a good and mighty person because he made a treaty of friendship with the Hebrew People.'"[31]

The author of this work gives a list of works he used and ones he did not use, and the reason for not using the Sadaqa Chronicle, cf. the Introduction; he comments upon the version of a letter he uses against a longer version he knows, but has not used, chapter 5.[32] Abu'l-Fath says that he omitted some "Greek expressions": "I have extracted the cream and cut down on such Greek expressions as I considered, on the whole, to be not worth including—as I feared the (possible) tedium—but without, however, spoiling the meaning, or embellishing it in any way,"[33] he states in the Introduction. The context of this sentence is a discussion of sources, and it would be odd to interpret it to the effect that Abu'l-Fath wanted to avoid individual words and expressions, as P. Stenhouse suggests.[34] It is more easily understood in the sense that he abbreviated his Greek sources, and did not include them verbatim. The Greek sources in question might be the NT, Josephus, and others.

J. Bowman states that "Abu'l Fath's basic source was the *Tolidah* chronicle with its priestly lists; on that ecclesiastical skeleton Abu'l Fath built his edifice."[35] Bowman also includes the (*Arabic*) *Book of Joshua*, but "Other sources used by Abu'l Fath have since disappeared."[36] It is possible to be more optimistic; large parts of the chronicle read as a paraphrase of the HB, and the use of Josephus is likely.

The origin of the Samaritan cult is to be sought in Joshua's construction of the altar and temple on Gerizim, according to the *Tarikh*:

---

[30] Stenhouse, *Kitab al-Tarikh*, 2.
[31] Ibid., 249.
[32] Ibid., 3.26.
[33] Ibid., 3.
[34] Stenhouse, "Samaritan Chronicles," 235.
[35] Bowman, *Samaritan Documents*, 115.
[36] Ibid., 115.

> It was at this time that Joshua built an altar of stones on Mount Gerizim, as Almighty God had told him (to do); and offered sacrifices upon it. Half the people stood facing Mount Gerizim, while the other half faced Mount Ebal. Joshua read out the Torah in its entirety in the hearing of all Israel, men, women, and children and of the stranger who was in their midst,[37]
>
> (Chapter 4.)

This is evidently taken from the Masoretic Josh 8:30–35, which refers in turn to Deut 27:2–8. There is evidence in two manuscripts that Deut 27:4 originally read הר גריזים, "Mount Gerizim," and this reading is preserved in the SP. "Ebal" in the MT was substituted for the original reading at a time when the cult on Gerizim was rejected by Jerusalem. I will return to this question in chapter 7. If half the people faced Gerizim and half the people faced Ebal, as we read in Josh 8:33, one might conjecture that the people must have been in Shechem, not on top of one of the mountains, and this is what *Tarikh* assumes. The renewal of the covenant took place in Shechem, Josh 24:1 ff., which in the *Tarikh* is the "plain of Nablus," chapter 8, where both Joshua and Eleazar perform covenant renewals.[38] The narrative of the origin of the cult on Mount Gerizim appears to have been built on Deut 27:4; Josh 8:30–35; 24:1 ff.

On this background, Abu'l Fath has the following version of how Samaritans and Jews became distinct groups:

> A terrible civil war broke out between Eli son of Yafnī, of the line of Ithamar, and the sons of Phinehas, because Eli son of Yafnī resolved to usurp the High Priesthood from the descendants of Phinehas. He used to offer sacrifice on the altar of stones. He was 50 years old, endowed with wealth and in charge of the treasury of the children of Israel. He continued for a time gathering a group around him to whom he said, "I am one to whom it is anathema to serve a child. I do not wish (to do) this myself, and I hope that you will not consent to it." They answered as a group and said, "We are at your command, and under your obedience: order us as you see fit, and we will not disobey." Accordingly, he made them swear that they would follow him in all his purposes. He offered a sacrifice on the altar, but without salt, as if he were inattentive. When the Great High Priest Ozzi learnt of this, and found that the sacrifice was not accepted, he thoroughly disowned him; and it is (even) said that he rebuked him. Thereupon he and the group that sympathized with him, rose in revolt and at once he and his followers and his beasts set off for Shiloh. Thus Israel split into factions. He sent to their leaders saying to them, "Anyone who would like to see wonderful things, let him come to me." Then he assembled a large group around him in Shilo, and built a Temple for himself there; he

---

[37] Stenhouse, *Kitab al-Tarikh*, 16.
[38] Ibid., 42 f.

constructed for himself a place like **the** Temple. He built an altar, omitting
no detail—it all corresponded to the original, piece by piece. Now, he
had two sons, Hophni and Phinehas, who rounded up young women of
attractive appearance and brought them into the Tabernacle which had
been built by his father. They let them savour the food of the sacrifices, and
had intercourse with them inside the Tabernacle. At this time the children
of Israel became three factions: A (loyal) faction on Mount Gerizim; an
heretical faction that followed false gods; and the faction that followed Eli
son of Yafnī in Shilo.[39]   (Chapter 9)

This story contains elements also known from 1 Sam 1–3; it centres on
Eli and his sons. Eli is here said to belong to the line of Ithamar, who was
the son of Aaron and the brother of Eleazar, Ex 6:23. In the HB Eli has
no genealogy, apart from scattered information seemingly pertaining to
his family, as the following survey will show.

Of the four sons of Aaron, Nadab and Abihu died because of the
"unholy fire," Lev 10:1 f., leaving behind no sons, Num 3:2, but Aaron's
son Eleazar formed the line of high priests according to 1 Chron 6:1 ff.,
leaving the fourth son, Ithamar, aside. Thus, Eli could be the descendant
of either Eleazar or Ithamar, according to the HB.

The following line of text combinations makes him the descendant of
Eleazar. Abiathar was expelled by Solomon from Jerusalem to Anathoth,
1 Kgs 2:26 f., "So Solomon banished Abiathar from being priest to the
Lord, thus fulfilling the word of the Lord that he had spoken concerning
the house of Eli in Shiloh," v. 27. The only candidate for such a prophecy
is found in 1 Sam 2:33, "The only one of you whom I shall not cut
off from my altar shall be spared to weep out his eyes and grieve his
heart; all the members of your household shall die by the sword." This
survivor can therefore be found in the Abiathar who was expelled by
Solomon. Now, Abiathar was the descendant of Aaron through the line of
Phinehas—if one combines 1 Sam 22:20 with 14:3. Because Phinehas is
the son of Eleazar, 1 Chron 6:4, this would make Eli's descendant Abiathar
connected to Eleazar. Thus, a combination of 1 Kgs 2:26 f.; 1 Sam 2:33;
22:20; 14:3 arrives at Eli being of the line of Phinehas, the son of Eleazar.
In 2 Esd 1:2 f. he is said to belong to the house of Eleazar, which is the
logical conclusion on the basis of these texts in the HB.

On the other hand, Ahimelek was Abiathar's father, according to 1 Sam
22:20. 1 Chr 24:3 attributes Ahimelek to the line of Ithamar. Another
combination of texts, ending with 1 Chr 24:3, therefore arrives at Eli

---

[39] Ibid., 47 f.

being of the line of Ithamar. Josephus, *Ant.* 5.361 f. tells us that Eli was the son of Ithamar, corresponding to this second combination of texts. Abu'l Fath sides with Josephus on this question, and not with 2 Esd 1:2 f.

In Abu'l-Fath's portrayal of the two sons, Hophni and Phinehas, he makes them worse than the description in the HB. According to 1 Sam 2 they took from the sacrifices more than the priests' share, and "they lay with the women who served at the entrance to the tent of meeting," v. 22. Abu'l Fath has a longer list of sins; the sons "rounded up young women of attractive appearance and brought them into the Tabernacle which had been built by his father. They let them savour the food of the sacrifices, and had intercourse with them inside the Tabernacle." He thus uses and reinforces elements from the HB, but his story is even more similar to that of Josephus, "They were arrogant to people and impious towards the Deity, refraining from no transgression. They carried off some shares of the sacrifices as an honor [due them], while others they took for themselves by way of spoil. They likewise outraged the women who came for worship, raping some, inflicting violence on others, and seducing still others with gifts," *Ant.* 5.339.[40] Abu'l Fath locates his description of the sons' behaviour to the situation after the new temple has been built at Shiloh, reinforcing the impression of an impious cult created by Eli there.

Abu'l Fath's whole story reminds us further of Josephus, *Ant.* 11. In building a temple and an altar at Shiloh as true copies of the ones at Mount Gerizim, Eli acts like Sanballat, who—according to Josephus, *Ant.* 11.310—built a temple on Mount Gerizim, modelled on the Jerusalem temple. This was done for the priest Manasseh, who was considered unwanted in Jerusalem because of a mixed marriage, *Ant.* 11.306 f. Just as Manasseh becomes the high priest at the new temple on Mount Gerizim, according to Josephus, Eli wants to usurp the high priesthood according to the *Tarikh*. The construction of the temple at Shiloh reads as a counter-story to Josephus' account in *Ant.* 11.310. Further, the priest who led the exodus and set up the schismatic cult is said to have been guilty of misconduct in his office, according to Josephus, *Ant.* 11.302 (exogamous marriage), and according to Abu'l Fath (sacrificing without salt). Just as Sanballat supplied the priests and Israelites from Jerusalem with money, land, and dwelling places, Eli promised wonderful things for the people who would follow him. In both cases, the schismatic priest is being followed by a whole group.

---

[40] Translated by Begg and Spilsbury, *Judean Antiquities Books 8–10*, 85.

The incident takes place during the office of the high priest Uzzi, at the time when God hid the Mishkan, according to the *Tolidah*, as quoted above. The *Tolidah* provided Abu'l Fath with the chronological framework, and with the catch-word for Abu'l Fath: the hiding of the Mishkan is developed into a story of the schismatic cult at Shiloh.

Abu'l-Fath here expands information from 1 Sam 1–3 by the genealogy of Eli, by information about his wealth and age, and most of all by a story of his misconduct as a priest: sacrificing without salt, which would be in violation of Lev 2:13. This latter, alleged religious offence by Eli is without a HB source, but reminds one of the biblical Eli's comment to his sons: "If one person sins against another, someone can intercede for the sinner with the LORD; but if someone sins against the LORD, who can make intercession?" 1 Sam 2:25. Abu'l-Fath bases his account of Eli's acts upon this logic, and reaches his goal by portraying a priestly misconduct at the altar and making it the central reason for the split. The acting high priest Uzzi is supposed to be justified in the way he addresses Eli's misconduct.

The rest of the story is solely the responsibility of Eli, who sets up a schismatic cult at Shiloh. It is difficult to avoid the impression that the story of Eli's exodus to Shiloh in the *Tarikh* is an imitation of Josephus' portrayal of Manasses' exodus to Sanballat and Mount Gerizim.

Abu'l-Fath adds to this material an authorial comment on the split: Eli wanted to usurp the High Priesthood from the legitimate High Priest, Uzzi. The effect is a civil war, and at the end we can see its result in the three factions: Samaritans, idolaters, and Jews. The mention of the idolaters reveals knowledge of 2 Kgs 17, for example vv. 33 f. The idea of three factions sounds like a self-defence. The Samaritans of the Middle Ages would know of the accusations that they worshipped other gods or false gods. By creating a third faction with this characteristic, they distanced themselves from this accusation. They belonged to the first party, those who were loyal to the ancient religion.

Thus the split really happened because of Eli's scheming, and his officiating contrary to the law was only the visible event that sparked off the split. His exodus with sympathizers from Mount Gerizim is termed a "revolt." Since it happened because he lost his wealth and—perhaps—was rebuked, he is indirectly accused of reacting to a loss of honour. The multifaceted blame is on Eli and his followers, and the High Priest Uzzi on Mount Gerizim is portrayed as a guardian of the Law.

In view of the fact that the Samaritans hold only the Pentateuch holy it might seem surprising that they have chosen a story from other books of the Hebrew Bible for explaining the split between Jews and Samaritans.

It need not mean that the Samaritans had a larger canon than the Pentateuch, but that they knew and were able to use the Jewish canon. The account of Eli and his two sons in 1 Sam 1–3 has certain elements that attracted their attention: the disrespect of the sons for regulations concerning the sacrificial meat and their sleeping with the temple personnel. Eli is a tragic figure in the HB, but his association with Shiloh is convenient for the Samaritans, because one could avoid mentioning Jerusalem directly. From this tragic figure Abu'l Fath created the wicked Eli, and the name "Shiloh" functioned as a transparent substitute for Jerusalem. Thus, to use Scripture which is holy to the Jews is to attack them with their own weapons without diminishing the value of one's own Holy Writ. Even though Abu'l Fath says that his audience is the Samaritans, this attack addresses the Jews of his own age.

Considering that Abu'l Fath based his chronicle on Greek sources, it is not unlikely that he used Josephus' account of the origin of the Samaritan cult on Mount Gerizim and turned it on its head. By using the same technique as Josephus, i.e., rewriting a biblical account, Abu'l-Fath based himself on material from which the Jews could not distance themselves. He included elements in his story similar to those of Josephus: the establishment of a schismatic cult on a mountain, the misconduct of the priest who did this, his promise of wonderful things for the people who followed him, and his being followed by a whole group, the new temple's construction as a copy of the original one, and the description of the conduct of the sons of Eli, cf. *Ant.* 11.302–347. The Samaritan version is, however, trapped in the same model as Josephus: the opposite party originated as the result of one singular event, and in the form of a split from the orthodox religion, which then remains in the form of the author's own party.

This is not the only case in the *Tarikh* where Josephus is echoed or rewritten or even twisted in the opposite direction. L. Grabbe mentions the following examples: Josephus has Alexander the Great doing obeisance to the Jewish high priest; Abu'l-Fath makes him do it to the Samaritan high priest. Josephus tells how John Hyrcanus destroyed Mount Gerizim and Shechem; the *Tarikh* has "King John," John Hyrcanus, destroy Samaria, but not Shechem, and even attempt to go on a pilgrimage to Mount Gerizim. "One could argue that it is his [i.e., Josephus'] version with a deliberate twist."[41]

---

[41] L. Grabbe, "Betwixt and Between," in *SBL Seminar1993 Papers* (ed. Eugene H. Lovering, Jr.; Atlanta, Ga.: Scholars, 1993), 341.

The *Tarikh* speaks of two returns from exile.[42] This presupposes the Jewish use of 2 Kgs 17 and Neh 13 as anti-Samaritan, or at least as speaking of the origins of the Samaritans. The knowledge of this use of these texts could lie behind the self-defence inherent in the idea of two returns from exile. According to the *Tarikh*, the Samaritans returned from an exile 70 years after the deportation under Nebuchadnezzar, and from another exile after a deportation under a Greek king. These accounts are easily understandable on the basis of Josephus: they are told as if admitting that there had been an influx of Israelites on these two occasions. But they are reformulated as having happened as returns from exile, and not as a result of expulsion from Jerusalem.

On the whole the *Tarikh* gives the impression of having been created to a large extent on the basis of the *Tolidah*, the HB, for example 1 Sam 1–3, and Josephus (at least *Ant.* 11), and maybe other genuinely ancient documents. The historical value of this creation for the biblical period is virtually nil, as the creation depends on the combination of older sources. Thus, these narratives in the *Tarikh* cannot be used for a reconstruction of Samaritan origins.

But perhaps there is old material to be found in the *Book of Joshua*?

The Arabic Book of Joshua

The *Arabic Book of Joshua* has come to us in one manuscript which J. Scaliger bought in Cairo in 1584, and is now in Leiden. It was published by T. Juynboll in 1848, and translated into English by O. Crane in 1890—a translation which was reprinted in a slightly modified form by R. T. Anderson and T. Giles in 2005.[43] Juynboll considered that chapters 1 up to the middle of chapter 46 had been created in A.H. 764 / 1362/3 C.E., on the basis of texts from an earlier period in the same century,[44] and that chapters 47 ff. were added in A.H. 919 / 1513 C.E. He suggested that

---

[42] Chapter 17; 18; Stenhouse, *Kitab al-Tarikh*, 78 f.

[43] T. G. J. Juynboll, *Chronicon Samaritanum, Arabice conscriptum, cui titulus est Liber Josuae* (Leiden: S. & J. Luchtmans, 1848); O. T. Crane, *The Samaritan Chronicle or The Book of Joshua the Son of Nun* (New York: John B. Alden, 1890); R. T. Anderson and T. Giles, *Tradition Kept: The Literature of the Samaritans* (Peabody, Mass.: Hendrikson, 2005), 67–142.

[44] F. Dexinger: at the latest from the beginning or middle of the thirteenth century, F. Dexinger, *Der Taheb: Ein "messianischer" Heilsbringer der Samaritaner* (Kairos: religionswissenschaftliche Studien 3; Salzburg: Otto Müller, 1986), 142, n. 26.

there were four sources behind this work: three Arabic and one Hebrew. If Juynboll is correct in his assumptions, this composition was made only a few years after the *Tarikh*. Abu'l Fath refers to an *Arabic Book of Joshua*, and this reference could have an early version of the book in mind.

The *Arabic Book of Joshua* covers the period from the death of Moses to Alexander the Great. The part on the schism and Eli are in chapters 41–43, and these chapters are younger than the *Kitab al-Tarikh*.[45]

A manuscript of an assumed Hebrew Book of Joshua was published by M. Gaster in 1908; this manuscript was acquired by M. Gaster in Nablus in 1907 and "... by the grace of Him who guides man's step, [...] He had enabled me [...] to recognize their true character."[46] He claimed that it was older than the Arabic version. P. Kahle and others alleged, however, that it was composed in Nablus in 1902.[47] This latter conclusion is confirmed by the linguistic analysis by M. Florentin. The Hebrew book of Joshua is identical in some parts with John Rylands ms. 257 (cf. *Chronicle II*, see below), and it must be dated on this basis.[48] This Hebrew Joshua can thus be left out of our consideration, even though scholars such as M. Gaster have supposed the material in it to be old.[49] It is, in fact, copied from the Masoretic Joshua, from the *Tarikh* and from other Samaritan sources. The *Arabic Book of Joshua* is, on the other hand, genuinely from the Middle Ages, and therefore of higher significance.

In the oldest part of the Scaliger manuscript we can read how the Jews split off from true Israel under Eli, chapter 43:

> Discord had arisen between the descendant of Phinehas (Uzzi) and his cousin Eli, whose name being interpreted means "The Insidious." This erring man was of the tribe of Ithamar, the brother of Eleazar the imam. Now the right of administration belonged to the tribe of Phinehas, and

---

[45] Stenhouse, "Samaritan Chronicles," 219 f.246, referring the viewpoints of Juynboll.

[46] M. Gaster, "On the newly discovered Samaritan Book of Joshua," *Journal of the Royal Asiatic Society of Great Britain and Ireland*, 1908, 795–809; quotation from 797; idem, "Das Buch Josua in hebräisch-samaritanischer Rezension. Entdeckt und zum ersten Male herausgegeben," *ZDMG* 62 (1908): 209–279. 494–549.

[47] P. Kahle, "Zum hebräischen Buch Josua der Samaritaner," *ZDMG* 62 (1908): 550–551; A. S. Yahuda, "Über die Unechtheit des samaritanischen Josuabuches," *SPAW* 39 (1908): 887–914; D. Yellin, "*spr yhws' 'w spr-hymym*," *Jerusalem Jahrbuch zur Beförderung einer wissenschaftlichen ganauen Kenntnis des jetzigen und des alten Palästinas* 6 (1902): 203–205; ibid., (1903): 138–155.

[48] Florentin, *Late Samaritan Hebrew*, 357–374.

[49] E. Tov thinks several readings agree with the LXX against MT, with reference to M. Gaster's edition, Tov, *Textual Criticism*, 81, note 56, where he is also positive to *Chronicle II*, containing material parallel to the biblical books of Joshua, Judges, 1–2 Samuel, 1–2 Kings and 2 Chronicles.

it was this tribe that was offering up the sacrifices upon the brazen altar and stone altar. And this man—The Insidious—was fifty years old and, being great in riches, had obtained for himself the lordship over the treasure house of the children of Israel; and he had obtained, through the knowledge of magic, what he had acquired of riches, proud rank, and wealth. And his self-importance being great in his own estimation, he gathered to himself a company and said unto them: "I am one to whom to serve a boy is impossible, and I will not reconcile myself to this, and I hope that you will not be content to have me do this." And the company answered him: "We are under your command, and under obedience to you; command us in whatever you will." And he put them under covenant that they would follow him unto the place where they purposed going on the morning of the second day (of the week). And he offered up offering on the altar without salt, as if he was ignorant, and immediately started out on the journey with his outfit and company, and cattle, and everything that he possessed, and settled in Shiloh. And he gathered the children of Israel into a factional sect, and held correspondence with their leaders, and said unto them: "Whoever desires to behold miracles, let him come unto me." And there was collected to him a multitude in Shiloh, and he built for himself a shrine there, and organized matters for himself in it on the model of the temple, and erected in it one altar, on which he might sacrifice and offer up offerings. And he had two sons, who used to gather the women into the temple in the morning and lie with them and would eat up all that was present of the offerings of wine and other things. And this man continued diverting the people by magic for the space of forty years.[50]

This story is similar to the version in the *Tarikh*, but with notable differences. The most conspicuous are the absence of Eli's resolve to usurp the High Priesthood, of his offering on Mount Gerizim, of Uzzi's rebuke, of the names of his sons, and of the three factions. Instead of an account of the intent to usurp the High Priesthood, the Book of Joshua explains that Eli purposed going to another place before the fatal offering. The *Book of Joshua* offers an explanation for the name "Eli" as "The Insidious," adds the element of magic to his abilities, emphasizes only his followers as a "factional sect," portrays the new cult in more reserved terms than the *Tarikh*, and describes the behaviour of the sons in a worse light.

If these two stories were written down only seven years apart, the differences are striking, and the *Arabic Book of Joshua* portrays Eli and his followers in a more derogatory way than the *Tarikh*. Eli did not act as a priest on Mount Gerizim at all and did not intend to usurp the High Priesthood in all Israel, but to set up a schismatic cult in Shiloh. He did not leave because he was rebuked, but because his intention was schism.

---

[50] Anderson and Giles, *Tradition Kept*, 127.

As a magician and as an insidious person he comes out worse in the *Arabic Book of Joshua* than in the *Tarikh*, and there are not three factions, but only one "factional sect" as a result of his exodus from the true Israel.

The impression gained from the three mediaeval chronicles is that the Samaritan version of the split between Jews and Samaritans was developed after the *Tolidah* of 1346 C.E. and before the *Tarikh* of 1355 C.E. If there had been such a version by 1346 C.E. one might expect an echo of it in the *Tolidah*—acknowledging that it is precarious to draw conclusions from the absence of evidence. But the *Tolidah* knows that the period of divine favour ended in the thirty-fifth year of Uzzi, and this is the point in history where it would have been natural to enter information on a schism. This was the time when the schism took place, according to the *Tarikh* and the *Arabic Joshua*. It is a fair assumption that the *Tolidah* had no further material available on the end of the *Rawuta*, and that in the years after 1346 C.E. the story was developed on the basis of Josephus' *Ant.* 11.302 ff. and 1 Sam 1–3. Slightly different versions of the schism created by Eli in the days of Uzzi went into the *Tarikh* and the *Arabic Book of Joshua*, and within seven years the description of the "civil war" of the *Tarikh* and the "discord" of the *Book of Joshua* became more negative towards Eli and his followers. The idea that the period of Divine Favour came to an end under the high priesthood of Uzzi (according to the *Tolidah*) was conducive to the notion of a schism, and the description of this schism can be found in texts from the middle of the 14th century C.E. (*Tarikh* and *Arabic Joshua*). All these texts are based on the HB, *Jubilees* and Josephus.

The New Chronicle / Chronicle Adler

A "New Chronicle" was published by E. N. Adler and M. Seligsohn in 1902–1903. It is printed from a manuscript that was transcribed by a German Jew, resident in Jerusalem, from a Samaritan manuscript. This New Chronicle, also called *Chronicle Adler*, was probably composed in 1899–1900,[51] as there was in Nablus at that time, in the words of P. Kahle, "a manufactory of chronicles."[52] In this chronicle the account of the split is as follows:

---

[51] Florentin, *Late Samaritan Hebrew*, 361–374.

[52] "Professor Paul Kahle has told me that at Nablus, at the end of he 19th century, there was 'a manufactory of chronicles' to supply the demand then current," Bowman, *Samaritan Documents*, 89.

Uzzi the son of Buhki, 25 years. In the days of his priesthood, the head of
the house of Ithmar was Eli the son of Yafni, of the sons of Ithamar, the
son of Aaron the priest. He was an old man far gone in days, while Uzzi
the son of Bukhi was a little lad; yet he sought to be installed in the high
priesthood instead of Uzzi. Now in those days the prince over Israel was
Samson, of the tribe of Dan, who was a mighty man in the land; he was the
last of the kings of the period of Divine grace, for in his days the LORD hid
the holy Tabernacle from the eyes of Israel. And so at that time Eli the son
of Yafni went and made for himself an ark of gold, wherein he placed the
books written in the handwriting of his ancestor, our lord Ithamar. He also
made for himself a tent and pitched it at Shiloh, because the children of
Israel who were at that time in Shechem and in other cities of Palestine,
had driven him from Mount Gerizim, together with those who joined
him. There in Shiloh he built an altar and offered sacrifices upon it, and
all the men of the tribe of Judah joined him, as well as many men from
other tribes. And all the things which Eli had done, are they not written
down in the Book of Chronicles? And the children of Israel in his days
were divided into three groups: one did according to the abominations
of the Gentiles and served other gods; another followed Eli the son of
Yafni, although many of them turned away from him after he had revealed
his intentions; and the third remained with the High Priest Uzzi the son
of Buhki, in the chosen place, Mount Gerizim Bethel, in the holy city of
Shechem, and in all the (other) cities. Then the LORD hid from the eyes of
all Israel the holy Tabernacle which Moses had made by the command of
the LORD in the wilderness. This happened at the end of the priesthood
of the aforementioned Uzzi.[53]

This version depicts Eli in considerably milder terms than the two mediaeval chronicles. Even here he is a usurper, but the usurpation reveals
itself in the act of making an ark for the books, perhaps the Law of
the common ancestor Ithamar. The theme of usurpation is thus further developed than in Abu'l-Fath, where it is only an authorial comment. One must assume that the making of the ark is the reason for the
expulsion from Mount Gerizim as there is no mention of an inattentive
or unknowing sacrifice. This also represents an understanding different
from that of the mediaeval chronicles; the reaction of Uzzi is here taken
to its consequence: expulsion. In Shiloh Eli builds a tent—neither a tabernacle nor a temple, as in the *Tarikh* and in the *Book of Joshua*—with an
altar. The Tabernacle remains on Mount Gerizim until it is hidden by
God. Perhaps this is a more subtle form of criticism: reducing the competing shrine to a tent. The followers of Eli are here primarily the tribe of

---

[53] Bowman, *Samaritan Documents*, 89 f.; diacritical dots under the letters k and h
omitted.

Judah. The story is set in a period of the history of Israel when Samson was the last king. There is no mention of the sons of Eli. In accordance with 1 Sam 2:22; 4:15 the *New Chronicle* emphasizes the old age of Eli, whereas Abu'l-Fath portrays him as 50 years old, possibly at the height of his career when he revolts. The old age of Eli adds a trait of folly to the usurper's illegitimacy.

The description of the three factions is dependent upon deuteronomistic language, and this is also visible in other parts of the story: some of Eli's followers turn away from him and join the correct faith. The phrase "is it not written in …" is reminiscent of deuteronomistic language. The reference to Samson in the story is also a deuteronomistic trait, from the Deuteronomistic History, but surprising, as Samson in the HB has no royal function at all. One would think Samuel to be a more likely reference; the ark played a role in his days. But Samuel is portrayed in the *Arabic Book of Joshua* as a magician trained by Eli, whereas Samson here is made into a royal hero. Despite the influence from the HB, the *New Chronicle* stays loyal to its Samaritan predecessors.

This account contains ideas from *Tarikh* and *Tolidah*. One notes the idea of the period of Divine grace (*Rawuta*), ending with the split, which inaugurated the period of Divine Wrath (*Fanuta*). The years for the High Priests in the *Tolidah* are taken over by the *New Chronicle*.

The story here is not so morally condemnatory as the other two, with less negative language, but the essence is the same: the blame for the split is upon Eli and his followers. The authors of the mediaeval chronicles felt free to portray their opponents in very negative terms, but at the end of the nineteenth century a Samaritan author did not feel the same freedom. There is some criticism of the Jews left in the *New Chronicle*, perhaps more subtle at times, but the overall picture is more cautious.

Chronicle II

Another version of the split is found in manuscripts 1142 and 1168 of the John Rylands library in Manchester, now renumbered as 257 and 259, respectively. On the basis of these and five other manuscripts, John Macdonald published a text which he termed *Chronicle II*, and hypothesized that there was once a book called *Sepher Ha-Yamim*, attested to in these manuscripts.[54] This *Sepher Ha-Yamim* would have been parallel to the

---

[54] J. Macdonald, *The Samaritan chronicle no. II; or, Sepher Ha-Yamim. From Joshua to Nebuchadnezzar* (BZAW 107; Berlin,: W. De Gruyter, 1969).

books of Joshua, Judges, 1 and 2 Samuel, 1 and 2 Kings, and 2 Chronicles in the HB. It would have been a text independent of the Masoretic tradition, coming from the old Northern Kingdom and preserved through the ages until the writing of the extant manuscripts 1142 (257) and 1168 (259). J. Macdonald read the colophon of ms. 1142 (257) to mean that it was first written in 1616, and then brought up to date century by century, until its final version of 1908. The other manuscripts he dated 1902, or left them undated.

Z. Ben-Hayyim's comment on this hypothesis was that ms. 1142 (257) was not copied, but created in 1908, written for M. Gaster by a Samaritan scribe on the basis of the HB.[55] This is the simplest explanation for the linguistic facts of the manuscript, and it means that there never was a *Sepher Ha-Yamim* in J. Macdonald's sense, but that this term was generic, used of different annals. Ms. 1142 (257) is written in Judaized Samaritan Hebrew for outside consumption.[56] The discussion about *Chronicle II* echoes the earlier controversies around the Samaritan *Book of Joshua*.

The colophon is written at the bottom of page 281B of ms. 1142 (257), a page containing a text referring to events in the late nineteenth century, and Z. Ben-Hayyim explained this fact by assuming that the ink dots in front of the word "thousand" means "300," which means that the dating then would read A.H. 1326/1908 C.E. and not A.H. 1026/1617 C.E., as J. Macdonald supposed.[57] Z. Ben-Hayyim's linguistic argument is conclusive for the age of the manuscript and the text, but there is also the possibility that the scribe intended to make readers assume that the text was from A.H. 1026/1617 C.E. by writing the enigmatic dots instead of the words "three hundred."

Manuscript 1168 of the John Rylands library, now renumbered 259, has been published by Friedrich Niessen.[58] The manuscript can be dated to the early years of the twentieth century, slightly earlier than 1142 (257),

---

[55] Z. Ben-Hayyim, *"nby'ym r'swnym nwsh swmrwn?"* Leš 35 (1971): 292–302. Cf. the comment by J. Purvis, "I have been informed by several members of the Samaritan community that the document was put together in the late nineteenth century. It is essentially a modern forgery of an alleged ancient document," J. Purvis, "The Samaritans and Judaism," in *Early Judaism and its Modern Interpreters* (ed. R. Kraft and G. W. E. Nickelsburg, Philadelphia, Penn.: Fortress; Atlanta, Ga.: Scholars Press, 1986), 82 f.

[56] Florentin, *Late Samaritan Hebrew*, 373.

[57] Ben-Hayyim, *"nby'ym r'swnym nwskh swmrwn?"* 297.

[58] Niessen, *Eine samaritanische Version des Buches Yehošua*, 2000.

and is to some extent a parallel text, but in Aramaic. The language is so heavily influenced by Arabic that this chronicle was shaped after Arabic became the vernacular of the Samaritans. It is therefore not useful as a source for the biblical period.

Ms. 1142 (257) repeats and greatly expands the account of the split between the High Priest Uzzi and the usurper Eli, but the backbone and the elements of the story are the same as in the *Tarikh*, the *Arabic Book of Joshua*, and in the *New Chronicle*.[59] The earlier story is enlarged with many details explaining how the split occurred.

The Samaritan chronicles reverse the story of Josephus in *Ant.* 11.302 ff. The story found in *Ant.* 9.278 f.288–291 seems not to have been utilized directly as material. It was also not countered directly, but the effect of it may have been addressed indirectly, by the introduction of the two returns from exile, and of three factions after the split occurred, one of which was the faction adoring false gods. By this third faction the chronicles were able to account for their own origin, that of the Jews, and the allegation that there were idolaters in the region.

J. A. Montgomery concluded in 1904 that the Samaritan chronicles "add nothing to our scanty knowledge … [they] at the best but illuminate the cruel history of the Byzantine period."[60] Other scholars have not followed his lead, and have been less circumspect. R. T. Anderson and T. Giles reconstruct the history leading up to the proto-Samaritans by using the Hebrew Bible, Josephus and *Kitab al-Tarikh* and *Chronicle Adler* together. They note that Abu'l Fath's chronicle was written in the fourteenth century C.E. and *Chronicle Adler* in the eighteenth, but still add data from the HB for understanding this Samaritan version of the origin.[61] H. G. Kippenberg does not include a discussion on the date and provenance of the Chronicles, but accepts the verdict of Montgomery that they are primarily of interest for the Byzantine period. Still, he refers to the *Tolidah* and *Chronicle Neubauer* in connection with the history of exile and return; for the chapter on the List of High Priests he uses the *Tolidah*, *Chronicle II*, and Josephus, and concludes that the list was

---

[59] In J. Macdonald's system: Judges § I – I Samuel § C.

[60] J. A. Montgomery, *The Samaritans: The Earliest Jewish Sect. Their History, Theology and Literature* (Philadelphia, 1904; repr. New York: Ktav Pub. House, 1968), 310.

[61] Anderson and Giles, *Keepers*, 10–13. They are aware that Josephus retells stories from the HB with an anti-Samaritan twist, but still use Josephus for much of the reconstruction.

created in the second century B.C.E.[62] According to R. J. Coggins, the Samaritan *Book of Joshua* and the *Tolidah* do not "preserve genuine historical information concerning the biblical period," but *Chronicle II* is "certainly one that deserved to be set alongside the biblical material as a basis for comparison." He refers to the chronicle extensively.[63] A parallel approach is taken by Jarl Fossum.[64] R. Pummer uses the Chronicles to infer that the Samaritans practised circumcision in times of persecution in the third or fourth century C.E., and accordingly also at the time of Hellenization.[65]

E. Noort's approach is slightly different.[66] He wants to study the image of Joshua in the Samaritan "Josua-Chroniken," because the Samaritans in several respects can be compared to groups from the second temple period. The relevant chronicles are mainly (1.) The *Arabic Joshua*, (2.) the *Tarikh*, (3.) John Rylands Library ms. 863, 864, and 1167 plus *Chronicle Adler*, and (4.) *Chronicle II*. He therefore does not attempt a dating of the Samaritan chronicles, but treats them as an a-temporal corpus of material for comparison with the HB and Josephus. As for the status of the tribes east of Jordan, he finds that Josephus represents a position to which the Samaritan chronicles join themselves seamlessly. This result corresponds to the view presented here in the case of the story of the origins of the Samaritans and Jews. However, Noort's approach cannot avoid the question of dating. Only when we know the temporal location of a text, are we able to assess the different theologoumena of the text and make use of them and of the methods visible in them as comparative material for other corpuses of text—perhaps from a different period.

It has often been said, in this connection as in others, that a manuscript may contain material from earlier ages. "Although the chronicles date from medieval times, they incorporate older material."[67] As we have seen,

---

[62] Kippenberg, *Garizim und Synagoge*, for exile and return, 36 f.; for "die Hohepriesterliste," 48 f.60–68.

[63] R. J. Coggins, *Samaritans and Jews: the Origins of Samaritanism Reconsidered* (Growing Points in Theology; Oxford: Blackwell, 1975), 117–131.

[64] J. E. Fossum, *The Name of God and the Angel of the Lord: Samaritan and Jewish Concepts of Intermediation and the Origin of Gnosticism* (WUNT 36; Tubingen: J. C. B. Mohr, 1985), 27–40.

[65] R. Pummer, "Genesis 34 in Jewish Writings of the Hellenistic and Roman Periods," *HTR* 75 (1982): 186.

[66] E. Noort, "Der reißende Wolf—Josua in Überlieferung und Geschichte," in *International Organization for the Study of the Old Testament: 18th Congress: Congress Volume* (ed. A. Lemaire; VTSup 109; Leiden: Brill, 2006), 153–173.

[67] Pummer, "Genesis 34 in Jewish Writings," 186.

this is indeed the case. The medieval texts are built upon older texts, but the crucial point is whether they also contain material independent of known texts, material which is just as reliable or more reliable than these texts. Until a method has been developed for finding such material, the information from these texts is basically to be treated as contemporary with the author. If it is possible to see antecedents for information in the chronicles, the more probable conclusion is that they borrowed from earlier literature or polemicized against it. The immediate impression is that the material is of a folkloristic type, developed as polemics or self-defence, created from older texts in order to substantiate contemporary self-understanding. This activity can be seen in two phases, one around the middle of the fourteenth century, and another around 1900. The methodological consequence is therefore to leave this material for the scholars of Samaritan history and folklore in the Middle Ages and later, and not use it for a reconstruction of their origins.

The two stories presented by Josephus on the origin of the Samaritans have not only influenced the thinking of the church fathers and the Samaritans, but have had a lasting impact on modern scholars up to the present. But the Samaritan story also has won supporters among scholars. Research on Samaritan origins has often taken some of this material as the starting point, and a review of this scholarship may be organized according to this influence. During the last decades, however, there have been tendencies to treat the subject independently of Josephus and the Samaritan chronicles, and see the traditional explanations more at a distance. Exciting explanations have been suggested on this basis, and opened the way for a new assessment. Both traditional and modern approaches teach a lesson by unveiling paths which lead somewhere, and by revealing cul-de-sacs. The next chapter is devoted to this topic.

CHAPTER THREE

STATE OF THE QUESTION

A review of research may start where we ended the previous chapter, with the Samaritan chronicles, and their influence on modern scholarship. A group of scholars have adhered to the Samaritan model of Samaritan origins, and this way of approaching the topic will be surveyed first.[1] Most scholars have not followed this lead, but have paid more attention to Josephus or are influenced by him, and this approach will be presented in the second part of this chapter. The third part will present scholars who depart from the Samaritan chronicles and Josephus, and create new theories. Keeping the investigation of relevant material in mind, this review of scholarship will pay attention to ideas which have been rendered obsolete by later investigation or new material, as well as to theories that are still open for a closer scrutiny. Without discarding all ideas in the section 3.1, it can be said on the basis of the previous chapter that the main ideas in the Samaritan chronicles cannot be considered relevant for my investigation. To omit a presentation of this line of investigation would not, however, be fair to the history of our subject.

3.1. *The Impact of the Samaritan Version*

The Samaritan version explains the origin of the Jews as a schismatic movement away from the true Israel, which itself continued and developed into the Samaritans. Scholars have usually not followed the Samaritans on the question of the origin of the Jews, but the continuation model has had a wide impact. It is inherently probable that there was a connection between the northern tribes and the later Samaritans, and the Samaritan model would seem attractive at the outset.

---

[1] 'Model' is used here in a loose sense of an explanatory way of thinking. After the material has been presented and evaluated, the scholar looks for some overarching system, some pattern known from other historical processes and events. Or, conversely, the scholar is embedded in a way of explanation, and applies this without, perhaps,

The clearest example of this approach is J. Macdonald, who bases himself primarily on the Samaritan *Chronicle II* for the origin of the Samaritans.[2] His version is therefore basically that the Samaritans were descendants of old Israel. This explanation is found, for example, in his famous *Theology of the Samaritans*.[3] The emphasis is on the continuity between old Israel and the Samaritans, not on the Samaritan version of the origin of the Jews.

A similar understanding is present in the work of I. Hjelm.[4] She uses the Samaritan *Arabic Book of Joshua* and the *Kitab al-Tarikh* for her understanding of the period before the turn of the era, and considers that other Samaritan chronicles also contain early material. The Samaritan chronicles are used as texts competing with the HB, which she thinks was a revision of older traditions in order to emphasize the position of Zion. Though not addressing the question of origin of the Samaritans in particular, her understanding implies that the Samaritan chronicles preserve genuine information on the early period.

One recent reviewer of research on the Samaritans, J. Davila, introduces us to two versions of their origin, viz. "their own traditions" and the "biblical account." His presentation is built on the work of J. Macdonald and I. Hjelm, both of whom take the Samaritan chronicles as their starting point.[5] As for the "biblical account" we noticed in the previous chapters that Josephus is the first author where we find a reading of the HB to the effect that it contains an account of the origin of the Samaritans. It is therefore questionable if there originally was a "biblical account;" at least the reading of the HB by Josephus should not be confused with the "biblical account." On the basis of his information on the question, J. Davila presumes that Jews and Samaritans existed as communities in the second temple period. "We may reasonably suppose that Samaritans were

---

making it overt. I do not intend to enter into a discussion on the definition of 'model' or other relevant expressions, as this is not a study of historical methodology, nor a contribution to discussion on the use of methods in historical research.

[2] J. Macdonald, "Samaritans, History, Until 1300," *EncJud* 14: 727–732.

[3] J. Macdonald, *The Theology of the Samaritans* (NTL; London: SCM Press, 1964), 15–21.

[4] I. Hjelm, *The Samaritans and Early Judaism: A Literary Analysis* (JSOTSup 303; Sheffield: Sheffield Academic Press, 2000), 237–254. Similarly in eadem, *Jerusalem's Rise to Sovereignty: Zion and Gerizim in Competition* (JSOTSup 404; London: T&T Clark, 2004), 184–187.

[5] J. R. Davila, *The Provenance of the Pseudepigrapha: Jewish, Christian, or Other?* (JSJSup 105; Leiden: Brill 2005), 51.

increasingly distinguishable from Jews during the closing centuries B.C.E. and into the early Common Era, as both groups shored up the boundaries between them."[6]

When J. Macdonald used the Samaritan version as a starting point and basic framework for the study, he followed a lead from M. Gaster.[7] J. T. Milik represents a second stage in this process, when he deals with the relationship between the Enochic tradition and the Samaritan book *Asatir*.[8] J. T. Milik had in his possession the earliest copy of the *Asatir* on parchment, and dated it to the thirteenth century, but he relied upon M. Gaster's edition and J. Macdonald's *Theology of the Samaritans* for his understanding of Samaritanism.[9] Based on theories about the date of the Samaritan material new theories were developed about its value for understanding the period before the turn of the era.

A corollary of the Samaritan model is the idea that a majority of the northern population stayed behind after the Assyrian conquest, and developed into the Samaritans; this is a common idea among scholars. Here belongs T. H. Gaster, who follows the Samaritan version in assuming that there were, after the fall of Samaria in 722, "(*a*) the remnant of the native Israelites; and (*b*) the foreign colonists."[10] The native Israelites would later become the Samaritans. In this thinking, the emphasis is not upon the idea that old Israel was true Israel, which developed into the Samaritans, but upon the presumption that the population that was left behind must have carried on their religion as long as they existed. This group of scholars also encompasses M. J. Bin-Gorion (= Berdyczewski) who considers the Gerizim covenant (Josh 24) older than the Sinai covenant, and I. Ben-Zvi and J. Bowman who suppose that the major part of the population was left behind in 722 and influenced the settlers; also, A. Mikoláŝek assumes that the connection between old Israel and Samaritans is certain.[11] Finding the roots of the Samaritans in earliest times, in line with the Samaritan self-understanding, and supplementing it with later material, is also the model suggested by N. Schur.[12]

---

[6] Ibid.

[7] Gaster, *Samaritans*; Macdonald, "Samaritans, History, Until 1300," 14:727–732.

[8] J. T. Milik and M. Black, *The Books of Enoch: Aramaic Fragments of Qumrân Cave 4* (Oxford: Clarendon, 1976), 64–69.

[9] M. Gaster, *The Asatir: The Samaritan Book of the "Secrets of Moses," together with the Pitron* (London: The Royal Asiatic society, 1927); Macdonald, *Theology of the Samaritans*.

[10] T. H. Gaster, "Samaritans," *IDB* 4: 192.

[11] For a more detailed review with full bibliography, Dexinger, "Ursprung der Samaritaner," 72–77.

[12] N. Schur, *History of the Samaritans* (BEATAJ 18; Frankfurt a. M.: Peter Lang, 1989).

This [the time of Ezra and Nehemiah] is perhaps the moment to start speaking of "Jews" and "Samaritans", each with a separate identity, though actually the continuity of neither side had been interrupted. The Samaritans regard themselves, as we have seen with some right, from an ethnic point of view, to this day as the direct continuation of the Ten Tribes of Israel … There was no "Samaritan Schism", the continuity of development was unbroken. Nor can one talk of a "final breach". There was a slow process of drawing apart in the religious sphere … It is true, however, that the direction and pattern of development in the religious sphere was changed from now on … When the editing of the next group of books of the Old Testament, the Prophets, was completed in Jerusalem, probably in the fourth or third century BC, the Samaritand [sic] were no longer prepared to include it in their canon … From now on it becomes possible to talk about two different sects (or shall we say religions? or people? or nations?) … the process of estrangement was a very slow one … J. L. Levin says on this subject: "… Only in the Middle Ages, when both the Jewish and Samaritan communities in Palestine had shrunk to insignificance, and their contacts had become enfeebled and finally disappeared, became the separation between them final."[13]

N. Schur does not make any distinction between the people of Samaria and the Samaritans, and on this point scholars like R. Pummer have made us aware of a possible fallacy (see below). N. Schur has great confidence in the sources, even though he speaks of the "biased account" of Josephus.[14] The difference between Jerusalem and Samaria, according to him, was that the latter had no Judas Maccabaeus, but both sides had hellenizing parties.

G. Knoppers seems to follow a Samaritan model of continuity when he describes "the Yahwistic Samarians of the Persian period as descendants of the Israelites who used to have their own kingdom centred in Samaria centuries earlier." He uses the term "Samarians," not "Samaritans" for this entity.[15]

That there was a connection between Old Israel and the Samaritans is also the position of F. Dexinger, who studied the sources and the different solutions thoroughly. He thought that the remnants of northern Israelites constituted the background for the development. The relation of these

---

[13] Ibid., 32 f.; quotation from J. L. Levin's contribution to volume 4 of *Ha-Historyah shel Erets-Yisra'el/History of Eretz Israel*, ed. J. Shavit, Jerusalem, 1981, 121 f.

[14] Schur, *History of the Samaritans*, 39 f.

[15] G. Knoppers, "In Search of Post-exilic Israel: Samaria after the Fall of the Northern Kingdom," in *In Search of Pre-Exilic Israel: Proceedings of the Oxford Old Testament Seminar* (ed. J. Day; JSOTSup 406; New York: T & T Clark, 2004), 172.

Yahwists to Jerusalem was so full of tension that they should be called proto-Samaritans in early post-exilic times. Then they developed into a group separated from Judean Yahwism, and the final break came with the recognition that Jerusalem was not relevant as a cult place any more, and the cult on Mount Gerizim gained its monopoly. This made the proto-Samaritans Samaritans, and it happened at the time of John Hyrcanus.[16] Dexinger considered that the "adversaries" mentioned in Ezra 4:1–5 were those pre-exilic Yahweh-worshippers who were not deported.[17] His emphasis upon the Maccabean period has gained momentum in scholarship during recent decades, and I will return to it in the third section.

The Samaritan version has provided scholarship with a model of continuity from Old Israel to the Samaritans, and this model still exerts its attraction. At the present, we do not have material which is old enough to verify or falsify the theory. It remains a dim possibility, but does not provide us with workable material.

3.2. *Josephus' Version Mirrored in Scholarship*

Josephus has been influential from early on, as briefly laid out in the previous chapter. His contention that the Samaritans stemmed from deportees from Assyria was echoed in different versions by the church fathers. There is thus no surprise in the fact that his theories have been followed also by many modern scholars, and that they have found their way into modern reference works.[18] Earlier scholars who embraced his theories include Chr. Cellarius, A. Brüll, and Y. Kaufmann.[19] More recently A. E. Cowley (who thought of a substratum of Israelites plus an element of foreigners), and S. Talmon (Yahwists were living in the countryside, syncretists in the cities of Bethel and Samaria) belong in this category.[20]

---

[16] Dexinger, "Ursprung der Samaritaner," 83.

[17] Those mentioned in Ezra 4:1–5 were "die nicht deportierten Angehörigen der vorexilischen Jahwereligion in Samaria." They were "Protosamaritaner." "Samaritaner sind sie erst ab dem Zeitpunkt, da Jerusalem keinerlei religiöse Relevanz mehr für sie hatte. Diese Entwicklung vollzog sich erst in der Makkabäerzeit," F. Dexinger, "Samaritaner," *TRE* 29 (1998): 752.

[18] For examples, cf. ch. 1, n. 1. Further examples of this approach, P. Henriksen, ed., *Aschehoug og Gyldendals Store Norske Leksikon* (Oslo: Aschehoug og Gyldendal,), 12 (1998): 726, s.v. "Samaritaner"; A. Gelston, "Samaritans," *NBD* 1131f.

[19] Details in Dexinger, "Ursprung der Samaritaner," 70ff.

[20] Details in Dexinger, "Ursprung der Samaritaner," 70ff.

R. Achenbach follows Josephus' descriptions closely, and provides Biblical references for the early period; but for these references to be relevant for the origin of the Samaritans one has to presuppose the understanding that Josephus has accorded to them.[21] He supposes syncretism for the original Samaritans. But their religion concentrates on the unity of God, Deut 6:4. This approach necessitates an explanation for the transition from syncretism to strict monotheism; but Achenbach has not addressed this problem. Another example where Josephus has directed modern scholarship is A. Zertal's interpretation of "the wedge-shaped decorated bowl" found in smaller settlements in Samaria from Iron age II. These are bowls with a "decoration" that is found in Mesopotamia from the third millenium B.C.E. on, and the finds in the territory of Manasseh in the period 700–530 B.C.E. mean that this decoration was imported by the resettled populace. "The deportees from Mesopotamia are the origin of the later Samaritans ... the first archaeological indications of the origin of the later Samaritans."[22] The supposed "decoration," however, is a common pattern in graters, found in modern and ancient societies. "... the artifact tells us more about the culinary arts of the inhabitants of Samaria than about their origin," according to G. London.[23]

The second explanation of the Samaritans' origin presented by Josephus is that the priest Manasses and his followers split off from Jerusalem and created the cult on Gerizim, thus supplying the already existing Samaritans with the essential elements of temple and priesthood. This idea of a split, a separation from Jerusalem, has influenced scholarship heavily. Often, the assumption of a split was used as a model, and it has turned up in expressions like 'schism' and 'sect'. As noted in chapter 1, scholars have supposed that there was a split, a rift, a *Herauslösung* of the Samaritans from the Jews. This idea ultimately goes back to Josephus. A surviving element from Josephus is therefore a separation model.

The most influential theory of this type was presented by J. Montgomery. One could say that modern study of the Samaritans started with his monograph *The Samaritans: The First Jewish Sect* in 1907, based on his 1906 lectures. Here, he made this classic observation:

---

[21] R. Achenbach, "Samaria. III. Religion, Geschichte, Literatur der Samaritaner," *RGG* 7: 817 f.

[22] A. Zertal, "The Wedge-Shaped Decorated Bowl and the Origin of the Samaritans," *BASOR* 276 (1989): 77–84; quotation from 82.

[23] G. London, "Reply to A. Zertal's 'The Wedge-shaped Decorated Bowl and the Origin of the Samaritans,'" *BASOR* 286 (1992): 89–90; quotation from 90.

When the present writer took up the study of the origin of the Samaritans, he naturally began with a consideration of the differences which distinguished the histories of the two sections of the Hebrew people, Israel and Juda, the North and the South. It seemed antecedently probable that the Samaritans must be the heirs of the peculiar religious characteristics of northern Israel; they would be the lineal successors of the church of Elija, Élisha and Hosea, and of those Yahwe-enthusiasts, the family of Jehu. But the results obtained in this field of investigation are entirely negative. When at last we come upon definite information concerning the Samaritans, of the kind that gives some description of them,—and these authorities belong to the Christian era, the New Testament, Josephus, the Talmud—the Samaritans appear as nothing else than a Jewish sect. The one essential difference between them and Judaism is that their cult centres on Gerizim, not on Zion; minor differences there are, but almost all of these can be shown to represent elder stages of Judaism and often to correspond with the tenets which distinguished the conservative Sadducees from the progressive and finally triumphant Pharisees.[24]

Montgomery further claimes that "The period in which we must look for data concerning the origin of the Samaritan sect is a lengthy one. It extends from the time, about 722 BC, to which the description given by 2 *Ki.* 17 of religious conditions in Samaria after the Assyrian conquest assumes to belong, down to the age of Alexander the Great, in whose reign the Jewish historian Josephus places the rise of the Samaritan sect and the building of its temple on Gerizim."[25] 2 Kgs 17, together with other HB texts and Assyrian records, is read by Montgomery in order to create a picture of a situation from 722 B.C.E. on, where there was considerable religious confusion and perhaps syncretism in the North, but a remnant of Yahweh-believers were loyal to Jerusalem and the temple there. Montgomery takes Josephus' account in *Ant.* 11 together with Neh 13:28 as testimonies of the event which created the Samaritans: there was a split in the Jerusalemite priesthood in the time of Nehemiah resulting in the construction of the rival sanctuary on Mount Gerizim. Josephus was right in his description of the split, according to Montgomery, but mistaken on the century in which it took place, because 1. Josephus is "absolutely irresponsible in Persian history and chronology,"[26] and 2. the Alexander Legend grew: the Jews had their story on Alexander's visit to Jerusalem and the Samaritans had theirs on the permission to build the temple. There might be a Samaritan source behind the story in Josephus.

---

[24] Montgomery, *Samaritans*, 46.
[25] Ibid., 48.
[26] Ibid., 68.

Summing up the Samaritans' origins, he states that

> For from all we know of Samaritanism there can be no doubt that it remained under the steady influence of Judaism, and that this spiritual patronage was so strong and so necessary that even after the complete excommunication of the schismatics in the IIIrd and IVth Christian centuries Rabbinism still infiltrated into Samaria. The proofs and fruits of this spiritual connection are found in the Samaritan possession of the Jews' priesthood, of the First Canon of the Jews' Scriptures, of most of those tenets that marked the Jewish Scriptures, earliest Sadducean Judaism in distinction from the Pharisaic development.

> But with the Jewish promulgation of the Second Canon, that of the Prophets, about 200 [B.C.E.], a definitive break must have separated the two sects on the question as to the extent of Scripture. The northern community could not accept the Second Canon with its pronounced proclivities for Juda, David, and Jerusalem.[27]

Montgomery thus sees the divisions in Jerusalem under Nehemiah as the start of the split, and the promulgation of the Prophets around 200 B.C.E. as its final stage. Thus there was a split, but the Samaritans represent the conservative elements: "... the Samaritan sect stands as a monument of early Judaism."[28]

Montgomery reasons that what unites Jews and Samaritans provides proof of their shared history or of Jewish influence, and what is particularly Samaritan stems from the split or later. Josephus is the main source for Montgomery, and his version was trusted, but the HB is considered more reliable in providing the century or time of the split. H. G. Kippenberg follows Montgomery in thinking that the cult on Gerizim started as a result of the expulsion of priests from Jerusalem who were attached to northern traditions, Deut 11; 27; Josh 8.[29] H. G. M. Williamson also reasons in the same direction, although he works from the books of Ezra, Nehemiah and Chronicles, not primarily from Josephus. His view is summarized thus:

> During the earlier reforms of Ezra and Nehemiah, it is clear that there were at least two groups in Jerusalem. Particularly amongst the priests and aristocracy, there were those who favoured a fully open attitude to the inhabitants of the land, whether truly Israelites or not. On the other hand, the reform party took a rigorously exclusive view for ideological reasons. Dur-

---

[27] Ibid., 72 f.
[28] Ibid., 73.
[29] Kippenberg, *Garizim und Synagoge*, 58 f.

ing the decades which followed, attitudes vacillated, but tended on the whole to polarize. The Chronicler's programme for reconciliation in the mid-fourth century BC failed, and not long after a group of the assimilationists found themselves forced out. What was more natural than that they should remove to the ancient and sacred site of Shechem to establish a new community more truly representative of Israel as they saw it ...?[30]

A similar model is presented by A. D. Crown.[31] "There is uncertainty about the beginnings of the Samaritan nation," we may read; we are presented with a nation, whatever that is—no definition is given. Taking Josephus as his starting point, he considers that

> In these circumstances Samaritan history begins in the eighth century B.C.E. and takes us through the exilic and postexilic periods. It is marked especially by the processes in the time of Ezra and Nehemiah, which see the Samarian state beginning to flourish as a rival to Judah.
>
> In establishing the Torah as state law, Nehemiah and Ezra ensured a distinct Judean national identity. The separatism forced on the heirs of Israel and Judah by the postexilic Judean leaders may well have been the major factor in the rift which led to the Samarians becoming the Samaritan nation ... The aftermath of the Hadrianic persecutions led to the final breach between Judeans and Samaritans.[32]

This understanding takes the eighth century as its starting point, in line with one of the explanations for the origin of the Samaritans given by Josephus. They were "settlers who replaced deported Samarians after 720 B.C.E."[33] Even so, he speaks of a "rift," because the Samaritans were Yahwists.

The focus upon the introduction of the Torah by Ezra and Nehemiah as state law may seem surprising if it is understood as excluding the Samarians and turning them into Samaritans. If there is one characteristic of Samaritan religion in addition to the concentration on Mount Gerizim, it is the Torah. In itself the Torah could hardly have created an offence to the Samaritans, only if it was interpreted with Jerusalem as an identity-marker.

---

[30] H. G. M. Williamson, "The Temple in the Books of Chronicles," in *Templum Amicitiae: Essays on the Second Temple Presented to Ernst Bammel* (ed. W. Horbury; JSNTSup 48; Sheffield: Sheffield Academic Press, 1991), 31; repr. in *Studies in Persian History and Historiography* (FAT 38; Tübingen: Mohr Siebeck, 2004), 161.

[31] Crown, "Samaritans," *EDSS* 2: 817 f.

[32] Ibid.

[33] Ibid.

The definition of "Samaritans" given by R. Pummer in 2002 operates with ideas that come close to the second story told by Josephus. According to this definition, the Samaritans were

> that religio-ethnic group that has its roots in Judaism, but split off from the latter, rejected the temple of Jerusalem and regarded its own temple on Mount Gerizim as the only legitimate sanctuary; eventually, they became an independent religion ... Research during the last three to four decades has shown that the split between Judaism and Samaritanism occurred gradually. In this process, the destruction of the temple on Mt. Gerizim by John Hyrcanus in 111 B.C.E. must have been a momentous event, even if it was not the end of the mutual relationships between the two branches of the biblical religion(s).[34]

This understanding of the origin of the Samaritans is not introduced *expressis verbis* as a consensus view, but the procedure of including it inside a definition of terms suggests that it is. R. Pummer refers to one book and two articles as a background for this view, and these scholarly contributions sum up much recent research.[35]

An important idea in R. Pummer's understanding is that the Samaritans split off from Judaism. This echoes what Josephus said on their origin. But Pummer alleges that they "rejected the temple of Jerusalem and regarded [their] own temple on Mount Gerizim as the only legitimate sanctuary," and that "the destruction of the temple on Mt. Gerizim by John Hyrcanus in 111 B.C.E. must have been a momentous event." An old idea from Josephus is here combined with modern ones, those of a gradual development (see the next section) and of a "momentous event."

According to Stefan Schorch in his *Habilitationsschrift* from 2004 there is at present a consensus on the time of separation: J. Purvis with his dissertation from 1968 (see the next part of this review) has created a consensus on the question of the time of separation between Samaritans and Jews. The final emancipation (German: *Herauslösung*) of the Samaritans from the common Israelite-Jewish culture was connected to John Hyrcanus's destruction of the Samaritan sanctuary on Mount Gerizim in 128 B.C.E. The Samaritans emancipated themselves from the larger Israelite-

---

[34] Pummer, *Early Christian Authors*, 1 f.

[35] The works in question are the following: Kippenberg, *Garizim und Synagoge*, 1971; Dexinger, "Ursprung der Samaritaner," 1992, and idem, "Samaritan Origins and the Qumran texts," In *Essays in Honour of G. D. Sixdenier: New Samaritan Studies of the Société d'études samaritaines* (ed. A. D. Crown et al., Sydney: Mandelbaum, 1995), 169–184.

Jewish culture, and formed the first distinct group within this tradition. This event was part of a longer process with a prehistory and a *Wirkungs-geschichte*.[36]

What S. Schorch terms a consensus applies to the time of the final separation, the second century B.C.E., when the Pentateuch was edited and the Samaritan temple was destroyed by John Hyrcanus. This was the "momentuous event" (Pummer) which brought about the separation between the groups. Josephus' model of schism or split therefore resurfaces in this thinking.

A special version of the Samaritans' origin is presented by F. Altheim and R. Stiehl.[37] They take as their starting point a story presented by the philosopher Porphyry of Tyre (died 304 C.E.) in his "On the Christians." This neo-Platonic philosopher claims to build his story on Philo of Byblos (floruit 100 C.E.), who claims in turn to have translated the 'Phoenician history' by Sanchuniathon (13th century B.C.E.) into Greek. Altheim and Stiehl render the relevant text in Porphyry's "On the Christians" in this way: the Samaritans were the successors of the people whom Nebuchadnezzar assigned to Syria after the capture and deportation of the Jews. The Samaritans had helped him by pointing out the weak points of the children of Israel. Therefore, he neither accused nor killed nor captured the Samaritans, but let them live in Palestine under his patronage. Altheim and Stiehl conclude that the Samaritans were the direct descendants of the people who worshipped at the high places of Northern Israel in the period after 721 B.C.E.[38]

---

[36] "In bezug auf die Frage nach dem Zeitpunkt der Trennung zwischen Samaritanern und Juden hat J. PURVIS mit seinem 1968 erschienenen Buch "The Samaritan Pentateuch and the origin of the Samaritan sect" insofern einen weitestgehenden Konsens herbeigeführt, als die endgültige Herauslösung der Samaritaner aus der gemeinsamen israelitisch-jüdischen Kultur in unmittelbarem Zusammenhang mit der wohl 128 v. Chr. durch Johannes Hyrcanus erfolgten Zerstörung des samaritanischen Heiligtums auf dem Garizim steht. In diesem Sinne sind die Samaritaner daher auch als die älteste distinkte Gruppe der israelitisch-jüdischen Tradition zu betrachten. Indes hat diese Trennung nicht nur eine Vorgeschichte und einen historischen Kontext, sondern auch eine Wirkungsgeschichte, die überhaupt erst zur Ausbildung der im eigentlichen Wortsinne "samaritanischen" Identität führt. Wie lange dieser Prozeß gedauert hat, ist nicht völlig klar und insofern der Aussagewert der genannten relativen Datierung unterhöhlt." S. Schorch, *Die Vokale des Gesetzes: die samaritanische Lesetradition als Textzeugin der Tora: 1. das Buch Genesis*, (BZAW 339, Berlin: de Gruyter, 2004), 17 f., footnotes omitted.

[37] F. Altheim and R. Stiehl, "Erwägungen zur Samaritanerfrage," In *Die Araber in der Alten Welt* (ed. R. Stiehl, F. Altheim, and A. Calderini; Berlin: de Gruyter, 1967), 204–224.

[38] Philo's text translated: "Sie sind die Nachfolger derer, denen Nebukadnezar Syrien zuteilte, als er die Juden gefangengenommen und es (Syrien) von ihnen geräumt hatte. Die Samaritaner hatten ihm geholfen und hatten ihn auf die Schwächen der Kinder

Philo's story seems to have been built upon 2 Kgs 25:11 f. in the version of Josephus. The biblical story says that Nebuzaradan took captive the rest of the inhabitants of Jerusalem and "those deserters who fell to the Babylonian king," left behind some of the poor in the land, and set Gedaliah (v. 22) to rule over them. Josephus retells this story but says that the Babylonian general left behind the poor and the deserters in the country, and appointed Gedaliah as governor over them, *Ant.* 10.155. The idea that the deserters were left behind under Gedaliah's governorship seems to have been created into the story in Porphyry/Philo of Byblos; the inspiration for this story would come from Josephus, not from more ancient sources. To identify these deserters with the Samaritans, as Porphyry/Philo does, is a polemical and anti-Samaritan version of their origin. To add to this the allegation that the Samaritans were the descendants of the worshippers at the high places of Northern Israel, as Altheim and Stiehl do, is to use Josephus's interpretation of 2 Kgs 17 about the origin of the Samaritans on top of the anti-Samaritan reading of 2 Kgs 25 presented by Porphyry/Philo.

The conclusion drawn from Porphyry/Philo by F. Altheim and R. Stiehl rests on an interpretation of his "On the Christians" alone. It supplements ancient anti-Samaritan polemics with another ancient polemical idea: that the Samaritans were worshippers of the gods of the sanctuaries at the high places. The model applied is one of continuity from the eighth century on, similar to Josephus' reading of 2 Kgs 17.

Another example of the impact of Josephus is the interpretation of the two limestone capitals found on the eastern slope of the archaeological site on Mount Gerizim, below the flight of steps that led visitors into the temple.[39] In this area a large concentration of fallen stones were found, with pillar sections and some inscribed stones, which the excavator thinks were part of the temple. The two limestone capitals "are most important for the tracing of a possible first stage of the Samaritan temple on the mount. These finds may originally have belonged to the building constructed on the mount by the people brought to Shechem and Samaria by the Assyrian kings to replace the exiled Israelites, during the

---

Israel hingewiesen. So hatte er sie (die Samaritaner) noch belangt, sie weder getötet noch gefangengenommen, sondern hatte sie in Palaestina weiterhin unter seiner Herrschaft wohnen lassen." Altheim and Stiehl's conclusion: "Diese Gemeinde ist die geradlinige Fortsetzung des Höhenkultes im israelischen [sic] Nordreich, nichts anderes. Wenn man ihren Beginn feststellen will, wird man auf die Jahre nach 721 verwiesen," ibid., 217.

[39] E. Stern and Y. Magen, "Archaological Evidence for the First Stage of the Samaritan Temple on Mount Gerizim," *IEJ* 52 (2002): 49–57.

seventh [sic] century B.C.E. (cf. 2 Kings 17:24)."[40] The stones belong to a class of "proto-Aeolic capitals (sometimes also termed 'proto-Ionic'), dating from the period of the Israelite monarchy."[41] They may be dated to the Persian period, along with all the other finds in their loci, but another interpretation is attempted: they may be "relics taken from a nearby Israelite sanctuary at Shechem ... which was previously destroyed by the Assyrians ... the stones were perhaps collected by the first Samaritan settlers brought by the Assyrian kings to replace the exiled Israelites ... we may ... perhaps identify these stones as a part of the earliest 'House of YHWH' built by the Samaritans on Mount Gerizim from the relics of the older Israelite temple."[42]

In this interpretation much hangs on the reading of 2 Kgs 17 in the version of Josephus, *Ant.* 9.278 f., 288–291. The character of this version is the topic in the next chapter, but here it suffices to say that Josephus cannot be taken at face value. The deportation myth is one of three explanations of Samaritan origins in *Antiquities*, and the construction of the Samaritan temple is part of the second story, which Josephus locates to the age of Alexander. The temple may have been older, but to suppose that the "first Samaritan settlers" built it means the pre-exilic period, and this is substantially earlier. The title of the paper includes the phrase "evidence for the first stage of the Samaritan temple on Mount Gerizim," and this may be what the authors think the stones are. If so, the evidence must come from archaeology, and not from a mix of Josephus and archaeological artefacts.

A similar dependence upon Josephus can be seen in the interpretation of the names of the inscriptions found during the excavations on Mount Gerizim. The editor of the Hebrew and Aramaic inscriptions found four "Arabic" names in the onomasticon of the inscriptions, and interprets this as evidence of the deportation by Sargon II of "Arabs" into Samaria.[43] The introduction to this edition of the inscriptions describes the construction of the temple on Mount Gerizim and the development before the turn of the era much along the lines drawn by Josephus, even if the author thinks Sanballat the Horonite, a contemporary of Nehemiah, was responsible for the construction. On the dating of the construction, the author has no

---

[40] Ibid., 49.
[41] Ibid., 50.
[42] Ibid., 55 f.
[43] Y. Magen, H. Misgav and L. Tsfania, *The Aramaic, Hebrew and Samaritan Inscriptions* (vol. 1 of *Mount Gerizim Excavations*; ed. Y. Magen, H. Misgav and L. Tsfania; Jerusalem: Judea and Samaria Publications, 2004), [27].

confidence in Josephus, because the finds of coins and building remains tell against him. But the general development is still described in terms formed by Josephus.[44] The inscriptions and their interpretation will be discussed in chapter 6.

A combination of the Samaritan and Josephan models is found with E. König and V. Tcherikover, who suppose that the ten tribes developed into a mixed race.[45] Similarly, the idea could be that the ten tribes and the newcomers formed the Samaritans. "The newcomers adopted the religion of the land; Shechem became their national shrine."[46] Here, the Samaritan model is combined with ideas developed from Josephus. Another combination is found in the dissertation of J. Zsengellér.[47] He considers the old Israelite element in the population after 722 b.c.e. to be a Yahwistic group, under the domination of immigrants—who were divided into two groups, a Yahwistic group and a syncretistic group, with the latter constituting the upper layer of society. An influx of recalcitrant priestly elements from Jerusalem led to the building of the temple on Gerizim at the time of Alexander the Great, and it was destroyed by John Hyrcanus.

Both the Samaritan and the Josephan versions present us with a breach or schism model; one where the Samaritans break away from the Jews, and one where the Jews break away from orthodox Israel. Josephus also has a deportation model, and this has loomed large in scholarship. Scholars have tended to view the development in the light of these models, continuity, deportation, and schism, or schism only. The character of the Samaritan model has been commented upon in the previous chapter, and the following chapter will delve into the material presented by Josephus. Even when his *Tendenz* is taken into account, he presents interesting material, still valuable for the present study.

In the latter part of the twentieth century, other views were introduced. The most influential is what we may term the Cross-Purvis hypothesis, and this will be presented first. R. J. Coggins' theory also has won support, and this comes next. A third theory is included more as a curiosity; it is what we may term the Cain and Abel model.

---

[44] Ibid., [1]–[13].

[45] Details in Dexinger, "Ursprung der Samaritaner," 70 ff.

[46] *New Catholic Encyclopedia* (ed. T. A. Caldwell; Detroit: Gale, 2003), 633 f., s.v. "Samaritans."

[47] J. Zsengellér, *Garizim as Israel: Northern Tradition of the Old Testament and the Early History of the Samaritans* (Utrechtse Theogogische Reeks 38; Utrecht: Faculteit der Godgeleerdheid, 1998), 180.

The Cross-Purvis Hypothesis

J. Purvis formulated this position as early as 1968: "The Samaritan Yah-wists of mixed ethnic descent, who had exercised political authority and cultural leadership in Samaria, were now disenfranchised. They could no longer maintain the status or exercise the authority they had enjoyed ... The solution to their dilemma was undoubtedly found in the develop-ment of a new Samaritan community at Shechem."[48] In 1986 he summed up this hypothesis in six points:

1. At the beginning of the Greek period, the ruling family and associated nobility of Samaria were deprived of political leadership of the city and the region by the Macedonians. They settled again at the ancient site of Shechem, a city which had been abandoned but which they now rebuilt ...

2. At the time of their settlement, the Samaritans of Shechem built a sanctu-ary to YHWH on the adjacent mountain, Gerizim. The Samaritans were thus making a conscious effort to relate themselves to the most ancient of Israel's traditions in order to maintain the support of the native Palestinian population of that region ...

3. Aside from the highly prejudiced account of Josephus, there is no evi-dence that the priesthood of the Samaritan temple was derived from the Jerusalem cultus ...

4. The action of the Samaritans in establishing their own sanctuary appears, then, to have been an independent activity on their part and not a schism from Jerusalem. But it (as well as the rebuilding of Shechem) was certainly undertaken with Jerusalem in mind, for it constituted, in the words of Coggins, "a kind of counterpoise to Jerusalem, an alternative center of loyalty ..."

5. During their time at Shechem (the Samaritan temple was destroyed by John Hyrcanus in 128 B.C.E.; the city of Shechem in 107 ...) relations between the Samaritans and the Jews badly deteriorated ...

6. At some time subsequent to the building of their temple, the Samaritans produced an edition of the Pentateuch in which their theological legiti-macy was decisively declared and through which the cultic traditions of Jerusalem were (in contrast) declared illegitimate. This was accomplished by deliberate textual manipulation to underscore the sanctity (and neces-sity) of Shechem/Gerizim as the divinely ordained center of Israel's cultic life ... It was this contention, not simply the existence of a Samaritan tem-ple, which drove the permanent wedge between the Samaritans and the Jews ... [49]

---

[48] Purvis, *Samaritan Pentateuch*, 108 f.
[49] Purvis, "Samaritans and Judaism," 87–89.

The full hypothesis with all its elements was formulated by J. Purvis on the basis of his own dissertation and several articles by F. M. Cross.[50] It is relatively independent from Josephus, and it developed in several stages as research progressed. The research behind the six points can be summarized in this way.

1. The first point in Purvis' theory builds on the following material. In 1962 N. and P. Lapp excavated a cave in Wadi Daliyeh, and found a collection of papyri and bullae from the fourth century B.C.E. together with a number of skeletons. In one of the papyri and one of the bullae the name "Sanballat" occurs, interpreted by F. M. Cross and others as the name of a person living in the first half of the fourth century B.C.E., father of the governor of Samaria. The papyrus WDSP 11 recto contains text written in Aramaic language and script. Line 13 reads [סנאבלט בר וע‏ חנן סגנא‏, "]w' son of Sanballat, Hanan the prefect." A sealing, WD 22, a bulla, attached to WDSP 16, contains text written in Hebrew and with palaeo-Hebrew letters, and reads [יהו‏, "[סנא[בלט בן [סנא פחת שמר]ן‏ ... yahu, son of [San]ballat the governor of Samari[a." Coin 55 from the 1999 hoard of Y. Meshorer and S. Qedar contains five letters, read by them as [סנאבל[ט‏, "Sanballa[t]."[51] This evidence is interpreted as proof of a second Sanballat in a series of three, of whom the first lived at the time of Nehemiah (Sanballat the Horonite), and the third at the time of Darius III and Alexander. The book of Nehemiah would refer to Sanballat I, the Daliyeh papyrus and bulla and coin 55 to Sanballat II, and Josephus to Sanballat III. A series of Sanballats is conceivable as a result of the practice of papponymy.[52] The papyri stem from wealthy people who had fled Samaria at the time of Alexander the Great. They hid in a cave, where the Greek troops found them and suffocated them by burning fires outside the cave, where their skeletons were found in 1962 together with remnants of clothing and papyri.

We learn from Curtius and other ancient authors that the inhabitants of Samaria burned alive the Greek prefect of Samaria, Andromachus,

---

[50] See e. g. F. M. Cross, "Aspects of Samaritan and Jewish History in Late Persian and Hellenistic Times," *HTR* 59 (1966): 201–211; repr. in *Die Samaritaner* (ed. F. Dexinger and R. Pummer; WdF 604; Darmstadt: Wissenschaftliche, 1992), 312–323; idem, "Papyri of the fourth Century BC from Dâliyeh," in *New Directions in Biblical Archaeology* (ed. D. N. Freedman and J. C. Greenfield; New York: Doubleday, 1971), 45–69.

[51] Transcriptions, translations and discussion in J. Dušek, *Les manuscrits araméens du Wadi Daliyeh et la Samarie vers 450–332 av. J.-C.* (Leiden: Brill, 2007), 254–265.321–331; plates XI.XL.

[52] Full presentation and discussion in J. C. VanderKam, *From Joshua to Caiaphas: High Priests After the Exile*, (Minneapolis, Minn.: Fortress, 2004), 75 f.

while Alexander campaigned in Egypt, and in retaliation Alexander punished the Samarians. According to this theory, this had the effect that one
group fled to Wadi Daliyeh and was discovered and killed. Another company of refugees fled to Shechem, and rebuilt the city, because archaeological evidence provided by the Drew McCormick excavations under
G. E. Wright shows that the city was rebuilt in the latter part of the fourth
century B.C.E.[53] This assumed group is thought to consist of the remnants
from the city of Samaria, who had been disenfranchised by the Macedonians, and therefore could not return to the city of Samaria or stay there.
A synthesis of this evidence from Josephus and other ancient authors,
the Wadi Daliyeh papyri and archaeology was presented by F. M. Cross.[54]
Among the scholars who adopt this view is M. Mor, who in 1989 wrote
the introductory chapter in the large volume *The Samaritans*.[55]

The idea of disenfranchisement was first presented by Albrecht Alt.[56]
His understanding was based upon the assumption that the territory of
Palestine in the Persian period was organized with a provincial capital
under a governor (*Statthalter*) in Samaria, and a religious centre with a
temple for Yahweh in Jerusalem. This ellipse with two focal points gave
the region a balance that lasted until the Persians granted Nehemiah
the status of governor in Jerusalem. A restoration on the model of the
old Davidic kingdom with a political and religious centre in Jerusalem
created an imbalance and deprived the ruling class in Samaria of their
southern sphere of influence, and of access to their religious centre.
Such development had to be counterbalanced by a temple in the north,

---

[53] G. E. Wright's report on the Drew-McCormick excavations at Shechem is summed
up in his *Shechem: The Biography of a Biblical City* (London: Duckworth, 1965).

[54] Cross, "Aspects of Samaritan and Jewish History," 201–211.

[55] M. Mor, "The Persian, Hellenistic and Hasmonean Period," in *The Samaritans*
(ed. A. D. Crown; Tübingen: Mohr, 1989), 1–18, esp. 4–11. He offers three different
possibilities for the origin of the Samaritans, viz. "the northern tribes of Israel," (the same
idea as Montgomery had), "the captives whom the Assyrians had transferred," (2 Kgs 17
in the reading of Josephus), and "these diverse populations living together side-by-side
intermingled, forming a new people who were eventually called Cuthaeans or Samaritans
… Our knowledge of the Samaritans begins at the time of Nehemiah's governorship in
Juda," when Sanballat "the Horonite" was one of Nehemiah's opponents.

[56] A. Alt, "Die Rolle Samarias bei der Entstehung des Judentums," in *Festschrift Otto
Procksch zum sechzigsten Geburtstag am 9. August 1943* (ed. A. Alt et al.; Leipzig: A. Deichert'sche Verlagsbuchhandlung, 1934), 5–28; repr. in *Kleine Schriften zur Gechichte des
Volkes Israel*, vol. II, (München: C. H. Beck) 316–337; idem, "Zur Geschichte der Grenze
zwischen Judäa und Samaria," *PJ* 31 (1935), 94–111; repr. in *Kleine Schriften zur Gechichte
des Volkes Israel*, vol. II, (München: C. H. Beck) 346–362.

and the mountain with old traditions was chosen: Mount Gerizim. This happened at the time of the last Persian king, Darius III, as Josephus connects the incident with Alexander the Great, Ant. 11.306 ff. Alt's thesis was adopted by M. Noth.[57]

Both Alt's theory and the Cross-Purvis theory operate with the model of disenfranchised nobility in the city of Samaria as the people creating the Samaritans. The latter can be seen as a revision of the former, inspired by new excavations in Shechem and the surprise discovery of the Wadi Daliyeh papyri.

This element of the theory rests upon the combination of G. E. Wright's excavation of Shechem and the Wadi Daliyeh papyri. The most recent report on the excavations in Shechem redates the beginning of the Hellenistic occupation to 325 B.C.E. instead of Wright's 331. A gap of half a decade thus exists between the burning of Andromachus in Samaria and the reoccupation of Shechem. Even if such a precise dating of archeological finds may be precarious, the fact remains that there was a reoccupation of Shechem shortly after the burning of Andromachus in Samaria. More importantly, there is nothing in the finds from Shechem to link the place to Samaria.[58] Also, the combination of textual studies and archaeology undertaken by Wright and resulting in the theory of Samaritan relocation to Shechem can be contested for methodological reasons; we may refer to the general discussions about Bible and archaeology.

The papyri and bullae from Wadi Daliyeh have now been studied thoroughly by J. Dušek.[59] His conclusions are the following: there is no confirmation in the papyri or the bullae of a Sanballat II nor of a Sanballat III as governor of Samaria. Only Sanballat the Horonite, during the reign of Artaxerxes I, 465–425 B.C.E., can be confirmed from bullae and papyri, and from the book of Nehemiah. His son Delayah is attested as governor by papyri from Elephantine and one bulla for the period of Darius II, 424–405 B.C.E. The last governor of Samaria who is attested is (H)ananiah, on coins from the fourth century B.C.E. and two papyri

---

[57] M. Noth, *Geschichte Israels* (Göttingen: Vandenhoeck & Ruprecht, 1950), 317–321.

[58] E. F. Campbell, Jr., *Shechem II: Portrait of a Hill Country Vale* (The Shechem Regional Survey; ASOR: Archaeological Reports 2; Atlanta, Ga.: Scholars Press, 1991); idem, *Shechem III: The Stratigraphy and Architecture of Shechem/Tell Balatâh* (ASOR Archaeological Reports 6, Vol I: Text; Vol. 2: The Illustrations; Boston, Mass.: ASOR, 2002).

[59] Dušek, *Manuscrits araméens*.

from Wadi Daliyeh, and he was a contemporary of Artaxerxes III, 359–338 B.C.E.[60] Josephus' Sanballat, by F. M. Cross termed Sanballat III, can not be confirmed.

J. Dušek understands WDSP 11 recto, line 13, ‏[ועֹ בר סנאבלט חנן סגנא‏, "]w' son of Sanballat, Hanan the prefect," as referring to Hanan as a prefect, but Sanballat is not given a title, and he is the father of someone who cannot have been governor, as this official was always presented at the head of the list of officials. Some 21–32 letters appear to have preceded the name "[...]w'," and the governor may have been mentioned there. Similarly, WD 22, the bulla attached to WDSP 16, with the text ‏[יהו בן‏ ‏[סנא]בלט פחת שמר]ן‏, "... yahu, son of [San]ballat the governor of Samari[a," is reconstructed as referring to "Delayahu, the son of Sanballat, the governor of Samaria." Following common practice in these documents, the title "governor" refers to Delayahu, whom we know from the Elephantine papyri, and his father was Sanballat the Horonite, known from the same papyri and the book of Nehemiah. Coin 55 from the 1999 hoard of Y. Meshorer and S. Qedar, was read by them as ‏[סנאבל[ט‏, "Sanballa[t]." Dušek observes that a different reconstruction of the letters is needed, and suggests ‏סנאבי‏, "Sin'abi," "Sîn is my father."[61] On the whole, Dušek's discussion is convincing.[62]

There is therefore at the present no vindication of Josephus' account and of the theory of Samaritan abandonment of Samaria and resettlement of Shechem during the days of Alexander the Great. A different understanding of Josephus on this point will be suggested in the next chapter. What can be said is that Samaria was converted into a Macedonian city, that the nobility of Samaria were killed in the cave in Wadi Daliyeh, possibly in 332–331 B.C.E., and that Shechem appears to have been repopulated around 325 B.C.E.

A. Alt's theory rests upon the assumption that there was no governor in Jerusalem before Nehemiah, but new finds of seals and bullae have been interpreted to the effect that Judah was a separate province from the sixth century or the early fifth century.[63] This would not invalidate the

---

[60] Ibid. 548 f.

[61] Ibid., 254–265.321–331.

[62] It appears that Dušek's arguments have not been taken into account by H. Eshel, "The Governors of Samaria in the Fifth and Fourth Centuries B.C.E.," in *Judah and the Judeans in the Fourth Century B.C.E.* (ed. O. Lipschits, G. N. Knoppers and R. Albertz; Winona Lake, Ind.: Eisenbrauns, 2007), 223–234. He therefore suggests a Sanballat II.

[63] N. Avigad, "Bullae and Seals from a Post-Exilic Judean Archive," *Qedem* 4 (1976) 36–52; N. Na'aman., "Samaria. II. Provinz," *RGG* 4 (2004): 816.

theory—it could apply for an earlier period; from A. Alt's theory and the Cross-Purvis-hypothesis, there is still left the idea of disenfranchisement.

2.–4. These parts of the theory follow from the first element.

5. A temple on Mount Gerizim and its destruction are mentioned by 2 Macc 6:2 and Josephus.

6. After suggestions by J. M. Jost and J. Taglicht of a split in the Maccabean period, W. F. Albright was the first to find an argument for a split in this period in the shape of the Samaritan letters: he dated this shape to the Hasmonean period; he was followed by F. M. Cross and G. E. Wright. The systematic investigation of the phenomenon of the script was done by J. Purvis. His work deserves a closer look.

J. Purvis' dissertation from 1968 focuses upon three phenomena of the SP. First, he studies its palaeography. This is done by comparing the earliest Samaritan inscriptions with the general development of the palaeo-Hebrew script from the sixth century B.C.E. to the second century C.E. The task seems to be a double one: first, to assess the palaeographic location of the script of the Samaritan inscriptions, second, to assess the relation between the Samaritan inscriptions and the Samaritan manuscripts. Purvis wrote the internal history of the script of the inscriptions. The Samaritan inscriptions, and one mosaic, are dated from the first century B.C.E. or C.E. to the fourth century C.E. His conclusion is that, "The earliest examples of Samaritan writing, known from inscriptions of the Roman period, indicate that the parentage of this particular script was the paleo-Hebrew of the Hashmonaean era."[64] "The Palestinian character of the proto-Samaritan is also indicated by its survival in the palaeo-Hebrew script (in 4Q Ex$^\alpha$)—the old national script of Palestine."[65] The underlying assumption is that the script of the inscriptions is similar enough to that of the SP-manuscripts to warrant conclusions about the age of the Samaritan version of the Pentateuch. Further, "it is not an archaizing sectarian creation in which an attempt has been made to bring into being a script comparable to the writing of ancient Israel."[66]

The second point is orthography. Purvis' conclusion is that the full orthography of the Samaritan Pentateuch manuscripts corresponds to the Hasmonean and Herodian manuscripts from Qumran, not to any earlier orthography, nor to the later MT orthography.

---

[64] Purvis, *Samaritan Pentateuch*, 21.
[65] Ibid., 80 f.
[66] Ibid., 20.

The third point in his study is the text type of the SP. As a full, or harmonistic, text it belongs to the Hasmonean period.

Earlier scholarship tended to consider the *construction* of the Samaritan temple as the decisive event in the relation between Samaritans and Jews, whether this took place in the Persian or the Hellenistic period. Purvis instead considers the *destruction* of the temple as the major event. "The complete and irreparable break in relations between the Samaritans and the Jews occurred neither in the Persian nor the Greek periods. It occurred in the Hasmonaean period as the result of the destruction of Shechem and the ravaging of Gerizim by John Hyrcanus."[67] The Samaritan script, the orthography of the SP and its text type all also point to the period. This development created Samaritanism of a type that no longer belonged to Judaism and did not return to it.[68]

Purvis was generally praised for his dissertation. J. Bright found it "extremely valuable—and, to this reviewer, convincing ... an important monograph ... highly commended," and he had no reservations.[69] R. Coggins thought that "Purvis has made a very convincing case for the redaction of the Samaritan Pentateuch during the Hasmonean age ... his basic conclusions will surely win general support."[70] E. Tov accepts the results of Purvis, but disagrees on the time the Samaritans became a sect.[71]

Other voices were more sceptical. Z. Ben-Hayyim:

> Conclusions drawn from orthography must be examined in relation to the Samaritan pronunciation ... whose antiquity goes back to the days of the Hasmoneans. In any event this requires proof ... Can one really come to an important historical and social conclusion such as the time of the formation of the Samaritan sect according to the orthographic form and the script of its Holy Writ? Can the Jewish version of the Torah with its square script testify as to the time of the crystallization of Judaism? Doesn't the existence of the Dead Sea Scrolls, with the differences in the writing even in the Torah, teach us the opposite of the supposition of the author?[72]

More sarcastic was B. Roberts: "Albright and Cross have spoken and that is that!" Roberts criticized Purvis for not giving "due emphasis

---

[67] Ibid., 118.
[68] Ibid., 86 f.
[69] J. Bright, review of Purvis, *Samaritan Pentateuch, CBQ* 31 (1969): 453 f.
[70] R. Coggins, review of Purvis, *Samaritan Pentateuch, JSS* 14 (1969): 273–275.
[71] Tov, *Textual Criticism*, 83 f.
[72] Z. Ben-Hayyim, review of Purvis, *Samaritan Pentateuch, Bib* 52 (1971): 255.

to the rather obvious hazard of comparing the script of inscriptions with that written on leather."[73]

The difference between formal (monumental inscriptions on stone) and cursive scripts (on ostraca, leather and papyrus) can be observed in Hebrew epigraphy,[74] and it is seen also in the charts provided by Purvis.[75] It is clear in the case of Chart VI "Early Samaritan Scripts," i. e. of the Samaritan inscriptions, and Chart VII "Late Samaritan Scripts," i.e. of Samaritan manuscripts from the 9th to the 16th century C.E. The general distinction between formal and cursive scripts now made by scholars is due to the difference in the inscribed materials and the tools for inscribing. The fundamental difference between stone on the one hand and clay, leather, and papyrus on the other influences opportunities to create the shape of letters. With the ever growing amount of texts, scholars are now able to see that what was earlier considered the result of development was in fact partly due to difference in materials and tools.[76]

A special case is the script on coins, seals, stamps, and bullae. These undergo separate developments, partly due to a conservative tendency, partly to the production methods of these artifacts.[77] Purvis only relies on the coins from the two Jewish revolts to prove the separation of Samaritan from Jewish script, but his observations here are easily explained as a difference in materials and in attitude (archaizing tendency in the coins).

In the study, Purvis considers script on all these materials without distinctions. This makes the results unreliable. There are clear differences between the scripts of the Samaritan inscriptions and those of the manuscripts, but these differences are not studied or commented upon by Purvis. "References to the later Samaritan inscriptions and manuscripts are made only when it seems advisable to note the further evolution of a trend which was begun, but not fully developed, in the

---

[73] B. Roberts, review of Purvis, *Samaritan Pentateuch*, *JTS* 20 (1969): 570.

[74] J. Renz and W. Röllig, *Die althebräischen Inschriften: Teil 1: Text und Kommentar* (vol. II/1 of *Handbuch der althebräischen Epigraphik*; Darmstadt: Wissenschaftliche, 1995), 96f.99.

[75] Purvis, *Samaritan Pentateuch*, Charts I–VII at the end of the book.

[76] Renz and Röllig, *Die althebräischen Inschriften*, 96. What is said here about the scripts of the tenth to the sixth century B.C.E. is transferable to later periods. Cf. also S. Talmon, "A Masada Fragment of Samaritan Origin," *IEJ* 47 (1997): 230.

[77] J. Renz and W. Röllig, *Materialien zur althebräischen Morphologie, Siegel und Gewichte* (vol. II/2 of *Handbuch der althebräischen Epigraphik*; Darmstadt: Wissenschaftliche, 2003), 106f.–108, for the seals and bullae.

early inscriptions."[78] This makes the connection between inscriptions and manuscripts uncertain, or at least not ascertained. In addition to these arguments of principle, come the new discoveries. Purvis's approach is set in a new light with the discovery of inscriptions on Mount Gerizim, cf. chapter 4. These are in different scripts, both palaeo-Hebrew and Aramaic.

4QpaleoExod[m] / 4Q22 is understood by Purvis to be pre-Hasmonean or early Hasmonean, but it is now on palaeographic grounds re-dated to late first century B.C.E., late Hasmonean or Herodian.[79] Only one of the relevant manuscripts, 4Q22, is in the palaeo-Hebrew script, the others are in the square script. If the Samaritans used a palaeo-Hebrew script from the second century B.C.E., they adopted the Pentateuch in a script that was preserved in the Qumran community both in a later variant of the palaeo-Hebrew script and in the square script, or they must have transcribed their Pentateuch into the Hasmonean script, perhaps as an archaism. If, as Purvis assumes, the adoption of the Pentateuch in a specific script is the expression of a sectarian process, we have problems explaining why this script was preserved and used in Qumran a century later. That the text of Exodus was in use at the end of the first century B.C.E., is seen from the repair of 4Q22: it was patched and re-scribed in col. XX because of wear and tear. The Qumran evidence shows that one text-type could have different graphic representations and that the 'full' or 'harmonistic' text-type was in use down to the turn of the era by other groups than the Samaritans.

The Cross-Purvis theory has two elements, the first part centring on the Wadi Daliyeh papyri, and the latter focusing on the destruction of the temple and the creation of the SP. In view of the relevant material and the discussion following the early publications on this theory, not much remains of it today. There may be material on the construction of the temple on Mount Gerizim and its destruction, and this will be considered later. The SP deserves closer scrutiny, and it will be treated in a separate chapter. The idea of disenfranchisement remains a possibility, which is difficult to verify.

---

[78] Purvis, *Samaritan Pentateuch*, 28.

[79] Purvis, *Samaritan Pentateuch*, 50; cf. J. Sanderson, "4QpaleoExodus[m]," in *Qumran Cave 4, IV: Palaeo-Hebrew and Greek Biblical Manuscripts* (ed. P. W. Skehan, J. E. Sanderson, and E. Ulrich; DJD 9; Oxford: Clarendon, 1992), 53–103.

R. J. Coggins' Model: Estrangement, and no Reconciliation

The fixed point in the consensus view, mentioned earlier, is John Hyrcanus's attack on the Samaritan temple, in 111 B.C.E. according to Pummer and in 128 B.C.E. according to Schorch. The importance of this attack
is, however, relativized if the development is viewed as a longish process.
This model was suggested by R. J. Coggins' *Samaritans and Jews* in 1975,
and he succeeded in creating a version which is more or less independent
of Josephus.[80]

R. J. Coggins' contribution from 1975 proposed to substitute the expression "process of estrangement"[81] for the older "schism." Samaritanism, according to him, "emerged from the matrix of Judaism," and
"differences concerning the priesthood and the true sanctuary were
among those that did most to ensure that reconciliation was unlikely."[82]
This does not exclude some "momentous event," as R. Pummer expresses
it, but the emphasis is on process and development, not on one event
in particular. The leading principle is one of estrangement, like partners sharing a common origin, but growing in different directions. This
understanding has contributed to the character of the "consensus view,"
perhaps because of the idea that Judaism constituted the origin out of
which Samaritanism developed. It is therefore not fundamentally different from the idea of a "split," since it also presupposes a common origin.
It results in emphasis upon a pre-history and *Wirkungsgeschichte* of the
late second century B.C.E. events.

R. J. Coggins' idea, that the Samaritans "emerged from the matrix of
Judaism," presupposes Judaism, and an emergence from this. One may
ask why it is natural to think in this way. Is it because Josephus and
the Samaritan chronicles both consider that one group split off from the
other? It is not necessary to suppose this, as we have seen. The Samaritans
could be the descendents of the earlier inhabitants of the north in a
continuous development, and even if frictions existed between Jerusalem
and the Samaritans, the development could have been more independent
in both parties.

---

[80] Coggins, *Samaritans and Jews*.
[81] Ibid., 7.
[82] Ibid., 164.

"Cain and Abel"

Both the Samaritan and the Jewish myth presuppose that the origins can be found in HB accounts. Attempts have been made to follow this up consistently, and at the upper end of the scale there is this peculiar idea:

> The history of the Samaritan people might be said to begin with the revolt of the Northern tribes from the rule of the House of David under the leadership of Jeroboam ... The original difference between the two sections of the people, due to the predominantly pastoral character of the tribe of Judah, in contrast with the widely spread agriculture of Ephraim and Manasseh, and the tribes that possessed the pre-eminently fertile plain of Jezreel, was accentuated during Solomon's reign, and after it, by a religious difference.[83]

That the Samaritans originally should have been tillers of the soil, and to this characteristic added a religious difference in relation to Solomon's son Rehoboam, is an explanation belonging to the realm of the curious. Even without appealing to scholars' treatment of the historical sources in the HB at the time this idea was presented, this cannot be considered an advantageous starting point for the quest for Samaritan origins. But it is an idea of continuity from earliest times and development from the starting point. It is most similar to the Samaritan myth, but with the twist of reading Cain and Abel into the North-South controversy. A modest reflection of this idea can be found in a recent book.[84]

Summing up, what remains from the different hypotheses still to be investigated is the material emerging from the excavations on Mount Gerizim and the SP. Even more important is, however, an investigation of a series of texts directed against the dwellers in Shechem. These texts have not received due attention in the research surveyed here. Also, there is material relevant for the Samaritan attitude towards prophets. The different ways of thinking, here labelled "models," will be kept in mind. But most of all, Josephus deserves another look. It is time to turn to his material.

---

[83] J. E. H. Thomson, *The Samaritans: Their Testimony to the Religion of Israel* (Being the Alexander Robertson Lectures, delivered before the University of Glasgow in 1916; London: Oliver & Boyd, 1919), 24–26.

[84] Anderson and Giles, *Keepers*, 16 f.: "The cultural differences between north and south reflect the historic conflict between the farmer and herdsman (highlighted in the biblical story of Cain and Abel) and it provides the backdrop of the Bible's suspicions of a religious sect claiming to be Israelite but not aligned with Jerusalem."

CHAPTER FOUR

JOSEPHUS ON THE ORIGIN OF THE SAMARITANS[1]

4.1. *Terminology and Sources*

"There can be little doubt of Josephus' prejudice against the Samaritans. In this, he reflects the general Jewish attitude of bitterness and contempt, as seen in rabbinic writings," L. Feldman wrote in 1989.[2] Doubt was raised, however, by R. Egger in her dissertation from 1986: she found that Josephus cannot be termed an anti-Samaritan author.[3]

The background for this difference of opinion is an important question: Which terms are used by Josephus to refer to the Samaritans? First, there are Σαμαρ(ε)ῖται (sing. Σαμαρ(ε)ίτης, fem: Σαμαρ(ε)ῖτις) and Σαμαρεῖς (sing. Σαμαρεύς, fem. Σαμαρῖτις)—do they both refer to the Samaritans or only one of them? In the latter case: which one? Then, there are Χουθαῖοι, Σικιμῖται, Ἑβραῖοι and Σιδώνιοι—to which groups do they refer? Clearly, the answer to these questions will influence our decision about which texts speak about the Samaritans.

Egger has undertaken to investigate the terminology of Josephus on this point. Σαμαρεῖς is found 49 times, Σαμαρεῖται 18 times, Σικιμῖται (including variants of this word) 17 times and Χουθαῖοι 8 times.[4] Are

---

[1] I am indebted to Steve Mason and Honora Howell Chapman for valuable comments and suggestions on my work in this chapter.

[2] L. H. Feldman, "A Selective Critical Bibliography of Josephus," in *Josephus, the Bible and History* (Detroit: Wayne State University Press, 1989), 330–448. Quotation from 420.

[3] Egger, *Josephus Flavius und die Samaritaner*, 311. She notes, however, a certain *Ambivalenz*, cf. 73, n. 176, referring to *Ant.* 9.291; 12.257; 11.340f. Cf. in general the important review by É. Nodet in *RB* 95 (1988): 288–294.

[4] Egger, *Josephus Flavius und die Samaritaner*, 48.247–249. A. Kasher, "Josephus on Jewish-Samaritan Relations under Roman Rule (B.C.E. 63 – C.E. 70)," in *Essays in honour of G. D. Sixdenier: New Samaritan Studies of the Société d'Études Samaritaines* (vols. 3 & 4; Proceedings of the Congresses of Oxford 1990, Yarnton Manor and Paris 1992, Collège de France with lectures given at Hong Kong 1993 as participation in the ICANAS Congress; ed. A. D. Crown and L. Davey; Studies in Judaica 5; Sydney: Mandelbaum, 1995), 217–236, seems not to make any distinctions between Σαμαρεῖται and Σαμαρεῖς, but treats all the occurrences as "Hellenic" designations (217, n. 4) referring to the Samaritans.

all the persons referred to by these designations really Samaritans, as the secondary literature will have us believe?[5]

Egger defines the Samaritans as "the Samaritan religious community" (*die Samaritanische Religionsgemeinschaft*), a group believing in YHWH, holding Mount Gerizim as the chosen place, sacrificing to YHWH in the temple there, and regarding only the Pentateuch as Scripture. Josephus refers directly to that community by the expression "those of Gerizim," (ἀπό ...) τῶν ἐν Γαριζείν, *Ant.* 12.7.[6] The other expressions may occasionally refer to the Samaritans. Thus, in her opinion, texts that speak of the Samaritan religious community are only *War* 3.307–315 (massacre under Cerealius); *Ant.* 12.7,10 (deportation to Egypt; discussions in Egypt about the temple site); 13.74f. (discussion in Egypt); 18.85–89 (Pilate stops the armed gathering to find the hidden temple vessels); these texts all mention "Gerizim." Possible other texts are: *War* 1.592 par *Ant.* 17.69 (Antipater); *War* 2.111 par. *Ant.* 17.342 (Archaelaus' brutality); *Ant.* 17.20 (Herod's wife Malthace); 18.30 (scattering of human bones in the Jerusalem temple); 18.167 (Agrippa borrows a million drachmas from a freedman).[7]

According to her, there are some clear tendencies: Josephus did not differentiate terminologically between the Samaritans and others.[8] Σαμαρεῖς refers to inhabitants of the city or region of Samaria, but not necessarily to them in their entirety.[9] For the Persian period, Σαμαρεῖται is the preferred term, as is Σαμαρεῖς for the period following the second century B.C.E. Some few texts refer to the Samaritans using the term Σαμαρεῖς.

An important observation is that the scribes who copied the manuscripts of *Antiquities* saw the two terms as synonyms: in the manuscripts Σαμαρεῖται is often substituted for Σαμαρεῖς.[10]

As for the Σικμῖται, Egger found that they were Sidonians settled to the west of Samaria in the time of the Persians, and therefore Josephus in *Ant.* 12.258ff. makes the mistake of identifying them with settlers from Media and Persia.[11]

---

[5] Egger, *Josephus Flavius und die Samaritaner*, 11.
[6] Ibid., 20.
[7] Ibid., 310.
[8] Ibid., 250.
[9] Ibid., 169.
[10] Ibid., 249.
[11] Ibid., 283 f.

The Χουθαῖοι were also Sidonians/Phoenicians, living at Gerizim. The Samaritans knew the origin of these Hellenistic Phoenicians, and named them Χουθαῖοι. This expression was taken over by the Jews and later extended to other foreigners.[12] John Hyrcanus destroyed the temple at Gerizim (*War* 1.63), which had been taken over by that time by the Sidonians, called Χουθαῖοι by Josephus—as he followed a Samaritan source at this point.[13]

One notices that two texts which have played a major role in the understanding of Josephus' account of the origin of the Samaritans, *Ant.* 9.278 f., 288–291 and 11.302–346, are absent from Egger's lists.

The assumption behind her investigation is that it is possible to find the Samaritans of her definition referred to by terms and expressions used by Josephus; but if she cannot find in the context the crucial element of her definition (Gerizim), the terms used must refer to some other entity, which may also be clearly definable. She assumes that the construction of the temple was done by a different group of Χουθαῖοι than the Χουθαῖοι whose temple was destroyed.

The pertinent question is then: is it appropriate to read the text of Josephus seeking consistent historical definitions? The danger is that one will read into the text only what is defined in advance. In Egger's case the material is reduced to only a few texts referring to the Samaritans of her definition. These texts contain little information in addition to her *a priori* definition of the Samaritans. Egger believes that a study of the terms will give us history—against the text of Josephus—a history she knows through her definition.

The topic that Egger has addressed is important, but the methodological question remains: is it possible to find such differences in the referents of the terms? A. Schalit listed Σαμαρεύς and Σαμαρείτης in one and the same entry in the *Namenwörterbuch zu Flavius Josephus*.[14] This may reduce the usefulness of the concordance at this point, but reveals another expert's thinking on the subject: the two terms were not used by Josephus to differentiate.

In considering this question one has to take into account the texts where Josephus identifies one designation with another. Of relevance are the following texts:

---

[12] Ibid., 300–302.
[13] Ibid., 287–300.
[14] A. Schalit, *Namenwörterbuch zu Flavius Josephus* (Leiden: Brill), 1968, 105.

Even now the name Χουθαῖοι continues to be used for these nations in the Hebrew language, whereas in Greek they are called Σαμαρεῖται. (*Ant.* 9.290)

Once Salmanasses had then deported the Israelites, he settled in their place the nation of Chouthaites (τὸ τῶν Χουθαίων ἔθνος), who previously were in the interior of Persia and Media. Thereafter, however, they were called the Samareians (Σαμαρεῖς) getting this name from the country in which they were settled. (*Ant.* 10.184)

... the Χουθαῖοι–it is by this name that the Σαμαρεῖται are called.[15]

(*Ant.* 11.88)

In the contexts of these three texts the Χουθαῖοι are twice equated with the Σαμαρεῖται and once with the Σαμαρεῖς. The identifications in these cases may not have been observed consistently by Josephus throughout his work, but they are indications that one cannot draw clear dividing lines between the words and assume that each of them has a distinct reference. The picture gained from these texts is that Josephus used three different designations for the Samaritans, and to some extent they seem interchangeable, and that at least one of them was derived from the country to which they were deported.

'Kuthaean' appears in a text from the second half of the first century B.C.E., the so-called 'Proto-Esther' found at Qumran, 4Q550[a-f]. Six fragments are supposed to belong together, and fragment c contains the following: "You know [... it is] possible to a Kutha[ean] man to return [...] your [kin]gdom, standing in the place where you stand [...] ... [...]." Unfortunately, we do not get much help to understand the name from this text, since it has many lacunae, as do the other 'Proto-Esther' fragments. There are no clear indications in the context what *Kuti* in 4Q550[c] I 5: *lgbr kwt[y]*, "to a Kutha[ean] man," might refer to.

A second group of texts from Josephus are those where the terminology varies in the same context. *War* 3.307–315; *Ant.* 11.114–118; 12.257–262; 18.85–89,118–135 oscillate between Σαμαρεῖται and Σαμαρεῖς. *Ant.* 11.302–346 uses all four terms, Σαμαρεῖται, Σαμαρεῖς, Χουθαῖοι, and Σικιμῖται. This last text has been subject to source analysis based upon this fact. There may be sources behind the text, but as it stands it bears the mark of Josephus, and even if the variation is due to the character of different sources, he did not reduce the number of terms

---

[15] Translation by Begg and Spilsbury, *Judean Antiquities Books 8–10.*

employed. *Ant.* 12.10 employs Σαμαρεῖς and Σικιμῖται. In these texts it seems that the different expressions were used for the same group of people, as Josephus wanted to portray them.

A third group of texts are the parallels in *War* and *Antiquities*. Josephus covers the period from Antiochus Epiphanes both in *War*, written in 75–79 C.E. and in *Antiquities*, completed in 93/94 C.E. The following table shows the actual terms in the incidents told in *War* and their counterparts in *Ant.*:[16]

Σαμαρεῖται		Σαμαρεῖς		Χουθαῖοι	
				War	*Ant.*
				1.62–63	13.254–256
	War 1.65	*Ant.* 13.275 ff.			
War 1.562		*Ant.* 17.20			
War 1.592	*Ant.* 17.69				
	War 2.111	*Ant.* 17.342			
	Ant. 18.118, 136	*War* 2.232 f., 237, 239 f., 242 f., 245	*Ant.* 18.118 f., 121 f., 125, 127, 129 f., 132, 134 f.		

Josephus' terminology is stable. In five cases he used the same terms; in one case he perhaps changed from Σαμαρεῖται to Σαμαρεῖς. In the case of Herod's wife, she is a Σαμαρεῖτις (from Σαμαρείτης or Σαμαρεύς) in *War* 1.562, but τοῦ Σαμαρέων ἔθνους in *Ant.* 17.20. The female form in *War* 1.562 could derive from any of the terms, therefore the case is not clear. In another case, *Ant.* 18 uses Σαμαρεῖς as in *War* 2, but supplements this term with Σαμαρεῖται. Οἱ Σαμαρεῖται is introduced at the beginning and end of the story about the difficulties arising from the killing in Ginaea, *Ant.* 18.118,136, in addition to the reuse of Σαμαρεῖς. Both terms are already present in *War* in the story of the killing of the 11,600 on Mount Gerizim, *War* 3.307–315 (no parallel in *Antiquities*).

---

[16] For the first two cases, cf. J. Sievers, *Synopsis of the Greek sources for the Hasmonean Period: 1–2 Maccabees and Josephus, War 1 and Antiquities 12–14* (*SubBi* 20; Roma: Pontificio istituto biblico, 2001), 209 f. 213.

In addition to these incidents *Antiquities* presents a number of others during the same period: Archelaus is accused by Judeans and Σαμαρεῖς in front of Caesar, 17.342; οἱ Σαμαρεῖται scatter human bones in the temple, 18.30; Pilate stops οἱ Σαμαρεῖς / οἱ Σαμαρεῖται in an armed gathering to find the hidden vessels on Mt Gerizim, 18.85–89; Agrippa borrows a million drachmas from a freedman, a Σαμαρεύς, 18.167. There are, accordingly, three cases with Σαμαρεύς and two with Σαμαρείτης.

It is not possible to conclude that Josephus had made his language more precise during the 14–19 years that had passed after the writing of the *War*, as there is one case where Σαμαρεῖται is introduced and one more case with Σαμαρεύς than with Σαμαρείτης in the parts found in one of the works only. The major difference between *War* and *Antiquities* is, of course, that *Antiquities* covers the history of Israel before the period covered by *War*. In this part of *Antiquities* Σαμαρεύς is used eleven times, and Σαμαρείτης ten times.

The occurrences of the two terms balance each other. There is no clear development from *War* to *Antiquities*, and the two terms are used in the same contexts and seem interchangeable. The only clear tendency that can be observed occurs after Josephus: in the manuscripts Σαμαρεῖται is often substituted for Σαμαρεῖς. The scribes tended to consider Σαμαρεῖται the natural choice in these contexts, and this may be taken as an indication that this term took on the meaning 'Samaritans' in a sense comparable to how modern readers would understand that term.

Taken together these observations show that it is futile to assume different referents for the different words. Josephus did not develop his terminology during the period between *War* and *Antiquities*, and he used the words interchangeably in both works. Where there are changes, they move in opposite directions, which means that he did not have any preference for one word over the other, and saw them as referring to the same group of people.

One may assume that Josephus did not use the different terms in a technical but in a broad way. This is one of the conclusions reached by R. Egger in her dissertation for the terms Σαμαρεῖς and Σαμαρεῖται,[17] but it may be generalized to encompass the other terms as well. Whether this broad use of the terms is due to the possible *Urtext* of Josephus, even if in Aramaic, to his own Greek text, to that of his possible secretaries

---

[17] Egger, *Josephus Flavius und die Samaritaner*.

or translators or to the text of the later scribes, is of course impossible to decide. What we have is a text extant in several manuscripts, and the tendency of the scribes was to a more extensive use of Σαμαρεῖται—perhaps because the Samaritan community was more and more referred to as Σαμαρεῖται in the vernacular after the time of Josephus.

As a result, we may look at all the texts traditionally assumed to deal with the Samaritans, and not confine ourselves to those chosen by Egger.[18]

Other scholars have also used the terminology as a starting point, and used this as a help to reconstruct Josephus' sources.[19] Especially the extensive treatment of the construction of the temple on Mount Gerizim in *Ant.* 11.302–346, with all four terms present, seems to invite scholars to do a *Literarkritik* in the sense of source criticism. In discussing A. Buchler's (also written Büchler) supposed three sources behind this text,[20] Kippenberg used the terminology as a criterion for a new source analysis. Buchler found one Samaritan source, one Jewish story modelled on the Samaritan source, and a third source, also Jewish. All of them are from the first century B.C.E.

Kippenberg rightly criticised Buchler for assuming a Samaritan source that contains inconsistencies, and suggested that only parts of it belongs to the supposed Samaritan source. Starting with the use of Σικιμῖται, and looking for material where the cult on Gerizim is considered to be the responsibility of a community and not of a family, he delimited a supposed Jewish source. This source uses Samaritan material that tells how Alexander legitimized the temple on Gerizim.

---

[18] For further criticisms of Egger, *Josephus Flavius und die Samaritaner*, see especially the reviews by R. Pummer, *JBL* 107 (1988): 768–772 and G. Brooke, *JSS* 37 (1992): 109–112, who both focus on other important aspects than those mentioned here.

[19] Kippenberg, *Garizim und Synagoge*, 50–57.

[20] A. Buchler, "Les sources de Flavius Josèphe dans ses Antiquités (XII, 5, 1–XIII)," *REJ* 32 (1896): 179–199; 34 (1897): 69–93. This analysis is adopted by M. Z. Segal, "נישואי בן כהן גדול עם בת־סנבלט ובניין מקדש־גריזים / The Marriage of the Son of the High Priest with the Daughter of Sanballat and the Building of the Temple of Gerizim," in *Simcha Assaf Anniversary Volume* (ed. M. D. Cassuto et al.; Jerusalem: Mossad Harav Kook 1952–1953), 404–414; repr. "Die Heirat des Sohnes des Hohenpriesters mit der Tochter des Sanballat und der Bau des Heiligtums auf dem Garizim," in *Die Samaritaner* (ed. F. Dexinger and R. Pummer; WdF 604; Darmstadt: Wissenschaftliche, 1992), 198–219. The analysis is basically adopted and extensively used also in Dexinger, "Ursprung der Samaritaner," 102–140.

However, this result falls down on the same criticism that Kippenberg
levelled against Buchler: the supposed source is inconsistent. In *Ant.*
11.345 f. it is claimed that the Jerusalemites who eat unclean food or
commit any other such sin flee to the Σικμῖται. The assumption that
this is in a Jewish source is conceivable. As Samaritan material it is
unthinkable. If Kippenberg's result is to be combined with Buchler's—
he is not clear on this point—there are two pro-Jewish sources and one
anti-Samaritan. But this is an impression one can also get by reading the
final text of Josephus: he is pro-Jewish and anti-Samaritan. It is simply the
text Josephus presents, whether he used sources for it or not. Feldman's
comment on Buchler's analysis is to the point: "... such a vivisection of
Josephus is hardly as likely as the view that Josephus had a single source,
which was more balanced than either BÜCHLER or SEGAL will admit."[21]
The significance of finding sources would be that it might open up the
possibility of dating the material to a specific period prior to Josephus,
but the tendencies are the same.

H. G. Kippenberg's idea that the word Σικμῖται reveals a Samaritan
source is faced with the fact that this term is used by Josephus in his
rendering of Gen 34, which will be discussed at the end of this chapter.
The idea of a Samaritan source is unlikely. Kippenberg also used the
occurrence of the term 'Argarizim' as an indication of a Samaritan source
in *War* 1.63, but there is no firm basis for this idea, as the discussion of
this term in chapter 6 will show.[22]

Feldman focused on the vocabulary of Josephus in studying the use
of ἔθνος and cognate terms to determine whether Josephus regarded
the Samaritans as Jews or as non-Jews.[23] His result was that Josephus is
ambivalent: he calls them an ἔθνος, distinct from the Jews, and at the
same time treats them as a Jewish sect: they are "Jews but rebellious in
their views," as he concluded with a nice rhyme.[24] "Josephus, like the

---

[21] L. H. Feldman, *Josephus and modern Scholarship (1937–1980)* (Berlin: de Gruyter,
1984), 534.

[22] Kippenberg, *Garizim und Synagoge*, 1971, 54 f., claims that 'Argarizim' is a sign of a
Samaritan source in *War* 1.63 (destruction of the temple on Gerizim), as the Samaritans
understood this to be one word and wrote it accordingly. But it may simply have been
a technical term at the time of Josephus, used by everyone as the proper designation
for Gerizim, cf. section 6.4 in this book. Further, it is not likely that a Samaritan source
would report on this destruction; there are no traces in later Samaritan literature of such
a report.

[23] L. H. Feldman, "Josephus' Attitude Toward the Samaritans: A Study in Ambivalence," in *Studies in Hellenistic Judaism* (AGJU 30; Leiden: Brill, 1996), 114–136.

[24] Ibid.,133.

rabbis, is ambivalent with regard to the Samaritans, at times referring to them as a separate national entity and at other times looking upon them as a variety of Jew."[25] Feldman's results may be correct, though he often argues from silence. The question is whether such an approach from the terms used should be supplemented by or even abandoned for a reading of those texts that most likely deal with the Samaritans.

This is what R. J. Coggins has done, without spending time on the question of which texts are relevant.[26] He is aware that "there are difficulties of terminology that still bedevil modern scholarly work on the subject," but does not elaborate on the topic. His comment that "to associate the Samaritans with Samaria ... may itself have been an example of Judahite polemic,"[27] is very much to the point, and if he is right in this assumption, this will make superfluous any speculations on which entities might be referred to by this or that designation. Coggins treats Josephus on the assumption that he used sources, but "such material has been developed into a basically consistent picture in the present form of the work,"[28] and "all the material has been worked into the overwhelmingly hostile pattern of the whole."[29] Thus, he reaffirms the traditional picture of the negative attitude of Josephus to the Samaritans, and this attitude is reflected in the terms. "Sidonians" is therefore not necessarily a description of their origins, but "had come to be a derogatory term,"[30] cf. Isa 23:2.4.

Coggins works with the traditional questions raised by a model working from the idea of conflict-and-schism, and ends his discussion with the assertion that "Samaritanism was essentially one variant within Judaism."[31] This model can be seen as one of estrangement, and is familiar from his book about the Samaritans,[32] but his open-minded approach to the texts of Josephus is a welcome contribution.

A few methodological observations can be made after this first survey of scholarship.

---

[25] Ibid., 136.
[26] R. J. Coggins, "The Samaritans in Josephus," in *Josephus, Judaism, and Christianity* (ed. L. H. Feldman and G. Hata; Leiden: Brill, 1987), 257–273.
[27] Ibid., 258.
[28] Ibid., 259.
[29] Ibid., 263.
[30] Ibid., 266.
[31] Ibid., 271.
[32] Coggins, *Samaritans and Jews*.

First, to read Josephus with *a priori* definitions may distort the material. We must listen to the voice of Josephus on its own terms. Oversimplifying the case, one could say that we have to read Josephus as if we had never heard of the Samaritans before, but knew his background and audience, his *Tendenz* and intentions.

Secondly, reading Josephus directly as history is not adequate, and ignores his overall plan and intentions. An attention to his *Tendenz* and his readers' presuppositions is necessary before addressing history. Only after the literary work is done, can one approach the historical questions.

Thirdly, we cannot be confident that Josephus will answer all our questions. He may be *überfragt*, but then we have to respect his territory, not insist on our own.

Fourthly, to delineate his sources on the basis of his terminology has proved to be difficult. Similarly, his different designations for groups are not used according to modern definitions. Trying to find clearly defined groups behind each designation has been a *cul de sac*.

4.2. *Josephus'* Tendenz

R. J. Coggins reads the text basically as literature and only secondarily as referring to history. His approach is careful and attentive in dealing with the passages about the Samaritans. Coggins reads them in the light of the *Tendenz* of Josephus: to provide a positive image of the Jews and to portray the Persians positively, possibly as an example of how a ruling nation should treat the Jews. Within this general picture the Samaritans are depicted as a group of dubious origins, consisting of base elements from Jerusalem. In the narrative about later times than that of John Hyrcanus, however, they appear in a more positive light.

It is doubtful whether A. Kasher is right in his assumptions about the *Tendenz* of Josephus. According to him, Josephus is pro-Roman and pro-Samaritan in *War*, but pro-Jewish and pro-Samaritan in *Ant.* 1–18 (until the time of Coponius) and anti-Samaritan in *Ant.* 18–20 (from the time of Coponius on)—because Josephus used a source by Nicolaus of Damascus for the time from the fall of the Gerizim temple to Archelaus' time.[33] This would be stretching Josephus' statements in the prologue to

---

[33] Kasher, "Josephus on Jewish-Samaritan Relations," 218; for the *Tendenz* of Josephus, cf. 224f. 228.232f.

War, where he presents himself as a proud Jew, loyal to the Romans, cf. *War* 1.1 ff. The account of Hyrcanus' conquest of Shechem and Gerizim, *War* 1.62 f., or of the unwise behaviour of Samaritans in *War* 3.307 ff., can hardly be considered pro-Samaritan. Kasher reads Josephus as an historical account together with other ancient documents, without due consideration of the overall project of Josephus and the other sources, and with too little attention to the problem of reconstructing history from written sources once one has diagnosed their purpose and *Tendenz*.

The *Tendenz* of Josephus is generally that he wishes to repudiate accusations against the Jews and to portray them as, for example, literate, cultured and benevolent. According to S. Mason, the main project in *War* and *Antiquities* is to present the Jews in a favourable light in order to counter the accusations levelled against them by Roman and Greek authors.[34] *War* was written while the victor over the Jewish people was still Emperor in Rome, and under his patronage. Josephus' idea is that only a part of the Jewish people rebelled against Rome, and the Romans acted as God's agents in punishing them. Conditions were almost intolerable under the later governors, so one can understand the rebel instincts, but the wiser leaders tried to keep the peace. The Jews had been able to defend themselves heroically under the Maccabees, as the figure of Hyrcanus showed. In *Antiquities* the antiquity of the Jews and their respectable origin is a major issue.

On the other hand, Josephus wants to respond to curiosity about the Jews, to create a readable, streamlined account of Jewish origins, laws and culture to a willing and attentive audience. There are different layers and levels in these works, several clusters of themes, many literary devices. These are complex works with several interests being followed at the same time. Still, if one considers the general framework, the Samaritans are used by Josephus as a group that forms a negative counterpart to the loyal Jews, an example of people who try to exploit the ruling powers and who are justly punished for that.[35]

---

[34] S. Mason, *Josephus and the New Testament* (2. ed.; Peabody, Mass.: Hendrickson, 2003), 55–121.

[35] M. Avioz, "Josephus' Retelling of Nathan's Oracle (2 Sam 7)," *SJOT* 20 (2006): 9–17, also discusses the tendency of Josephus—in this case in connection with a well-known biblical text.

Opportunism

The most conspicuous trait in Josephus' picture of the Samaritans is their opportunism—if we may use an anachronistic term for his portrayal of them.[36] This is emphasized three times in the form of comments on the stories of their origin and constitutes his *Tendenz* in this connection. The first occurrence of this allegation comes in connection with Josephus' retelling of 2 Kgs 17:

> [The Chouthaioi brought to Samaria their own gods and worshipped them and thereby] provoked the Most High God to anger and wrath ... And so they sent some elders to the king of the Assyrians and asked him to send priests ... and after being instructed in the laws and worship of this God, they worshipped him with great zeal ... They continue to practice these same customs even to this day, those who are called Chouthaioi in the Hebrew language, and Samareitai (Σαμαρεῖται) in the Greek; those who alternately (πρὸς μεταβολὴν) call themselves their relatives whenever they see things going well for the Jews, as if they were descendants of Joseph and had family ties with them in virtue of that origin; when, however, they see that things are going badly for them [i.e. for the Jews], they say that they are not at all close to them and that they have no claim to their loyalty or race; instead, they make themselves out to be migrants of another nation (μετοίκους ἀλλοεθνεῖς).[37]   (*Ant.* 9.288–291)

The crucial sentence here is χρώμενοί τε τοῖς αὐτοῖς ἔτι καὶ νῦν ἔθεσι διατελοῦσιν, "they continue to practice these same customs even to this day." Several understandings of the "customs" are possible. It may mean that the Samaritans kept their older cults while worshipping the Most High God; "practice the same customs" would then mean that they went on worshipping their original gods even after they had started to turn to the Most High God.[38] The idea expressed would then be that the Samaritans are primarily syncretists, as are the people mentioned in 2 Kgs 17:33: "So they worshipped the LORD but also served their own gods, after the manner of the nations from among whom they had been carried away." In the present text of 2 Kings there is confusion on this point, as

---

[36] Hanhart, "Zu den ältesten Traditionen," 106*-115*.

[37] Author's translation; cf. a different translation quoted in chapter 2, p. 18.

[38] Some translations of this passage may be understood in this way. See R. Marcus: "These same rites have continued ...," *Jewish Antiquities Books IX–XI*, 153; W. Whiston's translation from 1736: "they continue to make use of the very same customs," *The Works of Josephus: Complete and Unabridged* (new updated ed.; Peabody, Mass.: Hendrickson, 1987), 265.

the following verse states: "To this day they continue to practice their former customs. They do not worship the LORD and they do not follow the statutes or the ordinances or the law or the commandment that the LORD commanded the children of Jacob, whom he named Israel." The reader is given two pieces of information, the inhabitants worshipped Yahweh, and they did not worship him. Josephus may be interpreted to the effect that the Samaritans still worshipped their old gods, "Practising to this very day the same customs, they hold on to them," *Ant.* 9.290.

In the following sentence Josephus goes on to speak of the opportunism of the Samaritans in terms of their changing claims of ethnicity, not in terms of their religion, be it syncretism as in 2 Kgs 17:33 or the lack of worship of Yahweh, as in 2 Kgs 17:34. It seems therefore to be an adequate understanding of *Ant.* 9.288–290 that Josephus speaks of opportunism through this whole section, in the case of religion in the past, and in the case of claims of ethnicity in the present. The Samaritans saw how the wind blew, and set sails accordingly. The "customs" would simply mean their way of behavior, their opportunism.

The text continues with οἱ κατὰ μὲν τὴν Ἑβραίων γλῶτταν Χου-θαῖοι κατὰ δὲ τὴν Ἑλλήνων Σαμαρεῖται οἳ πρὸς μεταβολὴν συγγε-νεῖς ... ἀποκαλοῦσιν. Πρὸς μεταβολὴν is translated in different ways. If it describes the circumstances, R. Hanhart may be right in translating it "je nach der Lage."[39] C. Begg and P. Spilsbury connect the expression πρὸς μεταβολὴν to the following sentence: "Whenever, by turns, they see things going well for the Judeans ..." In the present translation it is connected to ἀποκαλοῦσιν, "they call," which is expressed in the translation "those who alternately [πρὸς μεταβολὴν] call themselves [by different names]," meaning that the Samaritans present themselves with different ethnic origins according to the changing situation. Their two names, one in Hebrew and one in Greek, may also be taken to under-line the inconsistent nature of the Samaritans. Their Greek name is not a transliteration of the Hebrew name, as in the case of the Jews, but a completely different name. Only one thing is consistent with them: their opportunism.

A syncretistic reading of *Ant.* 9.288 f. is therefore not suggested by *Ant.* 9.290, and there is no statement to this effect in the text of Josephus. Instead, the point in the context is that they are opportunists. "The

---

[39] Hanhart, "Zu den ältesten Traditionen."

Chouthaioi/Samareitai" are the grammatical subject of the practising of the customs, and this subject is continued in the expression οἱ πρὸς μεταβολὴν συγγενεῖς ... ἀποκαλοῦσιν. On this understanding they showed their opportunism in turning towards the Most High God at the time of the plague, and at present in pretending to be descended from Joseph when this is beneficial to them, but professing to be sojourners and foreigners unrelated to the Jews when they profit from this. The translation chosen here is supported by the following sentences, which describe the Samaritans as changing their claim of kinship according to circumstance.

They are not described as a mixed race, as for example in the Talmudic tractate *Masseket Kuthim* (partly quoted in chapter 2). Often they have been described as a mixed race with a syncretistic religion, but this is not what Josephus says. His agenda is their opportunism, and this agenda is felt in other texts as well.

The second time this portrayal of them is found is in connection with the retelling of Neh 13 and the establishment of the Samaritan temple at the time of Alexander the Great:

> For such is the nature of the Samaritans (εἰσὶν γὰρ οἱ Σαμαρεῖς τοιοῦτοι τὴν φύσιν), as we have already shown somewhere above. When the Jews are in difficulties, they deny that they have any kinship with them, thereby indeed admitting the truth, but whenever they see some splendid bit of good fortune come to them, they suddenly grasp at the connection with them, saying that they are related to them and tracing their line back to Ephraim and Manasseh, the descendants of Joseph. (*Ant.* 11.341)

The account stresses the opportunism of the Samaritans, to the extent that they deliberately use different names for themselves:

> [Alexander] inquired who they were that made this request [to remit the tribute in the seventh year]. And, when they said that they were Hebrews but were called the Sidonians of Shechem, he again asked them whether they were Jews. Then, as they said they were not, he replied, "But I have given these privileges to the Jews. However, when I return and have more exact information from you, I shall do as I shall think best." With these words, he sent the Shechemites away. (*Ant.* 11.343 f.)

The term "Sidonians" recurs in connection with Antiochus Epiphanes, *Ant.* 12.257–264, and Josephus might have done this in order to create an impression that the Samaritans use whatever means they can to obtain what they want from the different rulers. The allegation of opportunism also resurfaces:

But when the Samaritans saw the Jews suffering these misfortunes, they would no longer admit that they were their kin (συγγενεῖς αυτῶν) or that the temple on Garizein was that of the Most Great God (τοῦ μεγίστου θεοῦ), thereby acting in accordance with their nature (τῇ φύσει ποιοῦντες ἀκόλουθα), as we have shown; they also said they were colonists (ἄποικοι) from the Medes and Persians, and they are, in fact, colonists from these peoples.[40]   (*Ant.* 12.257)

As an historian, Josephus interprets his material and finds system and pattern. In the case of the Samaritans one of the patterns is that they were opportunists. The opportunism of the Samaritans shows itself mainly in the way they depict their origin, according to Josephus. In addition, it also shows itself in the way that they change their religion, depending on the plague that befalls them. Admittedly, this is the result of a divine oracle, so what might seem religious pragmatism is in fact the divine plan. But the pattern on the human level as far as the Samaritans are concerned is visible already here, and it is repeated several times in connection with their origin. Josephus thus makes two allegations at the same time: they profess ancestry depending on the situation, and this reveals a deeper phenomenon, their opportunism. He has a biblical source for the first instance of the opportunism, the religious one, and this he can spin into a longer yarn.

Josephus provides three stories on the origin of the Samaritans: they were brought in from the east; they were expelled from Jerusalem; and they were Sidonians.

4.3. *The First Story: An Eastern Origin*

The stories told by Josephus where the origin of the Samaritans from the east is mentioned, provide the following picture:

---

[40] Translations of *Ant.* 11.341, 343 f.; 12.257 quoted from R. Marcus, *Jewish Antiquities Books IX–XI*, 479.481, and idem, *Jewish Antiquities Books XII–XIII* (LCL 365; Cambridge, Mass.: Harvard, 1943), 133.

Ant.	Origin	Deportation of Israel?	Assyrian king	Possible HB parallel	Opportunism?
9.278f.,288–291	Chutha	Yes	Salmanassar	2 Kgs 17: Salmanassar	Yes
10.184	Persia and Media	Yes	Salmanassar	No	Not mentioned
11.19	Persia and Media	Yes	Salmanassar	Ezra 4:2: Asarhaddon (680–669); Ezra 4:10: Assurbanipal (668–629)	Not mentioned
11.302–347	Chutha	Not mentioned	No king	Neh 13	Yes
12.257–264	Colonists from Media and Persia; Sidonians	Not mentioned	No king	No	Yes

It is clear from this table that he streamlined the information on the Assyrian king who deported the Samaritans to Samaria. Ezra 4 refers to two different kings in the seventh century B.C.E., neither of them identical with the king in 2 Kgs 17; Josephus refers consistently to Salmanassar, the king of 2 Kgs 17. 'Chutha' and 'Persia plus Media' alternate; this is in line with his opening story in *Ant.* 9.278 that Chutha is in Persia. This origin story is therefore presented rather consistently. The Israelites were deported from Samaria and the Samaritans were imported there from Chutha/Persia. They were opportunistic in relation to their kinship with the Jews.

2 Kgs 17:29 refers to the שֹׁמְרֹנִים, LXX: Σαμαρεῖται. Josephus adopts Σαμαρεῖται in *Ant.* 9.290, and adds Χουθαῖοι as the corresponding Hebrew term. He is then able to use the whole biblical chapter as an explanation for the origin of the Samaritans. In 2 Kgs 17:24 Chutha is one of the place-names for the origin of the people deported by the Assyrian king into the northern kingdom after 722 B.C.E., and Josephus uses Χουθαῖοι throughout *Ant.* 9.278 f., 288–291. Σαμαρεῖται as used by Josephus most likely comes from the LXX rendering of שֹׁמְרֹנִים. All the more conspicuous is his Hebrew name for the Σαμαρεῖται as Χουθαῖοι, which is neither a translation nor a transliteration of שֹׁמְרֹנִים, but perhaps an adaptation of οἱ ἄνδρες Χουθ, 2 Kgs 17:30 LXX. It seems that the

Jewish usage of his day made it natural to use Χουθαῖοι, and that the name שמרונים for the Samaritans belongs to a later age. He thus adopted a polemical Hebrew term for this group and transliterated it, rather than providing a translation or transliteration of the more neutral שמרונים. Χουθαῖοι had a basis in 2 Kgs 17:30, and the application of this chapter to the Samaritans is clear in *Ant.* 9.278 f., 288–291, so indirectly he laid the foundation for the later use of שמרונים as a name for the Samaritans.

Compared with the biblical account of 2 Kgs 17, the story in *Ant.* 9.278 f., 288–291 has several distinctive features. The text is quoted in chapter 2, and not repeated here. 2 Kgs 17:6 says that the Assyrian king "carried the Israelites away to Assyria," but Josephus' expression is that he "transported the entire population to Media and Persia," *Ant.* 9.278. The HB also does not specify that the entire leadership was exterminated, but this is his version, perhaps in order to create a parallel to 2 Kgs 25:18–21 and *Ant.* 10.149.[41] The effect of these claims in *Ant.* 9 is that there can be no connection between the old Israelite population of the north and the Samaritans.

The deportees are all Chuthaeans, from Chutha in Persia or from the river Chutha in Persia,[42] even though 2 Kgs 17 mentions five different peoples. Josephus interprets these as five peoples within the category of Chuthaeans. This means that the population replacing old Israel are all Chuthaeans, that is, Samaritans.

In 2 Kgs 17:25–28 we read that the replacement population does not know how to worship the Lord, YHWH, so lions come and kill some of them. This is reported to the Assyrian king, and he orders one of the captured priests to return and teach them the religion of this god. A priest returns to Bethel and teaches them to worship YHWH. They continue in their old religion and become syncretists.

Josephus works this up into a story where the continued worship of their ancestral gods arouses the Most High God to wrath and rage, and a plague comes upon them. But an oracle, i.e. a divine message, informs them about this god and directs them to worship him in order to get rid of the plague. The settlers themselves ask for priests; this is not the initiative of the king. God directs them to salvation, and the solution is not the initiative of the Assyrian king as in 2 Kgs 17. After this divine information, they then send messengers to the Assyrian king and obtain priests, in the plural, not only one priest as in 2 Kgs

---

[41] Begg and Spilsbury, *Judean Antiquities Books 8–10,* 200, n. 1084.
[42] This is the understanding in the translation of Begg and Spilsbury, ibid., 200.

17:28. They then observe the worship of The Most High God lavishly, zealously, which perhaps means monolatry. The plague then ceases; a corresponding report is missing in 2 Kgs 17. In effect, the Most High God holds the initiative throughout this story.

Surprisingly, Josephus does not repeat the claim of syncretism levelled against the northern population in 2 Kgs 17:33, as I understand his text. Also surprisingly, he does not repeat the name Bethel, which in the HB is associated with the illegitimate worship set up by Jeroboam I against Jerusalem. Josephus is not interested in this association, but instead directs his story to fit the Samaritans, who are not associated with Bethel. The designation "The Most High God" recurs in 12.257 in connection with the Samaritans, as their temple is dedicated to this Deity. It seems to be a designation for the supreme God for Josephus, instead of the geographically limited Yahweh, "the god of the land" in 2 Kgs 17:26–27. The expression is surprising in so far as the association of the Samaritans with this supreme God runs counter to his portrayal of them as local and parochial. On the other hand, the interest here seems more to be the overall working of this Deity than the religion of the Samaritans. It is still interesting in that he indirectly admits that the Samaritans of his day were not syncretists or worshippers of their ancestral gods, but perhaps monolatrous.

Josephus tells of the worship of the ancestral gods before the plague, whereas 2 Kgs 17 relates this after mentioning the start of Yahweh-worship. In 2 Kgs 17 this creates the basis for the allegation of syncretism, but Josephus reverses the course of events to the effect that the Samaritans implicitly converted to The Most High God. He also has no need to spurn the conversion of the Samaritans from their old religion to Yahweh, as *Masseket Kuthim* does. There, the distinction is between 'lion converts' (cf. the attacking lions in 2 Kgs 17: 25) and 'real converts.' Rabbi Ishmael claims that they were real converts in the beginning, but later it was prohibited to have fellowship with them. Josephus seems to accept the shift in religion as genuine, without any need to deprecate it.

The basic story is found in 9.278 f.: καὶ μεταστήσας ἄλλα ἔθνη ἀπὸ Χούθου τόπου τινός ἔστι γὰρ ἐν τῇ Περσίδι ποταμὸς τοῦτ᾽ ἔχων τοὔνομα κατῴκισεν εἰς τὴν Σαμάρειαν καὶ τὴν τῶν Ἰσραηλιτῶν χώραν, "Moving other nations from a certain river called the Chouthas—for there is a river in the country of the Persians bearing this name—he settled them in Samareia and the country of the Israelites."[43] This story is

---

[43] Translated by Begg and Spilsbury, *Judean Antiquities Books 8–10*, 200.

repeated in 10.184, only with additional information on the derivation of the name 'Samaritans' from the name of the region 'Samaria':

> Once Salmanasses had then deported the Israelites, he settled in their place the nation of Chouthaites (τὸ τῶν Χουθαίων ἔθνος), who previously were in the interior of Persia and Media. Thereafter, however, they were called the Samareians (Σαμαρεῖς) getting this name from the country in which they were settled.[44]   (*Ant.* 10.184)

This text uses the Greek word Σαμαρεῖς and not Σαμαρεῖται as in book 9, but in both cases they are identified as Chuthaeans. The new information here is that the name Σαμαρεῖς was adopted "because they assumed the name of the country in which they were settled." Josephus interprets the name as a gentilicium formed from a geographical name, cf. the usage in the LXX.

At the time of the rebuilding of the temple in Jerusalem in the sixth century Josephus again returns to the story:

> While they [those who came to Jerusalem from the land of their captivity] were laying the foundations of the temple and very busily engaged in building it, the surrounding nations, especially the Chuthaeans, whom the Assyrian king Salmanesses had brought from Persia and Media and settled in Samaria when he deported the Israelite people, urged the satraps ...[45]
>   (*Ant.* 11.19)

Josephus elaborates on the problems for the temple builders described in Ezra 4, describing how they were able to bribe the local governors in order to hinder the building of the temple.

The long account 11.302–347 does not repeat the story, only the name 'Chuthaean' and the statement that the Σαμαρεῖς descend from them. But in connection with Antiochus Epiphanes the story resurfaces:

> But when the Samaritans saw the Jews suffering these misfortunes, they would no longer admit that they were their kin or that the temple on Garizein was that of the Most Great God, thereby acting in accordance with their nature, as we have shown; they also said they were colonists from the Medes and Persians, and they are, in fact, colonists from these peoples.[46]   (*Ant.* 12.257)

12.257 is a short repetition of the deportation from Media and Persia, with the new expression "colonist," ἄποικος.

---

[44] Quotation from Begg and Spilsbury, *Judean Antiquities Books 8–10*, 264.
[45] Translation by Marcus, *Jewish Antiquities Books IX–XI*, 323.
[46] Translation by Marcus, *Jewish Antiquities Books XII–XIII*, 133.

The full version of the story is told only once, in 9.278 f., 287–291, where Josephus expounds 2 Kgs 17, and this forms the basis for the short repetitions later in *Antiquities*. Four times the same story is told, even with the same king, Salmanassar, mentioned three times. Josephus is thus consistent in the telling of this 'myth.'

Already in his retelling of the split into two kingdoms after Solomon, Josephus announces that Jeroboam misled the people, something that led to the misfortunes of the Hebrews and their being defeated in war by other races and to their falling captive, *Ant.* 8.229. The general background for Josephus is constituted by the north-south tensions in the HB, and he is able to exploit these tensions in connection with the origin of the Samaritans.

4.4. *The Second Story: Origin from Jerusalem and Construction of the Temple*

Given that the Samaritans were deported from the east into Samaria, they receive a new element through the expulsion of the priest Manasseh and his followers from Jerusalem. This is how the cult on Mount Gerizim came into existence. Josephus presupposes that the Samaritans existed at this point. Manasseh was married to Nicaso, the daughter of "Sanaballetēs—he had been sent to Samaria as satrap by Darius, the last king, and was of the Cuthean race from whom the Samaritans also are descended," *Ant.* 11.302.[47] Still, the marriage of a Jerusalemite priest to a Samaritan woman occasions what amounts to a second story of the origin of the Samaritans, 11.302–347. A contracted version of this text is printed in chapter 2, and not repeated here; A. Buchler's and H. G. Kippenberg's source analyses of it have been commented upon in this chapter already. The *Tendenz* of this story is the transgression of the law by the people who went to Shechem, as the following excerpts will show (relevant expressions in italics):

> Now the elders of Jerusalem, resenting the fact that the brother of the high priest Jaddus was sharing the high priesthood while *married to a foreigner* (ἀλλοφύλῳ συνοικοῦντα), rose up against him, for they considered this marriage to be a stepping-stone for those who might wish to *transgress the laws* about taking wives and that this would be the beginning of *intercourse with foreigners*. They believed, moreover, that their former captivity and

---

[47] Translation by Marcus, *Jewish Antiquities Books IX–XI*, 461.

misfortunes had been caused by some who had *erred in marrying and taking wives who were not of their own country.* (*Ant.* 11.306 f.)

But, as many *priests and Israelites were involved in such marriages*, great was the confusion which seized the people of Jerusalem. For all these deserted to Manasses, and Sanaballates supplied them with money and with land for cultivation and assigned them places wherein to dwell, in every way seeking to win favour for his son-in-law. (*Ant.* 11.312)

The Samaritans, whose chief city at that time was Shechem, which lay beside Mount Garizein and was inhabited by *apostates* from the Jewish nation.[48] (*Ant.* 11.340)

Shechem is presented as the city of the Samaritans.

When Alexander died, his empire was partitioned among his successors (the Diadochi); as for the temple on Mount Garizein, it remained. And, whenever anyone was accused by the people of Jerusalem of eating *unclean food or violating the Sabbath, or committing any other such sin,* he would flee to the Shechemites, saying that he had been unjustly expelled.[49]
(*Ant.* 11.346 f.)

This story is not repeated, but alluded to in connection with the destruction of the temple:

And he captured Medaba after six months, during which his army suffered great hardships; next he captured Samoga and its environs, and, in addition to these, Shechem and Garizein and the Cuthaean nation, which lives near the temple built after the model of the sanctuary at Jerusalem, which Alexander permitted their governor Sanaballetes to build for the sake of his son-in-law Manasses, the brother of the high priest Jaddua, as we have related before. Now it was two hundred years later that this temple was laid waste.[50] (*Ant.* 13.255 f.)

The story seems to be built on a Hebrew Bible text, Neh 13:28, where Nehemiah claims: "And one of the sons of Jehoiada, son of the high priest Eliashib, was the son-in-law of Sanballat the Horonite; I chased him away from me." Neh 13:28 and *Ant.* 11.302–347 have in common that a member of the family of high priests in Jerusalem was married to a daughter of Sanballat and that he was expelled from Jerusalem because of this. The question of exogamous marriages is addressed in both texts. If one assumes that Josephus rewrote this brief account, one must also assume that he relocated it from the century of Nehemiah to that of

---

[48] All three quotations in the translation of Marcus, *Jewish Antiquities Books IX–XI,* 464 f.479.
[49] Ibid., 483.
[50] Marcus, *Jewish Antiquities Books XII–XIII,* 355.

Alexander the Great and that he renamed Jehoiada as Jaddus and called him the brother of the son-in-law of Sanballat instead of the father. He also has a new piece of information in providing the name of the son-in-law as Manasses. This is conceivable, as Josephus rewrote many stories from the Bible, and even his own stories in *War* were rewritten in *Antiquities* or *Life*.

Much effort has been put into proving the existence of different Sanballats, one at the time of Nehemiah and another at the time of Alexander the Great.[51] The Wadi Daliyeh papyri are held to prove the existence of a Sanballat in the mid-fourth century, a Sanballat II, and it is then surmised that a Sanballat III was in office at the time of Darius and Alexander. The theory has been commented upon in the previous chapter. A different possible explanation is the following.

Assuming that Josephus built his story upon Neh 13:28, he would use the additional information on the High priests provided by Neh 12:10f, 22. *Ant.* 11.297 offers a brief list similar to Neh 12:22f. Neh 12:10 presents us with the names of a series of Levites. V. 22 is very similar: "As for the Levites, in the days of Eliashib, Joiada, Johanan, and Jaddua, there were recorded the heads of fathers' houses; also the priests until the reign of Darius the Persian." The different lists may be compared in this way:

Neh 12:10f, 26	Neh 12:22	Neh 12:23	Neh 13:28	*Ant.* 11.297	*Ant.* 11.302
Jeshua					
Joiakim					
Eliashib	Eliashib	Eliashib	Eliashib	Eliashib	
Joiada	Joiada		Johoiada	Jodas	
Jonathan	Johanan	Johanan	unnamed son, son-in-law of Sanballat the Horonite	Joannes	Joannes
Jaddua	Jaddua				Jaddus, his brother: Manasses, married to Nikaso,
	until Darius the Persian				at the time of Darius, the last king

---

[51] Cross, "Aspects of the Samaritan and Jewish History," 201–211, and in several other articles, cf. the bibliography.

The fifth/third name in the series is 'Jonathan' in Neh 12:10 and 'Johanan' in vv. 22f., but this would not prevent ancient readers of Nehemiah from seeing the two lists as identical. 'Darius the Persian,' Neh 12:22, is Darius III Codomannus (338–331 B.C.E.), which means that this series of Levites at one point was contemporary with the king whom Josephus calls 'Darius, the last king,' *Ant.* 11.302. Neh 13:28 provides two names in this list, Eliashib and Jehoiada, and the son of Jehoiada is not named. If the book of Nehemiah is consistent on this point, the High priest's son who was the son-in-law of Sanballat was either the Jonathan/Johanan of Neh 12:10, 22, or his brother. Such a reading would have suggested itself to an ancient historian.

Josephus covers the high priests Eliashib, Jodas and Joannes in *Ant.* 11.297, and picks up the line in 11.302:

> When Joannes departed this life he was succeeded in the high priesthood by his son Jaddus. He too had a brother, named Manasses, to whom Sanaballetes .... gladly gave ... his daughter, called Nicaso, in marriage.[52]

Josephus therefore used the names in Neh 12:10, 22, only with a 'graecization' of the names, and 'Joannes' corresponds to 'Johanan' in Neh 12:22. If this list of names has any connection to Sanballat and Darius, it must have been through the last name on the list, Jaddua, 'Jaddus' in Josephus' text. Josephus therefore used this generation for the marriage to the daughter of Sanballat, moving it one generation down, and provided a brother and his name, Manasses. From Neh 12:22 he had good reason to locate the incident with Manasseh and Sanballat at the time of 'Darius, the last king' of the Persians. His story does not include the person of Nehemiah; so there is no acute chronological problem. In *Ant.* 11.174 he does not mention Sanballat, in distinction to Neh 4:7. Josephus may have modelled the whole incident upon the brief remark in Neh 13:28, and the time of the incident was provided by Neh 12:22. If this is correct, Josephus expounded Neh 13:28, and dated it according to Neh 12:22. In this way he made the construction of the temple on Gerizim take place in the time of Darius, the last king, and dependent upon the Greek king Alexander. This would have a negative ring to Roman ears in the days of Josephus; locating the story to the days of Alexander has an anti-Samaritan point. Josephus tacitly corrected the Biblical chronology on occasions when he

---

[52] Marcus, *Jewish Antiquities Books IX–XI*, 461.

thought it appropriate.[53] Thus, Josephus created his second story by
literary means, and it is futile to search for a Sanballat III. As J. Dušek has
shown, there is no evidence in the Wadi Daliyeh bullae for a governor
with this name at the time of the last Persian king.[54]

The expression 'Shechemites' is central to *Ant.* 11.302–347. H. G. Kippenberg supposes a Shechemite source in *Ant.* 11.302–347, which would
be a Samaritan source, but this is unlikely in view of the term's use earlier in *Antiquities*.[55] This expression occurs in *Ant.* 5.240 f., 243, 247, 248,
250 f., where Josephus deals with the rebellious kingdom in the North
under Abimelech, and the Shechemites. Here, the MT of Jud 9:2, 6, 7, 18,
20, 23, 24, 25, 26, 39 has שכם בעלי, or שכם אנשי, and the LXX οἱ ἄνδρες
Σικιμων/Συχεμ. Josephus changed to Σικιμῖται, thereby creating a link
to his contemporaries in Shechem. There are thus negative associations
to the name 'Shechemites' from early on. This expression cannot reveal
a Samaritan source, since it is negatively laden from the beginning. Josephus has a broad retelling of the Dinah story in Gen 34, and here also the
name Σικιμῖται occurs, *Ant.* 1.337–340 (see below). Josephus introduces
us to the Shechemites by retelling Gen 34 at the beginning of *Antiquities*,
then they appear at the time of Abimelech, and he further mentions that
the rebellion of Jeroboam against Jerusalem and the son of Solomon took
place in Σίκιμα, *Ant.* 8.212, 225. The later Samaritans are branded by the
use of the name Σικιμῖται for them. Josephus follows a practice that can
be found in a series of renderings of Gen 34 from the second century
B.C.E.

It would seem that Josephus through using this designation admits
that the Samaritans had a connection to the original inhabitants of the
city, and this runs counter to his first story that they are immigrants. The
underlying idea might be that the city conferred her characteristics on
her later inhabitants, irrespective of any direct descent. Josephus is not
consistent in this matter, as he offers three origin stories, so a genealogical
connection would not have been necessary for him. The expression was
negatively charged from book 5 of *Antiquities*, and this fits his purpose.

Scholars are today often inclined to believe this second explanation for
the origin of the Samaritans, combined with the archaeological evidence
from Tell Balata and the Wadi Daliyeh papyri, even if they realize the

[53] R. Marcus, "Josephus on the Samaritan Schism," appendix B in *Jewish Antiquities Books IX–XI* (LCL 326; Cambridge, Mass.: Harvard University Press, 1937), 510 f.
[54] See chapter 3.
[55] Kippenberg, *Garizim und Synagoge*, 50–57.

polemical nature of much of what Josephus writes.[56] Many scholars accept the account by Josephus and try to solve the problem of the short period of nine months for the construction of the temple.[57]

However, the question is whether Josephus here provides accurate history, or embellishes a biblical remark in order to deliver another blow at the Samaritans. He gives as the background for this story of the temple building on Gerizim Manasseh's ambitions and his mixed marriage, and as the result that "whenever anyone was accused by the people of Jerusalem of eating unclean food or violating the Sabbath or committing any other such sin, he would flee to the Shechemites, saying that he had been unjustly expelled," 11.347. A temple built for an ambitious priest living in a mixed marriage in violation of the law attracts unclean people from Jerusalem. This is the *Tendenz* of his story, and historical information would be hard to extract from it. If we realize this, it becomes unnecessary to explain the short construction period for the temple which Josephus' account implies. This may simply be another sign that his story is unreliable as historical information.

The actual construction of a sanctuary on Mount Gerizim may have taken place during the century of Nehemiah, if we are to believe the current excavator's reports, cf. chapter 5. If this was so, then Josephus may have realized this, but used the information in Neh 12:22 to date the construction to the century of Alexander. He would lower the age of the temple as much as he could, and not admit that it had an age that could compare in any way to the age of the Jerusalem temple, or to its solid foundations and splendour, *Ant.* 8.61 ff. The temple of Solomon existed for 470 years, six months and ten days, *Ant.* 10.147, and was rebuilt after 70 years of desertion, *Ant.* 10.184. The reconstruction of the temple happened according to the decree of the venerated king Cyrus, and it then existed for 639 years and 45 days; "the total period amounts to one thousand one hundred and thirty years seven months and fifteen days," *War* 6.269. 470 plus 639 years totals 1109 years, and an additional 70 years would give 1179 years. With a reconstruction of the temple in "the second year of the reign of Cyrus," *War* 6.270, we might end up with 1130 years, depending upon the calculation made by Josephus. In any case, the Jerusalem temple has a higher age in each of its two phases of existence—not to mention its total existence—than the Samaritan

---

[56] Kippenberg, *Garizim und Synagoge*, 52.57–59.
[57] Feldman, *Josephus and Modern Scholarship*, 537–539.

temple. Josephus could be suspected of lowering the latter's age as much as his sources would allow. Neh 12:22 offered the possibility of dating the construction to the period of Alexander. If the fixed date for Josephus was the destruction of the temple by John Hyrcanus, and he could admit that it had existed for two hundred years when it was destroyed, *Ant.* 13.256, this would result in the time of Alexander as the time of construction. He may have reached his result by a close reading of the book of Nehemiah, and by calculating backwards from the destruction.

4.5. *The Third Story: Sidonians*

The third origin story is found twice. First, it is embedded in the second story in the way that the Samaritans—here introduced by Josephus as Shechemites—request remission for taxes in the seventh year and Alexander asks who they are.

> And, when they said that they were Hebrews but were called the Sidonians of Shechem, he again asked them whether they were Jews. Then, as they said they were not, he replied, "But I have given these privileges to the Jews. However, when I return and have more exact information from you, I shall do as I shall think best." With these words, he sent the Shechemites away.[58]
>
> (*Ant.* 11.344)

At the time of Antiochus Epiphanes, this origin 'myth': Sidonians of Shechem, is repeated. Immediately after the passage where Josephus asserts that they are colonists from Media and Persia (12.257), we read how the Samaritans tried to alienate themselves from the Jews and pretended to be related to the Greeks:

> Accordingly, they sent envoys to Antiochus with a letter in which they made the following statements. "To King Antiochus Theos Epiphanes, a memorial from the Sidonians in Shechem. Our forefathers because of certain droughts in their country, and following a certain ancient superstition, made it a custom to observe the day which is called the Sabbath by the Jews, and they erected a temple without a name on the mountain called Garizein, and there offered the appropriate sacrifices. Now you have dealt with the Jews as their wickedness deserves, but the king's officers, in the belief that we follow the same practices as they through kinship with them, are involving us in similar charges, whereas we are Sidonians by origin, as is evident

---

[58] Translation Marcus, *Jewish Antiquities Books IX–XI*, 481.

from our state documents ... we are distinct from them [the Jews] both in race and in customs (ἡμῶν καὶ τῷ γένει καὶ τοῖς ἔθεσιν ἀλλοτρίων ὑπαρχόντων), and we ask that the temple without a name (ἀνώνυμον ἱερὸν) be known as that of Zeus Hellenios (Διὸς Ἑλληνίου), ..." To this petition of the Samarians (Σαμαρέων) the king wrote the following reply. "King Antiochus to Nicanor. The Sidonians in Shechem have submitted a memorial which has been filed. Since ... they are in no way concerned in the complaints brought against the Jews, but choose to live in accordance with Greek customs (ἀλλὰ τοῖς Ἑλληνικοῖς ἔθεσιν αἱροῦνται χρώμενοι ζῆν), we aquit them of these charges, and permit their temple to be known as that of Zeus Hellenios, as they have petitioned."[59]   (*Ant.* 12.258–263)

E. Bickermann and J. Goldstein claim that the documents in *Ant.* 12.258–264 are genuine.[60] In the words of Goldstein: "Bickerman solved most of the problems of these documents and proved them authentic."[61] Goldstein distinguishes between the descendants of old Israel still existing in the north after the fall of Samaria in the eighth century and the imported people. The reason why the latter used the term 'Sidonians' in the documents was the practice of the Graeco-Macedonian government: it considered them Sidonians, that is Phoenicians, which was the Greek equivalent of Canaanites. They would not have used this designation themselves, as the Canaanites were condemned in the Pentateuch and the Samaritans were tenaciously loyal to the Torah. But the government used it. The appearance of the term 'Sidonians of Shechem' in 11.344 would be anachronistic, because only after the time of Alexander were they forced to leave Samaria and settle in Shechem.[62] For this theory Goldstein builds upon the disenfranchisement theory launched by F. M. Cross.

One problem with this understanding is that Bickerman has to suppose that the exchange of documents happened according to the government policy of the day. It is not stated here that the king's reply was delegated to one of his officials; so this has to be assumed. Bickerman further thinks that a copy of it was handed on to the Samaritans, from whom it ended up, somehow, in the possession of Josephus; this constitutes a

---

[59] Marcus, *Jewish Antiquities Books XII–XIII*, 133–137.

[60] E. Bickermann, "Un document relatif à la persecution d'Antiochos IV Épiphanes," *RHR* 115 (1937): 188–223; repr. *Studies in Jewish and Christian History* (vol. 2; AGJU 9; Leiden: Brill, 1980), 105–135; J. A. Goldstein, "The Petition of the Samaritans and the Reply of Antiochus IV as Preserved by Josephus at *AJ* xii 5.5.258–264," in *II Maccabees: A New Translation with Introduction and Commentary* (AB 41A; New York: Doubleday, 1983), 523–539.

[61] Goldstein, *II Maccabees*, 524.

[62] Ibid., 534–536.

second assumption. In addition to these inherent problems comes the difficulty that the temple on Mount Gerizim was in fact not unnamed, as the documents claim, but consecrated to the same deity as the one in Jerusalem. This can now be assumed on the basis of the inscriptions found on Mount Gerizim, as one of them contains the divine name 'Yahweh', יהוה, and many of the personal names are Yahwistic.

The simpler understanding of the 'Sidonians'-story is that the Samaritans are portrayed by Josephus as opportunistic, even to the extent that they profess themselves Sidonians if they consider this opportune. I have mentioned the remark made by Coggins that 'Sidonians' may have had a negative ring to it at the time of Josephus. 'Sidon' occurs in the HB in the list of peoples in Gen 10:15.19; 1 Chr 1:13 as the son of Canaan; and further in the oracles against nations in Isa 23:2. 4.12; Jer 47:4; Ezek 27:8; 28:21 f.; Joel 4:4; Zech 9:2; and in the text on the cup of God's wrath in Jer 25:22. The simplest understanding of the phrase the 'Sidonians of Shechem' is to assume that negative sentiments attached to the expression in the HB are alluded to by Josephus. As 'Sidon' was the son of 'Canaan', it was not difficult to create the combination 'Sidonians of Shechem'. By this combination, the Samaritans were acknowledged as descendants of the Canaanites, according to the list of nations, but forming a group which had negative associations in the HB and could be connected to Greek customs and therefore seemed suspect in the eyes of the Romans.

Josephus' emphasis on the 'Sidonians' comes on top of his allegations that the Samaritans were Chuthaeans and apostates from Jerusalem. The three theories are hardly compatible. Taken together, these three origin 'myths' are confusing. The first and third compete with each other, while the second may be combined with either of them. When Josephus presents three different explanations of the origin it does not mean that they strengthen each other; on the contrary, they weaken each other. Polemics + polemics does not add up to truth, but shows that whatever was available was used. There will be facts behind this material, but they are not identical with it. Often, scholars have taken the first to be the true story of the origin, and more lately scholars have concentrated on the second. Josephus has been taken at face value by Jews and Christians, and even by the Samaritans, when in their chronicles they modelled their own origin 'myth' on Josephus.

Common to 2 Macc 6:2 and *Ant.* 12.257–264 is the assumption that the Samaritans accepted the hellenization of their temple, and even asked for it. 2 Macc 6:1–2 reads: μετ' οὐ πολὺν δὲ χρόνον ἐξαπέστειλεν ὁ βασιλεὺς γέροντα Ἀθηναῖον ἀναγκάζειν τοὺς Ιουδαίους μεταβαίνειν ἀπὸ τῶν πατρίων νόμων καὶ τοῖς τοῦ θεοῦ νόμοις μὴ πολιτεύεσθαι μολῦναι δὲ καὶ τὸν ἐν Ἱεροσολύμοις νεὼ καὶ προσονομάσαι Διὸς Ὀλυμπίου καὶ τὸν ἐν Γαριζιν καθὼς ἐτύγχανον οἱ τὸν τόπον οἰκοῦντες Διὸς Ξενίου, "Not long after this, the king sent an Athenian senator to compel the Jews to forsake the laws of their fathers and cease to live by the laws of God, and also to pollute the temple in Jerusalem and call it the temple of Olympian Zeus, and to call the one in Gerizim the temple of Zeus the Friend of Strangers, as the people who dwelt in that place had requested/as befitted the people who dwelt in that place."

2 Macc 6:2, together with Sir 50:25 f. and *Ant.* 12.257–264, has been studied by R. Hanhart.[63] He assumes that 2 Macc 6:2 is polemical, and its polemical attitude is shared by *Antiquities.* Josephus uses Διὸς Ἑλληνίου, which proves that he did not know 2 Maccabees with its Διὸς Ξενίου. This assumption may be true, but on the other hand there is a correspondence between the petition to the king from the Samaritans, which is provided by Josephus, and the information in 2 Macc 6:2. Josephus quotes the letter where the Samaritans asked for the hellenization, and καθὼς ἐτύγχανον, 2 Macc 6:2, may be a statement to the same effect: "as they requested."[64] If Josephus knew this claim in 2 Maccabees, he might have created the letter to the king and its response as a concrete elaboration of the brief allegation in 2 Macc 6:2.

In *Antiquities* the point is that the Samaritans wanted to follow Greek customs, but in 2 Macc 6:2 the idea is that the Samaritans were foreigners. This is an indication that at the time of 2 Maccabees the first or the third origin 'myth' presented by Josephus existed among the Jews of Jerusalem. As Josephus' report on the hellenization of the temple on Gerizim occurs inside the third origin story, the designation Διὸς Ἑλ-ληνίου would be appropriate. The Samaritans promise to live by Greek customs and, accordingly, are permitted to use a general Greek designation for Zeus. In 2 Maccabees, however, the hellenization happens at the two temples simultaneously, and the temple in Jerusalem receives the highest designation possible, but the Gerizim temple is designated in a way reminiscent of the foreign origin of its worshippers.

Both sources are here referring to the same information, perhaps independently of each other, or perhaps Josephus used 2 Maccabees. 2 Maccabees may have rendered the name of Zeus correctly, since the

---

[63] Hanhart, "Zu den ältesten Traditionen," 106*–115*.
[64] Ibid., with extensive discussion of this phrase.

author here was closer in time to the events told. Josephus created a name that would fit into the overall picture of opportunism. A possibility to be considered is that neither of them knew the correct names, but both authors created names that suited their polemical purposes. The information is polemical, aimed at portraying the Samaritans in a disgraceful light in the eyes of the readers, both of 2 Maccabees: the Jews, and of *Antiquities*: the Romans. Jews would despise them for their acceptance of hellenization, and Josephus could presume that bowing to Greek customs would be considered dishonourable by the Romans.

4.6. *The Destruction of the Temple*

The destruction of the temple on Gerizim has played a major role in recent Samaritan studies, cf. the presentation of the Cross-Purvis hypothesis in the previous chapter. This destruction is not mentioned in the books of Maccabees, nor is it reflected in Samaritan literature. Our only evidence for it is Josephus. It is in fact only mentioned once in ancient sources, in *Ant.* 13, as *War* 1 does not mention any destruction of the temple on Gerizim, as the following synopsis shows.

War 1.62f.		*Ant.* 13.254–256	
Subsequently, however, the campaign of Antiochus against the Medes gave him an opportunity for revenge.	Αὖθίς γε μὴν Ἀντίοχος ἐπὶ Μήδους στρατεύσας καιρὸν ἀμύνης αὐτῷ παρεῖχεν,	– Ὑρκανὸς δὲ ἀκούσας τὸν Ἀντιόχου θάνατον	So soon as he heard of the death of Antiochus,
He at once flew upon the cities of Syria, expecting to find them,	εὐθέως γὰρ ὥρμησεν ἐπὶ τὰς ἐν Συρίᾳ πόλεις,	εὐθὺς ἐπὶ τὰς ἐν Συρίᾳ πόλεις ἐξεστράτευσεν οἰόμενος αὐτὰς εὑρήσειν,	Hyrcanus marched out against the cities of Syria, thinking to find them, as indeed they were, empty
as he did, drained of efficient troops.	κενάς, ὅπερ ἦν, ὑπολαμβάνων τῶν μαχιμωτέρων εὑρήσειν.	ὅπερ ἦν, ἐρήμους τῶν μαχίμων καὶ ῥύεσθαι δυναμένων.	of fighting men and of any able to deliver them. And he captured Medaba after six months,
He thus captured Medabe	Μεδάβην μὲν οὖν	Μήδαβαν μὲν οὖν πολλὰ τῆς στρατιᾶς αὐτῷ ταλαιπωρηθείσης ἕκτῳ μηνὶ εἶλεν,	during which his army suffered great hardships;

War 1.62 f.		Ant. 13.254–256	
and Samaga with the neighbouring towns, also Shechem and Argarizin, besides defeating the Cuthaeans, the race inhabiting the country surrounding the [temple] modelled on that at Jerusalem.[65]	καὶ Σαμαγὰν ἅμα ταῖς πλησίον, ἔτι δὲ Σίκιμα καὶ Ἀργαριζεὶν αὐτὸς αἱρεῖ, πρὸς ἅις τὸ Χουταίων γένος, οἳ περιῴκουν τὸ εἰκασθὲν τῷ ἐν Ἱεροσολύμοις ἱερῷ.	ἔπειτα καὶ Σαμόγαν καὶ τὰ πλησίον εὐθὺς αἱρεῖ Σίκιμά τε πρὸς τούτοις καὶ Γαριζεῖν τό τε Κουθαίων γένος, ὃ περιοικεῖ τὸν εἰκασθέντα τῷ ἐν Ἱεροσολύμοις ἱερῷ ναόν, ὅν Ἀλέξανδρος ἐπέτρεψεν οἰκοδομῆσαι Σαναβαλλέτῃ τῷ στρατηγῷ διὰ τὸν γαμβρὸν Μανασσῆν τὸν Ἰαδδοῦς τοῦ ἀρχιερέως ἀδελφόν, ὡς πρότερον δεδηλώκαμεν. συνέβη δὲ τὸν ναὸν τοῦτον ἔρεμον γενέσθαι μετὰ ἔτη διακόσια.	next he captured Samoga and its environs, and, in addition to these, Shechem and Garizein and the Cuthaean nation, which lives near the temple built after the model of the sanctuary at Jerusalem, which Alexander permitted their governor Sanaballetes to build for the sake of his son-in-law Manasses, the brother of the high priest Jaddua, as we have related before. Now it was two hundred years later that this temple was laid waste.[66]

The background for the story of the destruction is the following. Hyrcanus had been attacked by Antiochus VII, and had been forced to break open the treasury to buy himself out of the siege of Jerusalem. Hyrcanus used the opportunity to take revenge while Antiochus was occupied with the war against the Medes (according to *War*), or after Antiochus was dead (according to *Antiquities*). He captured the Syrian Medabe, Samaga, Shechem and Aragarizin, and in addition to this τὸ Χουταίων γένος, "the people of the Cuthaeans," whose land surrounded the temple modelled on the temple in Jerusalem. From this region Hyrcanus went to "the middle of Samaria," and attacked the city now called Sebaste.

Read in the context, the victory over Shechem, Gerizim and the Chuthaeans is an example of the heroic war effort of the Jews, in this case exemplified by Hyrcanus. He is able to conquer enemy territory, the Syrian area, and as a reward he receives a laudatory comment for being

---

[65] H. St. J. Thackeray, *The Jewish War Books I–III* (LCL 203; Cambridge, Mass.: Harvard University Press, 1926), 31–33.

[66] Marcus, *Jewish Antiquities Books XII–XIII*, 355.

excellent in government, holding the offices of supreme commander, high priest and prophet, *War* 1.68 f. This praise of Hyrcanus is an important element in the history of Josephus, because it is a turning point in the Hasmonean narrative, after which things turn abruptly for the worse (with Aristobulus).

The report in *War* does not mention a sanctuary on Mount Gerizim at all; τὸ εἰκασθὲν τῷ ἐν Ἱεροσολύμοις ἱερῷ is short and reads as if avoiding the mention of a temple in addition to the one in Jerusalem. The reader might supply ἱερόν at the end of this sentence, but this word is conspicuously absent. The whole sentence is dependent upon the verb αἱρεῖ, so if there was something on Gerizim, it was captured, but there is no explicit mention of destruction. In *War* it is not explicitly stated that the temple was destroyed; this is only said in *Antiquities*, as noted long ago by Julius Wellhausen.[67] The expression is fuller in *Antiquities*: τὸν εἰκασθέντα τῷ ἐν Ἱεροσολύμοις ἱερῷ ναόν; the sentence uses a word for 'temple' or 'sanctuary' in both cases, and the verb is again αἱρεῖ. Here, therefore, the ναός of the Samaritans was captured, but no word for destruction is used. It is stated at the end that the temple ἔρημον γενέσθαι, "became desolate," either from destruction or abandonment. The translation of R. Marcus "was laid waste," quoted above, seems coloured by the Jerusalem temple's fate. Josephus does not state that Hyrcanus destroyed it, and there is at present no archaeological report from the Mount Gerizim excavations that can help us on this point.

It is amazing how *en passant* the attack on Shechem and the capture of the temple are presented. Compared to the weight attributed to it in recent scholarship, the information is meagre and casual.

Josephus refers to his story of the construction of the temple under Alexander, *Ant.* 11.302–347, and provides us with its life span, two hundred years. One would not expect Josephus to exaggerate the age of the temple, and the figure provided may therefore be lower than it actually was. High age had status in antiquity, and he would not admit more than absolutely necessary on this point. The temple of the Samaritans only existed for two hundred years, compared to the higher age of the Jerusalem temple, and it was only built as the result of the ambition of a renegade priest and a Chuthaean governor, and by permission from a king who conquered the world, but whose heritage was disliked by the

---

[67] J. Wellhausen, *Israelitische und jüdische Geschichte* (6. ed.; Berlin: Georg Reimer, 1907), 273, n. 1.

Romans. Another pagan king desecrated it on the request of its worship-pers, and only a Jewish hero, Hyrcanus, was able to put an end to its exis-tence. Victory over the Samaritans is an example of Hyrcanus's success, and for this he was rewarded with the highest privileges.

In *War*, the expression Ἀργαριζεὶν is found, and this will be treated in the framework of all cases where this contracted transliterated form of the name of the mountain is used; see chapter 6. Josephus in *War* used the imperfect, περιῴκουν, in *Antiquities* the present tense, περιοικεῖ. Whether he attached any significance to this difference, in *War* "they used to live, they lived," in *Antiquities* "they live (today)," is uncertain, and in any case he assumed the Samaritans to live in the area around Mount Gerizim in his day.

4.7. *Further Information on the Samaritans*

One story from the later history of the Samaritans might reveal a devel-opment in Josephus' attitude to the Samaritans. If we compare the story of the Galilean-Samaritan incidents in the two texts *War* 2.232–245 and *Ant.* 18.118–135, a more hostile attitude towards the Samaritans may be felt in the later version. *War* 2.232 f., 237, 239 f., 242 f., 245 tells how one Galilean on the way to Jerusalem was killed in Ginaea (Jenin); after revenge by the Jerusalemites, the Romans interfered and killed those responsible on both sides. This happened under Quadratus, governor of Syria, ca. 50 C.E. *Ant.* 18.118, 136 relates that many Galileans on the way to Jerusalem were killed in Ginaea; after revenge by the Jerusalemites, the Romans interfered and killed those responsible on both sides. In *Antiq-uities*, the Samaritans are said to have killed many Galileans, not only one, to have bribed the Romans and to have been punished justly after two extensive hearings performed by the Romans. The Galileans were on their way to "Jerusalem," *Antiquities*, not only to "the holy place," *War*. The changes may be part of Josephus' general tendency to provide new twists to stories, but in this case they produce a more negative portrayal of the Samaritans.

Similarly, the massacre on Gerizim at the hands of Cerealius throws a negative light on the Samaritans. The incident is due to the danger of insurrection by the Σαμαρεῖς gathered on Gerizim, *War* 3.307, and because they did not learn anything from the misfortunes of their neigh-bours in Joppa (Jaffa), and overestimated their forces. Their death was deserved for their rebellion against the Romans.

The texts surveyed here constitute the ideological backdrop to all that Josephus has to say on the Samaritans. I suggest that the other texts may be interpreted within this framework. In *Ant.* 12.7,10 Josephus tells us that the Ptolemaic king moved Samaritan troops to Egypt immediately after the death of Alexander. This is a later rationalization of the fact that there were Samaritans in Egypt; they occasioned discussion in Alexandria on where to send the offerings, to Jerusalem or Gerizim; we also read about discussions in Egypt in *Ant.* 13.74 f. According to *Ant.* 18.85–89 Pilate stops the Samaritan gathering to find the hidden temple vessels; *Ant.* 17.20 mentions that Herod had a Samaritan wife, Malthace; in *Ant.* 18.30 the Samaritans are said to have scattered human bones in the Jerusalem temple.

In the retelling of Ezra 4–5, Josephus does not change the overall picture, but relates the request to participate in the rebuilding of the temple, *Ant.* 11.84,88, and the hindering of its rebuilding, *Ant.* 11.19 f.; in *Ant.* 11.61, Darius orders the Samaritans to give up the villages to the Jews; in *Ant.* 11.97, the Samaritans write to Darius about the temple-reconstruction in Jerusalem, and in *Ant.* 11.116,118, Darius orders the Samaritans to support the funding of the temple in Jerusalem, but in *Ant.* 11.174, the Samaritans again hinder the temple building.

Josephus thus indirectly assumes that the Samaritans existed at the time of Ezra and Nehemiah in Samaria, and after the time of Alexander also in Egypt. The group was evidently large enough to cause harm to the temple reconstruction, to be treated separately by Antiochus Epiphanes, and to create irritation during the uprising against the Romans.

4.8. *Summing up so Far*

The terminology: Josephus made no clear distinction between the Samarians and the Samaritans, and he used all the following terms for the Samaritans: Σαμαρεῖται, Σαμαρεῖς, Χουθαῖοι, Σικιμῖται, Ἑβραῖοι and Σιδώνιοι. Σαμαρεῖται is said to be the Greek equivalent of the Hebrew term Χουταῖοι. Σαμαρεῖς is said to be used because they assumed the name of the country; he uses Σαμαρεῖτις and Σαμαρεῖτικον for the region. Χουθαῖοι links them to the imported peoples of 2 Kgs 17. Σικιμῖται is a term used to link them to ancient incidents like the rebellion against Jerusalem after the reign of Solomon, and Σιδώνιοι carries with it the negative associations this designation has in the HB.

Origin: The Samaritans are said to come from Mesopotamia, from

Jerusalem and from Sidon, in three different 'origin myths,' each of them referred to several times. They live in Shechem, and bear the characteristics of the original Shechemites, who rebelled against Jerusalem after the united kingdom.

The picture painted by Josephus of the Samaritans is one of opportunism, of renegade priests and laymen leaving Jerusalem for land and income in Samaria and worshipping at Mount Gerizim. In the overall story of the war between the Jews and the Romans, the Samaritans play the role of an opportunistic and untrustworthy group. The Samaritans' foreign origin is from lands belonging to the Romans' enemy, Babylon, and their opportunism stands out against the loyalty of Herod to the Romans (cf. *War*) and that of the majority of Jews. These were always loyal to common values, Roman and Jewish, and opportunism was evidently against these values.

Josephus' picture of the temple on Mount Gerizim is given in his story of the construction of the temple under Alexander, *Ant.* 11.302–347. Like the temple at Leontopolis, it was constructed in the likeness of that at Jerusalem, but he does not provide a description of it as he does of the Leontopolis temple, *War* 7.426–430. The temple on Mount Gerizim is not termed illegitimate, but its origin is highly dubious. Its destruction at the hands of one of Josephus' heroes, Hyrcanus, functions as an act of piety and valour. Its short, 200-year existence may be supposed to be due to this unlawful origin and unclean priesthood. Josephus would not give a high age for the temple of a group he dislikes, and he attributes the license to build the temple to an ambiguous figure in the eyes of Rome—Alexander the Greek—and its destruction to his hero—John Hyrcanus. If the temple was in fact from an earlier age than that of Alexander, it existed at the time of the Wadi Daliyeh papyri and bullae, and one element in the Cross-Purvis theory would be unfounded, namely that the temple was constructed by disenfranchised nobility from Samaria after the hellenization of that city at the hands of Alexander.

Josephus used 2 Kgs 17, Ezra 4 and Neh 12; 13 polemically and for his own purposes. His use of Neh 12; 13 implies that Jews living in mixed marriages joined the Chuthaeans, *Ant.* 11.302 f., paving the way for the allegation that they were a mixed race. The use of 2 Kgs 17 in *Ant.* 9 created the possibility that 2 Kgs 17:33 also spoke of the Samaritans: they had a mixed religion. This polemical use of Scripture might have had its origin in the attitude of the priests in Jerusalem.

Indirectly, Josephus testifies to a significant group of Samaritans, existing in his age, and probably much earlier. He presupposes that there were

Samaritans in Egypt shortly after Alexander, and that they had lived in
Samaria from early on. He does not criticize them for having a distinct
Torah, or *halakhah*; it seems that they were Jewish in these respects.
A distinct group with the later characteristics had not emerged at the
time of Josephus, but there were people living in Samaria, around Mount
Gerizim and focusing on this mountain, with a tradition that there had
been a temple there. The limits of this group were not yet fixed, but
they were committed to Mount Gerizim—enough to maintain hostility
to Jerusalem.

Josephus used the expression 'the Most High God' for the god of the
Samaritan temple. This may render the divine name in a way appropriate
to both Jews and Romans. The temple was 'unnamed,' but still dedicated
to the supreme God. As the inscriptions from Gerizim were made by
Yahweh-worshippers, and the name YHWH has been found on the
mountain, the sanctuary there was probably dedicated to this Deity.
Indirectly, Josephus allows for this.

4.9. *Genesis 34 in Josephus' Rendering*

In *Ant.* 1.157 Josephus does not mention Shechem in connection with the
journeys of Abraham.[68] On the other hand, he has a broad retelling of the
Dinah story in Gen 34, and here the name Σικιμῖται occurs, *Ant.* 1.337–
340. The story of Dinah is transformed by Josephus into a wonderful tale
of the king's son picking a girl of the invading tribe for his bride. Asked
for his daughter, the wobbling Jacob takes council with his sons, who are
mostly also at a loss what to do; only Simeon and Levi are capable of
taking action. Under the influence of the feast that the Shechemites hold,
they are all killed in the brothers' surprise attack.

> And Iakobos reached the place still now called "Booths," when he came
> to Sikimon—and it is a city of the Chananaians. And while the Sikimites
> were celebrating a festival, Deina—she was Iakobos' only daughter—came
> into the city in order to see the adornment of the indigenous women.
> And Sychemmes, the son of the king, Emmoros, catching sight of her,
> seduced [φθείρει] her through abduction; and being amorously disposed
> toward her, he implored his father to take the maiden in marriage for
> him. And he, having been persuaded, went to Iakobos asking him to give

---

[68] Cf. L. Feldman's footnote: "... perhaps out of anti-Samaritan motives ...," L. Feldman, *Flavius Josephus: Judean Antiquities 1–4* (vol. 3 of *Flavius Josephus: Translation and
Commentary*, ed. S. Mason; Leiden: Brill, 2000), 59, n. 506.

Deina in lawful marriage to his child, Sychemmes. And Iakobos, neither being able to refuse because of the rank of the one appealing to him, nor considering it lawful (νόμμον) to give his daughter in marriage to a foreigner (ἀλλοφύλῳ), decided to ask his permission to hold a council about the matters that he requested. Therefore, the king departed, hoping that Iakobos would permit the marriage, but Iakobos, revealing to his children the rape of their sister and the request of Emmoros, asked them to hold a consultation as to what it was necessary to do. Now, most of them kept quiet, being at a loss to decide, but Symeon and Leuis, the girl's brothers, born of the same mother, agreed with each other on some action. While there was a festival and the Sikimites had turned to relaxation and feasting, attacking first the guards at night, they killed them while they were asleep and entering the city killed every male, and the king and his son, together with them, but they spared the women. And having done these things without the consent of their father, they brought back their sister. And God, approaching Iakobos, who had been stricken with consternation at the enormity of the deeds and was angry with his sons, bade him to have courage, and purifying his tents to offer the sacrifices that he had vowed when he first departed to Mesopotamia upon the vision of his dream.[69]   (*Ant.* 1.337–341)

In his analysis of this text, L. Feldman interprets Josephus to a large extent by reviewing which parts of the biblical material have been omitted.[70] The guiding principle for Josephus would be on the one hand to avoid the impression that Jews were untrustworthy and that they zealously sought proselytes, and on the other hand to put the blame for the killing on Shechem and Hamor. He would remove all traits that could be interpreted as negative for the image of the sons of Jacob or positive for the Shechemites. By his sensitivity to what the Roman readers might infer from this story he would have carefully created a version which was intended to avoid fostering misconceptions about the Jews, such as aggressiveness in seeking proselytes, and to make the action taken by Simeon and Levi a parallel to a similar story from their own history, such as the revenge of the Romans on Tarquinius Superbus for the rape of Lucretia by Sextus Tarquinius, the son of king Tarquinius Superbus. Thus Josephus would build sympathy for Dinah and for the sons of Jacob's revenge for the rape.

L. Feldman may be right in this analysis, despite the problem arising from using evidence from silence. It would mean that Josephus had no

---

[69] Translation by L. Feldman, *Judean Antiquities* 1–4, 122–124.

[70] L. H. Feldman, *"Remember Amalek!" Vengeance, Zealotry, and Group Destruction in the Bible According to Philo, Pseudo-Philo, and Josephus* (Monographs of the Hebrew Union College 31; Cincinnati, Ohio: Hebrew Union College Press, 2004), 156–167.

problems with portraying the Shechemites negatively. This was part of his overall plan to invite sympathy with the Jewish nation, even if it entailed the sacrifice of their opponents' reputation. Josephus does not employ words from the LXX for the rape, but instead uses φθείρω, just as Demetrius and Theodotus had done two to three hundred years earlier in their retelling of the story; I will discuss their texts in the next chapter. He introduces the notion of a marriage according to the law, νόμος, which to Jewish readers would sound like a reference to Deut 7:3, cf. Theodotus. This is the idea also in the expression ἀλλόφυλος. In order to add verisimilitude to Dinah's trip to town and the attack by only two men, he introduces the feast, something found also in Theodotus.

Josephus introduces us to the Shechemites by retelling Gen 34 at the beginning of *Antiquities*, and he lets us meet them further in the rebellion of Jeroboam against Jerusalem and the son of Solomon. The later Samaritans are branded by the use of the name "Sikimites" for them. Josephus follows a practice that can be found in a series of renderings of Gen 34 from the second century B.C.E. There is so much material of this kind that a separate chapter is devoted to it. It constitutes some of the background for Josephus; we may even talk about his predecessors.

CHAPTER FIVE

JOSEPHUS' PREDECESSORS

The polemics of Josephus had predecessors in the third and second century B.C.E. in the form of a series of polemical texts directed at the inhabitants of the area in and around Shechem. Most of them are built upon the story of the rape of Dinah and the subsequent killing of the Shechemites in Gen 34.[1] This story is often associated with Deut 32:21. The texts in question are Demetrius, Theodotus, Sir 50:25 f., *Jub.* 30, *4QNarrative and Poetic Composition*[a-c], the *Aramaic Levi Document*, the *Testament of Levi*, and Judith. The interests and aims of these texts are different, and the mode of applying elements from Gen 34 varies in them. But it is interesting that so many texts from the same age show an awareness of this story. Without making too much of the quantity, one must say that it is conspicuous.

After the Hellenistic age, interest in Gen 34 continues. I have already treated Josephus' retelling of the story, and from Roman times I have chosen to include also *Joseph and Aseneth*, Philo, and Pseudo-Philo. These texts do not represent an end to interpretation of Gen 34, but I have chosen to stop there. The later Jewish readings of the biblical story in the Targums, the Midrashim and the Talmuds of course belong in a history of exegesis, but they have not been considered necessary for the period of Samaritan history which this investigation treats. A few remarks on Genesis 34 in the MT and the LXX introduce the treatment of the texts, and the SP version of the chapter is commented upon after the texts. A more or less chronological order is aimed at by this arrangement.

---

[1] Contemporary Western culture presupposes sexual intercourse to take place with mutual consent and by equal partners, and "rape" would then be one of the forms of sexual intercourse that do not comply with this presupposition. In cultures that do not necessarily share this presupposition, as for instance in ancient Israelite culture, "rape" would be an anachronistic or culturally displaced word. Most commentators of Gen 34 still use "rape" to render the act of Shechem against Dinah, and even as a translation of ענה. Voices have been raised against this understanding and rendering. For a recent presentation and discussion, see E. van Wolde, "Does *'innâ* denote rape?" *VT* 52 (2002): 528–544. The present book uses "rape" in line with traditional exegesis, but the author is aware that texts discussed here are more concerned with the defilement of Dinah than with the precise location of Shechem's act in a social-juridical system.

The relevant texts use phrases and motifs from Gen 34 and other bibli-cal texts. One method of studying this material was presented by L. Gins-berg in his famous *The Legends of the Jews* from the early 20th century, reprinted 1998.[2] His aim was to show that there existed a national lit-erature of the Jews, comparable to that of other peoples. He therefore retold the stories consecutively, thereby creating a new entity. This prod-uct, despite its large apparatus of notes, cannot constitute a basis for our investigation, even when it is supplemented with material discovered after Ginsberg wrote his volumes. Even though *The Legends of the Jews* is often referred to in scholarly literature, its purpose and method should be respected for what they were, and its aim should not be overlooked in our quest for relevant ancient sources.

Methodologically at the opposite extreme stands J. Kugel with his investigation of the motifs and traditions found in the literature which exploits Gen 34.[3] The study of motifs is interesting, but it has to be balanced by a reading of the whole text. Motif history as a method is productive for understanding the building blocks of a text, but runs the risk of creating a split image of the various texts. By reading texts as a whole we may arrive at their form and heart, taking into account all parts of them. To lay bare the way various elements of the mother text, in this case Gen 34, are understood, reused, developed, changed, twisted, and combined with new elements in the daughter texts is a valuable contribution to scholarship, but it cannot supplant the reading of individual texts in their entirety and with all their characteristics.

In this process one might be tempted to read too much into the later texts, by assuming that a word or a phrase from a biblical text carries with it larger implications from the biblical context. This might happen, but one must be aware of the possibility that notions from the context in the Bible have been passed over. In addition, a word or a phrase may have assumed a life of its own, somewhat detached from its original context; perhaps it also developed its own associations. Still, one has to check the source of the word or phrase, and in addition be aware that its employment in the new context may be dependent upon a development between the source and the present location. The texts treated in this

---

[2] L. Ginsberg, *The Legends of the Jews* (7 vols.; repr. ed.; Baltimore: Johns Hopkins University Press, 1998).

[3] J. Kugel, "The Story of Dinah in the *Testament of Levi*," *HTR* 85 (1992): 1–34; idem, *Traditions of the Bible: A Guide to the Bible as it was at the Start of the Common Era* (Cambridge, Mass.: Harvard University Press, 1998), 403–435.

chapter and the preceding one share the phenomenon that many phrases and motifs are taken over from the Bible, but some of these may have been given a new colouring by the later author, with which he has influenced others. We will have to reckon with several influences on an author, not only biblical ones.

5.1. Genesis 34[4]

The story in Gen 34 about the rape of Dinah and the subsequent killing of all the inhabitants of Shechem belongs with those biblical stories which seem relatively isolated in the larger context. The plot is not prefigured by earlier material, and only a few times is it referred to in subsequent texts. These are Gen 48:22; 49:5–7, and perhaps also Hos 6:9.

Quite differently, the location of the narrative, Shechem, receives due attention in the HB. In Genesis, Shechem is the first place which Abraham visits in the land that God will show him, Gen 12:6. Abraham builds an altar there, v. 7, and Jacob also does this, Gen 33:20. Further, Joseph is allotted land there, Gen 48:22. These narratives tend to set the locality in a positive light, and such an impression is strengthened by the account of the assembly of all Israel in Shechem, Josh 24. Josh 24:32 also tells us that Jacob was buried in Shechem. From this perspective, Gen 34 comes as a surprise with its two violent acts and the ambivalence thus created towards the location. Only in Judg 9 and 1 Kgs 12 are similarly controversial events located in Shechem: the reign of Abimelech and the division of the Solomonic kingdom. The burial of the idols under the oak near Shechem, Gen 35:4, adds another element of ambivalence: does it mean that idolatry is attached to the place, or is it parallel to the abrogation of idolatry told in Josh 24:14–28? The city of Shechem is thus given proper attention in the Bible, both as Abraham's first dwelling place, and as the place of violence, rebellion and idolatry. The story of Gen 34 is set in this

---

[4] The chapter is represented in one Qumran manuscripts and one or two Murabba'at manuscripts. The oldest, 4QGenesis-Exodusᵃ, fragm. 6 contains vv. 17–21, Mur(?)Gen contains vv. 1–3, and Mur Gen, Fragment 2 preserves parts of verses 5 and 6, and most of verse 7. All these manuscripts have the text of MT (with some orthographic differences). P. Benoit et al., eds., *Les grottes de Murabba'ât* (DJD 2; Oxford: Clarendon, 1961), plate XIX; E. Ulrich et al., eds., *Qumran Cave 4. VII: Genesis to Numbers* (DJD 12, Oxford: Clarendon, 1994), plates I–IV.

locale of ambivalence.[5] The story itself is also characterized by ambivalence: a negative assessment of the acts of Shechem is combined with a benign portrayal of the Shechemites, and the acts of the sons of Jacob are perhaps heroic, but considered tragic by their father.

The various literary techniques employed in the story invite comment. 'Hamor' is used as a name throughout, but at the end the word refers to the asses taken as booty by the Israelites, v. 28. This shift in meaning of the word suddenly throws some dubious light back on Hamor, the "prince of the land," v. 2. Jacob and his family arrive safely, שלם, 33:18, and later Hamor says that they are a "peaceful lot towards us," שלמים הם אתנו, 34:21. This verdict comes just before Simeon and Levi kill the men of Shechem. Dinah went out in order to "see" the daughters of the land, and immediately Shechem, the son of the prince of the land, "saw" her. Such a literary technique of sudden turnings creates a subtle ironical flair to the story. Further, there are open-ended sentences. Jacob's reaction to the news of the rape can only be guessed from the phrase "Jacob held his peace until [his sons] came" back from the field, v. 5.7. The implication of "they answered ... deceitfully and spoke," v. 13, is not clear. Was there some conversation not recorded or does the following reply, vv. 14–17, present the 'deceit' in the form of a device (circumcision) to make it possible for two men to kill many? Or is the 'deceit' introduced into the story post factum to cope with the idea that the reply was seriously meant, but then two of the respondents were carried away by emotion and broke the agreement? In the description of the rape, v. 2, two of the verbs from the law in Deut 22:28 f. occur, שכב and ענה, but the third verb in the law, תפש, is not found here. Instead, לקח, occurs, and this is taken from marriage law, cf. Gen 34:9.16.21. לקח is therefore used in this chapter with the meanings "seize," v. 2, and "take in marriage," vv. 9.12.21, but it also occurs with a third meaning, "retrieve," v. 17. In the marriage proposal of Shechem, vv. 11 f., he goes beyond the sum mentioned in the law in Deut 22, fifty pieces of silver, and leaves the sum open. The use of verbs in v. 2 describes Shechem as acting according to the case of Deut 22:28 f. by raping Dinah, but the first verb, לקח, shows that his intention was marriage. He was even willing to impose on himself a more generous payment than prescribed in the law of Deut 22:28 f. These and similar literary devices and open ends in the story provided the ground for exegetical efforts in the Hellenistic and Roman eras, and later.

---

[5] Relevant material presented in E. Nielsen, *Shechem: A Traditio-Historical Investigation* (Copenhagen: G. E. C. Gad, 1955); for archaeology, Wright, *Shechem*.

To the modern historical critics, however, such observations on the text, and the description of the roles of Jacob and his sons, of Shechem and Hamor, occasioned the idea that different stories were combined here, J and E.[6] Today, we may see that this source criticism was too *hellhörig*, even if many observations are still valid. We may, after all, find that the story reads well as a coherent whole. The author portrays Shechem first as aggressive, then as infatuated and eager to get Dinah as his wife; he sees the sons of Jacob as zealous, aggressive and deceiving; Jacob is described as a pale, distant figure, fearful of the consequences; Hamor is found to be the wise father with the overall view of the matter. In this way the author of the story has created a literary product which reflects the culture and sentiments of Israel's elite. These different 'personalities' are better seen as literary devices than as evidence of different sources.[7]

A central element in Gen 34 is that by the rape of Dinah Shechem "committed an outrage in Israel," נבלה עשה בישראל, v. 7 (LXX: ἄσχημον ἐποίησεν ἐν Ισραηλ). The whole expression "commit an outrage in Israel" appears in Deut 22:21; Josh 7:15; Judg 20:6; 2 Sam 13:12; Jer 29:23, in addition to Gen 34, and is a technical term for a special kind of sin: to be a bride without being a virgin, Achan's embezzling of the חרם, the Benjaminites of Gibeah's rape of the concubine until she dies, Amnon's rape of Tamar, prophesying lies in the name of Yahweh. The expression comes close to describing violation of divine justice. It is not a wisdom term, as the word "folly," נבלה, might suggest to modern readers. The use of this expression situates the story in a context of an especially serious violation of law and order.

Another important notion is that Shechem "defiled" Dinah, טמא, Pi., vv. 5.13.27 (LXX: μιαίνω). Although this is a general term, it has cultic overtones; the Qal means "to become ceremonially unclean." Through

---

[6] O. Eissfeldt, *Hexateuch-Synopse: die Erzählung der fünf BücherMose und des Buches Josua mit dem Anfange des Richterbuche in ihre vier Quellen zerlegt, und in deutscher Ubersetzung dargeboten, samt in einer in Einleitung und Anmerkungen gegebenen Begründung* (Leipzig: J. C. Hinrich, 1922; repr. Darmstadt: Wissenschaftliche, 1987), 69*-71*: E: v. 4.6.8.-10.13*.15–18.20–24.25b.27–29a; the rest is L(aienquelle), an earlier layer in J; G. von Rad, *Das erste Buch Mose: Genesis* (8. Aufl.; ATD 2/4; Göttingen: Vandenhoeck & Ruprecht, 1967), 288 f.

[7] The Hivites are the only people that deceive Joshua, Jos 9.3–27, as they inhabited Gibeon. This is the only place in the Bible where they are a single entity with a profile. If this has influenced Gen 34, then Hamor and Shechem were also crafty, not only the sons of Jacob.

such elements the story carries religious overtones. Circumcision is not
directly connected to worship of the God of Israel, as it is in Gen 17:9–14.
It is more of a cultural rite, in line with Josh 5:2–7, where it is associated
with possession of the promised land. Here it is said to be the condition
for becoming one people, vv. 16.22. Even if circumcision is not perceived
as a condition for relationship with the God of Israel, Dinah is said to
have been "defiled" by Shechem. There is a cultic element to this, and
the implication is that becoming one people through circumcision does
after all have to do with cult. An uncircumcised man will certainly "defile"
Dinah, something a circumcised man might do only under certain circumstances, cf. for example Ezek 22:11.

Although it is said that Shechem "defiled" Dinah, and "committed
an outrage"—clearly negative descriptions of his acting—the narrator is
not at all satisfied with the behaviour of the sons of Jacob. They speak
"deceitfully" to Shechem and Hamor, v. 13, a rare characterization of
actors in HB narratives. The ambiguity felt towards the killing of those
who agreed to circumcision and performed it, is also voiced through the
father's worried accusation: "You have brought trouble on me ...," v. 30.
The sympathy of the narrator is therefore not unambiguously on the side
of the Israelites.

This is also felt in the story's emphasis that Shechem fell in love with
Dinah, and wanted to pay a high bride price for her, as a voluntary fulfilment of the laws pertaining within Israel, Exod 22:15–16; Deut 22:28–29.
He and his father persuaded their fellow citizens to be circumcised, and
they all agreed and were circumcised. Apart from the act of rape, the Shechemites are portrayed benignly in the story.[8]

The topic of the land is present in the story. Hamor presents the land
as "open" to the sons of Jacob, so they may live and trade there, v. 10, 21;
it is "wide enough for them," v. 21. This offer is presented both before
and after the condition of circumcision, and would provide the Israelites
with an opportunity to acquire the land peacefully. The offer is implicitly

---

[8] Gen 34 is a story about the use of force against women, according to A. Standhartinger, "'Um zu sehen die Töchter des Landes': Die Perspektive Dinas in der jüdisch-
hellenistischen Diskussion um Gen 34," in *Religious Propaganda and Missionary Competition in the New Testament World: Essays Honoring Dieter Georgi* (eds. L. Bormann,
K. Del Tredici and A. Standhartinger; NovTSup 74; Leiden: Brill, 1994), 89–116. She is
aware, however, that this perspective on the story leaves many questions open. One must
agree that the opening sentence in v. 1 invites this understanding, but in what follows,
there is little interest in Dinah. On the contrary, the Shechemites would probably insist
that their fate is in focus. Simeon and Levi are certainly central.

rejected, however, by the course of events, and not commented upon by Jacob and his sons. A connection to Josh 9 may be seen in the "deceit" of the Hivites, Josh 9:22. If this connection is intended, the offer of land presents itself as another attempt at "deceit"—this time in the form of an offer which is a trap leading into idolatry, cf. Ex 34:16; Deut 7:3 f.; Judg 3:6. A connection to the deceit of the Hivites in Josh 9 may seem far-fetched, but it is conspicuous that the land theme is addressed twice by Hamor without any reply from the sons of Jacob. On the other hand, "they answered ... deceitfully and spoke," v. 13. If the two stories are related, and if the land offer is a trap, this time the sons of Jacob reply with equal guile.

Jacob criticizes Simeon and Levi for their slaughter of the Shechemites, v. 30, and this criticism is echoed in the curse, instead of a blessing, over these two tribes in Gen 49:5–7, and perhaps also in the omission of Simeon altogether in Moses' blessing, Deut 33. In the latter text, however, Levi is praised for his impartial application of the law, and there is no reproach, nor any reference to Gen 34 there. The HB texts already reveal ambivalence in their attitude to the acts of Simeon and Levi in Gen 34.[9] In the interpretations from the last centuries B.C.E. and the first century C.E., this ambivalence is not felt.

Gen 34 is considered polemical by Y. Amit. She sees "explicit polemic" over the issue of marriage with Canaanites in the text, and this "explicit polemic" is supported by indirect means: the plot is one of rape; specific designations are used; there are repetition and interpretation; the motif of circumcision occurs; there are allusive narrative interventions, and allusion to the language of law and rebuke.

In addition to this "explicit polemic," Amit finds "hidden polemic" in the account. Her method for finding "hidden polemic" is the following. First, there is no mention of the topic, the Samaritans, and relations with the Samaritans are a topic in other HB texts. Secondly, there are signs of polemic: the choice of Shechem as the locality, description of the Shechemites as Hivites, refraining from settlement in Shechem

---

[9] Criticism of Levi may also lie behind Hos 6:9. Here, the MT reads: "As robbers lie in wait for someone, so the priests are banded together; they murder on the road to Shechem, for they conceived evil thoughts." The LXX: "And thy strength is that of a robber: the priests have hid the way of the Lord, they have murdered the people of Sicima; for they have wrought iniquity (ἀνομίαν) in the house of Israel." The beginning of the translation is understandable from a different ordering of the consonants of the MT. The last sentence combines the MT with the beginning of v. 10, and seems to refer to Gen 34.

after the incident, circumcision as a motif, "marriage" connected to "[peoples of] the land," rape changed into a national issue, minority versus majority, and Jacob's attitude, different from that of his sons. Her third requirement for finding "hidden polemic" is that it is made visible in the exegetical tradition emanating from Gen 34, and this she finds in some of the texts that constitute the material for the present investigation. As a conclusion, she finds that groups hostile to the northern population, who later became the Samaritans, stood behind this text, and gave it its polemical traits. This was a school which bears a certain resemblance to the Priestly school, viz. "the Holiness School."[10] The polemic would be directed against the leaders of the people who were sympathetic towards intermarriage with foreigners. Both the explicit and the hidden polemic were hostile to the people of Shechem, both its earlier and later inhabitants. This understanding of Gen 34 leads her to assume a late date for its composition, or its present shape, at least as late as the books of Ezra and Nehemiah.

Some of the "signs" of Amit's hidden polemic in Gen 34 presuppose an anti-Samaritan reading of several HB texts, and build upon the assumption that Shechem in the time of the second temple had a mixed population. The evidence for these assumptions is debatable, therefore the theory rests upon uncertain ground.

Still, Gen 34 does raise the methodological question about polemics. Y. Amit's definition is this: "The description of a biblical text as polemical indicates its attitude toward an issue that lies at the center of some ideological struggle: one which generally—in one way or another—has some bearing upon reality."[11] It seems that this definition is too wide. Any disagreement on "an issue that lies at the center of some ideological struggle," and unbiased arguments in this connection, will be polemical, according to this definition. It will therefore embrace too much, and may be in need of more precision. A more precise definition might include a description of the means by which the attitude is expressed. Not every attitude in texts is polemical, but the way attitudes are expressed may be. I will return to the question of a definition of "polemic" later.

The history of "Levi" in the HB cannot be traced or described here, but some comments will be provided in connection with the discussion

---

[10] Y. Amit, *Hidden Polemics in Biblical Narrative* (Biblical interpretation series 25; Leiden: Brill, 2000),187–211.

[11] Ibid., 7.

of Gen 34 in SP. Mal 2:4–9 is one of the later texts relevant for the topic; K. W. Weyde's study of this text, overview of the biblical material, and research history is valuable.[12]

5.2. Genesis 34 Interpreted in the LXX

The LXX version of the rape of Dinah reveals a clearer bias in favour of Israel and the opposing party is less favourably described.

In the LXX Dinah is described as a παρθένος for נערה twice in v. 3, but she is a παῖς for the Hebrew ילדה in v. 4, and for נערה in v. 12. The use of παρθένος in the LXX has been discussed by James Barr in an article where he assumes that in the case of Is 7:14 "… the translator wrote παρθένος, and understood it to mean 'young woman'. But the same word could function also with the sense 'virgin', and was indeed better known with that sense. Some reader, or group of readers, read it in the latter way. We do not know when this took place, bur certainly before St Matthew's Gospel was written (Matt. 1:23)." Despite the fact that the word had a strong semantic component of "virgin," it was used in several cases with the meaning of "girl" or "maiden."[13]

If the renderings in Gen 34 were made in a similar vein, the possibility of reading the LXX's παρθένος as "virgin" was seen and exploited by later literature. If this was the "better known" sense of the word, then the greatest possibility is that the word was used and understood with this sense, and the sense "young woman" was the exception to the rule. A possibility mentioned but not discussed by Barr is that the LXX purposely interpreted the different Hebrew expressions in a desired direction. In Gen 34 this might well have been the case. It is therefore possible that the rendering παρθένος in v. 3 is used in order to emphasize the unacceptability of Shechem's action against her. In the following narrative the translation was not repeated, but a word closer to the Hebrew was chosen. Verse 3 sets the tenor of the translation of the whole chapter: Dinah was a virgin.

In v. 5 the LXX adds a subject for the verb "defiled": ὁ υἱὸς Εμμωρ, "the son of Hamor," where the MT only says "he defiled." Another possibility for the LXX would have been to add "Shechem," who is the person acting

---

[12] K. W. Weyde, *Prophecy and Teaching: Prophetic Authority, Form Problems, and the Use of Traditions in the Book of Malachi* (BZAW 288; Berlin: de Gruyter, 2000), 173–214.

[13] J. Barr, "The Most Famous Word in the Septuagint," JSSSup 16 (2005): 60.

in vv. 2–4. "The son of Hamor" sounds like a derogatory term for the man. In v. 12 the translation lacks an equivalent for "and a gift," leaving Shechem's promise to encompass the bride price only.

Through the addition in v. 14 of Συμεων καὶ Λευι οἱ ἀδελφοὶ Δινας υἱοὶ δὲ Λειας as a subject to "said," instead of "they" = the sons of Jacob, cf. v. 13 in MT, the LXX makes only Simeon and Levi responsible for the message to Shechem and his father Hamor. Verse 25 of the MT focuses on these two brothers, but this focus is found already in v. 14 in the LXX. It is a clarification of who spoke, but even more a way of putting these two brothers at centre stage.

The sons of Jacob end the description of the condition for marriage by saying that the parties will "become one people," v. 16, and Hamor repeats this phrase in v. 22. LXX renders the first case "become like one people," but the second "become one people." In this version the sons of Jacob envisage a one-people-result with some reservation, but in the report of the condition Hamor misses this finer point of the contract text and promises more than the sons of Jacob have done, "we will become one people," v. 22.

The addition of "Dinah" in v. 27 gives more emphasis to the statement: they defiled *Dinah* our sister. Similarly, the sentence in v. 31: "should they exploit our sister like a harlot?" is more explicit than the impersonal expression of the MT. The sentence is also more general: "they" refers to the Shechemites in general, instead of Shechem alone, who is in focus in the MT.

The change in v. 7 to καὶ οὐχ οὕτως ἔσται, "and so it must not be," instead of MT's "and so it must not be done" means that the statement is slightly more general in the LXX.

V. 9 has τοῖς υἱοῖς ὑμῶν i.e. as brides "for your sons," for MT's "for you." This is a more precise statement than the MT. In v. 16 ἀπὸ is added before "your daughters" and "as wives" is added, which makes this verse more precise. V. 17: "we will take our daughters and leave," is plural instead of the singular form of the MT, which refers to Dinah only. These readings are more precise, but also more general than the MT. They therefore point in the direction of general rules beyond the single case described in MT.

The booty taken in v. 29 is total in the LXX: "as much as was in the city" is added. The killing of the Shechemites has more devastating consequences in the LXX: "all" is added to "inhabitants"; in the LXX Jacob fears "all the inhabitants" of the land where MT has "the inhabitants" of the land.

The LXX made the story more general, and more precise in the expressions concerning exogamy. Simeon and Levi are more in focus, and Dinah is characterized as a virgin. Shechem's promise of a bride price lacks the additional gifts, and the city is completely emptied of its valuables. The narrative seems more negative towards the Shechemites than the MT. This tendency is carried further in the texts of the third and second century B.C.E.

5.3. Demetrius the Exegete and Chronographer[14]

Characteristic of Demetrius' version of the Dinah incident is the radical abbreviation of the story and the focus on the rape as the only motivation for the killings.

Demetrius wrote in the late third century B.C.E. His text was quoted by Alexander Polyhistor, whose work was in turn used by Eusebius.[15] Six fragments are preserved, all reflecting biblical material.[16] The literary style is lapidary and terse, with short narratives on a skeleton of chronology. The first fragment contains a short version of Abraham's sacrifice of Isaac, and the second devotes most attention to Jacob's story, including the marriages in Haran, the wrestling with the angel, the Dinah incident, the birth of Benjamin in Bethlehem, and the final sojourn in Mamre. The rest of fragment 2 is concerned with Joseph in Egypt. Fragment 3 discusses the marriage of Moses to Zipporah, and fragment 4 covers the incident at Marah, fragment 5 discusses why the Israelites had weapons, and the last fragment presents the chronology of Sennacherib's and Nebuchadnezzar's captivities in relation to each other and to the time of

---

[14] This title is suggested by U. Mittmann-Richert, "Demetrios the Exegete and Chronographer—a New Theological Assessment," in *The Changing face of Judaism, Christianity, and other Greco-Roman religions in antiquity* (ed. I. H. Herderson et al.; SJSHRZ 2; Gütersloh: Güthersloher, 2006), 186–209. Demetrius has for a long time been considered a chronographer and an exegete; accordingly, it is only appropriate to include both appellations within the title.

[15] Text in C. R. Holladay, *Historians* (vol. 1 of *Fragments from Hellenistic Jewish Authors*; TTPS 10; Chico, Calif.: Scholars Press, 1983), 51–91; introduction and translation by J. Hanson, "Demetrius the Chronographer (Third Century B.C.): A New Translation and Introduction," *OTP* 2: 843–854.

[16] Five fragments are provided by Alexander and Eusebius, the sixth fragment is found in Clement of Alexandria, *Stromata* I 141,1–2. The connection of this sixth fragment to the other five is still a matter of dispute. In the following, the parts of the text will be referred to by fragment and verse, as in *OTP* 2: 848–854.

Ptolemy IV (222/1–194 B.C.E.), which is the supposed time of the author. Chronology is a main concern of Demetrius, and the dates given are often added to the biblical account.

The question of the tribal system in Demetrius has been much debated, and U. Mittmann-Richert offers a new solution, which is also intended to shed light on the theology of the fragments.[17] She takes the status of the tribe of Dan as her starting point, and supposes that this tribe was suppressed because in Judaism it was associated with evil or the devil. Taken together with Demetrius' emphasis on migration Dan carries the responsibility for the dispersion of Israel in all the world. Israel should have been living as a nation in its own land, but is now exiled into many countries because of Dan. In Demetrius' hope for an eschatological restoration of Israel Dan is removed from the tribal system. Mittmann-Richert's idea is interesting, but builds more on inference from the text than on the text as it is. Her reflections on the academic traditions in Alexandria as formative for Demetrius' work are convincing, but if we are to understand his text, which displays efforts to read the Bible for his own times, we must primarily build on the extant text.

It seems that Alexander or Eusebius checked the text of Demetrius against the Bible, because it is stated that Demetrius accords with Scripture, fragments 3:1; 4:1. This means that we do not have Demetrius' text in front of us, but Alexander's and Eusebius' rendering of it. With the proviso that the extant text therefore may have suffered changes in relation to Demetrius' work, one may attempt an overall understanding of it.

The interests in the fragments of Demetrius are chronology and the solution of problems posed by the Bible, according to Hanson.[18] I do not disagree with this understanding, but want to add a few observations. Twice we read that "Abraham was chosen from among the gentiles and migrated (from Haran) to Canaan," fragment 2:16.18. The implication is that Israel is a chosen people, whose land is Canaan, where the three patriarchs lived for 215 years, fragment 2:18. Abraham was willing to sacrifice his son Isaac but an angel prevented him from doing this, fragment 1, and after his willingness to give up hope for any posterity, God provided Abraham with descendants. Isaac's son Jacob became the father of the tribes, fragment 2. Twice we read that Jacob was renamed "Israel," fragment 2:7.10. There is, therefore, emphasis on the election of

---

[17] Mittmann-Richert, "Demetrios."
[18] Hanson, "Demetrius," *OTP* 2: 845.

Abraham from the gentiles, on the divine grace embodying itself in this people, and on the renaming of Jacob. Israel is an elect people with its own land, Canaan.

This people sticks to endogamous marriages. Jacob marries his maternal uncle's daughters, fragment 2:3. Amram, Levi's grandson, marries his uncle's daughter, and by her begets Moses. Fragment 3 is concerned with the marriage of Moses to Zipporah. The author shows that she was descended from Jokshan, the son of Abraham by Keturah. The author evidently considers the marriage to an Ethiopian woman also as an endogamous marriage, fragment 3:3. Thus, Moses married endogamously, just like the patriarch Jacob in fragment 2. The defilement of Dinah is therefore found in a context of endogamous marriages.

We may therefore read Demetrius to the effect that this chosen people with an endogamous marriage system is set in the framework of a chronology starting with Adam, fragment 2:18, and ending with the author's time, fragment 6. The people of Israel are provided with an exact chronology within this framework, and major events in the people's life are highlighted. If this reading of Demetrius is on the right track, an image of the chosen and ethnically pure people with an exact chronology emerges. One may infer that such a people would be considered a worthy companion of the surrounding peoples in Alexandria towards the end of the third century B.C.E.

The Dinah incident is only a small part of the work, but it was evidently considered important enough to be among the selected stories, whereas other events in Jacob's life did not make it into Demetrius. We read in *Praeparatio Evangelica* (abbreviated *PE*), 9.21.8–10a about the arrival of Jacob with his ten sons and Dinah εἰς ἑτέραν πόλιν Σικίμων, "at another city of the Shechemites," emended by Hanson to "Salem, a city" in accordance with Gen 33:18 LXX. Their age on arrival is recorded. Fragment 2:9 is a brief summary of Gen 34.

> Now Israel lived beside Emmor for 10 years, and Israel's daughter, Dinah, was defiled (φθείρω) by Shechem the son of Emmor, when she was 16 years and four months old. And Israel's son Simeon, at 21 years and four months, and Levi, 20 years and six months of age, sprang up and killed both Emmor and Shechem, his son, and all the men because of the defilement (φθορά) of Dinah; and Jacob was 107 years old at the time. (*PE* 9.21.9)

The story focuses on the rape and the subsequent killing of the Shechemites; it is short and without any additions. Only Simeon and Levi take part in the killing. The inhabitants of the city are not named, but associated with Hamor and Shechem, who are not introduced as Hivites, as in the MT. Israel lives peacefully beside these people for a long time, and only when the daughter of Israel is defiled, do they kill the inhabitants of the land. Most of the biblical story is omitted, e. g. the negotiations between Jacob and his sons and Hamor, the circumcision of the Shechemites and the fatherly reproach of Simeon and Levi. The text thus is completely on the side of Simeon and Levi, and the killing of Hamor and Shechem is considered justified. The only reason provided for the killings is the rape. The technical terms, ἀσχήμων and μιαίνω, from Gen 34:7 do not occur, instead a term for seduction and destruction is used, φθείρω, common in late LXX texts and used also for decay of a concrete or abstract kind. Dinah's age—not found in the Bible—is supplied, together with other chronological and genealogical data.

There are no polemics against the contemporary inhabitants of Shechem in this text, which is understandable if it was produced in Egypt in the third century B.C.E., shortly after the Pentateuch was translated into Greek there.[19] But the topic of endogamous marriage was important also in that period, based on the patriarchs' endogamous marriages, and it probably also constitutes the background of the Dinah incident in Gen 34.

U. Mittmann-Richert understands Demetrius' main topic as being the question why Israel did not live in the Promised Land, but was dispersed into the whole world. If this is a correct understanding, there is also a conquest theme in Demetrius' rendering of the Dinah incident. Because of the defilement of Dinah, Hamor and Shechem are killed, and this also opens the way for a sojourn in their land.

Demetrius focuses on the defilement of Dinah and the immediate killings because of this, and the story is set in the context of the endogamous marriages of Jacob, Amram, and Moses. Israel, the elect people, keep themselves pure by the marriage policy, and Canaan being their land, they kill its former inhabitants only if this purity is endangered.

5.4. Theodotus

The most conspicuous traits of the poem of Theodotus are the extended description of the city of Shechem and the area around it in the first fragment, and the detail with which the killings are described in the last.

---

[19] Hanson, "Demetrius," OTP 2: 844.

The whole poem with its introductions centres on the Dinah incident, and it reads as an exposition of this story with an extended introduction in two parts, (1) the description of the Shechem area and (2) the sojourn in Haran. Also, the motivation for the killings includes—in addition to the rape of Dinah—the scriptural basis for endogamous marriage and for circumcision, as well as the promise of the land to Abraham.

Theodotus' epic poem is extant in eight fragments with 47 lines in hexameter verse. It was quoted and provided with introductions in prose by Alexander Polyhistor, and the poem with introductions is again quoted by Eusebius, *Praeparatio Evangelica* 9.22.[20] Since the text by Theodotus is in hexameter, one may assume that it has been faithfully transmitted by its two tradents, Alexander and Eusebius. The introductions by Alexander, however, may have a looser connection to the original text by Theodotus.

The eight fragments may be just fragments of a larger work, but these constitute the available text that we have to work with. It is commonly assumed that the poem uses Homeric form and phrases, in traditional Greek epic style. One must therefore suppose that many phrases were common stock, but the contents are biblical, in the form that these are represented in the LXX.

Alexander's introductions summarize or explain the contents of the following poetic fragments in the case of fragments 2, 3, 5, and 7. He provides additional information in his introductions to fragments 1, 4, 6, and 8, and adds a final note after fragment 8. Judging from the correspondence between the introductions to fragments 2, 3, 5, and 7 and the actual fragments 2, 3, 5, and 7, one may assume that his introductions to fragments 4, 6, and 8 are probably close to parts of the poem which he does not quote. There is reason to believe that his introduction to fragment 1, on the other hand, contains new information provided by himself, and this will be treated in what follows. We may therefore assume that we do not have a second layer of information in his introductions (except for the first), but merely a reworking in prose of the original poem. As a Greek philosopher he would probably not be able to make his own contribution on the topic, but would have to accept what he received.

---

[20] Introduction, text and translation with extensive notes in C. R. Holladay, *Poets: The Epic Poets Theodotus and Philo and Ezekiel the Tragedian* (vol. 2 of *Fragments from Hellenistic Jewish authors*; TTPS 12; Chico, Calif.: Scholars Press, 1989), 68–70; see also F. Fallon, "Theodotus (Second to First Century B.C.): A New Translation and Introduction," *OTP* 2: 785–793; N. Walter, "Theodotus der Epiker," *JHRSZ* 4: 154–171; G. S. Oegma, "Theodotos der Epiker," *JHRSZ* 6: 54–62.

Still, prose introductions by a Greek living in Rome in the middle of the first century B.C.E. are to be distinguished from the poem by Theodotus, and therefore the poetic fragments and the introductions are here treated separately. The third part of the text preserved in *Praeparatio Evangelica* is the contribution by Eusebius, which need not occupy us much, since he simply provides a superscription, "Theodotus' (Remarks) Concerning Jacob," to the following fragments with introductions. The contents of the poem and the introductions travelled from the HB to the LXX and then into Theodotus and Alexander, to end up in Eusebius.

In the following treatment the fragments of the poem are read separately and together, before I focus on Alexander Polyhistor's introductions to them. Since Eusebius clearly distinguishes between Theodotus and Alexander, it is possible to read the fragments of the poem on their own, before one studies the summaries and introductions by Alexander Polyhistor. Holladay's translation is used in the quotations (his capital letters at the beginning of lines are converted into lower case letters if quotations are in the format of continuous text).

The first fragment describes a "smooth wall" around the city of Shechem. Scholars have looked for this wall in the archaeological excavations of Shechem, as discussed by J. J. Collins and others.[21] Consequently, some commentators suppose that Theodotus wrote some time in the third century or the first half of the second century B.C.E., because of the archaeological evidence for a wall around Shechem. This wall was in good shape at that time, but fell into decay after ca. 150 B.C.E. This way of reasoning is, however, ill-founded, and cannot be maintained. The author of the poem praises Shechem in traditional terms that we should not take to be eyewitness descriptions of the city.[22] As scholars suppose that Theodotus created his poem after the model of Homeric poetry, it would not be natural to look for archaeological or historical references in it.

Similarly, the detailed description of the killing of Hamor and Shechem in fragment 8 could be traditional heroic language, and is not obviously "representative of the background of that action," viz. Hyrcanus' attack on Shechem.[23] Collins treats the poem by Theodotus and its introductions by Alexander as one unit, and sees a connection to the Mac-

---

[21] J. J. Collins, "The Epic of Theodotus and the Hellenism of the Hasmoneans," *HTR* 73 (1980): 100 f., cf. Fallon, "Theodotus," *OTP* 2: 787 f.

[22] Further arguments and discussion in Holladay, *Poets*, 68 f.

[23] Collins, "Epic of Theodotus," 102.

cabees: "... the passage would make excellent sense as a Jewish work from the time of John Hyrcanus."[24] "The poem of Theodotus could easily be read as a paradigmatic justification for the actions and policies of Hyrcanus."[25] "His [Theodotus'] vision of Judaism is covenantal nomism of the narrowest variety ... the epic form lent itself admirably to nationalistic propaganda, but it is striking that Jewish nationalism is comfortably clad in such an obviously Hellenistic dress. If this poem was written in support of John Hyrcanus, it offers a remarkable illustration of the Hasmonean blend of nationalism and Hellenization."[26] From general considerations and particularly because of the detailed description of the killings in fragment 8, Collins has suggested a date late in the second century B.C.E. for the poem. John Hyrcanus imposed circumcision on the Idumeans and attacked Shechem and Samaria, and the poem could have been created in his time.

In addition to the stylistic consideration that the poem is conventional heroic language, a fact to be remembered is that Josephus does not mention circumcision in the case of Shechem, and his testimony is later than Theodotus by two centuries or more. A reading from Josephus' perspective resulting in an exact dating is, therefore, precarious.

The question about Theodotus' provenance has received much attention. J. Freudenthal interpreted the interest in Shechem and its description as a Samaritan feature.[27] Given the overall impression of the language of the poem, however, this can be better understood in terms of praising the scenes where the events took place. The hero of the poem, Jacob, operates in a grand location, Shechem. The Samaritan holy place, Mount Gerizim, plays no part in the poem. After the study by J. Freudenthal, Theodotus was considered a Samaritan, but in a more recent study J. J. Collins has argued that he was "a militant and exclusivist Jew," representing "the anti-Samaritan propaganda of the Hasmoneans."[28] Collins has won general agreement for the idea that Theodotus was a hellenizing Jew, but not that his poem was anti-Samaritan.[29]

---

[24] J. J. Collins, *Between Athens and Jerusalem: Jewish identity in the Hellenistic diaspora* (2. ed.; The Biblical resource series; Grand Rapids, Mich.: Eerdmans, 2000), 58.

[25] Ibid., 59.

[26] Ibid., 59 f.

[27] Freudenthal, "Hellenistische Studien."

[28] Collins, "Epic of Theodotus," quotations from 102 and 92; further discussion in Holladay, *Poets*, 58–68, and in Fallon, "Theodotus," *OTP* 2:785–793.

[29] Holladay, *Poets*, 89 f., n. 41.

As for the location of the author, Palestine and Alexandria have been the most frequent suggestions. Mostly, the discussion has centred on the Homeric form and language as a help in this connection, but the LXX should also be taken into account. Then, Alexandria with its centre for classical Greek studies and as the home of the LXX of the Pentateuch is more likely than Palestine. A Jew with good classical training, living in Alexandria, is a possible author. This possibility is supported by the poem's affinity with Demetrius.

There are much the same interests here as in Demetrius, who is dated third century B.C.E., and whose provenance most probably is Alexandria. First, Theodotus' story follows that of the preserved fragments of Demetrius from the beginning of fragment 2, or to be precise he is close to *PE* 9.22.1–9. Admittedly, this is the biblical sequence, but the choice of biblical topics is much the same in the two works. Secondly, like Demetrius his vocabulary is close to that of the LXX, but neither of them uses the LXX word ἀσχήμων for the defilement of Dinah; both employ the word φθείρω. This word is found in the introduction to fragment 4 of Theodotus, but on the assumption that this introduction has a basis in the original poem, we cannot rule out the possibility that the wording is original. Thirdly, in line with Demetrius he has an interest in endogamous marriage. These observations taken together with the general affiliation to the LXX of Demetrius and Theodotus and the Homeric literary tradition in which Theodotus stands, make it not improbable that he worked in Alexandria. His audience seems to have been fellow Jews, whom he may have intended to strengthen in their discussion with the Samaritans. We know of such discussions in Egypt during the reign of Ptolemy VI Philometor (180–145 B.C.E.) from Josephus, *Ant.* 13.74 (*Ant.* 12.10 may refer to the same incident), and Josephus' information on these discussions is to be trusted as referring to a general phenomenon.

Another possibility is mentioned by L. H. Feldman: Theodotus was a Samaritan, living in Palestine, and perhaps "connected with Hasmonean politics, since the emphasis of the poem on circumcision would fit in with John Hyrcanus' forcible imposition of Judaism on the Idumeaeans."[30] This idea shows the problem of finding coherence in the seemingly conflicting observations scholars make on the poem. However, to make Theodotus into a Samaritan "connected with Hasmonean politics," which would have to be on the Hasmoneans' side, is to stretch our imagination

---

[30] Feldman, "*Remember Amalek!*," 171, n. 274.

too far. Feldman's evidence for this idea are here understood otherwise. The detailed description of Samaria could be a conventional way of portraying the setting of the story in grand scenery. The "ten peoples" are probably not the ten tribes, but a reference to Gen 15:18–21. "Hebrews" is a general term, not distinctive of the Samaritans. Feldman's suggestion cannot be followed.

The assumption that the poem was written in the early second century B.C.E. in Alexandria cannot be proved, and the question remains open, but there are arguments in favour of it. The other possibility is that Theodotus worked in Jerusalem, where he might have had his classical training at the gymnasium. He may have encouraged or supported the Hasmoneans or provided them with a heroic poem after their attack on Shechem; Collins' suggestion remains a possibility, even if we abandon the attempts at a precise dating on this basis. The Hasmoneans were opposed to Seleucid politics of their day, but not to foreign culture altogether. A Homeric-like poem might have been considered appropriate by them. On balance, therefore, it seems more probable that Theodotus was a Jew, probably working in Jerusalem, and siding with the Hasmoneans.

Theodotus lived before Alexander, who flourished in the middle of the first century B.C.E., and after the LXX of the Pentateuch was made, which was in the middle of the third century B.C.E. It is not possible to date him more precisely, but a date in the second century B.C.E. is not impossible.

In order to discover the *Tendenz* of the poem, one should first notice which elements are taken over from the LXX and which are new. The reworking of the contents of the LXX may reveal the interests of the author, and this together with the elements taken over forms a new entity. The combined result must be assumed to convey the message of the author.

The first fragment praises the country around biblical Shechem, employing terminology not taken from the LXX or the HB: "Now thus the land was indeed fertile, browsed by goats and well-watered, neither was it a long way to enter the city from the country ..." Perhaps the information in Gen 34:10.21 that the country was "wide" (LXX: πλατεία) inspired the impressive description of the country. Gen 34:5 says that Jacob's sons were tending their flock, which may have occasioned the mention of a fertile land and goats. Mount Gerizim and Mount Ebal are referred to: "And out of it very near two mountains appear quite steep, full of grass and trees." The praise of the city seems to build on traditional Greek or Hellenistic style: "... and on the other side the living (city of) Shechem appears, a holy city, built below at the base (of the mountain), and around (the city) a smooth wall running (in) under the foot of the mountain, on high, a defense enclosure." The characterization of Shechem as a "city," ἄστυ, which was the word used by Athenians for Athens, is in itself praise for the city.[31] When the expression is used about Shechem in the phrase ἱερὸν ἄστυ, "a holy city", it is therefore not necessarily a sign of the Samaritan provenance of the poem, as J. Freudenthal supposed. It is part of the generally hyperbolic language of the poem. The focus on Shechem instead of on Mount Gerizim, and on its characterization as "holy" reminds us of Gen 12, where Abraham arrives at Shechem and builds an altar to the Lord, or of Gen 33:20, where Jacob builds an altar near Shechem. But the Bible does not use the term "holy" for Shechem. This is a novelty in the poem. The Samaritans of the second century B.C.E. venerated "holy Argarizein," as in the Delos inscriptions. In a text from the Hellenistic period, the focus on Shechem instead of on Mount Gerizim is conspicuous, and even anti-Samaritan.

The name for the city is Σικιμα in fragment 1 and consistently throughout the poem and the introductions. The name of the person who attacks Dinah is Συχεμ, also consistently throughout. This distinction is not found in the HB, as only one word is used as the name for both the city and the person, שכם. In the LXX, however, the city is termed Σικιμα in Gen 33 and 35, but the person in focus in chapter 34 is Συχεμ. This distinction is not consistent throughout the LXX, but it is found in the chapters reflected in Theodotus, which brings him close to the LXX.

The second fragment builds on Gen 33:18–20; 34:1 and tells how Jacob arrived at "the shepherds' city," the "outstretched Shechem"—compare the "wide" country of the LXX. The expression "the shepherds' city" for Shechem is a brief allusion to the sons of Jacob tending their flock in that area in Gen 34:5, cf. also ch. 37, a theme picked up in the introduction to fragment 4. Hamor and Shechem are called "a very stubborn pair," a plus in relation to the LXX, and a prefiguring of the later accusations against them in fragment 7.

The author addresses the reader in fragment 2 as a "stranger," ξένος. The phenomenon of an address to the reader is, of course, traditional, but the word chosen here could carry some overtones. 2 Macc 6:2 is an anti-Samaritan text implying that the Samaritans were strangers in need of protection by Διὸς Ξενίου, "Zeus the friend of strangers." The theme of hospitality is addressed in fragment 7, where the Shechemites

---

[31] H. G. Liddell, R. Scott and G. R. Berry, *Greek-English Lexicon*, s.v. αστυ.

are said to lack hospitality. From these texts, one might infer that the Samaritans were themselves strangers in need of protection, but provided no hospitality to other strangers. If there is an anti-Samaritan tenor to the poem, the address of fragment 2 could be understood—in line with this tenor—as turning towards the Samaritans as readers, saying that Jacob is now about to occupy the city of Shechem and you, the contemporary occupants, are strangers. This reading would be strained, however, and an address to the general public with traditional language is a more probable understanding.

The third fragment refers to Jacob's sojourn in "Syria," Gen 27–31, and the sequence in Genesis is therefore recast: the allusions to Gen 33 precede the fragment which retells chapters 27–31. In this way, Jacob is associated with Shechem before his journey to "Syria." The story recounted in fragment 3 is not very different in content from the Genesis texts, but the persons are pictured in stylized phrases. If they were "round" figures in the Bible, they have become "flat" here.

Jacob's marriage to the two sisters is emphasized: he is endogamous. The two maids are not mentioned; the eleven sons plus Dinah all seem to be children from endogamous marriages.

A motif in fragment 3 which has not received attention in the scholarly debate is that of an initial friendly reception which later turns out to be deceit: "Graciously did Laban receive him unto his home … and to him the marriage of his daughter he promised, indeed committed his youngest … yet he did not at all intend for this to come to pass, instead he wound a skein of wile, and to the marriage bed sends to the man Leah, who was his elder daughter. Yet it did not at all escape Jacob's notice; instead he perceived the vile deed …" This motive is picked up in the introduction to fragment 4: "Hamor … received him hospitably and gave him a certain portion of land ….when Shechem … saw her, he loved her; and, seizing her as his own, he carried her away and raped her." It adds to the honour of Jacob and his sons that they are treated treacherously, but are able to cope with the treason and turn it into an asset for themselves. First, in spite of Laban's "vile deed," Jacob marries two sisters, his own kinsfolk. Second, after the rape of Dinah, the city of Shechem is emptied of its former inhabitants and the spoil falls to the sons of Jacob. This turning of the tables is in line with the character of the poem and its introductions as a heroic narrative.

Fragment 4 is close to Deut 7:3: "For indeed this very thing is not allowed for Hebrews to bring home sons-in-law and daughters-in-law from another place but only one who boasts of being of the same race."

It is not allowed to marry exogamously, neither with men nor women, cf. *Jub.* 30:11. The rule is not introduced here as a divine command, but that could be implied. This law is then explained in fragment 5, which retells Gen 17:9–27 in the form of a divine command to Abraham, which he obeys. Circumcision is the necessary requirement for a bridegroom if a marriage is to be endogamous. Abraham complies with the command to circumcise. The third and fourth fragments provide the reason why Dinah would have to marry a circumcised man, who by circumcision was "of the same race," γενεῆς ... εἶναι ὁμοίης, fragment 4, just as Jacob had married two women "of the same blood," ὅμαιμος, i.e. sisters from his own kinsfolk, according to the third fragment.[32] An exogamous marriage between Dinah and Shechem is forbidden by the law cited. The definition of endogamous marriage as based upon circumcision is important in Theodotus. In the HB there are texts naming forbidden peoples, like the Amalekites, Deut 25:17–19, and the Philistines and Ammonites, Neh 9:2. Theodotus does not provide a list of peoples who would not be eligible for marriage, but instead focuses on circumcision as a definition. Abraham complies with the divine command, and thus becomes a model for later generations.

Theodotus' use of "Hebrews" in fragment 4 is also Jewish usage. In Gen 14:13 Abraham is termed a "Hebrew," and in the HB the expression is confined to Gen 37–50; Ex 1–15; 1 Samuel. In Hellenistic and Roman times the expression meant a Jew, cf. Judith, 2 Maccabees and 4 Maccabees. The expression points in the direction of Jewish origin for the poem, as the self-designation of the Samaritans from this time is "Israelites" in the Delos inscriptions. The "Hebrews" of fragment 4 are Jacob and his sons, both in the poem and in the introduction where this word occurs.

Some commentators have seen in fragment 6 an allusion to the ten northern tribes of Israel, "For well have I heard a word of God; for he once said that he would give ten nations [ἔθνεα] to the sons of Abraham." Could this be an allusion to the population forming the background to the later Samaritans?[33] The assumption presupposes that the Samaritans formed the continuation of the ten tribes supposed to have constituted the Northern kingdom, or at least considered themselves to be such a

---

[32] Read as a sentence about Jacob's relation to the sisters, and not about their relation to each other as sisters, the problems described by Holladay, *Poets*, 170, are resolved.

[33] Freudenthal, "Hellenistische Studien," 100.

continuation. This would then lead in the direction of Samaritan provenance for the author. Such a reading is, however, now abandoned, because the later Samaritans do not consider themselves descendents of the ten tribes only but of all Israel, and thus there is no foundation in Samaritan self-understanding for this assumption. Neither is there a basis in Jewish thinking on the origins of the Samaritans for this theory. The reading of 2 Kgs 17 which is undertaken by Josephus considers them descendants of the imported peoples and not of the former inhabitants. 2 Kgs 17:23 seems to say that all Israel was deported, and Josephus spells this out clearly: "He [Salmanasser] utterly exterminated the leadership of the Israelites, and transported the entire population to Media and Persia, and along with them carried off Osees [Hoshea] alive," *Ant.* 9.278. J. Freudenthal has to presuppose an amalgamation of the former population and the imported peoples in order to arrive at his understanding of fragment 6, but this is a construction on the basis of his reading of the relevant texts and his theory that the Samaritans were syncretists.

Another way of understanding the "ten nations" is that the expression refers to the territory of the northern kingdom which was to be taken over by the later "sons of Abraham," viz. the Jews of the second century B.C.E.[34] The problem with this reading is that it presupposes that Theodotus bent Gen 15:18–21 in the direction of the later history of the two kingdoms, but there is no indication in the text for this association. Gen 15:18–21 names the ten nations, who are the inhabitants of the whole land before the Israelite conquest, "the land of the Kenites, the Kenizzites, the Kadmonites the Hittites, the Perizzites, the Rephaim, the Amorites, the Canaanites, the Girgashites, and the Jebusites." Fragment 6 seems to refer to this text with its enumeration of the former inhabitants of the land, not to a presumed ten-tribe-kingdom of the north. If this idea has to be abandoned, one of the important arguments for Collins' theory on the connection to Hyrcanus' attack on Shechem falls.

Gen 15:18–21 promises Abraham the inheritance of ten peoples in the land. Abraham's first stopping place in the land of Israel was Shechem, where he built an altar and received the promise to inherit the land. The combination of Abraham, land promise and Shechem is therefore taken from the biblical tradition in Gen 12, but the actual basis in fragment 6 for the land promise to Abraham is Gen 15:18–21. This is presented as a divine revelation, and functions as a second revelation to Abraham

---

[34] Collins, "Epic of Theodotus," 100.

after the divine word on circumcision in fragment 5. By implication, Abraham's obedience to the law of circumcision is the basis for the promise of the land.

Fragment 7 provides a third divine action, this time in the form of God's disabling of the Shechemites for reasons not found in the Bible:

> God disabled the inhabitants of Shechem, for they did not honour whoever came to them, the low, not even the noble; neither did they dispense justice (δίκας) nor enforce laws (θέμιστας) throughout their city. Their deadly deeds were their chief concern.   (*PE* 9.22.9)

The allegations are cast in Homeric language, and are also an addition to biblical traditions. A biblical background might be Joshua's setting of "law and justice" (LXX: νόμον καὶ κρίσιν) in Shechem, Josh 24:25. Fragments 6 and 7 provide new rationales for the killing of the Shechemites in addition to the rape of Dinah. According to Gen 34 the inhabitants were willing to circumcise themselves. If Theodotus took this into consideration, he deemed it more important that there was a divine command to inherit the land, based on the lawless and ungodly behaviour of the inhabitants. Fragment 6 echoes the promise of the land to the patriarchs, and the idea might be that the sons of Jacob are about to experience the realization of this promise. The claim that the Shechemites are ungodly is similar to one of the reasons for the transfer of the land to the Israelites in the Pentateuch: the former inhabitants are ungodly. They are to inherit the land from the impious, cf. Gen 15:16; Deut 9:4; 18:12. The "stubborn pair" Hamor and Shechem from fragment 2 are to lose their land and their lives. L. Feldman also reminds us of the parallel to the inhabitants of Sodom, who did not show hospitality to strangers, Gen 18:20; 19, which is reminiscent of Homer's Cyclopes, Odyssey 9.215.[35] This double reference would be in line with the interpretation offered here.

Fragment 8 details how Simeon killed Hamor and Levi Shechem, details not found in the Bible, but formed in Homeric language. Its tenor is the heroic act of the two, expressed in their strength and in their effectiveness in the slaughter of the enemies:

> So then Simeon lunged for Hamor himself
> And struck his head, seized his throat with his left hand
> But let go as it gasped, since another task arose.
> Meanwhile, Levi, with unbounded strength, grabbed (Shechem's) locks
>   of hair,

---

[35] Feldman, "*Remember Amalek!*" 172.

While Shechem, clutching his knees, raged furiously.
And he struck the middle of his collarbone, and the sharp sword
  pierced
The internal organs through the breastbone and his life left his body
  immediately. *(PE* 9.22.11–12)

The first and and the last of the fragments use short texts from Gen 33; 34 and develop them into a larger narrative in Homeric style. The other parts use the biblical material and recast it in Hellenistic style.

The eight fragments read together and in sequence contain a story which is built upon texts from Genesis, but is in fact a different story from the rape of Dinah. This narrative centres on Jacob and Abraham. First, the scene for the action is described: Shechem and its surroundings, fragment 1. In fragment 2 the hero Jacob enters this scene, but meets with Hamor and Shechem, a "very stubborn pair," perhaps implying that they are his enemies. He then goes to Syria in fragment 3, after fleeing from a second enemy, his unnamed brother. There he is well received by his own kin, the friendly Laban, who is a prosperous ruler with many descendents. However, Laban turns out to be a wolf in sheep's clothing, a traitor, but Jacob is able to cope with the deceit, and profits from it since he twice marries endogamously. In reward for this he is very successful, with eleven sons and "a daughter Dinah who had very beautiful appearance, a stunning figure and a noble heart too."

Endogamous marriage is commanded by law, probably of divine origin, fragment 4, and this law is made more precise as a law about circumcision. Abraham receives this law and complies with it, in reward for which his descendants are promised a land of ten peoples, fragment 5 and 6. In fulfilment of this promise God acts against the Shechemites in fragment 7, because of their lack of hospitality, their lawlessness and their sinful behaviour. Executors of the divine destruction of Shechem and Hamor are Simeon and Levi, fragment 8.

This narrative line in the poem centres on Jacob's conquest of Shechem as a fulfilment of the divine promise of the land to Abraham. It is not specified in these terms in the HB. After the attempt in the beginning he leaves for Syria and marries in accordance with the divine will. In reward for this he is prosperous, and his sons carry out the removal of the enemies in Shechem. The main events are in compliance with the divine will, and the conquest is therefore a divine act. Behind Jacob stands Abraham, who first enters Shechem and makes it into a holy city, who receives the divine command to practice circumcision and after adhering to this command is promised the land of the ten peoples.

Jacob, the territory to be conquered, his family and the divine commands and their execution are portrayed in positive and heroic language. The protagonist of the poem, Jacob, and his family receive praise through the adjectives and substantives used throughout the poem. The locations he visits, Shechem and Syria, are similarly described in impressive terms. Theodotus consistently uses positive language for the portrayal of the Hebrews. The danger, the enemies and the treason are all given negatively laden expression. In contrast to the praise for the city in fragment 1, her inhabitants are depicted as depraved. Simeon's and Levi's killing of Hamor and Shechem is described in heroic terms. As it is divinely motivated it hardly needs more justification.

Thus the major themes of the poem are the marriage laws and Jacob's conquest of Shechem, supported by fulfilment of the divine command of circumcision. The framework for the theme of the conquest is the lofty description of Shechem and surroundings.

The killing of the Shechemites could not be sufficiently justified by their uncircumcised condition: they agree to be circumcised in Gen 34; this is not repeated in the poem. The story in Gen 34 makes it clear that Simeon and Levi presuppose that the violation of their sister is reason enough to exterminate the Shechemites, perhaps since it happens when Shechem is uncircumcised. This is replaced in Theodotus by the divine oracle that Abraham shall inherit the land from the ten peoples, and the allegation that the Shechemites are evil. There is no divine word in Gen 34 for the action taken, but Theodotus provides such divine commands for the conquest. In this way he strengthens the case of the conquest significantly. To a Jewish (or even a Hellenistic) public these two additional reasons must have provided the necessary basis for the killings.

On the presupposition that the Samaritans of Theodotus' age identified with the Shechemites, it has been deemed inconceivable that a Samaritan would harbour the sentiments about the original inhabitants of Shechem evident in the poem, as Collins has emphasized.[36] Accordingly, the author of the poem could not be a Samaritan. If this presupposition is wrong, however, the picture changes. Gen 34; 49:5–7 in the SP reveal that the Samaritans sided with the sons of Jacob against the Shechemites (see below). Admittedly, this reflects a later historical period than Theodotus, but it is the oldest Samaritan witness we have for this

---

[36] Collins, "Epic of Theodotus," 91–104; idem, "Theodotus," in *Between Athens and Jerusalem*, 57–60.

question. Theodotus is milder in the assessment of Simeon and Levi than Gen 34, since in Gen 34 they waited until the Shechemites were defenceless before acting, and their plan is described as "treason." These two elements are lacking in Theodotus, and the divine authority behind their action is substituted. If the author identified with the people of Jacob as a whole, the poem would be conceivable as a Samaritan text, judging from Gen 34; 49 SP.[37] Seen on the basis of this particular point Theodotus may have been a Samaritan.

On the other hand, there are allegations against the Shechemites: "They did not honour whoever came to them," is the first statement in fragment 7, and this is not found in the HB. Josephus tells several stories about the the Samaritans' hostility to the Jews, and even if this is two centuries later than Theodotus, it continues in the same vein. Further, "neither did they dispense justice nor enforce laws throughout their city. Their deadly deeds were their chief concern." This is also reminiscent of later Jewish polemics against the Samaritans, cf. Josephus, *Ant.* 11:346 f.: "if anyone were accused by those of Jerusalem of having eaten things common or of having broken the Sabbath, or of any other crime of the like nature, he fled away to the Shechemites."

The most important point, however, is that these accusations are levelled against the population of Sikima, Σικίμων οἰκήτορας, fragment 7. The expression refers to the population without any specific time reference, "the phrase 'inhabitants of Shechem' would almost inevitably be applied to the present occupants ... lends itself readily to a typological application to the Shechemites of the Hellenistic age."[38]

It is therefore simpler to read Theodotus as a Jew focusing upon Jacob and his descendants' conquest of Shechem, and regarding with approval the action by Simeon and Levi against the ungodly Shechemites. Their ungodly behaviour is described in terms that we know from later Jewish polemics against the Samaritans. Jacob was then the first patriarch to actually conquer Shechem, after the initial "cultic conquest" performed by Abraham when he built the altar there, Gen 12:7. Long before Joshua, Jacob became master of the place.

---

[37] This possibility is discussed by van der Horst, "The Interpretation of the Bible by the Minor Hellenistic Jewish Authors," in *Mikra: Text, Translation, Reading, and Interpretation of the Hebrew Bible in Ancient Judaism and Early Christianity* (ed. M. J. Mulder and H. Sysling; Assen/Maastircht, van Gorcum, 1988), 527.

[38] Collins, "Epic of Theodotus," 95.

The emphasis is on conquest for Jacob and endogamy. This is clad in Homeric form, to an audience that would appreciate this, an educated public in Jerusalem or—also a possible provenance—Alexandria. In the second century B.C.E. it was primarily the Hasmoneans who were focused on conquest and circumcision. There could be some connection between the poem and the Hasmonean ideology, but not enough to pinpoint the date and location of the poem on this basis.

So much can be said for the poem itself. The summaries and introductions to each of the fragments continue in the same manner by using biblical material, but not the Homeric poetic style.

The first introduction presents the origin of the name of the city, again in Hellenistic fashion. In this overall introduction Σικιμίος is the eponymous originator of the city. This "Sikimios" is the son of Hermes. The presentation of the city's founder "Sikimios" as son of Hermes has occasioned much debate. The explanation that this eponymous hero is constructed on the basis of the names Shechem and Hamor as a hellenizing trait connecting the city to Greek mythology seems to be the best.[39] The point is to bring the city to higher esteem: it is of divine origin, thus creating a glorious origin for the city long before the time of Jacob, Hamor and Shechem, and evading the tricky question why the city was named after Hamor's son, and not after him. It would be natural for the Greek author Alexander to provide this link to Greek mythology, by twisting the names provided by Theodotus and introducing Hermes. In this way he was able to introduce the poem to a wider audience, an audience familiar with Greek mythology. For the following introductions, Alexander probably followed the original poem, with its affinity to the LXX.

The introduction to fragment 2 explains what the poem is about: the occupation of the land of Shechem by the Hebrews at the time of Hamor and Shechem.[40] Apart from this, it merely paraphrases the following fragment.

The introduction to the third fragment says that the poem is about Jacob, interprets the "Syria" of the poem as "Mesopotamia," and emphasizes that Jacob had only two wives. The combination of "Syria" and "Mesopotamia" is also found in Gen 33:18 LXX. The introduction to fragment 4 again focuses on Jacob, and retells Gen 34 in an abbreviated form, a story already indicated by fragment 8. The fragment uses

---

[39] Arguments and discussion in Holladay, *Poets*, 131–135.
[40] The sentence may mean "taken into possession by the Hebrews."

LXX-language: Hamor gives Jacob a portion, μέρος, of the land, cf. LXX Gen 33:19: μέρος. Dinah is presented as a παρθένος, as in Gen 34:3 LXX. Though relying on Gen 34:1–12 LXX, this introduction deviates from it, most notably in giving Shechem the active part in the approach to Jacob. The description of his act with Dinah is also more negatively charged. The remark about Jacob as a farmer and his sons as shepherds is occasioned by Gen 34:5; 37, and the name "the shepherds' city" is provided for Shechem in fragment 2.

This introduction says that Jacob was received hospitably by Hamor, against the allegation in fragment 7 that the Shechemites "did not honour whoever came to them."[41] The question of hospitality in Mount Gerizim or Shechem is also present in Pseudo-Eupolemus, fragment 1, and in 2 Macc 6:2. The Greek root used in this connection in these two texts is identical (ξένος), but Alexander employs the word ὑποδέχομαι.

The understanding of circumcision is that it means "becoming Jewish," ἰουδαΐζω, an interpretation of the fragment's sentence concerning "being of the same race."

The fragments do not contain a narrative of the actual rape of Dinah, and therefore lack the main point of the story. The introduction to fragment 4 summarizes this event, "When Shechem, the son of Hamor, saw her, he loved her; and, seizing her as his own, he carried her away and raped her." This summary was probably built on a part of the poem which is now missing, and as Alexander was neither a Jew nor a Samaritan, his use of LXX-language in this introduction must reflect Theodotus' reliance on the LXX.

The emphasis on "becoming Jews," however, should not be seen in the light of Samaritans supposedly being "Sidonians."[42] This hypothesis is based on the documents 'quoted' in Josephus, Ant. 12.257–264. E. Bickerman considered them authentic, and this was taken over by Goldstein (discussed in the previous chapter). They must, however, be a fabrication by Josephus. The temple on Mount Gerizim was dedicated to YHWH, and not "unnamed," as Josephus presupposes, cf. the next chapter dealing with the inscriptions from Mount Gerizim. The Samaritans were not

---

[41] Quoted from the translation by Holladay, Poets, 123. A different translation by Walter, "Theodotus," JHRSZ 4: 169 f.: "nicht musste bei ihnen büssen, wenn einer zu ihnen als Schlechter und Unedler gekommen war." The difference lies in the understanding of the form ἔτιον, but Holladay argues convincingly for his translation, Holladay, Poets, 194 f.

[42] Collins, Between Athens and Jerusalem, 59.

"Sidonians," but Josephus says that they were. To "become Jews" by circumcision is not directed against Samaritans in the capacity of being Sidonians, but a general statement.

Whereas the introduction to fragment 5 only makes clear that the enigmatic phrase in the poem "strip off the flesh" means "circumcision," the next introduction is more elaborate and specifies that Simeon took the initiative in the killing of Hamor and Shechem and even cited Gen 15:18 f. to persuade his brother to participate. Even though this introduction is built on Gen 34:18–25, the language is more negative towards Hamor and Shechem than Gen 34 is. Shechem had committed an "outrage," ὕβρις, according to this introduction. Hamor tries to persuade the Shechemites to accept circumcision, but before any action can be taken, "Simeon decided to kill both Hamor and Shechem." The theme of circumcision is thus not forgotten, but actual circumcision is evaded because Simeon cuts the story short and acts before the inhabitants may be circumcised. His initiative is not condemned, however, but buttressed by a divine oracle to Abraham in fragment 6.

The introduction to fragment 7 declares the Shechemites to be "impious," ἀσεβής. This expression summarizes the severe accusations against them in the fragment. The ideas of Simeon and Levi were "implanted" by God.

The introduction to fragment 8 summarises Gen 34:25 f. To the last fragment is added a sentence about the pillaging of the city and the rescue of Dinah by the other brothers—again reminiscent of Gen 34, this time vv. 26–29.

The introductions follow the general tenor of the poem, and spell out the negative descriptions of Shechem and Hamor. Admittedly, Hamor receives Jacob hospitably and persuades his countrymen to be circumcised, according to the introduction to fragment 4. This brighter picture of him is balanced by the emphasis upon Shechem's ὕβρις against Dinah, and the impiety of the population. Alexander in this way repeats the topic of "success in spite of deceit" from fragment 3.

The introduction to fragment 4 portrays Jacob as willing to accept intermarriage with the Shechemites, provided that it is based upon circumcision. At the same time Theodotus emphasizes the divine promise that the descendants of Abraham would inherit the place of the ten former peoples of the land. To tackle such opposing views one needs the action of the 'loose cannon' Simeon, who ignores Hamor's persuading the Shechemites to be circumcised. The tension is resolved by the independent action of Simeon. The promise to inherit the land is even repeated in the introduction to fragment 6, "God ordained to give to Abraham's descendants ten nations," so this must have been important in the eyes of Alexander (or his probable source, Theodotus).

The entire portion might be considered to refer to the history of the town of Shechem, and one could understand Theodotus as contrasting Shechem with Jerusalem, in polemics against Philo the Elder's praise of Jerusalem. Admittedly, the theme of the first fragment is Shechem, but this cannot determine our impression of the whole poem and its introductions. There is no mention of Jerusalem, so a contrast in this respect is not spelled out. The extant fragments taken together seem more to focus on Jacob and his two sons Simeon and Levi, and their dealings with the Shechemites. If this is correct, the poem sees things from the Israelites' point of view, and does not focus on the history of the city taken by itself.

R. Pummer has rejected Collins' idea that the poem with introductions are Jewish polemics against the Samaritans. Instead, he finds the intention to be "to underline the duty of circumcision and to militate against intermarriage between observers of the Law of Moses and Gentiles … Other motives, such as the whitewashing of the fathers, the emphasis on the zeal for God, and the justification of a ruse are sufficient explanations for the changes in the biblical account."[43] The elements in this understanding of Theodotus and Alexander have been adopted in my analysis of the text. But there is evidently some material here which is not covered by Pummer's summary: the focus on conquest and the nature of "the population of Sikima." It is difficult to avoid the impression that this has a target: the Samaritans of Theodotus' age. We know from Josephus that the Shechemites of his age were branded with the acts of the Shechemites in Gen 34. This technique was not invented by him, but is visible in the several re-tellings of Gen 34 in the second century B.C.E.

If the poem stems from Jerusalem, Collins' understanding would be logical. If the poem was written in Alexandria, however, the points mentioned by R. Pummer would have a general address, but the focus on the conquest of the territory of the "population of Sikima" would still have as its counterpart the Samaritans with their holy mountain. This mountain is only mentioned together with the other mountain, and not even by name, and instead Shechem is said to be a holy city. In the ears of Samaritans, this would have been offensive. Their holy mountain is

---

[43] Pummer, "Genesis 34," 187 f.

mentioned together with Ebal by Theodotus, and their city Shechem is considered Jewish territory. The discussions in Alexandria reported by Josephus centered on which place was holy, Jerusalem or Gerizim, and when Theodotus instead centers on Shechem, this type of polemics hits the Samaritans hard. If this poem was written in Jerusalem, much the same logic would apply. There seems to be an affinity to the book of *Jubilees*, which is considered close to the Hasmoneans, and this affinity would support Jerusalem as the provenance of Theodotus. He shows affinity to Demetrius and *Jubilees*, and this also explains his ideological position.

Theodotus thus might have had two audiences in mind: Hellenistic readers—whether Jewish or non-Jewish—would hear the word on circumcision and endogamy, the whitewashing of the biblical characters and the zeal for God. The Samaritans of Alexandria or Shechem would notice the emphasis on Shechem instead of on Mount Gerizim and the justification for the conquest of the land. Theodotus uses the actual interpretation of Gen 34 in Demetrius as a basis for recasting it in Homeric verse for an audience composed of Greeks, and Greek-speaking Jews and Samaritans.

5.5. *Sirach 50:25–26*

The earliest text which we know used the expression "fools" for the inhabitants of Shechem is Sir 50:25 f., and this description is echoed in two other texts from the second century B.C.E. This is a direct attack on the Samaritans.

The book of Sirach was written in Hebrew around 190 or 180 B.C.E.[44] Ben Sira lived in Jerusalem between the high priest Simeon II (the Just), 219–196 B.C.E., and Antiochus IV Epiphanes, 175–164 B.C.E. His work was translated into Greek by his grandson sometime after 132 or after 117 B.C.E.[45]

The famous passage Sir 50:25 f. is known in two main versions, one represented by the LXX, and one by the Hebrew and the Vulgate. The Hebrew reads:

---

[44] G. Sauer, *Jesus Sirach/Ben Sira* (ATD Apokryphen 1; Göttingen: Vandenhoeck & Ruprecht, 2000), 22: 190 B.C.E.; Di Lella and Skehan, *Ben Sira*, 10: 180 B.C.E.
[45] Di Lella and Skehan, *Ben Sira*, 8.

בשני גוים קצה נפשי   והשלישית איננו עם
יושבי שעיר ופלשת   וגוי נבל הדר בשכם

(Manuscript B, col. XX)[46]

With two peoples my soul is vexed, and the third is no people: Those who live in Seir, and the Philistines, and the foolish people that dwell in Shechem.   (Author's translation)

The Hebrew text is poetry with four cola of equal length, which one might suppose is the original form of the text. If the distinction between גוי and עם which became usual in late Hebrew is operative here, as in Sir 50:19, where the latter is used for the community of the Lord, the three peoples are designed as non-Jews: they are גוים and not an עם.[47] The Hebrew text is supported by the Vulgate in regard to the three peoples mentioned in the second line:

> Duas gentes odit anima mea tertia autem non est gens quam oderim qui sedent in monte Seir et Philisthim et stultus populus qui habitat in Sicimis

> Two peoples my soul hates but the third is not a people that I might hate it: Those who live in Mount Seir and the Philistines and the foolish people that lives in Shechem.   (Author's translation)

The textual tradition is not uniform on these three peoples. Against this textual tradition stands the LXX with a different triad in the second stanza:

> ἐν δυσὶν ἔθνεσιν προσώχθισεν ἡ ψυχή μου καὶ τὸ τρίτον οὐκ ἔστιν ἔθνος οἱ καθήμενοι ἐν ὄρει Σαμαρείας καὶ Φυλιστιιμ καὶ ὁ λαὸς ὁ μωρὸς ὁ κατοικῶν ἐν Σικιμοις

> With two peoples my soul is vexed and the third is no people: Those who live in the mountains of Samaria and the Philistines and the foolish people that lives in Shechem.   (Author's translation)

"Seir" in the Hebrew text and in the Vulgate is supported by the Old Latin, and this is probably the original reading over against "the mountains of Samaria" in the LXX.[48] R. Smend suggests various possibilities for a corruption in the LXX from "Seir" to "Samaria."[49] As the Syriac version

---

[46] P. C. Beentjes, *The Book of Ben Sira in Hebrew: A Text Edition of all Extant Hebrew Manuscripts and a Synopsis of all Parallel Hebrew Ben Sira Texts* (VTSup 68; Leiden: Brill, 1997), 90; according to Beentjes it was first published by S. Schechter & C. Taylor, *The Wisdom of Ben Sira* (Cambridge 1899), ibid., 16.

[47] For the development in meaning, cf. R. E. Clements, "גוי," ThWAT 1: 971–973.

[48] R. Smend, *Die Weisheit des Jesus Sirach Sirach: mit einem hebräischen Glossar* (Berlin: Georg Reimer, 1906), 491.

[49] Ibid.; followed by Hanhart, "Zu den ältesten Traditionen," 106*–115*.

in the Codex Ambrosianus reads "the inhabitants of Gebal" in this place, it indirectly testifies to the LXX reading: the Peshitta did not translate "the mountains of Samaria" in the plural, but named a single mountain, and chose the mountain of curse, Ebal. We are thus faced with a LXX-Peshitta tradition which did not necessarily originate in corruptions in the Greek transmission of the expression, as Smend suggests, but represents a continuous anti-Samaritan understanding of the text. That the Vulgate here adds *quam oderim*, "that I might hate it," shows a willingness to add elements for a better understanding of the text, but this did not occasion a deviation from "Seir" of the *Vorlage*.

Hanhart's understanding of the LXX as reflecting a differentiation between the inhabitants of the province Samaria (οἱ καθήμενοι ἐν ὄρει Σαμαρείας) and the inhabitants of the capital Shechem (ὁ λαὸς ὁ μωρὸς ὁ κατοικῶν ἐν Σικιμοις) is based upon his reading of Josephus. He interprets *Ant.* 11.323 as intending the inhabitants of the province Samaria, distinct from the Shechemites described in *Ant.* 11.342.[50] This distinction cannot be upheld, cf. chapter 4.

The "foolish people," גוי נבל of the Hebrew text, is sometimes traced to Deut 32:6, but there we read עם נבל and not גוי נבל.[51] Moreover, vv. 5–6 refer to Israel as "degenerate children" and a "crooked generation," and this does not fit the contents of Sir 50:25 f. This is not the model for Ben Sira. Cf. Psalm 74:18, where עם נבל describes the enemies of Israel.

The expression גוי נבל in Sirach is found in Deut 32:21, where it stands in parallel to לא־עם. The text of Deut 32:21 provides several points of contact.

Deut 32:21 is poetry with an elaborate pattern of repetitions and contrasts. Simultaneously, there is assonance between בהבליהם and נבל:

הם קנאוני בלא־אל כעסוני בהבליהם
ואני אקניאם בלא־עם בגוי נבל אכעיסם:

They made me jealous with what is no god, provoked me with their idols. So I will make them jealous with what is no people, provoke them with a foolish nation.[52]   (NRSV)

---

[50] Hanhart, "Zu den ältesten Traditionen," 107*.

[51] Hanhart, "Zu den ältesten Traditionen," 107*. The parallel to the expression "foolish people" of v. 6 is "not wise." The verb דור of the Hebrew text is found in the HB only in Ps 84:11, where it is used of "living with the godless"; it is used also in Sir 33:11; 50:26.

[52] The meaning of לא in both cases where it is used could be "non": "a non-God", "a non-people," and the translation would therefore perhaps rather have been "with what is a non-god" and "with what is a non-people."

Sir 50:26 uses the parallel לא־עם—גוי נבל from Deut 32:21, but the expressions are distributed over two lines. לא־עם is changed to איננו עם, implying that the intended people is not only a "non-people," but it does not really exist as a people. In the wisdom pattern "X plus one," Sir 50:26 focuses on the last case, "the foolish people that dwell in Shechem." The first two peoples are old enemies of Israel, the Edomites in Seir and the Philistines, but the target of the text really is the third entity: "the foolish people that dwell in Shechem." This must be the Samaritans of the second century B.C.E. The LXX has changed "Seir" into "Samaria," and thereby twice directed our attention to that area. It is tempting to see in this change a deliberate targeting rather than accidents of textual transmission.

J. Kugel supposes that Deut 32:21 was given an anti-Samaritan understanding very early on the basis of the expression "a non-people." 2 Kgs 17 reports that a mishmash of peoples was brought into the region. Since the Samaritans were associated with this conglomeration of different peoples, they accordingly were a "non-people," and this understanding is attested to in Sir 50:25 f.[53] It is not clear where the basis for seeing the Samaritans as a conglomeration of peoples might be in texts earlier than Josephus, and even he stresses that they were Chuthaeans, Χουθαῖοι. Further, Ben Sira does not repeat the expression "a non-people," לא־עם, from Deut 32:21, but changes it into איננו עם, "[the third] is no people." The idea that this would equal a mishmash of peoples sounds strained. On the other hand, the expression carrying weight in Sir 50:25 f. is the "foolish people," and the reading of איננו עם, even if we translate it "non-people," as referring to 2 Kgs 17:24–31 is not at all obvious.

The question of ancient exegesis was probably not "Why were the Samaritans said to be foolish?," as Kugel suggests,[54] but rather: who is this "foolish people" of Deut 32:21, and where do they live? The answer was found in a combination of Deut 32:21 and Gen 34:7; here I agree with J. Kugel. The first basis for Sir 50:25 f. was Deut 32:21, and the association with the story in Gen 34 was made because it contained the relevant expression: "foolish," נבל, of Deut 32:21 parallels "foolishness," נבלה, of Gen 34:7. Gen 34:7 is the only HB text which combines "Shechem" and נבלה. By combining Deut 32 and Gen 34 and creating a poem the author had the material for the text. The model for the poetic form of Sir 50:25 f.

---

[53] Kugel, *Traditions of the Bible*, 423.
[54] Ibid., 424.

may also have been provided by Deut 32. This is a sufficient explanation for Ben Sira's use of the two texts, which would be an old example of the principle *gezera shawa*, גזרה שוה.

The Shechemites were placed alongside the old enemies, the Edomites and the Philistines in the Hebrew text, and this polemic was intensified in the LXX and the Peshitta as "Seir" was replaced by "Samaria" and "Ebal" respectively.

The expression "foolish people" also occurs in Sir 49:5 in an expanded form, where the Hebrew text reads "a foolish, foreign people," גוי נבל נכרי, but the Greek and Vulgate only "a foreign people" (ἔθνει ἀλλοτρίῳ; alienae genti). In Sir 49:5 the expression refers to the Babylonians, and it has been suggested that the author in 50:26 parallels the Shechemites with this people.[55] There would then, at least in the Hebrew text, be an association with the "foolishness" of the people who destroyed Jerusalem, according to Sir 50:26. If so, then Sir 50:26 is the earliest text with the allegation that the Samaritans were immigrants into the region from the east. This association with the east is in line with the origin story in Josephus, cf. chapter 4. The plus נכרי in 49:5 against the simpler expression גוי נבל in 50:26 might, however, indicate that the author saw a difference between the people that burned the Holy city and made her streets desolate, 49:5 f., and the present inhabitants of Shechem. The former were נכרי, "foreigners," a word often associated to foreign worship, whereas the Shechemites were simply characterized by the shorter expression from Deut 32:21. But, if Sirach associated the reference to the Babylonians in 49:5 with the "foolish people" in 50:26, the author presupposed an anti-Samaritan reading of 2 Kgs 17.

In the Greek and Latin texts, however, there is no association between Sir 49:5 and Sir 50:25 f., as a reference to "a foreign people," perhaps the Babylonians, was kept, but not to their "foolishness." On the other hand, the Samaritans were targeted even more strongly in the LXX of Sir 50:25 f.

The enumeration of peoples in Sir 50:26 may have a parallel in 11Q14 Fragment 2. The text here reads

1 [...]טי הגוי הנב[ל ...] 2 [...]קומה גב[ור שבה פל]שתים ...] 3 [....]שומ[רונים[...]

This has been understood as "1 [...] ... of the stup[id] nation[...] 2 [... get up he]ro, take the Phil[istines] prisoner [...] 3 [... the Sama]ritans [...]."[56] The reconstruction is based upon Sir 50:25 f.; 1QM XII, and

---

[55] Hanhart, "Zu den ältesten Traditionen," 107*.

[56] F. García Martínez and E. J. C. Tigchelaar, *The Dead Sea Scroll: Study Edition* (Leiden: Brill, 1997), 2:1210 f.

is therefore not useful as a confirmation of the text of Sirach. 11Q14 Fragment 1,i–ii is a text on the offspring of David, the killing of the leader of the Kittim and the blessings following the eschatological community of Israel. 11Q14 overlaps with 4Q285, which in turn has a relationship to the War Scroll. 11Q14 Fragment 2 is too fragmentary to build any hypothesis upon, but the expression "the stup[id] nation" is the same as in Sir 50:26, and if the reconstruction "Samaritans" is correct, there is some affinity to the LXX version of Sir 50:26 with its ἐν ὄρει Σαμαρείας. At the time when this text was composed, שומרונים was most probably not used of the Samaritans in a narrow sense, but of the inhabitants of Samaria, as in 2 Kgs 17:24, and there would be a parallel expression to Sir 50:26 LXX. If the general tenor of the text is one of killing enemies ("Kittim"), there may here be an interest similar to that of Sir 50:25 f.

Sir 50:25 f. comes at the end of *Laus patrum* in Sir 44–50. It seems to be only loosely attached to the preceding and following sections of the Greek text, as the shift in topic from the admonition to praise God and the prayer for deliverance in verses 22–24 to the condemnation in verses 25 f. is abrupt. The following verses, 27–29, are an editorial note on the author of the preceding section of the book, Ben Sira. Vv. 25 f. stand out in the context, and seem to be a later addition; their present location after Laus Patrum and before the praise for the author of the book at least reveals that the editor thought it appropriate to include them with the work of Ben Sira.

The situation is different, however, in the Hebrew text, which is rather different from the Greek in this part of the chapter. V. 24 in the Hebrew version is translated in the NRSV in a footnote: "May his love abide upon Simeon, and may he keep in him the covenant of Phinehas; may one never be cut off from him; and as for his offspring, (may it be) as the days of heaven." This prayer concludes the prayer of vv. 22–24. In this context, vv. 25 f. are appropriate, as a concrete expression of the "covenant of Phinehas" (Num 25; Ps 106:31). The Simeon of this part of the chapter may be the Simeon of Gen 34, but the chapter in general centres on the high priest Simeon II. The prayer envisages that the descendants of this high priest should be able to act as Phinehas did in Num 25:7 f., which gave him a "covenant of peace," v. 11, and the priestly rights, v. 13.

Ben Sira deals with the zeal of Phinehas in 45:23–25 also, and reserves the high priesthood for his descendants alone, v. 25. In a final blessing, v. 26 turns to the present high priest, Simeon II, or more likely his son Onias III. This Onias III was assassinated, a fact that occasioned the different text of the Greek version of Sir 50:23 f. As the priestly line from Simeon II was out of the question at the time of translation, the text had to shift focus from the high priest to "May he [God] entrust to us his mercy, and may he deliver us in our days!"

If the original text of Sir 50:23 prays that God will enable the then high priest to practise the covenant of Phinehas, verses 25 f. become the recipe for the execution of this covenant. It is therefore not likely that "The couplet (50:25–26) on the three peoples that Ben Sira detests is in no way related to the preceding section or to the Postscript (50:27–29)."[57] If there is any point in mentioning this covenant twice, 45:24 and 50:24, with a blessing over the priest, 45:26, and a prayer that his offspring may prevail, 50:24, it must aim at some contemporary task, comparable to that of Phinehas. As the situation in Num 25 was one of idolatry and exogamous marriage, one would look for similar cases at the time of Ben Sira. Since the Shechemites are targeted in particular, they must have been seen by Ben Sira as performing similar abominable acts. "Those who dwell in Seir," the descendants of Esau, were Israel's enemies through the ages, as witnessed by the Bible, Ps 137:7; Obadiah, Jdt 7:8–18 etc. Samuel crushed the Philistines, according to Sir 46:18, and David did the same, Sir 47:7. In 50:25 f. the focus is on the third party and the zeal of Phinehas should be directed against them.

Laus patrum is an extensive eulogy on the prophets of the past and it leads up to the praise for Simon the high priest in chapter 50. But not all the persons mentioned in *Laus patrum* are prophets, and Ben Sira does not give such an impression, either. The portrayal of the high priest Simon in the last sequence of this eulogy is not in prophetical terms. His function was that he "in his life repaired the house, and in his time fortified the temple. He laid the foundations for the high double walls, the high retaining walls for the temple enclosure," 50:1 f. This is much the same as the work of Zerubbabel and Jeshua: "in their days they built the house and raised a temple holy to the Lord, prepared for everlasting glory," 49:11 f. "The memory of Nehemiah also is lasting; he raised for us the walls that had fallen, and set up the gates and bars and rebuilt our ruined houses," 49:13. Simon was also engaged in rebuilding the city, 50:3 f., just like Nehemiah. Simon's work compares with that of Zerubbabel, Jeshua and Nehemiah in the past.

---

[57] Di Lella and Skehan, *Ben Sira*, 558.

Laus patrum has been called "a theological etiology of Second Temple Judaism centered around the position of the High Priest Simon."[58] "... this primary interest is probably due to the increasing hellenization in Jerusalem."[59] The portion on Simon "... is the climax toward which the entire history has been moving."[60] The high priest in Jerusalem is praised for rebuilding the temple and city, just before the text shifts to the condemnation of the Shechemites. Chapter 50 could end with an anti-Samaritan bias, at the same time as it is directed against the hellenization of Jerusalem.

Two suggestions for the background of verses 25 f. are worth mentioning.

First, H. D. Mantel thinks that Ben Sira speaks of the Samaritans not as a separate people but as refusing reunion with their brethren by foolishly and stubbornly rejecting the Oral Law.[61] The Samaritan theological texts are too late, however, to substantiate this hypothesis.

Secondly, J. D. Purvis has tried to pin down accurately some historical event(s) to which the text might refer, and has proposed the harassment of the Jews by Samaritans at the time of the high priest Simon II (the just) under Antiochus III, recorded in *Ant.* 12.156.[62] The sentences in Sir 50:25 f. come after *Laus patrum* and form a rejoinder to the text's climax. They may be understood against the background of the preceding chapters and it is advisable to read them in a more general sense than referring to one event only or one part of Samaritan theology.

Verses 25 f. combine Gen 34 and Deut 32 in condensed poetry to declare the inhabitants of Shechem to be outside the Jewish community, the עם. They are associated with the terrible act of Shechem according to Gen 34 and with the foreigners whom God threatens to use as a provocation against his own people according to Deut 32. Because "Shechem" was given in the Biblical tradition, the name of the city was employed here also, but it might target the population of the wider region, the group later to be called Samaritans. Their problem in the view of the

---

[58] K. O. Sandnes, *Paul—One of the Prophets? A Contribution to the Apostle's Self-Understanding* (WUNT 2/43, 1991), 24.

[59] Ibid., 25.

[60] B. L. Mack, *Wisdom and the Hebrew Epic: Ben Sira's Hymn in Praise of the Fathers* (Chicago: University of Chicago Press, 1985), 54 f.

[61] H. D. Mantel, "The Secession of the Samaritans," *Bar Ilan* 7–8 (1969–1970): 162–177.

[62] J. D. Purvis, "Ben Sira' and the Foolish People of Shechem," *JNES* 24 (1965): 88–94; repr. in *Samaritan Pentateuch*, 119–129. This is criticized by Egger, *Josephus Flavius und die Samaritaner*, 85–93.

text lies in the area of religiously defined ethnicity. Gen 34 condemns exogamous marriages, and Deut 32 presents foreigners as a threat to Israel. The content of the critique in Sir 50:25f. is not that there was a sanctuary on Mount Gerizim, nor that the priests officiating there were illegitimate, nor that the Torah was not present there. The sting of the passage is that the Shechemites did not constitute a proper Jewish population, they were not part of the עם. Like the former Hivites of Gen 34 who committed a "foolishness," the present inhabitants of Shechem are to be described as "foolish."

There may be more to the text than the contents of vv. 25f. If we read it in the context created by the editor, we may see it in a wider perspective. Sir 49:10 lauded the twelve prophets for their comfort for Israel: "May the bones of the twelve prophets revive from where they lie, for they comforted the people of Jacob and delivered them with confident hope." This explicit mention of the corpus of Dodekapropheton is continued by the praise for Zerubbabel, Jeshua and Nehemiah, before Ben Sira continues with Simon and ends with the admonition to praise God and prayer for deliverance, followed by the negative remark about the three peoples. By reading the text in continuity one is led to assume that the whole context carries some meaning with it to the final verses. Prophets, temple and Jerusalem are the treasures for Ben Sira; a condemnation of a non-people without prophets, but with a schismatic temple and a holy place at Gerizim would constitute the appropriate counterpart to this list of favourite theologoumena. Whether one sees the focus of Sir 44–50 in the temple and priesthood of Jerusalem or in the prophets or in the totality of previous heroes up to Simon, it is conspicuous that the verdict on the Shechemites follows this long pericope. Within the pericope also there are negative statements about Ephraim (47:21.23). The condemnation of the Shechemites forms, by way of naming the contemporary adversaries in that area, the apt exclamation mark to the preceding portion.

Sir 50 thus testifies to the anti-Samaritan use of Gen 34 in the contemporary situation of the book. If we follow the Hebrew text of v. 24, and read it together with vv. 25f., it adds up to a prayer aiming at the killing of the Shechemites, just as Phinehas killed those who broke the law.

5.6. Jubilees *30*

The interpretation of Gen 34 in *Jub.* 30 centres on endogamous marriage and the priesthood of Levi. The rendering of Gen 34 is short, but supplied with a series of messages to be learned from the incident.

The book of *Jubilees* has been dated to different centuries B.C.E., currently to the second century B.C.E. J. VanderKam found that it was written between 160 and 150 B.C.E. by a priest, perhaps belonging to the Essenes.[63] K. Berger dates the book to 145–140 B.C.E., and most recently, M. Segal has identified the origin of the book in a redactional layer, and "*Jubilees* was therefore redacted following the formation of the Essene sect or stream, and it reflects the beginnings of the internal rift in the nation, which reaches its full expression in the sectarian literature preserved at Qumran."[64] Before the discovery of the Dead Sea Scrolls, R. H. Charles concluded that the book was "*written between 135 and the year of Hyrcanus' breach with the Pharisees*."[65]

The author or redactor used a Biblical text closer to the LXX and SP than to the Masoretic tradition.[66] 15 manuscripts with text from *Jubilees* have been found at Qumran, a fact taken to attest its popularity with the Qumran community, perhaps to its being regarded as holy text.[67] The Qumran-finds show that its Hebrew text is faithfully represented in the Ge'ez version considered canonical by the Ethiopian church.

Jubilees builds on Gen 1 – Ex 19, adds material from other parts of the Pentateuch, and shows an awareness of other biblical books, including Isaiah and the Psalms. Though it is selective in the material used, Gen 34 is covered in ch. 30. The narrative from the Bible is partly reproduced in 30:1–6.12.24 f. Vv. 6–11.13–23 contain new material explaining the present meaning of the story.

Jubilees is regularly seen as conveying a contemporary historical message. R. H. Charles found that the Maccabean victories over the Phili-

---

[63] J. C. VanderKam, *The Book of Jubilees* (Guides to Apocrypha and Pseudepigrapha; Sheffield: Shefffield Academic Press, 2001), 21.141–143. Cf. J. C. VanderKam, *Textual and Historical Studies in the Book of Jubilees*, (HSM 14; Missoula, Mont.: Scholars Press for Harvard Semitic Museum, 1977).

[64] K. Berger, "Jubiläen," *JSHRZ* 2: 300; M. Segal, *The Book of* Jubilees: *Rewritten Bible, Redaction, Ideology and Theology* (JSJSup 117; Leiden: Brill, 2007), 322.

[65] Charles, *Book of Jubilees*, lix, author's italics.

[66] VanderKam, *Book of Jubilees*, 137.

[67] J. VanderKam, "Authoritative Literature in the Dead Sea Scrolls," *DSD* 5 (1998): 400–401; idem, "Jubilees, Book of," *EDSS* 1: 434–438; E. Ulrich, "Our sharper Focus on the Bible and Theology Thanks to the Dead Sea Scrolls," *CBQ* 66 (2004): 1–24.

stines, Edom, and the Amorites are reflected or forecast in *Jubilees*; his method was to read passages from *Jubilees* as transparent allusions to historical events as described by Josephus.[68] S. Klein followed up this line of investigation; he thought that *Jub.* 34:4 enumerated sites and cities that Hyrcanus conquered, and *Jubilees* would be a defence of his campaign.[69] This approach presupposes the reliability of Josephus' account and the presence of historical references in *Jubilees*. The book may be a document of Essene-type Jerusalem theology from the mid-second century B.C.E. without any bias against outsiders, according to R. Pummer, but concerned with inner-Jewish discussions, a message from the Essenes, an explication of their imminent expectation.[70] A similar conclusion is drawn by M. Segal.[71]

The overall ideology of *Jubilees* is of significance for understanding the parts. The book reveals a particular interest in the observance of the law by the patriarchs, opposing the view that there was a period without the law. Further, it champions the solar calendar with 364 days per year, divided into 52 weeks, and into four quarters with 13 weeks each. The twelve months consist of 30 days each, and an extra day is inserted at the beginning of each quarter. Another important point is the priesthood, represented by Levi, but Adam already acts as a priest. There is also eschatology in the book, probably applied to the time of writing. A crisis will be followed by a period of salvation. Finally, an interest in marriage is seen at several points. Endogamous marriage is asserted for the patriarchs. Abraham's second wife, the Egyptian Hagar, is mentioned, but she is introduced as Sarah's maid, 14:22. Abraham's third wife Keturah is also mentioned, 19:11, with the justification that she came "from the daughters of his household servants because Hagar died before Sarah." Similarly, the two maids of Jacob's wives Leah and Rachel are included, 28:17.20. Moses' sojourn in Midian is mentioned, 48:1, but not his marriage to Zipporah; Moses' Cushite wife in Num 12:1 enters the biblical scene after the last incident recorded by *Jubilees* (Passover in chapter 49, cf. Ex 12; 'Sinai' in chapter 1 builds on Ex 19 ff.). In the case of Joseph's marriage to an Egyptian, *Jub.* 40:10 says that the king gave him a daughter of Potiphar, instead of the Bible's Potiphera, Gen 41:45. Potiphar

---

[68] Charles, *Book of Jubilees*, lvi.

[69] S. Klein, "Palästinisches im Jubiläenbuch," ZDPV 57 (1934): 18–20.

[70] R. Pummer, "Antisamaritanische Polemik in jüdischen Schriften aus der intertestamentarischen Zeit," *BZ* 26 (1982): 226 f.

[71] Segal, *Book of* Jubilees, 322.

is introduced as a priest at Heliopolis, just as Potiphera is in the Bible, so the wife of Joseph is the daughter of a heathen priest in *Jubilees* also. But *Jubilees* made Joseph's former master the father of his bride, perhaps as a small justification for the marriage. The main point, however, seems to be that the wife was given by Pharaoh.[72] The patriarchs thus married endogamously, according to *Jubilees*, except for Moses, whose marriages are not mentioned, and Joseph, whose foreign wife was given to him by Pharaoh himself.

The questions of law, eschatology and marriage are present in *Jub.* 30. The chapter retells Gen 34 in abbreviated form and interprets the story for the contemporary public. R. H. Charles saw anti-Samaritan sentiments in the chapter; it would encourage or endorse the attack of John Hyrcanus against Samaria in 109.[73] Charles was followed in this understanding by R. J. Coggins, who also thought that "there may be the beginnings of a warning against any inter-marriage with the Samaritans, a theme which frequently recurs at a later period, in the rabbinic writings …"[74] R. Pummer, on the other hand, found no anti-Samaritan bias in the text. Instead, he understood the chapter in terms of 1. opposition against marriages with gentiles, 2. support for Levi's and Simeon's zeal for God, and 3. an acquittal of the patriarchs of any possible guilt in connection with the Shechem incident. The omission of Jacob's demand for circumcision would be necessary for the use of Gen 34 as an occasion for prohibiting marriages with gentiles, according to Pummer.[75]

Charles may have been on the right track in seeing *Jub.* 30 as an encouragement to the Hasmoneans to attack Shechem, or an endorsement of this act. On the other hand, R. Pummer is correct in pointing to elements in the text which are more easily understood in general terms. Circumcision may be omitted in order to create a more general text, which could be turned against mixed marriages with gentiles. This omission has affected the demand for circumcision, Hamor's deliberations with his subjects on the topic, and the actual circumcision of the Shechemites in Gen 34. Instead, the sons of Jacob are quoted to the effect that "We will not give our daughter to a man who is uncircumcised because that is a reproach to us," *Jub.* 30:12. Except for the expression

---

[72] Later exegesis was embarrassed at the marriage of a patriarch to a foreign priest's daughter, and they made her the daughter of Dinah, Targum Pseudo-Jonathan on Gen 41:45; Pirqe de Rabbi Eliezer 38.

[73] R. H. Charles, *APOT* 2: 6, absent from earlier treatments.

[74] Coggins, *Samaritans and Jews*, 92.

[75] Pummer, "Antisamaritanische Polemik."

"daughter" instead of MT's "sister," this reproduces Gen 34:14. The theme of circumcision is therefore present in *Jub.* 30, but only to the effect that the Shechemites were uncircumcised.

On the other hand, there is more to say on the representation of Gen 34 in *Jub.* 30 than the three points emphasized by Pummer. The short version of Gen 34 found in *Jub.* 30:1–4 is characterized by a different tenor altogether from the source text.

> And in the first year of the sixth week he [Jacob] went up to Salem, which is east of Shechem, in peace in the fourth month. And there they carried off Dinah, the daughter of Jacob, to the house of Shechem, son of Hamor, the Hivite, the ruler of the land. And he lay with her and defiled her, but she was little, only twelve years old. And he begged her[76] father and her brothers that she be given to him as a wife, but Jacob and his sons were angry at the men of Shechem because they defiled Dinah, their sister. And so they spoke treacherously with them and defrauded them and seduced them. And Simeon and Levi entered Shechem suddenly. And they executed judgment upon all of the men of Shechem and killed every man they found therein and did not leave in it even one. They killed everyone painfully because they had polluted Dinah, their sister.[77] (*Jub.* 30:1–4)

Compared to the biblical text, we note that the following elements are missing: That Dinah on her own initiative went to see the "daughters of the land;" that Shechem fell in love with her; that Shechem approached his father and asked him to intercede and ask for her as his wife; Hamor's suggestion for general intermarriage and co-ownership of the land; Shechem's promise of a generous bride price; the promise to become "one people" on condition of the circumcision of all Shechemites; the positive attitude of Shechem and Hamor to the condition and their presentation of it to the population; the Shechemites' assent to the request and the following circumcision. A number of additions are conspicuous: the age of 12 for Dinah (cf. Demetrius: 16 years and four months); that she was a virgin (v. 6; not in the MT but in LXX; also in Theodotus); the repetition of the treacherous behaviour of Jacob and his sons; the definition of the killings as judgment; the emphasis that every Shechemite was killed (this seems to be the meaning, not only the males); the "pollution" of Dinah. The last element is present already three times in the biblical text: she was "defiled," v. 5.13.27 (טמא), but it is found five times here, v. 1.2.4.5.6.

---

[76] The feminine form is found in one ms. only, but it is preferred by VanderKam, *Book of Jubilees*, and Berger, "Jubiläen."

[77] This quotation and the following ones are from the translation by O. S. Wintermute, "Jubilees," *OTP* 2: 35–142.

Gen 34:2 makes Shechem alone responsible for the "taking" of Dinah; here, the whole city is made responsible: "they carried off Dinah."[78] As the whole city is responsible, so the whole city is judged. The city name "Salem" accords with the LXX translation of שלם, Gen 33:18, but the same word is here also translated "in peace," and there is no precedent for this double rendering in the LXX.

The biblical text says that Shechem "committed an outrage in Israel ... for such a thing ought not to be done," Gen 34:7, and quotes the sons of Jacob as saying, "We cannot do this thing, to give our sister to one who is uncircumcised," Gen 34:14. *Jubilees* expands these topics into the first lesson to be learnt (the expression is "and therefore") from the incident:

> And therefore let nothing like this be done henceforth to defile a daughter of Israel because the judgment was ordered in heaven against them that they might annihilate with a sword all of the men of Shechem because they caused a shame in Israel. And the Lord handed them over into the hand of the sons of Jacob so that they might destroy them with the sword and execute judgment against them, and so that nothing like this might therefore happen in Israel to defile an Israelite virgin.   (*Jub.* 30:5 f.)

The emphasis on the "judgment ordered in heaven" and that the Lord as judge handed them over to execution is a topic in accordance with the general theology of *Jubilees*, and serves here to acquit the sons of Jacob of guilt and to prevent future similar incidents. It also adds a deeper perspective to the event: the Lord is the judge over the Shechemites.

In addition to the almost verbatim quotation in v. 12 already mentioned, *Jubilees* returns to the biblical story towards the end of the chapter, vv. 24 f. Here, the taking of captives is omitted in accordance with the idea that everybody had been killed, v. 4. But *Jub.* 30:24 introduces the information that the sons brought the spoil to Jacob. Further, Jacob's worry about the "inhabitants of the land" is preserved, but the answer from his sons, "Should our sister be treated like a whore?" is omitted. Instead, the new answer to Jacob's worry is that the "terror of the Lord was in all the cities which surrounded Shechem and they did not rise up to pursue the sons of Jacob because a dread had fallen upon them," a topic introduced from Gen 35:5. Again, divine intervention is the important part of the events, and the weight of a reference to the treatment of Dinah as a motivation for the killings would be subject to discussion.

---

[78] This translation in Berger, "Jubiläen" is preferred to Wintermute's passive translation in "Jubilees."

The character of the *Jubilees* account is that the marks of sympathy towards the Shechemites, several times present in the Bible, are removed, resulting in a case of plain rape and violence without love or negotiations or acquiescence on the part of the Shechemites, elements which might have taken the edge off the nature of the act. The heavenly decision to exterminate the inhabitants adds weight to the unambiguously described sin and makes the judgment inescapable. Therefore, all the inhabitants are killed, not only the men as in the Bible. This story is in itself a much starker account than Gen 34; it is a story which creates antipathy towards Shechem and her inhabitants without regard for the possible change in the situation over time.

The message of *Jubilees* to be learned from this account is addressed already in vv. 5 f., and further spelled out in verses 7–23, centring on the proscription against intermarriage with "gentiles," vv. 7–17, the status of Levi, vv. 18–20, and the warning against breaching the covenant, vv. 21–23. The proscription against intermarriage deals first with the case of an Israelite girl given to a gentile bridegroom, vv. 7–10, and then with the case of taking a gentile girl as bride for an Israelite man, vv. 11–14. Vv. 15–17 describe the punishment affecting all of the people for such offences, which cannot be atoned for by sacrifice.

The law of stoning the man who gives his daughter to the uncircumcised is taken from Lev 20:2–4:

> Any of the people of Israel, or of the aliens who reside in Israel, who give any of their offspring to Molech shall be put to death; the people of the land shall stone them to death. I myself will set my face against them, and will cut them off from the people, because they have given of their offspring to Molech, defiling my sanctuary and profaning my holy name. And if the people of the land should ever close their eyes to them, when they give of their offspring to Molech, and do not put them to death, I myself will set my face against them and against their family, and will cut them off from among their people, them and all who follow them in prostituting themselves to Molech.

This law is the background for *Jub.* 30:7–10.[79] It is also the basis for v. 15, the treatment of those who close their eyes to this behaviour. The woman

---

[79] Moloch is interpreted as referring to mixed marriages in ps-Jonathan on Lev 20:2: "And of thy seed thou shalt not give to lie with a daughter of the Gentiles so as to draw him over to a strange worship." Same idea in *Sanh.* 82 a; ix. 6; *Meg.* 25a; *Meg.* iv. 9. R. H. Charles comments "It [the interpretation] may not be older than the Maccabean age. The circumstances of that time were such as to justify the extremest measures in order to save Judaism from annihilation," *Book of Jubilees*, 181, n. 10. The Latin version of *Jub.* reads *aliegenae* for "Moloch" in this place.

involved shall be killed according to the rule in Lev 21:9, "When the daughter of a priest profanes herself through prostitution, she profanes her father; she shall be burned to death." The application to Israel at large of a law concerning the daughter of a priest seems to assume that all Israel is considered "a nation of priests," as in Ex 19:6.[80] As J. Endres has pointed out, *Jub.* 30:8b emphasizes that "Israel is holy to the Lord," which is similar to Lev 19:2, "You shall be holy, for I the Lord your God am holy."[81] According to him, the essential element in marriage laws for this period was the regulations for the priests, *T. Levi* 14; 9; and the Damascus Document. For this purpose, one might add, *Jubilees* used the textual basis in Deut 7 and Lev 20 f. in accordance with Ex 19:6 and Lev 19:2.

The status of Levi as priest in Israel is described in vv. 18–20, resulting from his zeal, righteousness, judgment and vengeance "against all who rose up against Israel," v. 18. He will be blessed and "written down as a friend and a righteous one in the heavenly tablets," v. 20. Levi is given the priesthood because he killed the Shechemites, and this means a combination of violence and priesthood. This notion was not inappropriate in the Maccabean conception, and the book endorses the high priesthood of Levi to "the Most High God," 32,1—this was the title of the Maccabean priestly kings.

The elevation to priesthood for Levi on the basis of his zeal and execution of judgment as early as the Dinah episode is new in relation to the Bible. Deut 33:8–11 associates him with priesthood because God "tested [him] at Massah, with whom you [God] contended at the waters of Meribah," v. 7, referring by the names "Massah" and "Meribah" to the two incidents with water out of the rock, Ex 17:1–7; Num 20:2–13. Levi "said of his father and mother, 'I regard them not'; he ignored his kin, and did not acknowledge his children," Deut 33:9, which refers to the treatment of those who entice Israel to worship other gods in Deut 13:6. The Levites acted in such a way according to Exod 32.

> [Moses] said to them, "Thus says the LORD, the God of Israel, 'Put your sword on your side, each of you! Go back and forth from gate to gate throughout the camp, and each of you kill your brother, your friend, and your neighbour.'" The sons of Levi did as Moses commanded, and about

---

[80] J. C. Endres, *Biblical Interpretation in the Book of Jubilees* (CBQMS 18; Washington, D.C.: Catholic Biblical Association of America, 1987), 137 f. compares the legislation in case of the girl to the punishment for Tamar, Gen 38:24, and recalls Gen 34:31, "Should our sister be treated like a whore?" A harlot should be burned. But this sentence in Gen 34:31 is not quoted in *Jub.* 30.

[81] Ibid., 130–147.

> three thousand of the people fell on that day. Moses said, "Today you have ordained yourselves for the service of the LORD, each one at the cost of a son or a brother, and so have brought a blessing on yourselves this day."
>
> (Exod 32:27–29)

This might be the background for Deut 33:8–11, and the issue is idolatry, as in Deut 13:6. The zeal of Phinehas in Num 21:7 f. is another backdrop to *Jub.* 30:18–20.

> Phinehas son of Eleazar, son of Aaron the priest, has turned back my wrath from the Israelites by manifesting such zeal among them on my behalf that in my jealousy I did not consume the Israelites. Therefore say, "I hereby grant him my covenant of peace. It shall be for him and for his descendants after him a covenant of perpetual priesthood, because he was zealous for his God, and made atonement for the Israelites." (Num 25:11–13)

In *Jub.* 30:18 the speaking angel says that "Levi was chosen for the priesthood … and his sons will be blessed forever because he was zealous to do righteousness and judgment and vengeance against all who rose up against Israel." This dictum plays on expressions from the biblical texts mentioned, but locates the election to priesthood in the Dinah episode. J. Endres notes three similarities between Num 25:11–13 and *Jub.* 18–20: "(1) zeal for God is praised; (2) the reward is a perpetual share in the priesthood; (3) the focal issue is intermarriage with Gentiles."[82] Even though the topic in Num 25 is idolatry, Phinehas kills an Israelite man with the Midianite woman whom he brought into his family. Thus intermarriage is an issue also in Num 25. The zeal of Phinehas is the model for Mattathias in 1 Macc 2:24–26.54 as well; it was an ideal at the time of *Jubilees*.

Jub. 30:18–20 moves the motif zeal-resulting-in-priesthood back in time to the Dinah episode, and thus strengthens the historical basis for Levi's priesthood. The Testament of Levi argues in a similar way, as we shall see.

Vv. 21–23 give all Israel the choice between becoming "friends" or "enemies," depending upon their attitude towards the ordinances and the covenant "which was ordained for them." If they obey the ordinances and the covenant, they will be "written down as friends," but if they transgress and act in the way of defilement, they "will be recorded in the heavenly tablets as enemies." The killing performed by the children of Jacob provided an example, which probably was to be imitated, v. 23.

---

[82] Ibid., 150.

Three times Moses is addressed in particular. Each time the speaking angel refers to the written record of the Dinah story, and orders Moses to teach Israel an appropriate lesson from this record. The first case is centred on mixed marriages:

> And you, Moses, command the children of Israel and exhort them not to give any of their daughters to the gentiles and not to take for their sons any of the daughters of the gentiles because that is contemptible before the Lord. Therefore I have written for you in the words of the law all of the deeds of the Shechemites which they did against Dinah and how the sons of Jacob spoke, saying, "We will not give our daughter to a man who is uncircumcised because that is a reproach to us." *(Jub.* 30:11 f.)

Moses is given a commandment equivalent to Deut 7:3: "Do not intermarry with them, giving your daughters to their sons or taking their daughters for your sons," (cf. Theodotus). The precedent for this law is the dictum of the sons of Jacob in Gen 34:14: "We cannot do this thing, to give our sister to one who is uncircumcised." This dictum is changed into a sentence with general application; "sister" is altered into "daughter," referring to Israelite women in general. The notion of contemptible things is found in Gen 34:14 as well as in Deut 7:26. The account in Gen 34 is therefore written for Moses to provide an example of right conduct towards the gentiles: no intermarriage. The record of events before the time of Moses is written for him—not primarily as information, but as a basis for his legislation. This legislation is then provided in Deut 7:3.26.

This is not the first and best instance where rules like Deut 7:3 might have been given a narrative context, as R. Pummer presumes.[83] The marriages of the patriarchs might all have given opportunity to present the rule of endogamous marriage. For instance, the presentation of circumcision to Abraham would have been the logical place for emphasizing endogamous marriage as based upon circumcision, but *Jub.* 15 does not mention marriages. And the case of Esau's two Canaanite wives is treated in *Jub.* 25:1–10 without mention of circumcision. The extended treatment of the topic in chapter 30 is conspicuous.

In this way Moses' relation to Genesis is resolved: he receives from the angel the written record of Genesis, and in this way he becomes master also of this part of the Pentateuch. At the same time, his legislation is basically old, and what he transmits as revelation on Sinai is founded in patriarchal experiences and rules formulated in connection with these experiences.

---

[83] Pummer, "Antisamaritanische Polemik," 229.

The second example is concerned with the fate of the Shechemites and the righteousness of the sons of Jacob:

> Therefore I command you, saying, "Proclaim this testimony to Israel:" See how it was for the Shechemites and their sons, how they were given into the hand of the two children of Jacob and they killed them painfully. And it was a righteousness for them and it was written down for them for righteousness.   (*Jub.* 30:17)

Here, Moses is commanded to proclaim the Dinah episode; he is the transmitter of this part of the Pentateuch also. Moses' task is not only the retelling of the story, but it includes the proclamation of the message to be learned from the incident. The story shall serve as a testimony of capital punishment for the offence of mixed marriage, executed by Israel on the uncircumcised. The execution of the punishment provides the executioners with righteousness, much as with Abraham, who "believed the Lord; and the Lord reckoned it to him as righteousness," Gen 15:6. Jacob's children are to receive the same gift as Abraham, but by different means.

The third commission to Moses explains how Israel may become friends of God, or his enemies.

> All of these words I have written for you, and I have commanded you to speak to the children of Israel that they might not commit sin or transgress the ordinances or break the covenant which was ordained for them so that they might do it and be written down as friends. But if they transgress and act in all the ways of defilement, they will be recorded in the heavenly tablets as enemies. And they will be blotted out of the book of life and written in the book of those who will be destroyed and with those who will be rooted out from the land.   (*Jub.* 30:21 f.)

Moses is given a sermon to preach from the events and laws presented in chapter 30 up to this point. Texts like Deut 7 may provide background material also here: "Observe diligently the commandment—the statutes, and the ordinances—that I am commanding you today," Deut 7:11. The "covenant" leads in this connection in the direction of Abraham, whose covenant concerned circumcision, Gen 17, and the expression "friend" of God is in the Bible also connected to Abraham, Isa 41:8; 2 Chr 20:7; Dan 3:35 LXX.[84] As Levi obtained the status of being a "friend" by his zeal

---

[84] Also later, the expression "friend" was used for Abraham, and for the faithful generally. Examples in Charles, *Book of Jubilees*, 125 f., n. 9: Philo, *De Sobrietate*, 11; James 2.23; Clemens Romanus, x. 1; xvii. 2; *Tg. Yer.* on Gen 18.17; Wisd. vii. 27; Philo, *Fragment*, ii. p. 652. Cf. the philosophical idea that the wise man is God's friend, Plato, *Legg.* Iv. 8; cf. Max. Tyr. Xx. 6.

and his judgment on the Shechemites, *Jub.* 30:20, all Israel may obtain the same status by observing circumcision. Again, "defilement" is the result of not observing marriage laws based on circumcision, because Israel shall be holy, "For you are a people holy to the LORD your God; the LORD your God has chosen you out of all the peoples on earth to be his people, his treasured possession," Deut 7:6.

The task of Moses in these three instances is to convey the patriarchal story and explain its present meaning. His position on Sinai provides him with revelation covering earlier history, legislation received on the mountain, and the future meaning of these two in combination.

To pursue the question if chapter 30 is polemical against the Samaritans or not may end up in a cul de sac. To pose two alternatives, that the story is a transparent allusion to Hyrcanus' attack, or that there is no anti-Samaritan polemic, is too narrow a choice. Admittedly, there is no direct targeting of the Samaritans, but still, the city of Shechem is put in a bad light. The whole chapter serves to put the city under the spell of the rape of Dinah and the killing of all the Shechemites. The city is continuously marked by the old sin and heavenly judgment upon it, and therefore to be suspected at any time. Its reputation is blackened for ever. *Jub.* 34:1–9 describes a war taking place in the area of Shechem between Jacob and a series of kings. This story also contributes to the image created of the city.

Though the addressees of vv. 7–23 could well be fellow Jews who were not strict enough in their observance of the law, v. 22 points to a wider public: "But if they transgress and act in all the ways of defilement, they will be recorded in the heavenly tablets as enemies. And they will be blotted out of the book of life and written in the book of those who will be destroyed and with those who will be rooted out from the land/earth."[85] Combined with the emphasis on the lasting validity of the proscription against marriages with gentiles, v. 10, and the assurance that it cannot be atoned for by sacrifice, v. 16, these sentences carry weight. They would not only be applicable to hellenizers in Jerusalem, but to "gentiles" involved in such marriages. Both Jews and gentiles of mixed marriages are to be killed, "and there is no limit of days for this law," v. 10.[86] Though there is no specific targeting of contemporary Shechemites in

---

[85] Both "land" and "earth" are found in the translations of the text: Wintermute, "Jubilees": "land;" Berger, "Jubiläen": "Erde;" VanderKam, *Book of Jubilees*: "earth."

[86] Josephus, *Ant.* 11.312 can be interpreted as saying that all marriages between Jerusalemites and Shechemite women were mixed marriages.

the chapter, one cannot escape the feeling that the message is formulated so strongly because the existence of Shechemites was a reality at the time of composition of *Jubilees*.

Like Sir 50:25 f., *Jubilees* mentions hostility against Philistines and Edomites, *Jub.* 24:25–33; 37–38, and chapter 30 is concerned with the "third nation," the people of Shechem.

Another concept in *Jubilees* is relevant in this context. Zion has been elected for the temple, 1:17.27 f. This cannot have been a positive statement vis-à-vis the Samaritans at a time when there was a site for worship on Mount Gerizim, according to the oldest Delos inscription, 2 Macc 6:2 and 4Q372.

Jub. 30 reads as strong admonition for the community in Jerusalem to refrain from mixed marriages, and the fate of the Shechemites serves as a strong reminder of the consequences if this rule is not followed: "Proclaim this testimony to Israel: 'See how it was for the Shechemites and their sons, how they were given into the hand of the two children of Jacob and they killed them painfully!'" v. 17. And at a time when Shechem and Gerizim were populated the contemporary message would have been that the people still living there are under the spell of the old story. Thus it is not direct polemics or a message overtly directed against any contemporary Shechemites, but on a deeper level the population there would not feel reassured by *Jub.* 30. The concentration on Jerusalem and the pure people certainly implied unfriendliness or open hostility towards the other peoples, i.e. any people not inside the Essene or Jerusalem community. The thrust of *Jub.* 30 is that the acts of the Shechemites and their fate warn against intermarriage in general. But would it carry the same weight if there were no Shechem at the time of the composition of *Jubilees*? Would it have been a strong argument if the place were empty?

5.7. 4QNarrative and Poetic Composition[a-c]

The text known under this title (primarily 4Q371 and 4Q372) continues in the line of Sir 50:25 f. with a direct attack on contemporary Shechemites.[87] They are called "foolish," they are said to have built a במה on

---

[87] See also M. Kartveit, "Who are the 'Fools' in 4QNarrative and Poetic Composition[a-c]?" in *Northern Lights on the Dead Sea Scrolls: Proceedings of the Nordic Qumran Network 2003–2006* (ed. A. K. Petersen et al.; Studies on the Texts of the Desert of Judah 80; Leiden: Brill 2009) 119–133.

a high mountain, they are accused of attacking the temple in Jerusalem, and, consequently, the text prays that God may exterminate them from their land.

The texts under discussion are three fragments from two different manuscripts, 4Q371 and 4Q372. 4Q371 is made up of ten fragments and is dated to 100–75 B.C.E. 4Q372 consists of 26 fragments and is dated from the late Hasmonean to the early Herodian period. These two manuscripts belong together with two more manuscripts, 4Q373, represented by two fragments dated to the middle or late Hasmonean time, and 2Q22, which is Herodian. The dating by John Strugnell was mainly done on paleographic grounds.[88] Some of the text in each manuscript overlaps with text in at least one other manuscript, which suggests that the four manuscripts are related to each other. Hence, the manuscripts may be four copies of the same composition, or different compositions based on a common parent text; they could also be compilations based on a parent text or excerpts from it. Although the manuscripts are from 100–50 B.C.E., the original document may be older, stemming from the second century B.C.E. Since the text is very positive towards the temple in Jerusalem, it is tempting to use this as a means for dating it to a time prior to the possible exodus of the Teacher and his followers from Jerusalem.[89] This, however, is a fragile basis for dating. Another point of departure for dating the document is John Hyrcanus' destruction of Shechem and Gerizim, which took place in the latter third of the second century B.C.E. As the text does not seem to take this destruction into consideration, it might be older. However, such a procedure is an *argumentum e silentio*, and cannot provide a secure basis for dating.

The character of the underlying parent text is difficult to determine as the four manuscripts offer a mix of narrative parts, parts with hymnic or psalmic character, parts with sapiential character, hortatory texts, and a prayer. The manuscripts display military and priestly terminology, combined with halakhic and maybe even calendrical interests. Hence, the fragments do not seem to be unified in terms of content.[90] Despite these differences, the four manuscripts seem to have an interrelationship due to the overlapping text.

---

[88] E. Schuller and M. Bernstein, "371–373. 4QNarrative and Poetic Composition[a-c]," in *Wadi Daliyeh II: The Samaria Papyri from Wadi Daliyeh And Qumran Cave 4, XXVIII: Miscellanea: Part 2* (ed. D. M. Gropp et al.; DJD 28; Oxford: Clarendon, 2001), 151, n. 1.

[89] Different theories described by C. Hempel, "Qumran Community," *EDDS* 2: 746–751.

[90] Schuller and Bernstein, "4QNarrative and Poetic Composition," DJD 28:151–154.

Most fragments are small, but 4Q371 and 4Q372 include some larger fragments that are of particular interest to us. 4Q371 1a and 1b overlap with lines 5–14 of 4Q372 1.[91] Similarly, some letters in 4Q371 2, overlap with text in line 24. The overlapping text has allowed the editors to reconstruct a few words of text on different lines with some probability.

There are, however, differences between 4Q371 1 and 4Q372 1, particularly with regard to the tense of four verbs. In 4Q371 the verb form is *yiqtol*. Two of the verbs have correspondences in 4Q372, but here they are in the *wayyiqtol*-form. At first glance, this might indicate a different meaning of the text—a future perspective in 4Q371 and a past perspective in 4Q372—but *yiqtol* can also have a past meaning, especially where repetition or continuation is intended. If this explanation is not satisfying, one could side with the editors in DJD 28 and downplay the difference. They indicate that there may be circumstantial clauses in 4Q371, or that the forms may be poetic in their use. Accordingly, I conclude that 4Q371 and 4Q372 present the same basic meaning, and that 4Q371 refers to the past, as also 4Q372 1, 1–15 does.

After the initial publication of the text by E. Schuller, E. Qimron suggested improvements on the reading.[92] The editors, Schuller and Bernstein, have taken some, but not all, of his recommendations into account in DJD 28. The DJD-text is presupposed here. The first question to be addressed is the character of the text we have in these manuscripts.

Lines 1–3 in 4Q372 1 are fragmentary, but seem to describe the sins of the people in the form of idolatry. Lines 4–6 concern *Elyon* who is forcing the people into exile. Lines 7–8 refer to the predicament of Jerusalem in terminology echoing Isa 22:1.5 ("valley of Vision"), Ps 79:1 ("Jerusalem into ruins"), and Mic 3:12 ("the temple mount into a wooded height"). These lines pertain to the destruction of Jerusalem in 587 B.C.E. Lines 1–8 reflect on the destruction of Jerusalem and the exile as divine punishments for the sin of the people. Lines 10–15 seem to describe the present situation in the land of Joseph. According to lines 10 and 14 f., "Joseph" is in exile. Lines 16–32 is a prayer of Joseph for deliverance, with a short introduction in lines 15–16. The text is thus made up of a historical review of the sins of the people leading up to the exile and the destruction of Jerusalem, a second historical section about the exile of Joseph and the resulting situation in his land, which is followed by a

---

[91] Ibid., 151.
[92] E. Schuller, "4Q372 1: A Text about Joseph," *RevQ* 14 (1990); E. Qimron, "Observations on the Reading of 'A Text About Joseph' 4Q372 1," *RevQ* 15 (1992): 603–604.

prayer for divine deliverance and destruction of the enemy. The title "A text about Joseph" thus fits best in the case of lines 9–32, while the title "Prayer of Joseph" is appropriate for the lines 16–32.[93]

Line 9 mentions someone who stood at the crossroads and who was together with Judah. Line 10 says that someone was with his two brothers. Three brothers are named in line 14, Levi, Judah, and Benjamin, and it is reasonable to conclude that the same three tribes are alluded to in line 10. Schuller and Bernstein assume that the same three persons must be found also in line 9.[94] The text here, however, is in the singular and allows for only one companion of Judah, namely the unidentified companion who is standing at the crossroads. The three tribes identified in line 14, and possibly alluded to in line 10, refer to the southern part of the sons of Jacob, which at the time of the composition of the text must have meant the community centred on Jerusalem. A fourth tribe is identified in line 10, Joseph, who is in exile according to lines 10 and 15. This is an exile in "all the world," (line 11), and among a "foreign nation," or "foreigners" (lines 11 and 15). The expression in line 15, בני נאכר, is found both in the singular and the plural in the Bible, but גוי נאכר of line 11 is not known. גוי נאכר is, however, found in CD 14:15 and 11QTS 57:11, 64:7. נאכר carries a strong negative connotation in the Hebrew Bible where it is associated with idols. Thus, "Joseph" is in exile among "foreigners," who probably worship idols.

The most important part of the text for my discussion is found in lines 10–15. Underlined text is also found in 4Q371 1:

10.   And in all this, Joseph was cast into lands he did not k[now...]

11.   among a foreign nation (גוי נאכר) and dispersed in all the world. All their mountains were empty of them ... [w and fools were dwelling in their land (ונבלים ישבים בארצם)]

12.   and making for themselves a high place upon a high mountain to provoke Israel to jealousy (להקניא את ישראל); and they spoke with wor[ds of]

13.   the sons of Jacob and they acted terribly with the words of their mouth to revile against the tent of Zion; and they spoke ... [words of falsehood, and all]

14.   words of deceit they spoke to provoke Levi and Judah and Benjamin with their words. And in all this Joseph [was given]

[93] Schuller, "Text about Joseph;" H. Eshel, "The Prayer of Joseph, a Papyrus from Masada and the Samaritan Temple on ΑΡΓΑΡΙΖΙΝ," Zion 56 (1991): 125–136.
[94] Schuller, "Text about Joseph;" Schuller and Bernstein, "4QNarrative and Poetic Composition," DJD 28:174.

15. into the hands of foreigners (בני נאכר), who were devouring his strength
    and breaking all his bones until the time of the end for him. And he cried
    out ...

While Joseph is in "all the world" and among a "foreign people," his
mountains are completely "empty" of him (line 11). That all the mountains were desolate and empty is the same idea as in Josephus. 2 Kgs
17:23 seems to say that all Israel was deported, and Josephus spells this
out clearly: "He [Salmanasser] utterly exterminated the leadership of
the Israelites, and transported the entire population to Media and Persia, and along with them carried off Osees [Hoshea] alive," *Ant.* 9.278.
Joseph's area is occupied by "fools," נבלים (line 11, as reconstructed on
the basis of 4Q371). These occupants are described as "enemies," עם אויב,
in line 20. These "fools" or "enemies" have made a במה for themselves on
a high mountain, (line 12). This act is done in order to provoke Israel to
jealousy—"the sons of Jacob" in line 13 is most likely a parallel to "Israel"
in the previous line. These "fools" also act terribly by speaking against the
temple in Jerusalem, "the tent of Zion" (line 13), which appears to exist
in some form after the destruction described in line 8. The criticism of
Jerusalem is described as falsity and lies, and is said to provoke the three
tribes Levi, Judah, and Benjamin to anger in line 14.

The exile of Joseph has the effect that his enemies devour his strength
and break his bones (line 14), which is, again, biblical language, known
from Hosea, Lamentations and Isaiah. This will last until the time of his
redemption, עד עת קץ לו, (line 15). The meaning of עת קץ is "time of
redemption" as in Dan 8:17; 11:35.40; 12:4.9, and not "end time" or "time
of judgement," as in earlier literature. It is for this redemption from the
בני נאכר that Joseph prays in the following lines. Following the opening
prayer for deliverance is an extended description of God's justice, his
strength, non-violence, and mercy. This is followed by a repetition of the
claim that the enemy people took the land of Joseph and his brothers
and are now dwelling upon it (lines 19–20). This enemy speaks against
Jacob's sons, God's beloved, and enrages someone (line 21). Lines 19b–22
read:

19. [They took]my land from me and from all my brothers who

20. are joined with me. A hostile people is dwelling upon it and *k*.[ ].*p* and they
    [the people] opened their mouth against

21. all the sons of your friend Jacob with vexations to *l*[ ]

22. the time (when) you will destroy them from the entire world, and they will
    give [ ].

The root translated as "vexations" in line 21 is found also in line 14, כעס, followed by לל (possibly the preposition ל and the first letter of "Levi"). One may therefore assume that the subsequent text of line 21 would have referred to "Levi, Judah and Benjamin," as in line 14. Line 22 looks forward to the time when God will destroy the enemy from all the earth. This corresponds to the "time of redemption" of line 15, and thus represents the explanation of the kind of redemption for which the prayer asks. The rest of the prayer, or psalm, contains promises to do justice and praise God, to sacrifice and to teach the sinners God's laws. A new doxology rounds off the prayer and may be a declaration of personal insight, presumably into God's ways. The concluding promises contain elements known from the psalms of lament in the Hebrew Bible.

One notes the expression "your friend Jacob," whereas *Jub.* 30 speaks of Abraham as "friend." Isa 41:8 mentions Jacob in the same context as Abraham, so the association to Jacob as God's friend was not far away.

The MT of Gen 48:21 f. connects Joseph to Shechem. In the allotment of land to the tribes in the book of Joshua, the two Joseph-tribes are allotted land on the East and West of the Jordan. But in Gen 48:21 f. Joseph is connected to Shechem alone, which Jacob took with his sword and bow. This is an allusion to Genesis 34 through the word "sword," which occurs in connection with the killing of the Shechemites in Genesis 34. In Gen 48:21 f. there is a possible connection between Jacob and the killing of the Shechemites, and indirectly between "Joseph" and the killing.

Concerning the provenance of this text Schuller notes "nothing in the theology or vocabulary of the manuscript as a whole links it specifically to the Qumran community and writings such as *1QS, 1QM* or the *Pesharim*."[95] The text portrays the exiled tribes in the north as "Joseph" and the Samaritans as "fools" and an enemy people. F. García Martínez proposes that the author superimposed Joseph's experience in Egypt on to the northern tribes' dispersion experience.[96] In agreement with Schuller and Bernstein, M. Knibb argues that "Joseph" here does not correspond to traditions based upon the Joseph of Genesis, suggesting instead that the text has created "the representation of the tribes by their eponymous ancestor."[97]

---

[95] Schuller, "Text about Joseph," 350.

[96] F. García Martínez, "Nuevos Textos no bíblicos procedentes de Qumrán (I)," *EstBib* 49 (1991): 116–123: The text reflects the debate between Samaritan and non-Samaritan Jews over the identity of the true descendants of Joseph.

[97] M. Knibb, "A Note on 4Q372 and 4Q390," in *The Scriptures and the Scrolls: Studies in Honour of A. S. van der Woude on the Occasion of his 65th Birthday* (ed. A. Hilhorst,

J. Kugel claims, however, that "this broad consensus regarding the original aim of 4Q372 frg. 1 [referring to Schuller and Bernstein, DJD 28], though not without merit, ignores the receptive context in which we find the fragment." Instead, he perceives the character of Joseph "as an ideal figure at Qumran." Supporting his thesis with a wide range of references to the Scrolls and other texts, he claims that Joseph is primarily seen as a true mediator of God's truth and will, loyal to and beloved by the ancestors.[98]

Nevertheless, this interpretation fails to account for the exile of Joseph and his suffering under foreign rulers, as well as for his prayer for restoration of himself and the destruction of the enemies who are occupying his land. These elements in the text point towards a concrete understanding of Joseph rather than that of an idealized figure.

Based on Samaritan literature and writings from Josephus, Schuller and Bernstein argue that there was a discussion about who represented "Joseph" at the time of the writing of 4Q371–373. Since "Joseph" is a term of self-identification in Samaritan literature, a usage that is corroborated by two passages from Josephus (*Ant.* 9.291 and 11.341), the question was: Who is the real Joseph, the northern tribes now exiled or the present population of the North? This suggested literary context presupposes that the Samaritan literature can be used as comparative material. This is dubious because of the late date (Byzantine or mediaeval) of these texts, but the two passages from Josephus are early enough to produce comparable material.

Our text is concerned with the fate of the northern tribes. If one compares the perspective of 4Q372 with some biblical texts, which address the fate of the exiled northern tribes, the following picture emerges. Jer 31:8 f. looks forward to a return of "Ephraim, my firstborn." Ezek 37:15–23 prophesies that all Israelites will return to their own land from all the nations and be unified under one king (37: 21 f.); it is worth noting that verses 16 f. promise the unification of Joseph and Judah. According to Zech 10:6–10 the houses of Judah and Joseph will return and settle in the land of Gilead and Lebanon. Likewise, Zech 8:13 looks forward to the

---

C. J. Labuschagne and F. García Martínez; VTSup 49; Leiden: Brill, 1992), 164–177. According to him, the text reflects the debate between Samaritan and non-Samaritan Jews over the identity of the true descendants of Joseph.

[98] J. Kugel, "Joseph at Qumran: The Importance of 4Q372 Frg. 1 in Extending a Tradition," in *Studies in the Hebrew Bible, Qumran, and the Septuagint presented to Eugene Ulrich* (ed. E. Tov, J. C. VanderKam and P. W. Flint; Leiden: Brill, 2006), 261–278. Quotations from 272, 276 f.

restoration of the house of Judah and the house of Israel when they will be turning from being a curse among the nations to becoming a blessing. The text of Isa 11:13 expects a time when Judah and Ephraim, no longer a threat to each other, together will take spoils from Edom, Moab, Ammon and the Philistines. The rest of God's people will return from Assyria (11:16). In 1 Chr 5:1–3 Joseph is given the right of firstborn, but Chronicles does not operate with a deportation and return for the northern tribes; they are invited to participate in the cult in Jerusalem.

These texts are not concerned with the removal of contemporary dwellers in the land of Samaria or the Northern kingdom, only with the return of Joseph or Ephraim, and Judah. The same is the case in the prayer in Sir 36:1–19. The enemies, whom the petitioner asks to be destroyed, seem to be located in foreign lands, as are the tribes of Jacob. God is asked to "gather all the tribes of Jacob that they may inherit the land" in Sir 36:11.

More than two hundred years later, the *Testament of Moses* (first century C.E.), *2 Baruch* (early second century C.E.), and 2 Esdras (late first century C.E.), realizing that the Northern tribes are still in foreign lands, express a hope for their salvation. There is no mention of the removal of the contemporary inhabitants from the North of the land.

2 Esd 13:39–50 presupposes that ten tribes were exiled beyond the Euphrates by Salmanassar at the time of Josiah, from where they went even further to escape the pagan peoples. They are termed the "peaceful lot," who will be called by the Son of the Most High to return to him and to Zion, and be saved together with the people remaining in the holy land.

2 Bar. 78–86 contains a letter to the nine and a half tribes across the Euphrates. In this letter they are considered brothers of the tribes who were exiled from Jerusalem, as the writer asks, "are we not all, the twelve tribes, bound by one captivity as we also descend from one father?" (78:4). Whereas "the inhabitants of Zion were a comfort to you" (80:7), now most of them are in exile with no hope for a return to the land. God will punish the nations on behalf of his people, and the present era will come to an end. The writer admonishes the addressees: "remember Zion and the Law and the holy land and your brothers and the covenant and your fathers, and do no forget the festivals and the Sabbaths" (84:8). At the same time, there will be no return to the land, as the text states, "We have left our land, and Zion has been taken away from us, and we have nothing now apart from the Mighty One and his Law" (85:3).

The perspective of the *Testament of Moses* 3:4–4:9 is that the twelve tribes are in exile and "tribulation has come upon the whole house of Israel" (3:7). 4:5–9 clearly expects the return of the two tribes to Jerusalem, but its view on the fate of the ten tribes, who are to "grow and spread out among the nations during the time of their captivity," is less clear.[99]

Like 4Q372, these texts consider the northern and southern tribes as brothers. This is important given the background of Ps 78:67 f.: "He rejected the tent (אהל) of Joseph, he did not choose the tribe of Ephraim; but he chose the tribe of Judah, Mount Zion, which he loves." In this case, there is an explicit rejection of Joseph. This rejection (מאס) is not reflected in the later texts, which instead express solidarity with the northern tribes.

Against this background, the focus on the contemporary dwellers in the land of Joseph in our text (lines 11–14) deserves special attention. The psalm or prayer envisages a destruction of the enemies dwelling in the land of Joseph (line 22), but the extant text includes no hint of a return to the land, which would have been the logical consequence. It may have existed in text now lost. In contrast, the texts quoted from the Hebrew Bible, and texts two hundred years after 4Q372 do not even mention the existence of such dwellers in the land of Joseph. Even 2 Esdras, from the time of Josephus (who has a lot to say about these people), does not address the issue. Perhaps 2 Esdras expects a return to Zion, which would not affect the territory in the north.

Sirach, from the same century as the parent text of 4Q372 1, knows of such people in chapter 50, and prays that they be destroyed. But the enemies who are mentioned in chapter 36 are outside the land, and their destruction is prayed for, in order that all the tribes of Jacob will return to the land.

What is the picture painted of the people dwelling in the land of Joseph? The sympathy of 4Q372 is clear from the preserved fragments: the author looks favourably upon Jerusalem and its temple, and upon Joseph, and envisages that his predicament will come to an end. On the other hand, the texts express negative sentiments towards the "fools," i.e., the enemy people who are dwelling on his territory in the north. The description of them is therefore strongly polemical. In spite of the polemical portrayal of them we are able to discern some of the underlying assumptions.

---

[99] Translation by J. Priest, "Testament of Moses," *OTP* 1: 929.

The enemies are said to have made a במה on a high mountain. The expression ועשים להם במה may build on 2 Kgs 17:9, but the expression is closer to the wording of 2 Kgs 17:32 than to the text in v. 9. 2 Kgs 17 is derogatory towards the Assyrian settlers in Samaria, so either allusion to 2 Kgs 17 conveys negative overtones. The word במה denotes a sanctuary or an altar and may be a reference to the Samaritan temple on Mount Gerizim. If the point of our text is to reuse the critique against the settlers in 2 Kgs 17 and apply it to a new situation, then the negative connotations are important. If the text employs language from 2 Kgs 17, this is an indication that this chapter was interpreted as anti-Samaritan in the second century B.C.E., two hundred years before Josephus used the chapter in his explanation of the origin of the Samaritans (*Ant.* 9.288 ff.). In the case of 4Q372, however, there is no allegation of the foreign origin of the Samaritans, only possible allusions to 2 Kgs 17. 2 Macc 6:2 is a better case of such possible use of 2 Kgs 17 in the second century B.C.E. Much later, *Masseket Kuthim* mentions "the priests of the במות."

The *qal* participle referring to their building, עשים, does not necessarily mean "they are building right now," but could be timeless, just as the other participles in lines 11–12 are.[100] The temple existed at the time of composition of the text.

The construction of the במה is made להקניא את ישראל, "in order to provoke Israel," according to line 12. In line 14 we read of the present dwellers that "words of deceit they spoke to provoke (להכעיס) Levi and Judah and Benjamin with their words." The verbs קנא and כעס are adopted from Deut 32:21, "They made me jealous (קנא) with what is no god, provoked (כעס) me with their idols. So I will make them jealous (קנא) with what is no people, provoke (כעס) them with a foolish nation." The people provoke God and he will provoke them. In 4Q372 the provocation comes from the north against Israel, and against Levi, Judah and Benjamin.

The reference to "Israel" in 4Q372 is significant. The term does not appear in MT of Deut 32:21, as this verse appears inside the divine speech in Deut 32:20–35. Since this speech is addressed to Israel, the addition of "Israel" in 4Q371 and 4Q372 is not surprising. However, as an expression for the opponents of the "fools" of the north, "Israel" is significant. It may be parallel to the expression in line 14: "Levi, Judah, and Benjamin," or to all the descendants of God's beloved, Jacob, in line 21. In both cases it is a term denoting the opponents of the Samaritans. The

---

[100] Against Eshel, "Prayer of Joseph."

Samaritans from the early second century B.C.E. and onward called themselves "Israel," as the Delos inscriptions from the first half of the second century B.C.E. show (see the next chapter). The statement in 4Q371 that "they made for themselves a במה on a high mountain in order to provoke Israel" must then have sounded insulting in the ears of the Samaritans. Like the inhabitants of Jerusalem or all the descendants of Jacob, these inhabitants of the north considered themselves Israelites. The construction of the temple on Mount Gerizim was not intended to be a provocation to "Israel" but its pride. They termed the temple on the mountain, or even the mountain itself "holy," and "holy and sanctified" according to the Delos inscriptions (cf. the expression in Pseudo-Eupolemus, ἱερόν Ἀργαριζίν). Hence, there was a discussion not only concerning who were the true "Joseph"-ites, but also concerning who were the real "Israel."

4Q372 accuses the Samaritans of criticising Jerusalem and her temple. The people residing in the north mock Jerusalem: they revile the tent of Zion (line 13), producing lies and every kind of deceit in order to provoke Levi, Judah and Benjamin (line 13 f.). The background for this may be actual abuse against Jerusalem and the tribes around the city, but more likely the text expresses conventional, polemical language, as all the expressions are adopted from the Hebrew Bible. The uttering from the north is deemed a "terrible act." Most of all, it is characterized as "blasphemy," לגדף (Pi'el, line 13; cf. Sir 3:16; 48:18). The blasphemy is uttered in order to enrage "Levi, Judah, and Benjamin" (line 14). Nothing is preserved of such Samaritan polemics.

The strength of the allegation that the "fools" provoke Israel becomes evident in the light of the background in Deut 32:21. There, Israel provokes God with their non-gods and idols; here, the "fools" provoke Israel with their "high place" on the high mountain. To the degree that the "fools" call themselves "Israel," this claim is rejected by reserving this name for their opponents in the South. The construction of the במה in the North functions like the non-gods and idols of Deut 32:21.

The negative attitude toward the Samaritans in the text is strong enough for us to assume that the prayer in line 22 calls upon God to exterminate the Samaritans from all the earth.

4Q372 calls the Samaritans "fools," נבלים (line 11) as reconstructed on the basis of 4Q371. Schuller and Bernstein interpret the expression, נבלים, in 4Q372 on the basis of Deut 32:6.21.[101] The expression "fools" would be

---

[101] Schuller and Bernstein, "4QNarrative and Poetic Composition," DJD 28:174.

parallel to Deut 32:21, and 4Q372 uses other expressions from the same chapter. But the reference must be to Deut 32:21 alone, since Deut 32:6 uses the expression עם נבל; see above the discussion in connection with Sir 50:25 f.

In connection with Sir 50:25 f. I have discussed the question: How did the author of Sir 50:25 f. come to associate the "fools" of Deut 32:21 with the inhabitants of Shechem? The conclusion in that discussion, that the author combined Deut 32:21 with Gen 34, may hold also for 4Q372's association of the "fools" with the land of Joseph. This view is supported by a third text with roots in the second century B.C.E. that employs the expression "fools," namely *Testament of Levi 7*, to which I will now turn. The expression "fools" with reference to the Samaritans is found in three different texts from this period, and it amounts to a standard expression in the polemics levelled by Jerusalem against them. This is strong language against the Samaritans, some of whom may have come from Jerusalem, according to Josephus.

To sum up, 4Q372 can best be described as a polemical text about the Samaritans who are dwelling in Joseph's land in the second century B.C.E. They are considered descendants of the Shechemites and are associated with the sacrilege described in Genesis 34. Their criticism of the temple in Jerusalem amounts to blasphemy, in analogy with acts described in Deut 32:21. The controversy in the text is mainly over the temple site. The במה on Mount Gerizim is—so it seems—considered a foolish act, a sin. To speak against the temple in Jerusalem is blasphemy. If the whole text of Deut 32:21 is supposed to provide the background of the expression "blaspheme," then this expression is the closest any text from this period comes to accusing the Samaritans of idolatry. This remains, however, only a possibility.

5.8. Aramaic Levi Document *and* Testament of Levi

The Greek *Testament of Levi* summarizes Gen 34 and proclaims that Shechem "from this day forward" is a "city of fools." The perpetuation of the judgment over the city is here more clearly spoken out than in the other texts under consideration.

T. Levi is a Christian document, but it is assumed that it was composed on the basis of the Jewish *Aramaic Levi Document* (abbreviated *ALD*) or a text similar to it. This assumption is rejected by J. H. Ulrichsen, but he acknowledges that *T. Levi* contains traditions related to the Aramaic material.[102] On balance, it seems that he underestimated the degree of correlation between the Greek and Aramaic manuscripts, and the relevant Qumran material was published in full after he published his book. One may therefore reckon with the Aramaic material as an older version of *T. Levi*. On the other hand, it is recognized that the Aramaic material cannot be called a testament, as the manuscripts do not witness to this genre. In 1996 R. Kugler used the expression *Aramaic Levi* in his study of the material,[103] and the title chosen by J. Greenfield, M. E. Stone and E. Eshel for the material is the *Aramaic Levi Document*. They reconstructed the *ALD*, and the textual witnesses to *ALD* prove beyond doubt the existence of a Jewish substratum of *Testament of Levi*. This substratum was concerned with the story derived from Genesis 34.[104]

It is therefore necessary to start the investigation of the *ALD* before looking at *T. Levi*. The present form of *T. Levi* is preserved in 19 chapters in Greek.[105] *ALD* is reconstructed in 13 chapters, plus some unplaced fragments. We have proof for two stages in the development of the work, the *ALD* and *T. Levi*, but there may have been an intermediate stage, another Jewish *Testament of Levi*. Such a *Grundschicht* of *T. Levi* has been reconstructed by J. H. Ulrichsen. Without accepting his arguments and conclusions in detail, one must admit that he has made a case for the possibility of a Jewish version between the *ALD* and *T. Levi*.[106] The date of *T. Levi* is second century C.E. The *ALD* probably comes from the third century or early second century B.C.E.[107] A Jewish Testament would then have been created somewhere in between. *ALD* is close to *Jubilees*, and either *Jub.* 30–32 built upon *ALD*, or they used a common

---

[102] J. H. Ulrichsen, *Die Grundschicht der Testamente der zwölf Patriarchen: eine Untersuchung zu Umfang, Inhalt und Eigenart der ursprünglichen Schrift* (Historia religionum 10; Uppsala: Almqvist & Wiksell International, 1991), 186.

[103] R. A. Kugler, *From Patriarch to Priest: The Levi-Priestly Tradition from Aramaic Levi to Testament of Levi* (Early Judaism and its literature 9; Atlanta, Ga.: Scholars Press, 1996).

[104] J. Greenfield, M. E. Stone and E. Eshel, *The Aramaic Levi Document: Edition, Translation, Commentary* (SVTP 19; Leiden: Brill, 2004), 57.

[105] M. de Jonge, *Testamenta XII Patriarcharum: Edited According to Cambridge University Library Ms Ff. 1.24 fol. 203a–262b with Short Notes* (PVTG 1; Leiden: Brill, 1964); translations: H. W. Hollander and M. de Jonge, *The Testament of the Twelve Patriarchs: A Commentary* (SVTP 8; Leiden: Brill, 1985); H. C. Kee, "Testaments of the Twelve Patriarchs (Second Century B.C.)," *OTP* 1: 775–828; F. Schnapp and E. Kautzsch, "Die Testamente der 12 Patriarchen, der Söhne Jakobs," *APAT* 2: 458–506.

[106] Ulrichsen, *Grundschicht der Testamente*.

[107] R. A. Kugler, "Some Further Evidence for the Samaritan Provenance of *Aramaic Levi (1QTestLevi; 4QTestLevi)*," *RevQ* 17 (1996): 351–358; M. E. Stone, "Levi, Aramaic," *EDDS* 1: 486; Greenfield, Stone and Eshel, *Aramaic Levi Document*, 19.

source. An intermediate Jewish *Testament of Levi* would have been a further development of the tradition, and *T. Levi* is the last stage. In view of the difficulty in reconstructing an intermediate *Testament of Levi* no attempt is made here to speculate on which elements of Gen 34 it may have contained.

The *Aramaic Levi Document* is reconstructed on the basis of larger and smaller fragments in Aramaic, Greek and Syriac. The discovery of Aramaic fragments at Qumran confirmed its antiquity and it is now considered to be one of the oldest Jewish works outside the Hebrew Bible. It incorporates important ideas about the priesthood, sacrifice and wisdom and ideals of piety. J. T. Milik and R. A. Kugler think the work is of Samaritan provenance. Milik's argument was the presence of northern place names; Kugler found (1) similarities to Lev 1:6 SP; (2) the teaching on priestly marriages and personal purity; and (3) the status of Joseph and Levi.[108] The idea builds on Samaritan texts that at best date from the fourth century C.E., 5–600 years after the supposed composition of *ALD*. It presupposes that these texts contain information dating two centuries before the turn of the era, which is hard to prove in view of the present lack of sources.

The text of the *ALD* is fragmentary, but the publishers provide the following translation of "Chapter 1: The Story of Dinah":

> 1:1 ... you / she defiled the so[ns of (?) ac-]cording to the manner of all people [] to do according to the law (*or*: to do so) in all [... *took counsel with*] Jacob my father and Reu[ben my brother ...]

> 1:2 and we said to them: [...] "[I]f ⟨you⟩ desire our daughter so that we all become broth[ers] and friends,

> 1:3 circumcise your fleshly foreskin and look like us, and (then) you will be sealed like us with the circumcision [of tru]th and we will be br[others] for y[ou] ..."[109]

This translation is based on the only available manuscript for this passage, Cambridge Col. a. Lines 1–14 are supposed missing, and an amount of text is considered to have preceded the missing text. Due to the fragmentary nature of the text, reconstructions are debatable, and the details of these discussions are given in the apparatus of the edition.

The text contains טמאת in the first line, and this is a form of the verb meaning "to defile" which could be either second or third person;

---

[108] Kugler, "Further Evidence," 351–358.
[109] Greenfield, Stone and Eshel, *Aramaic Levi Document*, 57.

therefore it has received a double translation. There is here a concentration on the oldest son of Jacob, Reuben, instead of Simeon, who is next in line. "Brothers and friends," א[ח]ן [ן]וחברין, is, however, an interesting deviation from the expression "one people," Gen 34:16.22. The expression should perhaps be translated "brothers and partners," since there is a commercial interest in the dealings.[110] The description of the circumcision has occasioned some discussion by the editors of *ALD*.[111] Standard biblical terminology is to circumcise "the flesh of his foreskin," בשר ערלתו, but here we read עורלת בשרכן, "the foreskin of your flesh," or, in the translation of the editors, "your fleshly foreskin." The order of words is reversed, and the editors struggle to find an explanation. They suggest that the expression might have a metaphorical meaning and that "the Shechemites would have only a fleshly circumcision, not a spiritual one." They note, however, that the expression "circumcision [of tru]th" points in the opposite direction. The solution to the expression in *ALD* may be that "flesh," בשר, in some biblical texts denotes "the male organ," "the penis," Lev 15:2.7; Ezek 16:26; 23:20. A possible translation in *ALD* would be "the foreskin of your penis." Since the expression is preceded by the verb גזר, "to cut off," 1:3 would make good sense with this understanding of בשר: "cut off the foreskin of your penis and look like us, and you will be sealed like us with the circumcision [of tru]th and we will be br[others] for y[ou]."[112]

This text is close to *T. Levi* 6:3: "I took counsel with my father and Reuben my brother, in order that I should say to the sons of Hamor that they should be circumcised, because I was zealous because of the detestable/abominable act (βδέλυγμα) that they had performed in Israel." The occurrence of "Reuben" in both texts is one of the elements which make a literary connection between *ALD* and *T. Levi* likely.

ALD chapter 2 is reconstructed by E. Puech according to the story of the sale of Joseph, Gen 37, but this reconstruction is rejected by Greenfield, Stone and Eshel.[113] R. A. Kugler instead sees it as a continuation of the Dinah episode, and Greenfield et al. suggest the title "Chapter 2:

---

[110] Ibid., 113.

[111] Ibid., 113–115.

[112] The same understanding is presupposed in the translation of E. Cook, M. Wise, and M. Abegg Jr., *The Dead Sea Scrolls: A New Translation* (rev. ed.; San Francisco, Calif.: Harper, 2005), 252: "you must circumcise your penis."

[113] E. Puech, "Le Testament de Lévi en araméen de la geniza du Caire," *RevQ* 20 (2002): 511–556; Greenfield, Stone and Eshel, *Aramaic Levi Document*, 117–119.

The Wars of the Sons of Jacob (?)."[114] Chapter 2 includes as certain readings "Shechem" twice, "my brothers" twice, "Dan," "Judah," "Simeon," and "Reuben," so the association to the Dinah story is not impossible. The expression "[do]ers of violence," [עב]די חמסא], is not attached to any names, but in Cambridge Col. d, corresponding to T. Levi 12:5, the expression is parallel to "Shech[em]": ALD 12:6: "I was eighteen years old when I killed Shechem and annihilated the workers of violence"; T. Levi 12:5: "I was ... eighteen years old when I killed Shechem." The most likely understanding is that chapter 2 continues the re-telling of Gen 34. Cambridge column a seems to correspond to the part of the story represented in Gen 34:5–17, and column b would be part of the same material. The missing part between the preserved fragments of text may have expanded the same part.

The most interesting part is 2:1, translated thus by the editors:

> 2:1 [...] my brother(s?) at all times [...] who were in Shechem, [...] my brother(s?) and he told this [...] in Shechem and that [...do]ers of violence and Judah told them that I and Simeon my brother had gone [...] to Reuben our brother, which is to the east of Asher, and Judah leaped forward [to] leave the sheep [...][115]

If this text has to do with the Dinah episode, it would be building on the remark in Gen 34:5.7 that the brothers were tending their flock. The expression "doers of violence" would point in the direction of the Dinah narrative. The fragment may give the explanation for the occurrence of "Reuben" in chapter 1: Levi and Simeon went to Reuben for counsel.

In any case, there is enough preserved text in 1:1–3 to conclude that ALD contained the Dinah incident, but not enough to say anything about a certain ideological tendency in the material. The fragments preserved in 1:1–3 are more detailed than Gen 34, and thus there is a tendency to provide a longer text than Gen 34. The rest of ALD is parallel to Jubilees and T. Levi in many respects, and one may assume that the appointment of Levi as priest in ALD is connected to the events told in Gen 34: "I was eighteen when I killed Shechem and destroyed the workers of violence. I was nineteen when I became a priest ..." 12:6 f.

---

[114] Kugler, *From Patriarch to Priest*, 52 f. 63 f.; Greenfield, Stone and Eshel, *Aramaic Levi Document*, 58 f., and without the question mark, 117–122. Greenfield, Stone and Eshel criticize Kugler, "who perceives no need to demonstrate that 2:1 is part of the Shechem incident but assumes it," Greenfield, Stone and Eshel, *Aramaic Levi Document*, 117, n. 28.

[115] Greenfield, Stone and Eshel, *Aramaic Levi Document*, 59.

A third fragment is relevant to our subject, 4Q213 2 according to
R. Kugler, or 4QLevi^b, fragment 2, according to Greenfield et al.[116] The
readings in Kugler and in Greenfield et al. are quite different in a number
of cases. Kugler's translation is as follows:

> [ ] from the wom[a]n to [ ]°. And now °[]°° the pla[g]ues of men [ ] the
> ones incurring guilt [ ] your (or: wife?). And she profanes her name and the
> name of her father [ ] husband(s?) to bu[r]n her [ ]° °°°°[ ] and (the?) shame.
> And every virgin who ruins her name, and the name of her fathers, she also
> causes shame for all her brothers [and for] her father. And the reputation
> of her revilement will not be wiped out from among all her people forever.
> [ ]°[ ]° for all the generations of eternity. °°[ ]°° holy (pure?) from the people
> [ ]°° °[ ] a holy tithe, an offering to God from.

Greenfield et al. offer the following translation:

2.]he beswore us and [...] [...] men

3.]a wife and she desecrated her name and the name of her father

4.]with [...] shame and every

5.] who profaned her name and the name of her ancestors, and shamed all
   her brothers.

6.] her father; and the name of the righteous will not be wiped out from all
   her people for ever.

7.] for all the generations of eternity and [...] the holy ones from the people

8.]holy tithe a sacrifice for teaching (?)

The text is fragmentary and the readings are uncertain in lines 1–2, 4
and 8, but lines 3 and 5–7 are reasonably readable. DJD 22 and the
translation in the *DSS Study Edition* and in Abegg et al. in general support
the reading and translation of R. Kugler in these lines. This means that
the text seems to mention a young woman or virgin who defiles her name
and her family's name, and her disgraceful name will not be wiped out for
ever.[117] Greenfield et al. offer this text among the "Unplaced Fragments"
and Abegg et al. say the "the placement of this fragment is uncertain,"
but Kugler locates it inside Levi's vision. Greenfield et al. "regard them
[these fragments] with a measure of doubt." According to them, "Just how

---

[116] Kugler, *From Patriarch to Priest*, 36 f. 77–87; Greenfield, Stone and Eshel, *Aramaic Levi Document*, 219–222.

[117] Kugler, *From Patriarch to Priest*; García Martínez and Tigchelaar, *Dead Sea Scrolls: Study Edition*; Cook, Wise, and Abegg, *Dead Sea Scrolls: A New Translation*, all reconstruct בתלה here.

Dinah's rape could be related to the statements made here and how they can be related to the Dinah material in chapter 1, is quite obscure." Other scholars consider, however, this material as related to the Dinah story, much in line with *Jub.* 30, which after the re-telling of the first part of the story in Gen 34 provides a series of laws about intermarriage. Among these are the regulations for treating the daughter of a priest who has profaned her father, Lev 21:9, and this is probably the regulation behind what we read in 4QLevi[b], fragment 2.

There are probably three fragments in *ALD* which correspond to the Dinah story, two in the Cambridge manuscript and one in a Qumran text. The rendering of the story here is supplied with additional material, which may come from another source. This rendering is older than *Jubilees*, and there is no specific edge against the contemporary dwellers in the area around Shechem. Circumcision seems to be required of the Shechemites, and there is probably prohibition against exogamy in the form of an exegesis of Lev 21:9. If this understanding is correct, it means that all Israel is treated according to priestly laws, and circumcision is the definition of what "Israel" means. This ideology would be close to Theodotus with the combination of circumcision and endogamy, and to *Jubilees* with the understanding of all Israel as priests.

If we turn to *T. Levi*, we already in 2:2 find one of the main topics introduced: "I performed vengeance against Hamor because of our sister, Dinah." This is repeated in 12:5: "I was eight years old when I entered the land of Canaan, and eighteen years old when I killed Shechem," cf. *ALD* 12:6 quoted above. In the middle of this *inclusio*, the story itself is told.

Levi tells in *T. Levi* 2:3 ff. how he was tending his flock in Abel-Maoul, probably Abel Meholah, Judg 7:22, on the Jordan south of Bet Shan. When he was grieving over the sins of humans, sleep fell upon him, "and I beheld a high mountain, and I was on it. And behold, the heavens were opened, and an angel of the Lord spoke to me: 'Levi, Levi, enter!'" vv. 5 f. This "high mountain" is commonly supposed to be a standard expression for where revelation takes place, as in the HB. An additional note to v. 5 explains it as "the mountain of the Aspis ["shield"] in Abelmaul," thus connecting it to 6:1: "and when I was going to my father, I found a brass shield; therefore, also, the name of the mountain is Aspis ["shield"], which is near Gebal to the right of Abila." The location given in 6:1 is "to the right," i. e. south of Abila, Abel Meholah, and "near Gebal," i. e. Ebal. One would think of Mount Gerizim as a possible mountain fitting this geographical description, but the name "Aspis" is difficult to connect to Mount Gerizim or Argarizein. The city Sebaste, on the other hand, would also fit the description, and it is quite possible to imagine a development from "Sebaste" to "Aspis." With both sibilants intact, and a change from one labial to another, only the prosthetic vowel is added to arrive at "Aspis." The revelation in ch. 2 may therefore originally have been considered to take place in a natural location for revelations, according to tradition. A later interpretation of 2:5 identifies the revelatory place as "Aspis," the city of Sebaste on the mountain where Samaria was originally built, and where Herod rebuilt the city under the new name Sebaste. If the text originated in Samaritan circles, as Milik and Kugler suppose, it would be easy to imagine a general location in the original text. The probability of this provenance is slight, and a different explanation must be sought. In a Jewish version of the Testament, a revelation on Mount Samaria could carry an ironical note. The content of the revelation is vengeance because of the rape of Dinah, and this message is proclaimed on a mountain near Gebal, the mountain of curse. This is all rather hypothetical, however, and the easiest explanation is that the present, Christian, version of the text—probably created in Syria—built upon a general knowledge of the territory in question. Then, Samaria, Sebaste, "Aspis," came to the mind of the author: the "high mountain" was Sebaste.

T. Levi 2:7–4:6 is Levi's own report of his heavenly journey and reads to a large extent as a Christian text. It prefigures what is to come in the following chapters, as the focus in heaven is on human sin and divine retribution and vengeance. In chapter 5:2 God speaks, "Levi, to you I have given the blessings of the priesthood until I come and dwell in the midst of Israel." Then the angel brings Levi down to earth and gives him a shield and a sword and says, "Take vengeance on Shechem because of Dinah," 5:3. *T. Levi* 5:4 adds "And it was at that time that I killed the sons of Hamor, as it is written in the heavenly tablets." Apart from probable Christian elements here, the language recalls the "judgment" and "heavenly tablets" of *Jub.* 30.

After chapter 5 *T. Levi* 6:1 continues with the receiving of the shield and a geographical note. This seems awkward after 5:6 ("I am the angel that intercedes for Israel ...") or 5:7 (blessing of God and the interceding angel). If, however, 6:1 is a later addition, then 6:2 is a natural continuation, "And I kept these words in my heart." 2:5 and 6:1 seem to be additions to the earlier text.

After the heavenly commission to perform vengeance on Shechem and the execution of the commission in ch. 5, the story from Gen 34 is referred to once more in 6:3–5:

I urged my father and my brother Reuben to tell the sons of Hamor they must be circumcised, for I was zealous because of the abominable thing they had wrought in Israel. And I killed Shechem first, and Simeon killed Hamor. After that my brothers came and destroyed the city with the edge of the sword.

That Levi killed Shechem and Simeon Hamor is also found in Theodotus. The somewhat enigmatic connection between the demand for circumcision and the zeal because of the abominable act, may be understood in this way. The zeal for vengeance would result in making sure the enemy was weakened enough through circumcision before the attack itself. Against this background vengeance would be carried out successfully.

In vv. 6f. Jacob's reaction to the killings builds upon the circumcision having taken place, in accordance with the Bible.[118] In view of the lack of clarity or absence of circumcision in Theodotus and *Jubilees*, this is remarkable. "Father heard it and was angry and sorrowful, because they had received circumcision and died, and in his blessings did otherwise," v. 6. The last sentence reflects the reservations of the blessing in Gen 49 and perhaps the absence of a blessing of Simeon in Deut 33. The following concession of guilt stands out in the literature under study here: "We had sinned, because we had done the thing against his will, and he was ill that day," v. 7. Translations of the last sentence vary in saying that Jacob was ill at the moment of the killings (and could not be consulted), or that he became ill after the action (and if *post* means *propter, because* of the killings).

Levi defends himself against his own feeling of guilt and against his father's reproach by stating the reason for the action: "I saw that God's sentence upon Shechem was for evil because they wished to act against Sarah in the same way that they acted against Dinah our sister; but the Lord prevented them," v. 8. The heavenly judgment is also found in *Jub.* 30. The reference to Sarah seems to build upon Gen 20, where Abraham and Sarah are in Gerar, as all Canaanites are considered a group of enemies, *T. Levi* 7:1. A further reason is given: "In the same way they had persecuted Abraham our father while he was a stranger and trampled the flocks against him while they were big with young and maltreated very seriously Jeblae his home-born slave," v. 9. This was part of a general persecution of strangers, v. 10, as in Theodotus, fragment 7. "But the wrath of God came upon them, definitely," v. 11.

---

[118] Kee, "Testaments of the Twelve Patriarchs," *OTP* 1: 790, otherwise.

Like Theodotus, fragment 6, *T. Levi* 7:1 broaches the theme of conquest, "And I said to my father, 'Do not be angry, Lord, because by you the Lord will set at nought the Canaanites and he will give their land to you and your seed after you.'" It is worth noting that the conquest theme from Genesis emerges in the context of the Dinah episode. This is not the case in the biblical account, but is a creation of Theodotus and *T. Levi*. The combination of the sins of the Shechemites and the promise of land to Israel is also unique to these two documents. Even if *T. Levi* specifies the sins more precisely than Theodotus, the idea is similar. The biblical background for the land promise has been commented upon in connection with the discussion of Theodotus.

The text continues in the words of Levi, "from this day forward, Shechem shall be called 'City of Fools,' because as one mocks a fool, so we mocked them, because by defiling our sister they indeed committed folly in Israel," Ἔσται γὰρ ἀπὸ σήμερον Σικὶμ λεγομένη πόλις ἀσυνέτων· ὅτι ὡσεί τις χλευάσαι μωρὸν οὕτως ἐχλευάσαμεν αὐτούς· ὅτι καίγε ἀφροσύνην ἔπραξαν ἐν Ἰσραήλ μιᾶναι τὴν ἀδελφὴν ἡμῶν, 7:2–3. J. Kugel supposes that the Aramaic verb underlying χλευάζω might be the D-stem of נבל, meaning "to disgrace": "the rape of Dinah was called a *nĕbālâ* because, as a result of it, the sons of Jacob disgraced the Shechemites, and even today Shechem is known as a 'city of fools' in memory of this event."[119] As we do not have a basis for the Aramaic verb in the *ALD* texts, this reconstruction of the *Vorlage* of *T. Levi* is to be considered a possibility only.

J. Kugel has, however, sensed correctly that there is a connection between the name of the city as a πόλις ἀσυνέτων and the following sentence "because as one mocks a fool, so we mocked them." This connection is given by the particle ὅτι, "because." There is a second ὅτι in the text, in front of the following sentence, and this is emphasized by the expression καίγε, "because by defiling our sister they indeed committed folly in Israel." This second sentence seems to provide the basis for the preceding one, giving the reason for the action of the sons of Jacob. The first ὅτι therefore creates the link between the name and the reason for the name. The *tertium* between the name and the action of the sons of Jacob lies not in the verb χλευάζω, which has no equivalent in the name, but in the two expressions for "fools," μωρός and ἀσύνετος. "As one mocks a fool (μωρός), so we mocked them [who were called ἀσύνετοι in the name of

---

[119] Kugel, *Traditions of the Bible*, 424.

the city]" means that μωρός and ἀσύνετος are considered equivalents as in a parallel expression in poetry. The action of the sons of Jacob was a "mocking," which is a euphemism for the killing, but the victims were "foolish" as a common "fool," because they had defiled Dinah. As lightly as one scorns a fool, the Israelites easily killed the Shechemites.

Even if the original inhabitants were killed, their deed remains in the name of the city of Shechem. "From this day forward," i.e., after the killing, "Shechem shall be called 'City of Fools.'" The name "city of fools" will last through the generations.

The *Testament of Levi* condones the continued mocking of the Shechemites because of the detestable act, the "folly" committed according to Genesis 34. The word ἀσύνετος in the expression "a city of fools," creates an association with Deut 32:21. The LXX uses ἀσύνετος as a translation for נבל in Deut 32:21. The *Testament of Levi* thus combines Genesis 34 and Deut 32:21: by using an expression from Deuteronomy 32 LXX for the name of the city, and by referring to the events told in Genesis 34. This combination of Gen 34 and Deut 32 was also undertaken by the author of Sir 50:25 f., on the basis of the similarity of the Hebrew words נבל and נבלה. This was not exploited by *T. Levi*, as the "folly" was termed ἀφροσύνη, a wisdom term, which does not create a terminological link to ἀσύνετος in Deut 32:21 LXX. The LXX used ἄσχημον in Gen 34:7, and thus also missed the opportunity to create a word link between Gen 34 and Deut 32. The catchword connection between the texts must therefore have been made by an author using Hebrew, and therefore *T. Levi* took over the idea expressed in 7:2 f. from a Hebrew *Vorlage*. As a possible *Vorlage* we know of Ben Sira, but there may have been other texts.

T. Levi 8 continues the story by recounting the priestly inauguration of Levi taking place in heaven, and chapter 9 relates how Isaac blesses and instructs Levi in his capacity as priest, and Jacob pays tithes to him. Levi was therefore installed in his high priesthood after killing the Shechemites, and probably also because of this act.

John Hyrcanus was a high priest, according to Josephus, and *T. Levi* would provide an excellent justification of Hyrcanus' destruction of the temple, according to Josephus' logic, *War* 1.68 f.; *Ant.* 13.30,282, cf. 1 Macc 13:38–43.

T. Levi is a Christian document, and one cannot be sure which parts belong to the Jewish substratum of it and which parts are due to later editorial activity. Enough is preserved of the *ALD* to conclude that a version of the story in Gen 34 was present there, and *ALD* 12:6 indicates that the incident was central in this document: "I was eighteen years old when I killed Shechem and annihilated the workers of violence." It is no bold proposition that *ALD* provided *T. Levi* with basic parts of the Dinah episode. A Christian work would not have an axe to grind in this connection, as Gen 34 does not provide obvious material for Christological and similar prophecies and interpretations. A violent act as a basis for priesthood is the opposite of e. g. the letter to the Hebrews' understanding of priesthood. The most likely understanding of the situation is that *T. Levi* adopted what could not be dispensed with, and adapted it to its purposes.

A strongly negative attitude to the Shechemites is, on the other hand, not in line with Lukan and Johannine attitudes to the Samaritans. It may, however, be easier to combine it with the gospel of Matthew, where 10:5 reads, "These twelve Jesus sent out with the following instructions: 'Go nowhere among the Gentiles, and enter no town of the Samaritans, but go rather to the lost sheep of the house of Israel.'" If the gospel of Matthew originated in Syria and *T. Levi* has the same provenance, a connection might not be inconceivable.[120] The *Ascension of Isaiah* comes from Syria and contains anti-Samaritan material, which will be dealt with in chapter 7.

The Dinah episode is briefly reported in *ALD* and *T. Levi* with emphasis in the latter on the heavenly origin of the vengeance and the continuing situation of Shechem because of the rape and the vengeance. The latter text shares the expression "fools" with Sir 50:25 f. and 4Q372, and shows strong affinity to the Dinah-texts of Theodotus and *Jubilees*.

5.9. *Judith*

The book of Judith employs Gen 34 in a short form as a basis for a prayer which reads as a homily in chapter 9. The rape of Dinah is given emphasis, and it is considered re-enacted on a grand scale in the form of a military assault on Jerusalem and the temple. Simeon is the model for Judith's effort.

Scholars are mostly agreed that Judith was written in Hebrew in Jerusalem in the second century B.C.E., most likely between 150 and 102

---

[120] Kee, "Testaments of the Twelve Patriarchs," *OTP* 1: 778.

B.C.E.[121] The story takes place in the phantom city Bethulia, which probably reflects *Bet 'eloah*, "the house of God," and is a cover name for Jerusalem. The whole book is concerned with the temple and Jerusalem, 8:21; 9:13; 10:8; 13:4 etc.[122] The geographical horizon includes names like "Judaea," "Carmel," "Gilead," "Galilee," "Jizreel," "Samaria," and so on, but also "Betane," "Kelus," and other phantom names. Jdt 4:4 gives a good example of the mixture of fact and fiction: "So they sent word to every district of Samaria, and to Kona, Beth-horon, Belmain, and Jericho, and to Choba and Aisora, and the valley of Salem."[123] There is also phantom history: Nebuchadnezzar is king over the Assyrians, even after the Israelites' return from exile and their rebuilding and rededication of the temple. The main idea in the book is to save Jerusalem and the temple from the enemy. Scholars agree that historical situations like Sennacherib's assault on Jerusalem, and others, have provided the author with material for the novel, and that women like Jael and Esther have acted as role models for the shaping of Judith. It seems that the book condenses different historical situations into one, and locates it in a geography of Palestine which is partly real and partly figurative of reality.[124]

The book can be understood as a novel modelled on Hellenistic novels of the period. The contents are shaped on the basis of figures from the HB, e.g. Jael, Esther, David, Eglon, and Abraham, but also figures like Antiochus IV Epiphanes and Nikanor from the second century B.C.E. The theology centres on fear of God and courage, and Judith provides an example of these virtues.[125] Her name means "Jewess," and she is a model for good Jewish behaviour.

According to most scholars, the main inspiration for the book came from the events preceding and leading up to the Maccabean revolt, and

---

[121] Text: R. Hanhart, *Iudith* (vol. VIII, 4 of Septuaginta: Vetus Testamentum Graecum; Göttingen: Vandenhoeck & Ruprecht, 1979); translation: B. Otzen, *Tobit and Judith* (Guides to Apocrypha and Pseudepigrapha; Sheffield: Sheffield Academic Press, 2002), 132–136; E. Zenger, "Das Buch Judit," *JSHRZ* 1: 429–522.

[122] Zenger, "Buch Judit," 1:435.

[123] For a different reading of this verse, cf. C. A. Moore, *Judith: A New Translation with Introduction and Commentary* (AB 40B; Garden City, N.Y.: Doubleday, 1985), 69: "In fact, in the book of Judith *all* the inhabitants of the territory of Samaria were good Jews, ready to block Holofernes' path to Jerusalem (4:4–8) and prompt to join in the rout of the Assyrian army (15:3–5) .... Bethulia was in *Samaritan* territory! The author has a quite open and friendly attitude toward the Samaritans (cf. 4:4,6)."

[124] According to J. Montgomery, G. Hölscher considered that Judith in its geographical data assumed Jewish control of Samaria in the late Persian period, cf. Montgomery, *The Samaritans*, 74.

[125] Zenger, "Buch Judit," *JSHRZ* 1: 435.436–439.

persons and events from this period loom large in the story and the *dramatis personae* of the book. This understanding of the book leads to two new questions: (1) Why is a woman the heroine, and not a man, like the Maccabees? (2) What message, if any, would the book have for its audience? If the events around Antiochus IV Epiphanes and the Maccabees preceded the formation of the book, then the possible message of the author must have been meant for a later audience. These questions seem not to have received the attention they deserve.

The answer to the first question might be that there is an ironical edge against all the males of the Maccabean revolt. L. Alonso Schökel has argued for irony in Judg 5, and it may be found also at this point.[126] E. Zenger suggests that Judith acted non-violently, and the book's slogan is taken from Exod 15:3 LXX: God is "the Lord who crushes wars," Jdt 9:7; 16:2. The MT of Exod 15:3 testifies to the opposite idea, that God is a "man of war." Judith twice quotes the anti-war version of Exod 15:3, but it seems to be an exaggeration to take this as a form of non-violence or pacifism. God crushes the enemies' wars against Jerusalem, not every war, and Judith is the vehicle for this action by cutting the enemy's head from his body—not very non-violent. From this perspective she carries on the work of the Maccabees, but from another perspective she is the reversal of the Maccabees by being a woman. Her performance against the enemy also terminates the danger, and this may have reminded the audience of the fact that the Maccabean revolt was not a war to end all wars. If there is irony at this point, it is directed against the Hasmoneans. What they as men could not achieve, a lone woman accomplished.

The second question might be addressed by studying chapter 9, the prayer of Judith. This prayer comes at the centre of the book and at the height of tension. The enemy has surrounded Bethulia, and the population and their leaders are desperate and on the verge of surrender. In comes Judith in chapter 8 and promises salvation—but on what grounds can a single person, a woman at that, bring salvation in a situation which is out of control for the military and political leaders? Still, the leaders are reluctantly willing to let her try, and now she carries the responsibility for the people's, the city's and the temple's destiny. Then she prays, and the prayer reveals her strategy and her historical basis for the daring enterprise.

---

[126] L. Alonso Schökel, *A Manual of Hebrew Poetics* (*SubBi* 11; Roma: Editrice Pontificio istituto biblico, 1988), 163.

Chapter 9 contains the prayer of Judith before she goes to confront the leader of the enemy, Holofernes, in order to lure him to his death. The prayer builds upon Gen 34 by referring to some basic events from the episode, vv. 2–4, then by giving a homily on the text, in the form of a brief theology of history, vv. 5–7, and in the form of an explanation of the lasting message from Gen 34, vv. 8–14. Jdt 9:2–4 reads:

> O Lord God of my ancestor Simeon, to whom you gave a sword to take revenge on those strangers who had torn off a virgin's clothing to defile her, and exposed her thighs to put her to shame, and polluted her womb to disgrace her; for you said, "It shall not be done"—yet they did it. So you gave up their rulers to be killed, and their bed, which was ashamed of the deceit they had practiced, was stained with blood, and you struck down slaves along with princes, and princes on their thrones. You gave up their wives for booty and their daughters to captivity, and all their booty to be divided among your beloved children who burned with zeal for you and abhorred the pollution of their blood and called on you for help. O God, my God, hear me also—a widow.

Judith is herself introduced in some manuscripts as a descendant from Simeon, 8:1, but this may be a harmonization with 9:2.[127] The rape is described in three different phrases, all in the plural against the singular of the MT, and the act is performed by "strangers," "people of another race," ἀλλογενεῖς. Reaction comes from Simeon alone, against the majority reading of Gen 34 in the second century B.C.E. which focuses on Levi. The Israelite response takes the form of "revenge," cf. the "vengeance" of *T. Levi* 5. The sentence "It shall not be done" is a rule against rape, and it is introduced as a word from God. In the original location in Gen 34:7 it is also a rule pertaining to the crime committed, but presented as an editorial comment and not a divine command. That God "gave up their rulers to be killed," recalls the "heavenly tablets" of *Jub.* 30 and the divine commission in *T. Levi* 5. Simeon's act is not expounded in what follows, as everything is the act of God. The transmission of the text varies in the case of "Their bed, which was ashamed of the deceit they had practiced, was stained with blood," reflecting the different possibilities: The author of Judith may have had the bed in mind where Dinah was raped, or the bed where the circumcised were healing from their wounds. In both cases the situation was the result of "deceit," either the "deceit" ending in rape, or the "deceit" with which the sons of Jacob spoke about circumcision

---

[127] The name "Simeon" is found in parts of the textual tradition; for details, cf. Zenger, "Buch Judit," 1:485.

to the Shechemites, Gen 34:13. This bed is now once again stained with blood, but this time shed by Simeon's sword. The description of the booty expands the HB enumeration: "the women" includes also the daughters. On the other hand, the animals are left out. "Your beloved children" is rephrased from Hos 11:1. As in several texts, the "zeal" is important in the interpretation of the killing. Finally, endogamous marriage is again in the background, as the rape was a "pollution of their blood." Judith cries to God for similar intervention in the initiative she is about to take.

This brief version of Gen 34 (1) emphasizes the act of rape; (2) describes the rape as an act performed by all inhabitants of the city; (3) centres on Simeon instead of Levi and Simeon plus the sons of Jacob; (4) does not name the city or its inhabitants, but says that they are "of another race"; (5) asserts that the rape violated a divine command; (6) says that vengeance was ordained in heaven; (7) describes the avengers as God's beloved; (8) mentions their zeal; and (9) reckons with endogamy. The character of the story is therefore more universal and the opposition is not between the sons of Jacob and the Shechemites, but between God and those "of another race."

The brief theology of history in vv. 5–6 centres on God's rule over events, "you have done these things and those that went before and those that followed," v. 5. The heavenly judgment on the "strangers" is indicative of God's general dominance over the world. The emphasis in *T. Levi* and *Jubilees* on the heavenly decision to judge the Shechemites is paralleled in Judith by a general theology of history.

The last part of the chapter, vv. 7–14, expounds more specifically the paradigmatic character of the rape, and of Simeon's revenge on the strangers. The contents are as follows. Against the strength of the Assyrian army Judith recalls that God is "the Lord who crushes wars," v. 7, a quotation from Exod 15:3 LXX. The enemies "intend to defile your sanctuary, and to pollute the tabernacle where your glorious name resides, and to break off the horns of your altar with the sword," v. 8. The sentence repeats terms from the description of the rape ("defile," v. 2: μίασμα, v. 8: μιᾶναι; "pollute," v. 2: ἐβεβήλωσαν, v. 8: βεβηλῶσαι) and creates an impression of the expected attack on Jerusalem and the temple as a "rape." V. 10.13 predict the "deceit," ἀπάτη, of a woman, just like the ἀπάτη entrapping the strangers in v. 3, thus building on the "deceit" of the sons of Jacob, Gen 34:13. Verses 11–14 extols God as the helper of the oppressed, v. 11, as creator, v. 12, as God of power and might, v. 14, as the only protector of Israel, v. 14. Inside this doxology, Judith prays that her "deceitful words [may] bring wound and bruise on those who have planned cruel things against your covenant, and against your sacred house, and against Mount Zion, and against the house your children possess," v. 13. The "wound and bruise" recalls the "pain" of the Shechemites, Gen 34:25. This part of the homily places the rape of Dinah and the attack on Jerusalem in parallel, and this gives Gen 34 a paradigmatic character for the book of Judith as a whole.

Several scholars have suggested that Judith is not the equivalent of Dinah, but of Simeon, and this seems to be the case for the act of revenge. But Judith is facing a sexual assault by an uncircumcised man, just like Dinah, but unlike her, she knows what lies ahead and she will herself kill the aggressor and thus she will bring salvation to her people, like Jael and Esther. Thus there are parallels to both Simeon and Dinah. But the paralleling of Shechem's act against Dinah and Holofernes' attack on Bethulia means that what happened long ago prefigures the present situation in violence and abuse.

Judith does approach the enemy in a situation reminiscent of that of Dinah. But at the critical moment, she enters into the role of Simeon. Thus the novel ironically twists the plot of Gen 34 into the opposite. Where Dinah goes out to see the daughters of the land, Judith goes out to meet the general. Where Dinah is seized and violated, Judith cunningly chooses the moment for seduction and lures the man into drinking too much. Where Dinah is shut up in the house of the enemy, Judith kills the enemy and breaks out with his head and returns by herself to her people. Only towards the end is there symmetry. Just as the sons of Jacob take booty, the people of Bethulia do the same. Thus the whole book may be seen partly as reviving the situation of Gen 34 and partly as an ironical twist on the chapter.

The author of the book of Judith must have had some contemporary danger, some present threat in mind. The novel may of course be of general interest as a summary of past events through the ages, but without a contemporary message the implicit exhortation to practice Judaism's central tenets would be loose and only of general interest. The novel would then be half entertaining, half a general appeal to practice Judaism. What could the threat be at a time when the Hasmoneans were on top of events?

The concentration on Jerusalem and the temple would be expected at almost any time in post-exilic Jerusalem, but there is one external danger in the Hasmonean age which is worth considering. 4Q371/4Q372 alleges that the "foolish ones" in the territory of Joseph speak against the temple on Zion. Could the fear that the enemy "intend to defile your sanctuary, and to pollute the tabernacle where your glorious name resides, and to break off the horns of your altar with the sword," v. 8, refer to contemporary animosity from the Samaritans against Jerusalem? The danger would come from Shechem once more. This understanding need not mean that the book of Judith as a whole is concerned with the Samaritans, but the prayer of Judith contains language from the past, and might have present dangers of different kinds in mind.

An anti-Samaritan touch is not unlikely in view of some other parts of the book of Judith. Judith's husband's name was Manasseh, 8,2, "who belonged to her tribe and family." If she carries a symbolic name, "Jewess," then he may do the same, "the tribe Manasseh," or it may even be connected to verbs meaning "to deceive" or "to forget." Her tribe and family is ultimately "Israel," 8:1; the honorary name is used, not "Jacob." The husband's name and genealogy tells that he, i.e. the tribe Manasseh, belonged to Israel. Manasseh died from sunstroke, 8:2, perhaps not an honourable death? The story of Manasseh's death resembles the story in 2 Kgs 4:18–20: "When the child was older, he went out one day to his father among the reapers. He complained to his father, 'Oh, my head, my head!' The father said to his servant, 'Carry him to his mother.' He carried him and brought him to his mother; the child sat on her lap until noon, and he died." If this is the story in the background, the death of Manasseh was rather trivial, and not to be compared to the heroes who died for God or the people, and also not to the risk run by Judith. Manasseh was buried in the western territory of the tribe of Manasseh, "between Dothan and Balamon," 8:3.[128] The point of Judith's marriage to Manasseh may be that the tribe of Manasseh had belonged to "Israel," but had died out, and is now buried on ancestral territory. Samaritans of the second century B.C.E. termed themselves "Israelites," but this is contested by Judith. The people residing in 'Bethulia,' that is Jerusalem, is 'Israel,' and what belonged to 'Israel' in the north, is dead and buried.

A further indication of an anti-Samaritan attitude is provided by the enumeration of the peoples that the Israelites were to dispossess of their land. "They drove out before them the Canaanites, the Perizzites, the Jebusites, the Shechemites, and all the Gergesites, and lived there a long time," Jdt 5:16. This list of peoples contains traditional names from the

---

[128] G. Schmitt and S. Mittmann, *Tübinger Bibelatlas auf der Grundlage des Tübinger Atlas des Vorderen Orients (TAVO)* (Stuttgart: Deutsche Bibelgesellschaft, 2002), map B V 16.2.

HB, but it includes also τὸν Συχεμ, which is not to be found in any of the HB lists of peoples to be driven out from the land by Israel. Why, then, does "Shechem" appear here? Considering the possibilities the author had for finding an extra name, the choice of this name is conspicuous.

The area where the book of Judith locates the story is described with a mix of real and fictional names, giving the events a real-surreal atmosphere. Many of the known names are located in Samaria, and it seems that the battle of Bethulia takes place there. At the same time, the attack is defined as "intend[ing] to defile your sanctuary, and to pollute the tabernacle where your glorious name resides, and to break off the horns of your altar with the sword," Jdt 9:8. The attack seems to be directed against Jerusalem and the temple there, as v. 13 confirms, "against your sacred house, and against Mount Zion, and against the house your children possess." Accordingly, the battle is about Jerusalem, even though the phantom city Bethulia is located near Dothan, Jdt 7:3, in the northern part of Samaria.

This blend of real and fictional geography might be a literary technique for creating a novel, but as the area is not fictional, the story creates associations with the northern territory. At the time of the book of Judith, this territory was inhabited by the Samaritans, and their *bet 'eloah* was Mount Gerizim. By locating Bethulia further north, the author of Judith bypassed the sacred mountain, and thereby sidestepped it. But Shechem is there in the story, as the place for the attack on Dinah, and for the heroic act of Simeon, and as a place to be dispossessed by the invading Israelites.

The author of the book of Judith does not have "a quite open and friendly attitude toward the Samaritans," but considers them dangerous for Jerusalem and the temple.[129] Judaism did not only experience the dangers of hellenization, but of a Yahwistic cult close by.

5.10. Joseph and Aseneth

The story in *Joseph and Aseneth* 23:1–15 takes place after the Dinah episode, and exaggerates the act of Simeon and Levi.

---

[129] Moore, *Judith*, 69.

Joseph and Aseneth was written in Alexandria in Greek, some time between 200 B.C.E. and 200 C.E.[130] It belongs to the literature occupied with endogamous marriage, and in this booklet the case of Joseph is addressed. As he marries an Egyptian woman, and even the daughter of a heathen priest, this creates a problem for Jewish theologians advocating endogamy. The problem is here solved in that Aseneth converts to Judaism after a week of fasting and praying, and then Joseph marries her. A different solution was chosen by *Jub.* 40:10 (see above).

The book deals with the Dinah episode after Joseph has married Aseneth and when the son of Pharaoh sees Aseneth and becomes sick, wanting to have her. He says "thus it shall not be," inverting the idea in Gen 34:7 LXX, which refers to the rape, into a sentence directed at Aseneth's marriage to Joseph. He plans to kill Joseph and marry Aseneth, and in this plot he tries to drag in Simeon and Levi:

> I know today that you are powerful men beyond all men on the earth, and by these right (hands) of yours the city of the Shechemites has been overthrown, and by these two swords of yours thirty thousand fighting men were cut down. And behold, today I will take you as companions for myself, and give you plenty of gold and silver, and servants and maids and houses and big (estates as) inheritance. Only do this thing and show mercy on me, for I have been insulted very much by your brother Joseph, for he himself took Aseneth, my (envisaged) wife who was betrothed to me from the beginning. And now, come assist me, and we will make war on Joseph your brother, and I will kill him with my sword, and have Aseneth for (my) wife, and you will be to me brothers and faithful friends.[131]   (23:3–5)

The speech by the son of Pharaoh employs many of the ideas from Gen 34, in addition to referring to the story with exaggerated emphasis on the work of Simeon and Levi. He will reward them with "gold and silver, and servants and maids and houses and big (estates)," corresponding to the spoil which the sons of Jacob took from Shechem, Gen 34:27–29. Further, he will make them into "companions," "brothers and faithful friends," and this resembles the idea of the sons of Jacob and of Hamor to become "one people," Gen 34:16.22, and the idea of Hamor and Shechem to share land and cattle with the sons of Jacob, Gen 34:10.21.23. In Gen 34, the spoil is a result of the attack on the city, and the companionship is envisaged as a result of the circumcision and compliance with the demand of the

---

[130] C. Burchard, "Joseph and Aseneth (First Century B.C.-Second Century A.D.)," *OTP* 2: 187 f.

[131] Translation here and in the following, C. Burchard, "Joseph and Aseneth," 2:239 f.

sons of Jacob. The son of Pharaoh transforms these two ideas into an idea of reward for being hired killers of Joseph. Paralleling the insult offered by Shechem to Dinah and her father and brothers and the insult of the notion of giving Dinah to an uncircumcised man, Gen 34:7.14, the son of Pharaoh is insulted by Joseph's having married the woman he had desired for his wife, Aseneth. The object of the insult is not Israel, but the Egyptian. The author of Joseph and Aseneth thus creates a speech in the mouth of the son of Pharaoh from motifs in Gen 34 and twists them in such a way to become a parody on the original. The son of Pharaoh emerges as a comic figure, but with evil intent.

In the continuation of the story, Simeon is enraged and wants to kill the son of Pharaoh immediately, but Levi calms him and takes the initiative, "We are men who worship God, and it does not befit us to repay evil for evil," 23:9. Even so,

> Simeon and Levi drew their swords from their sheaths and said, "Behold, have you seen these swords? With these two swords the Lord God punished the insult of the Shechemites (by) which they insulted the sons of Israel, because of our sister Dinah whom Shechem the son of Hamor had defiled." And the son of Pharaoh saw their swords drawn and was exceedingly afraid and trembled over his whole body, because their swords were flashing forth (something) like a flame of fire, and he eyes of Pharaoh's son darkened and he fell on his face on the ground beneath their feet.
>
> (23:14–15)

That the punishment of Shechem was from God, is an idea in *Jub.* 30, *T. Levi* 5, and Jdt 9, and the focus on the swords is also found in Jdt 9. The flashing sword reminds one of the להט החרב המתהפכת, the "sword flaming and turning" of Gen 3:24. Simeon and Levi are able to produce swords like those of the Cherubim barring the entrance to the garden of Eden, and similar heavenly weapons were used in Shechem and threaten the son of Pharaoh.

Joseph and Aseneth thus enlarges the figures of Simeon and Levi by having them kill "thirty thousand fighting men," 23:3, and by providing them with heavenly swords like those of the Cherubim. Simeon is portrayed as the "daring and bold man," v. 7, and Levi as "a prophet ... sharp-sighted with his mind and his eyes," v. 8. The son of Pharaoh looks like a wicked fool with his twisted rendering of motifs from Gen 34, and falls on his face before Simeon and Levi.

The attack is planned against Joseph, and we are thus dealing with the eponymous ancestor of the territory around Shechem, Gen 48:21 f., where the "plot of ground that Jacob had given to his son Joseph" was located, Joh 4:5; we are in the land of Joseph, 4Q371/372. It is difficult, however, to see the figure of Joseph as a transparent symbol for the territory of Samaria or for Shechem. Joseph and Aseneth seems to be operating with the characters of a novel, and is not a figurative text for the Jerusalem-Shechem conflict. The message of the book seems to lie in virtues to be emulated by the Jews of Alexandria.

The reuse of Gen 34 displays motifs to be seen in much of the relevant literature from the second century B.C.E., but it presents them in a more developed or more general form. They evolved from the exegetical tradition of the chapter, as it was developed in an anti-Samaritan way, but uses it against the Egyptian fool, the son of Pharaoh, and not against the Samaritans.

5.11. *Philo*

The most extensive use of Gen 34 by Philo is found in *De migratione Abrahami* 1:224, where he exploits the Hebrew meanings of the names.[132] "Shechem" means "shoulder," which in turn is a "symbol of labour," 1:221. "Hamor" means "ass," which in turn stands for "an irrational being." "Dinah" means "judgment," corresponding to "the soul's court of justice," 1:223. "Israel" is several times presupposed to refer to a man who can behold God, 1:39.54.113, evidently because the name resembles the word ראה, and ends with אל. This "etymology" is *inter alia* substantiated by the story of the "seventy of the elders of Israel" who were to ascend the mountain, Ex 24:1. "And the meaning of this injunction is as follows, 'Go up, O soul, to the view of the living God.'"

The story about Abraham's journey to Shechem in Gen 12 is by these re-interpretations and many others explained as referring to the attaining of wisdom for the soul, against the constrictions of nature and irrationality.

> For the man who bears the name of this place, Shechem, being the son of Hamor, of an irrational being (for "Hamor" means "ass") practicing folly and being bred up with shamelessness and impudence, infamous man that he was, attempted to pollute and to defile the judicial faculties of the mind. But the hearers and pupils of sound sense, Simeon and Levi, were too quick. They made secure their own dwellings, and went forth

---

[132] F. H. Colson and G. H. Whitaker, *De migratione Abrahami* in *Philo* (vol. 4; LCL vol. 261; Cambridge, Mass.: Harvard University Press, 1968), 123–269.

against them in safety, and destroyed them while they were still involved in pleasure-loving, in indulgence of the passions, and in the labour of the uncircumcised. For though there was a divine decree that, "There shall never be a prostitute among the daughters of the seer, Israel," these men hoped to carry off unobserved the virgin soul. (*Migr.* 1:224)

Philo stays close to the text of the LXX, but changes the meaning or the context of the phrases:

	LXX	*Migr.* 1:224
διανοία	v. 3, (Shechem spoke to the) "heart" (of Dinah)	"mind," "understanding"
μιαίνω	v. 5, "pollute" (Dinah)	"pollute" (the understanding)
ἀσφαλῶς	v. 25, (Levi and Simeon entered Shechem) "safely"	Used twice: (Simeon and Levi made) "secure" (their dwellings, and went out) "safely"
πόνος	"pain"	"toil," "labour"

Shechem "attempted to pollute and to defile the judicial faculties of the mind," and did not really pollute them, contrary to Gen 34, which several times states that he polluted Dinah.

The "folly" in Gen 34:7, ἄσχημον, is not used by Philo, where "folly" is ἀφροσύνη. The emphasis on the folly, shamelessness and audacity of Shechem, resembles the emphasis on the wickedness of the Shechemites in Theodotus, *T. Levi*.

The motifs exploited are all set in the service of Philo's overall purpose, which is philosophical discussion of wisdom, folly, virtues etc. One notices, however, the very negative view of Shechem and Hamor, the virginity of Dinah, the quality of Israel, Simeon and Levi, and the justification of the victory of virtue over vice. This general reading of Gen 34 is the prerequisite for Philo's perusal of the story for his purposes. Compared to the material reviewed in this chapter, Philo does not change the general attitude towards the *dramatis personae*. Even though Philo does not attack the contemporary inhabitants of the city directly, he sets up a scenario which would not protect the Shechemites, but make them vulnerable. This negative picture of Shechem and Hamor and the positive image of Dinah and the sons of Jacob is also found in Philo's *De mutatione nominum* 193–200, and *De legum allegoria* 3:23–26. A slightly more positive portrayal of Shechem is found in *Quod deterius potiori insidiari soleat*

9, where "Shechem means 'shoulder' and is the symbol of patient striving." In the other three texts, however, Philo exploits the names "Hamor" and "Shechem" in purely negative categories.[133]

In *De mutatione nominum* 200 Philo explains why Jacob in Gen 49 treats Simeon and Levi in one unit: "because their minds are in concord and harmony and their purpose set in one and the same direction," and why Moses in Deut 33 only mentions Levi: "blending the two natures he makes them one, bearing the stamp of a single form, and unites hearing with action."[134] His etymology of the names provides him with the linguistic material for his philosophy. At the same time, he witnesses to the speculations going on in antiquity around the blessings in Gen 49 and Deut 33 and their relation to Gen 34.

5.12. *Pseudo-Philo*

The pseudonymous work *Liber Antiquitatum Biblicarum* 8:7 f. retells Gen 34 briefly without any bias, closely resembling Demetrius.[135] In 21:7 f.; 22:8 f. Joshua's efforts are located in Shilo, in Gilgal, and on Ebal, much as LXX replaces Shechem with Shiloh in Josh 24. *LAB* 25:10–12; 26:2–4 mentions artefacts of sin buried under Mount Gerizim and destroyed on its summit. Taken together these texts testify to a negative attitude to Samaritan places, and the short version of Gen 34 provides the ideological basis for this attitude, even though 8:7 f. is restrained and terse. Also *LAB* testifies to the anti-Shechemite reading of Gen 34.

5.13. *Genesis 34 in the Samaritan Pentateuch*[136]

The Samaritan version of Gen 34 is here considered after the apocryphal, Qumranic and pseudepigraphical texts which reflect this text because it is

---

[133] For a more detailed discussion, cf. Feldman, *"Remember Amalek!"* 149–155.

[134] F. H. Colson and G. H. Whitaker, *De mutatione nominum* in *Philo* (vol. 5; LCL vol. 275; Cambridge, Mass.: Harvard University Press, 1968), 128–281.

[135] C. Dietzfelbinger, "Pseudo-Philo: Antiquitates Biblicae," *JSHRZ* 2: 91–271.

[136] In the following, the readings used are from A. Tal's edition of ms. 6 from the Samaritan synagogue in Nablus, A. Tal, *The Samaritan Pentateuch Edited According to Ms 6 (C) of the Shekhem Synagogue* (Texts and Studies in the Hebrew Language and Related Subjects; Tel Aviv: The Chaim Rosenberg School for Jewish Studies / Tel Aviv University, 1994).

assumed that the form of SP as we know it from for example manuscript 6 from the Samaritan synagogue in Nablus is later than these texts. One may therefore look for traces of the exegetical tradition in the SP, either in the form of reception or rejection of this tradition. Surprisingly, these are not found; Gen 34 is not much different in the SP from the MT.[137] Most of the differences are of a nature known from the SP in general. The SP does not defend the Shechemites, but keeps the chapter's slant against the Hivite population, displays a pro-Simeon-and-Levi attitude, and does not twist it into something which would be based on a defence against attacks. It does this in an unexpected way, as we shall see.

First, there are a few differences of a linguistic nature in the SP: נערה is spelt with an ה at the end three times, vv. 3.12, against the Kethib of MT; the Masoretic cohortative is written as a regular imperfect: ואתן, v. 12, and נאות, v. 23; the *nota accusativi* is added in v. 14 before הדבר; instead of וישבו in v. 21 SP has ישבו, which perhaps reflects the transition from imperfect consecutive to perfect in later Hebrew, but not a difference in meaning. All cases are typical of the SP, and do not imply any differences in sense. They are due to linguistic change or dialectical differences.[138] The omission of כל before טפם in v. 29 could be deliberate or accidental; perhaps the scribes missed the second כל or felt that one was enough for the whole sentence—we can only guess. Similarly, the difference in v. 21 between רחבות ידים, SP, and רחבת ידים, MT, might be a variant without significance.

The same applies to the variation in laryngeals: SP: להראת, MT: לראת, v. 1; SP: וחריש, MT: והחרש, v. 5; SP: ואחזו, MT: והאחזו, v. 10. The different spellings in SP might imply differences in meaning, but often they do not, because the laryngeals were not pronounced. Thus, in v. 1, Dinah might go out to show herself (Hiphil) or be seen (Niphal), according to the SP. Similarly, there may be two Hiphils in MT where the SP has two Qal's, vv. 5.10. But this is uncertain.

The sequence of words is reversed in v. 12: SP: מהר מאד, MT: מאד מהר, so SP puts the emphasis slightly differently, "make a very high dowry and a gift." In the case of the phrase "become one people," vv. 16.22, SP displays the same text as LXX. V. 16 says "become like one people," כעם,

---

[137] Schorch, *Vokale des Gesetzes*, 192–194, discusses only 11 cases, all secondary in relation to MT.

[138] Cf. the grammars, Z. Ben-Hayyim, *A Grammar of Samaritan Hebrew* (Jerusalem: Magnes, 2000), and R. Macuch, *Grammatik des samaritanischen Hebräisch* (Studia Samaritana 1; Berlin: de Gruyter, 1969).

and v. 22 "become one people," לעם. There may also be a similar nuance in meaning, where Hamor is portrayed negatively by having him transmit the condition of co-existence incorrectly.

The change from singular טמא in MT to the plural טמאו in the SP, v. 13, may be taken to mean that according to the SP all the Shechemites were responsible for the rape or participated in it, in line with the tendency in some of the texts treated above. On the other hand, in v. 27 the same verb has the plural in the MT, and the plural in v. 13 of the SP might therefore be a harmonization with v. 27.

More important is the absence of "Hamor" in the SP, vv. 4.18. In the latter verse, SP reads "his son" instead of "Hamor's son." One may speculate that the use of a name with a pejorative meaning, "donkey," is avoided in these two places. It is present in all the other cases where MT has it, so the SP does not change the general picture, but only retouches it.

A substantial difference is to be found in the last verse.

MT: הכזונה יעשׂה את־אחותנו, "should our sister be treated like a prostitute?"

SP: הך זונה יעשׂו את־אחותנו, "See, they have made our sister into a prostitute."

In both texts, this is the justification for the violent action taken by Simeon and Levi, and it is strengthened in the SP. Those responsible are here put in the plural, in line with the plural of MT in v. 27 and the plural of SP in vv. 13.27, and the Aramaic particle הך—with the same consonants as MT—adds emphasis. A third element in the SP version here is the imperfect יעשׂו, implying that Dinah has been turned into a prostitute, which is stronger than saying, "Should our sister be treated like a whore?" In this last sentence of the chapter SP sides with Simeon and Levi against Shechem and Hamor, which shows which side of the conflict the Samaritans sympathized with.

The use of the Aramaic particle here shows the later date of SP. If the change from imperfect consecutive to perfect in v. 21 reflects a similar late tendency, we have traces of the relative lateness of SP in this chapter.

This stronger justification for the killing of the Shechemites in SP resonates in Gen 49 of the SP. The author of this chapter seems to have Gen 34 in mind when Simeon and Levi are called brothers, v. 5, and are treated together and not separately, as are the other brothers or tribes. "Instruments of cruelty *are in* their habitations," according to KJV, or "weapons of violence are their swords," NRSV. I will comment upon the difference between "habitations" and "swords" in a moment, but first we notice that both translations reflect the כלי חמס of the MT. The SP

instead reads כלו חמס in the context of šĕ'mūn wlibi 'ā'əm kallu âməs
makrētiyimma,[139] "Simeon and Levi are brothers; they have completed
violence," a reading shared by LXX, reflecting an understanding in line
with Gen 34:31 in all versions. Simeon and Levi were justified in their
action, and they wreaked complete retribution upon the Shechemites.
S. Schorch understands the verb כלו as "sie beendeten," "they put an end
to," which would fit the context as well. In both understandings the act of
Simeon and Levi is condoned.

This approval of the action is confirmed in v. 7, where the MT pronounces a curse upon the wrath of the brothers, ארור אפם. Here, the SP
has אדיר אפם, âdər abbimma kī' az,[140] "glorious is their wrath because it
is so strong / glorious is their strong wrath." In the square script, the waw
and yod may have been misread for each other, but hardly in the palaeo-
Hebrew script. The dalet and resh are more liable to confusion in both
scripts. This means that the variant in v. 5 is a real textual variation, but
in v. 7 the difference may have been the result of a confusion of dalet and
resh and a concomitant adjustment of the mater according to the contemporary understanding. This two-step development is, however, not
likely, and the SP may therefore contain a real variant to the MT also in
v. 7. If the SP contains the original text, the change may have taken place
in the tradition leading up to the Masoretic vocalization, which saw it
necessary to condemn the action by the brothers.

Schorch discusses this paragraph and translates Gen 49:5 "ihre Bun-
desschlüsse (מכרתיהם) beendeten Gewalt."[141] This understanding of
מכרתיהם as an elliptical expression for "their making [of a covenant]"
needs to be further substantiated from linguistic evidence. More likely
is the understanding "swords," from a Greek loan-word, μάχαιρα. The
translation in NRSV reflects this understanding.[142] The understanding
in SP would then be "Simeon and Levi are brothers; they completed (or:
put an end to) violence by their swords."

Another difference is found in the SP's reading יחר, resulting in "[be
not] angry [because of their assembly, my soul]," against MT's תחד, "[do
not] be united [in their assembly, my soul]," v. 6. Again, the SP seems to
condone the violence of Simeon and Levi.

---

[139] Z. Ben-Hayyim, Recitation of the Law (vol. 3/1 of The Literary and Oral Tradition
of Hebrew and Aramaic Amongst the Samaritans; The Academy of the Hebrew Language
Studies; Jerusalem: The Academy of the Hebrew Language, 1961) 33.
[140] Ibid.
[141] Schorch, Vokale des Gesetzes, 224–226.
[142] Kugel, "Story of Dinah," 6.

By these three different readings we have a different understanding of
the brothers' action against the Shechemites in Gen 49:5–7 SP. They were
justified in their action, and are even praised for it. S. Schorch sums up
the situation well:

> It is easily recognizable that the tendency of the Masoretic tradition stands
> in complete contradiction to the Samaritan tradition. While the former
> condemns Simeon and Levi severely, they appear in an extremely positive
> light in the latter. While, accordingly, the scattering of the Simeonites
> appears as a punishment in the Masoretic tradition (v. 7), it is evidently
> understood positively in the Samaritan tradition, with regard to the supra-
> tribal priestly service [translation mine].[143]

(The scattering pertains to both tribes, and this has the effect that Levi
may serve all the others.) S. Schorch considers this reading more original
than the MT here.[144] The Samaritan reading in Gen 49:5–7 means that the
SP identifies with the brothers against the Shechemites. They dissociate
themselves from the original Hivite population of the place, and identify
with Israel. The polemical readings of Gen 34 may linger on in the memory at the time when the finer nuances of the SP were introduced into the
text, and if so, they took care to side with the Israelite understanding of
the pericope: a pure people with no intermarriage. This accords well with
their oldest self-designation as "Israelites" in the Delos inscriptions. If the
Samaritans felt the weight of the polemics from the second century B.C.E.
when the SP was developed, the strategy was one of identifying with the
Jewish heroes and thereby drawing the sting of the polemics.

The third text relevant for this topic is Deut 33. MT here omits Simeon
altogether from the blessing, but devotes a longer passage to Levi. This
tribe is treated as the priestly tribe, and praised for the unbiased practice
and application of the law. This is the same in the SP; only philological
differences of a kind similar to those mentioned in connection with Gen
34 occur.

---

[143] "So wird leicht sichtbar, daß die Tendenz der masoretischen Überlieferung diejenige
der samaritanischen Tradition geradezu kontradiktorisch gegenübersteht. Während die
erstere Simeon und Levi hart verurteilt, erscheinen dieselben nach der samaritanischen
in äußerst positivem Licht. Während demzufolge die Zerstreuung der Simeoniten im
masoretischen Text als Strafe erscheint (V. 7), wird sie in der samaritanischen Tradition
offenkundig positiv im Hinblick auf den supertribalen Priesterdienst gedeutet," Schorch,
Vokale des Gesetzes, 226.

[144] Ibid., 227.

5.14. *Conclusions*

Gen 34 resonates in a number of texts from the third and second centuries B.C.E., some of which were written in Alexandria and some in Jerusalem, perhaps also one that was created in Syria. The amount of material shows that the rape of Dinah and the killing of the Shechemites had developed into a topos of contemporary ideology. In the texts the story is used for different purposes, but the understanding is much the same. Not all texts are directly polemical against the inhabitants of the northern region of their day, but Shechem is viewed negatively in all of them, and the Northerners would probably feel the weight of the legacy from Shechem and Hamor. Just as Josephus did, these texts brand the contemporary Shechemites with the acts committed by the Shechemites of Gen 34. What appears to be a re-telling of the old story is directed at the contemporary inhabitants of the city.

Gen 34 is ambiguous in the portrayal of Shechem and Hamor; the rape was a serious infringement on divine justice, but the intention was marriage, and this is followed up by sincere proposals and a willingness to meet the demand of the sons of Jacob. The chapter is also ambiguous in the portrayal of Simeon and Levi; they acted appropriately because of the sin committed, but exaggerated their revenge and were criticized for this by their father. In the *Wirkungsgeschichte* of this text the ambiguity in both respects is absent. Shechem and Hamor are portrayed negatively only, and other sins are added to the rape. Simeon and Levi are converted into heroes, and Levi in particular receives high honours, the priesthood, in reward for his violent act against the Shechemites (*Jubilees*, *T. Levi*).

Apart from the testimony of Josephus, later by two centuries, Ben Sira and *T. Levi* provide literary evidence for a settlement of the northern area, but *4QNarrative and Poetic Composition*[a-c] is new evidence for the same. Sir 50:25 f., and *T. Levi*, state that Shechem was populated; *4QNarrative and Poetic Composition*[a-c] confirms that there was a sanctuary on a "high mountain," Mount Gerizim. The evidence for a temple on Mount Gerizim has traditionally been 2 Macc 6:2 and Josephus, but now this 4Q-text confirms this. No name is provided for these inhabitants except "Shechemites," or "men of Shechem." "Samaritans" do not occur; "Israelites" and "Joseph" do not occur.

The most direct text is *4QNarrative and Poetic Composition*[a-c] with its picture of the north completely emptied of "Joseph" and presently inhabited by "fools." These "fools" have created a sanctuary on a high mountain, which is a blasphemy against Zion and her temple. Zion thus serves as an identity marker for the author of this text. The following prayer requests God to destroy these "fools." The text shares the expression "fools" with Sir 50:25 f. and *T. Levi* 7, two texts which also express negative sentiments against these "fools," and connect them to Shechem. All three texts seem to exploit a combination of Gen 34 and Deut 32 for the understanding of the Shechemites as "fools."

These three texts are the most direct in the request to God that he should annihilate the Shechemites. This is expressed by a combination of the Hebrew text of Sir 50:24 with vv. 25 f., and the implication of the author's hatred is some sort of action. *4QNarrative and Poetic Composition*[a-c] prays for such annihilation, and *T. Levi* 7 opens the way for action by stating that the city is "a city of fools" for ever.

The motivations for Simeon's and Levi's revenge vary. Demetrius' brief statement that Dinah was defiled is repeated in the other texts with various expressions, and other sins added. Theodotus mentions violation of justice and hostility to foreigners, *T. Levi* 6:8–7:1 the attempts to violate Sarah and Rebekah plus pregnant animals, and hostility to Abraham when he was a stranger. Philo mentions "shamelessness and impudence … pleasure-loving, indulgence of passions and the labour of the uncircumcised." In addition to the sins of Shechem, Theodotus and *T. Levi* also add the promise of land to Abraham. *Jubilees*, *T. Levi* and Judith make the whole city responsible for the rape. The revenge is, if considered more profoundly, ordained in heaven, according to Theodotus, Jdt 9:2; *Jub.* 30:6–7; *T. Levi* 5:1–5; 6:8.11; *Joseph and Aseneth*. Related to this idea is the zeal for God, which is found in Theodotus, Ben Sira, and *T. Levi*.

Scholars have noticed that circumcision is not mentioned in some of the texts, e.g. Josephus. This need not be interpreted as a conscious suppression of this element, but it is connected to the general interests of the text in question. Demetrius, Theodotus and *Jubilees* are concerned with marriage, and argue against exogamous marriages. The impediment to a marriage between Shechem and Dinah is first of all Shechem's lack of circumcision, as circumcision is required for an endogamous marriage. The expression used for the Shechemites, that they were "foreigners," found in Josephus, *Jubilees* and Judith is related to the question of marriage, although circumcision is not directly attached to this phrase.

Judith and *Joseph and Aseneth* are interested in the revenge of Simeon and Levi, and shape the story according to this interest. Judith constitutes a case on its own by describing the rape of Dinah in a way that opens up a paradigmatic reading of this event, prefiguring military attacks on Jerusalem and the temple. A military assault is an attempt at polluting and profaning city and temple. A concern for the temple in Jerusalem is shared by *4QNarrative and Poetic Composition*^*a-c* and *Jubilees*. These may also have a shared provenance in the group giving rise to the Qumran community.

Any one of these texts might have served as the ideological basis for the destruction of Shechem by John Hyrcanus. Such a function is claimed by J. J. Collins for the poem by Theodotus, an idea which is fully justified with regard to the text's multiple motivations for the act of Simeon and Levi.

Amid all the accusations against the Shechemites and the motivations for Simeon and Levi we do not find any accusation of idolatry or syncretism, nor of a canon consisting of the Torah only or a Torah with an unauthorized text. This is important in view of the allegations in this respect often made by scholars and others. The Samaritans in Delos term themselves "Israelites" and in the Gerizim inscriptions they worship Yahweh alone. Indirectly, this is confirmed by these texts: there is no specific name for the northerners—"Israel" or "Joseph" were too controversial to be mentioned and "Samaritans" was not yet applied to them—and there is no hint of idolatry or syncretism. Instead, the population is regarded as suspect because they had a dubious origin as descendants of the Hivites. This is implied in the continual use of Gen 34, and in particularly by the expression "fools."

Sometimes we may read that there would have been better reason to fear the gentiles or the Hellenizers inside Judaism than the Shechemites. In other words, the criticism levelled against Shechem seems in hindsight unjustified. But polemics often are most fierce against those who are closest. Considering the topic of intermarriage, this may have been very important in Jerusalem at this time; it constituted an identity marker. Marriage with the northerners had been practised before, and if they constituted a conservative element in the population, they may have seemed a likely party for marriage. Consequently, the attack was levelled where danger was most imminent. Gen 34 provided an excellent starting point for the topic of endogamous marriage, it was found in the canon common to south and north and addressed the important topic.

From early interpretation of Gen 34 in the LXX the *Wirkungsgeschichte* of this text became more and more anti-Samaritan in the course of the second century B.C.E. Demetrius is concerned with the endogamous aspects of the text, and this justifies the killing of Hamor and Shechem. On the basis of Gen 34 and Deut 32 Sir 50:25 f. introduces the expression "fools" for the inhabitants of Shechem, and this description is taken over by two later texts. The fragments of Theodotus' hexameter poem preserved by Eusebius concentrate on the patriarch Jacob and his endogamous marriages and the promise to Abraham of land on the condition that he practises circumcision. Alexander Polyhistor's introduction to the fragments of the poem reflects more directly Gen 34 and the land promise. Together with the other texts, they constitute a repository of anti-Shechem motifs that are not in the MT.

Indirectly, they witness to the existence of the Samaritans in and around Shechem with a sanctuary on Mount Gerizim. Jerusalem is concerned with the effect of this community on proper Jews, prohibits intermarriage with them, and prays for their annihilation.

Most of these texts from the second century B.C.E., and a few from the Roman period, employ Gen 34 and Deut 32 as material for anti-Samaritan polemics. This attitude was carried on by Josephus. Thus, there is a continuous flow of anti-Samaritan sentiments from before 200 B.C.E. until 100 C.E. Is it possible to find material from the same period that probably has a Samaritan provenance? Can we still hear a Samaritan voice amid these numerous accusations? The next two chapters will deal with this question, because there is now extant B.C.E. material from the Samaritans. What does it tell us?

CHAPTER SIX

SAMARITAN INSCRIPTIONS AND RELATED TEXTS

Early Samaritan material remains have been few and far between, derived mainly from archaeological excavations. Until recently, there have not been any Samaritan texts available from the Persian and Hellenistic periods, but two finds from the last two decades have changed this. Two inscriptions from the island of Delos in the Aegean Sea were found in 1979, and 395 Hebrew, Aramaic, and Samaritan inscriptions have come to light during the excavations on Mount Gerizim. In light of this new material, two texts known for some time have to be reconsidered, the so-called Pseudo-Eupolemus and Masada fragment 10. What kind of picture emerges from this new material, and what help will it provide for understanding Pseudo-Eupolemus and Masada fragment 10? A brief review of archaeological excavations will serve as an introduction to the material.

6.1. *Excavations*

A number of places related to the Samaritans have been excavated in the area around ancient Shechem. As our concern is with the origin of the Samaritans, the main sites of interest are Mount Gerizim (Arabic: *Jabal at-Tur*, map reference 175.178), *Tell er-Ras* (map reference 176.179), and Shechem (Arabic: *Tell Balatah*, map reference 176.179).

Shechem / Tell Balatah

Tell Balatah was excavated by an Austro-German team, mostly led by E. Sellin, in 1913–1914 and 1926–1933, and by the Drew-McCormick expedition under G. E. Wright during most of the years 1956–1973. Many of the records from the Austro-German excavation were destroyed by American fire-bombing of Berlin in 1943, and the Drew-McCormick expedition is only in recent years publishing reports, in memory of Wright, who died in 1974. His book, published in 1965, is the most comprehensive contribution to the subject from his hand.[1]

---

[1] Wright, *Shechem*, esp. ch. 10, "The Samaritans at Shechem," 170–184.

Since the publication of G. E. Wright's book theories about the origin of the Samaritans have often centred on the rebuilding of Shechem, around 331 B.C.E., and its destruction in 107 B.C.E. Wright found that the city had been unoccupied throughout most of the Persian period of the fifth and fourth centuries B.C.E., but that a great number of people had lived there during the third and second centuries B.C.E. The layers from the Hellenistic period could be dated by the help of pottery and coinage, resulting in the following stratification:

Stratum IV B and A	331 B.C.E.–ca. 250 B.C.E.
Stratum III B and A	ca. 250 B.C.E.–190 B.C.E.
Stratum II	ca. 190–150 B.C.E.
Stratum I	ca. 150–107 B.C.E.

The precise dates of beginning and end depend upon literary evidence, Josephus, Quintus Curtius, Eusebius, Jerome and Syncellus, combined with the papyri from Wadi Daliyeh. Wright accepts Josephus' account of the founding of the temple by permission of Alexander the Great, and the mention by Curtius of the burning to death of Andromachus in Samaria. The Samaritans were forced to establish a new capital, and the logical place was old Shechem. "This explains why so large a building program, the creation literally of a new city, was carried out in a comparatively brief period."[2]

Strata II and I are not well attested, as the surface layers have been destroyed by cultivation, and there is no evidence of a destruction of the city. Still, Wright thinks the end of the city "was evidently brought about by the Jews from Jerusalem … John Hyrcanus … in 128 B.C. … destroyed the Samaritan temple on Mt. Gerizim, and in 107 B.C. he campaigned successfully against Samaria. The final destruction of Shechem and the covering over of Wall A in the west and of the ruins of the Northwest Gate were probably his work at about the same time."[3]

E. F. Campbell, Jr., a member of the Drew-McCormick team 1957–1968, edited and wrote much of the official excavation reports of 1991 and 2002.[4] He laments the lack of publications at an earlier stage, while the leaders of the excavations were still alive, but sums up what can be said on the basis of the available material.

---

[2] Ibid., 181.
[3] Ibid., 183 f.
[4] Campbell, Jr., *Shechem II*; idem, *Shechem III*.

The stratification of Wright is repeated in this volume, except that the beginning of the Hellenistic period is given as 325 instead of 331. Campbell adds much detail on the excavations, and comments on some "Doubtful Speculations" by Wright. Among these is the question of soil outside Wall A, attributed by Wright to the destruction by John Hyrcanus. However, the investigation of these remains was imperfect, and "… the proposal that Hyrcanus was responsible must remain a conjecture."[5] Thus, we have very few remains from the last phase of occupation, and essentially no evidence for a destruction. Erosion, cultivation, and the employment of the site for graves and animal pens are among the phenomena that have affected the top layers of Tell Balatah.

Wright and Campbell correlate written records with their finds so that they mutually illuminate each other. This is not the ideal way to handle text and material remains, and their relationship to each other.[6] It is important to keep archaeological and literary studies apart. Archaeology and literary studies each have a different set of assumptions, which should be respected before a synthesis is attempted.

Tell er-Ras

Between 1964 and 1968 an excavation headed by R. J. Bull "located and excavated the probable site of the Samaritan sanctuary on Mt. Gerazim [sic]. Above fragmentary remains of a building of the 3rd cent. B.C.E. was a massive Roman temple. An inscription mentioning 'Zeus Olympius' connects this temple with the well-known Neapolis coins depicting a temple of Zeus on Mt. Gerazim and indicates that in the time of Hadrian (*ca.* A.D. 135) this building succeeded the Samaritan sanctuary erected earlier on the same spot."[7]

G. E. Wright's theories are here combined with certain ideas about the buildings whose remains were excavated on Tell er-Ras, the part of

---

[5] Campbell, Jr., *Shechem III*, 1:316.

[6] To mention one example from the debate: R. de Vaux, "On Right and Wrong Uses of Archaeology," in *Essays in Honor of Nelson Glueck: Near Eastern Archaeology in the Twentieth Century* (ed. J. H. Sanders; Garden City, N.Y.: Doubleday, 1970), 64–80, opts for separate investigation of texts and archaeological remains.

[7] W. Dever, "Excavations at Shechem and Mt. Gerazim [sic]," in *Eretz Shomron: The Thirtieth Archaeological Convention September 1972* (Jerusalem: The Israel Exploration Society, 1973), xi.

Mount Gerizim facing ancient Shechem. Building B on Tell er-Ras is supposed to have been the old Samaritan temple.[8]

These theories have had to be revised and completed as the excavations under the leadership of Y. Magen on the summit of Mount Gerizim have proceeded since 1982.[9] During these excavations Tell er-Ras was re-examined and re-excavated.[10] Y. Magen proposes the following explanations for the more recent finds. First of all, it is clear that building B on Tell er-Ras is not the old Samaritan temple, but a podium built over a watch-tower that was constructed at the time of Pontius Pilate or later. The fill for the foundation of this construction was taken from the area with Hellenistic remains south of the temple, and this led R. J. Bull to conclude that the first phase of construction was Hellenistic. On this podium was built a temple for Zeus during the time of the emperor Antoninus Pius (138–161), and this temple is building B. Early in the third century, during the time of Caracalla (211–217), the temple was reconstructed on foundations 2,5 m higher than the previous temple, and this is building A. The constructions at Tell er-Ras are thus not from the time when the Samaritans had a temple on the mountain. The temples were built much later, and were Roman temples. They were dedicated to Zeus Olympios, according to an inscription on a column (ΔΙΙ ΟΛΥΜ[ΠΙΩ], "For Zeus Olym[pios]") and another on a piece of flat copper (Διὶ Ὀλυμπίω. εὐπλοεις καὶ ἀμύτωρ, "for Zeus Olympios, supporter and helper").[11]

Mount Gerizim / Jabal at-Tur

Most important are the excavations on the summit of Mount Gerizim, done by Y. Magen and his team from 1982 on. The interpretation of the finds from the excavations will probably change as new finds are made, if one judges from what has happened until now; compare the account

---

[8] R. J. Bull, "Tell er-Ras (Mount Gerizim)," *EAEHL* 4: 1015.1017–1018.1020–1022; repr. *Die Samaritaner* (WdF 604; Darmstadt: Wissenschaftliche, 1992), 419–427.

[9] A summary of these excavations is found in R. Pummer, "Einführung in den Stand der Samaritanerforschung," in *Die Samaritaner* (WdF 604; Darmstadt: Wissenschaftliche, 1992), 56–63. Here, he has changed several of the conclusions he had drawn in his article "Samaritan Material Remains and Archaeology," in *The Samaritans* (ed. A. D. Crown; Tübingen: Mohr, 1989), 135–177.

[10] Y. Magen, "Mount Gerizim and the Samaritans," in *Early Christianity in context* (Studium Biblicum Franciscanum: Collectio maior 38; Jerusalem: Franciscan Printing Press, 1993), 122–129.

[11] Inscriptions supplied in Bull, "TELL ER-RAS," 1018, repr. 422; translations mine.

of Y. Magen from 1993 with his presentation from 2000 and his brief summary of archaeological findings in 2004.[12] To get a better picture one has to wait for the different volumes that will be published in the series which will present the excavations, *Mount Gerizim Excavations*.

For the origin of the Samaritans, the 395 Hebrew, Aramaic, and Samaritan inscriptions incised on stone that have been brought to light during this excavation are of significance. In order to put them in context, some quotations from the excavator, Y. Magen, may serve. On the basis of coins, pottery, and architecture the excavator in 2004 and 2007 assessed the finds as follows:

> The sacred precinct, centered around the temple, was built on the highest point on the mountain, overlooking the central crossroads of Samaria, Mt. Ebal, Shechem (Tell Balatah) and, to the east, the fertile Sukkar and Dajjan valleys. The excavations revealed two main construction phases: the precinct and the temple were first built in the fifth century B.C.E., during the Persian period, and survived until the end of Ptolemaic rule in the Land of Israel; the Seleucid conquest was followed by the rebuilding of the sacred precinct and the temple, in the early second century C.E. [sic: B.C.E.].[13]

> The many coins and pottery vessels discovered in the sacred precinct attest to the construction of the temple in the Persian period, during the fifth century B.C.E. The finds include pottery, as well as 68 coins from the fifth and fourth centuries B.C.E. (preceding the arrival of Alexander the Great in the Land of Israel). The earliest coin dates from 480 B.C.E.[14]

> Hundreds of coins dating to later than 128 B.C.E. were found on Mt. Gerizim, with the latest Seleucid coins dating from 112–111 B.C.E. In addition, many coins were found of "John the High Priest," that is, John Hyrcanus I himself, the first Hasmonean ruler to mint his own coins. The final conquest of Mt. Gerizim thus occurred in 112–111 B.C.E., during the reign of Antiochus IX.[15]

> The city then remained uninhabited, except for a part of the sacred precinct that was reconstructed by the Samaritans in the early fourth century C.E.,

---

[12] Magen, "Mount Gerizim and the Samaritans," 91–148; idem, "Mt. Gerizim—A Temple City," *Qad* 33 (2000), 74–119; idem, "Mount Gerizim," in *Mount Gerizim Excavations: Volume I: The Aramaic, Hebrew and Samaritan Inscriptions* (ed. Y. Magen, H. Misgav and L. Tsfania; Jerusalem: Judea & Samaria Publications, 2004), [1]–[13].

[13] Magen, "Mount Gerizim," [3]. The same assessment of the evidence is found in Y. Magen, "The Dating of the First Phase of the Samaritan Temple on Mount Gerizim in Light of the Archaeological Evidence," in *Judah and the Judeans in the Fourth Century B.C.E.* (ed. O. Lipschits, G. N. Knoppers and R. Albertz; Winona Lake, Ind.: Eisenbrauns, 2007), 157–211.

[14] Magen, "Mount Gerizim," [10].

[15] Ibid., [13].

during the Byzantine period. This area was severely damaged when the emperor Zenon demolished the interior of the precinct, replacing it (in 484 C.E.) with a church dedicated to Mary Theotokos ("Mother of God").[16]

Y. Magen thus envisages a city in existence from the early fifth century to the late second century B.C.E. He presupposes the existence of a holy place, a precinct, even if no traces of the temple or similar structures have been presented so far. What has been adduced as circumstantial evidence for a temple or an altar, are the hundreds of thousands of burnt animal bones which were found inside thick layers of ash. Most are from goats and sheep, but cattle and pigeons are also represented. The excavators evaluate this as evidence for the worship of the God of Israel.[17] These finds are interpreted in the light of written evidence, to produce the following picture, in the eyes of Y. Magen.

> The temple on Mt. Gerizim was thus built in the days of Sanballat the Horonite (Sanballat I), governor of Samaria in the days of Nehemiah, who arrived in the Land of Israel in 444 B.C.E. (Neh. 2:1–10). The temple remained in use during the Ptolemaic and Seleucid periods, as well, and also withstood the destruction of the city of Samaria and the construction of a Macedonian city on its ruins.[18]

> Josephus, however, wrongly ascribed its construction to the Sanballat who lived in the days of Alexander the Great; in fact, it was built by another Sanballat, who lived in the time of Nehemiah, some one hundred years earlier (Jos., *Ant.* 11: 302, 321–325).[19]

> In the third century B.C.E., in the Hellenistic period, the temple and the sacred precinct were rebuilt, and a city began to rise around them. The city expanded until it reached its maximal size in the second century B.C.E., with an overall area of about 400 dunams (800 m. long and some 500 m. wide), becoming the capital of the Samaritan people and its religious and cultic center.[20]

No *miqwes* were found, but a number of bath-tubs indicate that purification rites were observed. No human or animal images were found.—This summary of the excavator's report gives an impression of his thinking, but its evaluation will have to await the publication of the evidence.

---

[16] Ibid., [12].
[17] Ibid., [9].
[18] Ibid., [10].
[19] Ibid., [6.]
[20] Ibid., [1].

6.2. The Inscriptions from Mount Gerizim

From these excavations, 395 inscriptions have been published, and they constitute interesting evidence for the population living there.[21] The languages of the inscriptions are Hebrew and Aramaic, and the scripts are Aramaic, Palaeo-Hebrew, and Samaritan. The Samaritan inscriptions come from a later age. In other words, the languages and the scripts from the Hellenistic era are the same as those used in Jewish circles in that period. The conclusion which may be drawn from this material is that the onomasticon of the people worshipping on Mount Gerizim was the same as in the Jewish population of the Second Temple period. Many of the names are theophoric with elements of YHWH. No theophoric elements with foreign deities have come to light. Thus, the population worshipping on Mount Gerizim seems to have been a part of the general Jewish population of the country in the Persian and Hellenistic periods. Further, the deity worshipped there is the same as in Jerusalem. One inscription contains the name YHWH, two mention "Adonay," and a number of them use the general expression "God." No names of other deities occur. There is no trace of syncretism. Third, the place-names associated with the persons mentioned in the inscriptions are Samaria, Shechem, and some villages in the area. This means that we are able to discover the profile of the Gerizim-worshippers: it is the same cultural and religious profile as what is known of Jewish circles of the time. A closer look at the material will add detail to this impression.

146 inscriptions are in the Lapidary Aramaic script, 183 in the Proto-Jewish script (developed from the Aramaic script), and seven in the Palaeo-Hebrew script (termed "Neo-Hebrew" by the publisher). One is incised in a script mixed from Proto-Jewish and Palaeo-Hebrew/Neo-Hebrew.[22] Two 'special finds'—one a stone and the other a silver finger-ring—are very difficult to decipher. Four inscriptions are in the Samaritan script. In addition, a number of Greek inscriptions have emerged, from Hellenistic times, from the fourth century C.E. and from the Byzan-

---

[21] Briefly treated by B. Becking, "Do the Earliest Samaritan Inscriptions Already Indicate a Parting of the Ways?" in *Judah and the Judeans in the Fourth Century B.C.E.* (ed. O. Lipschits, G. N. Knoppers and R. Albertz; Winona Lake, Ind.: Eisenbrauns, 2007), 213–222.

[22] Tables in Magen, Misgav and Tsfania, *Mount Gerizim Excavations*, "Neo-Hebrew scripts," Fig. 13, [32], "Lapidary Aramaic scripts from the Mt. Gerizim inscriptions," Fig. 17, [38], "Proto-Jewish scripts," Fig. 18, [39], "Mixed (Lapidary Aramaic and Proto-Jewish) scripts from the Mt. Gerizim insriptions," Fig. 19, [40].

tine period. They have not yet been published. The Aramaic, Hebrew, and Samaritan inscriptions have been published with photographs, drawings, transcriptions into the square script, translations (if possible), and comments by H. Misgav.[23] The following discussion relates to the published inscriptions.

Most of the stones with inscriptions have been broken and most of the inscriptions are fragmentary. Some of the stones with inscriptions have been reused in new constructions. A number of the inscriptions contain only one letter or a few letters, and are impossible to decipher.

> The inscriptions in Aramaic [i.e. Lapidary and Proto-Jewish] and Neo-Hebrew script were all discovered in and around the sacred precinct ..., with the exception of three inscriptions found on construction rollers inside residential buildings (nos. 347–348, 373). It is noteworthy that except for a single inscription incorporated into the monumental staircase on the eastern slope (no. 223), none were found in situ, due to the destruction of the temple and the sacred precinct in different periods.[24]

> We believe that most of the early inscriptions should be dated to the Hellenistic period (third-second centuries B.C.E.), although some may belong to the earliest period of the sacred precinct (fifth-fourth centuries B.C.E.).[25]

This means that the scripts of the inscriptions confirm the results from Purvis' investigation of the Samaritan script of SP manuscripts (see the following chapter) in that the Palaeo-Hebrew/Neo-Hebrew script was found. But there are no inscriptions with Samaritan scripts from the period prior to the destruction of the city in the second century B.C.E., which means that a development into the particular script of the SP manuscripts cannot be confirmed from the inscriptions. All the Samaritan inscriptions are from the second century C.E. onwards, and the four which have been found on Mount Gerizim also come from the Common Era.[26] The scripts of the other inscriptions indicate that the people who made them belonged to the cultural milieu of Palestine before the turn of the era, and may even have belonged to the Jewish population.

What are the contents of the inscriptions?

The editor of the inscriptions interprets the inscriptions in the Neo-Hebrew and mixed scripts as coming from priestly circles. These inscriptions are very fragmentary, and seem—with one possible exception—

---

[23] Magen, Misgav and Tsfania, *Mount Gerizim Excavations.*
[24] Ibid., [13]f.
[25] Ibid., [14].
[26] Ibid., [36].

not to have been dedication or votive texts. The readable text is as follows: no. 382: "...] z°[...]priest ... [... p]riests [...] r bh[...]"; 383:
"...]h°°[... YHWH l[...]"; 384: "... P]inhas [...] which [...] the high";
388: "[That which offered PN] the priest so[n of PN for himself and] his
[wi]fe P°[... and for] his [s]ons"; 389 (mixed script): "...] son of Pinhas
the p[riest ...] their [br]others [the] priest[s .....]." "Pinhas" is mentioned
twice, nos. 384; 389.[27] Nos. 382, 384, 388 are in Hebrew; no. 389 in Aramaic; the others do not contain enough letters to make possible a decision
on this question.

The divine name YHWH in inscription no. 383, written in "Neo-
Hebrew" script, has been found in this inscription alone. Only this word
is preserved, so the language cannot be ascertained, but it is assumed by
the editor to have been Hebrew.

With the proviso that the material is meagre one may conclude that
the priests used the Hebrew language and the Palaeo-Hebrew script for
their inscriptions; they had a high priest; one inscription is of a dedicatory
nature (if the editor's reconstruction is correct).

As for the inscriptions in Aramaic language and Proto-Jewish scripts,
the publisher states the following,

> Most of the Mt. Gerizim inscriptions are dedication or votive inscriptions,
> in which the donor asks for God's blessing. In the great majority of cases,
> and as was common in all periods of antiquity, the names of the donors
> are mentioned, to which often the donation and a blessing or prayer for
> them are added. Two closely related formulae appear in the Mt. Gerizim
> inscriptions:
>
> (a) ... 'That [which] PN son of PN (from GN) offered for himself, his
>   wife and his sons.'
>
> (b) ... inscriptions that begin as in type (a), followed by the benedictory
>   formula ... 'for good remembrance.'[28]

The name "Adonay" occurs twice, nos. 150 and 151, in the Proto-Jewish
script, and in the Hebrew language. "God" occurs several times in the
Proto-Jewish inscriptions in the Aramaic language. There are no indications of names of other deities in the inscriptions.

Fifty-five different names of men and women can be identified. At least
35 of them are Hebrew, 13 Greek, four Arab, one Palmyrene, one Persian,
and two of uncertain origin.[29] Most of the Hebrew names are known from

---

[27] No.s 385, 386, and 387 are unintelligible.
[28] Magen, Misgav and Tsfania, *Mount Gerizim Excavations*, [16].
[29] Ibid., [25].

the Jewish onomasticon of the Second Temple period, and from the HB. A number of them are theophoric with a form of YHWH: Yehonatan, six times, Yehosef and Yosef, six times, Hanina and Honyah, four times; Yehohanan, twice; Yehudah and Yehud, twice; Delayah, a number of times; further Eliyahu, Ba'yah, and Shema'yah. Greek names include "Antipatros," three times; "Ploutas," three times; "Alexander," "Tryphon," and "Jason" once each.

"The predominant picture that emerges from the Aramaic inscriptions is one of typical common Jewish names of the Second Temple period … A similar reality is reflected in corpora of Jewish inscriptions."[30] These Jewish corpora are ossuaries and the Masada ostraca. The custom of adding a Greek name to a Hebrew or Aramaic one was common among the Jews at the time. "People with Arabic names, on the other hand, did not take an additional Hebrew one, leading us to conclude that the Arabic names are not a sign of cultural influence, but rather indicate Arab origin in an ethnically heterogeneous society."[31] The Arabic names are associated with "Assyrian annals and dedicatory inscriptions" which mention that those exiled to Samaria by Sargon II included Arabs, who "apparently assimilated into Samaritan society."[32] In view of the few names extant, however—only four are found—another explanation is more likely, that these names represent stray contemporary naming habits of the population.

The supposed Arabic names are "'Aslah" and "Zabdi" in inscription no. 20, "Maliku" in no. 46, and "Qimi" in no. 3. Inscription no. 20 is translated "That which offered 'Aslah son of Zabdi and Yehonatan his son Yehosef and Yeshua' Ba'yah Miriam and her son."[33] The commentary to this inscription informs us that "'Aslah" appears in Nabatean inscriptions, especially from Sinai and Petra, and in a document from Nahal Hever.[34] This means that these examples are contemporary with or later than the Mount Gerizim inscriptions. The name Zabdi occurs in the Bible, Josh 7:1; 1 Chr 27:27, and was popular in Palmyra and with the Nabateans. Thus, there is no reason to designate this an exclusively Arab name. It was common to the Bible and the later neighbours of Samaria.

---

[30] Ibid., [27].
[31] Ibid.
[32] Ibid.
[33] Ibid., [64].
[34] Ibid., [65].

Inscription no. 46 is translated "... PN] son of Maliku [...,]" with the commentary that the name "Maliku" was common in Nabatean and Palmyrene, and is also found in the Aramaic ostraca from Tell Arad and Tell Beersheba.[35] This is also contemporary or later material. Inscription no. 3 is translated "That which Haggai son of Qimi from Kfar Haggai offered," with the commentary that the name "Qimi" is also found in Nabatean and Palmyrene inscriptions.[36] Thus, this name is found in contemporary or later inscriptions. Qimi's son bears the name Haggai, known from the HB. Obviously, Qimi had no problems with giving his son a HB name.

All four names occur in contemporary or later inscriptions, or even in the HB. There is no reason to connect it, for example to Sargon II's inscription from 715 B.C.E.: "the tribes of Tamud, Ibadidi, Marsimanu, and Haiapa, the Arabs who live, far away, in the desert (and) who know neither overseers nor official(s) and who had not (yet) brought their tribute to any king. I deported their survivors and settled (them) in Samaria."[37] Such an interpretation seems to presuppose Josephus' reading of 2 Kgs 17, combined with "annals and dedicatory inscriptions" from the time of Sargon II—another example of the influence of Josephus upon research, cf. chapter 3. "Arabs" occur in late HB texts, 2 Chr 17:11; 21:16; 22:1; 26:7; Neh 2:19; 4:1; 6:1; and also in Isa 13:20; Jer 3:2, which are not necessarily old. There is therefore no obvious connection to the eighth century Assyrian inscription. The appearance of possible Arabic names in Transjordan and in the Negev would be due to migration and would have nothing to do with Assyrian deportations of the eighth and seventh centuries B.C.E.

The most frequent title in the Mount Gerizim inscriptions is "priest," five times. Priestly names that occur are Elazar, three times; and Pinhas, five times.

No names with theophoric elements representing other deities have been found. This is surprising in view of the frequency of this custom in other countries.

מקדש, "sanctuary," occurs in inscription no. 150, but several times the Aramaic expression "this place," אתרא דנה, is found, cf. nos. 147, 148

---

[35] Ibid., [83].

[36] Ibid., [51].

[37] "Sargon II (721–705): The Fall of Samaria: (b) From Annalistic Reports: 120–125," translated by A. L. Oppenheimer (ANET, 286); cf. "Sargon II. und die Araber (715 v. Chr.)," translated by R. Borger (TGI, 65).

(incomplete), 152 (incomplete), 154 (incomplete). אתר is a term for a cult place, cf. Ezr 5:15; 6:3, 5,7. In the Hebrew part of Ezra the term is מכון, 2:68; 3:3. It is interpreted by Misgav as a polemical term directed against Jerusalem.[38] This latter understanding would presuppose that the mode of expression of the inscriptions is a counter-move against that of the book of Ezra. The two expressions מקדש, "sanctuary," and אתרא דנה, "this place," indicate that there was an altar or a temple on the summit of Mount Gerizim.

The dedicatory inscriptions begin with a particle, זי, or די, referring to something not mentioned. The editor supposes that it refers to a stone or a part of the wall, which was built with financial support from the dedicator, cf. the practice in Neh 3:1–3. A stone is mentioned as dedicatory gift in nos. 147 and 148. The particle could be a demonstrative, "this is what [PN dedicated]." The verb for "dedicate" is קרב, in Hiphil or Aphel, depending on the language used; it could be taken to mean "present." This is a term for bringing sacrifice in Lev 1–7; 22:17 ff., and occurs here in a different sense—unless it means that the stone was equivalent to a sacrifice to the Lord. In Neh 3:1 קדש, Piel, is used for dedication or sanctification of the parts of the wall. In many of the inscriptions קרב is followed by a wish for good remembrance or memorial, דכרן טב, for the wife and children of the donor, sometimes also for himself. An almost full text is preserved in no. 147: "This is what Delayah, son of Shimon, presented for himself and for his children, [this] stone, for good remembrance before God in this place." The expression "remember PN for good" is known from late texts, Neh 5:19; 13:31, cf. the briefer expression in Neh 13:14. The negative counterpart is presented in Neh 6:14; 13:29, where Nehemiah's enemies should be remembered for their evil deeds against Jerusalem. Another case of "remembrance" or "memorial" is Neh 2:20, which tells how Nehemiah is approached by Sanballat, Tobiah and Geshem, and replies that they have no "portion, right, or memorial" in Jerusalem: לכם אין־חלק וצדקה וזכרון בירושלם. In connection with the cult, "remembrance" appears in Lev 23:24; Num 5:15.18; 10:10, denoting the effect of a festival or an offering. "Also on your days of rejoicing, at your appointed festivals, and at the beginnings of your months, you shall blow the trumpets over your burnt offerings and over your sacrifices of well-being; they shall serve as a reminder on your behalf before the Lord your God: I am the Lord your God," Num 10:10. Of special interest is the gar-

---

[38] Magen, Misgav and Tsfania, *Mount Gerizim Excavations*, [19].

ment of the high priest with the names of the Israelites on it, as a remembrance before the Lord, Exod 28:12.29; 39:7, and the silver half-shekel as temple tax, providing atonement for the donor, Exod 30:16, "You shall take the atonement money from the Israelites and shall designate it for the service of the tent of meeting; it will be a reminder of the Israelites before the Lord, to atone for your lives." The inscriptions on Mount Gerizim share the expression "a reminder before the Lord" with the language of the HB, לזכרון לפני יהוה, and Nehemiah shows that not only temple tax, but also good deeds were counted as grounds for a good remembrance in the eyes of God. The donor of the stones, which were parts of the temple or city walls, expresses the wish that his gift should serve the purpose of providing him with God's good remembrance, just as Nehemiah prays that his reconstruction of the wall around Jerusalem, Neh 5:16–19, and the expulsion of the exogamous priest from Jerusalem will serve the same purpose, Neh 13:28–31. Especially interesting is the combination of remembrance for good, Neh 13:31, with the negative counterpart, Neh 13:29, in connection with the expulsion of the priest living in an exogamous marriage, Neh 13:28.

The many inscriptions indicating that a stone or a part of the wall has been given by a named person reminds one of the scene described in Neh 3. Nehemiah's reconstruction of the wall is described as a continuous work from beginning to end, and even with the hindering mentioned in ch. 4, the wall is completed in a short period, 6:15. The construction on Mount Gerizim may have extended over a longish period, but the principle of participation by several named persons seems to be the same. In addition, the donors at Mount Gerizim address their gift to God in the hope of remembrance, perhaps for the forgiveness of sins or for a future existence, or for participation along the line of Neh 2:20 of "portion, right, or memorial."

The terminology and contents of the inscriptions lead in the direction of the books of Ezra and Nehemiah, and even though these books may be older than the inscriptions, there seems to be a linguistic connection. The construction and the activity on Mount Gerizim resemble that of Jerusalem as portrayed in these books, and the evidence from both sides seems to bear witness to an interest in polemics against the other party.

The term קרב provides one of the links to two other inscriptions from Hellenistic times, the Delos inscriptions. קרב could have a meaning similar to ἀπάρχομαι in these Greek inscriptions. In these texts we encounter a group of "Israelites" sending their temple tax to Mount

Gerizim, thus providing us with evidence that there was a sanctuary on the mountain, and that Samaritans living as far away as an island in the Aegean considered it their holy place.

6.3. *The Inscriptions from Delos*

According to Greek legend the island of Delos was the birthplace of Apollo and Artemis. It had an important temple of Apollo and was for a period an amphictyonic centre in the Aegean Sea. Its history proper began in the sixth century B.C.E. and lasted until the turn of the era. In the Hellenistic Period it was an important trade centre and home to people from many countries.

Among these was a Jewish colony on the island. This can be inferred from information in 1 Macc 15:15–24 and Josephus' *Antiquities* 14.10, from inscriptions mentioning "the supreme God," and from a building that was probably a synagogue.

In 1979 the architect of the École française d'Athènes, P. Fraisse, discovered two Greek inscriptions that were created by "Israelites who send their temple tax to Argarizein." This designation only fits the Samaritans. The inscriptions were cut on two marble stelae which at the time of the discoveries were lying in the debris near the remains of a wall. Together with an expert on Delian archaeology, P. Bruneau, Fraisse excavated them the following year and deposited them in the island's museum. Bruneau published the inscriptions in 1982, thus providing evidence for the existence of a Samaritan colony also on the island.[39]

Above the inscriptions are wreaths, with the inscriptions immediately below. The design is properly Greek.[40] Both stones have had the marble broken off at the top, and the second stone is broken also at the bottom. The first stela has preserved a complete inscription in six lines, but the second inscription is now incomplete: nine lines can be identified, and the first six contain readable text. This inscription has been made *in rasura*; whatever was cut on the surface originally has been hewn away and the present text carved in its stead.

---

[39] Ph. Bruneau, " 'Les israélites de Délos' et la juiverie delienne," *BCH* 106 (1982): 465–504.

[40] A. T. Kraabel: "As a classicist I was struck by how properly Greek both steles are. The same design is found time and again across the Mediterranean world; a rectangular shaft

Bruneau conjectured that both inscriptions adorned a wall of an important building, most likely a Samaritan synagogue or assembly hall.

Inscription no. 1:

1. ΟΙ ΕΝ ΔΗΛΩ ΙΣΡΑΕΛΕΙΤΑΙ ΟΙ Α
2. ΠΑΡΧΟΜΕΝΟΙ ΕΙΣ ΙΕΡΟΝ ΑΡΓΑ
3. ΡΙΖΕΙΝ ΣΤΕΦΑΝΟΥΣΙΝ ΧΡΥΣΩ
4. ΣΤΕΦΑΝΩ ΣΑΡΑΠΙΩΝΑ ΙΑΣΟ
5. ΝΟΣ ΚΝΩΣΙΟΝ ΕΥΕΡΓΕΣΙΑΣ
6. ΕΝΕΚΕΝ ΤΗΣ ΕΙΣ ΕΑΥΤΟΥΣ

Translation:

1. The Israelites in Delos who se-
2. nd their temple tax to sacred Arga-
3. rizein crown with a golden
4. crown Serapion, son of Iaso-
5. n, from Knossos, on account of the favour,
6. the favour unto them.

Inscription no. 2:

1. ΙΣΡΑΗΛΙΤΑΙ ΟΙ ΑΠΑΡΧΟΜΕΝΟΙ ΕΙΣ ΙΕΡΟΝ ΑΓΙΟΝ ΑΡ
2. ΓΑΡΙΖΕΙΝ ΕΤΙΜΗΣΑΝ   ΜΕΝΙΠΠΟΝ ΑΡΤΕΜΙΔΩΡΟΥ ΗΡΑ
3. ΚΛΕΙΟΝ ΑΥΤΟΝ ΚΑΙ ΤΟΥΣ ΕΓΓΟΝΟΥΣ ΑΥΤΟΥ ΚΑΤΑΣΚΕΥ
4. ΑΣΑΝΤΑ ΚΑΙ ΑΝΑΘΕΝΤΑ ΕΚ ΤΩΝ ΙΔΙΟΝ ΕΠΙ ΠΡΟΣΕΥΧΗ
    ΤΟΥ
5. ΘΕ[ΟΥ] ΤΟΝ
6. ΟΛΟΝ ΚΑΙ ΤΟ   ΧΡΥΣΩ ΣΤΕ[ΦΑ]
7. ΝΩ ΚΑΙ
8. ΚΑ
9. Τ

Translation:

1. Israelites who send the temple tax to sacred, holy Ar-
2. garizein honour Menippos, son of Artemidoros, from Her-
3. kleion, himself and his family, (him,) who bui-
4. lt and kept of his own means a synagogue to
5. Go[d], who
6. whole and the   with a golden cr[o]-
7. wn and
8. ??
9. ?

---

of white marble with a fine wreath carved in high relief, the inscription below it," idem, "New Evidence of the Samaritan Diaspora has been Found on Delos," *BA* 47 (1984): 45.

Those responsible for these two honorific stelae are the "Israelites who send the temple tax to sacred (or: sacred, holy) Argarizein." This designation for the Samaritans is not known from other ancient sources. There is no reason to doubt the authenticity of the inscriptions, so the designation is the Samaritans' own way of describing themselves in a Greek setting. From what period do they come?

In order to date the inscriptions, Bruneau considered the prosopography, without, however, reaching conclusive results. The two benefactors, Menippos from Herakleion and Serapion from Knossos had their origins in places close to each other on Crete. According to Thucydides, the islands in the Aegean were freed from sea-rovers by Minos of Crete.[41] It is therefore possible that such an origin would strike a note of the venerated past more than being a clue to dating the inscriptions.

It is also impossible to know whether or not they were two of the "Israelites who send temple tax to Argarizein." The idea that Serapion got his name because of some connection to the Hellenistic-Egyptian god Serapis, is understandable against the background of earlier scholarship's tendency to consider the Samaritans syncretists—and there was a shrine of Serapis, a Serapieion, on Delos. Today, scholarship is not inclined to do this. The names are not known from other texts and cannot be linked to specific dates or events.

After considering some relevant features of orthography—also without a conclusive result—Bruneau turned to palaeography. On this basis he dated inscription no. 1 to 150–50 B.C.E., and no. 2 to 250–175 B.C.E. The general impression of the script and some indicators (presence or absence of serifs, form of the *alpha*, and size of the *omicron*) led to this result. Bruneau warned against drawing strong conclusions on the basis of his dating; however, scholars have not come up with arguments against it, but seem to adopt it.[42]

Is it possible to make a few further remarks on the palaeography? I think so.[43] Both inscriptions have an old form of the *zeta*: like an I

---

[41] *The History of the Peloponnesian War*, book 1, ch. 1.

[42] This dating has been adopted by Kraabel," New Evidence"; Talmon, "Masada Fragment"; J. Zangenberg, ΣΑΜΑΡΕΙΑ: *Antike Quellen zur Geschichte und Kultur der Samaritaner in deutscher Übersetzung* (Texte und Arbeiten zum neutestamentlichen Zeitalter 15; Tübingen: Francke, 1994); and L. M. White, "The Delos Synagoge Revisited," *HTR* 80 (1987): 133–140, adds an argument for it, based on the variation between the longer and the shorter openings.

[43] I am indebted to Dr. Charles V. Crowther of the Center for the Study of Ancient Documents at the University of Oxford for discussing with me the inscriptions, and for valuable suggestions.

with extended horizontal lines, although inscription no. 1 is difficult to read at this point from the photographs alone. This form of the *zeta* is older than the familiar Z-form, which means that both inscriptions are early and may be dated to the first half of the second century B.C.E. The order between them could be reversed, because the arguments for dating adduced by Bruneau are not compelling. The engraving of inscription no. 2 is less carefully executed than no. 1, and thus does not invite precise judgments. This inscription is made *in rasura*, which means that the wreath originally adorned a different inscription or other object, now erased and replaced by the present one. Line 5 of the present inscription is again mostly erased, and preserved by some painted and some faintly visible incised text. On balance, inscription no. 2 seems to reveal a cheaper version of a stela, where an older marble was reused by keeping the ornament and replacing the other item.

Palaeographically, the inscriptions might therefore be from the same period in the second century B.C.E.

There are two more tools for dating which Bruneau did not mention.

One is the study of the wreaths. There are clear differences between them; no. 1 seems better executed than no. 2, a phenomenon which could provide a potential for precision of dating. Would the best executed be the older one? This stela also has the more carefully executed inscription.

Another tool for dating Greek inscriptions is to identify the letter cutter. In Athens there were 42 letter cutters during the years 229–160 B.C.E. and 56 between160 and 86 B.C.E. When Athens took over rule over Delos in 166 B.C.E., there was not enough work in Athens for all of them, and one may speculate that some of them went to Delos and took up work there.[44] If the inscriptions at Delos in general had been more thoroughly studied, it might have been possible to identify the letter-cutters who produced the two inscriptions and this would have made possible a more precise dating.

Unless the date of the wreaths and the identity of the stone-cutters are discovered, one is left with palaeography and the custom of creating wreaths with inscriptions as a means for dating. These elements point in the direction of the first half of the second century B.C.E.

From an exegete's point of view, the texts themselves might suggest which of them is the older one. A longer text normally is supposed to be later than a shorter (*lectio brevior anterior*), but this rule points

---

[44] S. V. Tracy, *Attic Letter-Cutters of 229 to 86 B.C.* (Hellenistic culture and society 6; Berkeley: University of California Press, 1990), 225.

in different directions in this case. The shorter opening of inscription no. 2 is counterbalanced by its longer description of the object of the worshippers' loyalty, ιερον αγιον αργαριζειν. The two phenomena may, however, be understood in that only a reference to "Israelites" was needed in a situation when the other islanders were familiar with them, and an addition of "holy" to "sacred Argarizein" might have been occasioned by disputes about the status of that temple. Josephus mentions such disputes in Egypt at the time of Ptolemy Soter (c. 300 B.C.E.), *Ant.* 12.10; 13.74, and a similar situation is not impossible on Delos. These obervations on the second inscription would reverse the order suggested by Bruneau. On the other hand, the rule of the longer reading applies to manuscripts, not to inscriptions. When other methods are exhausted, one is tempted to turn to whatever evidence there is, but we seem best advised to leave any conclusions from the length of the readings open.

The inscriptions seem to be genuine, perhaps dating from the first half of the second century B.C.E., and were created by a group which we would call Samaritans. They lived far away from Palestine, on an island that was a centre in the Aegean. Scholars have begun to recognize the importance of this fact.[45]

In a list of contributors to a temple on Delos for the Egyptian-Hellenistic god Serapis there is a Πραυλος Σαμαρευς, "Praulos the Samari(t)an," donating for the benefit of "his brothers and mother."[46] This list is from the end of the second or the beginning of the first century B.C.E. It is disputed whether this person was a Jew or a gentile.[47] If one follows a particular understanding of Josephus' *Ant.* 9.290 and presumes the Samaritans were syncretists, it would be natural to assume that Praulos was a syncretistic Samaritan. This reading of Josephus is not necessary, however, and the Samaritans were not syncretists. Praulos might have had his origins in Samaria and this is the background for the name.

A second case is ΡΟΔΟΚΛΗΣ ΜΕΝΙΠΠΟΥ ΣΑΜΑΡΙΤΑΣ, "Rodokles, son of Menippos, the Samari(t)an," a name figuring in an epi-

---

[45] Coggins, "Samaritans in Josephus," 264: "it is certainly probable from inscriptional evidence that a Samaritan group did exist on the island, perhaps around 100 BC." An earlier date is more likely.

[46] P. Roussel and M. Launey, *Inscriptions de Délos: décrets postérieurs a 166 av. J.-C. (No.s 1497–1524), dédicaces posterieures a 166 av. J.-C. (No.s 2220–2879)* (Paris: H. Champion, 1937), 390 f.

[47] Ibid.; Bruneau, "Les Israélites," 479.

taph from Thasos, dating to the second century B.C.E.[48] C. Fredrich suggests that the man came from Rhodes, but had an origin from the city Samaria.[49]

Whether or not these two inscriptions from different locations have anything to do with Samaria or the Samaritans, they form a backdrop to our inscriptions. It is conspicuous that none of these Greek expressions occur in these. We are in the fortunate position that the donors' identity is described not by an ambiguous σαμαρεύς or σαμάριτας, but by "Israelites" and the attachment to Mount Gerizim, a direct expression of Samaritan religion.

In the LXX the lemma Ἰσραηλίτης is found eleven times, eight of which are in the Pentateuch, and only in the singular, masculine and feminine. The plural is used only once, in 4 Macc 18:1. This might indicate that the plural form of this lemma is a late occurrence, against the overwhelming number of occurrences of the traditional υἱοὶ Ἰσραήλ as translation for בני ישראל in the HB.

In Justin's *Apology* I 53.4 Samaritans and Jews are both treated as peoples of Israel: τὸ δὲ Ἰουδαϊκὸν καὶ Σαμαρειτικὸν φῦλον Ἰσραὴλ καὶ οἶκος Ἰακὼβ κέκληνται, "but the Jewish and the Samaritan [races] are called tribe of Israel and House of Jacob."[50] This expression is three centuries later than the inscriptions, and shows that even in that period Jews and Samaritans may be called "tribe of Israel and house of Jacob." Justin writes long after Luke, John and Josephus, who all used "Jews" and "Samaritans" as opposing terms.

It has been suggested that the term "Israelites" should refer to people from the old Northern Kingdom, Israel. The association with Mount Gerizim was made lest the Jews lay exclusive claim to the title.[51] The first idea presupposes enough knowledge of the HB among the islanders to make the association with the Northern kingdom, and this cannot be assumed. "Israelites" is not found in other texts with the meaning "people from the Northern kingdom." The second statement implies that "Israelites" was a term also used by the Jews on the island. This is possible, and

---

[48] C. Fredrich et al., eds., *Inscriptiones insularum maris Aegaei praeter Delum* (Inscriptiones graecae 12, fasc. VIII; Berlin: Reimerum, 1909), No. 439.

[49] Ibid.

[50] Pummer, *Early Christian Authors*, 29 f.

[51] Kraabel, "New Evidence," 45; that the expression means that the Samaritans were remnants of northern Israelites is also the idea of Dexinger, "Ursprung der Samaritaner," 118.

then "Israelites" would have conveyed the general meaning "people from Israel," or "belonging to Israel," and to this expression was added the specification, "who send their temple tax to holy Argarizein," in order to separate the Samaritans from the other "Israelites," the Jews. The Samaritans on Delos considered themselves as "Israel" in the general sense of the HB. They did not refer to a geographical term as do Praulos of the Serapeion-list from Delos or Menippon in the Thasos-epitaph. "Israelites" must have been considered an appropriate term for communication on Delos. To be "Israel" would, however, need specification: Israelites who send their temple tax to Gerizim. Even though they were in a different location in the Mediterranean world, they kept their allegiance to Gerizim. How was this allegiance expressed?

The salient point is the understanding of the verb ἀπάρχομαι. In the edition of the inscriptions Bruneau translated it as "versant contribution"; later renderings include Kraabel's "make offerings," repeated by White in the translation of the inscription—but later in the article he changes it to "pay homage"—Zangenberg's "Opfer darbringen," Dexinger's "die ihre Erstlingsopfer dem Heiligtum am Garizim weihen," Talmon's modern Hebrew המנדבים, "who offer voluntary offerings," and Talmon's English "offer."[52] These translations may be understood in the sense to "bring sacrifices," and this would entail a conceivable, but unlikely, notion.

The basic meaning of the verb is "*to make a beginning*, esp. in sacrifice."[53] With a genitive it means to offer the firstlings or first-fruits; used absolutely, it means to begin a sacrifice, offer first-fruits or start the offering by cutting some hair from the forehead of the animal and throwing it on the flames. It seems improbable that the stelae were erected by people on a visit to the island; these honorific artefacts must have been sponsored by a group resident there, and it is inconceivable that persons in the Aegean sent the whole or parts of sacrificial animals to Palestine. Equally impossible is the idea that they would offer sacrifices on the island in the direction of Mount Gerizim. The sense of the word must have been

---

[52] Kraabel, "New Evidence," 44; White, "Delos Synagoge Revisited," 141.154; Zangenberg, ΣΑΜΑΡΕΙΑ, 325; Dexinger, "Ursprung der Samaritaner," 118; S. Talmon, "קטעי כתבים כתובים עברית ממצדה /Fragments of Scrolls from Masada," ErIsr 22 (1989), 284, in the translation of the inscription into modern Hebrew; idem, "Masada Fragment," 227; idem, "A Papyrus Fragment Inscribed in Palaeo-Hebrew Script," in *Masada: Yigael Yadin Excavations 1963–1965: Final Reports* (The Masada Reports 6; Jerusalem: Israel Exploration Society, 1999), 138–149.

[53] Liddell and Scott, *Lexicon*, s.v. ἀπάρχομαι.

transferred to the realm of money, and better understood in the more technical meaning to "*offer, dedicate,* χρυσάς (sc. δραχμάς)."[54]

To send money to the temple was the normal Jewish practice. It had a theological basis and provided the temple with the means for the everyday running of the sacrifices. The temple tax was half a shekel according to Exod 30:11–16, and in the period of the second temple the Tyrian shekel was used for payment.[55]

Israelites sending temple tax to Gerizim must have had strong objections to sending it to Jerusalem. From Josephus we learn of discussions in Egypt between diaspora Jews and Samaritans on the correct place for worship, and this would include the question of where to send the offerings, τὰς θυσίας πέμπειν, *Ant.* 12.10, under Ptolemy Soter (323–283 B.C.E.). *Ant.* 13.74 tells of a similar discussion under Ptolemy VI Philometor, 180–145 B.C.E., focusing upon which temple was built according to the law of Moses, which was the oldest and most celebrated in the world. In Jesus' conversation with the Samaritan woman in John 4 the question of the place of worship may have included the issue of the temple tax. At the least, it seems probable that the concrete outcome of such discussions was a decision on where to send the temple tax.

We may then make an assumption about what upset the Jerusalem priesthood about the temple on Gerizim: the Israelites who sent their money to Gerizim would not send it to Jerusalem, and her temple would suffer. Of course, it is not only a question of financial support as such. It is also a matter of acknowledgment, of honouring the traditions behind the Jerusalem temple. The ideological question is, Which temple is more holy and venerable? In the long run the consequence might be, Which temple will survive? Which will be more prosperous?

Whether there was a temple on Mount Gerizim at the time of the inscriptions does not necessarily need clarifying; as Bruneau argues, expressions may linger on after their referents have changed. It would, however, be a fair assumption that the Delian Israelites presumed that sacrifices took place. This may even have happened after the temple had been destroyed, as today's practice with the paschal lamb demonstrates.[56]

---

[54] Liddell and Scott, *Lexicon,* s.v. ἀπάρχομαι, meaning III, with reference to "IG2.652 B 19, cf. Plu. *Sull.* 27, AP 7.406 (Theodorid.)." The term ἀπαρχή, "firstling," is attested in the LXX and the New Testament, but the corresponding verb is not.

[55] On the theological meaning of the temple tax and its financial implications, J. Ådna, *Jerusalemer Tempel und Tempelmarkt in 1. Jahrhundert n. Chr.* (Abhandlungen des Deutschen Palästina-Vereins 25: Wiesbaden: Harrasowitz, 1999), 101–109.

[56] Pummer, "Samaritan Material Remains," 172 f.

Since the inscriptions were found 92,5 m north of a Jewish synagogue, and they may have originally adorned a Samaritan synagogue on the place where they were found,[57] one may reasonably infer that the particularisation οἵ ἀπαρχόμενοι etc. of the self-designation was necessary because of the proximity to the Jewish presence on the island. Did the Samaritans also have a synagogue?

The expression προσευχῇ τοῦ θε[οῦ] in inscription no. 2 I translated as "a synagogue to Go[d]," following White in his understanding of the phrase, against Bruneau's "en ex-voto" ("votive offering").[58] This leads in the direction of Bruneau's archaeological reconstruction. The two stelae were, perhaps, once attached to the wall where they were found, and the building could have been a synagogue or an assembly hall. If "synagogue" is the correct understanding, it would make good sense that the honorific stelae adorned its wall.

One more point should be made.

Inscription no. 2 seems to lack a proper beginning. At least the definite article OI should precede the noun ΙΣΡΑΗΛΙΤΑΙ, according to Bruneau.[59] Therefore, he assumes a line 0 over the wreath, with the words ΟΙ ΕΝ ΔΗΛΩ. Such an arrangement is not attested anywhere else, but he presumes it here, and argues that there would be space for it on the part of the stone that is now missing. The reason for the letter-cutter's locating a line above the wreath would be lack of space for the complete inscription below.[60]

This last argument is difficult, as the lower part of the stone has been broken off in all its breadth, and lines 8 and 9 therefore cannot be restored. There may even have been a line 10 or more. The argument from grammar is also difficult, as one can only make assumptions about scribal habits on inscriptions, even in cases where the language is well known. A line 0 cannot be ruled out, but with our present knowledge it remains hypothetical.

Another explanation has been offered by L. M. White. He thinks the short text ΙΣΡΑΗΛΙΤΑΙ comes from the period of independence for

---

[57] Bruneau thinks they may have belonged to the wall, at the foot of which they were found, "Les Israélites," 486 f.

[58] White, "Delos Synagoge Revisited," 142; Bruneau, "Les israélites;" "Ex-votos, sometimes called votive offerings, are gifts presented to a shrine as a sign of the pilgrim's devotion," N. C. Brockman, *Encyclopedia of Sacred Places* (vol. 1; Santa Barbara, Calif.: ABC-CLIO, 1997), 80.

[59] Bruneau, "Les Israélites," 474.

[60] Ibid.

Delos, before 166 B.C.E., when the people sponsoring the inscription would use this loose expression about themselves. The longer text of inscription no. 1, OI EN ΔΗΛΩ ΙΣΡΑΕΛΕΙΤΑΙ, reveals a situation when Athens had taken control of the island, which happened around 166 B.C.E. This gave status and proper designations to the different groups living on the island.[61] White therefore dates inscription no. 1 as later than 166 B.C.E. and inscription no. 2 as earlier.[62] This is possible. On the other hand, the less careful execution of inscription no. 2 would perhaps also have affected the opening and resulted in the lack of an article.

The implication of the Delos inscriptions for the origin of the Samaritans is that we know that the self-designation of the group was "Israelites," that there was probably, but not necessarily, a temple on Mount Gerizim in the first half of the second century B.C.E., and that diaspora Samaritans sent their temple tax to Mount Gerizim.

At the centre of the inscriptions stands the expression "Argarizein." The expression has been used for determining the provenance of Pseudo-Eupolemus and Masada fragment 10, and it is time to turn to this discussion. Before we do that, it is appropriate to throw a quick glance at some of the other early Samaritan inscriptions in order to check the understanding of the Mount Gerizim inscriptions. Do the later inscriptions also reveal a cult of Yahweh, or are they polytheistic or syncretistic?

Excursus: Later Samaritan Inscriptions

A number of inscriptions in Samaritan script have been found from the period after the turn of the era. They constitute four groups, those that quote the Shema, Deut 6:4, in an abbreviated form, with or without additions, those that quote the Decalogue in a short form, with the Samaritan tenth commandment added, those with the "ten words of creation" quotations from Gen 1, and inscriptions with other quotations from the HB.

The first group is constituted by 26 inscriptions and engravings which seem to refer to the Shema, stemming from the first or second century to the nineteenth century C.E.[63] The oldest inscription was found in

---

[61] White, "Delos Synagoge Revisited," 145 f.

[62] One may follow White's reconstruction of lines 5 and 6, but a discussion of this question is not necessary here as it has no bearing on the present investigation.

[63] See the list in G. Davies, "A Samaritan Inscription with an Expanded Text of the Shema'," *PEQ* 131 (1999): 3–19.

Emmaus by Clermont-Ganneau in 1881 and contains the two words, εἷς θεός, "one God" in Greek, and ברוך שם לעולם, "blessed be the name forever," in Samaritan script. The supposed date for this inscription is the first or second century C.E. The Greek expression εἷς θεός is also found on the door of a tomb from Bal'an, in a mosaic from Thessaloniki, in panels on mosaics from El Khirbe, in a graffito from Mount Gerizim, and on an amulet from Caesarea, all dated to the fourth century C.E. An amulet from Tel Barukh near Tel Aviv and a ring from Nablus contain Deut 6:4, also from the fourth century C.E. The later inscriptions and engravings continue the same praxis, but after the 5th century only texts using Deut 6:4 are found.

As an example the inscription published by G. Davies (Museum no. E.1–1870) may serve. It is dated by him "to a middle stage" between the fourth and the thirteenth century, and reads:

> YHWH
> (is) our God
> YHWH
> (is) one
> He alone (*lbdw*).[64]

Cf. also the silver coin with the inscription יהוה אחד from the Mount Gerizim excavations.[65]

The second group is the Decalogue inscriptions. The oldest is the Beit el-Ma-inscription, now in The Rockefeller Archaeological Museum/The Palestine Archaeological Museum/The Israel Museum:

> [I am YHWH] your God. You shall have no [oth]er God[s] before me. [Keep the] Sabbath [d]ay to sanctify it. Honour your [father] and your mother. [You shall not kill. You shall not com[mit adultery]. You shall not steal. You shall not bear fa[lse] witness against your neighbour. You shall [not] covet your neighbour's house. [This Law] which I command you to[day on mo]unt Gerizim.[66]

The Nablus Decalogue comes from a Samaritan synagogue, but is now in the Chizn Yakub mosque. It contains the Ten Commandments in a short form conflated from Exod and Deut, with the Samaritan tenth commandment and Num 10:35 f. added.[67]

---

[64] Ibid., 5.
[65] Magen, "Mt. Gerizim—A Temple City," table 4, opposite 89.
[66] Author's translation of the original inscription in the museum.
[67] Montgomery, *Samaritans*, plate I, and 273.

1. [You shall have no other] Gods
2. [in front of me.] You shall not [ta]ke the name of YHWH
3. your God in vain. Keep the day
4. of the Sabbath to sanctify it. Honour your father
5. and your mother. You shall not murder. You shall not commit adultery.
6. You shall not steal. You shall not witness against your brother
7. falsely. You shall not [co]vet the ho[use]
8. of your neighbour. [You shall not covet your neighbour's wife.]
9. And you shall build there [an altar to YHWH your God].
10. Arise YHWH, [return YHWH.] Num 10:35 f.[68]

The Leeds fragment of a Decalogue inscription contains the lower right-hand corner of a stone, probably with the same text as the Shechem Decalogue.[69] A fourth Decalogue inscription was discovered by J. Bowman in Sychar. The four inscriptions were studied by S. Talmon and J. Bowman who concluded that they might be pre-Hexapla texts, from a period when the Samaritan form of the tenth commandment was not yet fixed as in the SP.[70] A Gaza fragment of a Decalogue inscription is from the Islamic period.

Inscription no. 395 from Mount Gerizim is found in six stone fragments: "I am YHWH your God: You shall have no other gods before me: For YHWH, he is The God, besides him there is no other: For YHWH, he is The God, in heaven above and on the earth below, there is no other. YHWH is our [G]od, YHWH [is one], for YHWH [your God, h]e is God of [God]s and Lord of [Lord]s, and no fo[reign g]od is with him."[71] The text is made up of quotations from Deut 5:6/Ex 20:1; Deut 4:35.39; 6:4; 10:17; 14:12. "This stone was probably erected when the Samaritan cult was renewed at the site during the Crusader period."[72]

The third group of Samaritan inscriptions is the "Ten Words of Creation," also incised, and one example is from the Chizn Yakub mosque. It condenses Gen 1 to the ten cases of "and God said," plus God's self-presentation as "God of your father, the God of Abraham and the God of Isaac, and the God of Jacob. [margin] YHWH, YHWH, A God mer[ciful

---

[68] Translated after the text in J. Bowman and S. Talmon, "Samaritan Decalogue Inscriptions," *BJRL* 33 (1951): 218; cf. Montgomery, *Samaritans*, 273.

[69] Montgomery, *Samaritans*, plate 3, and 275.

[70] Bowman and Talmon, "Samaritan Decalogue Inscriptions," 235 f.

[71] Magen, Misgav and Tsfania, *Mount Gerizim Excavations*, 263; Magen, "Mt. Gerizim—A Temple City," plate 1, opposite 88.

[72] Magen, Misgav and Tsfania, *Mount Gerizim Excavations*, 264.

and] gracious, the Existent, YHWH."[73] The two inscriptions now in the Chizn Yakub mosque and the Leeds fragment were judged by Montgomery to be older than Justinian.[74]

A fourth group is inscriptions with miscellaneous quotations from the HB. Here belongs the second Emmaus inscription, which was found by Lagrange, and which reads: "YHWH is a hero in war, YHWH is his name, YHWH, you have led him, come you blessed by YHWH, there is none like the God of Jeshurun." The text is composed of quotations from Exod 15:3.13; Gen 24:31; Deut 33:26. The third Emmaus inscription was also found by Lagrange in 1896, and reads "YHWH will pass over the door. And will not allow the destroyer to enter," Exod 12:23. From Damascus come ten plus seven inscriptions with biblical texts.

All these inscriptions are pre-mediaeval and the concentration on the worship of YHWH is the most prominent feature. The decalogue inscriptions contain a prohibition against idolatry. There are no traces of worship of other gods than YHWH in any of these inscriptions, nor any syncretism. If the Samaritans before the turn of the era worshipped various gods, among whom was YHWH, the explanation for the later concentration must be that they changed their religion from polytheism to monotheism or monolatry, or that a monotheistic element in the population survived and the other elements disappeared.

A simpler explanation is that the Samaritans always were monotheists or monolatrists, worshipping YHWH, as attested by the Mount Gerizim inscriptions from before the turn of the era.[75] The allegations against them of being idolaters, syncretists, or polytheists—found in later literature—are without foundation in the earliest inscriptions.

6.4. Texts with "Argarizein"

The two Delos inscriptions use the expression ΑΡΓΑΡΙΖΕΙΝ, which renders the Hebrew הרגריזים, "Mount Gerizim," where the word הר,

---

[73] Montgomery, *Samaritans*, plate 2, and 274.

[74] Ibid., 275.

[75] Similarly, the liturgical poem by Marqe, published by Z. Ben Hayyim, once mentions *yhwh*, pronounced *šema*, verse IX, and twice "Lord," *mr*, pronounced *mār*, verse I; VII; Z. Ben-Hayyim, *Studies in the Traditions of the Hebrew Language* (Madrid-Barcelona: Instituto "Arias Montano," 1954), 123–130.

"mountain," is treated as part of the name.[76] The expression is not translated, but transliterated. This contracted form is found in several other texts as well, in this format or with small variations, and the discussion has centred on its use as a criterion for determining the provenance of texts. R. Hanhart, S. Talmon and H. G. Kippenberg have maintained that it reveals Samaritan provenance, R. Pummer is more cautious, and H. Eshel thinks on one occasion it may have been used in a text directed against the Samaritans.[77]

If all the texts with the expression "Argarizein" have a Samaritan provenance, then we are in the fortunate position that the material is much larger than the Mount Gerizim and Delos inscriptions alone. It is therefore necessary to treat seriously the claim to Samaritan provenance for these texts.

It has been suggested that two criteria need to be fulfilled if "Argarizein" is to be used as a criterion for deciding that a text is Samaritan. One is that the expression must be written as one word, and the second is that this custom must only have been used by the Samaritans.[78] The idea seems to be that if all known occurrences show the same pattern, one may use the expression as a criterion in new cases. The danger is, however, that the new case may have a different provenance, but still be classified by the investigator as a member of the known group. This shows the problem with one single expression as a criterion for determining provenance. On the other hand, the expression "Argarizein," with variants, is unique enough to provide us with an interesting fingerprint which perhaps reveals Samaritan provenance. To test this possibility, we have to take a look at the cases we have.

I will start with the texts whose provenance is undisputed. In addition to the Delos inscriptions, these are the Samaritan manuscripts of the

---

[76] Due to the elision of gutturals in Samaritan and Jewish pronunciation of Hebrew and Aramaic one cannot expect to find an equivalent of the ה in Greek or Latin transliterations.

[77] Hanhart, "Zu den ältesten Traditionen"; Talmon, "Papyrus Fragment," [138]–[149]: "The work from which it stems was most probably not written on the site, but rather was brought there by a Samaritan who sought refuge on the mountain fortress to escape the Roman army which by that time had already occupied most of Palestine," p. [146]; "... the identification of the Masada papyrus as a Samaritan document can be based only on the persuasive combination of scribal customs, cultic overtones and linguistic criteria," [147]; idem, "כתבי כתובים," 286–287; Kippenberg, Garizim und Synagoge, 54 f.; Pummer, "ΑΡΓΑΡΙΖΙΝ: A Criterion for Samaritan Provenance?" JSJ 18 (1987): 18–25; Contra: Eshel, "Prayer of Joseph," 125–136.

[78] Pummer, "ΑΡΓΑΡΙΖΙΝ."

Pentateuch, Pliny and the Christian sources. On this background it is possible to discuss the contentious cases, 2 Macc 5:23; 6:2, Josephus, *War* 1.63, Masada fragment 10, and Pseudo-Eupolemus. The occurrence of "Argarizim" in Papyrus Giessen 19 belongs to the discussion of the SP, and will be treated there.[79]

The transmission of the expression is uniform in MT. It is written as two words, and it is understood as "the mountain/Mount Gerizim" by LXX, Targum and Vulgate, and translated accordingly. The Samaritan manuscripts to the Pentateuch tend to write the expression as one word, but this is not consistent; in some instances it is written as two words.[80] In Samaritan inscriptions from Bet el-Ma (בה[רגריזים]) and Yabneh (בהרגרם) the expression is written as one word; the situation is the same in the Samaritan liturgy, in the Samaritan Targum, and in the Arabic Pentateuch.

The expression "Argarizein" with variations therefore originated in Samaritan circles, but it was also used in texts which in themselves are not Samaritan. The question is then if these texts reveal a Samaritan source or Samaritan allegiance through the expression.

Pliny the Elder, writing in 77 C.E., renders the name as *mons Argaris*, even though it seems to be located closer to the coast: "oppida Rhinocolura et intus Rhaphea, Gaza et intus Anthedon, mons Argaris," translated as "There are the towns of El-Arish and inland Refah, Gaza and inland Anthedon, and Mount Argaris."[81] This phraseology was continued by Christian writers: the Pilgrim of Bordeaux, 333 C.E. (*ibi est mons Agazaren*); Marinus *in* Damascius, first half of the 6th century

---

[79] A comprehensive list of occurrences is given by Pummer, "ΑΡΓΑΡΙΖΙΝ," 18–25.

[80] Ms. no. 6 (C) of the Samaritan synagogue in Shechem (1204 C.E.) writes the expression as two words in the tenth commandment, Exod 20:14b, and in Deut 11:29, but as one word in Deut 27:4.12, Tal, *Samaritan Pentateuch*, 75. 188.202. The Abisha Scroll writes it as one word in Deut 11:29; 27:4.12, cf. A. & R. Sadaqa, *Jewish and Samaritan Version of the Pentateuch with Particular Stress on the Differences between both Texts: Deuteronomium* (Jerusalem: Ruben Mass, 1966), 21.40; and also in the tenth commandment, A. & R. Sadaqa, *Jewish and Samaritan Version of the Pentateuch with Particular Stress on the Differences between both Texts: Exodus* (Jerusalem: Ruben Mass, 1964), 30.

[81] Pliny the Elder, *Naturalis historia*, V xiv 68. Pliny continues by calling "Samaria" the region with the cities Ascalon, Ashdod, two towns Iamnea, one of them inland, and Joppa. Further he mentions "inland Samaria" which includes "oppida Neapolis, quod antea Mamortha dicebatur, Sebaste in monte, et alteriore Gamala," V xiv 69, translated by H. Rackham in LCL as "the towns are Naplous, formerly called Mamortha, Sebustieh on a mountain, and on a loftier mountain Gamala."

C.E., quoted by Photius (πρὸς ὄρει ... τῷ Ἀργαρίζῳ καλουμένῳ); John Malalas, later 6th century C.E. (εἰς τὸ Γαργαρίζη/Γαργαζι ὄρος).[82] In all these cases the expression "Argarizin" is treated as the name for the mountain, and to the name was added "mountain," *mons*, ὄρος. As early as the first century C.E. "Argarizin" was considered a name, and if one wanted to make sure that the readers should know that it was a mountain, one had to add a word for "mountain."[83]

A similar explanation has been offered by H. Eshel. His model is that when the Hellenistic city was constructed around the temple on Mount Gerizim in the second century B.C.E., the Samaritans gave it the name "Hargerizim."[84] Eshel discusses only a part of the relevant evidence, and it seems that the name applied to the mountain rather than to the city. His idea would possibly also have to be pushed further back in time, since the city—as the excavator tells us—was founded earlier.

Chronicon Paschale, early seventh century C.E., has εἰς τὸ καλούμενον Γαργαρίδην, where the context is the Samaritan rebellion under the Emperor Zeno;[85] a story which is based upon Malalas' account, and the latter author's Γαργαρίζη/Γαργαζι. The name was then further changed by *Chronicon Paschale*, but without the addition of "mountain." The corrupted forms *Agazaren*, Γαργαρίζη/Γαργαζι and Γαργαρίδεν show how the original name was transmitted in settings where no attempt was made to understand the Hebrew behind it or to check what the correct form was. It had developed into a name, a technical term for the Samaritan Holy Mountain. In the case of the *Chronicon Paschale* the provenance of the text was so far away from Palestine that it was not natural to give information about the type of geographical phenomenon in question, so "mountain" was not added.

With the exception of *Chronicon Paschale*, in these Greek and Latin texts "mountain" is added to the expression. The name was only used for locating other phenomena, or else it occurs in a geographical account of Palestine, as in the case of Pliny. These authors evidently had no axe to grind in connection with "Mount Gerizim," and therefore are reliable witnesses to the contracted form of the name. "Argarizim" and variants

---

[82] Pummer, *Early Christian Authors*, 429 (Marinus).270f. (John Malalas).

[83] A modern parallel would be "Mount Kilimanjaro," where "Kilima Njaro" means "shining mountain" in Swahili. "Mount Kilimanjaro" is therefore a pleonasm, but this is not felt in contexts where the original meaning of the name is unknown.

[84] Eshel, "Prayer of Joseph," 135.

[85] Pummer, *Early Christian Authors*, 366.

are simply names for the mountain, without these authors necessarily drawing upon Samaritan sources, let alone taking any religious stance in favour of Samaritan claims.

With Procopius of Gaza (475–538) this is different; his anti-Samaritan attitude is outspoken. He writes a commentary on Deut 11:29 and quotes the name as ἐπ' ὄρους Γαριζὶν, just as in the LXX.[86] In the commentary he makes the point that the mountains Gerizim and Ebal of Deut 11:29 cannot be located where the Samaritans claim, near Neapolis. Two arguments are adduced for this. First, that the mountains there are so high that one would not be able to hear in the valley the blessing and curse pronounced from the mountains, and secondly, that the Book of Joshua locates them near Gilgal. Procopius therefore distinguishes the correct mountain Gerizim from "the mountain which they call Garizein," τὸ ὄρος ὃ φασι Γαριζεὶν (and similar expressions).[87]

Procopius offers two explanations for the name "Gerizim" and two for "Ebal." It may be that the first explanation for "Gerizim," "mountain of the redeemed," interprets the element *ger* as a form of הר, or as derived from this word.[88] On the other hand, "mountain" is there in the Biblical text in addition to "Gerizim" and "Ebal," and the second etymology for "Gerizim" interprets *ger* from גור. Since this is an explanation of a text on the basis of the LXX translation of the MT, there is no cause for Procopius to render the name as e. g. "Argarizein." Consequently, he treats the Samaritans' names for the mountains in Samaria on the basis of the given text. He might have known the expression "Argarizim," but we may speculate that this expression could be interpreted as condoning a claim to religious legitimacy, and so he refrained from using it.[89] This remains speculation in the case of Procopius, but such a tendency is evident in the Madaba map.

---

[86] Pummer, *Early Christian Authors*, 116.

[87] Cf. the rabbinical discussion in *y. Sotah* 7:3, where R. Eliezer explains that the mountains are not in Samaria, since the Israelites after crossing the Jordan made two heaps of stones and named them Mount Gerizim and Mount Ebal.

[88] The suggestion was made by Pummer, *Early Christian Authors*, 229.

[89] Editions with the relevant texts: Pliny the Elder, *Hist.* V. XIV. 68: LCL, ed. and translated by H. Rackham, 1949, 272; the Pilgrim from Bourdaux, *Itinerarium Burdigalense*, 587.3: Pummer, *Early Christian Authors*, 111–113; Marinus: *Life of Damascius*, quoted in Photius, *Bibliotheca* 242.345b.20: ibid., 429; John Malalas, *Chronicle/Chronographia* 15.383.1: ibid., 269 f.; the *Chronicon Paschale* 604.9: ibid., 366; Procopius of Gaza, *Commentarium* in Deut 11:29: ibid., 230 f.

The Madaba map was dated by M. Avi-Yonah to 542–565, perhaps to 560–565.[90] It offers ΓΕΒΑΛ and ΓΑ / PIZEIN near Jericho and Gilgal, but also ΤΟΥΡΓΩΒΗΛ and ΤΟΥΡΓΑΡΙΖΙΝ, one on each side of ΣΥΧΕΜ. In the case of ΓΕΒΑΛ and ΓΑPIZEIN near Jericho and Gilgal the orientation of the map is East-West, but in the case of ΤΟΥΡΓΩ-ΒΗΛ and ΤΟΥΡΓΑPIZIN on each side of ΣΥΧΕΜ it is possible that the orientation was North-South. The map is supposed in the main to reflect the Onomasticon of Eusebius (260–341).[91] Eusebius writes about the mountains:

> Gaibal, a mountain in the Promised Land, where an altar was built at Moses' command. It is said that there are two mountains near Jericho, facing one another and close [to each other], one of which is Garizein and the other Gaibal. However, the Samaritans point out others lying near Neapolis, but they are mistaken, for the mountains they indicate are too far from one another, so that those calling from each of them cannot hear each other.
>
> Garizein, a mountain where those who pronounced blessings were standing, near the aforesaid Gaibal.

Jerome's translation of this text is as follows:

> Gebal, a mountain in the Promised Land, where an altar was built at Moses' command. But there are two mountains near Jericho, facing one another and close [to each other], one of which is called Garizin and the other Gebal. However, the Samaritans think that these two mountains are near Neapolis, but they are grossly mistaken: mostly because they are far from one another, but also because the voice of anyone interchangeably blessing or cursing, as the Scripture says, cannot be reciprocally heard.
>
> Garizin, a mountain on which those who pronounced curses were standing, beside the aforesaid Gebal.[92]

---

[90] M. Avi-Yonah, *The Madaba Mosaic Map* (Jerusalem: Israel Exploration Society, 1954), 18.

[91] Avi-Yonah, *Madaba Mosaic Map*, 31 f.; L. di Segni, "The 'Onomasticon' of Eusebius and the Madaba Map," in *The Madaba Map Centenary 1897–1997: Travelling through the Byzantine Umayyad Period: Proceedings of the International Conference held in Amman, 7–9 April 1997* (Jerusalem: Studium Biblicum Franciscanum, 1999), 115–120.

[92] E. Klostermann, *Eusebius Werke* (Text und Untersuchungen zur Geschichte der altchristlichen Literatur. Neue Folge; Leipzig: Hinrichs, 1902), 64; texts edited and translated by di Segni in *Madaba Map Centenary*, 53; translation also in G. S. P. Freeman-Grenville, R. L. Chapman III and J. E. Taylor, *Palestine in the Fourth Century A.D.: The Onomasticon by Eusebius of Ceasarea*, (Jerusalem: Carta, 2003), 40 f. Translation here mine.

Eusebius finished his Onomasticon around 325 or 330 c.e.[93] One notices the more hostile attitude in Jerome's translation from around 390; he states that the correct location is near Jericho, not only that this "is said," and he adds that the Samaritans are "grossly" mistaken. The reference to Scripture for the voices of those cursing and blessing adds weight to his argument, and he terms Garizim the mountain for curses instead of blessings, contrary to Deut 11:29. This difference between Eusebius and Jerome shows a growing hostility towards the Samaritans in the course of the fourth century c.e. This hostility is even more pronounced in the sixth century Christian work dependent upon Eusebius, Procopius of Gaza, and it is visible in the Madaba map.

"The fact that the mosaicist has shown the two mountains twice proves that he had some doubts as regards the tradition followed by Eusebius."[94] This same fact can also be taken to prove that he followed Eusebius in his polemics against the Samaritan claims. The comments by Eusebius explain why the Madaba map presents two sets of mountains, and also why they receive different orthography.[95] The names of the mountains near Jericho and Gilgal are written according to the LXX, and the names around Shechem are transliterations of the current Samaritan pronunciation in Aramaic. The map shows that the Samaritan vernacular had changed to Aramaic, and that the Samaritans in the mid-sixth century used a contracted form modelled on the earlier Hebrew form: ΤΟΥΡ-ΓΩΒΗΛ and ΤΟΥΡΓΑΡΙΖΙΝ.

Thus there is no "second representation of the mountains Ebal and Gerizim ... in explicit disregard of Eusebius' statement."[96] The mountains near Jericho and Gilgal are evidently considered as the correct biblical ones with names taken from the LXX, and the mountains around Shechem are presented with their Samaritan names, which function as an argument against their legitimacy. The polemical nature of the map is spelled out in the case of Shechem, where the text on the map reads: "Sychem, which [is] also Sikima and Salem," ΣΥ / ΧΕΜ / ΗΚΣΙΚΙΜΑ / ΚΣΑΛΗΜ, corresponding to the Onomasticon's Συχὲμ ἡ καὶ Σίκιμα ἡ καὶ Σαλήμ, "Suchem, which also is Sikima or even Salem." In the Onomasticon, Eusebius continues by mentioning some incidents in the

[93] Freeman-Grenville, Chapman III and Taylor, *Onomasticon*, 4: 325 c.e.; Klostermann, *Eusebius Werke*, XII: 330 c.e.

[94] Avi-Yonah, *Madaba Mosaic Map*, 47.

[95] Cf. the discussion on the location of Ebal and Gerizim in *y. Meg.* 1:9, and the church fathers quoted above, p. 232 f.

[96] di Segni, "Onomasticon," 116.

HB connected to Shechem, and ends with the sentence: "There was also a Sychem in the mountain of Ephraim, a city of refuge." A "second Shechem" is a clear denigration of Shechem and without any biblical source. Under "Salem" Eusebius writes, "city of Sikimon, which is Sychem, as Scripture says. But there is also another village [*vacat*]." Σά-λεμ πόλις Σικιμῶν is a quotation from Gen 33:18 LXX (Σαλεμ πόλιν Σικιμων), and it may also be translated "Salem, city of the Sikemites." If Eusebius read the expression in this way, it may explain why he identified the place with Shechem. Again in the case of the lemmata "Suchem" and "Salem" in the Onomasticon the translation of Jerome is more anti-Samaritan than Eusebius. The Madaba map does of course not contain any of the extended comments by Eusebius or Jerome, but it simply treats Eusebius' series "Suchem, Sikima and Salem" as identical, and locates them at Shechem.

The modern Arabic name for Mount Gerizim is *Jabal at-Tur*, a mix of Arabic and Aramaic, meaning "Mount The Mountain." The first part of the Aramaic expression ΤΟΥΡΓΑΡΙΖΙΝ has been used in the Arabic name. This is a continuation of the old pattern of transcribing the expression and adding a geographical expression.

An attempt has been made to locate Salem in the vicinity of Shechem.

> Sites 12 and 13 are two parts of one ancient town, spread on two hills and the saddle between them. The modern village here carries the name Sâlim, a very likely pointer to the ancient name *Shālēm*, which comes down in English as Salem ... The cluster of Hellenistic references to Salem, on the other hand, fits very nicely with the evidence that a town developed here probably during Iron II and then flourished in Hellenistic times, at some point bearing the name Salem. By the third century B.C.E., when the plain was blossoming with new Samaritan settlements, a Salem here in the slopes of Jebel el-Kebîr is a virtual certainty, probably one of the three or four largest Hellenistic settlements in the greater Shechem region—after Shechem itself and Kh. El-Lozeh by Mount Gerizim.[97]

If a modern name reflects the name of a place in Hellenistic times, it seems strange that in the fourth and sixth centuries c.e., Eusebius, Jerome and the Madaba map identified Salem with Shechem instead of providing it with a separate location. All these witnesses reveal exact knowledge of the Holy Land, even if the representations on a mosaic map cannot be expected to be comparable to other materials for maps. The translation

---

[97] Campbell, *Shechem II*, 112.

of Gen 33:18 in the LXX was interpreted by Eusebius, Jerome and the Madaba map as identifying Salem with Shechem, and this would have been strange if Campbell's idea were correct.

On the background of Eusebius' Onomasticon the map makes the same impression as the slightly earlier text by Procopius of Gaza: there was a strong will among the Christians of the Byzantine period in the Holy Land to denounce the Samaritan claim for the legitimacy of their holy mountain. The Maria Theotokos church on the summit of Mount Gerizim was built around 484 C.E., perhaps on the spot where the Samaritan temple had once been. But even if it was not located exactly at the temple site, its construction on Mount Gerizim was a clear polemic against Samaritan claims for the mountain; compare the language in Eusebius' Onomasticon, in Procopius, and in the Madaba map. If "Gerizim" was changed to "Ebal" in Deut 27:4 MT, and if the altar-pericope in the Book of Joshua was relocated to chapter 8, these would be parallel phenomena.

In Pliny and the Christian sources the expression "Argarizim" is used as the name for the Samaritan Holy Mountain. In the Madaba map the name in its current Aramaic form was rendered in Greek transliteration, but with an anti-Samaritan purpose. The material with a known provenance shows that the contracted name "Argarizin/Argarizein/Argarizim" and variants was used by Samaritans, by a Roman author without any religious intention, and by Christians in neutral settings and also by Christians with an anti-Samaritan polemical purpose. It was not only used by Samaritans. The contracted form alone can therefore not function as a decisive criterion for Samaritan provenance of a text. On this basis it is possible to treat the disputed cases.

2 Maccabees 5:23 and 6:2

The majority of the manuscripts offer this text in the case of 2 Macc 5:22–23a:

κατέλιπεν δὲ καὶ ἐπιστάτας τοῦ κακοῦν τὸ γένος ἐν μὲν Ἱεροσολύμοις Φίλιππον τὸ μὲν γένος Φρύγα τὸν δὲ τρόπον βαρβαρώτερον ἔχοντα τοῦ καταστήσαντος ἐν δὲ Γαριζιν Ἀνδρόνικον πρὸς δὲ τούτοις Μενέλαον ὃς χείριστα τῶν ἄλλων ὑπερῄρετο τοῖς πολίταις

He left governors to oppress the people: at Jerusalem, Philip, by birth a Phrygian and in character more barbarous than the man who appointed him; and at Gerizim, Andronicus; and besides these Menelaus, who lorded it over his compatriots worse than the others did.

2 Macc 6:1–2 similarly in most manuscripts reads:

μετ᾽ οὐ πολὺν δὲ χρόνον ἐξαπέστειλεν ὁ βασιλεὺς γέροντα Ἀθηναῖον
ἀναγκάζειν τοὺς Ιουδαίους μεταβαίνειν ἀπὸ τῶν πατρίων νόμων καὶ
τοῖς τοῦ θεοῦ νόμοις μὴ πολιτεύεσθαι μολῦναι δὲ καὶ τὸν ἐν Ιεροσολύ-
μοις νεὼ καὶ προσονομάσαι Διὸς Ὀλυμπίου καὶ τὸν ἐν Γαριζιν καθὼς
ἐτύγχανον οἱ τὸν τόπον οἰκοῦντες Διὸς Ξενίου

Not long after this, the king sent an Athenian senator to compel the Jews
to forsake the laws of their ancestors and no longer to live by the laws of
God; also to pollute the temple in Jerusalem and to call it the temple of
Olympian Zeus, and to call the one in Gerizim the temple of Zeus-the-
Friend-of-Strangers, as did the people who lived in that place.

There are three Old Latin manuscripts and the Armenian translation
that render 2 Macc 5:23 with *argarizim*; and seven Old Latin manuscripts
plus the Armenian translation render 6:2 with *argarizim*; one manuscript
reads *arzarim* in 6:2.[98] The Vulgate follows the majority readings and
offers *Garizin*. In his edition of 2 Maccabees, R. Hanhart therefore reconstructed the text of 5:23 and 6:2 as Ἀργαριζίν.[99] The simple explanation
for the occurrence of *argarizim* in the Old Latin is that the translator read
it in his source, but did not understand what it meant, or understood it as
a name, and therefore transliterated it. His *Vorlage* therefore most probably had Ἀργαριζίν, and this seems to have been the original text here.[100]
2 Maccabees is dated around 100 B.C.E., so 5:23; 6:2 are also cases where
the expression was used in the second century B.C.E.

R. Hanhart supposes that the use of this expression in 2 Macc. 6:2
reveals a Samaritan source for the desecration of the temple on Mount
Gerizim, a source Jason of Cyrene or the epitomator of 2 Maccabees
twisted into an anti-Samaritan account of the origin of the Samaritans by
alleging that they were foreigners.[101] Hanhart does not explain the occurrence of the form in 2 Macc 5:23; the theory might require a Samaritan
origin for the account there as well.

However, another explanation is easier. It is not necessary to assume
a Samaritan origin for the account on the basis of the form of the name
alone. If Ἀργαριζίν was the regular Samaritan name for the mountain,
the expression could be used by people who had no religious attachment

---

[98] R. Hanhart, *Maccabaeorum liber II copiis usus quas reliquit Werner Kappler* (vol. 9,
fasc. 1 of *Septuaginta: Vetus Testamentum Graecum auctoritate Societatis Litterarum
Gotingensis editum*; Göttingen: Akademie der Wissenschaften in Göttingen/Vanden-
hoeck & Ruprecht, 1959), 9 f. 26. 69 f.

[99] Hanhart, *Maccabaeorum liber II*.

[100] D. D. de Bruyne, "Mélanges: I Notes de philologie biblique. II.—Argarizim (II Mach.
5, 23; 6, 2)," *RB* 30 (1921): 405–407.

[101] Hanhart, "Zu den ältesten Traditionen," 108 f.*.

to the mountain themselves. Pliny, and the Christian sources—including the Madaba map—all prove this. There was no allegiance to Mount Gerizim in using the name.

Jason of Cyrene, in the 2nd century B.C.E., had interpreted what he heard as one word as the name for the mountain. In both cases Ἀργαριζίν is paralleled with Ἱεροσόλυμα. Thus the name of the city of Jerusalem and the name Ἀργαριζίν corresponded to each other, perhaps already in the view of Jason, and most certainly in the mind of the epitomator who created 2 Maccabees. Later, the form of words at 5:23; 6:2 was adapted to that in the other four cases where the name occurs in the LXX, namely as Γαριζίν and, in the Latin version, *Garizin*. This may have happened at the time of the inclusion of 2 Maccabees into the collection of OT books, or as a result of changes in the historical situation. Ἀργαριζίν may have taken on such strong ideological overtones in the eyes of strict Jerusalem-oriented theologians that it became impossible to use it in 2 Maccabbes, a book which is a tribute to the Maccabeans who destroyed the temple on Gerizim, at least according to Josephus.

2 Macc. 5:23; 6:2 used Ἀργαριζίν in the second century B.C.E. in a text highly critical of the Samaritans: they were of foreign origin. J. A. Goldstein may be right in the assumption that the author of 2 Maccabees was not satisfied with the temple in Jerusalem, and tolerated temples at *Araq el Emir* and Leontopolis, and, by implication, may have been tolerant of the temple on Gerizim as well. J. A. Goldstein interprets the first occurrence of τὸ γένος in 5:22 to imply that the inhabitants of Jerusalem and Gerizim were "the same people."[102]

It is a fair assumption that there is a strong anti-Samaritan bias in the interpretation of the name Ζεύς Ξένιος in 2 Macc. 6:2: "as it befitted the inhabitants of the place," or "as the inhabitants of the place requested," καθὼς ἐτύγχανον οἱ τὸν τόπον οἰκοῦντες Διὸς Ξενίου.[103] An anti-Samaritan bias is there whichever understanding one chooses of the verb τυγχάνω here. The meaning of καθὼς ἐτύγχανον, may either be "as [the people] asked for" or "as it befitted [the people]."[104] The author of 2 Maccabees either says that the inhabitants of the place themselves decided which new name their temple should have, or that it was renamed by the Seleucids according to the character of the Samaritans as foreigners. Independent of whether the author of 2 Macc 6:2 thought

---

[102] Goldstein, *II Maccabees*, 261.
[103] Hanhart, "Zu den ältesten Traditionen," 108 f.*.
[104] Hanhart, "Zu den ältesten Traditionen," 107*.

that this renaming was the result of a Samaritan initiative or of Seleucid policies he in either case considered the Samaritans as foreigners; they needed a god who protected foreigners.

J. A. Goldstein has attempted to see "a punning translation" of "Garizin" in "Zeus the friend of strangers." *Zēn* was an alternative form of the name of Zeus and גר was mostly rendered προσήλυτος in Greek, but there is at least one case where it corresponded to ξένος (Job 31:32). "*Garizin* could thus be taken as 'sojourning stranger protected by Zeus.'"[105] This may have worked for "Gerizim," but would be difficult in the case of "Argarizin," which probably was the original form here. Jason or the epitomator may, however, have seen a connection between the element גר and ξένος, and this is what was needed for a pun on the name "Argarizin" and an anti-Samaritan reading of 2 Kgs 17. The allegation that the Samaritans were foreigners might be based on an anti-Samaritan reading of 2 Kgs 17, cf. the discussion of 4Q372 above.[106] Such an anti-Samaritan tendency in the reading of this text would then be two hundred years older than *Ant.* 9.288–291, where Josephus explicitly interpreted this biblical chapter in this way. The Samaritans were, at the time of Antiochus or of 2 Maccabees, considered "Jews," but also as descending from the deported people mentioned in that chapter.

The polemical nature of the verse is also borne out by the fact that a similar explanation for the renaming of the Jerusalem temple is not given, and that the dedication applied there was to Ζεύς Ὀλυμπίος. This is a more prestigious name than Ζεύς Ξένιος.

2 Macc. 5:23; 6:2 is therefore evidence that "Argarizim" could be used in a Jewish, anti-Samaritan setting in the second century B.C.E. It referred to the holy mountain of the Samaritans with a contracted expression understood as a technical term for the mountain with certain cultic implications. When, according to 2 Maccabees, Antiochus Epiphanes renamed the two temples, their locations are referred to under formal names, names used by the inhabitants in both cases.

2 Macc 6:1–2 is usually taken to mean that the Jews in Jerusalem were forced to abandon their customs and that only the temple in Jerusalem was defiled, cf. the NRSV translation quoted above. In fact, the syntax of

---

[105] Goldstein, *II Maccabees*, 274.

[106] Cf. the long insertion in the LXX of 2 Kgs 17:32: καὶ κατῴκισαν τὰ βδελύγματα αὐτῶν ἐν τοῖς οἴκοις τῶν ὑψηλῶν ἃ ἐποίησαν ἐν Σαμαρείᾳ ἔθνος ἔθνος ἐν πόλει ἐν ᾗ κατῴκουν ἐν αὐτῇ, preceded and followed by the same expression καὶ ἦσαν φοβούμενοι τὸν κύριον, showing it to be an insertion. This insertion is anti-Samaritan.

v. 2 is dependent on v. 1, and the verb ἐξαπέστειλεν of v. 1 governs the following infinitives: ἀναγκάζειν, μολῦναι, and προσονομάσαι. The Greek senator was sent in order to "compel the Jews to …., and also to pollute … and to rename …" If the finite verb ἐξαπέστειλεν governs these infinitives, the mission was to compel Jews in Jerusalem and Gerizim to desert their laws, and to pollute and rename both temples. J. A. Goldstein translates v. 2, "He was also to defile both the temple in Jerusalem and the temple on Mount Gerizim and to proclaim the former to be the temple of Zeus Olympios and the latter (in accordance with the … of the inhabitants of the place) to be the temple of Zeus Xenios."[107] It follows that the inhabitants on Gerizim were considered "Jews" by 2 Maccabees, and their laws were violated and their temple polluted in a way comparable to what happened in Jerusalem. J. A. Goldstein refers to המעוז in Dan 11:31, which Jason may have taken to be the Samaritan temple in the land of Ephraim, cf. Ps 60:9; 108:9. The idea is interesting, but presupposes a separation of המקדש המעוז, Dan 11:31, into two separate expressions and a link to the Psalm texts with their "Shechem" and "Ephraim" in subsequent verses.

Still, the anti-Samaritan bias is evident in the explanation of the name Ζεύς Ξένιος, and in the more prestigious name for the temple in Jerusalem. J. A. Goldstein is also clear on the point of an anti-Samaritan bias of 2 Maccabees. He thinks it possible that Jason considered Dan 11:32 to refer to the Samaritans: "those who violate the covenant."

2 Maccabees testifies to a temple, perhaps also a colony on Mount Gerizim, at the time of Antiochus IV Epiphanes. The colony was considered part of the Jewish nation, but they were nevertheless under Jason's criticism. "Argarizim" was used in 5:23 and 6:2 as a name for the mountain where the νεώς was located. It was therefore employed in a Jewish anti-Samaritan setting.

Josephus' War 1.63

Josephus offers Ἀργαριζείν only once, War 1.63, in the account of Hyrcanus' conquest of Shechem and Gerizim: Μεδάβην μὲν οὖν καὶ Σαμαγὰν ἅμα ταῖς πλησίον, ἔτι δὲ Σίκιμα καὶ Ἀργαριζείν αὐτὸς αἱρεῖ, "He thus captured Medaba and Samaga with the neighbouring towns, also Shechem and Argarizein." The parallel text in Ant. 13.255, however, is different: ἔπειτα καὶ Σαμόγαν καὶ τὰ πλησίον εὐθὺς αἱρεῖ Σίκιμά τε

---

[107] Goldstein, II Maccabees, 268. Goldstein's omission is due to the lack of clarity of the text in the case of the verb ἐτύγχανον.

πρὸς τούτοις καὶ Γαριζεὶν ...", "After this he at once captured Samoga and the neighboring places; and Shechem in addition to these, and Gerizim ..." In all other instances in *War* or *Antiquities* he used Γαριζεῖν. In this case also it has been suggested that the author used the contracted transliteration because he followed a source.[108] However, it is unlikely that the Samaritans provided him with an account of John Hyrcanus' capture of Shechem and "Hargarizim." The reason for Ἀργαριζεῖν in *War* 1.63 might be the same as it was for the author of 2 Macc. 6:2: the technical term for the Holy Mountain of the Samaritans is fitting in a context negative with regard to the Samaritans, in this case Hyrcanus' conquest. Hyrcanus was Josephus' hero, and the achievement was even greater if he conquered and destroyed the venerated mountain of the Samaritans. The different expression in the other instances, Γαριζεῖν, might rest upon the wish to avoid any recognition of Samaritan claims to legitimacy. Only where this misunderstanding was impossible because he explicitly mentioned the conquest, could he use Ἀργαριζεῖν. Another possibility is that he complied with standard Greek phraseology in all cases except one. The change in audience and purpose of *Antiquities* against *War* might also have played a role here.

So far we have seen "Argarizim" and variant forms used by the Samaritans themselves, in neutral contexts, Roman and Christian, and in Jewish and Christian polemics against them. The form seems to have a Samaritan origin, but its use does not necessarily entail religiously hostile or sympathetic attitudes by the authors. This insight will enable us to evaluate the following cases, which are even more contested.

Masada Fragment 10

A papyrus fragment with text on both sides has been found on Masada, Mas 10 or Mas pap paleo Unidentified Text, on the recto (obverse), and Mas 10 or Mas pap paleoText of Samaritan origin, on the verso (reverse).[109] The fragment is 4,0 × 3,8 cm, and contains two short Hebrew texts written by different hands in paleo-Hebrew, which are dated on palaeographical grounds before the common era. The texts are incom-

---

[108] Kippenberg, *Garizim und Synagoge*, 55.

[109] The fragment has not been published in the DJD-series, but by S. Talmon, "Papyrus Fragment," [138]–[149]. S. Talmon uses the expressions צד א and צד ב in "קטעי כתבים," and keeps the definitions in "Masada Fragment," and in "Papyrus Fragment," where צד א is "obverse" and צד ב is "reverse" in the caption to the photos of the texts, but then

plete, and among the few clearly readable words on the reverse side of the fragment is the double occurrence of לרנגה, "for praise," and הרגריזים. Because of the former word the text is considered hymnical. Apart from these words not much can be reconstructed. The fragment is important since it contains the oldest occurrence in a Semitic language of הרגריזים.

This short text has been considered a Samaritan text from a Samaritan who fled the Romans and joined forces with the insurgents on Masada, and also as an anti-Samaritan text.[110] Another possibility is that the text landed in Masada for unknown reasons and happened to end up together with the other hymnic material there. It is our task, however, to try to make sense of the material we have, so let us consider the two suggestions.

S. Talmon holds the former position on "the above persuasive combination of linguistic criteria, scribal tradition and cultic overtones."[111] His "linguistic criteria" is the custom to write "Hargarizim" as one word, which he considers a Samaritan phenomenon. As we have seen, this criterion does not on its own prove Samaritan provenance. The "scribal tradition" would refer to the texts' having been written by trained scribes, and the "cultic overtones" are the two occurrences of לרנגה, plus his reconstruction of other words indicating a liturgical setting. Against this one may assume that trained scribes and liturgy would have been present among both Samaritans and Jews, and are therefore inconclusive for provenance. S. Talmon's verdict is that "the work from which it [the fragment] stems was probably not written on the site, but rather was brought there by a Samaritan who sought refuge in the mountain fortress from the Roman army, which by that time had already occupied most of Palestine."[112] This is a possibility, but it remains without the necessary evidence.

H. Eshel has proposed to read the text as a fragment of a Jewish hymn praising God for his destruction of Mount Gerizim, and such a hymn would be a predecessor of the later "Day of Gerizim," when the Jews

---

reverses the definitions for the transcription, where "Obverse" heads the transcription of text on the reverse side and "Reverse" heads the transcription of text on the obverse side. This latter, however, is not reversed in the commentary. After the reversal in the captions, there is thus consistency of expressions.

[110] Talmon, "קטעי כתבים," 278–286; idem, "Masada fragment," 220–232; idem, "Papyrus Fragment," 138–149; he considers it a Samaritan text; Eshel, "Prayer of Joseph," 125–136 links it with 4Q372 and it, accordingly, is considered anti-Samaritan.

[111] Talmon, "Masada fragment," 231.

[112] Ibid., 230.

commemorated the assault by John Hyrcanus on the mountain.[113] This is a suggestion made on the basis of possible contacts between the fragment and the Prayer of Joseph from Qumran, 4Q371 and 4Q372. A hymn or a prayer to God could be combined with curses on the enemy, so this is a possibility. Where non-Samaritans use the contracted form elsewhere, they do not use it in connection with curses but rather in polemical contexts. H. Eshel's suggestion is the most probable, since it does not necessitate reconstructions of text, and it interprets the fragment in the Masada context, therefore in a Jewish context.

Pseudo-Eupolemus

There remains the text called Pseudo-Eupolemus, with its interesting information about Abraham and his attitude to Mount Gerizim. It has been suggested that the text is of Samaritan provenance, and if a case can be made for this, we have an important piece of evidence for one part of Samaritan ideology in the second century B.C.E.

The expression Ἀργαριζίν is found in the following story about Abraham in Pseudo-Eupolemus: ξενισθῆναί τε αὐτὸν ὑπο πόλεως ἱερόν Ἀργαριζίν, ὃ εἶναι μεθερμηνευόμενον ὄρος ὑψίστου· παρὰ δὲ τοῦ Μελχισεδὲκ ἱερέως ὄντος τοῦ θεοῦ καὶ βασιλεύοντος λαβεῖν δῶρα, "he [Abraham] was also received as a guest by the city Holy Argarizin, which translates as 'The Mountain of the Most High'. He also received gifts from Melchizedek who was a priest of God and reigned as a king as well." (*Praeparatio Evangelica* 9.17.2–9)[114]

The sentences are found in one of two fragments formerly believed to belong to Eupolemus; J. Freudenthal, on the other hand, argued that they are independent of Eupolemus, and therefore should be considered anonymous, or termed "Pseudo-Eupolemus."[115] The second fragment deals with Abraham in Babylon, Phoenicia and Egypt in a few sentences—perhaps as a summary of the first fragment—and throws no clearer light on the question of the provenance of the first fragment. The first fragment comes from the first half of the 2nd century

---

[113] Eshel, "Prayer of Joseph," 136.

[114] The text of Pseudo-Eupolemus with translation in Holladay, *Historians*, 157–187; translation in L. H. Feldman and M. Reinhold, *Jewish Life and Thought among Greeks and Romans: Primary Readings* (Minneapolis, Minn.: Fortress, 1996), 228; N. Walter, "Pseudo-Eupolemos," *JHRSZ* 1: 137–143; R. Doran, "Pseudo-Eupolemus," *OTP* 2: 873–882.

[115] Freudenthal, "Hellenistische Studien," 82–103.

B.C.E., and was conserved by Alexander Polyhistor, whence they came into Eusebius' *Praeparatio Evangelica* 9.[116]

The concentration on Abraham in the two fragments is the most prominent feature of the text. Pseudo-Eupolemus portrays Abraham as a descendant of the Giants who are saved from the flood. In accordance with this status he excells in wisdom, piety, and nobility above all men, and he—or Enoch—discovers astrology and Chaldean science. This he teaches the Phoenicians and the Egyptians. He comes to the assistance of the Phoenicians in the war with the Armenians, and defeats a numerous enemy with a few men. He is received by Melchizedek at Argarizin after this event. In Egypt, Sarah is miraculously kept from being violated by the king. His encounter with the king of the Egyptians turns out to benefit him. The other heroes in the story are compared to Greek figures: Belus is Kronos, Enoch is Atlas.[117]

This exalted picture of Abraham fits with the way the meeting with Melchizedek is described. In Gen 14:18 MT Melchizedek provides Abraham with bread and wine, but in v. 20 Abraham gives tithes to Melchizedek. In fragment 1 Abraham only receives gifts from Melchizedek. The question is which part of Gen 14 fragment 1 alludes to, and as the rest of the sentences here refers to v. 18 ("who was a priest of God and reigned as a king as well") it seems that the "gifts" refer to the "bread and wine" of the MT.

The first fragment builds upon Gen 6–9; 10; 11; 12; 14; 33. The sequence of the Bible is altered in this story. After Abraham on God's command has arrived in "Phoenicia"—compare Gen 12:5 f.—he teaches the Phoenicians astrology (no biblical equivalent), and assists the people in the war against the "Armenians"—a story reflecting Gen 14 even if the name of the enemy is different. After this, the text continues with the reception of Abraham by the city at Argarizin, probably once more building upon Gen 12:6, where Abraham enters Shechem.[118] Then it continues with Gen 14 in the sentence on Melchizedek. The report of the following famine and descent to Egypt again returns to Gen 12. Pseudo-

---

[116] C. R. Holladay gives 292–3 B.C.E. as terminus a quo and mid-first century B.C.E. as the terminus ante quem, *Historians*, 159 f. L. Grabbe sees the fragments as "apologetic historiography," "Betwixt and Between," 346, after G. E. Sterling, cf. ibid., 347, n. 40.

[117] As a further development along these lines: Melchizedek had Herakles as father and Astarte as mother, and lived at the time of Abraham, according to Epiphanius, *Pan.*, 55 II 517 Dind. (= Dindar's translation, Freudenthal, "Hellenistische Studien.")

[118] Ξενισθῆναι is pass. aor. inf., referring to the previous information: "having been received."

Eupolemus thus moves from Gen 12 to 14, back to 12, and then to 14, only to end in 12. Gen 12 and 14 are amalgamated. In this way, Abraham arrives from Mesopotamia in "Phoenicia," which equals "Canaan." The Melchizedek episode is transferred to the Shechem area. As Melchizedek in Gen 14 is king of Salem and priest of El Elyon, the question is how the author found Salem in this area, and how he found there an appropriate temple for Melchizedek.

This text shares with the two Delos inscriptions the expression ἱερόν Ἀργαριζίν, cf. ΙΕΡΟΝ ΑΡΓΑΡΙΖΕΙΝ in the first inscription and ΙΕΡΟΝ ΑΓΙΟΝ ΑΡΓΑΡΙΖΕΙΝ in the second. It is conspicuous, however, that this phrase occurs after a genitive πόλεως, governed by the preposistion ὑπο. If ἱερόν Ἀργαριζίν were in apposition to πόλεως, one would expect a genitive also in this expression, and if there is another reason for a neuter nominative or accusative, we miss an element that would justify this form. C. R. Holladay therefore in a footnote tentatively introduces the preposition εἰς before ἱερόν Ἀργαριζίν. This results in the translation "by the city at the temple Argarizin," and in the commentary it is added that perhaps the meaning is: "was admitted as a guest into a temple of the city called Argarizin." This latter translation would presuppose that "Argarizin" and "city" should be connected, bypassing the word "temple," which is difficult. It would also run counter to the explanation of "Argarizin" as "The Mountain of the Most High." Here, the author reveals that he knows the meaning of the element Αρ as הר, "mountain." One would therefore be more inclined to think that "Argarizin" in Pseudo-Eupolemus is the name of a mountain, and ἱερόν is either an adjective, "holy," or a noun, "temple." In the Samaritan sources the expression denotes the mountain, and this is confirmed by Pliny and some of the Christian sources which add a word for "mountain" to the expression. 2 Macc 6:2, with its τὸν ἐν Γαριζιν [νεώ], or, as reconstructed, τὸν ἐν Αργαριζιν [νεώ], takes "Argarizin" to refer to the mountain. Josephus is the only author to equate Shechem and Argarizin, as if they were both cities, *War* 1.63. C. R. Holladay's former translation is therefore more likely, "by the city at the temple Argarizin." The problem with this translation is that it also presupposes a preposition before ἱερόν Ἀργαριζίν, and this we do not have.

Another peculiarity with the sentence is that in the HB and the LXX Melchizedek is priest of אל עליון/τοῦ θεοῦ τοῦ ὑψίστου, but here he is priest of "God" only. The epithet ὕψιστος is applied to the mountain instead.[119]

---

[119] The Greek inscription with the phrase ΘΕΩ [ΥΨ]ΙΣΤΩ on a sundial found on

A third problem is that the explanation for the name "Argarizin" does not fit: "The Mountain of the Most High" cannot be easily connected to the name. The equation Ἀργαριζίν = הר עריץ, "mountain of the Fierce One," is possible, but presupposes some shifts in phonemes. If the author of this sentence knew Hebrew, it is strange that he came up with a translation which is difficult to connect to the Hebrew name.

A different solution therefore offers itself: this expression with its explanation could be an addition to the text. If ἱερόν Ἀργαριζίν, ὃ εἶναι μεθερμηνευόμενον ὄρος, "Holy Argarizin, which translates as 'Mountain,'" is removed, the text originally would have been ξενισθῆναί τε αὐτὸν ὑπὸ πόλεως ὑψίστου· παρὰ δὲ τοῦ Μελχισεδὲκ ἱερέως ὄντος τοῦ θεοῦ καὶ βασιλεύοντος λαβεῖν δῶρα, "he [Abraham] was also received as a guest by the city of the Most High. He also received gifts from Melchizedek who was a priest of God and reigned as a king as well." It is also possible that ὕψιστος originally belonged with "priest," as in Gen 14:18, and later was relocated to the present position. With this supposition the three problems mentioned would be resolved. The heavy syntax of the present sentence would then be easier, and the flow of the text better. Melchizedek would be introduced as a priest in the city of the Most High, or as a priest of the Most High. The translation of the name would pertain to the element Ἀρ, and no further etymological speculations need be assumed. As a result, Abraham sojourns (κατοικῆσαι) in Phoenicia in general and is received by the king and priest Melchizedek, who also supplies him with gifts. This picture has as its background Gen 12:6 LXX, "the Canaanites sojourned in the land," οἱ δὲ Χαναναῖοι τότε κατῴκουν τὴν γῆν. The original text would refer to events in the land of the Phoenicians, and behind the expression "the city of the Most High" one may even sense a reference to Jerusalem. The addition may have been a gloss explaining that this city was the holy "Argarizin," a name in need of a translation. This gloss eventually was included with the running text; a process which is well known from the HB.

Scholars have treated the two fragments as units, without considering the possibility of later additions. J. Freudenthal supposed both fragments to be Samaritan because their contents correspond to the "character" of the Samaritans as a mix of different peoples and religions, but with a propensity for Babylon, and because of the description of Gerizim

---

Mount Gerizim has not yet been published, but a photograph of it can be found in the upper right-hand corner of plate 4 in Magen, "Mt. Gerizim—A Temple City," 74–119.

as "Mountain of the Most High."[120] J. Freudenthal's image of the Samaritans was created from ancient polemics against them, so the appeal to the character of the people is spurious.[121] This "character" is often built upon Josephus' account in *Ant.* 11:343 f. about the Samaritans professing themselves "Sidonians," or their supposed syncretism, inspired by Babylonian religion.[122] As Phoenicia plays an important role in Pseudo-Eupolemus, this is taken to indicate Samaritan authorship (Phoenicia included Sidon), and an interest in Babylon is understandable if they were settlers from that area. J. Freudenthal has been followed by other scholars. J. Davila thinks the expression "mountain of the Most High" "would be unimaginable in the mouth of a Jew in the second century B.C.E. ... The working hypothesis that it was written by a Samaritan is robust and is our best starting point."[123] H. G. Kippenberg and N. Walter reason in the same way, but R. Doran argues for a non-Samaritan provenance.[124]— Josephus can be better understood in a different way, and there is no trace of other deities than YHWH in the Mount Gerizim inscriptions contemporaneous with Pseudo-Eupolemus. What remains of the arguments, therefore, is the description of Mount Gerizim as ἱερόν and as representing the Most High.

C. R. Holladay adds another argument. The war against the Armenians is understandable because the Shobach legend in Samaritan *Chronicle II* mentions Joshua's war against king Shobach and his allies, who include "Greater and Lesser Armina."[125] This argument can be dismissed. *Chronicle II* was created around the turn of the nineteenth and twentieth centuries C.E., and its testimony cannot be used to ascertain the provenance of a work which is older by two millennia. "Armina" seems to be a form of

---

[120] Freudenthal, "Hellenistische Studien," 87.96 f.

[121] M. Hengel, "Judaism and Hellenism Revisited," in *Hellenism in the Land of Israel* (ed. J. J. Collins and G. E. Sterling; Christianity and Judaism in Antiquity Series 13; Notre Dame, Ind.: University of Notre Dame Press, 2001), 6–37, argues for the monotheistic Yahwism of the Samaritans, 14–16.

[122] M. Hengel, *Judentum und Hellenismus: Studien zu ihrer Begegnung unter besonderer Berücksichtigung Palästinas bis zur Mitte des 2.Jh.s v.Chr* (WUNT 10; sec. rev. ed.; Tübingen: Mohr, 1973), 162–169. J. J. Collins, "Pseudo-Eupolemus?" in *Between Athens and Jerusalem*, 47–50, repeats the idea that Pseudo-Eupolemus used the expression "Phoenicia" because the Samaritans were Sidonians, and that it is easier to suppose that the author was a Samaritan. However, the fragment may be Jewish, and reflect a "remarkably ecumenical spirit ... in the pre-Hasmonean period."

[123] Davila, *Provenance of the Pseudepigrapha*, 55, cf. 66 f.

[124] Kippenberg, *Garizim und Synagoge*, 80–82; Walter, "Pseudo-Eupolemos," 1:137–143; Doran, "Pseudo-Eupolemus," 2:873–882.

[125] Holladay, *Historians*, 182, n. 16.

"Aramean," because Shobach is an Aramean general in 2 Sam 10:16.18.[126]
The same transition from "Aramean" to "Armina" could be reflected in
Pseudo-Eupolemus, without this indicating that this text is Samaritan.

R. Doran discusses four arguments in connection with the provenance
of the first fragment.[127] They deal with the relation between the genuine fragments from Eupolemus and the first fragment from Pseudo-
Eupolemus. His conclusion is that the latter stems from Eupolemus and
was created in Jerusalem ca. 158 B.C.E. Relevant for our purpose are
two of the arguments, (1) the supposed syncretism of the fragment, (2)
the attitude towards Mount Gerizim. I have commented upon the question of syncretism, and there remains therefore R. Doran's second argument, identical to one of J. Freudenthal's arguments, the attitude towards
Mount Gerizim represented by the sentences quoted above. As the form
"Argarizin" was used by Samaritans and by non-Samaritans, with or without an anti-Samaritan bias, the form alone does not provide us with a
conclusive argument. The idea that an occurrence of "Argarizin" means
Samaritan provenance, indirectly presupposes that any positive mention
of this place indicates Samaritan provenance, an understanding proposed
by J. Freudenthal and others. But this is not a necessary understanding,
and indeed not natural.

If we first deal with the supposed original text of Pseudo-Eupolemus, it
is acknowledged that the author used the LXX as a source in several cases,
and this is quite evident in the orthography of names. In addition he used
haggadic traditions (compare, for example, the Genesis Apocryphon and
the Enoch texts) and mythological traditions from Greek and Babylonian
sources (Berossos).[128]

The use of the LXX led scholars to infer that the author was not
a Samaritan. But J. Freudenthal finds in these fragments the evidence
that Samaritans read the LXX. Pseudo-Eupolemus would have to carry
the weight of this supposition alone. However, the older verdict is the
more probable: there is no evidence for the Samaritans using the LXX.
Samaritan use of Greek in the Samareitikon is possible, but from a later
period, and their use of Greek as a vernacular is later. Pseudo-Eupolemus'
use of the LXX and haggadic material would rather point in the direction
of a Jewish author. The evidence would fit a Jew, living in a Hellenistic
context perhaps other than Palestine and Egypt, in a milieu where the

---

[126] Ginzberg, *Legends*, 6.179, n. 45.
[127] Doran, "Pseudo-Eupolemus," 2:873–876.
[128] Holladay, *Historians*, 161, n. 4–6.

LXX was acknowledged. His use of sources is not literal, but followed the principle of a maximally favourable portrayal of Abraham, in accordance with a Hellenistic setting. It seems that the profile of the author is that of one who used the LXX and haggadic traditions on Enoch, and he had no objections to employing foreign mythology.

If the two fragments were written by a hellenizing Jew, the superscription of Alexander to fragment 1 would be partly correct. Eusebius introduces the fragment thus: "Eupolemus on Abraham, from the book 'On the Jews' by Alexander Polyhistor." Complicating the matter, however, he continues to say that "Eupolemus in his work 'On the Jews of Assyria' says ...," so readers are not sure who produced the book "On the Jews." Eupolemus' fragment 2 receives a similar introduction: "Alexander, who is called Polyhistor, in his book 'On the Jews' ...." Before the study by J. Freudenthal scholars were inclined to see all the fragments as coming from the same author, Eupolemus. J. Freudenthal argued for dividing the fragments into two groups, the first five in one group attributed to Eupolemus, and the last two in a second group attributed to an anonymous author, Pseudo-Eupolemus. His arguments for dividing the fragments into two groups may hold, but his arguments for Samaritan provenance for this latter group are not convincing. The information provided by Eusebius may be understood to the effect that Alexander created a work from different sources and entitled it "On the Jews." The opening of Pseudo-Eupolemus fragment 1 could be understood to mean that Alexander quotes from an author whom he wrongly believes to have been Eupolemus and whose work dealt with the Jews. Scholars have had a hard time explaining this information as an introduction to a Samaritan text, but if this premise falls, then the introduction to fragment 1 could simply be correct in the sense that the text had to do with the Jews. Alexander quoted a book on Abraham and termed it "On the Jews," and this became part of his own book "On the Jews."

Rather than considering Pseudo-Eupolemus a Samaritan, we are induced to see in him a hellenizing Jew, perhaps in the vein described in 1 Macc 1:11–15; 2 Macc 4:10–17. In regard to the original work of Pseudo-Eupolemus, M. Hengel's comments are to the point: "... the fragments which we have, apart from one statement about the sanctuary on Gerizim, could just as well come from a Jew with a Hellenistic education."[129] If the supposed original Pseudo-Eupolemus can be considered a

---

[129] Hengel, *Judentum und Hellenismus*, 167; my translation of "... die uns erhaltenen

Jew, it remains to discuss the provenance of the assumed gloss, ἱερόν Ἀργαριζίν, ὃ εἶναι μεθερμηνευόμενον ὄρος, "Holy Argarizin, which translates as 'Mountain.'" Does the occurrence of the form "Argarizin" reveal
Samaritan provenance?

The original text of Pseudo-Eupolemus rests on Gen 14:18–20, where
Abraham is received with honours by Melchizedek of Salem. The addition of "Argarizin" with an explanation can be understood from the LXX
translation of Gen 33:18a. The Hebrew text here reads: ויבא יעקב שלם
עיר שכם. This is usually taken to mean "Jacob came safely to the city of
Shechem." In the LXX, however, it is translated as καὶ ἦλθεν Ιακωβ εἰς
Σαλημ πόλιν Σικιμων, "Jacob came to Salem, the city of the Shechemites."
The understanding of שלם as a city rests upon Gen 14:18: ומלכי־צדק מלך
שלם, "And Melchizedek, the king of Salem," LXX: καὶ Μελχισεδεκ βασιλεὺς Σαλημ. By understanding שלם in both texts as a name for a city,
the LXX translators arrived at their version of Gen 33:18. But this understanding created a renaming of Shechem. There was in the Hebrew text of
Gen 33:18 the expression עיר שכם. If שלם was read as a name, this expression appeared to be in apposition to Salem, which resulted in the translation Σαλημ πόλιν Σικιμων, "Salem, the city of the Shechemites." Shechem
received the second name "Salem"; compare the identification of "Salem"
with "Sychem" and "Sikima" in Eusebius' Onomasticon and their location
at Shechem in the Madaba map.

After the LXX's identification of "Salem" as "Shechem," the author of
the addition to Pseudo-Eupolemus made the next move. He located the
Abraham-Melchizedek encounter to a place near Shechem. There was no
better choice than Mount Gerizim, which could add to the glorification of
Abraham his reception at a renowned temple mount. The association of
Shechem with Gerizim is traditional: Deut 11:29 f. combines Gerizim and
Ebal with "the oak of Moreh," Elon More, which in Gen 12:6 is located
in Shechem. The name of the mountain could then be interpreted on the
basis of Gen 14:18–20 as "The mountain of the Most High"; compare the
LXX rendering of the pertinent Hebrew expression for God in Gen 14 as
ὁ θεὸς ὁ ὕψιστος. If this epithet originally belonged with "God," it was
moved from "God" to "the mountain" when the addition was included
with the rest of the text.

The development could thus be that the LXX translation of Gen 33:18
implied that Melchizedek's city "Salem" was identified as "Shechem."

Fragmente bis auf den einen Satz über das Heiligtum auf dem Garizim ebensogout von
einem hellenistisch gebildeten Juden stammen könnten …"

Pseudo-Eupolemus amalgamated Gen 12 and 14 with the result that Abraham on his arrival in Canaan was received by the king. Fragment 1 first says that he found favour with the king of the Phoenicians because he taught them astrology, and after the war with the Armenians one must assume that this same king received him, and this time he is identified as Melchizedek. The author who created the addition, inserted "Argarizin" and translated Ἀρ as "mountain." The LXX is sufficient as an explanation for the occurrence of Mount Gerizim in the final text of Pseudo-Eupolemus.

The author of the assumed insertion knew the contracted name for the mountain, and transliterated it, and then translated one part of it. But the addition is more complex. To "Argarizin" is added ἱερόν, creating the expression ἱερόν Ἀργαριζίν, as in the two Delos inscriptions. The first Delos inscription uses the expression ΙΕΡΟΝ ΑΡΓΑΡΙΖΕΙΝ, which Bruneau translates as "sacré Garizim," Kraabel and White as "hallowed *Argarizein*," J. Zangenberg as "heiligen Argarizin," and S. Talmon as "holy *Argarizin*." As the second inscription shows, it may be combined with ἅγιος to give ΙΕΡΟΝ ΑΓΙΟΝ ΑΡΓΑΡΙΖΕΙΝ, and Bruneau then renders it "sacré et saint Gerizim," even though there is no καί between the words; Kraabel and White: "hallowed, consecrated *Argarizein*"; J. Zangenberg: "heiligen, geweihten Argarizin"; S. Talmon: "holy *Argarizin*."[130] ἱερόν in the Delos inscriptions is not translated as "temple" by any of these scholars, but in the case of Pseudo-Eupolemus C. R. Holladay translates it as "temple." This latter translation may have been inspired by the characterization of Melchizedek as priest. If the Delos inscriptions mention the temple tax, a similar understanding would be natural also in these texts.

The Greek and Latin renderings of the expression may be taken to attest the understanding that "Argarizein" is a name for a mountain, and we would be led to merely transcribe it as such in the Delos inscriptions also. But it would not be natural to contribute to or pay temple tax to a mountain, so the translation "temple Argarizein" seems justified.[131] This would presume a metonymic shift in meaning from the name of the mountain to the name of the temple upon the mountain. A similar

---

[130] This reflects his incomplete rendering of the Greek inscription at this point: he omits the word αγιον. For references, see below.

[131] Cf. Pummer's translation "the temple Argarizin" both in the Ps.-Eupolemus-text and in the Delos inscriptions, "ΑΡΓΑΡΙΖΙΝ," 19 and 20, n. 7; idem, "Samaritan Material Remains," 173 f., with reference to several translations with this translation, n. 211.

understanding in the supposed addition to Pseudo-Eupolemus is possible. Melchizedek was a priest and needed a temple.

The association of Abraham with a temple at Gerizim is found with Marinus *in* Damascius, first half of the 6th century C.E., quoted by Photius: "Then the impious writer uttered the blasphemy that on this mountain there is a most holy sanctuary of Zeus the Highest, to whom Abraham the father for the old Hebrews consecrated himself, as Marinus himself maintains."[132] This report may be based upon the consecration of the Roman temple on Tell er-Ras to ΔΙΙ ΟΛΥΜ[ΠΙΩ], "For Zeus Olym[pios]," or on the renaming of the Mount Gerizim temple according to 2 Macc 6:2 and Josephus, *Ant.* 12.257–264.[133] The attachment to Abraham may be dependent upon Pseudo-Eupolemus, and consequently cannot carry any weight of the identification of the provenance of the addition in Pseudo-Eupolemus. The whole attitude to Mount Gerizim in the addition must be seen in the light of what we know about the Samaritans' theology.

Shechem is the first place Abraham arrives at in the promised land, Gen 12:6. Accordingly, it would not have been surprising to find an interest in Abraham among the Samaritans. Strangely enough, the Abraham of Gen 12 does not play a significant role in later Samaritan tradition. Admittedly, this is working from silence, but at least one could say that the Samaritans did not exploit the SP systematically for justification of their holy places. Abraham would provide them with a good case for Shechem. Much later, probably, they identified the site of Gen 22 with Mount Gerizim, perhaps as a late counter-move to the identification of Mount Moriah with Zion, 2 Chr 3:1. The Samaritans concentrated on Moses, a figure who never entered the land. The concentration on Abraham in the two fragments of Pseudo-Eupolemus is not a typically Samaritan trait. The same can be said for Enoch and Melchizedek. These figures play a role in the literature of the second temple period, but a similar interest is not reflected in later Samaritan literature. Thus there is no basis for stating that the assumed addition to Pseudo-Eupolemus is an expression of Samaritan interest in Abraham. This would pertain to the creation of the assumed addition and to the interest in the text as a whole.

If the assumed addition builds upon the LXX, the profile of this translation in the case of Shechem comes into focus. The possible use of the LXX by the Samaritans has been commented upon already. If there is

---

[132] *Bibliotheca* 345b.21–24, quoted from Pummer, *Early Christian Authors*, 429.
[133] Bull, "TELL ER-RAS."

an anti-Samaritan tendency in the LXX, their use of it is unlikely. The city of Shechem seems not to have been a test case for the LXX. In Josh 24:1.25 "Shechem" of the MT is changed into "Sēlo" in the LXX, possibly an anti-Samaritan rendering. But Josh 24:25 LXX has "Sēlo," with the addition "in front of the tent," in harmony with Josh 18:1; 19:51 LXX, so it might be an inner-LXX harmonization. In the Pentateuch, all five cases of "Shechem" are rendered as "Shechem" by the LXX. Most cases in Joshua show the same pattern. "Shechem" is a city of refuge and the bones of Joseph are brought to Shechem. The books of Judges and 1 Kings in the LXX display the same pattern as the earlier books. Jer 48:5 LXX is a special case. MT Jer 41:5 "Shechem and Shilo and Samaria," is rendered in the LXX as: "Shechem and Salem and Samaria," but this could be a case of dittography (ומ in ומשמרון read twice by the LXX, creating "Salem" from שׁ and ל in "Shilo," plus מ). There is not, therefore, a clear anti-Shechem tendency in the LXX, but even against this background a Samaritan use of the LXX is not likely.

J. Freudenthal did not like the idea that a single case of Samaritan Hellenistic text could be the result of his investigation. He therefore also adduced the poem by Theodotus, texts by Cleodemus Malchus, Sibylline XI, Marinos, Thallos, a possible Samaritan in Chronicon Paschale, and the Samareitikon as hellenizing Samaritan literature.[134] Most of these supposed hellenizing Samaritan documents are fragmentary and spurious. As Theodotus' poem is clearly anti-Samaritan (cf. the previous chapter), J. Freudenthal's major evidence falls. The evidence for Samaritan provenance for Cleodemus Malchus is the similarity to the ideology of Pseudo-Eupolemus. If the poem by Theodotus is anti-Samaritan, "There is no need to regard Cleodemus as a Samaritan."[135] Thallus' work is referred to in several ancient authors and his work may be reconstructed from these, but it is impossible to tell exactly what his work may have included. The main arguments for his Samaritan provenance are his supposed euhemeristic tendencies, which he shares with Pseudo-Eupolemus, and his identification as the Samaritan mentioned in Josephus, Ant. 18.167, or with a Tiberius Claudius Thallus in Augustus 67,2. This is possible, but not certain. It seems that his possible Samaritan material is reduced to a part of a sentence in Pseudo-Eupolemus.

---

[134] Holladay, "Cleodemus Malchus," in Historians, 245–259; idem, "Thallus," ibid., 343–369.

[135] Collins, Between Athens and Jerusalem, 51.

The author of the assumed addition might have been a Samaritan, but the indications for this are meagre. The main argument is the occurrence of ἱερόν Ἀργαριζίν. "Argarizin" in itself is not conclusive, but the full expression is only found in the definitely Samaritan texts from Delos. Against this stands the use of the LXX and the general interest in Abraham, neither of which can be ascertained for the Samaritans. Could the author have been a Jew who used honourable traditions to elevate the status of Abraham? The addition's identification of the place for Melchizedek builds on the LXX, and the author might have created his insertion at a time when the identification of Salem with Shechem was acceptable, before the identification with Jerusalem became fixed, as in 1QapGen^{ar} XII 13, Josephus, *Ant*. 1.180. 1QapGen^{ar} XII 13 and Josephus might have directed their identification against the identification in the LXX (and Pseudo-Eupolemus). But before that, is it conceivable that the assumed addition was created by a Jew?

In order for the sentence to be unthinkable in the writing of a Jew, one must assume that the attitude to the expression "Argarizin" was negative among all Jews. On the basis of such an attitude the use of the contracted and transliterated form and a positive interpretation of it implied recognition of Samaritan claims, and the attitude demanded complete avoidance of the expression. It is not necessary, however, to assume such attitudes everywhere in Jewish literature of the period, least of all with an author who used Greek and other equations for his heroes liberally. It is possible to imagine a situation or an author without an anti-Samaritan attitude to Mount Gerizim whose intention it was to glorify his Israelite ancestors with the help of the material available. We have seen a neutral use of "Argarizim" in Roman and Christian texts. As witnessed by Pliny and the Christian writers, the contracted form was used by non-Samaritans. The origin of the contracted form is Samaritan, but its use is not limited to them. There is no compelling reason to consider an author a Samaritan on account of this name alone. As far as the expression "Argarizim" is concerned, it is possible that the insertion was made by a Jewish author. Even the anti-Samaritan author Josephus used this expression. The interpolation can therefore be seen as an anti-Samaritan move. The text extols Abraham, a Jewish hero, but not a Samaritan one. This hero is treated with honours by Melchizedek in the city of the Most High God, according to the original text, and this site was identified as the holy Argarizin, according to the interpolation. At a time when "Argarizin" had become the name for the Samaritan temple mountain, the interpolation said that even this Samaritan holy site was inferior to the ancient hero of the text, Abraham. Melchizedek of "holy Argarizin" paid tribute to Abraham by giving him gifts. Considering that Ps 110 connects the king of Zion to Melchizedek, without locating the latter in Jerusalem, this understanding gains in probability. Ps 110 appears to be earlier than Pseudo-Eupolemus, and a pro-Jerusalem application of Melchizedek was followed up by 1QapGen^ar and Josephus. In the intermediate period, the insertion in Pseudo-Eupolemus takes the opportunity to exploit the original text to say that "holy Argarizin" stood in the service of Abraham. He had no location of Melchizedek in Jerusalem to take into account, but instead built upon the identification in the LXX of Salem as a Shechemite city.

It is also possible that the addition was made outside Palestine, where the negative associations of Gerizim were not prevalent. If the interpolation was done by a Jew, it would have been an authorial device for achieving the goal, *ad majorem gloriam Abrahae*. He did not necessarily share the prejudices of Sirach, the *Book of Jubilees* or other literature from Jerusalem against the Samaritans. He would be part of the movement that had a positive attitude to the outside world and did not consider differences in relation to the Samaritans a priority.

One final possibility must be mentioned: the author of the assumed addition may have been a Christian. The Septuagint was the first Bible of the Christians, and the identification of Salem with Shechem is attested in the Christian documents Onomasticon by Eusebius and Jerome, and in the Madaba map, long after Josephus had identified it with Jerusalem. A Christian author need not have harboured anti-Samaritan sentiments; a friendly attitude is witnessed in the gospels of Luke and John, and in Acts. Christian interest in Abraham is visible in many NT texts. The use of ἱερόν Ἀργαριζίν by a Christian is conceivable, though not attested by other texts. The syncretistic character of the original Pseudo-Eupolemus would not have been offensive enough to a Christian author to discard the use of this text altogether. Even if Pseudo-Eupolemus as a whole is introduced by Eusebius as a book "On the Jews," a small element of Christian provenance may have been included with the originally Jewish text. In any case, the text was included in a Christian setting by Eusebius.

The original text of Pseudo-Eupolemus was thus, most likely, created by a hellenizing Jew, extolling Abraham by telling a story based on the LXX, with elements of Greek and Babylonian myths. The assumption that this text is Jewish is partly due to the fact that an origin in Jerusalem or another Jewish milieu is conceivable, since we know of centres capable of creating such texts, whereas we are not informed about possible

Samaritan centres where this might have taken place. This text perhaps received an addition created by a Samaritan, a Jewish or a Christian author, who included the Samaritan name for Mount Gerizim as the place where Abraham met with Melchizedek and added a translation of the first part of the name. In that way the whole text continued as a Jewish text, or was "samaritanized" or "Christianized." There is also a possibility that the original text was Jewish and the interpolation was anti-Samaritan. In that case, the text would be one of the many polemical texts from the second century B.C.E.

6.5. *Summary*

The oldest occurrence of the phrase "Argarizein" and variants is therefore the two Delos inscriptions. Here, the contracted expression reveals that "Argarizein" was seen as the name for the mountain, as a special case of terminus technicus. When the expression was heard or read by people without knowledge of Hebrew, they perceived the whole of it as the name of the mountain. Presumably, the Israelites of Delos were in this position, and they therefore did not translate הר, but transliterated it.

Thus, in Samaritan contexts where the users knew Hebrew, they would not add an extra word for "mountain," but render the expression as one word. In contexts where the users probably did not know Hebrew, they would perceive the contracted expression as the name, and add a word for "mountain." This explains why we read ΤΟΥΡΓΩΒΗΛ and ΤΟΥΡ-ΓΑΡΙΖΙΝ in the Madaba-map in the cases near Shechem. In Samaritan circles הר had been replaced by טור in Aramaic and was transcribed in the map with Greek letters in one word. The two names occur also on the map near Jericho, but only as "GARIZEIN" and "GEBAL," probably in deference to the location in Josh 8.

In the Samaritan sources it occurs as one word, even in the Aramaic, Greek and Arabic translations. The Samaritan sources never attach הר to the following name in other instances, which means that the special status of Gerizim occasioned the expression as one word. Thus, it seems that the contracted expression refers to the temple-mount Gerizim, and as such it attained a technical meaning. As a terminus technicus for the temple-mount Gerizim it appears in non-Samaritan texts that wish to refer to the special status of Mount Gerizim.

It was considered neutral in the Roman and most of the Christian sources, but there are cases where it was used in Christian and Jewish polemical texts against the Samaritans. The context decides if it was negative or positive. Circles in Jerusalem made it negative.

Pseudo-Eupolemus is probably a hellenizing Jew's text, which perhaps was adopted by a Jewish, Samaritan or Christian author who inserted the phrase with "Argarizin" and the explanation for the name. The high evaluation of the mountain by the Samaritans is thus reflected in the final text of Pseudo-Eupolemus. The provenance of the Masada-papyrus is impossible to ascertain. The chances are that it is part of a Jewish hymn thanking God for the destruction of Mount Gerizim.

The Samaritans of the early second century b.c.e. called themselves "Israelites" and sent their temple tax to Mount Gerizim. The use of "Argarizim" and variants in the second century testifies to the importance of the site, as there was a temple and a city there in that period. It is impossible to state that the expression originated in the second century b.c.e.

The prosography of the Mount Gerizim inscriptions is the same as for the Jewish population of the time. Their originators worshipped YHWH on the mountain, and no other deities are named in these inscriptions.

CHAPTER SEVEN

THE PENTATEUCH THAT THE SAMARITANS CHOSE

The Samaritans had a choice when they selected their version of the Pentateuch. This is a fair assumption as several versions of the Pentateuch are represented among the Dead Sea Scrolls—also a series of pre-Samaritan text-type manuscripts. This means that the SP is not solely the product of Samaritan revisions from later times, but that its character existed before the Samaritans made it their own and revised it according to their theology. They also had a choice of scripts for their Pentateuch, as the pre-Samaritan manuscripts use both the proto-Hebrew and the square script. The question is what profile the Pentateuch of their choice had, and if this version can tell us anything about their early theology. This is the topic of the present chapter.

7.1. *The Samaritan Pentateuch in the West*

For a long period, the Samaritan version of the Pentateuch was considered of no importance in the West for text-critical studies. Rabbinical literature included passages with comments upon the differences between the MT and the SP. *Y. Sotah* 7:3 says that R. Eleazar b. Simeon accused the Samaritan scribes of having forged the Torah by adding "Shechem" to "near the oak of Moreh"; *b. Sotah* 33b says that R. Eleazar ben Jose accused the Kutheans of falsifying the Torah, by saying that Elon More is Shechem in Deut 11:30. Perhaps such negative assessments of the SP were not conducive to taking an interest in it.

However, the breakthrough to European attention camewhen Pietro della Valle brought a complete manuscript of the SP to Europe in 1616.[1] It took only forty years for this text to become widely accessible: it was printed in volume four of the Paris Polyglot of 1632,[2] which was used

---

[1] And another with the Samaritan Targum to the Pentateuch.

[2] J. Morinus, vol. 6 of *Biblia. 1. Hebraica,2. Samaritana, 3. Chaldaica, 4. Graeca, 5. Syriaca, 6. Latina, 7. Arabica. Quibus textus originales totius Scripturae Sacrae* (Paris: Antoine Vitray, 1629–1645).

in turn as a base text for the London Polyglot of 1655–1657.[3] Here, the whole Samaritan text was printed in Samaritan characters, and the Samaritan Targum underneath, with a Latin translation of it.

A good century later, the London Polyglot's presentation of it became in turn the source for Benjamin Kennicott's edition which appeared in 1776.[4] Kennicott printed only the variants in a left hand column with the Masoretic text in the right hand column. And some 140 years later again, it was one of the major manuscripts on which A. von Gall based his edition of 1914–1918.[5] The manuscript is now in the possession of the Bibliothèque Nationale in Paris.[6]

This single manuscript has thus served to make scholars aware of the Samaritan textual tradition and it has played a major role in the study of the text of the Hebrew Bible in Europe. It was written in 1345/6 and accordingly was less than 300 years old when it appeared here.

Its arrival in Europe happened at a time of disputes between Catholic and Protestant scholars about the original text of the Old Testament, and it was trapped in questions about the original and authoritative text, a situation which became the fate of the SP for a long time. Pope Clement VIII declared in 1592 the canon of the LXX and the text of the Vulgate to be decisive for faith and life (Editio Sixto-Clementina). Forty years later, Jean Morin/Iohannes Morinus not only published the Samaritan text in the Paris Polyglot, but also considered it to be "of considerable purity, . . . a witness to the fragility of the Massoretic text and a proof of the authenticity of the Septuagint."[7] This conclusion was criticized by the Protestant

---

[3] B. Walton, E. Castellus and J. Lightfoot, "Animadversiones Samariticae, Textum hebraeum et samaritanum," in vol. 1 of *S.S. Biblia Polyglotta Completentia Textus Originales: Hebraicos cum Pentat. Samarit. etc.* (London: Roycroft, 1657).

[4] B. Kennicott, *Vetus Testamentum Hebraicum, cum variis lectionibus* (vol. 1; Oxford: Clarendon, 1776). Kennicott used Walton's polyglot, but in all he used 18 Samaritan manuscripts from different libraries, 11 that were "per totum collati" for Gen (p. 106), Exod (p. 203), Num (p. 360) and Deut (p. 443), and 10 for Lev (p. 266), and 7 that were "in locis selectis collati" for all the books. Cf. B. Blayney, *Pentateuchus Hebraeo-Samaritanus charactere Hebraeo-Chaldaico editus* (Oxford: Clarendon, 1790).

[5] A. Fr. von Gall, *Der Hebräische Pentateuch der Samaritaner* (Giessen: Töpelmann, 1914–1918).

[6] No 2 in the Bibliothèque nationale, *Manuscrits orientaux: Catalogues des Manuscrits Hébreux et Samaritaines de la Bibliothèque impériale* (Paris: Imprimerie impériale, 1866).

[7] G. Firmin/P. L. Stenhouse, "Morin, Jean (1591–1659)," in *A Companion to Samaritan studies* (ed. A. D. Crown, R. Pummer, and A. Tal; Tübingen: Mohr, 1993), 160; Morin's main works on the SP include the *Excercitationes* from 1631, his *Diatribe* from 1639 and his *Opuscula*, published 1657.

scholars Johannes Buxtorf in 1620, Simon de Muis in 1631, and Henricus Hottinger in 1644, all of whom defended the Masoretic tradition. The Protestants even claimed infallibility and inspiration for the Masoretic text, and the attacks on the Catholic position were vehement.[8]

The disputes came to a preliminary end when W. Gesenius in 1815 published his investigation of the SP.[9] Gesenius placed the particular readings of the SP in eight categories, to be described briefly as 1. grammatical corrections, 2. glosses or interpretations, 3. emendations of difficulties, 4. corrections and additions based on parallel texts, 5. large additions from parallel passages, 6. emendations of (logically) objectionable passages, 7. morphological alterations in favour of the Samaritan dialect, and 8. alterations because of Samaritan theology, cult and hermeneutics. The names of the categories are telling: They imply that the SP mainly contains secondary readings in relation to the MT.

Gesenius' conclusion is famous: only in four instances is the SP to be considered an old text: Gen 4:8 (Cain said to his brother, "*Let us go out to the field.*" [MT: nil]); 14:14 (Abram *counted* [MT: *armed*] his followers in order to free Lot); 22:13 (Abraham saw *one* [MT: *behind*] ram); 49.14 (Issachar is a *bony*, i.e. strong, donkey [MT: donkey of *bones*, i. e. of strength]).[10] In all other cases he found the text to be inferior to the MT.

Gesenius was a part of the Protestant-Catholic discussion, and sided with the Protestants in their high esteem of the MT. The earlier counting of variants also has this discussion as its background: it was estimated that the SP has 6000 variants in relation to the MT.[11] In 1900 of these cases the SP agrees with the LXX against the MT. A. Geiger's study seems to build on Gesenius' investigation and on the counting of differences.[12]

This treatment of the SP as an element in the discussion on the oldest, "best" and most authoritative text has been maintained and can be seen in

[8] R. T. Anderson, "Jean Morin as a Prime Catalyst in Modern Textual Criticism," in *For a Testimony: Essays in Honor of John H. Wilson* (ed. M. Haykin; Toronto: Central Baptist Seminary and Bible College, 1989), 62–73.

[9] W. Gesenius, *De Pentateuchi Samaritani origine, indole et auctoritate: commentatio philologica-critica* (Halle: Regenerianae, 1815).

[10] Gesenius, *Pentateuchi Samaritani*, 1815, 61–64.

[11] Cf. Walton, Castellus and Lightfoot, *Biblia Polyglotta*.

[12] A. Geiger, *Urschrift und Übersetzungen der Bibel in ihrer Abhängigkeit von der innern Entwicklung des Judentums* (2. ed.; Frankfurt a. M.: Madda, 1928), 98–100. As Geiger has no references to literature and no bibliography, it is impossible to tell on what he founds his arguments; only an assumption can be made.

B. Waltke's dissertation on the SP from 1965, and even in J. Sanderson's dissertation on 4QpaleoExod^m from 1986 and her publication of it in DJD, vol. 9, in 1992.[13]

By the time of Gesenius, a number of Samaritan manuscripts were known in Europe, mainly through Kennicott's listing of variants from 1776–1780.[14] When von Gall published his *Pentateuch der Samaritaner* in 1914–1918, he gave the number of manuscripts and fragments as "circa 80."[15] W. Gesenius had already noted that the Samaritan manuscripts varied considerably among themselves and von Gall concluded that it was impossible to reconstruct textual families, and even the idea of an archetype was difficult to retain. Therefore, his edition became an eclectic text, created by him on the basis of the manuscripts and by preferring *scriptio defectiva*, by following the rules of Hebrew (i.e. Masoretic) grammar, and by preferring older forms to later ones.[16] Thus, the edition does not give the reader an impression of the original manuscripts, and the character of Samaritan manuscripts has to be recreated from the apparatuses.

The variation among Samaritan manuscripts together with their differences from the other textual witnesses laid the foundation for the thesis advocated by P. Kahle, G. Gerleman and S. Talmon. They held that the SP constituted a vulgar version compared to the standard text of the Masoretes. "S[P] is originally a vulgar version of the Torah in which popular trends were systematised and which, at the crucial point of its history, was provided with a "typical Samaritan" superstructure."[17] S. Talmon here continues in the vein of Gerleman and refines the studies by Kahle. "Vulgar" refers to a text which is smooth and reworked to suit the popular need to understand the text.

A shift from Gesenius is evident here: Gesenius considered the Samaritans as critics, scholars, who worked on the text to make it acceptable to the critical mind of its day. This idea was followed up by Waltke, even

---

[13] B. Waltke, "Prolegomena to the Samaritan Pentateuch" (Ph.D. diss., Harvard, 1965); J. Sanderson, *An Exodus Scroll from Qumran: 4QpaleoExod^m and the Samaritan Tradition* (HSS 30; Atlanta, Ga.: Scholars Press, 1986); eadem, "4QpaleoExodus^m."

[14] Tov, *Textual Criticism*, plate 17, gives an impression of Kennicott's procedure.

[15] Gall, *Der Hebräische Pentateuch der Samaritaner*: "etwa 80," Preface, dated Christmas 1913, p. VII*.

[16] Ibid., LXVIII f.

[17] S. Talmon, "The Samaritan Pentateuch," *JJS* 2 (1950), 150; cf. G. Gerleman, *Synoptic studies in the Old Testament* (Lunds universitets årsskrift, N. F. avd. 1, vol. 44:5; Lund: Gleerup, 1948); P. Kahle, "Untersuchungen zur Geschichte des Pentateuchtextes," *Theologische Studien und Kritiken* 38 (1915).

though they both supposed that the MT was the more original text, and therefore to be preferred. The idea of the SP as a vulgar text is a different approach to the SP. It relegates it to the status of an old textual witness which is interesting, but long superseded as far as its quality is concerned.

All the earlier observations lie behind F. M. Cross's hypothesis of textual families. SP was seen as a Palestinian text, the LXX as an Egyptian or even Alexandrian text, and the MT as a Babylonian text.[18] The geographical distance would explain the textual distance, and the import of texts to Palestine would explain the similarities.

7.2. The Predecessors of the Samaritan Pentateuch in Qumran

The study of the SP entered a new stage when 4QpaleoExod[m] was presented in an article by P. Skehan in 1955. The title of the article announced that there was a book of "Exodus in the Samaritan Recension from Qumran."[19] Skehan for the first time presented the major expansions in this Qumran scroll, expansions that were known from the SP, e.g. in the form of Gesenius' category 5. Skehan called the Qumran text "Samaritan," but it has later been termed "pre-Samaritan."[20] It was given a comprehensive study by J. Sanderson in 1986, published in *An Exodus Scroll from Qumran*.[21] 4QpaleoExod[m], now termed 4Q22, is still the main text in this connection.

With this publication the quest for the oldest, best and most authoritative text was replaced by the realization that whether the SP could be termed a scholarly edition, a vulgar text or a Palestinian text, its predecessor was—first of all—one among several versions of the Pentateuch current at the turn of the era. It became clear that 4Q22 do not include the typical Samaritan pericopes, e. g. the Samaritan tenth commandment and the בהר-variant in Deuteronomy, but many of the other characteristics of the text are there. These are distinctive features, and they can no

---

[18] F. M. Cross, "The Evolution of a Theory of Local Texts," *1972 Proceedings* (ed. R. A. Kraft; Septuagint and Cognate Studies 2; Missoula, Mont.: Society of Biblical Literature, 1972).

[19] P. Skehan, "Exodus in the Samaritan Recension from Qumran," *JBL* 74 (1955): 182–187.

[20] E. Tov, "Rewritten Bible Compositions and Biblical Manuscripts, with Special Attention to the Samaritan Pentateuch," *DSD* 5 (1998): 65 ff.

[21] Sanderson, *Exodus Scroll from Qumran*.

longer be suspected of being the result of the Samaritans tampering with
the text at some unknown period of history. They are earlier than the
textual consolidation on the part of the Jews.

As the scrolls were published, it was realised that more manuscripts are
of the same type as 4Q22. 4QNum[b] = 4Q27 is seen as another manuscript
of a similar type. Scholars very often link these texts to 4Q158 and 4Q175,
to the question of a Reworked Pentateuch, and further to 4QEx-Lev =
4Q17. All these texts include major expansion or display a reworking
known from the SP.

These texts are now seen as "pre-Samaritan" texts, as they share important features with the SP, and exclusively so compared to other texts.
This means that even if "texts such as these must have been current in
ancient Israel,"[22] there are not many texts that witness to this unique feature of major expansions. Many small variations are found in the Dead
Sea scrolls compared to the MT, variations that witness to a tendency
to modernize grammar, vocabulary and orthography, but not larger harmonizations. Each manuscript of the pre-Samaritan texts at Qumran has
its own distinctive features, but they share a set of common traits which
make them a group. Manuscripts have affiliations in different directions,
but the major expansions point in one direction only.[23]

Which texts are pre-Samaritan? In addition to 4Q17, 4Q22,[24] and
4Q27, the group 4QRP is relevant. It consists of 4Q158, 4Q364, 4Q365,
4Q366, and 4Q367. All these texts are part of the same composition.
"4Q364–367 belong to what once were four different scrolls, supposedly representing different copies of 4QRP."[25] 4Q158 and 4Q364 reflect
the text of SP, according to E. Tov, and this is visible in the deviating
sequences of the biblical passages in 4Q158, frgs. 6–8, as well as in small

---

[22] Tov, *Textual Criticism*, 100.

[23] M. Kartveit, "The Major Expansions in the Samaritan Pentateuch—The Evidence
from the 4Q Texts," in *Proceedings of the Fifth International Congress of the Société
d'Études Samaritaines: Helsinki, August 1–4, 2000* (ed. H. Shehadeh & H. Tawa with the
collaboration of R. Pummer; Paris: Geuthner, 2005), 117–124.

[24] The book of Exodus is represented in these DSS: Mur 1.4–5 is Masoretic. 2QExodus[a]
= 2Q2 and 4Exodus[b] = 4Q13 are of the Septuagint type. Paleo-Genesis-Exodusl =
4Q11 and 4QExodus[c] = 4Q14 lack affiliation." It is probable that the scant fragments
of Exodus[j] [= 4Q20] should also be reconstructed according to this expansionistic
tradition," J. R. Davila, "Exodus, Book of," *EDSS*, 1:278.

[25] E. Tov, "Biblical Texts as Reworked in Some Qumran Manuscripts with Special
Attention to 4QRP and 4QparaGen-Exod," in *The Community of the Renewed Covenant*
(ed. E. Ulrich and J. VanderKam; Christianity and Judaism in Antiquity Series; Notre
Dame, Ind.: University of Notre Dame Press 1994), 125.

details in other fragments of 4Q158. Tov estimates that the complete 4QRP could have been 22–27 metres long. The RP is therefore termed thus: 4Q158: 4QRP^a, 4Q364: 4QRP^b, 4Q365: 4QRP^c, 4Q366: 4QRP^d, 4Q367: 4QRP^e.

7.3. *The Major Expansions*

Already W. Gesenius distinguished between minor and major insertions from another biblical text. The major insertions constitute his category 5, a separate group from the minor cases in category 4.[26] As many of the minor variants but none of the major ones are shared with the LXX, it may be supposed that the text had a longer history behind it, and that some of the variants are prior to the stage when the major insertions were made. The major insertions and transpositions were, accordingly, introduced into the text in a period following the LXX and preceding the 4Q-texts. Further, they reveal the same formal characteristic, that they are all insertions into the text from another Pentateuchal text. From a formal or external point of view, we seem to be dealing with a specific phenomenon in the pre-Samaritan manuscripts and the SP.

Gesenius enumerated the following cases with large additions from parallel passages, his category 5: Exod 6:9; 7:18.29; 8:19; 9:19; 10:2; 11:3; 18:24; 20:17.21; Num 4:14; 10:10; 12:16; 13:33; 20:13; 21:11.12.20; 27:23; 31:24; Deut 2:7; 4:21; 10:6.[27] There are some more cases, however, and taken together, there are 40 large expansions in the SP, 30 of which are also found in the Dead Sea Scrolls (DSS). The most conspicuous absence in the DSS is the Samaritan tenth commandment, Exod 20:17+, the first of three large additions in this chapter. The other 39 expansions are listed in the two charts at the end of this chapter.

The two charts list 37 major insertions and two transpositions. The two cases where text is moved from one place to another are included because they are represented in the pre-Samaritan texts and may reveal some of the logic behind the reworking.

---

[26] Gesenius, *Pentateuchi Samaritani*, 45–48. Thomson, *Samaritans*, 283, claims that "It is redundant; class 5 is contained under class 4," but Gesenius considered the difference between them to be significant.

[27] It is not clear why Num 31:24; Deut 4:21 are included in the list, yet the other cases are considered major expansions.

It is appropriate to mention that the differing genealogical frameworks of Gen 5 and 11 are not treated here. The reason for this is that they constitute a different type of problem. In these chapters the MT, the LXX and the SP all have different numbers for the lives and deaths of the patriarchs. A sound approach to this material is to assume that the numbers all resulted from calculations made in order to remove difficulties seen by some reader or editor.[28] There are no insertions of text from other passages.

J. Sanderson presents a number of cases where expansions are "preserved" in 4Q22.[29] This terminology is not so simple if one looks at the texts. We may categorize these cases as follows. A. Cases in which extant text represents an expansion which is preceded and/or followed by text known from the MT; B. Cases in which extant text is supposed to belong to an expansion or transposition on the basis of line and column calculation; and C. Cases in which no expansionist text is extant, but an expansion or transposition is assumed on the basis of line and column calculation alone. This taxonomy is used in the following overview of the individual cases.

A remark is necessary on the use of the "+" in this overview. It has the same significance as in the textual apparatuses of BHS, Hebrew University Bible, and others. This is an attempt to overcome the ambiguity of the letter "b," commonly used for this phenomenon; compare the three different meanings of the letters "a" and "b" in von Gall's edition of Exod 20: "19[b]" means the latter half of v. 19 in MT, "21[a]" means all of v. 21 of the MT, and "21[b]" means the plus in SP against MT. As he follows the versification of MT, and references to this text use letters "a" and "b" to signify the first and the second halves of verses, this is confusing. Despite the general adoption of von Gall's usage, it is unfortunate.[30] The system adopted here is therefore different. There is text before, within and following relevant MT text. "A" and "b" are used for verse halves divided by *atnach*. "+17" means an addition connected to and preceding verse 17,

---

[28] R. Klein, "Archaic Chronologies and the Textual History of the Old Testament," *HTR* 67 (1974): 255–263.

[29] Sanderson, "4QpaleoExodus[m]."

[30] N. Jastram uses the system of von Gall, and accordingly uses '2b' for a supposed addition to Num 36:2, "4QNum[b]," in *Qumran Cave 4. VII: Genesis to Numbers* (ed. E. Ulrich et al.; DJD 12, Oxford: Clarendon, 1994), 263 f., an addition not found in von Gall and the SP.

"17*" means additional text within the verse, and "17+" means after the verse. In each case the expansion discussed is described as "number XX," referring to the two charts.

4QExod-Lev^f = 4Q17[31]

Category A. *Cases in Which Extant Text Represents an Expansion Which is Preceded and/or Followed by Text Known from the MT*

This is one of the oldest DSS, dated on palaeographical grounds to the mid-third century B.C.E.[32]

Col. II, lines 5 f. contain text from Exod 28:30, preceded by Exod 39:20–21 and followed by Exod 39:22–23. This is Exod 39:21+, number 21.

4QpaleoExod^m = 4Q22[33]

4Q22 has been dated on palaeographical grounds to 100–25 B.C.E. It has also been subjected to radiocarbon dating, the "1-σ 1997 Decadel Calibration," at the Tucson facility, with the result "164–144 B.C.E. or 116 B.C.E. – 48 C.E." A special feature of the scroll is a patch in col. VIII, meaning that it was repaired. This repair patch has been dated paleographically to 100–25 B.C.E. also, and the Tucson facility dated it "51 B.C.E. – 47 C.E." by the radiocarbon method.[34]

Category A. *Cases in Which Extant Text Represents an Expansion Which is Preceded and/or Followed by Text Known from the MT*

Col. II, lines 6–11 have text from Exod 7:16–18 between Exod 7:18 and 19 of MT. There are three repeated words: line 1 repeated in line 7, line 2 in line 8, line 4 in line 10. Thus, the source text in 7:16–18 is repeated in an expansion, v. 18+, and followed by v. 19. Number 4.

---

[31] F. M. Cross, "4QExod-Lev^f," in *Qumran Cave 4. VII: Genesis to Numbers* (ed. E. Ulrich et al.; DJD 12, Oxford: Clarendon, 1994), 133–144.

[32] Ibid., 134.

[33] Sanderson, "4QpaleoExod^m."

[34] McLean *apud* Sanderson, "4QpaleoExod^m," 62; B. Webster, "Chronological Index of the Texts from the Judaean Desert," in *The Texts from the Judean Desert: Indices and an Introduction to the Discoveries in the Judaean Desert Series* (ed. E. Tov; DJD 39; Oxford: Claredon, 2002), 366.

Col. IV, lines 4–9 have 18 words, completely or partially extant, from Exod 8:16b–19. They are preceded in col. III, lines 30–33 by Exod 8:16–18, and followed by Exod 8:20–22, col. IV, lines 10–13. V. 19 is not extant, but col. IV, lines 1–3 would have contained the rest of v. 18 and all of v. 19. Line calculation needs to assume a large interval between source and expansion,[35] but this is no decisive obstacle to assuming the presence of the expansion. Two words that are extant in col. III, lines 31 and 32 recur in col. IV, lines 5 and 6. We therefore have Exod 8:19+. Number 7.

Col. V, lines 28–31 represent Exod 9:17–19, followed in lines 32 f. by Exod 9:20 f. Lines 15–18 offer v. 13–16. Lines 19–26 are missing, but they would have had v. 16–19. There must have been an open space in the column for eight lines for this to have been a continuous text. This is not likely, on the basis of what these MSS look like in other cases. The simplest explanation, then, is that lines 15–18 represent v. 13–16 and that lines 27–31 represent the expansion of v. 19+. There is no overlap in this case. Number 9.

Col. VI, lines 27–29 have only four letters, followed in lines 30–33 by six letters from Exod 10:3–5 and one unidentified *he*, only seven letters. No text precedes, as lines 23–26 are missing. The letters on lines 27–29 are either from Exod 10:5–6, or from the expansion, v. 2+. Since lines 30–33 are from 10:3–5, and no text in 10:6bff fits the letters in lines 30–33, lines 27–29 must be from text preceding 10:3–5, and this would be the expansion, v. 2+. Number 10.

Col. XIX, lines 1–6 represent Exod 18:21–24, and lines 21–24 contain Exod 18:26 f. Lines 18–20 are missing. The remaining lines 7–17 do not correspond to Exod 18 at all, but contain Deut 1:9b–16. The missing lines 18–20 probably had the rest of the expansion, Deut 1:17 f., and the beginning of Exod 18:26. We thus have the expansion Exod 18:25 SP, where v. 25 of the MT is replaced by Deut 1:9b–18. Number 13.

Col. XXI, line 20 has one word from Exod 20:18, and lines 21–28 represent text from Deut 5:24–27, corresponding to the second expansion in this chapter in the SP, v. 19*. Line numbering is based upon calculation of lines and arrangement of text in cols. XXI and XXII. One fragment from col. XXI contains parts of three letters from Exod 20:18 and 11 letters from Deut 5:24, thus making it certain that an expansion based on Deut 5 was present in the scroll.[36] Number 14.

---

[35] Sanderson, "4QpaleoExod^m," 78.
[36] Ibid., plate XVII, top.

Col. XXX, line 9 contains most of one word from Exod 27:19+, preceded in line 7 by one word and one letter from v. 18 and line 8 with most of one word from v. 19. No text follows. Number 17.

Col. XXXVIII, line 2 is from Deut 9:20, followed by Exod 32:11 in lines 2 ff. Col. XXXVII, line 31 and col. XXXVIII, line 1 have letters and words from Exod 32:9.10. We thus have Exod 32.10+ here. Number 20.

Category B. *Cases in Which Extant Text is Supposed to Belong to an Expansion or Transposition on the Basis of Line and Column Calculation*

Col. III, lines 2–5, parts of four words, and no text preceding. The last word is from Exod 8:1. The three other fragmentary words could be from Exod 7:28 f. or from v. 29+. Only line calculation on cols. II and III makes it probable that these words are from the expansion and not from the source text. Accordingly, we probably have Exod 7:29+. Number 5.

Col. V, lines 1–3 present us with six words from Exod 9:3, six from Exod 9:4 and four from v. 5. There is no preceding text; lines 4 ff. have Exod 9:6 ff. This fragment is at the top of the column, thus line calculation on col. IV makes it probable that this text is from Exod 9:5+ and not from Exod 9:3–5. Number 8.

Col. XXX, lines 12 f. are reconstructed from a fragment representing text from Exod 30:10, which logically belongs in col. XXXV, where much of Exod 29:34–30.18 occurs. Col. XXXV is well represented in the extant fragments, but unfortunately lines 13–21 are missing, exactly where Exod 30:10 would belong. However, the extant fragments allow a reconstruction of the whole column, and then there is not enough space for Exod 30:1–10. The fragment with Exod 30:10 thus has to be placed somewhere else, and a fair assumption is that it belongs in col. XXX, corresponding to its place in SP. An indication that this is correct is the thinness of the ink strokes on this fragment and on the other fragments of col. XXX, against the thicker ink strokes on the fragments from col. XXXV.[37] The text Exod 30:1–10 would thus have been located after Exod 26:35, and was transposed from its place in ch. 30 of MT. We have Exod 26:35+. Number 16.

---

[37] Ibid., 113.

Category C. *Cases in Which no Expansionist Text is Extant, but an Expansion or Transposition is Assumed on the Basis of Line and Column Calculation Alone*

Col. III, lines 2–4 might have contained Exod 8:1+. Number 6.

Col. VIII, lines 11–16 and lines 19–20 would have had two expansions: Exod 11:3* and Exod 11:3+. Numbers 11 and 12.

Col. XXII, lines 1 ff. would have contained Exod 20:21+, = Deut 5:28b–29; 18:18–22; 5:30–31, according to Sanderson's reconstruction.[38] This is the third expansion in this chapter in the SP. Number 15.

Col. XXXIV, lines 6–7 present Exod 29:20 and 22, but omit v. 21. Line calculation makes it probable that v. 21 was transposed to approximately lines 22–24. We would then have Exod 29:28+. Number 19.

4QNum^b = 4Q27[39]

The palaeography of the scroll suggests a date in the latter half of the first century B.C.E., or 30 B.C.E.–1 B.C.E.[40]

Category A. *Cases in Which Extant Text Represents Text from Deuteronomy and is Preceded and/or Followed by Text Known from the MT of Numbers*

Col. XI, lines 25–30: Deut 3:24 f.26b.27aα, preceded by (some letters from) Num 20:12 f. Accordingly, we have Num 20:13+. Number 28.

Col. XIII, lines 13–15 are from Deut 2:9, followed by Num 21:12 in line 15. Thus, Num 21:+12. Number 30.

Col. XIII, lines 16 f. are from Deut 2:17–19, preceded by Num 21:12 in line 15. We have Num 21:+13. Number 31.

Col. XIII, lines 27–29 are from Deut 2:24, preceded by Num 21:20 in line 26, corresponding to Num 21:20+. Number 32.

Col. XXI, line 31 is from Deut 3:21, following Num 27:23. This would be Num 27:23+. Number 36.

---

[38] Ibid., 101–103; Sanderson, *Exodus Scroll*, 13.208.
[39] Jastram, "4QNum^b," 205–267.
[40] Ibid., 211.

Category C. *Cases, in Which no Expansionist Text is Extant, but an Expansion or Transposition is Assumed on the Basis of Line and Column Calculation Alone*

Col. I, lines 24–28 are not extant, but the editor reconstructs them with Deut 1:20–22. This would be Num12:16+. Number 24.

Col. XII, lines 1–9 would have included Deut 3:27aβ.b.28; Deut 2:2–6 = Num 20:13+ (cf. number 28), second expansion. The top of col. XII is missing, but the extant lines 13 ff. contain Num 20:16 ff. and this means that the rest of the expansion is needed to fill in lines 1–9, unless something else would have been there or the top of the column were empty. Number 29.

Col. XIV, lines 2–4 would have had Deut 2:28–29a inside Num 21:22; thus Num 21:22*. Number 34.

Col. XIV, lines 4–7 are reconstructed with Deut 2:31 inside Num 21:23; so: Num 21:23*. Number 35.

Col. XXVI, lines 3–7 reconstructed would have had Num 31:21–24, corresponding to Num 31:20+. Number 37.

RP = 4Q158: a, 4Q364: b, 365: c, 366: d, 367: e[41]

4Q158 (RP[a]) and 4Q364 (RP[b]) include relevant text, and the fragments of this manuscript are characterized paleographically as displaying "a late Hasmonean or transitional formal script."[42] The manuscript fragments would thus be dated 75–25 B.C.E.

Category A. *Cases in Which Extant Text Represents an Expansion Which is Preceded and/or Followed by Text Known from the MT*

4Q364, frg. 4b–e, col. II, lines 21–26 have Gen 31:11–13 following Gen 30:36. No text follows. Thus, we have Gen 30:36+. Number 1.

---

[41] 4Q158: J. Allegro, "158. Biblical Paraphrase: Genesis, Exodus," in *Qumran Cave 4. I: (4Q158–4Q186)* (ed. J. Allegro; DJD 5; Oxford: Clarendon, 1968), 1–5, with important improvements in J. Strugnell, "Notes en marge du volume V des 'Discoveries in the Judean Desert of Jordan,'" *RevQ* 26 (1970): 163–229; the other fragments: E. Tov and S. White [Crawford], "4QReworked Pentateuch[b-e]," in *Qumran Cave 4. VIII: Parabiblical Texts, Part 1* (ed. H. Attridge et al. in consultation with J. VanderKam; DJD 13; Oxford: Clarendon, 1994), 197–351.

[42] Tov and White [Crawford], "4QReworked Pentateuch[b-e]," 201.

4Q158, fragment 6, line 1 possibly contains one word from Deut 5:27 (אתה), followed in lines 2–4 by fragments of words and whole words from Exod 20:19–21, in lines 4–6 by text from Deut 5:28–29, and in lines 6–9 by text from Deut 18:18–22. If the one word in line 1 is accepted as belonging to Deut 5:27, this fragment represents the Samaritan sequence in Exod 20:19–22+, containing expansions number 14 and 15. If this is not accepted, only expansion number 15 is represented.

4Q158, fragments 7–8, have text from Exod 20:12–17 in lines 1–2, from Deut 5:30–31 in lines 3–4, introduced by "And Yahweh said to Moses," and followed in line 5 by "And the people returned, each man to his own tent, but Moses remained before [Yahweh]." Lines 6–9 correspond to Exod 20:22–26. The last part of expansion number 15 is therefore present here, but attached directly to the last commandment of the Decalogue, and supplied with an introduction and a follow-up sentence, neither of which is present in the HB nor in the SP.

4Q364, frg. 23a–b col. I, lines 1–4 present us with Num 20:17–18, preceding Deut 2:8–14 of lines 5–16. Thus, this is the last part of Deut 2:7+. Number 38.

4Q364, frg. 27, lines 3–4 have a text similar to Deut 10:6* SP. Number 39.

4Q175

This text is a special case, but included here since it contains Deut 5:28–29 followed by Deut 18:18–19 in lines 1–8, which corresponds to the first part of expansion number 15. It is introduced by "....[= Yahweh] spoke to Moses, saying," and this is the introduction to Deut 5:28–29 of Exod 20:21 SP, whereas MT, LXX and SP has a different wording as an introduction in Deut 5:28. The rest of 4Q175 contains Num 24:15–17; Deut 33:8–11; Josh 6:26, this last text followed by an explanation. 4Q175 is dated to the beginning of the first century B.C.E.

17 of the insertions and transpositions in the biblical 4Q-texts belong to category A, 3 to category B, a further 10 are of the category C, and were reconstructed by the editors of DJD 9 and 12, making a total of 30 out of the 39 major SP variants. In the remaining 9 cases no DSS-text is extant.

May we reconstruct the parts missing in the pre-Sam texts with the help of the SP? This is certainly not an ideal situation, but on the one hand we have so much pre-Samaritan text preserved that we may infer what the pre-Samaritan text looked like with a certain amount of confidence. We may deduce that it included most of—or even all—the major expansions except for the tenth commandment with temple building on Mount Gerizim; compare the two charts of the major insertions. These are all insertions into the text from another Pentateuchal text.

7.4. Explanations

Why were these additions and transpositions made? The idea of harmonization was launched already in the 19th century. W. Gesenius suggested that they represent "the endeavour of the Samaritans to render their text more plain and more complete."[43] Later assessments of these additions have ranged from J. Purvis' characterization of them as an "unnecessary redundancy," "They are the result of the growth of a textual tradition whose development covered several centuries,"[44] to E. Tov's idea that "the nature of the exegesis" is such that "It seems that a single text must be assumed at the base of the SP texts reflecting the work of a single person,"[45] and it was in circulation in Israel.[46] As we have seen, the text-type is represented by different manuscripts, and the theory of a single person at work presupposes that his work was adopted by several scribes and reworked. This leads us back to the beginning, on the basis of the present manuscripts.

J. Sanderson has based her explanation on the major expansions in Exod 7–11 and suggests that they were made because "This is a narrative of warfare between two deities ... This particular scribe decided to make major expansions to enhance the central plot of the conflict between Yahweh and Pharaoh."[47] This explanation does not take into account the other expansions, and it is not further substantiated. It is an interesting insight, however, that the expansions may be seen in the light of a communication between Yahweh and Pharaoh. She makes an attempt at understanding the expansions from a theological viewpoint.

---

[43] Gesenius, *Pentateuchi Samaritani*, 47; translation by B. Waltke, "The Samaritan Pentateuch and the Text of the Old Testament," in *New Perspectives on the Old Testament* (ed. J. Barton Payne; Evangelical Theological Society: Supplementary Volumes: Symposium Series; Waco, Tex.: Word Books, 1970), 224.

[44] Purvis, *Samaritan Pentateuch*, 72, with reference to F. M. Cross, *The Ancient Library of Qumran*, 193.

[45] Tov, "Rewritten Bible Compositions," 351.

[46] Ibid., 334–354; Purvis, *Samaritan Pentateuch*, 72.

[47] Sanderson, *Exodus Scroll*, 204.

A. D. Crown has made an original suggestion:

> Comparisons result in the redating of some of the "expansionist" Samaritan readings and interpretations. It may well prove to be the case that expansions in the pre-Samaritan and Samaritan texts will be found to have nothing to do with matters of late, textual harmonization but rather reflect and preserve the halakhic traditions of those Jews who did not accept the Oral Law. In other words, they are the textual deposit of shared laws agreed by "One Torah" Jews in their common past.[48]

These Jews would be the Qumran community and the Samaritans. However, it is difficult to see any *halakhic* interest in these expansions. One of the conspicuous traits about them is that they have not affected the legal material in the Pentateuch.

H. G. Kippenberg has suggested that these additions were made in order to counter the prophetic movement in Samaritanism, The Dositheans.[49] The difficulty with his explanation is that Dositheus probably lived in the first century C.E. and the pre-Samaritan texts are B.C.E. It is therefore an older phenomenon, and this explanation cannot be upheld. The focus on prophecy is, however, worth investigating.

The most common explanation is that of W. Gesenius: the additions are harmonizations.[50] To use the words of E. Ulrich: they are "major harmonistic expansions," "intentionally systematically developed."[51] This is further made precise as follows, the expansions "reflect a tendency not to leave in the Pentateuchal text any internal contradiction or irregularity which could be taken as harmful to the sanctity of the text."[52] A. Tal suggests that a large number of the variants are of a literary nature, designed to make the text more comprehensible, Exod 7:18.29; 8:19; 9:5.19; 10:2; 11:3, whenever the redactor considered the narrative too

---

[48] Crown, "Samaritans," *EDSS* 2:818.

[49] Kippenberg, *Garizim und Synagoge*.

[50] E. Tov, "The Nature and Background of Harmonization in Biblical Manuscripts," *JSOT* 31 (1985): 3–29; Tov and White [Crawford], "4QReworked Pentateuch[b-e]," 193.195.

[51] E. Ulrich, "The Dead Sea Scrolls and the Biblical Text," in *The Dead Sea Scrolls after Fifty Years: A Comprehensive Assessment* (ed. P. W. Flint and J. C. VanderKam; Leiden: Brill, 1998), 87.

[52] Tov, *Textual Criticism*, 85 f.; idem, *Der Text der Hebräischen Bibel: Handbuch der Textkritik* (Stuttgart: Kohlhammer, 1997), ch. 2, I, B, 4, alfa (3): the expansions "zeig[en] die Absicht der Revisoren, die exakte Durchführung der Anordnung zu betonen." Cf. F. Dexinger, "Das Garizimgebot im Dekalog der Samaritaner," in *Studien zum Pentateuch: Walter Kornfeld zum 60. Geburtstag* (ed. G. Braulik; Vienna: Herder, 1977): "Man wird nicht fehlgehen, wenn man—ganz allgemein gesprochen—eine Tendenz zur (theologischen) Systematisierung mittels Textwiederholung sieht," 130.

segmental.[53] F. M. Cross's assessment of the SP was that "The Palestinian family is characterized by conflation, glosses, synoptic addition and other evidences for intense scribal activity, and can be defined as 'expansionistic.'"[54] These mere formal descriptions of the phenomenon are very accurate, but the next question is: why this "scribal activity"?

The work was done in specific places and with "pedantic precision" to quote E. Tov again.[55] The "pedantic precision" did not mean that every unevenness was removed. Tov has also used the term "content editing" for this type of activity,[56] and perhaps we may add: editing done at specific places and under a certain perspective. Even if we assume that Moses as a mediator was in focus in the reworking, this was not done consistently. Divine messages to Moses in Exod 6:6–8; 19:3–5 are not repeated. Harmonization do not take place in the narrative on the plagues; the two stories of the death of the animals in Egypt are not harmonized; the firstborn of the cattle die twice in the SP also, Exod 9:6 compared with Exod 9:25; 12:29. Moses is to meet Pharaoh a last time in Exod 10:29, but there is another meeting in Exod 11:8. The people believe Moses according to Exod 4:31, and yet in 6:9 he complaints that they do not listen to him. A number of inconsistencies are not harmonized in the SP.

After Exod 7:29+ (insertion number 5) one would expect a report that Pharaoh rejects the offer, or the threat, because in v. 29+ = v. 27 it is said, "If you refuse to let them go, I will plague your whole country with frogs." This creates the impression that Pharaoh had a choice, and an answer would be expected; but no answer to this threat is reported. Only a new command via Moses to Aaron to execute the plague follows, and in this case the command to Moses is repeated by him to Aaron. In this context of two insertions Pharaoh's answer is conspicuous by its absence. A harmonization process would be assumed to explain this and similar cases.

Two problems arise in connection with the idea of harmonization. First, it presupposes that texts should be consistent—but according to what standards? When is e. g. the presumed sanctity of the text affected?

---

[53] A. Tal, "Pentateuch," in *A Companion to Samaritan Studies* (ed. A. D. Crown, R. Pummer and A. Tal; Tübingen: Mohr, 1993), 179.

[54] F. M. Cross, "The Contribution of the Qumrân Discoveries to the Study of the Biblical Text," *IEJ* 16 (1966): 86; repr. in *Qumran and the History of the Biblical Text* (ed. F. M. Cross and S. Talmon; Cambridge, Mass.: Harvard University Press, 1975), 278–292.

[55] Tov, "Rewritten Bible Compositions," 342.

[56] Ibid., 340f. This a development from the phrase "harmonizing additions," Tov, *Textual Criticism*, 99.

Secondly, why is there no harmonization in other texts or everywhere? Why is there no consistent reworking of the Pentateuch? Why is the legal material not fundamentally reworked? Why not the creation accounts? We have to look for a different explanation for the existence of the major expansions.

7.5. A Layer of Major Expansions

The additions and transpositions share the same formal characteristic. They are all insertions into the text from another Pentateuchal text. From a formal or external point of view, we seem to be dealing with expansions in the pre-Samaritan manuscripts and the SP that share a specific external characteristic.

Formally, these expansions can be compared to Exod 32:9, a verse that is present in the MT, SP and 4Q22, but not in the LXX. It is copied from Deut 9:13. Further, one would think of the additions in MT Jer, and of the recensional activity in MT and LXX in the case of Joshua, Ezekiel, 1 Sam. 16–18, Proverbs, etc. Thus, there are models in the tradition for this recension.

The *terminus ante quem* of these major expansions is given by the Qumran-texts. 4Q17 has been dated mid-third century B.C.E. 4Q22 is dated 100–25 B.C.E., and the patch in col. VIII is of the same date. Radiocarbon analysis confirms this dating. The patch in 4Q22 was necessary because of use, wear, or damage, and the repair reveals that the scroll was valuable. 4Q27 is dated the last decades of the last century B.C.E. 4Q364 might be late Hasmonean or early Herodian, 75–25 B.C.E. The manuscripts belong to the third—first century B.C.E., so the expansions must be older. None of them are included in the LXX, so their *terminus post quem* is probably the LXX; probably, because it is difficult to make an assumption from silence. The absence of the expansion in Exod 32:9 in LXX could mean that this translation had a *Vorlage* without this type of reworking; compare also books like Jeremiah in the LXX.

One conspicuous phenomenon about these expansions is that the laws in Exod 21–23; Leviticus; Num 1–10 (with one exception) and Deuteronomy have not received any major interpolations. The narratives in Genesis are in a similar situation, but here two instances can be found.

Further, the expansions are unevenly distributed: ten of them are concentrated in Exod 6–11, and 15 are copied from Deut 1–3, one into Exodus, the rest into Numbers. Exod 20 has received two long insertions, together covering 13 verses. Expansions and transpositions numbers 16–19 and 21 are in the large section dealing with the construction of the tabernacle, Exod 25–40. Expansion number 22 also has to do with the tabernacle, this time supplementing a regulation for its transport. In the main, we are, therefore, dealing with four sets of expansions and transpositions: the plague narrative, the theophany at Sinai, the tabernacle construction, and the narrative counterparts of the historical survey in Deut 1–3.

The first 12 insertions are listed on chart 1, and apart from the two in Genesis, they are all concentrated in Exod 6–11, the first section with a concentration of expansions. The insertions here are mostly found in places where divine messages are brought verbatim to the ear of Pharaoh. In two cases they are placed where Moses receives them. Seven cases contain the prophetic formula כה אמר יהוה, (numbers 4, 5, 7, 8, 9, 10, 12) and in another case (number 11) the insertion is made into a divine speech and the following repetition of the divine message is introduced by the formula. As a result of the expansions, all God's messages to Pharaoh are received by Moses and faithfully transmitted, introduced by the prophetic formula "Thus says the Lord." In Exod 8:1+ (number 6) the insertion repeats the divine message that Moses receives for Aaron, so that in this case also the reception corresponds to its delivery. Insertion No. 3 creates a basis for the people's assertion after the exodus that they had earlier asked to stay in Egypt. This desire is—according to the SP, no DSS text is extant—uttered already at the first encounter with Moses.

The first expansion is a divine revelation through a dream to Jacob, and it is a basis for his referring back to it in a later conversation with his wives. The second insertion similarly creates a basis for Joseph's brothers' argument that they had earlier made Joseph aware of the reason why Benjamin should not be brought to Egypt.

Of the twelve expansions ten have to do with divine revelations, in nine of the cases they are given to Moses, in one case to Jacob. In eight cases we find the prophetic formula כה אמר יהוה, and a further two instances contain a similar expression. The remaining two expansions create a basis for Joseph's brothers' and the people's references back to previous words.

Many small unevennesses are not smoothed out, however, e.g. the descriptions of the plagues are often more detailed than the announcements of them. Nor is there exact correspondence between Pharaoh's petition for prayers and the prayers themselves. It is not a "full" or harmonious text in the sense that every supposed omission is restored or every non-alignment is aligned. It is reworked or edited at specific points. An interesting phenomenon is that Moses is called an 'elohim in Exod 7:1, and from then on the text has been expanded.

If we turn to chart 2, we have 25 insertions and two transpositions. Of these, 15 are insertions copied from Deut 1–3, where Moses narrates previous history (numbers 13, 23, 24, 25, 26, 27, 28, 29, 30, 31, 32, 33, 34, 35, and 36). Here he refers to many incidents and revelatory occurrences that are not found in LXX and MT where we might expect them in Exodus and Numbers. But in the pre-Samaritan texts and the SP we can read them—supplemented from Deut 1–3. Insertion no. 38 has been made into Deut 2 from Num 20, creating a correspondence between Deut 1–3 and the previous story in the opposite way. In some of these insertions divine speech is introduced by "Yahweh [The Lord] spoke to Moses." The result of these 16 cases is that Moses in Deut 1–3 is depicted as a truthful history-teller. He does not report an event or a divine revelation in Deuteronomy unless it actually took place according to Exodus and Numbers. Moses himself starts out by saying in Deut 1:6 that "God spoke to us," and in 1:42; 2:2.9.17. (24[dependent upon v. 17].) 31 he states that "God said to me." In 2:4 he says that "God commanded the people," and in 1:9.20.29 he refers to what "I [Moses] said," in 1:27 he reminds the people that "You grumbled and said …" With so many references to divine revelation in the past, and a number of other reminders of previous events it was natural to create the text that Deut 1–3 could refer to. And this is what the hand that worked on the pre-Samaritan texts did.

Insertions numbers 14 and 15 in Exod 20 from Deut 5 serve specific purposes in the latter chapter. But they also have the side effect that Moses is a truthful history-teller in Deut 5 according to the SP, since Deuteronomy is a recapitulation of former events. The same is the case with Deut 10 (No. 39), which has been partly supplemented from Num 33. In this latter case, Moses is consistent in his information about where Aaron died and was buried.

According to insertion no. 20 Moses prays for Aaron, and this prayer is the reason why Aaron is pardoned in the following verse. Praying for other persons is a prophetic activity; in the Pentateuch we encounter the idea in Gen 20:7.17. This concept is important in the corpus of the prophets in the HB, but such texts cannot have served as a theological basis for SP expansions.

Nos. 17, 18, and 21 are found in the divine laws for the tabernacle. In the first two cases commands that seem to be lacking are supplied, and number 21 supplies us with the information on the execution of a command, which happened "as the Lord had commanded Moses." The two transpositions are also in the section in Exodus where God gives commands to Moses about the tabernacle.

The transposition of Exod 30:1–10 to 26:35+ (number 16) can be understood on the basis of the sequence of commandments to produce the tabernacle and its equipment in chapters 25–31, and the actual reports on it, one in chapters 35–39, and two in chapter 40, verses 1–15 and 16–33. Chapters 35–39 emphasize that the production was done in execution of God's command to Moses. But the incense altar is number five in the sequence of execution in chapters 35–39 and in both sequences of chapter 40, whereas it is number 11 in the commands of chapters 25–31 (30:1–10). Thus, the execution does not correspond to the command in the MT and the LXX. In the SP, however, it holds the same sequential place in the commands given and in the execution of the commands, due to the transposition of the command from Exod 30:1–10 to Exod 26:35+. The second transposition, number 19 in chart 2, is understandable on the principle that it is logical to command the sprinkling of the attire of Aaron and his sons after the attire has been mentioned in Exod 29:28. The expansion Num 4:14+, number 22, belongs to the category of tabernacle texts, as it streamlines the laws for moving the tabernacle by inserting text from Exod 31:9. The same principle can be observed here as in the section Exod 6–11: God's commands are truthfully transmitted and executed by Moses.

In expansion no. 37, Num 31:20+, Moses gives Eleazar the command which the latter is to pass on to the troops, thus creating the basis for the MT of Num 31:21, where Eleazar refers to a divine command given to Moses. This case is especially telling. The expansion is taken from the following verses and adapted where necessary, and is a divine command to Moses, transmitted to Eleazar. In the MT it is said that Eleazar commanded the men going to war by employing a law given by God to Moses. There is no report of a divine revelation of such a law, so the SP supplies us with the necessary revelation to Moses. The reason seems clear. We should not be left with the impression that an alleged divine revelation to Moses did not take place. The guiding principle behind the insertion in Num 31:20+ is not that the laws should be consistent and flawless, but that a divine revelation said to have been given to Moses should actually be reported as given.

In all these cases consistency between revelation to Moses and his transmission of this revelation is obtained and the authority of Moses is

strengthened. In the second set of insertions, in Exod 20, his own authority and that of his successor as prophet are in focus. The third location of
expansions and transpositions in the commands and their execution in
the tabernacle pericope Exod 25–40, plus Num 4:14+, operates on the
same principle as the expansions in the first section with expansions,
Exod 6–11. Moses truthfully communicates the divine regulations, and
they are executed. This is the case also for number 37, Num 31:20+. The
fourth batch of expansions provides the necessary background for Moses'
history-telling in Deuteronomy. This includes number 20, where Moses
prays for Aaron. Most of the insertions have the effect that Moses is portrayed as a reliable mediator of divine messages to Pharaoh and to the
people, and that he relates history to the people in a correct and truthful
manner.

In the remaining cases, Jacob is furnished with a divine message, Gen
30:36+, number 1, to which he can refer in Gen 30:11–13. The idea seems
to be the same as in the case of Moses: Jacob needs a revelatory background for his later report to his wives. Expansion number 2 creates consistency in the Joseph narrative. The same effect is obtained by expansion
number 3. Number 39 smoothes out a difference in an itinerary report,
partly with text from Num 33:31–37. In the last three cases (numbers 37,
38 and 39) consistency seems to be the principle.

If we look at the two charts, it is striking that we so often find the
prophetic formula כה אמר יהוה in the first, and so often the introduction
to prophetic words [משה] וידבר/ויאמר יהוה אל in the second. These expressions are present in the original places, but it is important that they are
copied and used in their new locations also. By the time the insertions
were made, the formulas must have had behind them a long history in
oral and written prophecy. Against this backdrop the editor found them
in the Pentateuch in connection with Moses and meticulously copied
them in the insertions. Thus Moses is depicted as a mediator who introduces his message to Pharaoh by the prophetic "Thus says the Lord" and
who repeatedly experienced that "The Lord spoke to me." When he prays
for Aaron, he performs a prophetic activity.

The internal evidence of the expansions corresponds well to the external: they share the same characteristics as far as contents are concerned.
The impression is that they form one distinct layer in the pre-Samaritan
texts and in the SP. This layer had Moses as its primary figure, and we
may term it a 'Moses layer.'

This editing of the Pentateuch is in line with a series of other texts
in the same corpus emphasizing the status of Moses as a prophet. They

are in presumed historical order, starting with the latest: Deut 34:10; Num 12:6–8; Deut 18:9–22; Num 11:14–17.24b–30.[57] They have a lone parallel in the prophetic corpus, Hos 12:14; compare Moses as a prophet in Wis 11:1. Common to these texts is Moses as a point of reference for prophecy, *eine Instanz*—a point from which legitimacy and authority has to be received or borrowed, and in comparison with whom the others do not come off well.

The Moses layer in the pre-Samaritan texts brings the Mosaic victory home by its own means: by using existing authoritative text to expand the Pentateuch at certain points, by repeating what is already there and thus making it even more evident that Moses had prophetic authority: כה אמר יהוה. In this way the Moses layer followed up the intentions of the Pentateuchal texts about the prophetic primacy of Moses. This was also done explicitly with the help of one of the texts in question, Deut 18:18–22, to which we now turn.

Expansions number 14 and 15 are present in 4Q22, 4Q158, and 4Q175, but with different representations. The following chart will clarify the relations.

Exod 20 SP	4Q158, fragment 6	4Q158, fragments 7–8	4Q175	4Q22
The commandments		The six last commandments		
The Samaritan tenth commandment				
Exod 20:18				Exod 20:18
Expansion no. 14 Deut 5:24–27	אתה			Deut 5:24–27
Exod 20:19–21	Exod 20:19–21		Exod 20:21*	
Expansion no. 15 Deut 5:28–29	Deut 5:28–29		Deut 5:28–29	Deut 5:28–29
Expansion no. 15 Deut 18:18–19	Deut 18:18–19		Deut 18:18–19	Deut 18:18–19
Expansion no. 15 Deut 18:20–22	Deut 18:20–22			Deut 18:20–22

---

[57] L. Perlitt, "Mose als Prophet," *EvT* 31 (1971): 588–608.

Exod 20 SP	4Q158, fragment 6	4Q158, fragments 7–8	4Q175	4Q22
Expansion no. 15 Deut 5:30–31		Deut 5:30–31		Deut 5:30–31
Exod 20:22–21:10		Exod 20:22–21:10		

As the chart will illustrate, the two expansions nos. 14 and 15 in Exod 20 are found in three different manuscripts from the first century B.C.E. 4Q158, fragments 7–8, has a different arrangement of texts, and 4Q175 combines the beginning of expansion 15 with other texts and an explanation, probably applied to contemporary events.[58] There are also an introduction and a conclusion in 4Q158, fragments 7–8, not found in the other textual witnesses. This means that Exod 20 was reworked in several manuscripts, and both expansions, using text from Deut 5 and 18, are attested.

Deut 18:18–22 is found in the second main location for insertions, at the centre of the Pentateuch, the theophany at Sinai or Horeb, Exod 20. This chapter has received three insertions in the SP, two of which are also found in other Qumran texts. The Samaritan tenth commandment has not been verified in any of those, and the Dead Sea manuscripts seem not to have contained it.[59] But both 4Q22 and the SP display two insertions, number 14 (category A) and number 15 (category C), and 4Q158 contains, perhaps, expansion no. 14, and clearly no. 15 (category A). The relationship between the Gerizim commandment and expansions number 14 and 15 is therefore of a secondary nature and the Gerizim commandment cannot be seen together with expansion number 15, as F. Dexinger presupposed.[60] Expansions number 14 and 15 have text copied from the parallel account in Deut 5, and in the second case Deut 18:18–22 is found inside the expansion copied from Deut 5. Expansion number 14 is the people's request that Moses should mediate between

---

[58] Cook, Wise, and Abegg, Jr., *Dead Sea Scrolls*, 229–231: The standard model of identification: The Wicked Priest and Jonathan or Simon; instead, Wise suggests Alexander Jannaeus and his two sons, Aristobulus and Hyrcanus.

[59] Sanderson, *Exodus Scroll*; eadem, "4QpaleoExodusᵐ," 68–70.

[60] F. Dexinger, "Der 'Prophet wie Mose' in Qumran und bei den Samaritanern," in *Mélanges bibliques et orientaux en l'honneur de M. Mathias Delcor* (ed. A. Caquot, S. Légasse and M. Tardieu; Kevelaer: Butzon & Bercker, 1985), 97–111.

God and man, a feature already present in Exod 20:19–21 of the MT, but the version in Deuteronomy is more elaborate in this respect. By inserting Deut 5:24–27 into Exod 20:19, the pre-Samaritan text and SP create an unambiguous and elaborate picture of Moses as the only divine mediator. Insertion no. 15 is found immediately after this expansion, cf. chart 2. In this expansion God sanctions the request of the people for a mediator and points to Moses for this function, and to a prophet like Moses as the subsequent mediator or the permanent mediator between God and Israel. Expansion number 15 consists of text copied from two different locations, Deut 5:28 f.; 18:18–22; 5:30 f. They seem to have been amalgamated into one expansion and introduced into Exod 20 in one operation. The rationale for this combination of texts seems to have been a catchword principle; see below. What does the promise to raise up a prophet like Moses, Deut 18:18, mean as part of this second addition to Exod 20?

Deut 5:29, introduced into Exod 20:21+, raises the question how the whole law of God—אֵת כָּל מִצְוֹתַי—may be observed permanently—לְעוֹלָם—in Israel. The last verse from Deut 5, v. 31, says that Moses is about to receive the sum total of laws that are needed for life in the land. In the text-flow of Deut 5, these laws are the response to the wish in v. 29: "If only they had such a mind as this, to fear me and to keep all my commandments always." In other words, Moses had the task of initiating law-obedience and securing its permanence. In the Exod 20 combination with Deut 18:18–22, however, the promise for a prophet like Moses is introduced between these verses. This means first that Moses here is explicitly called a prophet, secondly that the prophet's task is defined as having God's words in his mouth and speaking all that God will command him, and thirdly that Moses will have a successor who will carry on this task. A prophet will speak everything that God commands him, אֲצַוֶּנּוּ, Deut18:18. In the root צוה, reflected in מִצְוֹתַי, Deut 5:29, and אֲצַוֶּנּוּ, Deut 18:18, the two texts have a terminological link that could be used when they were knitted together. A prophet is thereby defined as a preacher of the law in the connected texts. A prophet like Moses is a preacher of the law.

There is a twofold corollary to this promise in the following verses from Deut 18: he who will not listen to the prophet's words shall be held accountable;[61] and the prophet who speaks presumptuously shall die. The

---

[61] Or even expelled from Israel, depending on the understanding of the Hebrew אנכי אדרש מעמו.

two corollaries mean in the context of Exod 20 that persons not observing the Mosaic laws as presented in later times will be held accountable, and that prophets who prove to be false in this respect will be put to death. To put prophets to death means in terms of the writings of the prophets that they will be abolished. At the time when this insertion was made the last sentence from Deut 18, לא תגור ממנו, could best be read as "do not have religious respect for it," referring to the word of the false prophet.

The promised prophet will be a preacher of the law, of the law given to Moses at Sinai. Together with the other groups of expansions, nos. 14 and 15 mean: (1) Moses was a truthful mediator, a true prophet, and he holds the primacy among prophets; (2) The prophets to succeed him will be preachers of the law. Thus a double defence against intruders is built up: Moses is the reference point of prophecy, and his successors are preachers of the law revealed to him.

If the guidelines for prophets after Moses were given in this way, and if the standard of prophecy was Moses himself, it would emerge as imperative that Moses had an impeccable record in this respect. This record was given by the Pentateuch, and it would be here that his impeccability had to be proved. In order to create this record, the insertions were made. Thus, the insertion of Deut 18:18 into Exod 20 would be a clue to understanding the nature of the other expansions.

This expectation of a prophet like Moses, interpreted as a preacher of the law, distinguishes itself from the expectation of a prophet found in 1 Macc 4:44–46; 14:41. In these cases a prophet who delivers new prophecies is in focus, but not a new interpreter of the law of Moses. 4Q22, 4Q158, 4Q175 share with 1 Maccabees, however, an expectation for a coming figure of prophetic character.

In the first section with expansions, Exod 6–11, Moses emerges as an accurate mediator of divine messages to Pharaoh and Aaron. In the second section, the theophany after the Decalogue in Exod 20, he is the true and only mediator between God and the people; he is described as a prophet; a prophet is defined as a preacher of the law; and Moses will have a successor with the same profile; he is the model for all succeeding prophets. In the third section, Exod 25–40, his reception of divine commands for the construction of the tabernacle and their execution is consistent. In the last series of expansions, Moses is provided with the necessary background for appearing as a narrator of historical truth in the sermon in Moab. We have observed that most of the major expansions in the pre-Samaritan texts and the SP are Moses-centred. The insertions have been made in places where Moses plays a pivotal role.

This portrayal of Moses has been carried further in the later editing of the SP. In the SP the idea that Moses could be under God's displeasure is not present in Deut 4:21. Here, the SP lacks the expression "and swore," meaning that God did not swear that Moses should not cross the Jordan and enter the land. The remaining sentence only says that God was angry with Moses because of the people.

At three places the SP has introduced a "today": "You shall not add to the word which I command you *today*," Deut 4:2. "Be careful to heed *and do* all these words which I command you *today*," Deut 12:28. "Everything that I command you *today* you shall be careful to do; you shall not add to it or take from it," Deut 13:1 (ET 12:32). Seen together, these small additions give an impression of emphasis on the original Law of Moses over against newer revelation. The additions may have been earlier than the Moses layer. Compare the adding of "today" in Deut 4:1.2 (2×); 12:11.28; 13:1 in the LXX. In any case they are congenial with the Moses layer.[62]

The Samaritan Pentateuch contains the major expansions of the DSS plus some that are not extant in these texts, together forming the Moses layer. Among the DSS there are texts with expansions of a type that are not found in the SP, and some examples of such expansions are the following.

4Q27 in its last column, col. XXXII, lines 16–19, contains text from Num 36:5–7, preceded by two and a half lines of text where the readings "Eleazar the [priest]" and "Nun and K[aleb]" occur.[63] "[Ele]azar the priest" occurs also in line 30 of the preceding column, col. XXXI, where the text seems to correspond to Num 36:1. But "Eleazar" is not found in Num 36:1 MT, and occurs only in Num 27:2 MT in connection with the laws for the inheritance of the daughters of Zelophehad. N. Jastram has reconstructed the text of the last two columns of 4Q27. He starts with Num 36:1–2, extant in col. XXXI, lines 29–31, and supposes that "Eleazar the priest" belonged to the original text of Num 36:1, preserved in col. XXXI, line 30. Col. XXXII, lines 1–13, supposedly contained the rest

---

[62] For the development of the image of Moses, cf. H. Najman, *Seconding Sinai: The Development of Mosaic Discourse in Second Temple Judaism* (JSJSup 77; Leiden: Brill, 2002).

[63] Jastram, "4QNum^b," 259–264; idem, "The Text of 4QNum^b," in The Madrid Qumran Congress: Proceedings of the International Congress on the Dead Sea Scrolls, Madrid 18–21 March, 1991 (ed. J. Trebolle Barrera and L. Vegas Montaner; Leiden: Brill, 1992), 177–198; idem, "A Comparison of two 'Proto-Samaritan' Texts from Qumran: 4QPaleoExod^m and 4QNum^b," *DSD* 5 (1998): 264–289.

of Num 36:2; then he uses text from Num 27:2–11 for a reconstruction, followed by text from Num 36:3–4. This would have been followed by an expanded Num 36:1b in lines 14–16, and Num 36:5–7 in col. XXXII, lines 16–19. The reconstruction of col. XXXII therefore assumes that the pericopes on the daughters of Zelophehad in Num 27:1–11 and 36:1–13 were combined here, as they are in RP^c: 4Q365, fragment 36 offers Num 27:11 followed immediately by Num 36:1 f.[64] That Eleazar was included in 4Q27's rendering of Num 36:1 is certain, col. XXXI, line 30; the presence of his name some 16 lines later, col. XXXII, lines 16–19, is used by Jastram to make it probable that Num 27 and 36 were combined in 4Q27. If Jastram's reconstruction is correct, this is an example of a reworked law, a reworking which is not present in the SP.

4Q37 (4QDeut^j), col. IX–X, adds Exod 12:43–51; 13:1–5 (circumcision is the condition for eating the paschal lamb) to Deut 11:21 (you will live in the country for a long time if you keep my commandments). This is an expansion found in no other manuscript, and represents another example of reworked laws.[65]

4QRP^d, 4Q366, Frg. 4, col. i contains Num 29:32–30:1 followed by Deut 16:13 f., two laws dealing with Sukkot.[66] E. Tov and S. White [Crawford] see this in connection with 4Q365, Frg. 23.[67] In the latter text, Lev 23:42–24:2 is present, plus a new text, not found in the HB. Thus, laws about Sukkot are followed by new laws, including a law about an oil festival and a wood festival. This new material is presented in a different language or dialect from the preceding biblical text, as seen in the forms -kæmma of beboakæmma and lakæmma, against the -kæm of abotekæm in line 2. This non-biblical material is not found in the Masoretic Pentateuch, but it is more in line with the Temple Scroll, and Y. Yadin published it as a part of this scroll. E. Tov and S. White Crawford, however, think it belongs with 4QRP.

Another example is 4Q366, fragment 2, which probably contains Lev 24:20–22 followed by Lev 25:39–43, a combination of the law of retribution and the law for the status and manumission of persons who sell themselves because of poverty.[68] The combination resembles that of Exod 21:24–25 (law of retribution) followed by Exod 21:26–27 (slave laws).

---

[64] Tov, "Rewritten Bible Compositions," 353 f.

[65] J. A. Duncan, "4QDeut^j," in Qumran Cave 4: IX: Deuteronomy, Joshua, Judges, Kings (ed. E. Ulrich et al.; DJD 14; Oxford: Clarendon, 1995), 88–89.

[66] Tov and White [Crawford], "4QReworked Pentateuch^b-e," 341 f.

[67] Ibid., 290–296.

[68] Ibid., 339.

There are therefore examples of rewritten laws, but these examples are not found in the SP apart from the expansions and transpositions in the tabernacle texts. Instead, the SP steered a middle course between MT and RP, and it also did not follow 4Q27 completely. None of these manuscripts are generally harmonizing. The pre-Samaritan manuscripts were reworked on one principle, Moses the prophet and his successor, and the other manuscripts reworked some of the laws. The sections that have been reworked are to do with divine revelations, divine messages. That Moses prays for Aaron (expansion no. 20) is a prophetic activity, and even though the rationale for this expansion is to provide the background for the history in Deuteronomy, the side effect is that a prophetic mandate is observed.

N. Jastram has tried to use this situation as a basis for dating the split between Samaritans and Jews by assuming that the Samaritans chose the pre-Samaritan version of the Torah before the development witnessed by 4Q27 and the RP took place. The split accordingly happened in the first half of the first century B.C.E., after John Hyrcanus conquered Shechem and Mount Gerizim in 128 B.C.E. or when Pompey released them from Jewish control in 64 B.C.E.[69] This model presupposes a split, which is not immediately clear from the sources, and a rather mechanical development in the editing of the Pentateuch in the Hasmonean and Roman periods. Judging from the biblical manuscripts from the Judean Desert, the manuscript situation was volatile, and the development was not necessarily linear.

We may conclude that 4Q22 is close to SP in the question of major expansions, that 4Q27 provides much of the same material, but has additional features, and that 4QRP constitutes another way of approaching pentateuchal text. Seen in the wider perspective, SP contains the major expansions dealing with some of the Moses texts, and none of the expansions in the law corpora, nor the reworking of texts by using non-biblical text.

"In the case of Judaism, the Torah's *ritual* authority seems to have preceded its authority on other matters." "... I wonder if the priest and the book travelled to Mount Gerizim together."[70] There is one piece of evidence for this idea in the reworking of the tabernacle texts in Exodus

---

[69] Jastram, "Text of 4QNum[b]," 196–198.

[70] J. W. Watts, "Ritual Legitimacy and Scriptural Authority," JBL 124 (2005): 412.414; idem, *Ritual and Rhetoric in Leviticus: From Sacrifice to Scripture* (Cambridge: Cambridge University Press, 2007), 209. 211.

and Numbers. Here, we encounter an interest in cultic matters, as well as in the true transmission of divine orders for the construction of the tabernacle.

7.6. Script

The Samaritans write their Pentateuch in characters developed from the old Hebrew script. The palaeo-Hebrew script in the inscriptions on Mount Gerizim, termed "Neo-Hebrew" by the publisher, is an older example of the same development, though they are incised, not written, characters. The reason for the use of the old Hebrew script in the inscriptions has been guessed at as revealing a priestly background.[71]

15–16 biblical manuscripts in the palaeo-Hebrew script have been found at Qumran and one at Masada.[72] E.g. 4QpaleoGen-Exod[l] and 4QpaleoDeut[r] do not "seem to share the same text-type or orthography as the SP" according to E. Ulrich.[73] 11QpaleoLev[a] does not contain additions to the text as in SP, according to the editors.[74] 4Q22 is written in palaeo-Hebrew script, but it is not identical with the script of the SP manuscripts. 4Q27 is in the Assyrian script. This means that the pre-Samaritan text-type is reflected in manuscripts with different scripts, and that the palaeo-Hebrew texts belong to different text-types.[75] The Samaritans standardized and archaized their Pentateuch version over against the pre-Samaritan manuscripts.

The Qumran manuscripts in the palaeo-Hebrew script include the following only: pentateuchal manuscripts, one of Joshua, three unidentified, and one manuscript of the book of Job. The theory is that the Pentateuchal books and Job were thought to have been written by Moses, and therefore were rendered in the ancient script. This could well be the case for the choice of the palaeo-Hebrew script for the Samaritan manuscripts also, and be another sign of the emphasis upon Moses as the most important

---

[71] Magen, Misgav, and Tsfania, *Inscriptions*, [35]: priestly script.

[72] Tov, *Textual Criticism*, 105; cf. the list in *The Texts from the Judean Desert: Indices and an Introduction to the Discoveries in the Judaean Desert Series* (ed. E. Tov; DJD 39; Oxford: Claredon, 2002), 214.

[73] Ulrich, "Dead Sea Scrolls and the Biblical Text," 97.

[74] D. N. Freedman, K. A. Mathews, and R. S Hanson, *The Paleo-Hebrew Leviticus Scroll (11QpaleoLev)* (Winona Lake, Ind.: American Schools of Oriental Research; distributed by Eisenbrauns, 1985), 13.

[75] A table of the Old script: Tov, *Textual Criticism*, 104.

person in the Pentateuch. If so, the Samaritans chose the palaeo-Hebrew script to emphasize the Mosaic character of the Pentateuch, and they used it for a specific version of the Pentateuch where the prophetic status of Moses was made explicit. The script seems therefore to be the result of a choice and not due to the manuscript situation of the time. The use of the Samaritan script later spread to other Samaritan texts, which may be another sign of the fundamental Mosaic character of Samaritan religious literature. Eventually, the original significance of the script was lost.

Their choice of script occasioned condemnation from the rabbis, who prohibited the use of the old script.

> Mar Zutra or, as some say, Mar 'Ukba said: Originally, the Torah was given to Israel in Hebrew characters and in the sacred [Hebrew] language; later, in the times of Ezra, the Torah was given in *Ashshurith* script and Aramaic language. [Finally], they selected for Israel the *Ashshurith* script and Hebrew language, leaving the Hebrew characters and Aramaic language for the *hedyototh*. Who are meant by the '*hedyototh*'?—R. Hisda answers: The Cutheans. And what is meant by Hebrew characters?—R. Hisda said: The *libuna'ah* script.[76]
>
>   (*b. Sanh.* 21b)

The *hedyototh* would correspond to the נבלים, "fools" of Sir 50:25 f.; 4Q372. Such an idea of the history of scripts would leave the Samaritans with a good argument: their script was the older of the two. It is therefore interesting that later in the same context it is said that

> It has been taught: Rabbi said: The Torah was originally given to Israel in this [*Ashshurith*] writing. When they sinned, it was changed into *Ro'az*. But when they repented, the [Assyrian characters] were re-introduced, as it is written: *Turn ye to the stronghold, ye prisoners of hope; even today do I declare that I will bring back the Mishneh unto thee.* Why [then] was it named *Ashshurith*?—Because its script was upright [*me'ushshar*].[77]
>
>   (*b. Sanh.* 21b)

The *Ro'az*, the "broken script," "the rugged script," is the palaeo-Hebrew script, so called because of the shape of the characters; and the name of the Assyrian script is given an explanation designed to avoid the impression that it was imported from Assyria. This seems to reflect a discussion on the original script of the Torah, and the development was in the direction of declaring the square script the original one, and to see

---

[76] J. Schachter, chs. I–VI of *Sanhedrin Translated into English with Notes, Glossary and Indices* (vol. 3 of *Seder Nezikin in Four Volumes*; *The Babylonian Talmud*, ed. I. Epstein; London: Soncino, 1935; repr. 1987), 119.

[77] Ibid., 120.

the palaeo-Hebrew script as a result of sin. With a quotation from Zech 9:12 the return of the square script is bolstered, evidently playing with the wording of this text. The anti-Samaritan tendency here is evident, both in the older declaration that the '*hedyototh*' were given the palaeo-Hebrew script, and in the later discussion resulting in the notion that this script was not original but a result of sin.

In the famous discussion on the question of which manuscripts "defile the hands," מטמאים את הידים, *b. Meg.* 9a also refers to the scripts: "[A Scriptural scroll containing] a Hebrew text written in Aramaic or an Aramaic text written in Hebrew, or [either] in Hebraic script, does not defile the hands; [it does not do so] until it is written in Assyrian script upon a scroll in ink," cf. *y. Meg.* 1.9. *M. Yad.* 4:5 further discusses this topic, and also whether the books of Ecclesiastes and the Song of Songs defile the hands. The ruling in *m. Yad.* 3,5 is that "the Aramaic sections in Ezra and Daniel render unclean the hands. If an Aramaic section was written in Hebrew, or a Hebrew section was written in Aramaic, or Hebrew script, it does not render unclean the hands. It never renders unclean the hands until it is written in the Assyrian script, on hide, and in ink." The discussion about which manuscripts render the hands unclean has to do with the question of the canon of the HB, and this we may leave aside for the moment.[78] Of interest here is the decision of the rabbis to emphasize the Assyrian script, and also the nature of the manuscripts; they must be scrolls, from hide, and written in ink. The rule may have had several opponents in mind, but the Samaritans seem to have been one of them. The discussion on the script, seen in *b. Sanh.* 21b, has here resulted in a focus on the square script, combined with other physical characteristics necessary for a manuscript to be proper for use. In this way the Samaritan choice of script is robbed of legitimacy.

7.7. *The Samaritan Tenth Commandment*

The Samaritan tenth commandment is not found in any of the pre-Samaritan manuscripts. 4Q22 is deemed not to have had any room for this insertion, and accordingly it is assumed that this commandment belongs to a stage of development later than that witnessed to by the

---

[78] J. Barton, *The Spirit and the Letter: Studies in Biblical Canon* (London: SPCK, 1997), 106–130.

DSS.[79] The Samaritans reorganized the Decalogue by considering the first commandment of the Jewish tradition as a preamble to the Decalogue, and furnished their Pentateuch with a new tenth commandment, about the building of an altar on Mount Gerizim. They did this by quoting existing text, in a method similar to that of the major expansions.

SP:	MT:
Exod 20:17+ When the Lord your God has brought you into the land of the Canaanites that you are entering to possess, set up some large stones for yourself and cover them with plaster. Write on *the stones* all the words of this law.	Deut 11:29a When the Lord your God has brought you into the land that you are entering to possess, Deut 27:2b set up some large stones for yourself and cover them with plaster. 3 Write on *them* all the words of this law when you have crossed over, to enter into the land that the Lord your God is giving you, a land flowing with milk and honey, as the Lord, the God of your ancestors, promised you.
And when you have crossed the Jordan, set up these stones on Mount *Gerizim*, as I command you today. Build there an altar to the Lord your God, an altar of stones. Do not use any iron tool upon them. Build the altar of the Lord your God with unhewn stones and offer burnt offerings on it to the Lord your God. Sacrifice whole offerings and eat them there and rejoice in the presence of the Lord your God.	4 And when you have crossed the Jordan, set up these stones on Mount *Ebal*, as I command you today, and cover them with plaster. 5 Build there an altar to the Lord your God, an altar of stones. Do not use any iron tool upon them. 6 Build the altar of the Lord your God with unhewn stones and offer burnt offerings on it to the Lord your God. 7 Sacrifice whole offerings and eat them there and rejoice in the presence of the Lord your God.
This mountain is across the Jordan, westwards towards the setting sun, in the territory of the Canaanites who dwell in the Arabah facing Gilgal, near the large *tree* of Moreh, facing Shechem.	Deut 11:30 *As you know, these* are across the Jordan, westwards towards the setting sun, in the territory of the Canaanites who dwell in the Arabah facing Gilgal, near the large *trees* of Moreh.

The insertion is composed of parts of Deut 27:2b–7, enclosed in—or framed by—parts of Deut 11:29 f. Immediately after Exod 20:17 comes Deut 11:29a. This verse has some similarity to Deut 27:2a (in the MT

---

[79] Sanderson, *Exodus scroll*; eadem, "4QpaleoExodus^m," 68–70.

there are catch-words: "to the land that …") and this explains both the association of these two texts and why 27:2a is not quoted in addition to 11:29a.

In the quotation from Deut 11:29a SP says "the land of the Canaanites" instead of "the land." The reason could be quite simple: The expansionist tendency of the pre-Samaritan texts had taught the interpolator to fill in what naturally belonged there. The expression "the land of the Canaanites" is present in Deut 11:30, quoted at the end of this insertion, and the interpolator could simply have copied it from there.

The combination of Deut 11:29 with 27:2 ff. is very natural: in both texts Ebal is the mountain of curse and Gerizim that of blessing, 11:29b; 27:12 f. In the MT of Deut 27:4 (and Josh 8:30) the altar shall be built on Ebal—this must be a Jewish change of the text after it was used by the Samaritans.[80] In Josh 8:30–33 Joshua builds the altar as prescribed by Moses on "Ebal": Many of the words are taken from Deut 27. The Jewish text "Ebal" must be a reaction to the Samaritan use of Mount Gerizim; it may have been changed at any time after the Samaritans had built their sanctuary on that mountain and after the special status of the mountain made "Mount Gerizim" into the fixed name "Argarizim" and variants. The question of the text of Deut 27:4 and the location of the altar-pericope in the Book of Joshua is discussed in the excursus on Papyrus Giessen 19 and the Lyon Old Latin manuscript at the end of this chapter.

The last sentence has been changed at three places: "They" (= the two mountains Gerizim and Ebal in Deut 11:29) has been altered into "that mountain" = Gerizim. The Samaritan text focuses on Gerizim throughout. The question-form of Deut 11:29 ("Are they not …?" = "As you know, …") is changed into a statement ("This mountain is across …"). At the end is added "vis-à-vis Shechem" to make the localization of the altar quite clear. This addition could have been inspired by Gen 12:6, or it may have been occasioned by the localization of the mountains near Gilgal in Josh 8.

Of the three expansions in Exod 20 only this one is present also in Deut 5 of the SP. There are small textual differences between these two interpolations. This insertion is not known from any other text—apart from the fact that it is also to be found in Deut 5 in the SP. It is therefore

---

[80] In this long-disputed question I agree with among others Dexinger, "Garizimgebot," 127 f. Cf. the discussion in the excursus.

often considered to be the main characteristic feature of the SP, the one exclusively sectarian alteration of the text. In addition, the בחר–version in Deuteronomy is a Samaritan phenomenon.

There are catch-words in Exod 20:24 f. that made this insertion natural: v. 24 speaks of an earthen altar and v. 25 of a stone altar. The regulation for the altar of earth is followed in the MT by a promise that God will bless at every place where he will have his name commemorated. MT is difficult: "at the whole place"; the versions therefore have "at every place." In the SP this has been changed into "at the place," intending Mount Gerizim. This change must be simultaneous with the inserting of the tenth commandment. The insertion is, therefore, natural in a context that already spoke of altars, and on the other hand it occasioned a small change of the text about the altars in Exod 20:24 f.

According to J. Sanderson, "... all of the characteristics of that 'sectarian' expansion about Gerizim had their precedent in those shared expansions."[81] This means that the procedure behind the Gerizim commandment, doing theology by internal, biblical quotations, is the same as in the Moses layer; it could have been learnt from the expansionist and reordering activity in 4Q22 and the other pre-Samaritan texts.

F. Dexinger has suggested that the destruction of the Samaritan temple was the reason why the tenth commandment was inserted.[82] Its insertion is attributed to the time of the Maccabees or earlier by J. Purvis, or to the third century C.E., at the time of Baba Rabba, by A. D. Crown.[83] Z. Ben-Hayyim suggests that it was introduced as a reaction against Christian ideas that the Decalogue consisted in supreme moral precepts only. Therefore they linked "what the heretics considered a sublime principle with the observance of a practical commandment."[84] G. Hepner theorizes that the reason for the inclusion of the Samaritan tenth commandment

---

[81] Sanderson, "4QpaleoExodus^m," 70.

[82] Dexinger, "Garizimgebot": "Sucht man nach einem konkreten historischen Sitz im Leben dieser Interpolation, so würde sich am besten die Zerstörung des Tempels auf dem Garizim durch Joh. Hyrkan (129 v. Chr.) anbieten. An sich könnte es auch bereits früher geschehen sein, um gleichsam einen konzentrierten "Schriftbeweis" für die Legitimität des Garizimkultus zu haben," 132. "Hier suchte eine religiöse Gruppe einen zentralen Artikel ihres Credos mit Offenbarungsautorität zu versehen," 133.

[83] A. D. Crown, *Samaritan Scribes and Manuscripts* (TSAJ 80; Tübingen: Mohr 2001), 11 f.

[84] Z. Ben-Hayyim, "The Tenth Commandment in the Samaritan Pentateuch," *New Samaritan Studies of the Société d'Études Samaritaines* (vols. 3 and 4; ed. A. D. Crown and L. Davey; Studies in Judaica 5; Sydey: Mandebaum, 1992), 487–491.492.

is to be found in Exod 34:23, where "covet," חמד, is used, just as it is
found twice in the ninth (in the MT Decalogue: last) commandment. A
commandment about the "holiness of space" was appropriate for those
who had not experienced the exodus, against the exodus community who
tended to neglect this notion for another, the holiness of time, expressed
in the Sabbath and the festivals.[85] These are valuable suggestions, but
remain in the domain of suggestions, and we have to look for more data
that may help us further.

"The fact that the scroll was repaired indicates that *Exodus* in this
form continued to be used and treasured at Qumran despite the damages
it had suffered."[86] The date of the repair patch of 4Q22 has on palaeographical grounds been set to 100–25 B.C.E., and the Tucson facility
dated it "51 B.C.E. – 47 C.E." by the radiocarbon method. This would
imply that the pre-Samaritan text was still used at Qumran at a time
when the Samaritans existed. If the Samaritan tenth commandment is
older than this patch or older than the pre-Samaritan manuscripts, we
would have to assume a situation where this text type was used in circles other than the Samaritans at a time when it was adopted and used
as a Samaritan text. Either the Samaritans were a wider phenomenon
than could be assumed from the texts we have, or the tenth commandment is later than the turn of the era. Is it conceivable that the pre-
Samaritan texts were used at Qumran at a time when this text-type was
used in Shechem or at Gerizim? The strong anti-Samaritan sentiment of
4Q371 can be considered as incompatible with a favourable attitude to
the Samaritan community on the part of those residing at Qumran. The
probability is then that the tenth commandment is later than the turn
of the era, and that the pre-Samaritan texts were used more widely in
Israel before that point in time. This commandment uses Deut 27:2–7,
a text that is referred to several times in the altar-pericope in the Book
of Joshua, Josh 8:30–35 MT. I will return to this question in the excursus.

It has often been thought that the Pentateuch was finished and ready
for canonization at a certain point in time, and that after that the Samaritans broke off from the Jews and took with them what was canonical at the time of the breakaway, or the split, or the schism, whichever

---

[85] G. Hepner, "The Samaritan Version of the Tenth Commandment," *SJOT* 20 (2006):
147–151.
[86] J. Sanderson, "The Contributions of *4QPaleoExodᵐ* to Textual Criticism," *RevQ* 13
(1988): 550.

expression seems most appropriate to the different scholars. What S. L. Leiman calls the "modern scholarly consensus," referring to Pfeiffer, Bentzen, Weiser and Eissfeldt, holds that: "The Prophetic books (Joshua-Twelve Minor Prophets) were canonized in the third century BC, i.e. shortly after the Samaritan schism. Had any of the Prophetic books been canonized prior to the schism, they would have been included in the Samaritan canon."[87] Slightly different is the opinion of A. C. Sundberg: the Samaritans returned in the second century B.C.E. to the earlier Jewish canon, using the archaizing script of the time.[88]

On the other hand, the schism is used as an argument for the dating of the canonization of the Pentateuch. Thus G. Wanke: "Sollte die Loslösung der Samaritaner von Jerusalem—wie vielfach angenommen—in das ausgehende 4. Jh. fallen, so wäre dies ein weiterer Beleg für die kanonische Geltung des Pentateuchs [sc. at that time]."[89] On this notion, the Samaritans passively received what was canonical at the time of the schism, and their canon is simply the original HB/OT canon.

S. L. Leiman rejects this: "The Prophetic canon may have been closed long before the schism; when the schism occurred, the Samaritans may have rejected the Prophetic canon along with normative Judaism."[90] In a similar vein, R. Beckwith supposes that the schism took place after the destruction of Samaria, Shechem and the Samaritan temple, around 120 B.C.E. This was well after the canonization of the Prophets took place in the third century B.C.E.—thus the Samaritans must have deliberately repudiated them.[91] It seems that the pre-Samaritan texts compared to the contemporary material would point in the direction of Leiman's and Beckwith's suggestions. The Samaritans chose the text-type that had a clear pro-Moses tendency, and after the turn of the era they supplemented this text with the tenth commandment and made other changes that were related to the altar on Mount Gerizim. In later Samaritan literature the status of Moses as prophet and sole mediator was in focus.

---

[87] S. L. Leiman, *The Canonization of Hebrew Scripture: The Talmudic and Midrashic Evidence* (Transactions of The Connecticut Academy of Arts and sciences 47; Hamden, Conn.: Archon, 1976), 17.26f.

[88] A. C. Sundberg, *The Old Testament of the Early Church* (HTS 20; Cambridge, Mass.: Harvard University Press, 1964).

[89] G. Wanke, "Die Entstehung des Alten Testaments als Kanon," *TRE* 6 (1980): 3.

[90] Leiman, *Canonization*, 27.

[91] R. Beckwith, *The Old Testament Canon of the New Testament Church and its Background in Early Judaism* (London: SPCK, 1985), 128–131.

7.8. *Moses as a Prophet in the Durran*

If we ignore the Samaritan inscriptions for the moment, the oldest Samaritan document after the SP and, perhaps, the Samaritan Targum,[92] is some parts of the Samaritan liturgy.[93] In this liturgy the portion called the Defter is older than the 14th century C.E., and A. E. Cowley dated this to the fourth century C.E. A series of Aramaic texts in the Defter, the so-called Durran, is supposed to be earlier than the fourth century: H. G. Kippenberg has suggested the second century C.E.[94] On linguistic grounds, Z. Ben-Hayyim has argued for a fourth century C.E. dating of the Durran.[95] Whether the arguments based on contents or those founded on linguistic data should prove to be the stronger in the end, it seems that the Durran is the oldest Samaritan text next to the SP.

A few examples from this text will suffice to show the teaching of the Samaritans on the subject of Moses as a prophet. The texts here chosen from the Durran in the Samaritan liturgy are possibly anti-Dosithean polemics, but this is not of special concern in our context.[96]

> Because He (God) has said "A prophet like Moses" he (Moses) will see what His greatness is.[97]

> There is no other God than our Lord,
> and no Scripture like the Torah,

---

[92] The Samaritan Targum could be "contemporary with the Jewish targums … IIId and IVth Centuries," according to Montgomery, *Samaritans*, 292.

[93] Edited by A. E. Cowley, *The Samaritan Liturgy in two Volumes* (Oxford: Clarendon, 1909). In the following footnotes reference is made to the first volume.

[94] H. G. Kippenberg, "Ein Gebetbuch für den samaritanischen Synagogengottesdienst aus dem 2. Jh. n. Chr.," *ZDPV* 85 (1969): "Da der Durran vor Amram Darrah aber nach Auftreten der Dositheaner entstanden ist, wird man ihn am ehesten dem 2. Jh. n. Chr. zuweisen," 79; "Da er die Vorgänge dieser Zeit [Hadrian; Zeus-Tempel auf dem Garizim] aber deutlich reflektiert, wird man ihn in dieser Zeit ansiedeln müssen," 80; "Somit liegt im Durran das älteste Literaturwerk der Samaritaner vor, schaut man von der Tora ab," 103.

[95] Z. Ben-Hayyim, "Einige Bemerkungen zur samaritanischen Liturgie," *ZDPV* 86 (1970): 87–89.

[96] In addition to the edition by Cowley, see Z. Ben-Hayyim, *The Recitation of Prayers and Hymns* (vol. 3, part 2 of *The Literary and Oral Tradition of Hebrew and Aramaic amongst the Samaritans*; The Academy of the Hebrew Language: Texts and Studies 6; Jerusalem: The Academy of the Hebrew Language, 1967).

[97] Kippenberg, "Gebetbuch," 78, translates, "Wer sagt, dass der Prophet wie Mose ist, soll schauen, was seine (sc. Mose) Grösse ist." Against this, Ben-Hayyim, "Einige Bemerkungen," 87, has objected that the correct understanding should be, "Nachdem (oder da) er (sc. Gott in Deut 34,10) "Prophet … wie Mose" gesagt hatte, möge (oder: darf) er (sc. Mose) sehen was seine (sc. Gottes) Grösse ist."

and no true prophet like Moses,
and no perfect religion
and no truth apart from his.[98]

If it is correct that the expression "a prophet like Moses" refers to Deut 34:10, and the idea "of seeing God's greatness" plays on Exod 33:17–23, this means that the author of the Durran held Moses to be the only prophet allowed to see God, and that no one after him in fact did that.[99] Later prophets are qualitatively different from Moses.

> Behold, the Scriptures are as
> the hand-writing of God.
> Moses was entrusted with them for ever,
> and he will entrust them to you for ever.
> And who can erase them?[100]

This text plays on Num 12:7. Moses is entrusted with stewardship over everything, i.e. every relation, and this applies to the Scriptures, i.e. the Torah.

> There is no prophet like Moses the prophet[101]
> and no book like the Torah,
>
> the holy one,
>
> And no other devotion than to Yahweh
> in front of Hargerizim, the house of God,
> the elected, the holy, the selected part of
> the dry land.[102]

On Kippenberg's understanding, the text here plays on Num 12:6f., and that is why he uses "your servant" ("dein Knecht") in the translation. This is possible, but one might equally well think of Deut 34:10. "The dry land" reminds one of Gen 1:9f., where the earth is called "the dry land." Gerizim is a selected part of the earth.

---

[98] Cowley, *Samaritan Liturgy*, 38–39; Ben-Hayyim, *Recitation of Prayers and Hymns*, 42.

[99] Ben-Hayyim, "Einige Bemerkungen," 87: "Damit spielt der Verfasser auf Exod 33,17–23 an. Nur Mose durfte Gott sehen."

[100] Cowley, *Samaritan Liturgy*, 39; Ben-Hayyim, *Recitation of Prayers and Hymns*, 43.

[101] Kippenberg here translates "dein Knecht," "Gebetbuch," 81; Ben-Hayyim, *Recitation of Prayers and Hymns*, "הנביא."

[102] Cowley, *Samaritan Liturgy*, 40; Ben-Hayyim, *Recitation of Prayers and Hymns*, 50.

A great God, and none is like him,
a great community, and none compares to it,
a great prophet and none arose like he did–
they gathered at Mount Sinai
on the day the Book descended.
The trumpet began to sound
and the voice of the prophet became strong
and the Good One said: "May my prophet become exalted!"
May the prophet become great and make himself beautiful
and grow and reach the dark cloud!
Verily, he was dressed in a garment that
no king could be dressed in.
Verily, he was hidden in the cloud
and his face was dressed in the horn of light
in order that all people know
that Moses was the servant of God
and His entrusted one.[103]

In this case Moses is described in terms of the Servant of Isa 52:13–53:12. This could be directed against Jewish or Christian use of this text. Moses is often mentioned in the Durran, apart from the places here cited. For example, the Durran calls Deut 32 "the great song," it says that the Sabbath was revealed through the most elevated prophet, and speaks of two Lords of Divine favour: Joseph the king and Moses the prophet.[104] This teaching could be directed against the prophets in general or against the prophets of Judaism or Christianity.[105] In any case, these phenomena are "prophetical," just as the Dositheans were a movement centred on prophets. According to the Durran, a prophet cannot arise, or can hardly arise, who would be on a par with Moses. This is, possibly, directed against the Dositheans, but in any case we here get an indication of how the Samaritans would actually react when they met a prophetic movement in their own midst or elsewhere.

The liturgical poem by Marqah, published by Ben-Hayyim, mentions "Moses, the greatest of the prophets, bore us the following message in his book: 'And thou shalt return to the Lord'. [cf. Deut 30:8.20] Blessed is he who returns and finds his Lord," verse IX.[106]

---

[103] Cowley, *Samaritan Liturgy*, 40–41; Ben-Hayyim, *Recitation of Prayers and Hymns*, 53–54.

[104] Cowley, *Samaritan Liturgy*, 42.44.47; Ben-Hayyim, *Recitation of Prayers and Hymns*, 63.67.84.

[105] S. Lowy, *The Principles of Samaritan Bible Exegesis*, (StPB 28; Leiden: Brill, 1977), 261 f., n. 818.

[106] Ben-Hayyim, *Traditions of the Hebrew Language*, 144.

"The rigid exclusiveness of the Samaritans was dependent upon a priestly type of legalism … … other sects, like the Essenes and the Dead Sea Scroll Sect, were also based on … a 'prophetic' trend, which exerted a strong influence upon these sects, kindling in them a deep interest in 'prophesying.'"[107] This may be a correct way of describing the Samaritans and their difference in relation to, e.g. the Qumran community. The Samaritans were centred on Moses in the Durran, and later in the Memar Marqah, and rejected other forms of prophecy. In the oldest liturgical texts of the Samaritans they reveal an interest in Moses as a prophet much in line with the Moses layer in their Pentateuch.

7.9. Conclusion

The Samaritans chose one text-type in particular among the different texts available, but avoided some of the major expansions in some of the texts, as witnessed by the last two columns of 4Q27. The pre-Samaritan texts and the SP contain a layer highlighting Moses as prophet and defining later prophecy as fundamentally a preaching of the law. The tabernacle texts were adjusted also, revealing an interest in cultic matters. This makes the SP a deliberately chosen text. This text-type was created before the writing of the oldest manuscript in this group, 4Q17 from the middle of the third century B.C.E., and it was in use down to the turn of the era. This means that this text-type was formed at a time when the prophetic corpus was gaining in importance. The focus on Moses defied this latter process.

One may hear behind these texts the discussion between Moses and the prophets, between the traditions behind the Pentateuch and later prophecy. In the pre-Samaritan texts and in the SP the result of the discussion is clear: Moses is the absolute authority from which the other prophets had to derive theirs.

This type of text has become the canon of the Samaritans and later expansions have been made according to the same pattern. Later Samaritan liturgical texts show the same picture, and they are understandable as a continuation of the interest displayed in the SP.

---

[107] Lowy, *Samaritan Bible Exegesis*, 220, cf. also 256.

Excursus: Deuteronomy 27:4 in the Old Greek Papyrus Giessen 19 and in the Old Latin Lyon Manuscript, and the Altar-Pericope in Joshua 8:30–35

"Gerizim" occurs only four times in the MT, and only in the expression הר גריזים, "Mount Gerizim," Deut 11:29; 27:12; Josh 8:33; Judg 9:7. The SP follows this wording in the Pentateuchal cases, and uses "Mount Gerizim" even in Deut 27:4, where MT offers "Mount Ebal."

In Deut 11:29f. Moses commands the people: "(v. 29a) When the LORD your God has brought you into the land that you are entering to possess, (v. b) you shall set the blessing on Mount Gerizim and the curse on Mount Ebal. (v. 30) As you know, they are across the Jordan, westwards towards the setting sun, in the territory of the Canaanites who dwell in the Arabah, facing Gilgal, near the large tree of Moreh." V. 29a and most of v. 30 are used in the Samaritan tenth commandment, with the following addition at the end: "facing Shechem," Exod 20:17+ SP. "Gilgal" and "Moreh" could cause confusion since they were located at different places; but the addition clarifies that it is in the vicinity of Shechem.[108]

Deut 27:12 resumes the topic of "blessing" from Deut 11:29f., and specifies that six tribes shall stand on Mount Gerizim to bless: Simeon, Levi, Judah, Issachar, Joseph, and Benjamin. V. 13 has a slightly different form of expression: "And these shall stand on Mount Ebal for the curse (על־הקללה): Reuben, Gad, Asher, Zebulun, Dan, and Naphtali." The combination of Gerizim with blessing in both these cases lends positive connotations to the expression הר גריזים.

The context of Deut 27:12 f. is Moses' law to the elders about the stones to be erected on Mount Ebal (MT). Plastered stones inscribed with the Torah shall be raised, vv. 1–4; vv. 5–7 deals with the altar of unhewn stones; v. 8 commands them to write the law on the stones, and vv. 9–10 are an admonition to obey the law. Vv. 12f. are introduced by v. 11: "The same day Moses charged the people as follows ..." We are not sure which stones are meant in v. 8, separate stones as vv. 2–4 seem to indicate, or the stones of the altar mentioned in vv. 5–7? As v. 5 specifies that the altar shall be built "there," obviously referring to "Ebal" in the preceding verse, it is of some consequence whether the law shall be written on the

---

[108] There are no DSS variants in this case. 1Q4 = 1QDeut[a] contains Deut 11:27–30 with גריזים ואת, and that is all in this MS. 4Q45 = 4QpaleoDeut[r] contains 11:28.30–32, and there is no space for מול שכם in 11:30. These manuscripts do not contain a Samaritan text.

stones of the altar—which is on Ebal—or on the other stones, which are not located. Mount Ebal is a place for curse in Deut 11:29; 27:13 and therefore a surprising place for the altar.

Deut 27:2b.3a.4–7 are quoted in the tenth Samaritan commandment inside the quotations from Deut 11:29a.30, but with Mount Gerizim as the place of the stones instead of Mount Ebal. Since v. 8 is not quoted—the text is almost identical to v. 3a which is quoted—there is no ambiguity on which stones belong where: there are only stones used for the altar. Deut 11:29b with "Mount Gerizim" is omitted, but the name is supplied in the quotation from Deut 27:4 SP.[109]

The account in MT of how Joshua builds the altar on Ebal, Josh 8:30–35, mostly uses phrases identical to Deut 27:1–13. The theme of blessing is also followed up:

> Then Joshua built on Mount Ebal an altar to the LORD, the God of Israel, just as Moses the servant of the LORD had commanded the Israelites, as it is written in the book of the law of Moses, "an altar of unhewn stones, on which no iron tool has been used"; and they offered on it burnt offerings to the LORD, and sacrificed offerings of well-being. And there, in the presence of the Israelites, Joshua wrote on the stones a copy of the law of Moses which he had written. All Israel, alien as well as citizen, with their elders and officers and their judges, stood on opposite sides of the ark in front of the levitical priests who carried the ark of the covenant of the LORD, half of them in front of Mount Gerizim and half of them in front of Mount Ebal, as Moses the servant of the LORD had commanded at the first, that they should bless the people of Israel.   (Josh 8:30–33)

There is no mention of any curse in this last verse, but in the following verse Joshua reads aloud the law, the blessing and the curse, but without any specific location. The surprising element here is the location of the altar and the ceremony when Israel is encamped at Gilgal—right after the occupation of Ai and before the ruse of the Gibeonites. This is far from Mount Gerizim and Mount Ebal, and the location makes no sense.

These three cases depict Gerizim as a place for blessing, and two of them Ebal as a place for curse. Judg 9:7 strikes a different note: "When it was told to Jotham, he went and stood on the top of Mount Gerizim, and cried aloud and said to them, 'Listen to me, you lords of Shechem, so that God may listen to you.'" Mount Gerizim is in focus here also, and it looks as though the author has chosen a mountain of his liking.

---

[109] 4QDeut[c] includes 27:1–2, 4QDeut[f] has 27:1–10, 4QDeut[k] perhaps has 27:1; no relevant text.

Thus there are few cases with the expression "Mount Gerizim" in the HB, but they are important. The two cases in the Pentateuch have formed the basis of the Samaritan tenth commandment, and highlight a fundamental problem in Deuteronomy: an altar at Ebal or Gerizim is at variance with the demand for one place only for worship, Deut 12, if Jerusalem is the correct place. If, however, one of the places mentioned in the Pentateuch is the right place, then Deuteronomy is consistent. What, then, is the earlier reading in Deut 27:4, "Ebal" or "Gerizim"?

In the case of Deut 27:4 an Old Greek and an Old Latin manuscript support the reading "Mount Gerizim" of SP.[110] Papyrus Giessen 19 has εν αρ(?)γαρ[ι]ζιμ. Since the original document was destroyed in 1945 and only a photograph of it exists, it is impossible to determine on the basis of the extant photograph if the expression is written as one word or as two words, but P. Glaue and A. Rahlfs, who saw the manuscript before it was damaged, considered it was written as one word.[111] The same fragment has ε]πι αρ γαριζ[ιμ] in Deut 27:12, where αρ and γαριζ[ιμ] are on different lines. Words are frequently divided and written on different lines in this manuscript, so this occurrence does not help decide if the expression was contracted or not. We note that in both cases in this papyrus the whole expression is transliterated, not translated. In view of the material discussed in the previous chapter, the probability of the contracted version is higher than for the version with two separate words. There are no cases with the expression written as two words.

Further, one Old Latin manuscript (now in Lyon) has *in monte Garzin* in Deut 27:4, which is a regular translation of הר, and also containing "Gerizim" instead of "Ebal" in the MT.[112] On the basis of these two manuscripts, one in Greek and one in Latin, scholars tend to consider "Gerizim" the original reading in Deut 27:4, preserved by the SP. If

---

[110] In 2008 a Hebrew fragment with the text of Deut 27:4b–6 was announced, J. H. Charlesworth, "An Unknown Dead Sea Scrolls Fragment of Deuteronomy." Cited 29 Aug 2008. Online: http://www.ijco.org. This text reads הרגרזים. Its evaluation can take place after the full publication.

[111] P. Glaue und A. Rahlfs, "Fragmente einer griechischen Übersetzung des samaritanischen Pentateuchs," *Nachrichten der Königlichen Gesellschaft der Wissenschaften zu Göttingen, Phil.-hist. Klasse* (vol. 2; Berlin: Weidmann, 1911), 167–200; E. Tov, "Pap. Giessen 13, 19, 22, 26: A Revision of the LXX?" *RB* 78 (1971): 360. The article includes a full report of the earlier evaluation of the manuscript by P. Glaue and A. Rahlfs, pictures of the fragment, a text edition and a detailed discussion.

[112] U. Robert, *Heptateuchi partis posterioris versio Latina antiquissima e codice Lugdunens: Version latine du Deutéronome, de Josué et des Juges antérieure a saint Jérôme, publiée d'après le manuscrit de Lyon avec des observations* (Lyon, 1900), 30.

Papyrus Giessen 19 is of Samaritan provenance, as earlier scholarship was inclined to favour, the burden of proof would rest more heavily on the Lyon manuscript as the only non-Samaritan manuscript with this reading.

After the presentation of Papyrus Giessen 19 by P. Glaue and A. Rahlfs in 1911 it was considered a Samaritan Greek translation, part of the Samareitikon. E. Tov investigated the papyrus anew in 1971, and claimed that it was a revision of a translation in the LXX-tradition in order to bring it closer to the MT, or to a *Vorlage* earlier than MT. But there is one major obstacle to this explanation: the occurrence of αρ γαριζιμ in Deut 27:4, which seems to indicate Samaritan provenance. Tov would not completely rule out that it is a Samaritan text, but leans towards the solution that "Argarizim" "is an ancient, not yet sectarian, variant reading"; he states this also in his *Textual Criticism of the Hebrew Bible*.[113] This view is also presented by C. McCarthy in BHQ with reference to several scholars of the same opinion.[114]

הרגרייזים rendered as αρ γαριζιμ or αργαριζιμ in Papyrus Giessen 19 includes two problems. One is the reading "Gerizim" instead of "Ebal"; another is the translation technique, that is, the transliteration of הר.

The first problem can be addressed in this way. Papyrus Giessen 19 and the Lyon Latin manuscript are independent witnesses to the presence of "Mount Gerizim" in Deut 27:4. The Greek is a transliteration and the Latin a translation, which proves that they are independent witnesses to the same text. They both testify to the same name, but in different ways. This is the case whether Papyrus Giessen 19 is of Samaritan provenance or not. One may therefore conclude that there once was a Hebrew text with "Mount Gerizim" in Deut 27:4. This was the earlier reading. The change to "Ebal" must have been made at the hands of the Jews and could be a polemical alteration: an altar in the North was to be built on the mountain of curse.[115]

The second problem is posed by the probably contracted version of the expression, and this might diminish the importance of Papyrus Giessen 19. The contraction could reveal Samaritan provenance. But, as we have seen in a number of cases, this is not so. One could imagine a similar

---

[113] Tov, "Pap. Giessen," 374, cf. 376; idem, *Textual Criticism*, 95, n. 67.

[114] C. McCarthy, *Deuteronomy* (vol. 5, *Biblia Hebraica Quinta editione cum apparatu critico novis curis elaborato*; Stuttgart: Deutsche Bibelgesellschaft, 2007), 122*f.

[115] Altheim und Stiehl, "Erwägungen zur Samaritanerfrage," 218, mentions this possibility, but on the premise that the textual difference took shape in 621 B.C.E., ibid, 223.

situation to the one for 2 Macc 5:23; 6:2: the translator did not understand the expression and transliterated it. Or, and this is perhaps the more likely development, the Greek translation was made under the impression that αργαριζιμ was the common name for the mountain. When the revision of the text was made to bring it into accordance with the MT, this expression survived the revision. The revisers obviously did not feel the need to carry the revision through at this point, or they would have corrected "Garizim" into the name found in the MT and LXX: ἐν ὄρει Γαιβαλ, "on Mount Ebal." Josephus, *War* 1:63, is also a case in point. His disposition towards the Samaritans did not prompt him to alter the contracted version of the name according to his later custom, "mount Gerizim." Obviously, the contracted expression could be used by authors not at all amicably disposed towards the Samaritans.

The translation technique should be seen as part of this general picture. Tov's problem with the rendering of הרגריזים as αρ γαριζιμ or αργα-ριζιμ builds on the assumption that this is a sectarian reading. He further assumes that all "*tendentious* sectarian" (italics his) readings were originally non-sectarian. Since there is no testimony for a non-sectarian reading of such an important variant as הרגריזים he has his doubts about the conclusion that Papyrus Giessen 19 is a non-sectarian translation, even though he decided in favour of it.[116] The premise for this idea is that the expression is "*tendentious* sectarian."[117] Since the reading is found in Samaritan texts, this seems a natural inference, but it is not a necessary conclusion.

First, one must question the basic premise. In the SP there are some readings which are "*tendentious*[ly] sectarian." Many of them are found in non-sectarian texts from Qumran, but not all. The tenth commandment in the SP is composed of non-sectarian readings, as we have seen, but the complete text of the commandment is "*tendentious*[ly] sectarian," not found anywhere outside the SP. Similarly, the 21 cases where SP reads בחר instead of MT's יבחר may be found in a few places outside the SP, but it seems to be a tendentious sectarian reading without any prehistory.[118]

Secondly, granted that the framework sectarian versus non-sectarian fits the data, is it possible that the form הרגריזים was considered the name

---

[116] Tov, "Pap. Giessen," 374.376.

[117] Tov, "Pap. Giessen," 374, n. 21.

[118] The eight cases referred to by Pummer, "ΑΡΓΑΡΙΖΙΝ," 25, are late and may even have been influenced by the SP.

for the mountain without any sectarian bias in the expression itself? As we have seen in some of the other cases with "Argerizim," the answer is in the affirmative.

Applied to Papyrus Giessen 19 this would mean that the translation was made without any sectarian bias, but by rendering the expression as the name of the mountain. It was the acknowledgment of the cult on Mount Gerizim that was tendentiously sectarian, not the use of the expression as a name. Texts in Greek and Latin tend to understand the expression as a name, and this could be the case here as well. A Jewish translation of Deut 27 would treat the expression as a name and render it accordingly.

My supposition is that Pap. Giessen 19 was not a Samaritan document, but a Jewish translation made from a Hebrew manuscript that contained the expression הרגריזים. The Hebrew text could have been a Jewish text at a time when there was no temple on Mount Gerizim. Gerizim is the mountain for blessing, and it was only natural that the altar should be built there, and not on the mountain for curse, Ebal. At the time of translation into Greek, this was considered a name for the mountain, and so Papyrus Giessen 19 rendered it αϱ γαϱιζειν or αϱγαϱιζειν. The Latin translator of the Lyon Old Latin manuscript knew Hebrew, and translated הר as *mons*, or he translated a Greek text with ὄϱος. In any case he presented it together with *Garzin*. The reading is possible before the Gerizim-cult became an object of criticism for groups in Jerusalem. With the change from "Gerizim" to "Ebal," two textual traditions may have existed side by side for some time, and the "Ebal" version eventually outnumbered the "Gerizim" texts, as with the development in 2 Macc 5:23; 6:2. Thus, Tov would be right in judging Papyrus Giessen 19 to be a revision of a LXX-version to bring it in closer harmony with the MT, but with one notable exception. Two textual witnesses have preserved the original reading "Mount Gerizim" in Deut 27:4, and the SP carried on this reading. "Argarizim" was used as a technical term without overtones of loyalty to the (later) temple there. Is this conceivable as a Jewish phenomenon? There was a tendency in some LXX manuscripts to render the names of mountains as one word.[119] Thus, we have to consider the possibility for such a tradition in Papyrus Giessen 19.

The conclusion is that the reading "Gerizim" in Deut 27:4 is older than the reading "Ebal" of the MT.

---

[119] Pummer, "ΑΡΓΑΡΙΖΙΝ," 23.

The textual transmission of Deut 27:1 ff. may have been complex.[120] For our purpose it does not seem necessary to enter into the development behind Deut 11:29 f. and Deut 27:1 ff., but the altar-pericope at the end of Josh 8 in the MT, and in Josh 9:2+ in the LXX is of interest. In addition to these textual witnesses we have 4Q47 (4QJosh[a]), where it is located before Josh 5:2, and a similar context is considered to be presupposed by Josephus' *Ant.* 5.16–20. Against this background several scholars have reconstructed the relevant parts of the book of Joshua and of Deut 27, and have traced the history of the context of this pericope. Of the different solutions, E. Ulrich's takes more of the relevant data into consideration than any other.[121] His solution is this: in the first stage there was no name for the place of the altar in Deut 27:4; it was only said that the building should take place immediately after the crossing of the Jordan. In correspondence with this, the narrative with the building of the altar in the Book of Joshua constituted the end of chapter 4. This arrangement is witnessed to by 4Q47 and Josephus' *Ant.* 5.16–20.

In the second stage the Samaritans inserted בהר גריזים into Deut 27:4, as witnessed by Vetus Latina and the SP.

The final stage is represented by the MT and LXX, which introduced בהר עבל into Deut 27:4 and into the narrative with the building of the altar in the Book of Joshua as a counterclaim to the Samaritan version. The pericope with the altar-building was then transposed to its present location in Jos. 8 in MT and in Jos. 9 in the LXX.[122] The altar at Ebal "seems to make sense only as a countermove to the Samaritans' claim for Mt. Gerizim."[123]

Josephus describes two altars, one at Gilgal, *Ant.* 5.16–20, and one at Ebal near Shechem, *Ant.* 5.69. The texts are here offered in the translation of C. Begg:[124]

> When they had advanced fifty *stadia*, they pitched camp ten *stadia* from Jericho. Iesous, having erected an altar from the stones that each of the

---

[120] M. N. van der Meer, *Formation and Reformulation: The Redaction of the Book of Joshua in the Light of the Oldest Textual Witnesses* (VTSup 102; Leiden: Brill, 2004), 479–522, offers a full report on the discussion of the problem and presents his own suggestions for a resolution. It seems that he is not aware of Papyrus Giessen 19, cf. 501.

[121] E. Ulrich, "4QJosh[a]," in *Qumran Cave 4: IX: Deuteronomy, Joshua, Judges, Kings* (ed. E. Ulrich et al.; DJD 14; Oxford: Clarendon, 1995), 145 f.

[122] Ibid.

[123] Ibid., 145.

[124] C. Begg, *Judean Antiquities Books 5–7* (vol. 4 of *Flavius Josephus, Translation and Commentary*; Leiden: Brill, 2005), 7.

tribal rulers had pitched up from the river-bed in accordance with the
prophet's directions as a future memorial of the stoppage of the current,
sacrificed to God on it. They also celebrated the Phaska in that region ...
(*Ant.* 5.20)

Iesous, having moved his camp from Galgala into the hill country, erected
the holy tent at the city of Silo, for he thought the site suitable—given
its beauty—until the situation would allow them to build a sanctuary.
Proceeding from there to Sikima with all the people, he erected an altar
where Moyses had foretold. Then dividing the army, he stationed one half
on Mt. Garizeis, and the other half on Mt. Hebel (on which the altar was
as well), together with the Levitical tribe and the priests. Having sacrificed
and pronounced curses that they left behind inscribed on the altar, they
returned to Silo.   (*Ant.* 5.68–70)

Ant. 5:20 is seen in Begg's commentary as building on Josh 4:19–5:10,
and as adding that Joshua erected an altar from the stones he had had
brought from Jordan, and sacrificed to God on this altar. Josephus might
have been influenced by Deut 27:1–8, where the building of an altar and
sacrifice is prescribed immediately after the crossing of the Jordan. We
may add to Begg's comments that Josephus' description fits well with the
location of the altar-pericope witnessed to by 4Q47. 4Q47 is dated to
the Hasmonean period, and it is possible that the tradition which this
manuscript witnesses to was known to Josephus.

In the commentary to *Ant.* 5:69 Begg refers to *Ant.* 4.305, where
Josephus relates "And when they had fully conquered the land of the
Cananeans and destroyed all the populace in it, as was fitting, they should
set up an altar turned toward the rising sun, not far from the city of
the Sikimites, [and] bring it around between two mountains, Garizaeus
lying on the right and that called Counsel on the left." In accordance
with this location of the altar, *Ant.* 5.69 locates it near "Sikima." The anti-
Samaritan tendency in the latter passage emerges from the topic of the
curses written on the altar, in place of the law, which Deut 27:3.8 wants
inscribed on the stones or the altar. Ebal is therefore a mountain of curse,
as in Deut 11:29 and Deut 27:13, but this time the curse is spoken "not
far from the city of the Sikimites." This latter expression is adequate in
view of Gen 34, but sounds a contemporary note as well.

Josephus' second altar is built later than the first, but not near Gilgal,
where the Israelites were encamped according to MT and LXX. *Ant.* 5.69
reproduces the situation described in Josh 18:1, where the Israelites are
assembled at Shilo, but on the other hand, his description of the altar-
building at Ebal uses the division of the people into two camps from
Josh 8:33. The parallel account in *Ant.* 4.305–308 builds on the same

division and much more material from Deut 27:1 ff. His stories of the
altar at Ebal therefore know of these two biblical accounts. He does not
mention two sets of mountains, one near Gilgal and one near Shechem,
as do the Christian writers and the Madaba map from the Byzantine
period; see the previous chapter. Josephus sticks to the biblical location of
Mount Gerizim: Deut 11:30 combines Gerizim and Ebal with "the oaks
of Moreh," אלוני מרה, and אלון מורה is in Gen 12:6 located at Shechem. But
still, his *Ant.* 5.68–70 is given an anti-Samaritan twist. Why?

The Samaritans' temple on Mount Gerizim and their connection to
Shechem were reasons enough to denounce them by leaving an altar
with inscribed curses on Mount Ebal. But Josephus refers to the erection
of an altar on Ebal with words from Deut 27, the same text that forms
the core of the Samaritan tenth commandment. Is there any connection
between his use of this text and the Samaritans' use of it? We do not know
when this commandment was created, but if we take the patch in 4Q22
as a point of reference, this patch is slightly older than the turn of the
era, and I assumed earlier that the Samaritan tenth commandment was
created after the situation behind this repair of the text. If it was made
before Josephus wrote his *Antiquities*, the date of the commandment
would be first century C.E. If it happened in that century, Josephus would
have occasion to counter the Samaritan claim, and he did it by using the
same text, locating it on the mountain of curse, and leaving the curses on
Mount Ebal, "not far from the city of the Sikimites," *Ant.* 4.305.

Returning now to the question of the altar-pericope, we know that
Josephus knew its location according to 4Q47 and the Masoretic or LXX
text of Josh 8 or 9. He is witness that both traditions existed at the end
of the first century C.E. But he did not follow the latter tradition on
the location of the altar; instead he adhered to the older version which
located Mount Ebal near Shechem. As I interpret the textual situation
of Deut 27:4, the earlier version referred to Mount Gerizim, and the
change to Mount Ebal was an anti-Samaritan move. When the tension
in Jerusalem ran high against Mount Gerizim, Deut 27:4 was changed
into "Ebal." Was the narrative about the building of the altar transferred
to Josh 8 in the MT and ch. 9 in the LXX at the same time? This is a
logical place because Mount Gerizim and Mount Ebal are located "over
against Gilgal" in Deut 11:30, and the Israelites were encamped at Gilgal
according to Josh 9:6. The location immediately after the conquest of
Ai and before the expected attack of the peoples of the land in MT is
a natural setting, but the LXX ordering is also understandable: closer
to the remark about the camp at Gilgal. Also the location in Josh 4

has something to commend it. The erection of the altar should happen immediately after the crossing of the Jordan, and there is the story of the memorial stones from the river in Josh 4. Josephus makes these memorial stones into an altar, *Ant.* 5.20, and the same rationale may have occasioned the altar-pericope to land there. A. G. Auld has made a remark about the text as "A latecomer looking of a suitable home."[125] He and other scholars have suggested that the text was created after the bulk of the Book of Joshua was finished, so late that it became located at different places in the three textual witnesses. If this was the case, then one may speculate that the whole text is anti-Samaritan, made in order to counter their claim to the status of Mount Gerizim. Josh 8:30–35 is made up of text from Deut 27:2–13 and includes several references to the law book of Moses, so the whole text presents itself as an application of Deut 27:2–13. Then, the altar-pericope itself may have been an anti-Samaritan move, similar to the change from "Gerizim" to "Ebal" in Deut 27:4. If these two processes were simultaneous, they both witness to Jerusalem sentiments towards the Samaritans at a time when the relation between them was strained. We may be speaking of the time of the erection of the sanctuary on Mount Gerizim, and this would be in the fifth or fourth century B.C.E.

---

[125] A. G. Auld, "Reading Joshua after Kings," in *Words Remembered, Texts Renewed: Essays in Honour of John F. Sawyer* (JSOTSup 195; ed. G. Harvey, J. Davies, and W. G. E. Watson; Sheffield: Sheffield Academic Press, 1995), 167–181.

Chart 1: Major Expansions in the Samaritan Pentateuch: Gen 1 – Exod 11

No.	Expansion	Source	God's word received	God's word transmitted to Pharaoh	כה אמר יהוה	DSS: Category	Plague
1	Gen 30:36+	Gen 31:11–13	x		("The angel of the Lord spoke … to Jacob")	4Q364: A	
2	Gen 42:16+	Gen 44:22				(4Q9 without expansion)	
3	Exod 6:9+	Exod 14:12aβb				No extant text	
4	7:18+	7:16–18		x	x	4Q22: A	1: Blood
5	7:29+	7:26–29		x	x	4Q22: B	2: Frogs
6	8:1+	8:1 (partly)		(x: to Aaron)		4Q22: C	
7	8:19+	8:16b–19		x	x	4Q22: A	4: Insects
8	9:5+	9:1–5		x	x	4Q22 : B	5: Pestilence
9	9:19+	9:13–19		x	x	4Q22: A	7: Hail
10	10:2+	10:3–6	x		x	4Q22: A	8: Locusts
11	11:3*	11:4b–7	x			4Q22: C	10: Firstborn
12	11:3+	4:22 f.		x	x	4Q22: C	

Gen 30:36+, number 1, is a revelation to Jacob. ואיטיב עמך is added and ארץ מלדתך is changed to ארץ אביך.

Gen 42:16+, number 2: Joseph's brothers' argument against bringing Benjamin to Egypt. In Gen 43:28 SP Joseph honours Jacob in an added sentence: "He said, 'Blessed be this man by God!'" This addition is without any source.

Exod 6:9+, number 3: "They [the people] said to Moses, 'Please, let us alone and let us serve the Egyptians, for it is better for us to serve the Egyptians than to die in the wilderness.'"

Plagues 3 (Lice), 6 (Boils) and 9 (Darkness) are not introduced by a message to Pharaoh, but only by a command to Moses and Aaron.

Exod 10:2+, number 10, and v. 5 add עשב הארץ ואת כל פרי from Exod 10:12 SP (cf. Gen 1:11 f.).

Exod 11:3*, number 11, quotes 11:4b–7, but not v. 8, where Moses speaks his own words to Pharaoh. Exod 4:22 f. is a divine message to Pharaoh, introduced by calling Israel "my firstborn son." Its delivery to Pharaoh in 11:3+, number 12, comes—appropriately— before the tenth plague.

Chart 2: Major Expansions in the Samaritan Pentateuch: Exod 12 – Deut 34

No.	Expansion	Source	Contents	וידבר/ ויאמר יהוה אל משה	DSS: Category	Comments
13	Exod 18:25 SP, replacing MT's v. 25	Deut 1:9b–18	Appoint judges		4Q22: A	Moses' words
14	Exod 20:19*	Deut 5:24–27	Who can hear God and live?		4Q22: A	People's words
15	Exod 20:21+	Deut 5:28f.; 18:18–22; 5:30f.	A prophet like Moses	x as in v. 22 MT	4Q22: C	
16	Exod 26:35+	Exod 30:1–10	Make the incense altar	(x: speech starts in 25:1)	4Q22: B	Transposition
17	Exod 27:19+	Exod 39:1	Make vestments	(x: idem)	4Q22: A	
18	Exod 28:29+	Exod 28:30	Make Urim and Thummim	(x: idem)	4Q22 not extant, not re-constructed in DJD IX	
19	Exod 29:28+	Exod 29:21	Sprinkle blood and oil on the attire of Aaron and his sons	(x: idem)	4Q22: C	Transposition
20	Exod 32:10+	Deut 9:20	Moses prays for Aaron		4Q22: A	Narrative
21	Exod 39:21+	Exod 28:30	They made Urim and Thummim		4Q17: A	Narrative
22	Num 4:14+	Num 4:13f.; Exod 31:9	They shall cover the basin and its stand	(x: speech starts in 4:1)	No extant text	
23	Num 10:10+	Deut 1:6–8	Conquer Canaan	x	No extant text	
24	Num 12:16+	Deut 1:20–22	Conquer Canaan; spies		4Q27: C	Moses' words; people's response

No.	Expansion	Source	Contents	וידבר / ויאמר יהוה אל משה	DSS: Category	Comments
25	Num 13:33+	Deut 1:27–33	God hates us; God will fight for you		No extant text	People's words; Moses' reply
26	Num 14:40+	Deut 1:42	No invasion	x	No extant text	
27	Num 14:45+	Deut 1:44b–45 (partly)	Like bees		No extant text	Narrative
28	Num 20:13+	Deut 3:24–25.26b–28	Let me enter Canaan. No.		4Q27: A	Moses-God.
29	Num 20:13+	Deut 2:2–6	Pass through Edom	x	4Q27: C	
30	Num 21:+12	Deut 2:9	No trouble with Moab	x	4Q27: A	
31	Num 21:+13	Deut 2:17–19	No trouble with Ammon	x	4Q27: A	
32	Num 21:20+	Deut 2:24f.	Conquer Sihon's land	x (cf. Deut 2:17)	4Q27: A	
33	Num 21:+21	Deut 2:26f.	Request to pass through Sihon's land		4Q27 not extant, not re-constructed in DJD 12	Moses' words changed to Israel's words
34	Num 21:22*	Deut 2:28–29a	Request to Sihon		4Q27: C	Idem
35	Num 21:23*	Deut 2:31	Conquer Sihon's land	x	4Q27: C	
36	Num 27:23+	Deut 3:21b–22	Blessing on Joshua		4Q27: A	
37	Num 31:20+	Num 31:21–24	Handling of booty	(x: Divine law)	4Q27: C	
38	Deut 2:7+	Num 20:14,17f.	Request to pass through Edom		4Q364: A	Moses' message to the king of Edom
39	Deut 10:6*	Deut 10:7 (partly); Num 33:31–37	Extended itinerary		4Q364: A	Narrative

CHAPTER EIGHT

THE SAMARITAN ATTITUDE TO THE PROPHETS

The previous chapter concluded that the Samaritans chose their version of the Pentateuch because it provided Moses with an enhanced status as prophet, and they decided to write this version in palaeo-Hebrew script as an expression of its Mosaic character. The status of Moses as a prophet is a central element in later Samaritan theology, as witnessed already in the oldest liturgical texts, some of which were quoted in the previous chapter.

The topic of this chapter is to look at texts that may have a bearing on the Samaritan attitude to prophets and the books of the prophets. Deut 18:15.18 promise a "prophet like Moses"—a promise whose relevance was emphasized in the SP through expansion no. 15. A brief look at this promise as reflected in literature from the Hellenistic and Roman periods is necessary before the pertinent texts are discussed.

8.1. *A Prophet like Moses*

Deut 18:9 ff. has undergone several editorial revisions, but this phenomenon belongs to a stage before the period covered in the present investigation. Our starting point is the final text with its two promises for a prophet like Moses, first in the mouth of Moses, v. 15, then in the words of God, v. 18. There are several possibilities for the understanding of this expectation. It could envisage a prophet like Moses at any and every time in history—a permanent prophetic institution or phenomenon. Secondly, it might be an eschatological hope for a figure like Moses, with all the different possibilities for the understanding of "eschatological." Thirdly, it could represent an expectation for a renewed prophecy in opposition to existing, contemporary, prophecies and prophets. A fourth interpretation is that it was a text with a certain person in mind: scholars have guessed at Joshua or Jeremiah. Most likely, different groups have made use of these different possibilities for interpretation.[1]

---

[1] H. M. Teeple, *The Mosaic Eschatological Prophet* (JBL Monograph Series 10; Phila

The process of defining true prophecy did not stop with the law in Deut 18. Deut 13:2–6 (MT; v. 1–5, ET) reads, to some extent, as a commentary on Deut 18:21 f. Even if prophecies should come true, their speaker has to be tested by the criterion of the first commandment, and the law of God as a whole. This law would, most likely, be the Torah, the law as spoken by Moses. If we read Deut 13:2–6 as a companion piece to Deut 18:21 f., the two texts would emerge as expressing two sides of what true prophecy is. The first commandment is emphasized as barring any adherence to non-Yahwistic prophets, and the prophet will be tested on his ability to create new reality.

When these laws for the prophets are read together with Deut 34:10, we understand that the Torah is explicitly given a primary status in relation to the prophets. The prophets have to be like Moses, and not like the diviners of the neighbouring peoples, Deut 13:9–15. They have to be tested, not only heard, Deut 18:16–22. This test includes not only the first commandment, but the Torah as a whole, Deut 13:2–6. And, finally, no prophet like Moses arose, Deut 34:10, not in his lifetime, and not at any time before the Deuteronomic law was made.

The attitude to the truth of prophecy found in Deut 18:21 f. has clearly influenced later passages in the Deuteronomistic history, as is evident for example in the pericope 1 Kgs 13:1–6.32. It is probable that the Deuteronomistic History contains a prophetic layer distinct from the historical and nomistic layers.[2]

"We do not see our signs; there is no longer any prophet, and there is none among us who knows how long," Ps 74:9. This is the only mention in the Psalter of "prophets," a fact that may be interpreted as a conspicuous lack of interest in prophets in the poetic literature, that is in the temple service and among the persons creating liturgical and other poetic works. But this sole occurrence of the "prophet" is not without significance: it has a sore tone. It is not stating that prophecy has ceased, and it does not say that such cessation is necessary or welcome. Prophecy is seen as something good, but it is wanting in the present situation. The complaint also addresses the fact that the return of "signs" and "prophets" is uncertain: "there is none among us who knows how long." The feeling

---

delphia: Society of Biblical Literature 1957); W. A. Meeks, *The Prophet-King: Moses Traditions and the Johannine Christology* (NovTSup 14; Leiden: Brill, 1967).

[2] W. Dietrich, *Prophetie und Geschichte: eine redaktionsgeschichtliche Untersuchung zum deuteronomistischen Geschichtswerk* (FRLANT 108; Göttingen: Vandenhoeck & Ruprecht, 1972).

of the author of Lam 2:9 is much the same as in Ps 74: "Her gates have sunk into the ground; he has ruined and broken her bars; her king and princes are among the nations; the law is no more, and her prophets obtain no vision from the LORD."

The expectation of a prophet in Ps 74:9; Lam 2:9 is also evidenced by 1 Macc 4:46; 9:27; 14:41. This expectation is paralleled at about the time of 1 Maccabees by an expectation of a prophet like Moses, 4Q158; 4Q175; 4Q22. The expectation of a prophet like Moses may be a variant of the expectation of a prophet, but it may also have carried an anti-prophetic overtone in the sense that it concentrated on the Torah rather than on a continuation of prophecy. The SP stands in the Moses tradition.

In Samaritan circles the expectation for a prophet like Moses later found expression in the different versions of the expectation for the Taheb, "The Returning One" or "The Repenting One." Clear evidence of this figure is found in the Durran from the fourth century C.E.[3] Despite the effort by F. Dexinger to emphasize the originally prophetic elements in this figure, the most conspicuous traits are the messianic. The Johannine understanding in John 4:25 of the Samaritan expectation may be on the right track: "The woman said to him, 'I know that Messiah is coming' (who is called Christ). 'When he comes, he will proclaim all things to us.'" Such messianic interpretation in the Gospel of John may not be too far away from the—admittedly much later—attestation of the Samaritan Taheb in the Durran. The name Taheb is not inconceivable as a Messianic title, as Jewish and Christian Messianism had ample time to influence the Durran passages and later texts. At the same time, a figure who will "proclaim all things to us" is a prophet and not a Messiah. Thus there is an indication of a Samaritan expectation for a prophet in John 4:25. W. Meeks' investigation uses late texts and does not distinguish between the prophetic and royal traits in the figure of the Taheb.[4]

This expectation also led to the phenomenon of the Dositheans, which S. J. Isser supposes existed in the first century C.E., and whose leader, Dositheus, purported to be the promised prophet from Deut 18:18.[5]

---

[3] F. Dexinger, "Die fruhesten samaritanischen Belege der Taheb-Vorstellung," *Kairos: Zeitschrift für Religionswissenschaft und Theologie* 26 (1984): 224–252; idem, *Taheb*; idem, "Taheb," in *A Companion to Samaritan Studies* (ed. Crown, Pummer, Tal; Tübingen: Mohr, 1993), 224–226.

[4] Meeks, *Prophet-King*.

[5] S. J. Isser, *The Dositheans: A Samaritan Sect in Late Antiquity* (SJLA 17; Leiden: Brill, 1976).

The evidence for this dating is meagre, however, consisting of Origen, the *Clementina* and the Samaritan chronicles. These later texts cannot carry the burden of proof, in view of the lack of evidence in earlier texts, especially in Josephus. Dositheus and the Dositheans are a possible, but elusive, first century C.E. phenomenon.

These two effects of the expectation for a prophet like Moses are not our concern here, but rather texts that deal more directly with the canon of the prophets, or with the attitude to the HB prophets in general.

8.2. *The Canon of the Prophets*

The reverse side to the status of Moses as a prophet and the expectation for a prophet like him is the attitude taken towards the prophets, in particular towards the former and latter prophetic books of the HB. The Samaritans ended up with a canon without these books, and some scholars have supposed that this was a result of a conscious rejection of the prophetic corpus. Explicit statements about this question are found in the writings of the early church, e.g. in Epiphanius' *Panarion* from C.E. 370: "The Samaritans ... differ from the Jews in this first, that no writing of the prophets after Moses was given them (οὐχ ἐδόϑη αὐτοῖς), but only the Pentateuch ..." Other church fathers have the same type of statements on the Samaritan canon, cf. Irenaeus, *Adv. Haer.*,1 23,3; Hippolytus, *Philosophoumena*, IX, 24; Pseudo-Tertullian, appendix to *De praescriptione haereticorum*; Origen, *Contra Celsum*, I, 49.[6]

There are no earlier direct witnesses to the Samaritan attitude to the prophets, but in the *Ascension of Isaiah* (*Ascen. Isa.*) there is the figure of a prophet from Samaria who accuses Isaiah of being in conflict with Moses. This looks like a caricature of a possible Samaritan attitude, and if it can be made probable that the *Ascension of Isaiah* contains relevant material on this point, it may provide us with an insight into an actual discussion between Jews and Samaritans on the prophetic corpus. The figure of a prophet from Samaria in the *Ascension of Isaiah* has links to two Jewish documents, to 4Q339 from before the turn of the era, and to the Talmud. These Jewish texts make it likely that there is an old Jewish nucleus in the pertinent part of the *Ascension of*

---

[6] Texts are found in Pummer, *Early Christian Authors*, 149.156.53.36.

Isaiah, which means that we have here Jewish polemics from the first or second century B.C.E. Even if the portrayal of the prophet from Samaria should be polemical, we may discern behind it a discussion in the real world.

8.3. *The* Ascension of Isaiah

The story of the prophet from Samaria is found in the first part of the booklet, 2:12–5:16.[7] The text of the *Ascension of Isaiah* is extant in three different versions, which makes it a complex task to find the date and provenance of the relevant portions of the text. We have to know which parts constituted the oldest version of the work, and which parts were added in the course of the textual transmission, if we are to have any possibility of utilizing the *Ascension of Isaiah* for our purpose.

Literary Analysis

First, the complete text of the *Ascension of Isaiah* has been preserved in four Ethiopic manuscripts dating from the 14th to the 18th century. Two Coptic versions are available in manuscripts with fragments from chs. 1, 3, 5, 6, 7, 8, 9, 10 and 11 and they are supposed to date to the fourth century. A Greek manuscript with 2:4–4:4 stems from the fourth or fifth century, and is generally supposed to bear witness to the original language of the complete *Ascension of Isaiah*.[8] Then there are two Latin versions, one of which comes from the fifth or sixth century, covering 2:14–3:13 and 7:1–19 and termed Lat1. No two manuscripts agree on the text, but there is enough agreement between these manuscripts to convince scholars that they form one group, the Ethiopic-Coptic-Greek-Lat1 group, which one might abbreviate as the Ethiopic group.

Secondly, the second Latin manuscript is older than 1522, and testifies only to chs. 6–11, and in a shorter version than the manuscripts of the Ethiopic group. It is called Lat2. A similar version of chs. 6–11 is also available in Slavonic or Palaeobulgaric; the manuscripts testifying

---

[7] M. Knibb, "Martyrdom and Ascension of Isaiah," *OTP* 2: 143–176.

[8] B. P. Grenfell and A. S. Hunt, *The Amherst papyri: Part I The Ascension of Isaiah, and Other Theological Fragments with Nine Plates* (London: H. Frowde, 1900; repr. Milano: Istituto Editoriale, 1975).

to it represent a translation dating from the tenth or eleventh century. Together these manuscripts form the Slavonic-Lat2 group, abbreviated as the Latin2-group.[9]

Thirdly, the story in the *Ascension of Isaiah* has been recast completely in a work called The Greek Legend, which we know from two manuscripts, one from the eleventh century and one from the twelfth century. In this version, the contents of chapters 6–11 precede the story of chapters 1–5. There is no equivalent to 3:13–5:1; 11:2–22 in the Greek Legend.[10]

Attempts have been made to solve the textual problems through literary criticism in the traditional sense (*Literarkritik*), but it has proved impossible to distinguish between textual criticism and literary criticism. When manuscripts contain extra portions of text compared to other relevant texts, it is a fact to be handled by textual criticism. But it might also be a testimony to the growth of the text, which is a phenomenon to be handled by literary criticism. The situation is familiar from biblical studies, especially in the case of the book of Jeremiah, and many of the Dead Sea biblical texts add new material which has to be investigated from both a textual and a literary point of view.

On the basis of the manuscript situation R. H. Charles in 1900 suggested that there was originally a Greek *Ascension of Isaiah*, attested by some quotations in the church fathers (Epiphanius, *Adv. Haer.* 47:3; Jerome, *Commentary* on Isa. 64:3), which was the basis for the restructuring of the material in The Greek Legend. This original received two recensions in Greek. One recension is represented by the Ethiopic and Greek (and now one may add by the subsequently published Coptic) manuscripts and by Lat1. He called this the G^1 recension. The other is represented by the Slavonic manuscripts and by Lat2, termed by him G^2.[11]

---

[9] The study of *Ascen. Isa.* has been much facilitated through the edition of the different versions, supplied with an introduction, a synopsis and an extensive commentary, by E. Norelli, *Ascensio Isaiae: Textus* (vol. 7 of *Corpus Christianorum: Series Apocryphorum*; ed. Association pour l'étude de la littérature apocryphe chrétienne; Turnhout: Brepols, 1995); idem, *Ascensio Isaiae: Commentarius* (vol. 8 of *Corpus Christianorum: Series Apocryphorum*; ed. Association pour l'étude de la littérature apocryphe chrétienne; Turnhout: Brepols, 1995).

[10] O. von Gebhart, "Die Ascensio Isaiae als Heiligenlegende," *ZWT* 21 (1878): 330–353.

[11] R. H. Charles, *The Ascension of Isaiah: Translated from the Ethiopic version, which, together with the New Greek Fragment, the Latin Versions and the Latin Translation of the Slavonic, is here Published in full* (London: Adam & Black, 1900).

As for Epiphanius, *Adv. Haer.* 47:3, the correspondence with Lat2 consists in one word only, περιπατῶν = *ambulans*, 9:35, and this is very meagre evidence for a G² recension reflecting an original G. Jerome's commentary on Isa. 64:3 testifies to the inclusion of 1 Cor 2:9 in *Ascen. Isa.* 11:64 according to the Lat2 group, but this does not mean that he knew more than chs. 6–11. He might have known chs. 6–11 only and not any larger work. The church fathers offer very thin evidence for a G² recension. Charles further adduces quotations in Ignatius, *To the Ephesians* 19, *Protoevangelium Iacobi* and *Actus Petri* 24.[12] This material proves the existence of ch. 11 in the second century C.E., but not the existence of an original G of the *Ascension of Isaiah*.

The first question is the relation of the larger text of the Ethiopic group to chapters 6–11 of the Lat2-group. It is natural to start a literary analysis with a look at the synopsis.[13] The question is whether chs. 6–11 were once an independent unit or were cut off from an already existing *Ascension of Isaiah*. If they were cut off, the reason might have been that the first part of the *Ascension of Isaiah* lost relevance in the communities where this process took place. The separated texts were then edited and supplied with the redactional notes at the end of ch. 11.[14]

However, it is more likely that chs. 6–11 existed independently before they were incorporated into the *Ascension of Isaiah*. The arguments for this are the following. The second Latin and the Slavonic versions contain only chs. 6–11, and they form one common tradition, over against the Ethiopic and the first Latin versions. Further, the former manuscripts have an introduction and an ending, and—except for 7:37*; 9:15–23*; 11:1*. 2*. 34* and some words in different places—they present a shorter version of the text. The introduction is the same in all versions: "The vision that the (holy) prophet Isaiah, the son of Amos, saw," in the heading to 6:1. The ending of the second Latin runs as follows: "But he ceased to speak and went away from king Hezekiah," 11:40; and of the Slavonic: "And he ceased to speak and went away from king Hezekiah. But unto him, our God, be glory, now and always and forever and ever. Amen."

In addition, there is an admonition toward the end of this narrative: "As for you, be in the Holy Spirit that you may receive your robes, and

---

[12] Ibid., xxxii.

[13] Norelli, *Ascensio Isaiae: Textus*, 357–344.

[14] Ibid., 15–21; P. C. Bori, "L'Estasi del profeta: 'Ascensio Isaiae' 6 e l'antico profetismo cristiano," *CNS* 1 (1980): 367–389.

the thrones and crowns of glory, which are placed in the seventh heaven,"
11:40. The admonition addresses the audience by referring to the robes
and to the thrones and crowns of glory, as described in 7:2–11:35, i.e.
the second and longest "vision" in the book. There is no reference to the
contents of the first vision, 3:13–4:22, where we hear much more about
earthly matters than celestial ones, and where the saving ministry of Jesus
on earth is in focus—rather than his descent and ascent, of which we hear
in the second "vision."

We are able to observe the editor of the text of the Ethiopic group at
work. He removed whichever of the endings quoted above that he had
before him, and created a new ending which binds the two different parts
together: "Because of these visions and prophecies Sammael Satan sawed
Isaiah the son of Amoz, the prophet, in half by the hand of Manasseh.
And Hezekiah gave all these things to Manasseh in the twenty-sixth year
of his reign. But Manasseh did not remember these things, nor place
them in his heart, but he became the servant of Satan and was destroyed,"
11:41–43. The new ending reveals that 6:1–11:40 was connected with
material in chs. 1–5 simultaneously with the editing of 6:1–11:40, and
the result was a new book.

It is thus likely that there was originally an independent version of chs.
6–11, complete with an introduction and an ending, preserved in chs. 6
and 11, respectively. It had in addition an admonition to the audience on
the basis of Isaiah's vision in 7:2–11:35.

This version of chs. 6–11 was a Christian product. One cannot assume
that the version we have before us in the second Latin and the Slavonic
translations is identical with the original, independently existing text in
chapters 6–11. But the correspondence with the Ethiopic version, the first
Latin translations and the Coptic fragments of chs. 6–11 is high enough
to convince us that the changes due to transmission and revision cannot
be very substantial.

The theological pluses in the Latin2-group are the emphasis on the
angel Michael, 9:23.29.42, the assertion that God's name has not been
revealed, 7:37; 10:6, the expression "the Son of God," 9:12; 10:7, the
descent to hell, 9:15 f.; 10:8.15, the mission, 9:17, the idea that no one has
seen God earlier or later like Isaiah, 11:1.34, the expression "rex gloriae,"
11:24, and the revelation to the king, 11:40.

On the other hand, the *Sondergut*-passages in the Ethiopic group are
explanations, clarifications and similar exegetical material, understandable as development on the basis of the original behind the Latin2-group.
One may assume that texts were hardly ever shortened, unless an epitome

should be created, and where we have shorter texts not designed as epit-
omes, they will betray mechanical or human factors at work. The Latin2-
group is not an epitome, and it does not betray mechanical or human
factors, and thus reflects an independently existing text.

The Ethiopic text that we have may also be deficient, as the Coptic
texts in 11:36 and 40 show. In 11:36 they both have "they heard," which
is lacking in the Ethiopic text, but extant in the Latin2-group. In 11:40
the extant Coptic text has had some text restored by Norelli as "except
….in parables." This is not identical with the Latin2-group, but at least
shows that the Ethiopic may lack text here, which would explain why the
present text is so terse.

The assumption is, therefore, that 6:1–11:40 existed as an independent
work and that the Latin2-group reflects this text with some, but not many,
changes.

We may envisage the relations between the two groups of text in
the case of chs. 6–11 in this way. There existed a supposed original
version of chapters 6–11—probably without 11:2–22. This version is
represented by the Latin2-group and the Ethiopic group, but neither
of them contains the original unaltered. The Latin2-group has some
theological interpretations, and the Ethiopic group reveals editing based
on parts of chapters 1–5 as well. At this stage, the Ethiopic group had not
incorporated 3:13–5:1. The text of this latter group was the basis for the
Greek Legend, which created a more logical order of events, where the
execution of Isaiah comes last. The evidence of the Greek Legend tells
us that there was once a version of the book without 3:13–5:1; 11:2–22.
After this stage of editing the additions in 3:13–5:1; 11:2–22 were made
in the Ethiopic group.[15]

The secondary character of 3:13–4:22 is indicated by the repetition of
the formula: "Beliar was angry with Isaiah because of this/these vision/s,"
3:12 and 5:1a. 3:13–4:22 is an insertion, circumscribed by this introductory and concluding formula.

---

[15] Knibb, "Martyrdom and Ascension of Isaiah," 2:150, supposes that 3:13–4:22 was
first combined with the rest of chapters 1–5, and then this text was combined with
chapters 6–11. This theory presupposes that the Greek Legend retells the whole story
of *Ascen. Isa.* in a format without 3:13–4:22; 11:2–22, and that such a version must
have been created. The simpler explanation is that ch. 6:1–11:1.23–40 were attached
to ch. 1:1–3:12; 4:23–5:16, and that this state is reflected in the Greek Legend. After
this version was made, 3:13–4:22; 11:2–22 were added to the version of the Ethiopic
group.

We may therefore reduce the oldest part of the *Ascension of Isaiah*
to 1:1–3:12; 5:2–16. Scholarly approaches employing literary criticism
(*Literarkritik*) have several times tried to delineate the extent of a Jewish
nucleus in chs. 1–5. The analysis made by A. Dillmann[16] on the basis of
studies undertaken by H. Ewald has been accepted by other scholars.[17]
According to this analysis, 2:1–3:12 and 5:2–14 constitute the oldest and
Jewish parts of the work. R. H. Charles, on the other hand, held that this
Jewish part started in 1:1 (1:2b–6a being a later interpolation).[18] More
recently, M. A. Knibb concluded that 1:1–3:12; 5:1–16, "minus a number
of obvious editorial additions," was the original extent of chs. 1–5.[19]

These critical analyses have been made mainly on the basis of content—the question is what can belong together and what cannot. As an
example A. Dillmann's analysis may serve; he argues that 2:1–3:12; 5:2–
14 (1.) belong well together and contain a purely Jewish story taken from
the Misdrashim, (2.) contain some Jewish names, and (3.) do not show
any Christian traces.[20]

Presently, the study of the *Ascension of Isaiah* is moving away from a
literary-critical approach (in the traditional sense) with its resultant split-
ting up of the text towards a more "holistic" reading. But even in this
scholarly climate, it is acknowledged that the *Ascension of Isaiah* is composed from diverse materials, perhaps from different written sources that
were woven together by an author. In the words of D. D. Hannah: "In the
past the *Ascension of Isaiah* was often viewed as a composite document
made up of two or three sources pasted rather clumsily together. Today
the trend is toward viewing the apocalypse as a unity, composed by one
author who, while perhaps utilizing written or oral sources, clearly left
his or her stamp on the work as a whole."[21] Hannah mentions several
studies of this type and writes about R. G. Hall that his study "fits best
into this category. Although he finds evidence for a number of written
sources behind the Ascension, he emphasizes its final unity as the work

---

[16] A. Dillmann, *Ascensio Isaiae Aethiopice et Latine cum prolegomenis, adnotationibus criticis et exegeticis additis versionum latinarum reliquiis edita* (Leipzig: Brockhaus, 1877), X.

[17] According to R. H. Charles, *APOT* 2: 157, *by* Harnack, Schürer, Deane and Beer; see for example G. Beer in Kautzsch, *APAT*, 119 ff.

[18] Charles, *APOT* 2: 156 f.

[19] Knibb, "Martyrdom and Ascension of Isaiah," *OTP* 2: 148.

[20] Dillmann, *Ascensio Isaiae*, x.

[21] D. D. Hannah, "Isaiah's Vision in the Ascension of Isaiah and the Early Church," *JTS* 50 (1999): 80–101; quotation from 84.

of one author."[22] Still, Hannah suspects "that the legend of Isaiah's martyrdom at the hands of Manasseh may have existed in written form and was used by the Ascension's author."

According to this account, the difference between old and new interpretation is that the former saw the work as pasted clumsily together, whereas the latter sees it as the unified work of one author. Both approaches assume sources. If one assumes that the sources were written, one is doing literary criticism,[23] if oral, the method would be called tradition history or tradition analysis.[24] To think that an author used written documents is in fact exactly the same as the literary critics' assumption that an editor used written sources. If we assume that "the author" is referring to the same phenomenon as the earlier "redactor" or "editor," we realize that the change from old to new approach is not so great after all. Perhaps we today would characterize the literary critic's view of the text as "a patchwork of various sources."[25] An assumption that the author used written sources and "left his or her stamp on the work as a whole" which has "similar themes and language ... throughout"[26] is, however, nothing else than literary criticism supplemented with redaction criticism. One may ask whether the difference here is merely verbal—how one describes the *Ascension of Isaiah*, as a patchwork or a unity. What constitutes the work and how it came into existence is seen in the same way by both parties, old and new.

At present, one may see three different attitudes in the study of the *Ascension of Isaiah*. One is represented by A. M. Schwemer and J. Knight, according to whom the work is a unity, produced by one person or group in one operation.[27] The second is represented by E. Norelli, who holds that there were two authors behind the work, both coming from the same milieu, and representing the same Christian prophetic and apocalyptic interests. Chs. 6–11 were produced first, and as they were rejected by the ecclesiastical establishment, a second author produced

---

[22] R. G. Hall, "The *Ascension of Isaiah*: Community Situation, Date, and Place in Early Christianity," *JBL* 109 (1990): 289–306.

[23] J. Barton, *Reading the Old Testament: Method in Biblical Study* (London: Darton, Longman & Todd, 1996), 20 ff.

[24] H. Barth and O. H. Steck, *Exegese des Alten Testaments: Leitfaden der Methodik: ein Arbeitsbuch für Proseminare, Seminare und Vorlesungen* (8. ed.; Neukirchen-Vluyn: Neukirchener, 1978), 40.

[25] Hannah, "Isaiah's Vision," 85.

[26] Hannah, "Isaiah's Vision," 84 f.

[27] A. M. Schwemer, *Studien zu den frühjüdischen Prophetenlegenden Vitae prophetarum* (TSAJ 49–50; Tübingen: Mohr, 1995); J. Knight, *The Ascension of Isaiah*, 1995.

chs. 1–5 in defence of the first work. The third tendency is found in Hannah's scholarship, where we find different written sources used by one author in the production of the booklet.

None of these three approaches seems adequate. My approach is more in line with the older analysis, based upon the manuscript situation and the extent of the Christian material.

The date of the *Ascension of Isaiah* has been difficult to agree upon, but the late first century c.e. seems probable for the first five chapters, except for the later addition 3:13–5:1a. Justin Martyr and Tertullian knew the tradition that Isaiah was sawn in half, and Hebrews 11:37 may testify to the same tradition. The second part of the book (chs. 6–11*) is later, but the second century is a not unlikely date.[28]

Ascen. Isa. 3:13–4:22 has since R. H. Charles' analysis been called the *Testament of Hezekiah*, as he assumed that this section was the vision that the king himself had seen and that he wanted to transmit to his son Manasseh, 1:2–4. But 3:13–4:22 is clearly presented as the vision of Isaiah, 3:13; 5:1, so this name will not fit. But the text is obviously the last portion added to the work. This addition probably occasioned some Christian interpolations in ch. 1.

This result may be summed up by the earlier designations for the parts of the *Ascension of Isaiah*, the *Martyrdom of Isaiah* (1:1–3:12 and ch. 5), the *Testament of Hezekiah* (3:13–4:22) and the *Vision of Isaiah* (5–11). Even if the name *Testament of Hezekiah* is misleading, the division into three parts still has some merit.

But 1:1–3:11; 5:1b–16 is not necessarily one piece. What material did the editor have and what changes were made to the first five chapters?

Ch. 1 contains several Christian portions, and one may ask whether the whole chapter is a work of the editor. Charles' argument that 2:1 proves the existence of parts of ch. 1 is invalidated by the close correspondence between ch. 1 and 2:1. The editor may have created these texts together.

But there is a small remark in 1:6 that reveals the existence of part of ch. 1 before it was united with chs. 6–11: "[Hezekiah] was giving his commands [to Manasseh]." This corresponds to the intention expressed in 1:2, but there it is said that he would hand over "words of righteousness which the king himself had seen." In 2 Kgs 20:1; Is 38:1 we read "set your house in order," NRSV; the Hebrew text is צו לביתך; we might say:

---

[28] Knibb, "Martyrdom and Ascension of Isaiah," *OTP* 2: 149 f.

"give מצות, 'commands,'" as in *Ascen. Isa.* 1:6.[29] We have the giving of "commands" in *Ascen. Isa.* 1:6.7, and this information is not followed up in the rest of the book. The expression bears witness to something earlier than the Christian elements in ch. 1 (e.g. 1:2–4).

It is, therefore, a fair assumption that there was a story which the editor of the *Ascension of Isaiah* used in ch. 1, removing some elements and adding others, so that the present ch. 1 is largely Christian. The extent of the Jewish material in the earliest part of the *Ascension of Isaiah* can be found by using criteria similar to those employed by Dillman.[30] There is a story similar to Jewish texts, there are some Jewish names, and there are parts that do not show any specific Christian traces. To the older analysis we may add that 4Q339 (see below) contains the name Zedekiah ben Chanaanah; compare *Ascen. Isa.* 2:12 ff. Using these criteria we are led to see parts of chapter 1, and 2:1–3:12; 5:1b–12/13 as a Jewish substratum[31] that is probably older than the Christian reworking of chapters 1–5.[32] We are thus speaking about the first century c.e., or an earlier date. E. Norelli's supposition that chapters 6–11 were produced first, and then chapters 1–5, cannot be upheld, in the light of our literary analysis, and because the first chapters contain Jewish material.

The Oldest Stratum

This oldest part of the *Ascension of Isaiah* contains relevant material for our purpose. The narrative in 2:1–6 first depicts king Manasseh as very wicked, in line with the portrayal in 2 Kgs 21:1–18; 2 Chr 33:1–10. The alternative story in 2 Chr 33:11–20, where Manasseh repents of his sins, is not reflected here. In 2 Kings Manasseh serves the gods of Canaan and Assyria; in the *Ascension of Isaiah* he instead serves Sammael/Satan/Beliar. According to *Sib. Or.* 3:63 Beliar will come from the Σεβαστήνοι, and this is interpreted by J. J. Collins as "Nero will come from the line of Augustus." He also mentions another interpretation,

---

[29] From the *Opus Imperfectum* (an incomplete work on Matthew from the sixth century) we learn that Hezekiah fell ill and summoned Manasseh with the purpose of giving him commands about the fear of God and about how he should rule.

[30] Dillmann, *Ascensio Isaiae.*

[31] Norelli, *Ascensio Isaiae: Commentarius*, 66: "lettura targumica dell'Antico Testamento."

[32] "There are good reasons to believe that the book as a whole is of Jewish origin and that all the clear Christian references belong to a later editor or interpolator," I. Gruenwald, *Apocalyptic and Merkavah Mysticism* (AGJU 14; Leiden: Brill, 1980), 62, n. 119. This is an exaggeration.

that Beliar is an anti-Messiah coming from the city of Samaria, which was renamed "Sebaste" by Herod in 25 B.C.E.[33] Beliar is mentioned also in *Ascen. Isa.* 4:2–13 in terms reminiscent of Nero, that is, in the last addition to the work. "Beliar" in the *Sibylline Oracles* and *Ascen. Isa.* 4:2–13 would most likely refer to Nero, but in 2:4; 3:11 it is just a name for the devil. There is some information in the *Ascension of Isaiah* to associate the name with Samaria; in 3:11 Beliar dwells in the heart of king Manasseh, who is pleased with Belkira, the false prophet from Samaria. The late addition 4:2–13 seems to interpret Nero in terms of Manasseh: Beliar dwells in Manasseh, 1:8 f.; 3:11, and later he appears in human form, in the king, 4:2. In the Damascus Document, CD XII, 2 f., the prophet who preaches apostasy under the influence of the spirits of Belial, shall be punished according to Lev 19:31; 20:27, and Deut 13 is specified as pertaining to prophecy under Belial. Belkira is portrayed in such a way in the *Ascension of Isaiah* that the verdict in his case would be capital punishment according to the Damascus Document.

Next, the narrative focuses on Isaiah, son of Amoz, with the other prophets, Micah, the aged Ananias, Joel, and Habakkuk. Isaiah leaves Jerusalem because of the king's iniquities and arrives in Bethlehem. That place is also full of iniquities, so he withdraws and dwells on a mountain "in a desert place." M. Knibb thinks this trait was influenced by the story of Elijah, 1 Kgs 19:1–8.[34] Micaiah and Eljiah are considered models for Isaiah; the latter reproved king Ahaziah and Samaria, *Ascen. Isa.* 2:14, and the former is killed at the instigation of the false prophets, *Ascen. Isa.* 2:16. If we look for parallels in the Book of Isaiah, the withdrawal to "a desert place" in *Ascen. Isa.* 2:8 could, however, reflect the preparation of the way of the Lord in the desert, Isa 40:3 f., and "sackcloth" and "naked" of *Ascen. Isa.* 2:10 are reminiscent of Isa 20:2. Isaiah in the *Ascension of Isaiah* is not said to be the teacher of the other prophets, but he provides the example in the choice of a dwelling place, of clothing, and of food, all of which are taken from the Book of Isaiah.

In *Ascen. Isa.* 2:12–16 we read about the false prophet Zedekiah son of Chenaanah, whom we know from 4Q339 (see below). He is said to be the teacher of four hundred Baal prophets, and a contemporary of Micaiah son of Amida, the prophet.[35]

---

[33] J. J. Collins, "Sibylline Oracles," *OTP* 1: 360.363.

[34] Knibb, "Martyrdom and Ascension of Isaiah," 2:158, n. l.

[35] Hannah, "Isaiah's Vision," 86, thinks of the the language of the Greek fragment as coming from the LXX, but it seems more directly influenced by the Hebrew.

M. Knibb thinks the "writer has confused the 400 prophets of Yahweh of 1 Kgs 22:6 with the prophets of Baal mentioned in 1 Kgs 18:19, 22."[36] Zedekiah prophesied by Yahweh, 1 Kgs 22:11, but Micaiah ben Imlah revealed that it happened through the "spirit of lies," vv. 20–23. Thus, there is a problem of the spirit involved in 1 Kgs 22. The *Ascension of Isaiah* develops this conundrum into a clear cut situation: Zedekiah was a false prophet; and the *Ascension of Isaiah* creates a link to the prophets of 1 Kgs 18: he was the teacher of the Baal prophets, 2:12. One may here see not so much a confusion of texts as a solution of the problem of the spirit in 1 Kgs 22.

Ahaziah was "the son of *alamerem balalaaw*," an enigmatic phrase. "Alam" is usually taken to represent Ahaziah's father Ahab, but "balalaaw" is unsolved.[37] The different roots considered here, are *'lm*, "black," or "hidden," in the Ethiopic "signify." But it could be *ba'alaw*, "his master," i.e. Ahaziah, the son of Ahab, his teacher (in injustice). A. Caquot's idea that the expression is infamous, would fit the context.[38]

Compared to the bare name of Zedekiah son of Chanaanah in 4Q339 (see below), he is here presented as teacher and leader of four hundred other false prophets. The name is a Yahweh-name in the HB, and this is not changed or corrupted here. He is further presented as the uncle of Belkira/Melcheira, Isaiah's opponent. The name of this false prophet from Samaria is given in a variety of forms, but they belong to two main groups, "Belkira" and "Melcheira." The latter is a transcription of מלכירע, "the king of evil," and the former of בחררע, "the elect of evil." Both forms are denigrating. Belkira might be a pun on the question of the election of the place for worship. The Samaritans of the common era read בחר, "has elected," in 21 instances in Deutoronomy, referring to Mount Gerizim as elected already at the time of Moses' sermon before the conquest of the land, and the Jews יבחר, "will elect," referring to the future status of Jerusalem. The false prophet from Samaria is named *Behira'*, a form bringing the question of election down upon the heads of the Samaritans, "The Elect of Evil." The question of election could have been an issue

---

[36] Knibb, "Martyrdom and Ascension of Isaiah," 159, n. t.

[37] Norelli: "Il testo, corrotto, constituisce un enigma insoluto." The Greek SEMMOO could easily be read as SELLAAOO and this was again misread in Ethiopic as lala'aw and further corrupted, "e corromporsi ulteriormente," *Ascensio Isaiae: Commentarius*, 142; Charles, *Ascension of Isaiah*, 87: balaaw = baliseoos, meaning 'Ahab, the king'; A. Caquot, "Bref commentaire du 'Martyre d'Isaïe'," 80: suggests a Hebrew *ba shemamah*, "en dévastation, horreur," which would be "un sobriquet infamant."

[38] Caquot, "Bref commentaire."

some time before the present text of Deuteronomy was codified on both sides of the controversy. We notice the distortion of names connected with Samaria here.

It is emphasized that the accusing prophet comes from Samaria, 3:1, cf. 2:12; 3:3. He operates in Jerusalem, 3:1, as he has escaped the deportation in the North under Shalmaneser, and fled to Jerusalem. There he spreads his false prophecies, "and there were many from Jerusalem who joined with him." This story is the reverse of that of Josephus, according to which the northern population were made up of deportees from Mesopotamia and refugees from Jerusalem. No influx from Samaria to Jerusalem is reported by Josephus, but here it is alleged. Might this mean that the false prophet had a wider audience than that found in Samaria?

From Jer 23:13 we know that Samarian prophets were ill-reputed: they were foolish, they prophesied by Baal and led the people into idolatry. Ezek 16:46–56 mentions Samaria and Sodom as sinful sisters of Jerusalem. *Paralip. Ier.; Ant.* 8.236, 243–245, 401–410 mention prophets from Samaria and Judah who are corrupt. The false prophet from Samaria is thus a variation on an HB theme. Belkira/Melcheira could have been created on the basis of the OT passages about false prophets from the North.

J. Knight thinks that he was given ancestry from Samaria in order that this pseudoprophet should be denigrated as much as possible. He stands for Jewish exegesis, and thus this exegesis is denigrated. Moreover, Moses (= Judaism) is said to not see God, but Isaiah (= Christianity) can see him.[39] This understanding presupposes that the passage is a Christian text, which I dispute. Rather, the *Ascension of Isaiah* introduces the accusing prophet from Samaria, not in order to attack rabbinical theology, but either because false prophets come from Samaria according to Jeremiah, or because of some contemporary phenomenon, which might be reflected in the story of Simon in Acts 8—called the "great power" and connected to magic; in later literature, he became the father of all heresies;[40] or Dositheus might have provided raw material here.

That the false prophet from the North preaches in Jerusalem would mean that the accusations against the canonical prophets had some support in circles in Jerusalem also, not only among the Samarians.

---

[39] J. Knight, *Disciples of the Beloved One: The Christology, Social Context and Theological Context of the Ascension of Isaiah*, (JSPSup 18; Sheffield: JSOT Press, 1996), 43 f.192 f.

[40] Kippenberg, *Garzim und Synagoge*, 328–349.

The teacher of the false prophets in 2:15 f. is called Jalerias from mount Joel. The latter name is also given as "Efrem" in Lat1, which is supposed to be the original name for the mountain, and this was changed to "Israel" ("islal" in the Greek fragment), and corrupted to "Joel" in the other manuscripts. The reference to the North is evident in both versions. Jalerias is said to have been the brother of Zedekiah. Jahleel, Jehallelel and Jehiel are possible equivalents from the HB, and as we know that the onomasticon of the worshippers at Mount Gerizim is typical of the Jews in the third and second century B.C.E., the name "Jalerias" or a Hebrew equivalent might well be a Samaritan name. Another possibility is that this name also is denigrating, and composed with רע at the end. If the first element is from the root ילד, the name would mean "child of evil." Belkira/Melcheira seems to be a part of the Jewish version behind the present *Ascension of Isaiah*.

The Accusations against Isaiah

Belkira/Melchira brings accusations against Isaiah and other prophets in front of king Manasseh in the following way:

> And Melcheira accused Isaiah and the prophets, saying, "Isaiah and the prophets who are with Isaiah prophesy against Jerusalem and [th]e cities in Judah [and] Be[nj]amin, that th[ey] w[il]l go into cap[ti]vi[ty, and] in iron chains, [and you, O King], that you will go away [in iron chains]. But they prophesy falsely and they hate Israel and Judah and Benjamin and their word is evil against Judah and Israel. And Isaiah has himself said to them, 'I see more than Moses the prophet.' For Moses said, 'Man cannot see God and live.' But Isaiah has said, 'I have seen [God], a[nd] behold, I live'. [Re]alize therefore, O ki[n]g, that he is a lia[r]. He has called J[e]rusalem Sodo[m]a a[nd] de[clar]ed [the] leader[s of Judah] and Israel [to be the people of Go]morrah." [Th]us he brought many accusations [against Isaiah] and the prophets before Manasseh.[41] (3:6–10)

Isaiah is asked to withdraw his alleged teaching, but refuses and Manasseh has him killed, 5:1b–11.

Ascen. Isa. 3:6–10 is paralleled by some texts in the Talmud, all of them dealing with conflicts perceived within the HB. *B. Yebam.* 49b addresses

---

[41] Translated on the basis of the Greek text of *Ascen. Isa.* in Grenfell and Hunt, *Amherst Papyri*. The Ethiopic version is slightly different, cf. Knibb, "Martyrdom and Ascension of Isaiah," *OTP* 2: 159f.

the relation of Isaiah to Moses, and—just like the *Ascension of Isaiah*—locates Isaiah anachronistically to the time of king Manasseh:[42]

> Said R. Simeon B. Azzai etc. [A tanna] recited: Simeon b. Azzai said, "I found a roll of genealogical records in Jerusalem and therein was written 'So-and-so is a bastard [having been born] from a forbidden union with] [sic] a married woman' and therein was also written 'The teaching of R. Eliezer b. Jacob is small in quantity but thoroughly sifted.' And in it was also written, 'Manasseh slew Isaiah.'"
>
> Raba said: He brought him to trial and then slew him. He said to him: Your teacher Moses said, "*For men shall not see Me and live*" and you said, "*I saw the Lord sitting on a throne, high and lifted up.*" Your teacher Moses said, "*For what [great nation is there, that hath God so nigh unto them], as the Lord our God is whensoever we call upon him,*" and you said, "*Seek ye the Lord when he may be found.*" Your teacher Moses said, "*The number of thy days I will fulfil*" but you said, "*And I will add unto your days fifteen years.*" "I know," thought Isaiah, "that whatever I may tell him he will not accept; and should I reply at all, I would only cause him to be a wilful [homicide]." He thereupon pronounced [the Divine] Name and was swallowed up by a cedar. The cedar, however, was brought and sawn asunder. When the saw reached his mouth he died. [And this was his penalty] for having said, "*And I dwell in the midst of a people of unclean lips.*"[43] (b. Yebam. 49b)

The text then continues with a detailed discussion of the three points where Isaiah and the Torah contradict each other: Exod 33:20 versus Isa 6:1; Deut 4:7 against Isa 55:6; Exod 23:26a versus Isa 38:5b (= 2 Kgs 20:6aα). In each case an explanation is given—in the last even two—in order that Isaiah no longer should be in conflict with his Rabbi (in the translation above "teacher") Moses.

This is not the only case in the Talmud where a prophet is said to be in conflict with the Torah. Another instance concerns Ezekiel, and this case is recorded at two different places in the Talmud:

---

[42] A different set of texts that has been used in the discussion as comparative material are a Persian legend about king Jamshed who flees before Dhaak. An Adonis myth behind the Jewish legend has been suggested by O. Eissfeldt, "Martyrium und Himmelfahrt Jesaias (Martyrium et Ascensio Isaiae)," *Einleitung in das Alte Testament* (4. ed.; Tübingen: Mohr), 825 f., after an idea of K. Galling, "Jesaja-Adonis," *OLZ* 33 (1930): cols. 98–102. O. H. Steck has suggested that the Jewish story had its home in the hassidic movement, *Israel und das gewaltsame Geschick der Propheten: Untersuchungen zur Überlieferung des deuteronomistischen Geschichtsbildes im Alten Testament, Spätjudentum und Urchristentum* (WMANT 23; Neukirchen: Neukirchener Verlag, 1967).

[43] I. W. Slotki, *Yebamot translated into English with Notes, Glossary and Indices* (vol. 1 of *Seder Nashim in Four Volumes*; *The Babylonian Talmud*; I. Epstein, ed.; London: Soncino, 1936; repr. 1984), 324.

Rab Judah said in Rab's name: In truth, that man, Ananiah son of Hezekiah
by name, is to be remembered for blessing: but for him, the Book of Ezekiel
would have been hidden [footnote: "The technical term for exclusion from
the Canon."], for its words contradicted the Torah [Footnote: "E. g. Ezek.
XLIV,31; XLV,20, q.v."]. What did he do? Three hundred barrels of oil were
taken up to him and he sat in an upper chamber and reconciled them.[44]

(b. Shabb. 13b)

Rab Judah said in the name of Rab, That man is to be remembered for
good, and Anina b. Hezekiah is his name; for were it not for him the
Book of Ezekiel would have been suppressed, since its sayings contradicted
the words of the Torah. What did he do? He took up with him three
hundred barrels of oil and remained there in the upper chamber until he
had explained away everything.[45]   (b. Menach. 45a)

This text comes in the middle of a series of quotations from the Book of
Ezekiel, taken from chapters 44–46, concerning offerings, and followed
by a discussion about their meaning. They were said to conflict with the
Torah: compare Ezek 46:11 to Num 28, and Ezek 45:18 to Num 28:11. In
some cases, Ezekiel is at variance with the Torah, and in others, Ezekiel
is able to explain what to do if the Torah cannot be followed: the answer
lies with the Prophet.

Of a similar nature is the discussion in the Talmud about the story in
1 Kgs 13, where two prophets receive different messages, and about Jonah
and Micaiah ben Imlah. The problem is resolved in this way:

Or a prophet who transgresses his own words. E. g. Iddo the prophet, as
instanced by the following verses, [i] For so it was charged me by the word
of the Lord [saying, Eat no bread, nor drink water, nor turn again by the
same way that thou camest], [ii] And he [the self-styled prophet] said unto
him. ...

... But perhaps they [sc. the Heavenly Court] repented thereof?—Had
they repented, all prophets would have been informed. But in the case of
Jonah they did repent, yet Jonah himself was not informed!—Jonah was
originally told that Niniveh would be turned, but did not know whether
for good or for evil.

He who disregards the words of a prophet. But how does he know [that
he is a true prophet], that he should be punished?—If he gives him a

---

[44] H. Freedman, *Shabbat Translated into English with Notes and Glossary* (vol. 1 of
Seder Mo'ed in Four Volumes; *The Babylonian Talmud*, ed. I. Epstein; London: Soncino,
1938, repr. 1987), 55.

[45] E. Cashdan, *Menahot Translated into English with Notes, Glossary and Indices* (vol. 1
of *Seder Kodashim in Three Volumes*; *The Babylonian Talmud*, ed. I. Epstein; London:
Soncino 1948; repr. 1989), 272.

sign. But Micah [ben Imlah, MK] did not give a sign, yet he [i.e. his colleague] was punished!-If he was well established [as a prophet], it is different. For should you not admit this, how could Isaac listen to Abraham at Mount Moriah, or the people hearken to Elijah at Mount Carmel and sacrifice without [the Temple]? Hence the case, where the prophet is well established is different.[46]   (b. Sanh. 89a)

In all these four texts one can see how the rabbis were able to reconcile conflicting information in the Hebrew Bible, whether this was within one text as in the instances alluded to in b. Sanh. 89a, or between different texts, as in the three other texts. The whole thrust is towards solving problems on a given basis, that is, the—more or less—canonical text. But in the first three texts the problem is even more severe: a prophetic book is found not to be in accordance with the Torah. But fortunately this problem can also be resolved by the rabbis' reasoning.

R. Johanan seems to have criticized those who based their opinion on tradition deriving from Haggai, Zecharaiah and Maleachi, b. Hul. 137b, b. Bek. 58a.[47] He also held that, "In every matter, if a prophet tells you to transgress the commands of the Torah, obey him, with the exception of idolatry," b. Sanh. 90a,[48] and he said that "this passage [Ezek 45:18] will be interpreted by Elijah in the future," b. Menach. 45a.[49] The reference to Elijah reflects Mal 3:23 MT; the prophets are in these texts considered as providers of relevation that had to be in accordance with the Torah if they should be considered prophets like Moses.

This relationship between the Torah and the prophet is aptly described by E. E. Urbach:

> … the Amoraim came and elevated the Sages of the Oral Torah to the level of the Prophets and even gave the former precedence over the latter. At the close of the third century R. Avdimi of Haifa declared: "Since the destruction of the temple, prophecy was taken away from the Prophets and given to the Sages" (T. B. Bava Batra 12a).

---

[46] H. Freedman, chs. VII–XI of Sanhedrin Translated into English with Notes, Glossary and Indices (vol. 3 of Seder Nezikin in Four Volumes; The Babylonian Talmud, ed. I. Epstein; London: Soncino, 1935; repr. 1987), 594f.

[47] E. Cashdan, Hullin Translated into English with Notes and Glossary (vol. 2 of Seder Kodashim in Three Volumes; The Babylonian Talmud, ed. I. Epstein; London: Soncino 1948; repr. 1989), 787; L. Miller and M. Simon, Bekorot Translated into English with Notes and Glossary (vol. 3 of Seder Kodashim in Three Volumes; The Babylonian Talmud, ed. I. Epstein; London: Soncino 1948; repr. 1989), 396.

[48] Freedman, Sanhedrin, 599.

[49] Cashdan, Menahot, 271.

As a result of this approach they [the Sages] denied the prophets who were active in the past the possibility of initiating or amending anything in the conduct of life by Divine injunction, and if we find that innovations and enactments were ascribed to them, these were not only given at Mount Sinai together with all "that a senior disciple was due to originate," but just as the disciple innovates by dint of his reasoning, so, too, the Prophets established what they did as a result of their argumentation (T. B. Temura 16a) … The teachings of prophecy are included in the Torah, and they, too, are Torah.[50]

It is important in our connection that such variance inside Scripture is recorded and discussed in the Talmud. On the basis of this fact alone we are able to state that the story in the *Ascension of Isaiah* is possible inside a Jewish milieu. The recording in the Talmud of discrepancies between the Torah and Isaiah or Ezekiel makes it likely that the nucleus of the story in *Ascen. Isa.* 3:6–10; 5:1b–11 has a Jewish origin. This assumption is confirmed by the anachronistic dating of Isaiah to the reign of Manasseh found both in the *Ascension of Isaiah* and in *b. Yebam.* 49b; this must be due to the common origin of the story.

There are other elements common to the *Ascension of Isaiah* and *b. Yebam.* 49b. First of all, they are both created on the basis of biblical material. Two of the main characters, Isaiah and Manasseh, are known from the HB, and the persons speak in quotations from the HB. Some of the quotations are identical in the two texts. The problem of inconsistencies between Torah and prophets is also common to the *Ascension of Isaiah* and *b. Yebam.* 49b: the HB reveals tensions and inconsistencies between these two groups of biblical texts. The conflict between king and prophet is also common—a well-known issue in the HB, e. g. Jer 37; 38; Isa 7. Jeremiah and perhaps Isa 53 may have given rise to the notion of prophets as martyrs.[51] Thus, the *Ascension of Isaiah* and *b. Yebam.* 49b share a stock of motifs from the HB.

From common roots the two texts developed in different directions. *B. Yebam.* 49b focuses on the theological differences between Moses and Isaiah, by offering three cases of inconsistencies. In the *Ascension of Isaiah* there is one main case in point, but other accusations focus upon other aspects of the prophetic preaching.

It is also an important difference that *b. Yebam.* 49b tells of a trial: Manasseh brings Isaiah to trial before he decides to kill him. But Manasseh is

---

[50] E. E. Urbach, *The Sages: Their Concepts and Beliefs* (Jerusalem: Perry Foundation, 1987), 306.

[51] Steck, *Geschick der Propheten*.

not completely vindicated since he has Isaiah killed without urging him to explain himself. Only after the prophet's death are explanations given for the discrepancies; thus Manasseh remains in a somewhat ambiguous light. Another point in *b. Yebam.* 49b is that Isaiah is pious in that he does not defend himself, in order not to make Manasseh into a wilful homicide. Isaiah also pronounces the divine name and is swallowed up by a tree. As this is his last resort, God saves him, but the evil king finds him and kills him. Isaiah dies when the saw reaches his mouth. This is a theodicy, there is some justification in his dying, because he was a person with unclean lips. Or else he dies for having accused his own people of having a bad character. In *b. Yebam.* 49b Isaiah comes out fairly well, and Manasseh fairly badly.

It is also conspicuous what is *not* found in *b. Yebam.* 49b but extant in the *Ascension of Isaiah*.

First of all, it is the accusing prophet. In *b. Yebam.* 49b the king himself is both accuser and judge. In the *Ascension of Isaiah* Melcheira is the accuser and king Manasseh only the judge.[52] By introducing another prophet, the *Ascension of Isaiah* makes use of the old conflict between prophets, so well known from Jeremiah, Ezekiel, Micah, Zechariah, etc.

This is clear because the *Ascension of Isaiah* uses the term "prophet" of Moses, whereas *b. Yebam.* 49b entitles him Rabbi, "teacher" in the translation cited above. The *Ascension of Isaiah* confronts Isaiah with the real prophet, Moses; the Talmud sets him against his teacher, *the* Rabbi Moses. In the Talmud the hierarchy is established as that of Teacher and prophet, whereas the *Ascension of Isaiah* creates inner-prophetic discussions and strife.

The villain of the story in the *Ascension of Isaiah* is the Samarian prophet Melcheira. There were three problems with Isaiah in *b. Yebam.* 49b, and Melcheira levels three allegations against Isaiah. First, Belkira/Melcheira gives a rough summary of HB prophetic preaching about Jerusalem, the cities of Judah, and Benjamin, "that th[ey] w[il]l go into cap[ti]vi[ty, and] in iron chains, [and you, O King], that you will go away [in iron chains] ... He has called J[e]rusalem Sodo[m]a a[nd] de[clar]ed [the] leader[s of Judah] and Israel [to be the people of Go]morrah," *Ascen. Isa.* 3:6.10. This allegation is focused on the judgment without

---

[52] The conversion of Manasseh that we hear about in 2 Chr 33 and his attitude according to the Prayer of Manasseh are very different from the portrayal in *Ascen. Isa.* Thus, *Ascen. Isa.* represents a different tradition, as does *b. Yebam.* 49b.

mentioning the verdict on the sins of the people. If Melcheira refers to specific prophecies, we might think of Isa 1:10; 5:13; 6:12; Amos 7:11.17, maybe also 2 Chr 33:11 in the case of the oracle against the king.[53] This proof from prophecy will substantiate the claim that the prophets are ill-willed against their addressees. The prophets "hate Israel and Judah and Benjamin and their word is evil against Judah and Israel," *Ascen. Isa.* 3:7. The words used in the original Greek text here are μισέω and κακός.

Even if all prophets are accused, "they prophesy falsely and they hate Israel and Judah and Benjamin," *Ascen. Isa.* 3:7, Melcheira particularly aims at Isaiah: "[Re]alize therefore, O ki[n]g, that he (Isaiah) is a lia[r]," *Ascen. Isa.* 3:10, and this constitutes the second accusation. King Manasseh was not taken into captivity according to the Book of Kings, but he was taken prisoner according to 2 Chr 33. There was a lack of correspondence between prophecy and later history, but this is not expounded in the allegation. On the basis of the Book of Kings, Isaiah is a liar, and according to Deut 18:21 f. the prophet is false if his sayings do not come true. *Ascen. Isa.* 3:7.10 allege that Isaiah is a false prophet, and there could be HB texts that would substantiate the claim. This is the tenor of the accusation: they are false prophets who hate their audience and speak evil words.

This appeal to the king comes right after what might be called the third and central accusation against Isaiah. Melcheira asserts here that Isaiah has said, "I see more than Moses the prophet," and, "I have seen [God], a[n]d, behold, I live!" 3:8 f. What makes these statements into a forceful accusation is the Mosaic rule in Exod 33:20b that "no one can see [God] and live," as opposed to Isa 6:1: "I saw the Lord sitting on a throne, high and lifted up."

We notice that *b. Yebam.* 49b and *Ascen. Isa.* 3:8 f. both use the MT in the case of Exod 33:20b, and not the expanded version of the LXX.[54] Moses is quoted according to the MT. But when it comes to quoting Isaiah, they are very different. *b. Yebam.* 49b again simply cites the MT of Isa 6.1: "I saw the Lord sitting on a throne, high and lifted up." The *Ascension of Isaiah*, on the other hand, has a free rendering, "I have seen

---

[53] A. Caquot has noted that the word γαλεάγρα in *Ascen. Isa.* 3:6 is found in the LXX only in Ezek 19:9 (in an oracle against king Jehoiakin) and this fact could indicate that the prophet Ezekiel is also included. Caquot, "Bref commentaire," 83. Cf. the Prayer of Manasseh, 10, for the expression "iron chains."

[54] The LXX has an addition: "No one can see <u>my face</u> and live," οὐ γὰρ μὴ ἴδῃ ἄνθρωπος <u>τὸ πρόσωπόν μου</u> καὶ ζήσεται.

[God], a[nd] behold, I live," and this is preceded by the assertion, "I see more than Moses the prophet"–a sentence without any clear precedent in the HB. The former sentence reads as direct polemics against Exod 33:20b, and the second provides Isaiah with a higher status than Moses. The false prophet makes his "citations" from Isaiah into a more direct contradiction of Moses than what is the case in *b. Yebam.* 49b. Moses is quoted correctly by Melcheira, but Isaiah is not.

Here, we must say that Melcheira betrays a certain *Tendenz.* His aim is not to produce exact quotations for the sake of theological discussion of the differences between Moses and Isaiah, but to create an Isaiah who directly contradicts Moses.

The problem of "seeing God" and the discrepancy between Moses and Isaiah at this point may lie behind the LXX rendering of Exod 33:20b with the addition of "my face": "No one can see my face and live." According to the LXX, Isaiah was perhaps not violating the Torah. Similarly, John 5:37: "You have never heard his voice nor seen his form (εἶδος)."

The theological interest revealed by the Talmud tells us that the project was to save the integrity of the two parts of the HB, the Torah and the Prophets. There is a 'canon-saving' undertaking behind these discussions. This aim is not shared by the the *Ascension of Isaiah.* Here, it is more important to portray the false prophet in as negative a light as possible, and the heightened conflict between Moses and Isaiah was only a weapon in his mouth for reaching this goal. A caricature of a position would exaggerate it, perhaps to the point where it is diametrically opposed to the favoured position. Polemics functions in this text in the way that names are distorted and made into words of abuse. Points of view are exaggerated and distorted and made into nasty pictures. Heroes are more heroic; Isaiah is an unblemished martyr; villains are worse; Belkira is completely bad. The distorted quotations in the mouth of Isaiah illustrate this. Moses is quoted correctly, Isaiah not. The result reached by this literary method is extended to a wider circle: the *Ascension of Isaiah* is not only interested in one prophet against one false prophet, but in the prophets and the company of false prophets; Belkira accuses Isaiah and the prophets, 3:6.

The prophet from the North not only accuses Isaiah by distorting Isa 6:1 and adding a statement to the effect that he claims a higher status than Moses; he adds other arguments against Isaiah. The first accusation is that the prophets proclaim judgment on Jerusalem, Judah, and the king, and they "hate Israel and Judah and Benjamin and their word is evil against Judah and Israel," *Ascen. Isa.* 3:7. The Book of Isaiah presents us with judgment oracles against Jerusalem because of her sins, but it also contains Zion-theology, a positive assertion of the status of the city. Isa 2:3; 28:16 may serve as examples of the long series of statements on Zion, most of them in the context of salvation oracles. Melcheira's summary of Isaian teaching on this point is one-sided.

The second accusation against him and the other prophets is that they are false prophets, *Ascen. Isa.* 3:7.10; the expressions are ψευδοπροφη-τεύουσιν and ψευδή[ς] ἐστίν. In 3:7 the reason for this designation is the accusations against the city and the king, and in 3:10 the rationale for the designation is the conflict with Moses. These two accusations are not found in the Talmudic texts, yet they belong to the Jewish parts of the *Ascension of Isaiah*.

The Greek Legend, chapter 3, has a different portrayal of the conflict around Isaiah. Isaiah is consistently made into a prophet of Christ. There is the false prophet Melchias accusing "the great Isaiah" in front of king Manasseh, as in the *Ascension of Isaiah*. The accusation does, however, not mention Moses or the conflict with the Torah at all. Only Isaiah's preaching against "the beloved and elect city" Jerusalem and against the king is in focus, and because of this he is killed. The hero here is Isaiah, as in the *Ascension of Isaiah*, but there is no animosity against the North. The origin of Melchias is not mentioned. The Greek Legend thus gives a different interpretation of the martyrdom of Isaiah. It is not the conflict with Moses that is the reason for his death, but his true prophecy about the fate of the beloved and elect city Jerusalem and his prediction of the exile of king Manasseh and his family. In relation to the *Ascension of Isaiah* the whole northern background for false prophets is absent.

The northern ancestry of Melcheira is a prominent feature in the *Ascension of Isaiah*. This northern or foreign origin of false prophets was observed by the author of an *Aramaic List of False Prophets*, found at Qumran, 4Q339.

8.4. 4QList of False Prophets ar/4Q339

4QList of False Prophets ar, 4Q339, consists of two fragments, which probably originally formed one single manuscript, which was torn in the middle. Together the two fragments are part of a leather fragment of 8.3 × 5 cm. The original size was 8.5 × 7 cm. The fragment has been folded twice, and the right hand part of the lines is missing.

It is written in a normal Herodian hand, with no traced lines. This means that the date of the fragment is late first century B.C.E. Some modern paper on the back prevents us from telling if there was text on the back.

The text and a translation are published in DJD 19.[55] It has an Aramaic heading in line 1, a Hebrew list of names in lines 2–8, and line 9 is reconstructed in Aramaic.

1 נביאי [ש]קרא[די קמו ב]ישראל[
2 בלעם]בן[בעור
3]ה[זקן מביתאל
4]צד[קיה בן כ]נ[ענה
5]אהא[ב בן ק]ול[יה
6]צד[קיה בן מ]ע[שיה
7]שמעיה נח[למי
8]חנניה בן עז[ור
9]נביאה די מן גב[עון

Line 9 contains three letters only, ʿayin, waw, and nun. M. Broshi and A. Yardeni reconstructed a waw at the beginning of lines 3–9, and line 9 as "Johanan son of Simeon," = John Hyrcanus I (135–104). Hyrcanus held three offices, supreme command, high priesthood and prophecy, Josephus, War 1.68–69. "The author … might have regarded him as a false prophet."[56] In this reconstruction, they were influenced by E. Qimron.[57] But this reconstruction was abandoned altogether in the DJD edition of the text, and line 9 was changed by the same authors into "a prophet from Gibeon."

Much reconstruction of the text is necessary. Reconstruction is a question of the size of letters as written by individual scribes, but also of orthography. There was no Academy of the Hebrew language at the time—so orthography is in principle uncertain. Reconstruction is not only a question of scribal habits, but also which letters we should look for.

I think the simplest reconstruction is to assume an Aramaic heading in line 1, followed by quotations from the Hebrew Bible in lines 2–9. There is

---

[55] A. Yardeni and M. Broshi, "4QList of False Prophets ar," in *Qumran Cave 4: XIV Parabiblical Texts, Part 2* (ed. M. Broshi et al.; DJD 19; Oxford: Clarendon, 1995), 77–79.

[56] M. Broshi and A. Yardeni, "On *netinim* and false prophets," in *Solving Riddles and Untying Knots: Biblical, Epigraphic, and Semitic Studies in Honor of Jonas C. Greenfield* (ed. Z. Zevit, S. Gitin, and M. Sokoloff; Winona Lake: Eisenbrauns, 1995), 37.

[57] E. Qimron, "On the Interpretation of the List of False Prophets," *Tarbiz* 63 (1994): 273–275.

enough space in line 9 to reconstruct it in Hebrew, which would make all lines after the heading into Hebrew. Line 9 would then be reconstructed as הנביא אשר מגבעון.

With this reconstruction the text can be translated in this way:

1. The [fa]lse prophets who arose in [Israel] [:]
2. Balaam [son of] Beor
3. [the] old man of Bethel
4. [Zede]kiah son of Cha[na]anah
5. [Aha]b son of Q[ol]iah
6. [Zede]kiah son of Ma[a]seiah
7. [Shemaiah the Neh]lemite
8. [Hananiah son of Az]ur
9. [the prophet from Gib]eon

The names on the list are familiar ones from the HB. Their distribution can be seen from the following table, where 4Q339 is located according to the supposed chronological order: MT, the LXX, 4Q339 and the Targum. Since 4Q339 provides all the names under the heading "false prophets," it is interesting to note which designations they receive in the different versions:

MT	LXX	List of False Prophets	Tg.
Num 22–24: בלעם בן־בעור No designation	= MT	Balaam [ben] Beor	= MT
1 Kgs 13: 11 נביא אחד זקן	προφήτης εἷς πρεσβύτης	[The] old man of Bethel	נבי שקרא חד
1 Kgs 22: 24: צדיהו בן־כנענה No designation	= MT	[Zede]kiah ben Cha[na]anah	= MT
Jer 29:1.8: אל־הנביאים Verses 21–23: אחאב בן־קוליה צדקיהו בן־מעשיה	Jer 36:1: πρὸς τοὺς ψευδοπροφήτας Verse 8: οἱ ψευδοπροφήται Verses 21–23 only first names	[Aha]b ben Q[ol]iah [Zede]kiah ben Ma[a]seiah	Jer 29:1: ולות ספריא Verse 8: נבייכון דשקרא Verses 21–23 = TM
Jer 29:24 שמעיהו הנחלמי	Jer 36:24 = MT	[Shemaiah the Neh]lemite	שמעיה דמן חלים

MT	LXX	List of False Prophets	Tg.
Jer 28:1: חנניה בן־עזור הנביא אשר מגבעון	Jer 35:1: Ανανιας υἱὸς Αζωρ ὁ ψευδοπροφήτης ὁ ἀπὸ Γαβαων	[Hananiah ben Az]ur [the prophet from Gibe]on	חנניה בר עזור נבי שקרא דמגבעון

Balaam was considered an ambiguous figure in Jewish circles.[58] On the one hand his prophecy in Num 24:17–19 was interpreted as a prediction of the Messiah in the LXX, and in Targum Onkelos, Targum Neofiti and Targum Pseudo-Jonathan. In the DSS there is a positive use of this oracle, 4Q175; 1QM 11:4–6; CD 7:18–21 MS A, and this is the case also in *T. Jud* 24:1–6; *T. Levi* 18:2–3; also in *b. B. Bath.* 15b and Pseudo-Philo's *Biblical Antiquities* Balaam is viewed positively.

On the other hand, the NT sees in him a mercenary prophet, Jude 11; 2 Pet 2:15 f., and a preacher in favour of eating food sacrificed to idols and a preacher of fornication, Rev 2:14. At the same time, he was considered a predictor of the incarnation. This tension was resolved by attributing his prophecy to Isaiah, and by quoting him alongside Isa 11, Justin, *Apol.* I. 32.12–13, cf. 1QSb 5:27. Ambrose and Augustine considered him evil, but Origen and Jerome created a repentant prophet out of him. In order to save him from being a false prophet, two strategies were chosen, to attribute his oracle to Isaiah, or have him repent.

This ambiguity in Jewish and Christian circles is not present in 4Q339. Here, he is a false prophet, even though MT does not even call him a prophet, nor a seer. He is able to see, חזה, Num 24:4.16, but no specific designation is given him.

The old man of Bethel is the prophet who deceives the man of God from Judah and causes his death, 1 Kgs 13:11. On the one hand he is the deceiver, כחש לו, v. 18, on the other hand he buries the man of God in his own grave. The old man truthfully predicts the death of the man of God, but he also affirms the fulfilment of the prophecies of the man of God "against the altar in Bethel, and against all the houses of the high places which are in the cities of Samaria," v. 32. This ambiguity is impossible to

---

[58] K. J. Cathcart, "Numbers 24:17 in Ancient Translations and Interpretations," in *Interpretation of the Bible: The Slovenian Academy of Sciences and Arts, Section Two: Philological and Literary Sciences* (Sheffield: Sheffield Academic Press, 1998), 511–520.

feel in 4Q339: the old man of Bethel was a false prophet. The man of God, who spoke against king Jeroboam I and in favour of king Josiah of Judah, is vindicated.

Zedekiah ben Chanaanah, 1 Kgs 22:24, on the other hand, is clearly viewed negatively in the MT. He speaks against Micaiah ben Imlah, the true prophet of God, after Micaiah has said that all the four hundred other prophets, including Zedekiah, had a lying spirit in their mouths, v. 22.

The four prophets from Jer 28; 29 are clear cases of false prophets in the MT. They do not receive special designations, but are condemned by Jeremiah and said to speak lies, Jer 28:11; 29:9.21.31.

4Q339 contains all the named prophets of MT who spoke lies in the name of Yahweh.

There is no such term as "false prophet" in the MT, but the terms "prophets" and שֶׁקֶר occur together. One only has to combine the two in order to get the expression used by the LXX, ψευδοπροφήτης. In Zech 13:2–3, for example, both terms are present in the Hebrew text, and LXX attaches the שֶׁקֶר from v. 3 to הנביאים in the MT of v. 2, and gets τοὺς ψευδοπροφήτας in v. 2. The term is new in the LXX, but it also occurs in the Targum, in the form נבי שיקרא, which is the expression we find as heading to 4Q339.

The three names taken from Jer 29MT/36LXX (Ahab, Zedekiah, and Shemaiah of lines 5–7) are given the heading ψευδοπροφήται in vv. 1.8 of the LXX. The fourth name from the book of Jeremiah (line 8: Hananiah, Jer 28:1) is also called ψευδοπροφήτης in Jer 35:1 LXX. If line 9 is read as in the MT of Jer 28:1, as an attribute of Hananiah of line 8, then four out of the seven names are termed ψευδοπροφήται in the LXX, so an influence from the LXX is possible. Very little Hebrew text from Jeremiah has been found at Qumran—Jer 28 and 29 are not represented at Qumran—so at present we cannot prove a Hebrew *Vorlage* of a LXX-type behind 4Q339.

The LXX has a more widespread use of ψευδοπροφήτης than the cases quoted in 4Q339. It introduced the term at ten places where the MT has "prophets" only: Zech 13:2; Jer 6:13; 33:7.8.11.16 (MT 26:7 etc.); 34:9 (MT 27:9); 35:1 (MT 28:1); 36:1.8 (MT 29:1.8). The change is easily understandable since the book of Jeremiah puts Jeremiah in opposition to other prophets, and contains extensive portions on the question of true and false prophets: Jer 23:9–40; 26:7–24; 27:9–22; 28; 29. Zech 13:2 speaks of the expulsion of prophets at the end of time, so the change to "false prophets" there is natural and prompted by the Hebrew text. 4Q339 contains names only, and all the named "false prophets" in the LXX of the book of Jeremiah occur on the list. Zech 13 contains no names, and this may be the reason why the *List of False Prophets* has no allusions to that text.

The Targum has followed the LXX in only four of the ten instances: Jer 27:9 (= MT-counting) נבייכוא דשקר; 28:1 נביי שקר; 29:8 נבייכוא דשקר; Zech 13:2 נביי שקר. But the Targum introduced the term in other cases: in Ezek 13 the Targum has replaced the "prophet(s)" of the MT with "prophet(s) of lie." The old man of Bethel is also a "false prophet." The vocabulary from the LXX was thus taken over and used more extensively by the Targum. It also proved useful for the Peshitta and the Vulgate, but this lies outside the scope of the present inquiry. In the other six of the ten LXX instances with "false prophets" the Targum reads ספר, "scribe," instead of MT's נביא—no less significant, as the critique then falls upon the scribes. The Targum thus parallels 4Q339 in terming the second and the last four names on the list as "false prophets."

The term ψευδοπροφήτης was probably an invention of the LXX. Texts like Zech 13:2 f. made this invention easy; it was only a question of combining two words already in the text: נביא and שקר. The LXX invented the term ψευδοπροφήτης in order to be able to differentiate false from true prophecy. This is a defence of prophecy itself, effected by the introduction of a distinguishing term. The phenomenon of prophecy was not a mistake *per se*, only the false parts of it. The invention of the distinguishing term in the LXX is a major contribution to the defence of prophecy. For the first time it was possible to speak precisely about prophets and prophets: by using ψευδοπροφήτης for the false ones, leaving only the true ones as "prophets." The defence of the prophets was continued and reworked in the LXX by introducing the term "false prophets," which facilitated this defence greatly.

If 4Q339 was compiled from the LXX, it happened on the basis of a recension older than the MT. The introduction of ψευδοπροφήτης is an older phenomenon than the MT, but it was not taken over by the MT. Why was this List of False Prophets produced?

"... perhaps the list of false prophets (4Q339) was used didactically to provide examples of those who could serve as a measure of false prophecy for the Qumran community," according to G. J. Brooke, who also mentions *4QApocryphon of Moses B^a* (4Q375 1.4–9) which "is full of the phraseology of both *Deuteronomy* 13 and 18."[59] The anointed priest

---

[59] G. J. Brooke, "Prophecy," *EDSS* 2: 698.

determines the truth of the prophet's declarations. "Prophetic activity is subsumed under priestly authority."[60] Thus, 4Q375 is another 4Q text with restrictions on prophecy; in this case the priest is the institution for making decisions. If so, the *List of False Prophets* would deal with the historical prophets, and the priest of 4Q375 would decide in future cases on possible false prophets.

Considering that it is a series of foreign and northern names on the list, another explanation is possible. Of these seven names four are located outside Israel (Balaam, Ahab, Zedekiah, Shemaiah) and the other three are from the North, where Gibeon was also (the old man, Zedekiah, Hananiah).[61] The list contains a complete repertoire of the named false prophets in the Hebrew Bible, and there are no names present in the other LXX texts where the term ψευδοπροφήτης is used. With the help of the Bible, a list of false prophets is set up, and it then becomes evident that they were all foreign or northern prophets. The list therefore carries the message that false prophets were foreign or of northern origin. Those from the old Southern kingdom or Jerusalem proper may by inference be considered true prophets. Admittedly, this is reading what is not stated expressly. The explicit information given by the list is that the prophets named were false. But as there are only names from the Hebrew Bible on the list, the biblical prophets not mentioned would probably be considered true prophets. A second purpose of the list may have been didactic.

May I suggest that the list was influenced by the terminology of the LXX, and reveals a tendency to defend the prophets by identifying the false ones? This might be a continuation of HB discussion on the topic, but by giving names it takes a more robust approach than by looking for different criteria.

Could this have happened at a time when the prophets of old were under attack? By naming the prophets from the North and from outside Israel, the Judean prophets were defended against attacks.

---

[60] Ibid.

[61] The false prophets in Jer 29 have arisen among the Judean exiles of 597, but their ministry took place outside the land of Israel.

8.5. *False Prophets from the North*

One of the names on the list in 4Q339 occurs also in the *Ascension of Isaiah*: "Zedekiah the son of Chenaanah, the false prophet," 2:12. He is presented as a teacher of four hundred Baal prophets, and as the uncle of Belkira/Melcheira, who is the opponent of Isaiah. Isaiah lives in the desert together with other HB prophets, Micah, the aged Ananias,[62] Joel, and Habakkuk, 2:9. The *Ascension of Isaiah* thus introduces true and false prophecy in the form of groups of true prophets and false prophets. The opposition between these groups escalates in the story of how the true prophet Isaiah is killed by king Manasseh at the instigation of the false prophet Belkira/Melcheira, as chapters 2, 3 and 5 narrate. The *Ascension of Isaiah* would be the oldest witness to an idea which rejected the Prophets of the HB. The Talmud discusses the hermeneutical problem: Is Scripture not consistent? Can Moses and Isaiah contradict each other? The *Ascension of Isaiah* has a different pupose: to present northern opposition to the prophets in a bad light, and in this way indirectly to defend the prophets and their books in the HB. This purpose made the originally Jewish work into a useful tool for presenting Christian ideas about prophecy, and about Messianic predictions.

4Q339 may be a defence of true prophecy by way of identifying the false ones. Again, the false prophet from the North in the *Ascension of Isaiah* has no project of this kind. He is portrayed as a preacher who proves the inadequacy and fallibility of prophets, and their basic character as opposing the true prophet, Moses. Seen in the context of the positive appreciation of prophets in *b. Yebam.* 49b and 4Q339 Belchira/Melcheira in the *Ascension of Isaiah* is only evil-minded and devious.

What associations would Belkira/Melcheira and his accusations have evoked in a Jewish milieu, say around the turn of the era? I would propose that "Samaria" in the *Ascension of Isaiah* had a contemporary meaning, and that it was meant to evoke sentiments connected with the Samaritan community at the time. Some Jews had a polemical attitude to the Samaritans, from Ben Sira of the early second century B.C.E. to Josephus, and it would thus fit in well with such Jewish polemics. "Samaria" in this period could hardly mean anything else than the place of the Samaritans. The exaggerated statements put in Melcheira's mouth

---

[62] Cf. the prophet Jehu, son of Hanani, 1 Kgs 16:7 = 2 Chr 19:2 under king Baasha, and Hanani, the seer, 2 Chr 16:7, under king Asa.

would be statements that had a factual basis in Samaritan opposition to the prophets. In this way one did not attack the Samaritans *expressis verbis*, but on the other hand it was easy to recognize Samaritan attitudes behind the twisted statements of the story, and these attitudes were discredited through a rather dubious ancestry.

The Jewish substratum of *Ascen. Isa.* 2:1–3:12 seems to be a polemical story directed against the Samaritans. The historical element behind it would be their opposition to the prophets. Being a (part of a) Jewish story from a time when we have Jewish polemics against the Samaritans, the information in the *Ascension of Isaiah* about the Samarian, accusing prophet, his sayings and behaviour, cannot be expected to represent Samaritan ideas objectively. Polemical texts would not render correctly the viewpoints of their adversaries, but some connection there should be. It would be reasonable to infer from the polemics that (1.) the Samaritans had objections to the prophets, (2.) these objections were built on common Jewish discussions about the prophets' preaching in relation to the Pentateuch, and (3.) the objections emphasized the preaching of judgment by the prophets—perhaps the condemnation of Judah and Jerusalem in particular. The viewpoint of Melcheira is that Isaiah only had judgment oracles against Jerusalem and Judah, but this neglects the Zion theology presented in the Book of Isaiah. The prophet not only condemned Jerusalem and Judah, but also condoned the Zion-theology. The Samaritans may have felt an uneasiness with Isaiah (and other prophets) because of the Zion-theology; this theology may have fallen on barren ground with the Samaritans. Their attitude expressed itself in emphasizing the negative view of Jerusalem and Judah, which is also found in the book of Isaiah.[63] This last point is then exploited by Melcheira, and he neglects completely the Zion-theology of Isaiah and the other HB texts. The Samaritan interest in Moses as a prophet and in the future prophet like Moses understood as a preacher of the law, cf. the expansions no. 14 and 15 in the SP, may lie behind the words put into the mouth of Melcheira in the *Ascension of Isaiah*.

Melcheira also accuses Isaiah and the other prophets of being false prophets. The reasons for this are the judgment oracles and the conflict

---

[63] Samaritan attitudes to the prophets in M. Kartveit, "The *Martyrdom of Isaiah* and the Formation of the Samaritan Group," in *Samaritan Researches* (vol. 5; Proceedings of the Congress of the SES (Milan July 8–12 1996) and of the Special Section of the ICANAS Congress (Budapest July 7–11 1997); ed. V. Morabito, A. D. Crown, and L. Davey; Studies in Judaica 10; Sydney: Mandelbaum, 2000), 3.15–3.28.

with Moses. This accusation may reflect actual arguments against the prophets and their books, not only as these are represented in the Talmud, but also among the Samaritans. The *Ascension of Isaiah* locates Melcheira and his ancestry in the North, which seems to reflect polemics against the Samaritans: false prophets come from the area of the earlier Northern Kingdom. The accusation of being a false prophet is therefore turned around and levelled against Melcheira and his northern counterparts. All polemics are directed against the North in the texts discussed in chapter 5. There is a pattern of criticism of the northern area. The true prophets in the HB were persecuted by the false prophets in the HB.[64] In the same manner the true prophets were persecuted by false prophets, according to the *Ascension of Isaiah*. Isaiah has the chance to save his life by revoking his preaching, but instead he curses Belkira/Malcheira, and is killed. All the false prophets watch the execution, 5:11 f. The hero of the story is killed, and the false prophets survive. But they cannot save their reputation by accusing Isaiah and the others of being false. It is just this statement that makes them into false prophets. The author of the Jewish nucleus of the *Ascension of Isaiah* turns the accusation back on the Samaritans: their criticism of the prophets makes them into false "prophets" themselves.

8.6. *True and False Prophets*

A conspicuous aspect of HB prophetical texts is that there is so much criticism of false prophets. The attacks on illegitimate prophecy found in the books of prophets presuppose a differentiation between legitimate and illegitimate prophecy. There is not yet developed a fixed terminology for this distinction, but different terms and varying criteria are used. It is significant that the criticism of the prophets is found in the books of the prophets. We have a situation of prophet-against-prophet. This cannot have strengthened the authority of the prophets in general, and we must assume that in some circles it weakened it. In addition, Deut 13 and 18 were sceptical of the prophets in general and sought to develop criteria to handle the phenomenon. Two late prophetic texts testify to the problem, and to different atttitudes taken.

---

[64] Cf. Eupolemus, Fragment 4: Jonachim (Jehoiachim) wished to burn Jeremiah because he prophesied against the Baal-cult in Judah.

Joel 3:1 (ET 2:28) solved this problem by envisaging new prophecy in the future: "And it shall come to pass afterward, that I will pour out my spirit on all flesh; your sons and your daughters shall prophesy, your old men shall dream dreams, and your young men shall see visions." In this text the outpouring of the spirit is an eschatological sign, when prophesying will be for all. This does not mean that prophecy was lacking in the time of Joel, nor that there was criticism of prophecy as such. Rather, the text is positive towards this phenomenon, and foresees a democratization of it.

Quite a different attitude is taken in Zech 13:2–6.

> On that day, says the LORD of hosts, I will cut off the names of the idols from the land, so that they shall be remembered no more; and also I will remove from the land the prophets and the unclean spirit. And if any prophets appear again, their fathers and mothers who bore them will say to them, "You shall not live, for you speak lies in the name of the LORD"; and their fathers and their mothers who bore them shall pierce them through when they prophesy. On that day the prophets will be ashamed, every one, of their visions when they prophesy; they will not put on a hairy mantle in order to deceive, but each of them will say, "I am no prophet, I am a tiller of the soil; for the land has been my possession since my youth." And if anyone asks them, "What are these wounds on your chest?" the answer will be "The wounds I received in the house of my friends."

This text has been read as directed against all forms of prophecy. Since it is found in a prophetic book, a more likely understanding is that it advocates a differentiation between false and true prophecy, and thus is a defence of the phenomenon of prophecy. The purpose is not to stop all prophecy, but to refine, to purify this mode of revelation and to discern right from wrong. Illegitimate prophecy could be false Yahweh-prophecy or prophecy in the name of other gods. Zech 13:2–6 may also be read as directed against Joel 3:1. No democratization will take place, but a refinement of the phenomenon.[65]

The first unit, v. 2, mentions prophecy in connection with idols and an unclean spirit, and is thus directed against foreign prophecy. It could be a nucleus, defined and described more closely in the following verses, or it could be a late superscript, specifying the attack on prophets as a rejection of foreign prophets. The whole unit 13:2–6 is embedded in a promise

---

[65] A review of the different attitudes in M. Kartveit, "Das Ende der Prophetie—aber welcher?" in *Text and Theology: Studies in Honour of Prof. Dr. Theol. Magne Sæbø* (ed. K. A. Tångberg; Oslo: Verbum, 1994), 143–156.

of future purity, v. 1 and vv. 7–9 with reference to the pure remnant. In this context, vv. 2–6 functions as a warning to purify the phenomenon of prophecy.

The attitude to the prophets that we found in the Jewish legend behind the *Ascension of Isaiah* and in the SP is very much the same as that in Deut 13; 18, cf. Deut 34. The prophetic books criticized other prophets with various words and arguments, but they did not convey a critical attitude in principle to them. This we find in Deuteronomy, and this attitude is continued and pursued to a logical conclusion by the Samaritans. In addition to the double assurance in Deut 18 of the coming of a prophet like Moses there is also the prophecy in Mal 3:23 (ET 4:5): "Behold, I will send you Elijah the prophet before the great and terrible day of the LORD comes." The promise of a return of Elijah could be a late variation on the theme from Deut 18. A person so inextricably connected to the Torah as Moses is the model for the coming prophet in Deut 18. In Mal 3:22–24 we are dealing with a prophetic text that refers to the Law of Moses, the servant of the Lord, v. 22, and the mission of Elijah may, according to v. 24, be to bring the Torah into effect. The figure of Elijah in Mal 3:22–24 seems to be a continuation of the promise of a prophet like Moses. At the same time, law and prophets are here seen in harmonious cooperation, just as in Deut 18.[66]

8.7. *Conclusion*

4Q339 is an indication that the oldest story in the *Ascension of Isaiah* is Jewish, and *b. Yebam.* 49b makes this a probable assumption. It is possible that this story existed before the turn of the era. Several passages in the Talmud reveal how the discussion on the relation of the prophets to Moses was resolved, and in particular *b. Yebam.* 49b shows how the tension between the Book of Isaiah and the Pentateuch was handled and resolved. In distinction from these discussions the *Ascension of Isaiah* builds on a story of a false prophet from Samaria who accuses Isaiah, and occasions his death. This may be another case of Jerusalem polemics against the Samaritans. The polemical texts from the second century discussed in ch. 5 reveal a situation where such polemics abound. Still, the Jewish nucleus of the *Ascension of Isaiah* shows how the Samaritans

---

[66] Weyde, *Prophecy and Teaching*, 391–393, has a slightly different understanding of Mal 3:22–24.

were opposed to the prophets. This opposition was the reverse side of their reverence for Moses understood as the greatest of all prophets, and their expectation for a prophet like him, who would preach the Torah. An inner-Jewish discussion on the relation between the prophets and the Torah, as found in the Talmud, was turned into an anti-Samaritan polemical portrayal of Samaritan opposition to the prophets. Under the caricature of the Samaritan attitude we may discern a real antagonism against the prophets' preference for Zion.

4Q339 appears to be a defence of the true prophets by naming the false ones. If this was the case, there was an inner-Jewish discussion on prophecy. The Samaritans eventually combined their reverence for Moses with a rejection of the prophets. In doing this, they embodied general attitudes evident in the major expansions of the pre-Samaritan Pentateuchal manuscripts, and in 4Q339, the *Ascension of Isaiah* and *b. Yebam.* 49b. They started as a group centred on the temple on Mount Gerizim, and later emerged with a combination of general Jewish sentiments on the prophets of the last centuries B.C.E.; later this was developed into a distinct group theology.

CHAPTER NINE

THE ORIGIN OF THE SAMARITANS

The moment of birth of the Samaritans was the construction of the temple on Mount Gerizim. The people who erected it did exist before that moment, but they were not Samaritans until the temple project got under way. They may have had diverse origins—as many people in the area probably would—they would have lived in Samaria and elsewhere, and they would have had other characteristics. But they cannot be termed Samaritans before the temple project was in progress, as we do not know of any other distinguishing characteristics that made them Samaritans. It may therefore be considered a cul-de-sac in scholarship to look for the Samaritans before the construction of the temple. Much energy has gone into this project, but what can be found out in that way? Has Josephus lured us into believing that the Samaritans had a continuous history from the time of Shechem, the son of Hamor, or from that of the Assyrian deportees of 2 Kgs 17? This may be true, but is there any reason to assume that ethnic origins were decisive for creating the Samaritan temple on Mount Gerizim? The more likely assumption is that Josephus reflects polemics rather than history on this point, and this suspicion is strengthened by the fact that he does not refer to the Samaritans as natural successors of the former Northern kingdom, but only describes backgrounds considered even more dubious.

Josephus' works constitute one of our main sources. Moving back in time to the other main document, the HB, we encounter the same difficulty: the negative attitude of the HB towards the North. The overall impression of the HB is that it presents viewpoints from the south and criticism of the north. Not only Ezra-Nehemiah is negative towards the north; the book of Chronicles deletes the Northern kingdom altogether, but invites conversions from the north—join in with the worship in Jerusalem! The opposite strategy, that of the Deuteronomistic History, was to criticize the Northern kingdom as illegitimate in itself, emerging from a rebellion against Jerusalem. This strategy was not followed by the Chronicler, or else it was not considered enough for his purpose. Even the northern prophets, Amos and Hosea, were brought to Jerusalem, their criticism of the northern kings and kingdom was preserved, and to it was added a Jerusalem layer of new material, as if God spoke from Jerusalem against the north. There is so much negative sentiment against the north in the HB, that it is difficult to isolate specific parts as more relevant for the Persian and Hellenistic periods. An example is 2 Kgs 17, which may have been directed against a situation before the exile, but it also provided the necessary basis for a general mistrust of the Northerners of the Persian and Hellenistic ages, and it was expanded with new anti-northern additions.

One may see in this phenomenon an attitude in Jerusalem dating back to the time when the picture of the Northern kingdom was shaped, or one may see here layers of later anti-northern sentiments added as time went by and conditions changed. In other words, it is difficult to decide whether an actual text aims at an early situation or reflects later conditions. The different attempts at finding evidence for the backgrounds of the temple builders are hampered by the HB bias and by the lack of external documents early enough to be of any help. This overall impression gained from the HB makes it notoriously difficult to trace the origins of the Samaritans beyond the construction of the temple. The result of such attempts is a series of speculations—another indication that Josephus leads us astray with his allegations.

These considerations lead to the conclusion that the search for the origin of the Samaritans cannot profitably move very far behind the construction of the temple, because we do not have material, and it may be doubted that we can expect to find any distinctive feature which is earlier. The construction of the temple, on the other hand, is evidenced by different types of material, some of which is external to the HB and Josephus.

The Samaritans were not the only "Israelites" to have a temple located outside Jerusalem—we may think of Elephantine, Leontopolis (Egypt) and Araq el-Emir—but they constitute the only community with a continued existence down to our own age. It may be considered unfair to the other, more short-lived communities, but the Samaritans have existed until the present day and were more important in the eyes of the NT and Josephus, so we focus upon their origin. Because they drew such heavy criticism from Jerusalem in the second century B.C.E. we also know that they were important in the eyes of the community there, and other ancient texts like the Talmud see in them an important group. For these two reasons, importance in antiquity and survival to the present, we are interested in finding their origin.

9.1. *The Construction of the Temple*

The decisive moment was the erection of the temple, described by Josephus (under the term ναός), but its existence in the second century B.C.E. is also attested by 2 Macc 6:2 (νεώς) and by 4Q372 (under the polemical term במה, "a high place"). A temple is probably also referred to by the Mount Gerizim inscriptions (מקדש, "a sanctuary," and אתר, "a cult place") for the Hellenistic period. From the Mount Gerizim inscriptions we know that there were priests on the mountain, and the many bones found north of the sacred precinct indicate that sacrifices were offered. Archaeological, epigraphic and literary material all attest the existence of a cult in a shrine on Mount Gerizim in the Hellenistic period. With the cult on Mount Gerizim, the "breach of unity," Zech 11:14, was a fact.

The Delos inscriptions from the first half of the second century B.C.E. confirm that there was a Samaritan self-consciousness in the Aegean at that time, and the information of Josephus that there were discussions in Egypt among Jews and Samaritans in the early Hellenistic age on where to send the temple tax indicates that in that area also there were Samaritans. The focus upon the temple on Mount Gerizim in the Delos inscriptions lends credence to the report in Josephus that the controversies in Egypt had to do with the temple site. Both the Delos inscriptions and Josephus' report connect the Samaritan identity to the temple on Mount Gerizim. The contents of these two types of documents means that a Samaritan identity must have developed long enough before the early second century B.C.E. to have spread into the diaspora by then.

When is it conceivable that the Samaritans chose Mount Gerizim for a cult site and thereby laid the foundation for this self-consciousness? Archaeology is not yet able to help on this point, but the excavators of the summit site of the mountain think of the Persian period rather than the Hellenistic.[1] Also, a general consideration of Josephus leads in the same direction. Josephus may be suspected of giving as late a date as possible for the building of the temple on Mount Gerizim when he says that it took place at the time of the last Persian king, Darius, and of Alexander the Great; we may confidently assume that the temple was erected in the Persian age. His *Tendenz* in connection with the Samaritans would make him use the opportunity that Alexander gave him to have a Greek king give the permission for temple building—the Greeks were not favoured

---

[1] See part 6.1 in this book.

by the Roman readers of his works. There are two reasons to doubt the
dating of the temple building provided by Josephus: his intention to
provide the temple with a short life span, and the possibility of attributing
the building permission to a Greek king. The real construction probably
took place earlier than Josephus would have us believe. Is it possible to
be more precise?

It seems to me that a relevant question in connection with the temple
is this: Why was the temple built on Mount Gerizim and not in Shechem?
Shechem was an old place of worship according to archaeology. Gen 12
reports that it was the first place where Abraham arrived in the promised
land, and that it was a מקום, a "cult-place" when he arrived there. From
an historical and scriptural point of view, Shechem would have been a
natural choice. Shechem was not chosen, but rather Mount Gerizim.

> Mt. Gerizim lacks any natural attributes conducive to the construction of
> a large city. The city was established on top of a high, cool, and bare moun-
> tain with no springs, nor any sources of livelihood; the harsh nature of the
> land precluded the development of agriculture; commerce, as well, was not
> viable, because the city was not centrally located and did not control any of
> the main trade routes. The inaccessibility of the high mountain prevented
> its inhabitants from enjoying the same quality of life experienced by the
> inhabitants of other Hellenistic cities, and [it] was clearly established for
> exclusively religious and cultic considerations.[2]

If this pertains to the construction of a city, it would apply to the founding
of a cult site as well. In other words, the erection of a temple or a place of
worship on Mount Gerizim is unexpected. From a topographical point
of view, the only argument is that the mountain is easily defensible.

What "religious and cultic considerations" may have led to the choice
of temple site? J. Purvis offers this reason for the choice:

> At the time of their settlement, the Samaritans of Shechem built a sanctu-
> ary to YHWH on the adjacent mountain, Gerizim. The Samaritans were
> thus making a conscious effort to relate themselves to the most ancient
> of Israel's traditions in order to maintain the support of the native Pales-
> tinian population of that region … The action of the Samaritans in re-
> establishing the Gerizim cultus relates well to what is otherwise known of
> political-religious establishments in the eastern Mediterranean region.[3]

Purvis does not specify what evidence there is for an earlier cult on
the mountain; in fact, we do not know of any such evidence. An effort

---

[2] Magen, Misgav, and Tsfania, *Inscriptions*, [1]f.
[3] Purvis, "Samaritans and Judaism," 87.

to relate to ancient traditions is, however, witnessed in the final text of Pseudo-Eupolemus, where Melchizedek is said to be priest and king at "holy Argarizin." This text is from the second century B.C.E., but could it reflect earlier ideas? There are no indications that the Samaritans later claimed Melchizedek or Abraham for themselves, and they do not bring these figures into connection with Mount Gerizim. Gen 14 SP is the same as in the MT. Pseudo-Eupolemos may even be anti-Samaritan in the final version, and we cannot trace the ancient tradition appealed to here back to the moment of the choice of temple site. Ps 110 is more likely to be contemporary (in the Jewish context) with the temple construction, or even older, and this psalm connects Melchizedek to Zion.

The "most ancient of Israel's traditions" that we know of are found in the HB. Mount Gerizim is only mentioned in Deut 11:29; 27:12; Josh 8:33; Judg 9:7 MT, plus Deut 27:4 SP. In the first three of these texts Mount Gerizim is proclaimed as the place for pronouncing the blessing over the people, and in Judg 9:7 it is the location for Jotham's speech. In comparison to Shechem, and the other locations in tradition, Mount Gerizim can hardly be said to belong to one of "the most ancient of Israel's traditions." It was not to our knowledge an old and venerated place of worship.

The only argument for the choice of the mountain seems therefore to have been the supposed original reading in Deut 27:4; compare our discussion of the locus in the Samaritan version, supported by Vetus Latina and Pap. Giessen 19 (chapter 7, excursus). This text contains the only indication in the Pentateuch of where future worship shall take place in the promised land, and Mount Gerizim is appointed as the cult site:

> So when you have crossed over the Jordan, you shall set up these stones, about which I am commanding you today, on Mount [Gerizim], and you shall cover them with plaster. And you shall build an altar there to the LORD your God, an altar of stones on which you have not used an iron tool. You must build the altar of the LORD your God of unhewn stones. Then offer up burnt offerings on it to the LORD your God, make sacrifices of well-being, and eat them there, rejoicing before the LORD your God.
>
> (Deut 27:4–7)

For the temple builders, Shechem may have been the first place where Abraham built an altar in the land, but the Mosaic command to Joshua in the original Deut 27:4 had the greater authority. Moses would also outrank David as authority on the choice of cult site. The choice of the mountain would also explain the origin of the form 'Argarizim' in documents and inscriptions from the early second century B.C.E.

onwards. Deut 27:4 in the original used the expression הר גריזים, and this has been the name of the place from the moment it was decided to build the temple there. The choice of Mount Gerizim rather than Shechem would also explain the expression אתר, "cult place," in the Mount Gerizim inscriptions, as this Aramaic word corresponds to the Hebrew מקום. If Shechem was a מקום according to Scripture, Mount Gerizim attained the same status.

If this assumption is correct, the model offered by A. Alt can be left aside. A. Alt supposed that after the installation of Nehemiah as governor in Jerusalem, the need was felt for a temple in the north. If there was a governor in Jerusalem already before Nehemiah, the model still functions, but for an earlier age. But the model also needs to answer the basic question, why Mount Gerizim? One would rather think of Samaria as a natural choice for a cult place of strategic importance. But the decision to build on Mount Gerizim was not a strategic one, as the place lacks basic elements important for strategy, as shown by the description of the place by the excavators quoted above. It seems to me that the choice was done in adherence to a Mosaic command, against the arguments in favour of Samaria (strategy), or Shechem (Abraham), and it would even beat David's choice of Jerusalem on the basic question of the most ancient authority.

Also, Josephus' allegation that Sanballat built a temple for his son-in-law, a member of the high priest's family in Jerusalem, can be dismissed. That the building happened at the time of Sanballat, meaning Sanballat the Horonite, is conceivable—if the governor for some reason wanted to have worship on Mount Gerizim—but the motive for the construction was not to please a son-in-law, but to follow a Mosaic command.

"It is also significant that the author [of the Ezra source in Ezra-Nehemiah] assumed Ezra's arrival to have taken place in the mid fifth century B.C.E. In other words, he implied that the inhabitants of Judah/Yehud lived without the Torah more than half a century after the rebuilding of the temple."[4] It is difficult to conceive of an ancient author who would have assumed this. Any cult site in Jerusalem would need regulations for the cult, at least orally transmitted.[5] Ezra did not introduce a new

---

[4] J. Pakkala, *Ezra the Scribe: The Development of Ezra 7–10 and Nehemia 8* (BZAW 347; Berlin: Gruyter, 2004), 294.

[5] On this question I disagree with R. Kratz, "Temple and Torah: Reflections on the Legal Status of the Pentateuch between Elephantine and Qumran," in *The Pentateuch as Torah: New Models for Understanding Its Promulgation and Acceptance* (ed. Gary Knoppers and B. M. Levinson; Winona Lake, Ind.: Eisenbrauns, 2007), 77–103.

law in Jerusalem; he brought with him a law which was commonly known in Judah. His mission was to secure its implementation on specific points. Its status was therefore not introduced by Ezra to the area, but it may have been confirmed by him on the question of mixed marriages.[6] The corollary to the assumption of Deut 27:4 in the original as the necessary and sufficient theologoumenon for the founding of the cult on Mount Gerizim is that this part of the Pentateuch was held in high esteem by the people who chose the temple site. The fatal division between Jerusalem and Samaria was motivated by one specific commandment in the Pentateuch. The profile of the bones found north of the sacred precinct on Mount Gerizim is interpreted by the excavators as "consistent with the distribution of sacrifices mentioned in the Pentateuch (Lev 1–6)."[7] If ἀπαρχόμενοι in the Delos inscriptions refers to the temple tax as described in Ex 30:11–16, this would indicate that this part of the Pentateuch was important to the Samaritans of the Hellenistic age. It could therefore be that the temple constructors had a version of the Pentateuch that comprised these elements (Deut 27:4; Lev 1–6; Ex 30:11–16), and similar parts would be necessary for the cult in Jerusalem. The status of this material was common to Israelites in the land and abroad in the Persian period.[8]

The construction of a temple on Mount Gerizim in the Persian period would mean that it was built at a time when there was probably a sanctuary in Samaria. Archaeology has not found remains of a temple there from the Iron Age, nor the Persian period, but it is generally assumed that there was one during the Iron Age, and that the names of Sanballat's sons, Shemaiah and Delaiah, prove that Yahweh was worshipped there in the second half of the fifth century.[9] If it can be assumed that there was Yahweh-worship in Samaria in the Persian period, then another Yahweh-

---

[6] S. Mowinckel, *Studien zu dem Buche Ezra-Nehemia III: Die Ezrageschichte und das Gesetz Moses* (Skrifter utgitt av Det norske vitenskaps-akademi i Oslo. Hist.-filos. klasse. Ny serie; Oslo: Universitetsforlaget, 1965), 124–136.

[7] Magen, Misgav, and Tsfania, *Inscriptions*, [9].

[8] C. Nihan, "The Torah between Samaria and Judah: Shechem and Gerizim in Deuteronomy and Joshua," in *The Pentateuch as Torah: New Models for Understanding Its Promulgation and Acceptance* (ed. Gary Knoppers and B. M. Levinson; Winona Lake, Ind.: Eisenbrauns 2007), 187–223, presents an interesting discussion of "the intended audience of the Pentateuch during the main stages of its composition," 189, but reaches results different from those presented here, partly due to a different view of the origin of the Samaritans.

[9] M. Köckert, "Samaria," *TRE* 29 (1998), assumes an Iron Age Yahweh temple, 746, and that Sanballat worshipped Yahweh, 748. N. Na'aman, "Samaria," *RGG* (4. ed., 2004) 7:815, assumes a Yahweh-temple for the Iron Age.

temple was erected on Mount Gerizim while the former was in operation. If Sanballat the Horonite wanted a Yahweh-temple, Samaria was the site for it, not Mount Gerizim, but he may have endorsed a new project inside his jurisdiction.

The five letters and one memorandum from Elephantine now designated TAD A4.5–10, are commonly taken to reveal—among other things—the situation in Israel 410–405 B.C.E. The temple to Yehu on Yeb/Elephantine was destroyed in the summer of 410, and Yedoniah and his priestly colleagues there turned to the governor and the high priest of Jerusalem for help, but without any reply, TAD A4.7: "Also before this, at the time when this evil was done to us, we sent a letter to your lordship [Bigvai, the governor of Yehud] and to Johanan the high priest and his colleagues the priests who are in Jerusalem, and to Ostanes the brother of Anani, and the nobles of the Jews. They have not sent any letter to us." TAD A4.7 therefore addresses Bigvai once more, and this letter also informs him that the letter writers have written to "Delaiah and Shelemiah the sons of Sanballat governor of Samaria." The reply to these requests seems to be TAD A4.9, in which Bigvai and Delaiah instruct the recipient to say to Arsames, the satrap of Egypt, that he should have the temple rebuilt, and this was probably effected around 405 / 404 B.C.E.[10] Two things here are of importance to us. One, the priests turn to the high priest in Jerusalem and to the governors of Jerusalem and Samaria for help. The first request was sent to the high priest and to the governor in Jerusalem simultaneously, as it seems; a second was sent to the governor of Samaria, and the third, TAD A4.7, to the governor of Jerusalem alone. The reply came from the governors of Jerusalem and Samaria in a joint letter. The addressees of the requests indicate that the temple in Elephantine was considered to be under the twin jurisdiction of high priest and governor. The second important phenomenon is that the governors of Jerusalem and Samaria together take responsibility for the matter.

The construction of a temple on Mount Gerizim in the Persian period would on this evidence need the support of the governor in Samaria, so in this respect Josephus may be correct. As late as the last decade of the fifth century B.C.E. the two governors were on speaking terms, which is quite different from the situation described by Ezra-Nehemiah and Josephus. Both governors attended to the case of a Yehu-temple, which would be difficult if the governor of Samaria did not worship this deity.

---

[10] Discussion of the letters in VanderKam, *From Joshua to Caiaphas*, 55–63.

But as it is, his name in the letters, Delaiah, contains Yahweh. If there was Yahweh-worship in Samaria in the last half of the fifth century, it is conceivable that the governor would approve a temple project on Mount Gerizim for Yahweh also, as the builders could argue with Deut 27:4 as scriptural basis for the project. It seems, however, that a deterioration of relations with Jerusalem is a more likely backdrop to the Gerizim project, and Ezra-Nehemiah testifies amply to such a situation. This book could therefore belong to the period following the amicable relations between Jerusalem and Samaria, and the temple project may have been embarked upon in the first part of the fourth century. It would then be a new Yahweh-temple in the region, probably sanctioned by the governor in Samaria, and constituting an archaizing tendency in the choice of temple site.

On this assumption, the resettlement of Shechem in the late fourth century was not decisive, as presumed in the Cross-Purvis hypothesis. Argarizim existed at the time of the resettlement, and it would have functioned for the people living in the surrounding area also. A revival of Shechem would contribute to the population for whom Argarizim was important, but the place names found in the inscriptions on Mount Gerizim indicate that the area of cultic interest was wider than Shechem only.

On the basis of the inscriptions found on Mount Gerizim, dating to the Hellenistic period, we can infer that there was worship to Yahweh on the mountain, and no other divine names are found in these inscriptions. There is thus no support for the idea that there was "a syncretistic tendency, which was especially, though not exclusively, characteristic of Samaritan Hellenism."[11] The inscriptions witness that the Samaritans worshipped Yahweh only. The description of the renaming of the temple in 2 Macc 6:2 is polemical, but it presupposes that the temple was dedicated to a deity different from Zeus, and in the light of the Mount Gerizim material the assertion that the Samaritans endorsed the Zeus-cult appears unjustified.

In the second century B.C.E., 4Q372 used the expression במה for the temple on Mount Gerizim, evidently a polemical description. This phrase is an indication of the attitude in the south towards the cult on Mount Gerizim: it was illegitimate. Further, this text alleges that the inhabitants

---

[11] Feldman, "*Remember Amalek!*," 171, n. 274.

of the north treat Zion in a way that is described as blasphemy, highlighting the question of temple site. 4Q372 can be understood as referring to the current population in the north as "enemies" and "foolish," whereas "Joseph" has been removed totally from his area. In other words, this text seeks to undermine the legitimacy of the temple and of the people worshipping there by branding the temple as illegitimate and the population as "enemies" and "foolish." The latter expression is attached to Shechem, Sir 50:25 f.; *T. Levi*. If Shechem had the authority of Abraham behind it, according to the Pentateuch, the site was provided by these texts with associations to a different ancestry.

In the second century B.C.E. a number of texts with their origin in Alexandria or Jerusalem polemicize against the contemporary population in Shechem. Even if these texts were created for the home market, they reveal the attitude on the Jewish side. In addition to the interest in the temple witnessed by 4Q372, the texts are concerned with the question of mixed marriages. Mostly, the Samaritans are accused of living in mixed marriages, but foreign origin is indicated by 4Q372 and 2 Macc 6:2. The accusation that they were foreigners may thus be older than Josephus, and is probably attested also by 2 Macc 6:2. The accusations move in different directions—ξένιος, cf. 2 Macc 6:2, is different from living in mixed marriages—but together they reveal the same attitude to the Shechemites: they were of dubious background. Josephus accused the Samaritans of opportunism, and his predecessors accused them of living in mixed marriages, so the dubious character of the people is the common element to all the polemics of the second century B.C.E. and to Josephus in the first century C.E. The polemics endorse continued violence against the Samaritans.

In the same century there were people on Delos who used the expression "Israelites" about themselves and sent their temple tax to Mount Gerizim. The polemical texts from the same age define the boundaries between Jerusalem and the Samaritans. Their claim to being "Israel" or "Joseph" is countered by accusations of living in mixed marriages, of having a foreign origin and an illegitimate temple site, in short, of being "enemies" and "fools."

Archaeologists tell us that the city around the Samaritan cult site on top of Mount Gerizim was expanded in the beginning of the second century B.C.E.; it is tempting to link this expansion to the polemical texts against the Samaritans from this century. Certainly, the attitude expressed in these texts is older than the texts, and the dwellers in Shechem may have felt the heat from Jerusalem and looked for a more secure place than a city located at the bottom of a valley. Such a place was found on the mountain nearby, where they already had their cult, and they expanded the place and lived there until the site was razed by John Hyrcanus some time after 130 B.C.E.

In addition to the controversy over the temple site came the discussion about Moses in relation to the prophets. The issue appears to have been the question of whom to trust the more, Moses or the later ones. This problem is visible in the HB, e.g. in the texts depicting Moses as a prophet, and where the prophetic corpus ends in a reference to the law of Moses, Mal 3:22 MT. The discussion in the HB is older than the supposed date for the "canonization" of the prophets around 200 B.C.E., and the material discussed in the present book (chapters 7 and 8) is later than the "canonization." The biblical witness to the discussion, seen together with the material discussed here, indicates that the disagreements continued down to the turn of the era, and the prophetic corpus was adopted while the discussion was going on. Those favouring Moses eventually won the discussion on who was the greatest prophet, as Moses prevailed over the other prophets in the HB. But the price for this victory was that the prophetic books became included in the canon, and the consistent attitude against the prophets survived only in Samaritanism.

The pre-Samaritan manuscripts reveal that the discussion in the HB on Moses and the prophets continued in the form of a redaction of the Pentateuch and that this version of the Pentateuch was used down to the turn of the era. This was not a point at issue in the polemics against the Samaritans before that time. In this respect the latter participated in a wider phenomenon, but they eventually ended up as the only group embodying the kind of concentration on Moses that also entailed consistent opposition to the prophets; the Saduccees were another group, but the evidence needs closer scrutiny before they can be included as completely anti-prophetic. Later, the Samaritans added to the conflict with Moses the sympathy for Zion in the books of the prophets and their failure to predict the future correctly, as indicated by the *Ascension of Isaiah*. Their opposition to prophets was fuelled by the concentration on Zion in these books. This attitude can only have been developed after Mount Gerizim was chosen as the cult site. The list of false prophets from Qumran, 4Q339, contains names familiar to us from the HB. They all operate in foreign nations or come from Northern Israel. One of these names occurs also in the *Ascension of Isaiah*, in which a pre-Christian nucleus seems to be Jewish and anti-Samaritan, caricaturing Samaritan accusations against the prophets. The arguments presented by the false prophet

Melcheira/Belchira of the *Ascension of Isaiah* indicate that the concentration on Moses occasioned a discussion on the status of the other prophets.
This discussion was inner-Jewish and involved the question of false and
true prophecy, cf. 4Q339. The question of Moses versus the prophets
was resolved on the Jewish side, *b. Sanh.* 89a and other tractates. On the
other hand, the caricature of the false prophet in the *Ascension of Isaiah* reveals what the arguments ending in the rejection of the prophets
looked like.

As the Samaritan community continued in existence after the Persian
age, new theological factors may have become significant. The decisive
moment was the construction of the temple, but controversies over the
prophets may have developed, and the Moses-alone party eventually
sided with the Mount Gerizim community and they grew into one. A
fusion of different theological elements led to the situation at the time of
the NT and Josephus. The texts found in Qumran illustrate the situation:
the manuscripts there included a Moses-oriented Pentateuch and a list of
false prophets—two tenets shared with the Samaritans—but also a text
with a strong attack on the worship on Mount Gerizim and a prayer for
the divine removal of the inhabitants in Samaria, 4Q372.

9.2. *The Biblical Evidence*

Is it possible to align the development described here with the biblical
evidence from the period? Ezra 4 offers itself as describing a situation
conducive to a separate development in the north. According to this
text, the people deported by Esarhaddon wanted to participate in the
reconstruction of the temple in Jerusalem in the sixth century, because
they also worshipped Yahweh and sacrificed to him.[12] They were rejected
because of the Persian mandate. Only we are authorized by Cyrus to build
here, say Zerubbabel, Jeshua, and the rest of the heads of families in Israel.
Josephus adds to this story that the only thing which the Samaritans
might have in common with the temple builders in Jerusalem was to
come and worship, like all humanity, *Ant.* 11.87.

---

[12] Ezra 4:2 Qere appears to be the original reading; one would expect a לו after
זבחים if the Kethib were correct; J. Blenkinsopp, *Ezra-Nehemiah: A Commentary* (OTL;
Philadelphia: Westminster, 1989), 105, assumes the Kethib to be an anti-Samaritan
reading.

The rejection by Jerusalem occasioned action from the enemies to obstruct the reconstruction, according to Ezra 4–6. Can it be inferred from the book of Ezra that the enemies did not have a sanctuary of their own, that they had not yet built a shrine on Mount Gerizim? But how could they sacrifice without a shrine? And if they had a shrine of their own, why would they wish to participate in the rebuilding of Jerusalem? Such questions reveal the anachronistic character of Ezra 4:2, which comes from a situation where the division was a fact in need of justification. For the author the events take place during the first period of reconstruction. He appears to have been inspired by the account in 2 Kgs 17, only that the king of the deportation is different. The important point is that the controversies are said to have happened in the Persian period, and that the descendants of the assumed deportees are rejected. It is not inconceivable that such a rejection in the end also occasioned the construction of a separate temple in the north. If the whole account is unhistorical, and its only aim is to justify the contemporary situation, a different series of events must have taken place.

Given the chronological difficulties in the book of Ezra, it is not easy to pinpoint the date of the purported rejection of the people from the north. On the face of it, Ezra 4 takes place in the sixth century B.C.E., but is often assumed to reflect a situation in the late Persian or early Hellenistic periods. The different literary divisions and reconstructions of the books of Ezra and Nehemiah do not affect the point made here. Scholars commonly assume that these books reveal the mental climate of the times, and this mental climate made a concentration on Jerusalem the condition for participating in the cult and the community. The rejection by the בני הגולה of the עם־הארץ and of the adversaries of Judah and Benjamin is the attitude reflected in all the supposed different layers of the books of Ezra and Nehemiah, and this rejection may have occasioned the construction of the temple on Mount Gerizim. When this happened, we do not know, but general considerations point towards the Persian period. Ezra 4:2 mentions that the adversaries worshipped and sacrificed to the God of the returnees; this could be an indirect witness to the Yahweh-cult assumed by the excavators of Mount Gerizim and evidenced by the inscriptions found there.

An echo of this text is the following: "And thereafter I saw while the shepherds pastured for twelve periods; and behold, three of those sheep returned and came and entered and began to build up all that had fallen down of that house; but the wild boars hindered them, so that they could not." 1 En. 89:72. "There is no problem about the identification here of wild boars; they are unmistakably the Samaritans and the mixed peoples who supported them of Ezr. 4–5, Neh. 4–6."[13] Apart from the idea of the "mixed peoples," M. Black's understanding seems justified; for the wild boars, cf. Ps 80:14.

The question of exogamous marriages was the main thrust of the polemics in the second century B.C.E., and the corresponding idea of a pure people is among the most important in the books of Ezra and Nehemiah. Both Ezra-Nehemiah and the second century B.C.E. texts reckon with intermarriage between pure Israel and the Canaanite population. Wives and children of men from Jerusalem and Judah were ejected from the city, Ezra 9–10; Neh 9; 13. It is tempting to see a connection here, and consider the information in these two books as providing a background for the second century polemics against the Shechemites. Ezra and Nehemiah expelled the people living in exogamous marriages, and Gen 34 provided the second century with an old model, in the action of the sons of Jacob, for similar protective measures, which made Gen 34 into an important text in the fight against the Samaritans. The use of Gen 34 could imply the foreign origin of the Shechemites: Shechem was a Hittite; the women of Shechem survived; Jacob did not colonize Shechem, so it remained a foreign city.

If it is correct that the restoration under Zerubbabel, Joshua, Ezra and Nehemiah is described in Ezra-Nehemiah as resembling the exodus, perhaps also the wilderness wandering, a parallel to the conquest would also be expected. If so, the description of the peoples of the land, or the adversaries of Judah and Benjamin, would follow that model. We could not, in that case, expect accurate expressions which we could identify in some reconstruction of history, but rather inaccurate expressions. In Ezra 4:4 עַם הָאָרֶץ, "the people of the land," is found, and 9:1 uses "the peoples of the lands," עַמֵּי הָאֲרָצוֹת, as a designation, and specifies them as "the Canaanites, the Hittites, the Perizzites, the Jebusites, the Ammonites, the Moabites, the Egyptians, and the Amorites." The expressions used in the Deuteronomistic History to refer to the peoples of the land at the time of Joshua's invasion, cannot be used to identify specific elements in the Persian period. "Foreign women," נָשִׁים נָכְרִיּוֹת, is found in Ezra 10 six times, and once in Neh 13:27; in the HB, the expression is only found once more, for the many wives of Solomon, 1 Kgs 11:1. This appeal to

---

[13] M. Black, O. Neugebauer, and J. C. VanderKam, *The Book of Enoch or I Enoch: A New English Edition with Commentary and Textual Notes* (SVTP 7; Leiden: Brill, 1985), 273.

traditional models (Joshua's invasion and Solomon's wives) was carried on by the second century texts, where the issue was possible associations to Shechem. Then Gen 34 was employed—an even older and more effective model for the criticism of exogamous marriages than the wives of Solomon. Theodotus also used the land promise to Abraham, Gen 15:18–21, against the Shechemites in what could be a counter-move in case somebody hit upon the idea to use Gen 12 in favour of Shechem.

Did the Samaritans descend from mixed marriages and did they practice exogamous marriages in the second century B.C.E.? Taking into account that the information we have is polemical, one would tend to answer in the negative. On the other hand, mixed marriages were found inside Jerusalem, according to Ezra-Nehemiah. The standard used was the genealogical lists current at the time, and by this standard, it is likely that many marriages would qualify for divorce, without their necessarily being formed with foreigners of some kind or other. The בני הגולה defined a correct marriage, and those not married in conformity with this definition would have to divorce in order to participate in the congregation. Seen from this perspective, the people of the land must have constituted a dubious lot, and polemics against them can be found in Ezra-Nehemiah and in the second century texts, where the contemporary inhabitants of Shechem were branded as followers of the original inhabitants of the city in this practice.

Josephus considered the Samaritans to be descendants of the peoples deported by the Assyrians. There was an import of peoples to Samaria at the time of Sennacherib, as witnessed by the Assyrian royal inscriptions. In the HB this is connected to the fall of the Northern kingdom in 2 Kgs 17 and to Esarhaddon in Ezra 4, which means that both texts think that it happened before the fall of Jerusalem, generally agreeing with the Assyrian royal inscriptions. Whether these imported peoples intermingled with the locals, or kept themselves separate, we do not know; there is A. Alt's theory, that it is unlikely that the upper echelons would intermarry with common people. If my assessment of Ezra-Nehemiah and the second century texts is valid, it is unnecessary to look for any confirmation or falsification of A. Alt's theory. The pure seed was defined by the בני הגולה in the fifth and fourth centuries, and by Jerusalem in the second. The Samaritans were branded as Shechemites, whose practice from earliest times was against the Torah.

Josephus calls Sanballat a Cuthean, a descendant of the deported peoples. But in Nehemiah his name is "Sanballat the Horonite." Papyri from Elephantine and Wadi Daliyeh only provide the name and the title "governor," פחה. From a Jerusalem perspective, therefore, he received two derogatory appellations, a Cuthean in Josephus' eyes and a Horonite to Nehemiah. If Sanballat actually came from Upper or Lower Bet-Horon, he was local. He was perhaps not from either of these cities, but could be described in this way, denigrated by this name as a person from a place of no renown. Josephus renames him and moves him to a different century, but carries on the practice of giving him a derogatory appellation.

In a later period, late first or early second century C.E., the *Paralipomena Ieremiae*, chapter 8, recounts the beginning of the Samaritans as related to the question of mixed marriages. In a twist of the problem described in Ezra-Nehemiah and by the second century B.C.E. polemics, where the forbidden spouses come from the local population, the *Paralipomena* describes returnees from Babylon married to Babylonians. When the persons living in such marriages refuse to separate from their spouses, Jeremiah denies them access to Jerusalem, whereupon they return to Babylon, but are refused there because of their secret departure from the city. Then they turn to a deserted place at some distance from Jerusalem, build a city there and call it Samaria, and receive a benign message from Jeremiah.[14] Motifs from 2 Kgs 17, as read by Josephus, and from Ezra-Nehemiah are here blended into this version of the origin of the Samaritans. The forbidden spouses come from the east; here the *Paralipomena* agrees with Josephus; because of exogamous marriages they are denied access to Jerusalem; here the text is in line with Ezra-Nehemiah. The *Paralipomena* seems to be a late version of an ancient theme, that the Samaritans are of mixed origin; it also strikes a note of Samaritan conflict with prophets.

Ethnicity seems not to have been constitutive to the Samaritans. They were accused of exogamous marriages, but this may only have been a general trait in the population of Palestine. Gen 34 was used in an unspecific way against any exogamous marriages, but this was aimed at the population of Shechem in particular. The polemical use of Gen 34 in the second century B.C.E. was followed up by Josephus, who also connected the original Shechemites to the contemporary Samaritans. I suspect that the question of ethnicity is a cul-de-sac.

Readers of the books of Ezra and Nehemiah have tended to consider

---

[14] Cf. the discussion by P. W. van der Horst, "Anti-Samaritan Propaganda in Early Judaism," in *Jews and Christians in their Graeco-Roman Context: Selected Essays on Early Judaism, Samaritanism, Hellenism, and Christianity* (WUNT 196; Tübingen: Mohr, 2006), 134–150.

the returnees, the בני הגולה, as a natural continuation of old Israel. These books would therefore describe the normal prolongation of "Israel," and the Samaritans would develop out of this standard Jewish group. M. Noth and J. Jeremias summarize the development from the fourth century B.C.E. to the second century C.E. as if the Samaritans freed themselves from the Jewish community.[15] This understanding has led to the view that after all, the Samaritans split off from Jerusalem, or that they created "eine samaritanische Gegenorthodoxie in Sichem."[16] Then Jerusalem would represent the standard, against which the Samaritans should be seen and evaluated.

The people of the books of Ezra and Nehemiah portray themselves as the underdogs, against the overwhelming inimical majority of the people in the land, of the local governors, of an enemy in the north and east. They evidently need some justification for their acts, and this is found in the Persian royal decrees and in Scripture. If one reads the books from the perspective of the indigenous population, the בני הגולה, "the children of the captivity" (KJV), "the returned exiles" (NRSV), would appear to be intruders. What if the Samaritans belonged to a wider circle of Yahweh-believers living in the country?

If we consider the material from the perspective of the Israelite/Jewish population living in the country at the time when the בני הגולה arrived, a different picture emerges. Denied access to the reconstruction of the temple in Jerusalem, a group instead turned to Mount Gerizim and constructed a sanctuary there. They used the Pentateuch in deciding where to build their altar, a sign that they shared Israel's foundation document with the returnees of the Persian period. This Pentateuch already contained traces of the discussion on the relation of the prophets to Moses, and before the middle of the third century (the time of the earliest pre-Samaritan manuscript) this discussion led to the creation of a Pentateuch where the preference for Moses was expressed in a layer of expansions, without showing signs of preference for Mount Gerizim or Shechem. The Samaritans shared this version also with wider elements in Israel; a situation which lasted at least until the turn of the era (4Q22). After the turn of the era this Pentateuch was provided with the Samaritan

---

[15] M. Noth, *Überlieferungsgeschichtliche Studien: die sammelnden und bearbeitenden Geschichtswerke im Alten Testament* (Tübingen: Niemeyer, 1943), 166; J. Jeremias, *Jerusalem zur Zeit Jesu: eine kulturgeschichtliche Untersuchung zur neutestamentlichen Zeitgeschichte* (3. ed.; Göttingen: Vandenhoeck & Ruprecht, 1969), 388.

[16] M. Oeming, *Das wahre Israel: die "genealogische Vorhalle" 1 Chronik 1–9* (BWANT, Folge 8, 7; Stuttgart: Kohlhammer, 1990), 46.

tenth commandment and the 21 בחר variants in Deuteronomy, resulting in the SP proper. Did the Samaritans have a choice of Pentateuchs? The Qumran biblical manuscripts seems to indicate this. The Samaritans did not accidentally end up with the SP, but they chose the 'Moses text-type' for their holy text. The traditional discussion about Samaritan origins and the 'canonization' of the Pentateuch can therefore be considered obsolete. There was one version of the Pentateuch in circulation at the time when Deut 27:4 provided the temple founders with their necessary *hieros logos* for the project, but their version of the Pentateuch was deliberately chosen around the turn of the era or later. It is impossible to date the Samaritan 'schism' after the supposed 'canonization,' or to date the 'canonization' before the 'schism.' Also, to find in the Samaritan Passover celebration a pre-deuteronomistic form in the way J. Jeremias did, is problematic because it presupposes a critical evaluation of the HB material which can no longer be upheld.[17]

The effect in Jerusalem of the construction of a YHWH-temple on top of Mount Gerizim may have been strong, as 4Q372 suggests. M. Noth assumed that the books of Chronicles were written against the Samaritan community with its own cult on Mount Gerizim.[18] The concentration in Chronicles on the temple in Jerusalem is clear, and H. G. M. Williamson thinks Chronicles was a mission call to the north, before the construction of the temple on Mount Gerizim.[19] This call failed, and in the early years of the Hellenistic age Ezra-Nehemiah was written in order to bolster the Jerusalem attitude. The new, separate temple was built by priests who felt themselves forced out of Jerusalem.[20] S. Japhet thinks the North was included as "Israel" by the books of Chronicles, as part of "the basic relationships between people, land and God of Israel."[21]

Of the different suggestions for the relationship between Ezra-Nehemiah and the books of Chronicles the most convincing appears to be that these books originally formed one continuous history of Israel or that Chronicles were written after Ezra-Nehemiah, and ended with the edict

---

[17] J. Jeremias, *Die Passahfeier der Samaritaner und ihre Bedeutung für das Verständnis der alttestamentlichen Passahüberlieferung* (BZAW 59; Giessen: Töpelmann, 1932).

[18] Noth, *Überlieferungsgeschichtliche Studien*, 174; idem, *Geschichte Israels*, 320.

[19] H. G. M. Williamson, *Israel in the Books of Chronicles* (Cambridge: Cambridge University Press, 1977), 110–118.

[20] Williamson, "Temple in the Books of Chronicles," 15–31; repr. in idem, *Studies in Persian History and Historiography*, 150–161.

[21] S. Japhet, "Conquest and Settlement in Chronicles," *JBL* 98 (1979): 205–218, repr. in idem, *From the Rivers of Babylon to the Highlands of Judah: Collected Studies on the Restoration Period* (Winona Lake, Ind.: Eisenbrauns, 2006), 38–52.

of Cyrus, where Ezra begins, implying: you know where you can find more about the following story.[22] If this work was created in the fourth century B.C.E., as many commentators assume, it was written at a time when the temple on Mount Gerizim existed, or at the time when it was built, and directed against this, as M. Noth suggested.

Crucial in this debate is the understanding of Abijah's speech in 2 Chr 13. H. G. M. Williamson refers to H. G. Kippenberg's argument that Abijah's focus upon the "sons of Aaron" cannot be anti-Samaritan, since Aaronite priests were one of the Samaritans' strongest points.[23] Kippenberg uses the *Tolidah* for his understanding of the Samaritan priesthood, and this chronicle was written in 1149 / 1346 C.E. No proof has been presented that this chronicle contains material from the Persian or Hellenistic periods, and in my opinion, the *Tolidah* cannot be considered relevant for the period in question. Accordingly, I am not able to take this as an argument against the anti-Samaritan profile of 2 Chr 13, and its direction against the Samaritans remains the most probable reading. In addition to the question of the temple, the other main focus in Chronicles is the Davidic dynasty, which H. G. M. Williamson considers more of interest for the home market than a question of foreign affairs. This dynasty is carried on by Jerusalem, according to Abijah: Jerusalem not only has the Davidic dynasty, but "the kingdom of the LORD in the hand of the sons of David," 2 Chr 13:8. But the phrasing here is of importance. This understanding focuses on the divine legitimation of the Davidic dynasty, not on the perpetuation of it into Persian times or later. The focus on legitimation would also have been aimed at the northerners. "The kingdom of the LORD" was a contentious issue, and Abijah locates this in Jerusalem, not elsewhere.

According to 1 Chr 9:3 and Neh 11:4, people from Judah and Benjamin lived in Jerusalem. To this information common to both texts, 1 Chr 9:3 adds "people from Ephraim and Manasseh," which means that Chronicles included northerners also among the inhabitants of Jerusalem. If Chronicles is later than Neh 11 and quotes from it, it can be taken to mean that Chronicles asserts that some of the northerners already lived in

---

[22] S. Japhet, "The Supposed Common Authorship of Chronicles and Ezra-Nehemiah Investigated anew," *VT* 18 (1968): 330–371, repr. in idem, *From the Rivers of Babylon to the Highlands of Judah*, 1–37, discusses the problem; for a different view, M. Kartveit, "2 Chronicles 36.20–23 as Literary and Theological 'Interface,'" in *The Chronicler as Author: Studies in Text and Texture* (ed. M. P. Graham and S. L. McKenzie; JSOTSup 263: Sheffield: Sheffield Academic Press, 1999), 395–403.

[23] Kippenberg, *Garizim und Synagoge*, 48–50. 60–68.

Jerusalem, giving emphasis to the invitation to the rest to turn in the same direction, as in the following chapters in Chronicles. If the northerners considered themselves successors of a Northern kingdom, the existence of this phenomenon was deleted by the Chronicler, and therefore a possible rationale for continuing existence in the north was removed. If the temple builders had found a theologoumenon in the Pentateuch that would beat the claim to Jerusalem as the legitimate cult site, the book of Chronicles employed the opposite technique: to obliterate the history of the Northern kingdom altogether in order to remove possible attachments to history.

The two points of temple and exogamous marriages may qualify as identity markers, important enough to term the conflict as ethnic in a relational sense, and constituting boundaries which could not be violated. In this relational sense the conflict between Jerusalem and the Samaritans was an ethnic question: Jerusalem defined boundaries around herself.

The criticism of the Samaritans and the destruction of the temple in 129 or 109 B.C.E., may have constituted "one momentous event" (R. Pummer, see chapter 3) in the development, but the decisive moment was the rejection by Jerusalem of the Northerners, and the concomitant construction of the temple on Mount Gerizim. The Samaritans were at that time and later Yahweh-worshippers like the returnees, but had a profile which was not accepted by Jerusalem. Their basic flaw might have been that they had not been exiled, they did not possess the quality of exile and restoration. The idea of a separation or schism or split presupposes that there was a unity, which is doubtful. If anything, the returnees created the split or the separation by not cooperating with the people of the land. The former developed into the Jews of Jerusalem and elements of the latter eventually became the Jews of Samaria, better known as the Samaritans.

BIBLIOGRAPHY

Ådna, J. *Jerusalemer Tempel und Tempelmarkt in 1. Jahrhundert n. Chr.* Abhandlungen des Deutschen Palästina-Vereins 25. Wiesbaden: Harrassowitz, 1999.

Allegro, J. M. "158. Biblical Paraphrase: Genesis, Exodus." Pages 1–5 in *Qumrân Cave 4. I: (4Q158–4Q186)*. Edited by J. Allegro. Discoveries in the Judaean Desert of Jordan 5. Oxford: Clarendon, 1968.

Alonso Schökel, L. *A Manual of Hebrew Poetics.* Subsidia Biblica 11. Roma: Editrice Pontificio istituto biblico, 1988.

Alt, A. "Zur Geschichte der Grenze zwischen Judäa und Samaria." *Palästina-Jahrbuch* 31 (1935): 94–111. Repr. pages 346–362 in idem, *Kleine Schriften zur Gechichte des Volkes Israel*, vol. 2. München: C. H. Beck, 1959.

——, "Die Rolle Samarias bei der Entstehung des Judentums." Pages 5–28 in *Festschrift Otto Procksch zum sechzigsten Geburtstag am 9. August 1943.* Edited by A. Alt et al. Leipzig: A. Deichert'sche Verlagsbuchhandlung, 1934. Repr. pages 316–337 in idem, *Kleine Schriften zur Gechichte des Volkes Israel*, vol. 2. München: C. H. Beck, 1959.

Altheim, F., and R. Stiehl. "Erwägungen zur Samaritanerfrage." Pages 204–242 in *Die Araber in der Alten Welt.* Edited by R. Stiehl, F. Altheim, and A. Calderini. Berlin: de Gruyter, 1967.

Amit, Y. *Hidden Polemics in Biblical Narrative.* Biblical Interpretation Series 25. Leiden: Brill, 2000.

Anderson, R. T. "Jean Morin as a Prime Catalyst in Modern Textual Criticism." Pages 62–73 in *For a Testimony: Essays in Honor of John H. Wilson.* Edited by M. Haykin. Toronto: Central Baptist Seminary and Bible College, 1989.

——, "Samaritans." Pages 938–947 in vol. 5 of *Anchor Bible Dictionary.* Edited by D. N. Freedman. New York: Doubleday, 1992.

Anderson, R. T., and T. Giles. *The Keepers: An Introduction to the History and Culture of the Samaritans.* Peabody, Mass.: Hendrikson, 2002.

Anderson, R. T., and T. Giles. *Tradition Kept: The Literature of the Samaritans.* Peabody, Mass.: Hendrikson, 2005.

Auld, A. G. "Reading Joshua after Kings." Pages 167–181 in *Words Remembered, Texts Renewed: Essays in Honour of John F. Sawyer.* Edited by G. Harvey, J. Davies, and W. G. E. Watson. Journal for the Study of the Old Testament: Supplement series 195. Sheffield: Sheffield Academic Press, 1995.

Avigad, N. "Bullae and Seals from a Post-Exilic Judean Archive." *Qedem* 4 (1976): 36–52.

Avioz, M. "Josephus' Retelling of Nathan's Oracle (2 Sam 7)." *Scandinavian Journal of the Old Ttestament* 20 (2006): 9–17.

Avi-Yonah, M. *The Madaba Mosaic Map.* Jerusalem: Israel Exploration Society, 1954.

Barr, J. "The Most Famous Word in the Septuagint." *Studia Semitica Supplement.* Jubilee Volume, 16 (2005): 59–72.

Barth, F. *Ethnic Groups and Boundaries: The Social Organization of Culture Difference.* Bergen: Universitetsforlaget, 1969.

Barth, H., and O. H. Steck. *Exegese des Alten Testaments: Leitfaden der Methodik: ein Arbeitsbuch für Proseminare, Seminare und Vorlesungen.* 8., rev. ed. Neukirchen-Vluyn: Neukirchener Verlag, 1978.

Barton, J. *Reading the Old Testament: Method in Biblical Study.* London: Darton, Longman & Todd, 1996.

——, *The Spirit and the Letter: Studies in Biblical Canon.* London: SPCK, 1997.

Becking, B. "Do the Earliest Samaritan Inscriptions Already Indicate a Parting of the Ways?" Pages 213–222 in *Judah and the Judeans in the Fourth Century* B.C.E. Edited by O. Lipschits, G. N. Knoppers and R. Albertz. Winona Lake, Ind.: Eisenbrauns, 2007.

Beckwith, R. T. *The Old Testament Canon of the New Testament Church and its Background in Early Judaism.* London: SPCK, 1985.

Beentjes, P. C. *The Book of Ben Sira in Hebrew: A Text Edition of all Extant Hebrew Manuscripts and a Synopsis of all Parallel Hebrew Ben Sira Texts.* Vetus Testamentum Supplements 68. Leiden: Brill, 1997.

Begg, C. *Judean Antiquities Books 5–7.* Vol. 4 of *Flavius Josephus: Translation and Commentary.* Edited by S. Mason. Leiden: Brill, 2005.

Begg, C. and P. Spilsbury, *Judean Antiquities Books 8–10.* Vol. 5 of *Flavius Josephus: Translation and Commentary.* Edited by S. Mason. Leiden: Brill 2005.

Ben-Hayyim, Z. *Studies in the Traditions of the Hebrew Language.* Madrid: Instituto "Arias Montano", 1954.

——, *Recitation of the Law.* Vol. 3/1 of *The Literary and Oral Tradition of Hebrew and Aramaic amongst the Samaritans.* The Academy of the Hebrew Language Studies 3. Jerusalem: The Academy of the Hebrew Language, 1961.

——, *The Recitation of Prayers and Hymns.* Vol. 3/2 of *The Literary and Oral Tradition of Hebrew and Aramaic amongst the Samaritans.* The Academy of the Hebrew Language: Texts and Studies 6. Jerusalem: The Academy of the Hebrew Language, 1967.

——, "Einige Bemerkungen zur samaritanischen Liturgie." *Zeitschrift des deutschen Palästina-Vereins* 86 (1970): 87–89.

——, *"nby'ym r'swnym nwsh swmrwn?" Lešonénu* 35 (1971): 292–302.

——, Review of J. Purvis, *The Samaritan Pentateuch. Biblica* 52 (1971): 255.

——, "The Tenth Commandment in the Samaritan Pentateuch." Pages 487–492 in *New Samaritan Studies of the Société d'Études Samaritaines: Essays in Honour of G. D. Sixdenier.* Vols. 3 and 4. Edited by A. D. Crown and L. Davey. Studies in Judaica 5. Sydney: Mandelbaum, 1995.

——, *A Grammar of Samaritan Hebrew.* Jerusalem: Magnes, 2000.

Benoit, P. et al., eds. *Les grottes de Murabba'ât.* Discoveries in the Judaean Desert 2. Oxford: Clarendon, 1961.

Berger, K. "Das Buch der Jubiläen." Pages 273–575 in *Unterweisung in erzählender Form.* Vol. 2 of *Jüdische Schriften aus hellenistisch-römischer Zeit.* Edited by H. Lichtenberger et al. Gütersloh: Gütersloher Verlagshaus, 1981.

Betz, H. D. et al., eds. *Religion in Geschichte und Gegenwart*. 4th ed. 8 vols. and index vol. Tübingen: Mohr, 1998–2005. Translated as *Religion Past and Present*. A—Haz, 5 vols. Boston, Mass.: Brill, 2005–

Bibliothèque nationale. *Manuscrits orientaux: Catalogues des Manuscrits Hébreux et Samaritaines de la Bibliothèque impériale*. Paris: Imprimerie impériale, 1866.

Bickermann, E. J. "Un document relatif à la persecution d'Antiochos IV Épiphanes." *Revue de l'histoire des religions* 115 (1937): 188–223. Repr. pages 105–135 in vol. 2 of *Studies in Jewish and Christian History*. Arbeiten zur Geschichte des antiken Judentums und des Urchristentums 9. Leiden: Brill, 1980.

Black, M., O. Neugebauer, and J. C. VanderKam. *The Book of Enoch or I Enoch: A New English Edition with Commentary and Textual Notes*. Studia in Veteris Testamenti pseudepigrapha 7. Leiden: Brill, 1985.

Blayney, B. *Pentateuchus Hebraeo-Samaritanus charactere Hebraeo-Chaldaico editus*. Oxford: Clarendon, 1790.

Blenkinsopp, J. *Ezra-Nehemiah: A Commentary*. The Old Testament Library. Philadelphia: Westminster, 1989.

Bori, P. C. "L'Estasi del profeta: 'Ascensio Isaiae' 6 e l'antico profetismo cristiano." *Cristianesimo nella storia*. 1 (1980): 367–389.

Botterweck, G. J. and H. Ringgren, eds. *Theologisches Wörterbuch zum Alten Testament*. 10 vols. Stuttgart: Kohlhammer, 1973–2000. Translated by J. T. Willis et al. as *Theological Dictionary of the Old Testament*. Grand Rapids: Eerdmans, 1974–.

Bowman, J. *Transcript of the Original Text of the Samaritan Chronicle Tolidah*. Leeds: Leeds University Oriental Society, 1954.

——, *The Samaritan Problem: Studies in the Relationships of Samaritanism, Judaism, and Early Christianity*. Pittsburg Theological Monograph Series 54. Pittsburg, Penn.: Pickwick, 1975.

——, *Samaritan Documents Relating To Their History, Religion and Life: Translated and Edited*. Pittsburg Original Texts and Translations Series 2. Pittsburg, Penn.: Pickwick, 1977.

Bowman, J. and S. Talmon. "Samaritan Decalogue Inscriptions." *Bulletin of the John Rylands Library of Manchester* 33 (1950–1951): 211–236.

Bright, J. Review of J. Purvis, *The Samaritan Pentateuch*. *Catholic Biblical Quarterly* 31 (1969): 453–454.

Brockman, N. C. *Encyclopedia of Sacred Places*. Santa Barbara, Calif.: ABC-CLIO, 1997.

Brooke, G. Review of R. Egger, *Josephus Flavius und die Samaritaner*. *Journal of Semitic Studies* 37 (1992): 109–112.

Broshi, M. and A. Yardeni. "On *netinim* and false prophets." Pages 29–37 in *Solving Riddles and Untying Knots: Biblical, Epigraphic, and Semitic Studies in Honor of Jonas C. Greenfield*. Edited by Z. Zevit, S. Gitin, and M. Sokoloff. Winona Lake, Ind.: Eisenbrauns, 1995.

Bruneau, P. "'Les Israélites de Delos' er la juiverie délienne." *Bulletin de correspondance hellénique* 106 (1982): 465–504.

Bruyne, D. D. de. "Mélanges: I. Notes de philologie biblique II.—Argarizim (II Mach. 5, 23; 6, 2)." *Revue biblique* 30 (1921): 405–407.

Buchler, A. "Les sources de Flavius Josèphe dans ses Antiquités (XII,5 - XIII,1)." *Revue des études juives* 32 (1896): 179–199; 34 (1897): 69–93.

Bull, R. J. "Tell er-Ras (Mount Gerizim)." Pages 1015.1017–1018.1020–1022 in vol. 4 of *Encyclopedia of Archaeological Excavations in the Holy Land*. Edited by M. Avi-Yonah and E. Stern. Jerusalem: Massada, 1978. Repr. pages 419–427 in *Die Samaritaner*. Edited by F. Dexinger and R. Pummer. Wege der Forschung 604. Darmstadt: Wissenschaftliche Buchgesellschaft, 1992.

Burchard, C. "Joseph and Aseneth (First Century B.C.–Second Century A.D.)." Pages 177–247 in vol. 2 of *The Old Testament Pseudepigrapha*. Edited by J. H. Charlesworth. New York: Doubleday, 1985.

Buttrick, G. A. *The Interpreter's Dictionary of the Bible: An Illustrated Encyclopedia*. 4 vols. and supplementary volume. Nashville, Tenn.: Abingdon, 1962–1976.

Caldwell, T. A., ed. "Samaritans." Pages 633–634 in vol. 12 of *New Catholic Encyclopedia*. Detroit: Thomson/Gale, 2003.

Campbell, E. F., Jr. *Shechem II: Portrait of a Hill Country Vale*. The Shechem Regional Survey. American Schools of Oriental Research Archaeological Reports 2. Atlanta, Ga.: Scholars Press, 1991.

———, *Shechem III: The Stratigraphy and Architecture of Shechem/Tell Balatâh*. Vol. 1: Text; Vol. 2: The Illustrations. American Schools of Oriental Research Archaeological Reports 6. Boston, Mass.: American Schools of Oriental Research, 2002.

Caquot, A. "Bref commentaire du 'Martyre d'Isaïe." *Semitica* 23 (1973): 65–93.

Cashdan, E. *Menahot Translated into English with Notes, Glossary and Indices*. Vol. 1 of *Seder Kodashim in Three Volumes*. *The Babylonian Talmud*. Edited by I. Epstein. London: Soncino 1948. Repr. 1989.

———, *Hullin Translated into English with Notes and Glossary*. Vol. 2 of *Seder Kodashim in Three Volumes*. *The Babylonian Talmud*. Edited by I. Epstein. London: Soncino 1948. Repr. 1989.

Cathcart, K. J. "Numbers 24:17 in Ancient Translations and Interpretations." Pages 511–520 in *Interpretation of the Bible*. The Slovenian Academy of Sciences and Arts, Section Two: Philological and Literary Sciences. Sheffield: Sheffield Academic Press, 1998.

Charles, R. H. *The Ascension of Isaiah: Translated from the Ethiopic Version, which, together with the New Greek Fragment, the Latin Versions and the Latin Translation of the Slavonic, is here Published in Full*. London: Adam & Charles Black, 1900.

———, *The Book of Jubilees, or, The Little Genesis*. London: Adam & Charles Black, 1902.

———, *The Apocrypha and Pseudepigrapha of the Old Testament in English, with Introductions and Critical and Explanatory Notes to the Several Books*. 2 vols. Oxford: Clarendon, 1913.

Charlesworth, J. H. "An Unknown Dead Sea Scrolls Fragment of Deuteronomy." Cited 29 August 2008. Online: http://www.ijco.org.

Coggins, R. J. Review of J. Purvis, *The Samaritan Pentateuch. Journal of Semitic Studies* 14 (1969): 273–275.

——, *Samaritans and Jews: The Origins of Samaritanism Reconsidered*. Growing Points in Theology. Oxford: Blackwell, 1975.

——, "The Samaritans in Josephus." Pages 257–273 in *Josephus, Judaism, and Christianity*. Edited by L. H. Feldman and G. Hata. Leiden: Brill, 1987.

Cohen, A. *Minor Tractates Translated into English with Notes, Glossary and Indices*. Vol. 29 of *Hebrew-English Edition of the Babylonian Talmud*. Edited by I. Epstein; London: Soncino, 1984.

Collins, J. J. "The Epic of Theodotus and the Hellenism of the Hasmoneans." *Harvard Theological Review* 73 (1980): 91–104.

——, "Sibylline Oracles." Pages 317–472 in vol. 1 of *Old Testament Pseudepigrapha*. Edited by J. H. Charlesworth. New York: Doubleday, 1983.

——, *Between Athens and Jerusalem: Jewish Identity in the Hellenistic Diaspora*. 2. ed. The Biblical Resource Series. Grand Rapids, Mich.: Eerdmans, 2000.

Colson, F. H. and G. H. Whitaker. *De migratione Abrahami*. Pages 123–269 in vol. 4 of *Philo*. Loeb Classical Library 261. Cambridge, Mass.: Harvard University Press, 1968.

Colson, F. H. and G. H. Whitaker. *De mutatione nominum*. Pages 128–281 in vol. 5 of *Philo*. Loeb Classical Library 275. Cambridge, Mass.: Harvard University Press, 1968.

Cook, E. M., M. O. Wise, and M. G. Abegg. *The Dead Sea Scrolls: A New Translation*. Rev. ed. San Francisco, Calif.: Harper, 2005.

Cowley, A. E. *The Samaritan Liturgy in two Volumes*. Oxford: Clarendon, 1909.

Crane, O. T. *The Samaritan Chronicle or The Book of Joshua the Son of Nun*. New York: John B. Alden, 1890.

Cross, F. M. "The Contribution of the Qumrân Discoveries to the Study of the Biblical Text." *Israel Exploration Journal* 16 (1966): 81–95. Repr. pages 278–292 in *Qumran and the History of the Biblical Text*. Edited by F. M. Cross and S. Talmon. Cambridge, Mass.: Harvard University Press, 1975.

——, "Aspects of Samaritan and Jewish History in Late Persian and Hellenistic Times." *Harvard Theological Review* 59 (1966): 201–211.

——, "Papyri of the Fourth Century BC from Dâliyeh." Pages 45–69 in *New Directions in Biblical Archaeology*. Edited by D. N. Freedman and J. C. Greenfield. New York: Doubleday, 1971.

——, "The Evolution of a Theory of Local Texts." Pages 108–126 in *1972 Proceedings*. Edited by R. A. Kraft. Septuagint and Cognate Studies 2. Missoula, Mont.: Society of Biblical Literature, 1972.

——, "4QExod-Lev^f." Pages 133–144 in *Qumran Cave 4. VII: Genesis to Numbers*. Edited by E. Ulrich et al. Discoveries in the Judaean Desert 12. Oxford: Clarendon, 1994.

Crown, A. D. *Samaritan Scribes and Manuscripts*. Texte und Studien zum Antiken Judentum 80. Tübingen: Mohr, 2001.

Crown, A. D., ed. *The Samaritans*. Tübingen: Mohr, 1989.

Crown, A. D. and R. Pummer. *A Bibliography of the Samaritans*. 3. ed.: Revised, Expanded and Annotated. ATLA Bibliography 51. Lanham, Md.: Scarecrow Press, 2005.

Crown, A. D., R. Pummer, and A. Tal, eds. *A Companion to Samaritan Studies*. Tübingen: Mohr, 1993.

Davies, G. "A Samaritan Inscription with an Expanded Text of Shema." *Palestine Exploration Quarterly* 131 (1999): 3–19.

Davila, J. R. *The Provenance of the Pseudepigrapha: Jewish, Christian, or Other?* Journal for the Study of Judaism in the Persian, Hellenistic and Roman Periods: Supplement Series 105. Leiden: Brill, 2005.

Dever, W. "Excavations at Shechem and Mt. Gerazim [sic]." Pages ix–xi in *Eretz Shomron: The Thirtieth Archaeological Convention September 1972*. Jerusalem: Israel Exploration Society, 1973.

Dexinger, F. "Das Garizimgebot im Dekalog der Samaritaner." Pages 111–133 in *Studien zum Pentateuch: Walter Kornfeld zum 60. Geburtstag*. Edited by G. Braulik. Vienna: Herder, 1977.

——, "Die frühesten samaritanischen Belege der Taheb-Vorstellung." *Kairos: Zeitschrift für Religionswissenschaft und Theologie* 26 (1984): 224–252.

——, "Der 'Prophet wie Mose' in Qumran und bei den Samaritanern." Pages 97–111 in *Mélanges bibliques et orientaux en l'honneur de M. Mathias Delcor*. Alter Orient und Altes Testament 215. Kevelaer: Butzon & Bercker, 1985.

——, *Der Taheb: Ein "messianischer" Heilsbringer der Samaritaner*. Kairos: religionswissenschaftliche Studien 3. Salzburg: Otto Müller, 1986.

——, "Der Ursprung der Samaritaner im Spiegel der frühen Quellen (Originalbeitrag 1991)." Pages 1–66 in *Die Samaritaner*. Edited by F. Dexinger and R. Pummer. Wege der Forschung 604. Darmstadt: Wissenschaftliche Buchgesellschaft, 1992.

——, "Samaritan origins and the Qumran texts." Pages 169–184 in *New Samaritan Studies of the Société d'Études Samaritaines: Essays in Honour of G. D. Sixdenier*. Vols. 3 and 4. Edited by A. D. Crown and L. Davey. Studies in Judaica 5. Sydney: Mandelbaum, 1995.

Di Lella, A. A. and P. W. Skehan. *The Wisdom of Ben Sira: A new Translation with Notes, Introduction and Commentary*. The Anchor Bible 39. New York: Doubleday, 1987.

Dietrich, W. *Prophetie und Geschichte: eine redaktionsgeschichtliche Untersuchung zum deuteronomistischen Geschichtswerk*. Forschungen zur Religion und Literatur des Alten und Neuen Testaments 108. Göttingen: Vandenhoeck & Ruprecht, 1972.

Dietzfelbinger, C. "Pseudo-Philo: Antiquitates Biblicae." Pages 89–271 in *Unterweisung in erzählender Form*. Vol 2 of *Jüdische Schriften aus hellenistisch-römischer Zeit*. Edited by H. Lichtenberger et al. Gütersloh: Gütersloher Verlagshaus, 1973–1999.

Dillmann, A. *Ascensio Isaiae aethiopice et latine cum prolegomenis, adnotationibus criticis et exegeticis additis versionum latinarum reliquiis edita ab Augusto Dillmann*. Leipzig: F. A. Brockhaus, 1877.

Doran, R. "Pseudo-Eupolemus." Pages 873–882 in vol. 2 of *The Old Testament Pseudepigrapha*. Edited by J. H. Charlesworth. New York: Doubleday, 1985.

Douglas, J. D. *The New Bible Dictionary*. London: Inter-Varsity, 1962.

Duncan, J. A. "4QDeutʲ." Pages 75–91 in *Qumran Cave 4. IX: Deuteronomy, Joshua, Judges, Kings*. Edited by E. Ulrich et al. Discoveries in the Judaean Desert 14. Oxford: Clarendon, 1995.

Dušek, J. *Les manuscrits araméens du Wadi Daliyeh et la Samarie vers 450–332 av. J.-C.* Leiden: Brill, 2007.

Egger, R. *Josephus Flavius und die Samaritaner: eine terminologische Untersuchung zur Identitätsklärung der Samaritaner.* Novum testamentum et orbis antiquus 4. Freiburg: Universitätsverlag, 1986.

Eissfeldt, O. *Hexateuch-Synopse: die Erzählung der fünf Bücher Mose und des Buches Josua mit dem Anfange des Richterbuches, in ihre vier Quellen zerlegt, und in deutscher Übersetzung dargeboten, samt einer in Einleitung und Anmerkungen gegebenen Begründung.* Leipzig: J. C. Hinrich, 1922. Repr. Darmstadt: Wissenschaftliche Buchgesellschaft, 1987.

———, "Martyrium und Himmelfahrt Jesaias (Martyrium et Ascensio Isaiae)." Pages 825–826 in *Einleitung in das Alte Testament.* 4. ed. Tübingen: Mohr, 1976.

Encyclopaedia Judaica. 16 vols. Jerusalem: Encyclopaedia Judaica, 1971–.

Endres, J. C., S.J. *Biblical Interpretation in the Book of Jubilees.* Catholic Biblical Quarterly Monograph Series 18. Washington, D.C.: Catholic Biblical Association of America, 1987.

Eshel, H. "The Prayer of Joseph, a Papyrus from Masada and the Samaritan Temple on ΑΡΓΑΡΙΖΙΝ." *Zion* 56 (1991): 125–136.

———, "The Governors of Samaria in the Fifth and Fourth Centuries B.C.E." Pages 223–234 in *Judah and the Judeans in the Fourth Century B.C.E.* Edited by O. Lipschits, G. N. Knoppers and R. Albertz. Winona Lake, Ind.: Eisenbrauns, 2007.

Fallon, F. "Theodotus (Second to First Century B.C.): A New Translation and Introduction." Pages 785–793 in vol. 2 of *Old Testament Pseudepigrapha.* Edited by J. Charlesworth. New York: Doubleday, 1985.

Feldman, L. H. *Josephus and Modern Scholarship (1937–1980).* Berlin, New York, 1984.

———, "Josephus' Attitude Toward the Samaritans: A Study in Ambivalence." Pages 114–136 in *Studies in Hellenistic Judaism.* Arbeiten zur Geschichte des antiken Judentums und des Urchristentums 30. Leiden: Brill, 1996.

———, *Judean Antiquities Books 1–4.* Vol. 5 of *Flavius Josephus, Translation and Commentary.* Edited by S. Mason. Leiden: Brill, 2000.

———, *"Remember Amalek!" Vengeance, Zealotry, and Group Destruction in the Bible According to Philo, Pseudo-Philo, and Josephus.* Monographs of the Hebrew Union College 31. Cincinnati, Ohio: Hebrew Union College Press, 2004.

Feldman, L. H. and G. Hata. "A Selective Critical Bibliography of Josephus." Pages 330–448 in *Josephus, the Bible, and History.* Detroit: Wayne State University Press, 1989.

Feldman, L. H. and M. Reinhold. *Jewish Life and Thought among Greeks and Romans: Primary Readings.* Minneapolis: Fortress, 1996.

Florentin, M. *The Tulida: A Samaritan Chronicle: Text. Translation. Commentary.* Jerusalem: Yad Izhak Ben-Zvi, 1999.

———, *Late Samaritan Hebrew: A Linguistic Analysis of its Different Types.* Studies in Semitic Language and Linguistics 43. Leiden: Brill, 2005.

Fossum, J. E. *The Name of God and the Angel of the Lord: Samaritan and Jewish*

Concepts of Intermediation and the Origin of Gnosticism. Wissenschaftliche Untersuchungen zum Neuen Testament 36. Tübingen: Mohr, 1985.

Fredrich, C. et al., eds. *Inscriptiones Graecae.* Vol. 12, fasc. VIII of *Inscriptiones insularum maris Aegaei praeter Delum.* Berlin: Reimerum, 1909.

Freedman, D. N., editor in chief. *The Anchor Bible Dictionary.* 6 vols. New York: Doubleday, 1992.

Freedman, D. N., K. A. Mathews, and R. S. Hanson. *The Paleo-Hebrew Leviticus Scroll (11QpaleoLev).* Winona Lake, Ind.: American Schools of Oriental Research, 1985.

Freedman, H. *Shabbat Translated into English with Notes and Glossary.* Vol. 1 of *Seder Mo'ed in Four Volumes. The Babylonian Talmud.* Edited by I. Epstein. London: Soncino, 1938. Repr. 1987.

———, Chapters VII–IX of *Sanhedrin Translated into English with Notes, Glossary and Indices.* Vol. 3 of *Seder Nezikin in Four Volumes. The Babylonian Talmud.* Edited by I. Epstein. London: Soncino, 1935. Repr. 1987.

Freeman-Grenville, G. S. P., R. L. Chapman III, and J. E. Taylor. *Palestine in the Fourth Century A.D.: The Onomasticon by Eusebius of Ceasarea.* Jerusalem: Carta, 2003.

Freudenthal, J. "Hellenistische Studien: Heft I: Alexander Polyhistor und die von ihm erhaltenen Reste jüdischer und samaritanischer Geschichtswerke." In *Jahresbericht des jüdisch-theologischen Seminars "Fraenkel'scher Stiftung."* Breslau: Grass, 1874.

Gall, A. Fr. von. *Der Hebräische Pentateuch der Samaritaner.* Gießen: Töpelmann, 1914–1918.

Galling, K., E. Edel, and R. Borger. *Textbuch zur Geschichte Israels.* 3., durchgesehene Auflage. Tübingen: Mohr, 1979.

García Martínez, F. "Nuevos Textos no bíblicos procedentes de Qumrán (I)." *Estudios bíblicos* 49 (1991): 116–123.

García Martínez, F. and E. J. C. Tigchelaar. *The Dead Sea Scrolls: Study Edition.* Leiden: Brill, 1997.

Gaster, M. "Das Buch Josua in hebräisch-samaritanischer Rezension. Entdeckt und zum ersten Male herausgegeben." *Zeitschrift des deutschen morgenländischen Gesellschaft* 62 (1908): 209–279. 494–549.

———, "On the newly discovered Samaritan Book of Joshua." *Journal of the Royal Asiatic Society of Great Britain and Ireland* (1908): 795–809.

———, *The Samaritans: Their History, Doctrines and Literature: With Six Appendices and Nineteen Illustrations.* Schweich Lectures on Biblical Archaeology 1923. München: Kraus Reprint, 1980.

———, *The Asatir: The Samaritan Book of the "Secrets of Moses," together with the Pitron.* London: The Royal Asiatic society, 1927.

Gebhardt, O. von. "Die Ascensio Isaiae als Heiligenlegende." *Zeitschrift für wissenschaftliche Theologie* 21 (1878): 330–353.

Geiger, A. *Urschrift und Übersetzungen der Bibel in ihrer Abhängigkeit von der innern Entwicklung des Judentums.* Breslau: J. Hainauer, 1857. 2. ed. Frankfurt a. M.: Madda, 1928.

Gerleman, G. *Synoptic Studies in the Old Testament.* Lunds universitets årsskrift, N. F., Avd. 1, 44:5. Lund: Gleerup, 1948.

Gesenius, W. *De Pentateuchi Samaritani origine, indole et auctoritate: commentatio philologica-critica*. Halle: Regenerianae, 1815.

Ginzberg, L., H. Szold, and P. Radin. *The Legends of the Jews*. Johns Hopkins paperbacks ed. 7 vols. Baltimore: Johns Hopkins University Press, 1998.

Glaue, P. and A. Rahlfs. "Fragmente einer griechischen Übersetzung des samaritanischen Pentateuchs." Pages 167–200 in vol. 2 of *Nachrichten der Königlichen Gesellschaft der Wissenschaften zu Göttingen, Phil.-hist. Klasse*. Berlin: Weidmann, 1911.

Goldstein, J. A. "The Petition of the Samaritans and the Reply of Antiochus IV as Preserved by Josephus at *AJ* xii 5.5.258–264." Pages 523–539 in *II Maccabees: A New Translation with Introduction and Commentary*. The Anchor Bible 41A. New York: Doubleday, 1983.

Grabbe, L. L. "Betwixt and Between: The Samaritans in the Hasmonean Period." Paper presented at the Society of Biblial Literature, Washington D.C., November 20–23, 1993. Pages 334–347 in *SBL Seminar Papers 1993*. Edited by E. H. Lovering, Jr. Atlanta, Ga.: Scholars Press, 1993.

Greenfield, J. C., M. E. Stone, and E. Eshel. *The Aramaic Levi Document: Edition, Translation, Commentary*. Studia in Veteris Testamenti pseudepigrapha 19. Leiden: Brill, 2004.

Grenfell, B. P. and A. S. Hunt. *The Amherst papyri: Part I The Ascension of Isaiah, and other Theological Fragments with Nine Plates*. London: H. Frowde, 1900.

Gruenwald, I. *Apocalyptic and Merkavah Mysticism*. Arbeiten zur Geschichte des antiken Judentums und des Urchristentums 14. Leiden: Brill, 1980.

Hall, R. G. "The Ascension of Isaiah: Community Situation, Date, and Place in Early Christianity." *Journal of Biblical Literature* 109 (1990): 289–306.

Hanhart, R. *Maccabaeorum liber II copiis usus quas reliquit Werner Kappler edidit Robert Hanhart*. Vol. 9, fasc. 1 of *Septuaginta: Vetus Testamentum Graecum auctoritate Societatis Litterarum Gotingensis editum*. Göttingen: Akademie der Wissenschaften in Göttingen / Vandenhoeck & Ruprecht, 1959.

———, *Iudith*. Vol. 8, 4, of *Septuaginta: Vetus Testamentum Graecum*. Göttingen: Vandenhoeck & Ruprecht, 1979.

———, "Zu den ältesten Traditionen über das samaritanische Schisma." *Eretz-Israel* 16 (1982): 106*–115*.

Hannah, D. D. "Isaiah's Vision in the Ascension of Isaiah and the Early Church." *Journal of Theological Studies* New Series 50 (1999): 80–101.

Hanson, J. "Demetrius the Chronographer (Third Century b.c.): A New Translation and Introduction." Pages 843–854 in vol. 2 of *Old Testament Pseudepigrapha*. New York: Doubleday, 1985.

Harviainen, T. and H. Shehadeh. "How did Abraham Firkovich Acquire the Great Collection of Samaritan Manuscripts in Nablus in 1864?" *Studia Orientalia* 73 (1994): 167–192.

Headland, T. N., K. L. Pike, and M. Harris, eds. *Emics and Etics: The Insider/Outsider Debate*. Frontiers of Anthropology 7. Newbury Park, Cal.: Sage, 1990.

Heidenheim, M., "Die samaritanische Chronik des Hohenpriesters Elasar aus dem 11. Jahrhundert übersetzt und erklärt." *Deutsche Vierteljahrsschrift für englische theologische Forschung* 4 (1870): 347–389.

Hengel, M. *Judentum und Hellenismus: Studien zu ihrer Begegnung unter besonderer Berücksichtigung Palästinas bis zur Mitte des 2. Jh.s v. Chr. 2.*, durchgesehene und ergänzte Auflage. Wissenschaftliche Untersuchungen zum Neuen Testament 10. Tübingen: Mohr, 1973. Translated by J. Bowden as *Judaism and Hellenism: Studies in Their Encounter in Palestine during the Early Hellenistic Period*. London: SCM Press, 1981.

——, "Judaism and Hellenism Revisited." Pages 6–37 in *Hellenism in the Land of Israel*. Edited by J. J. Collins and G. E. Sterling. Christianity and Judaism in Antiquity Series 13. Notre Dame, Ind: University of Notre Dame Press, 2001.

Henriksen, P., ed., *Aschehoug og Gyldendals store norske leksikon*. 16 vols. Oslo: Aschehoug & Gyldendal, 1995–1999.

Hepner, G. "The Samaritan Version of the Tenth Commandment." *Scandinavian Journal of the Old Testament* 20 (2006): 147–151.

Hjelm, I. *The Samaritans and Early Judaism: A Literary Analysis*. Journal for the Study of the Old Testament: Supplement Series 303. Sheffield: Sheffield Academic Press 2000.

——, *Jerusalem's Rise to Sovereignty: Zion and Gerizim in Competition*. Journal for the Study of the Old Testament: Supplement series 404. London: T & T Clark International, 2004.

The Hodder and Stoughton Illustrated Bible Dictionary. See Lockyer, H., Sr., *Nelson's Illustrated Bible Dictionary*.

Holladay, C. R. *Historians, Text and Translations*. Vol. 1 of *Fragments from Hellenistic Jewish Authors*. Text and Translations Pseudepigrapha Series 10. Chico, Calif.: Scholars Press, 1983.

——, *Poets: The Epic Poets Theodotus and Philo and Ezekiel the Tragedian*. Vol. 2 of *Fragments from Hellenistic Jewish Authors*. Text and Translations Pseudepigrapha Series 12. Chico, Calif.: Scholars Press, 1989.

Hollander, H. W. and M. de Jonge. *The Testament of the Twelve Patriarchs: A Commentary*. Studia in Veteris Testamenti Pseudepigrapha 8. Leiden: Brill 1985.

Horst, P. W. van der. "The Interpretation of the Bible by the Minor Hellenistic Jewish Authors." Pages 519–546 in *Mikra: Text, Translation, Reading, and Interpretation of the Hebrew Bible in Ancient Judaism and Early Christianity*. Edited by M. J. Mulder and H. Sysling. Assen/Maastricht: van Gorcum, 1988.

——, "Anti-Samaritan Propaganda in Early Judaism." Pages 134–150 in *Jews and Christians in their Graeco-Roman Context: Selected Essays on Early Judaism, Samaritanism, Hellenism, and Christianity*. Wissenschaftliche Untersuchungen zum Neuen Testament 196. Tübingen: Mohr, 2006.

Hylland Eriksen, T. *Us and Them in Modern Societies: Ethnicity and Nationalism in Mauritius, Trinidad and Beyond*. Oslo: Scandinavian University Press, 1992.

Isser, S. J. *The Dositheans: A Samaritan Sect in Late Antiquity*. Studies in Judaism in Late Antiquity 17. Leiden: Brill, 1976.

Japhet, S. "The Supposed Common Authorship of Chronicles and Ezra-Nehemiah Investigated anew." *Vetus Testamentum* 18 (1968): 330–371. Repr. pages 1–37 in eadem, *From the Rivers of Babylon to the Highlands of Judah: Collected Studies on the Restoration Period*. Winona Lake, Ind.: Eisenbrauns, 2006.

———, "Conquest and Settlement in Chronicles." *Journal of Biblical Literature* 98 (1979): 205–218. Repr. pages 38–52 in eadem, *From the Rivers of Babylon to the Highlands of Judah: Collected Studies on the Restoration Period*. Winona Lake, Ind.: Eisenbrauns, 2006.

Jastram, N. R. "The text of 4QNum^b." Pages 177–198 in *The Madrid Qumran Congress: Proceedings of the International Congress on the Dead Sea Scrolls, Madrid 18–21 March, 1991*. Edited by J. Trebolle Barrera and L. Vegas Montaner. Leiden: Brill, 1992.

———, "4QNum^b." Pages 205–267 in *Qumran Cave 4. VII: Genesis to Numbers*. Edited by E. Ulrich, et al. Discoveries in the Judaean desert 12. Oxford: Clarendon, 1994.

———, "A Comparison of Two 'Proto-Samaritan' texts from Qumran: 4Qpaleo-Exod^m and 4QNum^b." *Dead Sea Discoveries* 5 (1998): 264–289.

Jaubert, A. "The Calendar of Jubilees." Pages 15–30 in *The Date of the Last Supper*. Translated by I. Rafferty. Staten Island, N.Y.: Alba House, 1965.

Jeremias, J. *Die Passahfeier der Samaritaner und ihre Bedeutung für das Verständnis der alttestamentlichen Passahüberlieferung*. Beihefte zur Zeitschrift für die alttestamentliche Wissenschaft 59. Gießen: Töpelmann, 1932.

———, *Jerusalem zur Zeit Jesu: eine kulturgeschichtliche Untersuchung zur neutestamentlichen Zeitgeschichte*. 3. neubearbeitete Auflage. Göttingen: Vandenhoeck & Ruprecht, 1969.

Jones, S. *The Archaeology of Ethnicity: Constructing Identities in the Past and Present*. London and New York: Routledge, 1997.

Jonge, M de. *Testamenta XII patriarcharum: Edited according to Cambridge University Library Ms Ff. 1.24 fol. 203a–262b with Short Notes*. Pseudepigrapha Veteris Testamenti Graece 1. Leiden: Brill, 1964.

Josephus. Translated by H. St. Thackeray et al. 10 vols. Loeb classical library. Cambridge, Mass.: Harvard University Press, 1926–1965.

Josephus. The Works of Josephus: Complete and Unabridged. Translated by W. Whiston. Peabody, Mass.: Hendrickson, 1987.

Juynboll, T. G. J. *Chronicon Samaritanum, Arabice conscriptum, cui titulus est Liber Josuae*. Leiden: S. & J. Luchtmans, 1848.

Kahle, P. "Zum hebräischen Buch Josua der Samaritaner." *Zeitschrift der deutschen morgenländischen Gesellschaft* 62 (1908): 550–551.

———, "Untersuchungen zur Geschichte des Pentateuchtextes." *Theologische Studien und Kritken* 38 (1915): 399–439.

Kartveit, M. "Das Ende der Prophetie—aber welcher?" Pages 143–156 in *Text and Theology: Studies in Honour of Prof. Dr. Theol. Magne Sæbø*. Edited by K. A. Tångberg. Oslo: Verbum, 1994.

———, "2 Chronicles 36.20–23 as Literary and Theological 'Interface.'" Pages 395–403 in *The Chronicler as Author: Studies in Text and Texture*. Edited by S. L. McKenzie and M. Patrick Graham. Journal for the Study of the Old Testament: Supplement series 263. Sheffield: Sheffield Academic Press, 1999.

———, "The Martyrdom of Isaiah and the Formation of the Samaritan Group." Pages 3.15–3.28 in *Samaritan Researches: Proceedings of the Congress of the SES (Milan July 8–12 1996) and of the Special Section of the ICANAS Congress*

(Budapest July 7–11 1997). Vol. 5. Edited by V. Morabito, A. D. Crown, and L. Davey. Studies in Judaica 10. Sydney: Mandelbaum, 2000.

———, "The Major Expansions in the Samaritan Pentateuch—The Evidence from the 4Q Texts." Pages 117–124 in *Proceedings of the Fifth International Congress of the Société d'Études Samaritaines: Helsinki, August 1–4, 2000*. Studies in Memory of Ferdindand Dexinger. Edited by H. Shehadeh & H. Tawa with the collaboration of R. Pummer. Paris: Geuthner, 2005.

———, "Die älteste samaritanische Kanonauffassung." Pages 219–226 in *"Und das Leben ist siegreich!" "And Life is Victorious!" Mandäische und samaritanische Literatur/Mandaean and Samaritan Literatures: Im Gedenken an Rudolph Macuch/In Memory of Rudolph Macuch (1919–1993)*. Edited by R. Voigt. Mandäistische Forschungen 1. Wiesbaden: Harrassowitz, 2008.

———, "Who are the 'Fools' in 4QNarrative and Poetic Composition[a-c]?" Pages 119–133 in *Northern Lights on the Dead Sea Scrolls: Proceedings of the Nordic Qumran Network 2003–2006*. Edited by A. K. Petersen et al. Studies on the Texts of the Desert of Judah 80. Leiden: Brill 2009.

Kasher, A. "Josephus on Jewish-Samaritan Relations under Roman Rule (B.C.E. 63 –C.E.70)." Pages 217–236 in *New Samaritan Studies of the Société d'Études Samaritaines: Essays in Honour of G. D. Sixdenier*. Vols. 3 and 4. Edited by A. D. Crown and L. Davey. Studies in Judaica 5. Sydney: Mandelbaum, 1995.

Kautzsch, E. *Die Apokryphen und Pseudepigraphen des Alten Testaments: in Verbindung mit Fachgenossen*. Hildesheim: Olms, 1962.

Kee, H. C. "Testaments of the Twelve Patriarchs (Second Century B.C.)" Pages 775–828 in vol. 1 of *The Old Testament Pseudepigrapha*. Edited by J. H. Charlesworth. New York: Doubleday, 1983.

Kennicott, B. *Vetus Testamentum Hebraicum, cum variis lectionibus*. Vol. 1. Oxford, 1776.

Kippenberg, H. G. "Ein Gebetbuch für den samaritanischen Synagogengottesdienst aus dem 2. Jh. n. Chr." *Zeitschrift des deutschen Palästina-Vereins* 85 (1969): 76–103.

———, *Garizim und Synagoge: Traditionsgechichtliche Untersuchungen zur samaritanischen Religion der aramäischen Periode*. Religionsgeschichtliche Versuche und Vorarbeiten 30. Berlin: de Gruyter, 1971.

Klein, R. W. "Archaic chronologies and the textual history of the Old Testament." *Harvard Theological Review* 67 (1974): 255–263.

Klein, S. "Palästinisches im Jubiläenbuch." *Zeitschrift des deutschen Palästina-Vereins* 57 (1934): 7–27.

Klostermann, E. *Eusebius Werke*. Text und Untersuchungen zur Geschichte der altchristlichen Literatur. Neue Folge. Leipzig: Hinrichs, 1902.

Knibb, M. "Martyrdom and Ascension of Isaiah." Pages 143–176 in vol. 2 of *The Old Testament Pseudepigrapha*. Edited by J. H. Charlesworth. NewYork: Doubleday, 1985.

———, "A Note on 4Q372 and 4Q390." Pages 164–177 in *The Scriptures and the Scrolls: Studies in Honour of A. S. van der Woude on the occasion of his 65th Birthday*. Edited by A. Hilhorst, C. J. Labuschagne, and F. García Martínez. Vetus Testamentum Supplements 49. Leiden: Brill, 1992.

Knight, J. *Disciples of the Beloved One: The Christology, Social Context and Theological Context of the Ascension of Isaiah.* Journal for the study of the Pseudepigrapha: Supplement series 18. Sheffield: Journal for the study of the Pseudepigrapha Press, 1996.

Knoppers, G. "In Search of Post-Exilic Israel: Samaria after the Fall of the Northern Kingdom." Pages 150–180 in *In Search of Pre-Exilic Israel: Proceedings of the Oxford Old Testament Seminar.* Edited by J. Day. Journal for the Study of the Old Testament: Supplement series 406. London: T & T Clark International, 2004.

Kraabel, A. T. "New Evidence of the Samaritan Diaspora has been Found on Delos." *Biblical Archaeologist* 47 (1984): 44–46.

Kratz, R. "Temple and Torah: Reflections on the Legal Status of the Pentateuch between Elephantine and Qumran." Pages 77–103 in *The Pentateuch as Torah: New Models for Understanding Its Promulgation and Acceptance.* Edited by G. Knoppers and B. M. Levinson. Winona Lake, Ind.: Eisenbrauns, 2007.

Krause, G. and G. Müller, eds. *Theologische Realenzyclopädie.* 36 vols. and 2 index vols. Berlin: de Gruyter, 1977–.

Kugel, J. "The Story of Dinah in the Testament of Levi." *Harvard Theological Review* 85 (1992): 1–34.

——, *Traditions of the Bible: A Guide to the Bible as it was at the Start of the Common Era.* Cambridge, Mass.: Harvard University Press, 1998.

——, "Joseph at Qumran: The Importance of 4Q372 Frg. 1 in Extending a Tradition." Pages 261–278 in *Studies in the Hebrew Bible, Qumran, and the Septuagint Presented to Eugene Ulrich.* Edited by E. Tov, J. C. VanderKam, and P. W. Flint. Leiden: Brill, 2006.

Kugler, R. A. *From Patriarch to Priest: The Levi-Priestly Tradition from Aramaic Levi to Testament of Levi.* Early Judaism and its Literature 9. Atlanta, Ga.: Scholars Press, 1996.

——, "Some Further Evidence for the Samaritan Provenance of 'Aramaic Levi' (1QTestLevi; 4QTestLevi)." *Revue de Qumran* 17 (1996): 351–358.

Leiman, S. Z. *The Canonization of Hebrew Scripture: The Talmudic and Midrashic Evidence.* Transactions / The Connecticut Academy of Arts and Sciences 47. Hamden, Conn.: Archon Books, 1976.

Levy-Rubin, M. *The Continuatio of the Samaritan Chronicle of Abū l-Fath al-Sāmirī al-Danafī: Text, Translated and Annotated.* Studies in Late Antiquity and Early Islam. Princeton, N.J.: Darwin, 2002.

Liddell, H. G., R. Scott, and G. R. Berry. *Greek-English Lexicon.* 26. ed. Classic dictionaries. Chicago, 1958.

Lockyer, H., Sr., general editor. *Nelson's Illustrated Bible Dictionary: An Authoritative One-Volume Reference Work on the Bible, with Full Colour Illustrations.* Consulting editors F. F. Bruce ... [et al.]. Cover and spine titles read: *The Hodder and Stoughton Illustrated Bible Dictionary.* Nashville: Nelson; Dunton Green: Hodder & Stoughton, 1986.

London, G. "Reply to A. Zertal's 'The Wedge-shaped Decorated Bowl and the Origin of the Samaritans.'" *Bulletin of the American Schools of Oriental Research* 286 (1992): 89–90.

Lowy, S. *The Principles of Samaritan Bible Exegesis*. Studia Post-Biblica 28. Leiden: Brill, 1977.

Macdonald, J. *The Theology of the Samaritans*. New Testament Library. London: SCM Press, 1964.

——, *The Samaritan chronicle no. II; or, Sepher Ha-Yamim: From Joshua to Nebuchadnezzar*. Beihefte zur Zeitschrift für die alttestamentliche Wissenschaft 107. Berlin: de Gruyter, 1969.

Mack, B. L. *Wisdom and the Hebrew Epic: Ben Sira's Hymn in Praise of the Fathers*. Chicago: University of Chicago Press, 1985.

Macuch, R. *Grammatik des samaritanischen Hebräisch*. Studia Samaritana 1. Berlin: de Gruyter, 1969.

Magen, Y. "Mount Gerizim and the Samaritans." Pages 91–148 in *Early Christianity in Context*. Studium Biblicum Franciscanum: Collectio maior 38. Jerusalem: Franciscan Printing Press, 1993.

——, "Mt. Gerizim—A Temple City." [In Hebrew] *Qadmoniot* 33 (2000): 74–119.

——, "Mount Gerizim." Pages [1]–[13] in *The Aramaic, Hebrew and Samaritan Inscriptions*. Vol. 1 of *Mount Gerizim Excavations*. Edited by Y. Magen, H. Misgav and L. Tsfania. Judea & Samaria Publications 2. Jerusalem: Israel Antiquities Authority, 2004.

——, "The Dating of the First Phase of the Samaritan Temple on Mount Gerizim in Light of the Archaeological Evidence." Pages 157–211 in *Judah and the Judeans in the Fourth Century B.C.E.* Edited by O. Lipschits, G. N. Knoppers and R. Albertz. Winona Lake, Ind.: Eisenbrauns, 2007.

Magen, Y., H. Misgav, and L. Tsfania, eds. *The Aramaic, Hebrew and Samaritan Inscriptions*. Vol. 1 of *Mount Gerizim Excavations*. Judea & Samaria Publications 2. Jerusalem: Israel Antiquities Authority, 2004.

Mantel, H. D. "The Secession of the Samaritans." [In Hebrew] *Bar Ilan* 7–8 (1969–1970): 162–177.

Marcus, R. "Josephus on the Samaritan Schism." Pages 498–511 in *Josephus: Jewish Antiquities Books IX–XI*. Translated and edited by R. Marcus. The Loeb Classical Library 326. Cambrigde, Mass.: Harvard University Press, 1937.

Mason, S. *Josephus and the New Testament*. 2. ed. Peabody, Mass.: Hendrickson, 2003.

McCarthy, C. *Deuteronomy*. Vol. 5 of *Biblia Hebraica Quinta editione cum apparatu critico novis curis elaborato*. Stuttgart: Deutsche Bibelgesellschaft, 2007.

Meeks, W. A. *The Prophet-King: Moses Traditions and the Johannine Christology*. Novum Testamentum Supplements 14. Leiden: Brill, 1967.

Meer, M. N. van der. *Formation and Reformulation: The Redaction of the Book of Joshua in the Light of the Oldest Textual Witnesses*. Vetus Testamentum Supplements 102. Leiden: Brill, 2004.

Milik, J. T., and M. Black. *The Books of Enoch: Aramaic Fragments of Qumrân Cave 4*. Oxford: Clarendon, 1976.

Miller, L. and M. Simon. *Bekorot Translated into English with Notes and Glossary*. Vol. 3 of *Seder Kodashim in Three Volumes*. The Babylonian Talmud. Edited by I. Epstein. London: Soncino 1948. Repr. 1989.

Mittmann-Richert, U. "Demetrios the Exegete and Chronographer—a New Theological Assessment." Pages 186–209 in *The Changing Face of Judaism, Christianity, and other Greco-Roman Religions in Antiquity.* Edited by I. H. Hen-
derson et al. Studien zu den Jüdischen Schriften aus hellenistisch-römischer
Zeit 2. Gütersloh: Gütersloher Verlagshaus, 2006.

Montgomery, J. A. *The Samaritans, the Earliest Jewish Sect: Their History, Theology, and Literature.* The Bohlen lectures 1906. Repr. New York: Ktav Publishing House, 1968.

Moore, C. A. *Judith: A New Translation with Introduction and Commentary.* The
Anchor Bible 40B. New York: Doubleday, 1985.

Mor, M. "The Persian, Hellenistic and Hasmonean Period." Pages 1–18 in *The
Samaritans.* Edited by A. D. Crown. Tübingen: Mohr, 1989.

Morinus, J. Vol. 6 of *Biblia 1. Hebraica, 2. Samaritana, 3. Chaldaica, 4. Graeca, 5.
Syriaca, 6. Latina, 7. Arabica. Quibus textus originales totius Scripturae Sacrae
...* Paris: Antoine Vitray, 1629–1645.

Mowinckel, S. *Studien zu dem Buche Ezra-Nehemia: III. Die Ezrageschichte und
das Gesetz Moses.* Skrifter utgitt av Det norske vitenskaps-akademi i Oslo:
Hist.-filos. klasse. Ny serie. Oslo: Universitetsforlaget, 1965.

Najman, H. *Seconding Sinai: The Development of Mosaic Discourse in Second
Temple Judaism.* Journal for the Study of Judaism in the Persian, Hellenistic
and Roman Period: Supplement Series 77. Leiden: Brill 2002.

Neubauer, A. "Chronique samaritaine, suivie d'un appendice contentant de
courtes notices sur quelques autres ouvrages samaritains." *Journal asiatique*
14 (1869): 385–470.

Nielsen, E. *Shechem: A Traditio-Historical Investigation.* Copenhagen: G. E. C.
Gad, 1955.

Niessen, F. *Eine samaritanische Version des Buches Yehosua' und die Sobak-
Erzählung: die Samaritanische Chronik Nr. II, Handschrift 2: JR(G) 1168 =
Ryl. Sam. MS 259, Folio 8b–53a.* Texte und Studien zur Orientalistik 12.
Hildesheim: Olms, 2000.

Nihan, C. "The Torah between Samaria and Judah: Shechem and Gerizim in
Deuteronomy and Joshua." Pages 187–223 in *The Pentateuch as Torah: New
Models for Understanding Its Promulgation and Acceptance.* Edited by
G. Knoppers and B. M. Levinson. Winona Lake, Ind.: Eisenbrauns,
2007.

Nodet, É. Review of R. Egger, *Josephus Flavius und die Samaritaner. Revue
biblique* 95 (1988): 288–294.

Noort, E. "Der reißende Wolf—Josua in Überlieferung und Geschichte." Pages
153–173 in *International Organization for the Study of the Old Testament.
18th Congress. Congress volume Leiden, 2004.* Edited by A. Lemaire. Vetus
Testamentum Supplements 109. Leiden: Brill, 2006.

Norelli, E. *Ascensio Isaiae: Textus.* Edited by Association pour l'étude de la littérature apocryphe chrétienne. Corpus Christianorum: Series Apocryphorum 7.
Turnhout: Brepols, 1995.

———, *Ascensio Isaiae: Commentarius.* Edited by Association pour l'étude de la
littérature apocryphe chrétienne. Corpus Christianorum: Series Apocryphorum 8. Turnhout: Brepols, 1995.

Noth, M. *Überlieferungsgeschichtliche Studien: die sammelnden und bearbeiten-den Geschichtswerke im Alten Testament.* Tübingen: Niemeyer, 1943.
———, *Geschichte Israels.* Göttingen: Vandenhoeck & Ruprecht, 1950.
Oegma, G. S. "Theodotos der Epiker." Pages 54–62 in *Supplementa.* Vol. 6 of *Jüdische Schriften aus hellenistisch-römischer Zeit, Neue Folge.* Edited by H. Lichtenberger et al. Gütersloh: Gütersloher Verlagshaus, 2002.
Oeming, M. *Das wahre Israel: die "genealogische Vorhalle" 1 Chronik 1–9.* Bei-träge zur Wissenschaft vom Alten und Neuen Testament, Folge 8, 7. Stuttgart: W. Kohlhammer, 1990.
Otzen, B. *Tobit and Judith.* Guides to Apocrypha and Pseudepigrapha. Sheffield: Sheffield Academic Press, 2002.
Pakkala, J. *Ezra the Scribe: The Development of Ezra 7–10 and Nehemia 8.* Beihefte zur Zeitschrift für die alttestamentliche Wissenschaft 347. Berlin: de Gruyter, 2004.
Perlitt, L. "Mose als Prophet." *Evangelische Theologie* 31 (1994): 588–608.
Pliny the Elder, Natural history. Translated by H. Rackham and W. H. S. Jones. The Loeb Classical Library. Cambridge: Harvard University Press, 1949.
Powels, S. "The Samaritan Calendar and the Roots of Samaritan Chronology." Pages 691–742 in *The Samaritans.* Edited by A. D. Crown, Leiden: Brill, 1989.
Priest, J. "Testament of Moses." Pages 927–934 in vol. 1 of *The Old Testament Pseudepigrapha.* Edited by J. H. Charlesworth. New York: Doubleday, 1983.
Pritchard, J. B. *Ancient Near Eastern Texts Relating to the Old Testament.* 3. ed. Princeton, N.J.: Princeton University Press, 1969.
Puech, E. "Le Testament de Lévi en araméen de la geniza du Caire." *Revue de Qumran* 20 (2002): 511–556.
Pummer, R. "Antisamaritanische Polemik in jüdischen Schriften aus der inter-testamentarischen Zeit." *Biblische Zeitschrift* Neue Folge 26 (1982): 224–242.
———, "Genesis 34 in Jewish Writings of the Hellenistic and Roman Periods." *Harvard Theological Review* 75 (1982): 177–188.
———, "Argarizin: A Criterion for Samaritan Provenance?" *Journal for the Study of Judaism in the Persian, Hellenistic and Roman Periods* 18 (1987): 18–25.
———, Review of R. Egger, *Josephus Flavius und die Samaritaner. Journal of Biblical Literature* 107 (1988): 768–772.
———, "Samaritan Material Remains and Archaeology." Pages 135–177 in *The Samaritans.* Edited by A. D. Crown. Tübingen: Mohr, 1989.
———, "Einführung in den Stand der Samaritanerforschung." Pages 56–63 in *Die Samaritaner.* Edited by F. Dexinger and R. Pummer. Wege der Forschung 604. Darmstadt: Wissenschaftliche Buchgesellschaft, 1992.
———, *Early Christian Authors on Samaritans and Samaritanism: Texts, Transla-tions, and Commentary.* Texts and Studies in Ancient Judaism 92. Tübingen: Mohr, 2002.
———, "The Samaritans and their Pentateuch." Pages 237–269 in *The Pentateuch as Torah: New Models for Understanding Its Promulgation and Acceptance.* Edited by G. Knoppers and B. M. Levinson. Winona Lake, Ind.: Eisenbrauns, 2007.
Purvis, J. D. "Ben Sira' and the Foolish People of Shechem." *Journal of Near East-ern Studies* 24 (1965): 88–94. Repr. in idem, *Samaritan Pentateuch,* 119–129.

————, *The Samaritan Pentateuch and the Origin of the Samaritan Sect.* Harvard Semitic Monographs 2. Cambridge, Mass.: Harvard University Press, 1968.

————, "The Samaritans and Judaism." Pages 81–98 in *Early Judaism and its Modern Interpreters.* Edited by R. A. Kraft and G. W. E. Nickelsburg. The Bible and its Modern Interpreters 2. Philadelphia, Penn.: Fortress, 1986.

Qimron, E. "Observations on the Reading of 'A Text About Joseph' 4Q372 1." *Revue de Qumran* 15 (1992): 603–604.

————, "On the Interpretation of the List of False Prophets." *Tarbiz* 63 (1994): 273–275.

Rad, G. von. *Das erste Buch Mose: Genesis.* 8. ed. Altes Testament Deutsch 2/4. Göttingen: Vandenhoeck & Ruprecht, 1967.

Renz, J. and W. Röllig. *Die althebräischen Inschriften: Teil 1 Text und Kommentar.* Vol. 2/1 of *Handbuch der althebräischen Epigraphik.* Darmstadt: Wissenschaftliche Buchgesellschaft, 1995.

————, *Materialien zur althebräischen Morphologie: Siegel und Gewichte.* Vol. 2/2 of *Handbuch der althebräischen Epigraphik.* Darmstadt: Wissenschaftliche Buchgesellschaft, 2003.

Robert, U. *Heptateuchi partis posterioris versio Latina antiquissima e codice Lugdunensi: Version latine du Deutéronome, de Josué et des Juges antérieure à saint Jérôme, publiée d'après le manuscrit de Lyon avec des observations par U. Robert.* Lyon, 1900.

Roberts, B. Review of J. Purvis, *The Samaritan Pentateuch. Journal of Theological Studies* 20 (1969): 570.

Roussel, P. et M. Launey. *Inscriptions de Délos: décrets postérieurs à 166 av. J.-C. (No.s 1497–1524), dédicaces posterieures à 166 av. J.-C. (No.s 2220–2879).* Paris: H. Champion, 1937.

Sadaqa, A. & R. *Jewish and Samaritan Version of the Pentateuch with Particular Stress on the Differences between both Texts: Exodus.* Jerusalem: Ruben Mass, 1964.

————, *Jewish and Samaritan Version of the Pentateuch with Particular Stress on the Differences between both Texts: Deuteronomium.* Jerusalem: Ruben Mass, 1966.

Sanderson, J. E. *An Exodus Scroll from Qumran: 4QpaleoExod^m and the Samaritan Tradition.* Harvard Semitic Studies 30. Atlanta: Scholars Press, 1986.

————, "The Contributions of 4QPaleoExod^m to Textual Criticism." *Revue de Qumran* 13 (1988): 547–560.

————, "4QpaleoExodus^m." Pages 53–103 in *Qumran Cave 4. IV: Palaeo-Hebrew and Greek Biblical Manuscripts.* Edited by P. W. Skehan, J. E. Sanderson, and E. Ulrich. Discoveries in the Judaean Desert 9. Oxford: Clarendon, 1992.

Sandnes, K. O. *Paul, one of the Prophets? A Contribution to the Apostle's Self-Understanding.* Wissenschaftliche Untersuchungen zum Neuen Testament, Reihe 2, 43. Tübingen: Mohr, 1991.

Sauer, G. *Jesus Sirach/Ben Sira.* Altes Testament Deutsch Apokryphen 1. Göttingen: Vandenhoeck & Ruprecht, 2000.

Schachter, J. Chapters I–VI of *Sanhedrin Translated into English with Notes, Glossary and Indices.* Vol. 3 of *Seder Nezikin in Four Volumes. The Babylonian Talmud.* Edited by I. Epstein. London: Soncino, 1935. Repr. 1987

Schalit, A. *Namenwörterbuch zu Flavius Josephus*. Leiden: Brill, 1968.

Schiffman, L. H. and J. VanderKam, editors in chief. *Encyclopedia of the Dead Sea Scrolls*. 2 vols. Oxford: Oxford University Press, 2000.

Schmitt, G. and S. Mittmann. *Tübinger Bibelatlas auf der Grundlage des Tübinger Atlas des Vorderen Orients (TAVO)*. Stuttgart: Deutsche Bibelgesellschaft, 2002.

Schnapp, F., and E. Kautzsch. "Die Testamente der 12 Patriarchen, der Söhne Jakobs." Pages 458–506 in vol. 2 of *Apokryphen und Pseudepigraphen des Alten Testaments*. Edited by E. Kautzsch. Darmstadt: Wissenschaftliche Buchgesellschaft, 1962.

Schorch, S. *Die Vokale des Gesetzes: die samaritanische Lesetradition als Textzeugin der Tora: 1. Das Buch Genesis*. Beihefte zur Zeitschrift für die alttestamentliche Wissenschaft 339. Berlin: de Gruyter, 2004.

Schuller, E. "4Q372 1: A Text about Joseph." *Revue de Qumran* 14 (1990): 349–376.

Schuller, E. and M. Bernstein. "371–373. 4QNarrative and Poetic Composition[a-c]." Pages 151–200 in *Wadi Daliyeh II: The Samaria Papyri from Wadi Daliyeh. Qumran Cave 4. XXVIII: Miscellanea, part 2*. Edited by D. M. Gropp et al. Discoveries in the Judaean Desert 28. Oxford: Clarendon, 2001.

Schur, N. *History of the Samaritans*. Beiträge zur Erforschung des Alten Testaments und des antiken Judentums 18. Frankfurt am Main: Peter Lang, 1989.

Schwemer, A. M. *Studien zu den frühjüdischen Prophetenlegenden Vitae prophetarum*. Texte und Studien zum antiken Judentum 49–50. Tübingen: Mohr, 1995.

Segal, M. *The book of* Jubilees: *Rewritten Bible, Redaction, Ideology and Theology*. Journal for the study of Judaism: Supplement Series 117. Leiden: Brill, 2007.

Segal, M. Z. "נישואי בן כהן גדול עם בת־סנבלט ובניין מקדש־גריזים"/The Marriage of the Son of the High Priest with the Daughter of Sanballat and the Building of the Temple of Gerizim." Pages 404–414 in *Simcha Assaf Anniversary Volume*. Edited by M. D. Cassuto et al. Jerusalem: Mossad Harav Kook 1952–1953. Translated by F. Dexinger and repr. as "Die Heirat des Sohnes des Hohenpriesters mit der Tochter des Sanballat und der Bau des Heiligtums auf dem Garizim." Pages 198–219 in *Die Samaritaner*. Edited by F. Dexinger and R. Pummer. Wege der Forschung 604. Darmstadt: Wissenschaftliche Buchgesellschaft, 1992.

Segni, L. di. "The 'Onomasticon' of Eusebius and the Madaba Map." Pages 115–120 in *The Madaba Map Centenary, 1897–1997: Travelling through the Byzantine Umayyad Period: Proceedings of the International Conference held in Amman, 7–9 April 1997*. Jerusalem: Studium Biblicum Franciscanum, 1999.

Sievers, J. *Synopsis of the Greek Sources for the Hasmonean period: 1–2 Maccabees and Josephus*, War 1 and Antiquities 12–14. Subsidia Biblica 20. Roma: Pontificio istituto biblico, 2001.

Skehan, P. W. "Exodus in the Samaritan Recension from Qumran." *Journal of Biblical Literature* 74 (1955): 182–187.

Slotki, I. W. *Yebamot Translated into English with Notes, Glossary and Indices*. Vol. 1 of *Seder Nashim in Four Volumes*. *The Babylonian Talmud*. Edited by I. Epstein. London: Soncino, 1936. Repr. 1984.

Smend, R. *Die Weisheit des Jesus Sirach mit einem hebräischen Glossar.* Berlin: Georg Reimer, 1906.

Standhartinger, A. "'Um zu sehen die Töchter des Landes': Die Perspektive Dinas in der jüdisch-hellenistischen Diskussion um Gen 34." Pages 89–116 in *Religious Propaganda and Missionary Competition in the New Testament World: Essays Honoring Dieter Georgi.* Edited by L. Bormann, K. Del Tredici and A. Standhartinger. Novum Testamentum Supplements 74. Leiden: Brill, 1994.

Steck, O. H. *Israel und das gewaltsame Geschick der Propheten: Untersuchungen zur Überlieferung des deuteronomistischen Geschichtsbildes im Alten Testament, Spätjudentum und Urchristentum.* Wissenschaftliche Monographien zum Alten und Neuen Testament 23. Neukirchen: Neukirchener Verlag, 1967.

Stenhouse, P. "The Kitab al-Tarikh of Abu 'l-Fath." Ph.D. diss., Sydney University, 1980.

———, *The Kitab al-Tarikh of Abu 'l-Fath Translated into English with Notes by Paul Stenhouse, M.S.C. Ph. D.* Studies in Judaica 1. Sydney: Mandelbaum, 1985.

———, "Samaritan Chronicles." Pages 218–265 in *The Samaritans.* Edited by A. D. Crown. Tübingen: Mohr, 1989.

Stern, E. and Y. Magen. "Archaeological Evidence for the First Stage of the Samaritan Temple on Mount Gerizim." *Israel Exploration Journal* 52 (2002): 49–57.

Strugnell, J. "Notes en marge du volume V des 'Discoveries in the Judaean Desert of Jordan." *Revue de Qumran* 26 (1970): 163–229.

Sundberg, A. C. *The Old Testament of the Early Church.* Harvard Theological Studies 20. Cambridge, Mass.: Harvard University Press, 1964.

Tal, A. *The Samaritan Pentateuch Edited According to Ms 6 (C) of the Shekhem Synagogue.* Texts and Studies in the Hebrew Language and Related Subjects. Tel Aviv: The Chaim Rosenberg School for Jewish Studies / Tel Aviv University, 1994.

Talmon, S. "The Samaritan Pentateuch." *Journal of Jewish Studies* 2 (1950–1951): 144–150.

———, "קטעי כתבים כתובים עברית ממצדה/ Fragments of Scrolls from Masada." *Eretz-Israel* 22 (1989) 278–286.

———, "A Masada Fragment of Samaritan origin." *Israel Exploration Journal* 47 (1997): 220–232.

———, "A Papyrus Fragment Inscribed in Palaeo-Hebrew Script." Pages 138–149 in *Masada: Yigael Yadin Excavations 1963–1965: Final Reports.* The Masada Reports 6. Jerusalem: Israel Exploration Society, 1999.

Teeple, H. M. *The Mosaic Eschatological Prophet.* Journal of Biblical Literature: Monograph series 10. Philadelphia: Society of Biblical Literature, 1957.

Thomson, J. E. H. *The Samaritans: Their Testimony to the Religion of Israel.* Being the Alexander Robertson Lectures, delivered before the University of Glasgow in 1916. London: Oliver & Boyd, 1919.

Tov, E. "Pap. Giessen 13, 19, 22, 26: A Revision of the LXX?" *Revue biblique* 78 (1971): 355–383 and plates X–XI.

——, "The Nature and Background of Harmonization in Biblical Manuscripts." *Journal for the Study of the Old Testament* 31 (1985): 3–29.

——, "Biblical Texts as Reworked in Some Qumran Manuscripts with Special Attention to 4QRP and 4QParaGen-Exod." Pages 111–134 in *The Community of the Renewed Covenant*. Edited by E. Ulrich and J. VanderKam. Gregory E. Sterling Christianity and Judaism in Antiquity Series. Notre Dame, Ind.: University of Notre Dame Press, 1994.

——, *Der Text der Hebräischen Bibel: Handbuch der Textkritik*. Stuttgart: Kohlhammer, 1997.

——, "Rewritten Bible Compositions and Biblical Manuscripts, with Special Attention to the Samaritan Pentateuch." *Dead Sea Discoveries* 5 (1998): 334–354.

——, *Textual Criticism of the Hebrew Bible*. 2. rev. ed. Minneapolis, Minn.: Fortress, 2001.

Tov, E. and S. White [Crawford]. "4QReworked Pentateuch[b-e]." Pages 187–352 and plates XIII–XXXXVI in *Qumran Cave 4. VIII: Parabiblical Texts, Part 1*. Edited by H. Attridge et al., in consultation with J. VanderKam. Discoveries in the Judaean Desert 13. Oxford: Clarendon, 1994.

Tracy, S. V. *Attic Letter-Cutters of 229 to 86 B.C.* Hellenistic culture and society 6. Berkeley: University of California Press, 1990.

Ulrich, E. "4QJosh[a]." Pages 143–152 and plates XXXII–XXXIV in *Qumran Cave 4. IX: Deuteronomy, Joshua, Judges, Kings*. Edited by E. Ulrich et al. Discoveries in the Judaean Desert 14. Oxford: Clarendon, 1995.

——, "The Dead Sea Scrolls and the Biblical Text." Pages 79–100 in vol. 1 of *The Dead Sea Scrolls after Fifty Years: A Comprehensive Assessment*. Edited by P. W. Flint and J. C. VanderKam. Leiden: Brill, 1998.

——, "Our sharper Focus on the Bible and Theology Thanks to the Dead Sea Scrolls." *Catholic Biblical Quarterly* 66 (2004): 1–24.

Ulrich, E., et al. eds. *Qumran Cave 4. VII: Genesis to Numbers*. Discoveries in the Judaean Desert 12. Oxford: Clarendon, 1994.

Ulrichsen, J. H. *Die Grundschrift der Testamente der Zwölf Patriarchen: eine Untersuchung zu Umfang, Inhalt und Eigenart der ursprünglichen Schrift*. Historia religionum 10. Uppsala: Almqvist & Wiksell International, 1991.

Urbach, E. E. *The Sages: Their Concepts and Beliefs*. Jerusalem Publications of the Perry Foundation in the Hebrew University of Jerusalem, 1987.

VanderKam, J. C. *Textual and Historical Studies in the Book of Jubilees*. Harvard Semitic monographs 14. Missoula, Mont.: Published by Scholars Press for Harvard Semitic Museum, 1977.

——, "Authoritative Literature in the Dead Sea Scrolls." *Dead Sea Discoveries* 5 (1998): 382–402.

——, *The Book of Jubilees*. Guides to Apocrypha and Pseudepigrapha. Sheffield: Sheffield Academic Press, 2001.

——, *From Joshua to Caiaphas: High Priests after the Exile*. Minneapolis: Fortress Press, 2004.

Vaux, R. de. "On Right and Wrong Uses of Archaeology." Pages 64–80 in *Essays in Honor of Nelson Glueck: Near Eastern Archaeology in the Twentieth Century*. Edited by J. H. Sanders. New York: Doubleday, 1970.

Vilmar, E. *Abulfathi Annales Samaritani quos ad finem codicum manu scriptorum Berolinensium Bodleijani Parisini edidit et prolegomenis instruxit Eduardus Vilmar.* Gothae: Sumtibus Frederici Andreae Perthes, 1865.

Walter, N. "Pseudo-Eupolemos (Samaritanischer Anonymus)." Pages 137–143 in *Historische und legendarische Erzählungen.* Vol. 1 of *Jüdische Schriften aus hellenistisch-römischer Zeit.* Edited by W. G. Kümmel et al. Gütersloh: Gütersloher Verlagshaus, 1981.

———, "Theodotos der Epiker." Pages 154–171 in *Poetische Schriften.* Vol. 4 of *Jüdische Schriften aus hellenistisch-römischer Zeit.* Edited by W. G. Kümmel et al. Gütersloh: Gütersloher Verlagshaus, 1974–1983.

Waltke, B. K. "Prolegomena to the Samaritan Pentateuch." Ph.D. diss., Harvard University, 1965.

———, "The Samaritan Pentateuch and the Text of the Old Testament." Pages 212–239 in *New Perspectives on the Old Testament.* Edited by J. Barton Payne. Evangelical Theological Society: Supplementary Volumes: Symposium Series. Waco, Tex.: Word Books, 1970.

Walton, B., E. Castellus and J. Lightfoot. "Animadversiones Samariticae: Textum hebraeum et samaritanum." In vol. 1 of *S.S. Biblia Polyglotta Completentia Textus Originales: Hebraicos cum Pentat. Samarit: etc., 1653–1657.* London 1657.

Watts, J. W. "Ritual Legitimacy and Scriptural Authority." *Journal of Biblical Literature* 124 (2005): 401–417.

———, *Ritual and Rhetoric in Leviticus: From Sacrifice to Scripture.* Cambridge: Cambridge University Press, 2007.

Webster, B. "Chronological Index of the Texts from the Judaean Desert." Page 366 in *The Texts from the Judean Desert: Indices and an Introduction to the Discoveries in the Judaean Desert Series.* Edited by E. Tov. Discoveries in the Judaean Desert 39. Oxford: Clarendon, 2002.

Wellhausen, J. *Israelitische und jüdische Geschichte.* 6. Aufl. Berlin: Georg Reimer, 1907.

Weyde, K. W. *Prophecy and Teaching: Prophetic Authority, Form Problems, and the Use of Traditions in the Book of Malachi.* Beihefte zur Zeitschrift für die alttestamentliche Wissenschaft 288. Berlin: de Gruyter, 2000.

White, L. M. "The Delos Synagoge Revisited: Recent Fieldwork in the Greco-Roman Diaspora." *Harvard Theological Review* 80 (1987): 133–160.

Williamson, H. G. M. *Israel in the Books of Chronicles.* Cambridge: Cambridge University Press, 1977.

———, "The Temple in the Books of Chronicles." Pages 15–31 in *Templum Amicitiae: Essays on the Second Temple Presented to Ernst Bammel.* Edited by W. Horbury. Journal for the study of the New Testament: Supplement series 48. Sheffield: Journal for the Study of the Old Testament Press, 1991. Repr. pages 150–161 in idem, *Studies in Persian History and Historiography.* Forschungen zum Alten Testament 38. Tübingen: Mohr, 2004.

Wintermute, O. S. "Jubilees." Pages 35–142 in vol. 2 of *The Old Testament Pseudepigrapha.* Edited by J. H. Charlesworth. New York: Doubleday, 1985.

Wolde, E. van. "Does 'innâ denote rape?" *Vetus Testamentum* 52 (2002) 528–544.

Wright, G. E. *Schechem: The Biography of a Biblical City*. London: Duckworth, 1965.

Yahuda, A. S. "Über die Unechtheit des samaritanischen Josuabuches." *Sitzungsberichte der preussischen Akademie der Wissenschaften* 39 (1908): 887–914.

Yardeni, A. and M. Broshi. "4QList of False Prophets ar." Pages 77–79 of *Qumran Cave 4. XIV: Parabiblical Texts, Part 2*. Edited by M. Broshi et al. Discoveries in the Judaean Desert 19. Oxford: Clarendon, 1995.

Yellin, D. "*spr yhws' 'w spr hymym.*" *Jerusalem Jahrbuch zur Beförderung einer wissenschaftlichen genauen Kenntnis des jetzigen und des alten Palästinas* 6 (1902): 203–205; (1903): 138–155.

Zangenberg, J. *ΣΑΜΑΡΕΙΑ: Antike Quellen zur Geschichte und Kultur der Samaritaner in deutscher Übersetzung*. Texte und Arbeiten zum neutestamentlichen Zeitalter 15. Tübingen: Francke, 1994.

Zenger, E. "Das Buch Judit." Pages 427–534 in *Historische und legendarische Erzählungen*. Vol. 1 of *Jüdische Schriften aus hellenistisch-römischer Zeit*. Edited by W. G. Kümmel et al. Gütersloh: Gütersloher Verlagshaus, 1981.

Zertal, A. "The Wedge-Shaped Decorated Bowl and the Origin of the Samaritans." *Bulletin of the American Schools of Oriental Research* 276 (1989): 77–84.

Zsengellér, J. *Garizim as Israel: Northern Tradition of the Old Testament and the Early History of the Samaritans*. Utrechtse Theologische Reeks 38. Utrecht: Faculteit der Godgeleerdheid, 1998.

——, "Kutim or *Samarites*: A History of the Designation of the Samaritans." Pages 87–104 in *Proceedings of the Fifth International Congress of the Société d'Études Samaritaines, Helsinki, August 1–4, 2000*. Studies in Memory of Ferdindand Dexinger. Edited by H. Shehadeh & H. Tawa with the collaboration of R. Pummer. Paris: Geuthner, 2005.

INDEX OF ANCIENT SOURCES

HEBREW BIBLE

Genesis

1	227
3:24	191
14:18–20	244, 250
15:18–21	131
33:18	235, 250
34	111–117
34 LXX	117–119
34 SP	194–198
48:21 f.	165
49:5–7	114
49:5–7 SP	196–198

Exodus

15:3	184
20	226–227, 281–282
20:24 f.	293
30:11–16	223
30:16	215
32:9	276
32:27–29	155–156
33:17–23	297
33:20	330, 335–336

Leviticus

20:2–4	154

Numbers

10:10	214
12:7	297
25:11–13	156

Deuteronomy

5	226–227
5:24–31	281–284
6:4	226
11:29 f.	300
13:2–6	314
18:15–22	313–316
18:18–22	281–284

27:4	29, 292, 302–309, 355–357
27:12 f.	300–301
32:21	142, 169
33 SP	198
34:10	297

Joshua

8:30–35	29, 292, 294, 301–309
9:2 LXX	306

1 Samuel

1–3	30–32

2 Kings

17	1, 17–22, 51, 57, 86–90, 239
17:33 f.	82–83
25:11 f.22	56
25:18–21	18

Isaiah

6:1	330, 335–336
11:13	167
52:13–53:12	298

Jeremiah

23:13	328

Ezekiel

37:15–23	166

Hosea

6:9	115

Joel

3:1	347

Zechariah

8:13	166
10:6–10	166

Zechariah (*Continued*)
13:2–6   347

Malachi
3:22–24 (ET: 4:4–6)
           348

Psalms
74:9   314
78:67 f.   168

Lamentations
2:9   315

Daniel
11:31   240

Ezra
4–5   104
4:2   362–363

Nehemiah
2:20   214
3:1–3   214, 215
12   92
13:28   3, 23, 51, 91, 215

1 Chronicles
9:3   369

2 Chronicles
13   369

ELEPHANTINE TEXTS

TAD A4.5–10   358

APOCRYPHA AND PSEUDEPIGRAPHA

2 Esdras
13:39–50   167

Sirach
36:1–19   167
50:25–26   140–149

Judith
4:4   183
5:16   188
9:2–4   185
9:5–6   186
9:7–14   186, 189

1 Maccabees
15:15–24   215

2 Maccabees
5:23   236–240
6:2   64, 98–100,
           236–240

Aramaic Levi Document
1:1–3   173
2:1   175
12:6   175

2 Baruch
78–86   167

Jubilees
30:1–4   152
30:5 f.   153
30:11 f.   157
30:17   158
30:21 f.   158

1 Enoch
89:72   363

Sibylline Oracles
3:63   325–326

Testament of Levi
2:2   177
2:3 ff.   177
5:2–4   178
6:3–7   179
7:1–11   179–181
12:5   177

Testament of Moses
3:4–4:9   167

Ascension of Isaiah
3:6–10   329

Joseph and Aseneth
23:3–5   190
23:14–15   191

Paralipomena Ieremiae
8   366

DEAD SEA SCROLLS

Damascus Document (CD)
              326
4Q17   267
4Q22   267–270
4Q27   270–271, 285
4Q37   286
4Q47   306
4Q158   271
4Q175   272
4Q213   176
4Q339   337–344
4Q364   271–272
4Q365   271–272
4Q366   271–272, 286
4Q367   271–272
4Q371   160–171
4Q372   160–171, 359–
              360
4Q375   342–343
4Q550   74
11Q14   144–145

NEW TESTAMENT

Matthew
10:5   182

John
4:25   315

ANCIENT JEWISH WRITERS

Demetrius
2:9   121

Theodotus
Fragment 7   132
Fragment 8   132–133

Pseudo-Eupolemus
              243–256

Josephus
War
1.62 f.   100–101, 240–241
2.232–245   103
3.307   103
Antiquities
1.337–340   106–107
4.305   307–308
5.16–20   306–308
5.69   307
9.278 f   17, 131, 164
9.278 f., 288–291
               1, 57, 86–90
9.288–291   18, 74, 82
10.155   56
10.181   74
10.184   89
11   51
11.19   89
11.88   74
11.302 f.   23
11.302–346   77–78, 90–91
11.302 f., 306–312
               2
11.306–312   23
11.341   84
11.343 f.   84
11.344   96
11.346 f.   135
12.257   85, 89
12.257–264   98–100
13.254–256   100–101
13.255 f.   91, 240–241
14.10   216
18.118–135   103

Philo
De migratione Abrahami
  1:224   192–193

Pseudo-Philo
Liber Antiquitatum Biblicarum
  8:7 f.   194

RABBINIC TEXTS

Masseket Kuthim
                19, 88

Y. Sotah
  7:3   259

B. Shabbat
  13b   331

B. Megillah
  9a   290

B. Yebamot
  49b   329–330

B. Sotah
  33b   259

B. Sanhedrin
  21b   289
  89a   332
  90a   332

B. Menachot
  45a   331, 332

CHRISTIAN AUTHORS

Chronicon Paschale
                231

Epiphanius of Salamis
Haereses / Panarion
                20, 316, 318–319
Anacephalaiosis 21

De XII gemmis   21

Eusebius of Caesarea
Onomasticon   20, 233–236
Praeparatio Evangelica
  9.17.2–9   243–256
  9.21.9   121
  9.22   127–139
  9.22.9   132
  9.22.11–12   132–133

John Malalas   231

Justin
Apology
  I 53.4   221

Marinus   230–231, 252

Origen
Commentarii in evangelium Johannis
                20

Procopius of Gaza
                232

GREEK AND LATIN TEXTS

Philo of Byblos   55

Pliny the Elder
Naturalis historia
  V xiv 68   230

Porphyry of Tyre
                55

SAMARITAN TEXTS

Manuscript 6 (C) of the Shekhem
  synagogue
                195–198

Arabic book of Joshua
                2, 34–37, 46

Chronicle Adler 37

Chronicle II 39, 46

Kitab al-Tarikh 2, 27–34, 46

The New Chronicle
37

Tolidah 24–27

INDEX OF MODERN AUTHORS

Achenbach, R., 50
Adler, E. N., 37
Ådna, J., 223
Albright, W. F., 64
Alonso Schökel, L., 184
Alt, A., 61–63, 356
Altheim, F., 55
Amit, Y., 115–116
Anderson, R. T., 6–8, 41, 69
Auld, A. G., 309
Avi-Yonah, M., 233

Barr, J., 117
Barth, F., 12
Beckwith, R., 295
Begg, C., 306, 307
Ben-Hayyim, Z., 40, 65, 197, 293, 296–299
Berger, K., 149
Bernstein, M., 162, 166
Bickerman, E., 97
Black, M., 364
Bowman, J., 24–26, 28, 227
Bright, J., 65
Brooke, G. J., 342
Broshi, M., 338
Bruneau, P., 216–217
Buchler, A., 77–78
Bull, R. J., 205

Campbell, Jr., E. F., 204, 235–236
Chapman, H. H., 71 n1
Charles, R. H., 26, 149, 318, 322
Coggins, R. J., 42, 65, 68, 79–80, 151
Collins, J. J., 124–125, 135, 325
Cowley, A. E., 296
Crown, A. D., 7, 53, 274, 293
Crowther, C. V., 218 n43
Cross, F. M., 59–67, 263

Davies, G., 226
Davila, J., 46
Dever, W., 205 n7
Dexinger, F., 7, 10–11, 48–49, 282, 292, 315
Di Lella, A. A., 1 n1
Dillmann, A., 322
Dušek, J., 62–63, 94

Egger, R., 7, 71–77
Endres, J. C., 155
Eshel, E., 172–177
Eshel, H., 169, 229, 231, 242

Feldman, L., 71, 78, 107, 126
Florentin, M., 24–26, 35
Fossum, J., 42
Freudenthal, J., 1 n1, 125, 243–253

García Martínez, F., 165
Gaster, M., 35, 47
Gaster, T. H., 47
Gebhart, O. von, 318 n10
Gesenius, W., 261, 265, 273
Giles, T., 6, 41, 69
Ginsberg, L., 110
Glaue, P., 302–303
Goldstein, J., 97, 238–240
Greenfield, J., 172–177

Hanhart, R., 83, 99, 142, 229, 237
Hannah, D. D., 322, 324
Hengel, M., 249
Hepner, G., 293–294
Hjelm, I., 46
Holladay, C. R., 124, 245–247
Horst, P. W. van der, 366 n14
Hylland Eriksen, T., 12

Isser, S. J., 315

Japhet, S., 368
Jastram, N., 285, 287
Jeremias, J., 367, 368
Jones, S., 12
Juynboll, T., 34

Kahle, P., 35, 37
Kasher, A., 80
Kippenberg, H. G., 14, 41, 51,
  77–78, 229, 274, 296–299
Klein, S., 150
Knibb, M., 165, 321 n15, 322, 327
Knight, J., 323, 328
Knoppers, G., 48
Kraabel, A. T., 216 n40, 222
Kratz, R., 356 n5
Kugel, J., 110, 143, 166, 180
Kugler, R. A., 172–180

Lapp, P., 60
Lapp, N., 60
Leiman, S. L., 295
London, G., 50
Lowy, S., 298–299

Macdonald, J., 39–40, 46
Magen, Y., 56–57, 206–208
Mantel, H. D. , 147
Mason, S., 71 n1, 81
Meeks, W., 315
Milik, J. T., 47, 173
Misgav, H., 210–214
Mittmann-Richert, U., 119–120
Montgomery, J., 50–53, 227–228
Moore, C. A., 183 n123
Mor, M., 61
Mowinckel, S., 357 n6

Niessen, F., 40
Noort, E., 42
Norelli, E., 318 n9, 323
Noth, M., 62, 367, 368

Oeming, M., 367

Pakkala, J., 356
Puech, E., 174

Pummer, R., 5 f., 42, 54, 139,
  150–152, 229, 370
Purvis, J. D., 54, 59–67, 147, 210,
  354

Qimron, E., 162

Rahlfs, A., 302–303
Renz, J., 66 n74
Roberts, B., 65–66
Röllig, W., 66 n74

Sanderson, J., 266, 273, 292
Sandnes, K. O., 147
Schalit, A., 73
Schorch, S., 54–55, 195 n137, 197
Schuller, E., 162, 166
Schur, N., 47–48
Schwemer, A. M., 323
Segal, M., 149
Seligsohn, M. , 37
Sellin, E., 203
Skehan, P. W., 1 n1, 263
Smend, R., 141
Standhartinger, A., 114 n8
Stenhouse, P., 27–28
Stern, E., 56–57
Stiehl, R., 55
Stone, M. E., 172–177
Strugnell, J., 161
Sundberg, A. C., 295

Tal, A., 194–198, 274
Talmon, S., 218–222, 227, 229, 242,
  263
Tov, E., 1 n1, 65, 264–265, 273, 286,
  303

Ulrich, E., 306
Ulrichsen, J. H., 171–172
Urbach, E. E., 332–333

VanderKam, J. C., 149, 358 n10
Vilmar, E., 27

Weyde, K. W., 117
White, L., 218–225

White [Crawford], S., 286
Williamson, H. G.M., 52–53, 368
Wright, G. E., 61, 203

Yardeni, A., 338

Zangenberg, J., 218 n42
Zenger, E., 184
Zertal, A., 50
Zsengellér, J., 9, 58

SUBJECT INDEX

Abraham, 244–252
Abu'l Fath, 27–34
Alexander Polyhistor, 119, 123
Andromachus, 60, 62, 204
Antiochus IV Epiphanes, 183–184,
    239–240
Arabs, 212
Argarizim, Argarizein, 228–256
Asatir, 47
'Aspis', 177–178

Balaam, 340
Beit-el-Ma-inscription, 226
Beliar / Satan, 325–326
Belkira / Melcheira, 326–327,
    344–346
Bene haggola / בני הגולה, 363–367
Bethulia, 183–184
Blasphemy, 170–171

Calendar, 26, 150
Circumcision, 11, 126, 130,
    137–138, 151–152, 177, 179
'City of Fools', 180–181
Chronicle II, 247
Curtius, 60

Daliyeh, *see* Wadi Daliyeh
Decalogue inscriptions, 226–227
Demetrius, 119–122, 126
Defter, 296
Dinah, 111–116
Disenfranchised population, 60–61,
    97
Divine Favour, *Rawuta*, 26, 39
Divine Wrath, *Fanuta*, 39
Dositheus, Dositheans, 274,
    296–299, 315, 328
Durran, 296–299, 315

Ebal, mount, 302
Edomites, 141–144

El elyon, The Most High God, 162,
    243–251
Elephantine, 358
Emmaus inscription, 226
Endogamous marriages, 121–122,
    129, 149–151, 186, 190
Ephraim, 166–167
Exogamous marriages, 130, 148,
    154–157, 177, 364–265
Ethnicity, 10, 78, 83, 121, 129, 148,
    366, 370
Eusebius, 119, 123

False prophets
    general, 338–343
    from the North, 328, 344–346
'Fools', μωροί, נבלים, 140–145,
    160–171, 180–181, 289

Gezera shawa, 144
Gerizim, mount, 302, 354

Hargerizim, Qumran text, 302
    n110
Hivites, 113 n7, 115
Holofernes, 185

Identity marker, 201, 370
Israel, 169–170
Israelites, 221–222

John Hyrcanus, 101, 149–151, 161,
    181, 201, 204, 287, 338, 361
Joseph, 162–168, 190
Jubilees, calendar, 26

'Kuthim', 4, 19

Levi's priesthood, 149–151,
    155–159, 175, 181
Literary criticism / *Literarkritik*, 317,
    323

Maccabees, 183, 238
Madaba map, 233–236
Manasseh, king, 325–329
Maria Theotokos church, 236
Marqah, 298
Martyrdom of Isaiah, 324
Masada, 241–242
Melchizedek, 243, 355
Mixed population, 1, 360
Morin, Jean / Iohannes Morinus, 260
Moses
    general, 157–159
    as prophet, 277–288

Names, onomasticon, 211–213
Nikanor, 183

Onias III, 145

Pietro della Valle, 13, 259
Philistines, 141–144
Phinehas, 156
Pilgrim of Bordeaux, 230
Place of worship, במה, 160–161, 164, 169
Polemics, 115–116, 171, 336, 345
Polyglot Bibles, 259–260
Pre- / proto-Samaritans, 7
Pre-Samaritan texts, 263–265
Prophet after Moses
    expectation, 283–284
    like Moses, 313–316
Proto-Esther, 74
Pseudo-Eupolemus, 243–255, 355

Race, 10, 19, 129, 185
Reworked Pentateuch, 264–272

Salem, 234–235, 250–255
Samareitikon / Samaritan targum, 303
Samaria (region) / Σαμάρεια, 5, 59–63
Samaria / Sebaste, 61, 178
Samaritan inscriptions, 226–228

Samaritan Pentateuch
    general, 64–67
    disputes in Europe over, 260–261
    text-critical value of, 261
    as a vulgar text, 262
    as a Palestinian text, 263
    major expansions in, 265–280
        as harmonizations, 273–274
        as expressions of divine warfare, 273
        as halakhic traditions, 274
        as anti-prophetic, 274
        added for comprehension, 274
        as a Moses layer, 280
Samaritan script, 64–67, 288–290
Samaritan self-consciousness, 353
Samaritan temple, 91–95, 100–103, 351, 353–357
'Samaritans'
    השמרנים, 1, 5, 86–87
    Σαμαρεύς, Σαμαρεῖς
        general, 5
        used by Josephus, 71–77
    Σαμαρίτης, Σαμαρῖται,
        general, 4
        used by Josephus, 71–77, 86–87
    Σικμῖται, Shechemites
        used by Josephus, 71–77, 94, 96, 106–108
    Χουθαῖοι, Chouthaioi
        general, 2, 5, 74
        used by Josephus, 71–77, 86–87
    Ἰσραηλίτης, 221
    in NT, 3
    definitions of, 4–9, 71–77
    perhaps referred to in 2 Kgs 17, 169
    as used in this book, 10
Samaritans' origin
    sources for, 1–4
    descendants of Old Israel, 46–49
    deportees from the east, 49–50
    estrangement theory, 68
    split off from Jerusalem, 50–55, 287

Cross-Purvis hypothesis, 59
Samaritans in Egypt, 104, 126, 223
Sanballat, 59–63, 94, 208
Schism, 50, 68
Scripts, 209–210, 288–290
Seir, 141–144
Sect, 50
Shechem
    general, 59–63, 91, 111
    in Theodotus, 122–123, 124, 128
Simeon II, 140, 145, 146
Simon (Acts 8), 328
Société d'Études Samaritaines (SES),
    15
Syncretism, 1, 19, 50, 82–83, 88,
    209, 220, 228, 359

Tabernacle, 277, 278–279
Taheb, 315
Temple
    in Jerusalem, 164, 168

at Araq el Emir, 238, 352
at Leontopolis, 238, 352
at Elephantine, 352
at Mount Gerizim, 91–95,
    100–103, 351–355
Temple tax, 223
Tenth commandment, Gerizim
    commandment, 281–282, 291,
    308
Testament of Hezekiah, 324

Vetus Latina / Old Latin, 302–309
Violence, 154–158, 180–182

Wadi Daliyeh, 60–63, 94

Zeal, 186
Zedekiah, false prophet, 326–335,
    341, 344
Zeus, 205–206, 237–240
Zion, 164, 167–170, 187, 337, 345